CW01497150

THE EDINBURGH NEW TOWN GARDENS

'Blessings as well as beauties'

THE EDINBURGH NEW TOWN GARDENS

'Blessings as well as beauties'

Connie Byrom

Birlinn

First published in 2005 by
Birlinn Limited
West Newington House
10 Newington Road
Edinburgh
EH9 1QS

www.birlinn.co.uk

ISBN10: 1 84158 402 9
ISBN13: 978 1 84158 402 7

British Library Cataloguing-in-Publication Data
A catalogue record for this book is available from the British Library

The publisher gratefully acknowledges support from

Scottish
Arts Council

and

EDINBURGH WORLD HERITAGE

towards the publication of this book

Designed and typeset by Brinnoven, Livingston
Printed and bound by Antony Rowe Ltd, Chippenham

For John
who opened my eyes to Architecture and Landscape

and to

Simon, Thomas, Sarah, Calum and Robbie
who opened them still further

16 July 1848: Sunday and broiling. It was so hot yesterday we did not go out till quite late, just before tea when we strolled for an hour in the Queen Street Gardens. These beautiful shrubberies at intervals all over the town are blessings as well as beauties.

Elizabeth Grant of Rothiemurchus: *The Highland Lady in Ireland*

Elizabeth was on a visit to her mother, staying at 24 York Place. The stroll was probably taken in the East Queen Street Gardens, the closest to York Place. In the earlier part of her diary (*Memoirs of a Highland Lady*) she tells of sometimes joining her sister Jane at Mr Wilson's art classes held in his studio, and gaining much from his 'reading' of a drawing or print. This would have been some time before Andrew Wilson's involvement in the design of the Central and West Queen Street Gardens.

CONTENTS

LIST OF ILLUSTRATIONS

Colour Illustrations

FOREWORD

This great book chronicles and illustrates the origins, planning, development and management of the gardens and pleasure grounds of Edinburgh's New Town, and tells us about the skill and perseverance given, over 235 years, by successive experts, enthusiasts and authorities – advice still needed today for this World Heritage Site.

To visit, or better, to live in Edinburgh is to experience a city close to hills and sea, whose core is bounded, north and south, by the parklands of Inverleith and the Meadows, and whose historic centre, north of the Castle, has many precious and beautiful open spaces.

The grass, trees and flowers of 'The Gardens of the North Loch', known as Princes Street Gardens, have delighted visitors for well over a century, while residents enjoy thirty-four smaller gardens throughout Georgian Edinburgh. Few of the classical terraces and crescents do not have a glimpse of foliage; a welcome foil to disciplined masonry.

This book, meticulously researched, and the achievement of a lifetime, will inspire those who agree that gardens are living ornaments requiring constant attention; sometimes ruthless pruning; sometimes redesigning.

Edinburgh, a university city and the pinnacle of Scottish justice, has always produced citizens willing to give their time and knowledge freely in a good cause. Dr Connie Byrom provides many such examples – City Councillors, Garden Committee Members, landscape designers, gardeners, people such as Lord Cockburn and many others, including now the author of this work.

Desmond Hodges
Edinburgh
October 2005

PREFACE

Is it going too far to suggest that the New Town is, as it were, a realisation of an ideal landscape of this kind, combining the intellectual order of classical architecture and regular planning with a prospect of nature, fields and trees and hills, laid out for man's delight like a gentleman's park? Some such idea was surely in Craig's mind when he incorporated in his plan the views south of Princes Street, and north of Queen Street. There is the same sort of vision where the Queen Steet gardens are retained, where the Calton Hill is kept as a walk and open space, where Lord Moray's pleasure grounds still slope, steeply wooded, to the banks of the Water of Leith: the vision of an earthly paradise, of the harmony between man and nature which the Enlightenment felt was both natural and desirable: man in touch with nature, and yet distinct.

A.J. Youngson, 1967[1]

This book is about the pleasure gardens attached to the New Town of Edinburgh: the subscription gardens, sometimes referred to as pleasure grounds, or simply as the New Town Gardens. Never before have they been considered together or in relation to the building developments to which they are attached. Created for the benefit of those living adjacent or close by, their contribution to the overall appearance of Edinburgh's Georgian New Town and its later Victorian additions is nevertheless considerable. As we pass them by, the sight of green refreshes, and the rhythm of seasonal change never fails to excite. The gardens have enriched the city and have added to the enjoyment of those who live, work or visit the capital of Scotland.

At the same time these gardens, which include the ones along Princes Street, St Andrew Square, Charlotte Square, Queen Street, Moray Place, Drummond Place and so on have become taken for granted; they are there, they seem to have always been there, and somehow, as if by magic, they continue to survive without apparent effort. Moreover, it has always been the buildings that have stolen the limelight with just a cursory nod at the gardens which provide them with such a splendid foil. But how did these 'foliaged compartments' – so aptly described by Lora Cockburn – come into being? Who was involved in having them formed, who designed them, how were they laid out, what was planted, how were they maintained and paid for, what uses were made of them and what changes and difficulties have they encountered over time? To find answers to these questions has been the inspiration behind these writings; and the picture to emerge has been far more complex and arbitrary than ever expected. The gardens did not happen in the neat way that maps and plans suggest, but rather they involved a lot of people putting in a great deal of time, effort and negotiating skills; and on occasions a fair bit of fighting spirit to preserve their patch of open space for the benefit of the wider community and the lasting benefit of Edinburgh.

This book can be approached on various levels – as a reference source, for information on specific gardens or groups of gardens, for background on particular developments and how the gardens relate to them and so on. It is designed to follow a general progression in time, from the first Georgian Gardens to later Victorian ones of similar character. The first chapter provides an overall introduction to the gardens and the personalities and features common to many of them. Thereafter you can wander in whatever direction you please: 'Bon Voyage'. May your journey through the gardens of Edinburgh's New Town be as pleasurable and rewarding as mine has been.

Note

1. A.J. Youngson, 'The City of Reason and Nature', in *Edinburgh in the Age of Reason* (Edinburgh, 1967), p.21.

ACKNOWLEDGEMENTS

This book originated from the discovery that many of the clerks and secretaries of the Edinburgh New Town garden committees had in their safekeeping old records, including early garden minute books. The material first came to light during a brief study of the gardens carried out in 1970 by landscape students attached to the Department of Architecture, Edinburgh University, under the supervision of John Byrom, Director of Studies. This complemented a larger survey then underway by several Edinburgh architects (on behalf of the Scottish Civic Trust), focusing on the exterior condition of the Georgian buildings within the New Town of Edinburgh. Signs of physical decay and insensitive alterations having given cause for considerable alarm. The results were presented at a conference on *The Conservation of Georgian Edinburgh* in June 1970[1] and led ultimately to the formation of the Edinburgh New Town Conservation Committee (ENTCC). Under the direction of Desmond Hodges, the Committee became responsible for initiating a major programme of repair and rehabilitation of the buildings. In 1995 both Edinburgh New Town and Old Town were designated World Heritage sites by UNESCO. Similar work but covering this enlarged area continues and under the renamed title Edinburgh World Heritage. Zoë Clark is the present Director.

My first and foremost thanks must start with all the many clerks and secretaries to the garden committees, past and present, who gave me access to their archival material and often went to considerable trouble hunting missing items or answering pressing questions. I would like to think that their spirit of benevolent stewardship lives on in this book, for certainly without their willing support there would have been no book. Equally helpful and appreciated was the interest shown by many members of the garden committees, and I hope that the discoveries made during my researches will enhance their enjoyment of the gardens and indeed allow everyone to better appreciate how precious and valuable they are.

In addition, the archives of the George Heriot Trust and those of the City of Edinburgh Council produced a lot of valuable material. Over the years I have had contact with many staff in both institutions and remember with pleasure the periods spent working there and making my various discoveries. Memories of a very helpful Mr Smiley at the George Heriot Trust and the useful comments and pondering of Dr Walter Makey, late City Archivist, remain rooted in my mind. Their successors have been equally accessible, and my sincere thanks go to both organisations and especially to Arnott Wilson (now archivist of Edinburgh University Special Collections), Richard Hunter, his successor as City Archivist, and Elspeth Third, City Development Department.

Further information has been culled from a wide range of sources including the Edinburgh Royal Botanic Garden Library (Mr Matthew, Dr Colin Wills and Jane

Hutcheon have all been most supportive); the National Library of Scotland; Edinburgh University Library; the Royal Commission on the Ancient and Historical Monuments of Scotland, including the National Monuments Record of Scotland; the Scottish National Services Library (now the National War Museum); the Royal College of Physicians Library; the National Galleries of Scotland; Huntly House Museum (now the Edinburgh Museum); the Writers Museum; the City Art Centre (where the efforts of Ian O'Riordan and David Paterson to track down possible illustrations have been most helpful); Edinburgh World Heritage and particularly the support of all the staff both past and present; the National Trust for Scotland; the Cockburn Association (the Edinburgh Civic Trust); the Walker Trust; the Culture and Leisure Department, City of Edinburgh Council; the Hopetoun Trust archives; Victoria and Albert Museum archives; the Witt Library, the Courtauld Institute; and the Sir John Soane's Museum, London. In all these places I have been met by helpful and interested staff. I have left for special mention the Edinburgh Room attached to the Edinburgh City Library where I have spent many fulfilling hours poring over old newspapers and other items. How fortunate Edinburgh is to have such riches so readily to hand, and meted out by a most dedicated, efficient and friendly staff. Thank you all indeed!

And to many other people who over the years have kept faith and given support. In particular I would like to mention Ted Ruddock, who supervised my early researches; Kitty Cruft, one of the first people I met in my early days of tracking down information, and formerly curator of the NMRS; Ian Gow, senior curator, National Trust for Scotland who looked through an early draft of the book and made encouraging noises; Andrew Fraser and Allen Simpson, who co-edited Chapter 7 which first saw the light of day as an article in the *Journal of the Old Edinburgh Club*; Roland Paxton, who generously gave me an early receipt slip for the West Princes Street Gardens and later made available some useful illustrations; Joanna Soden, librarian, the Royal Scottish Academy, who tracked down some interesting material about the artist Andrew Wilson; Pat Crichton, archivist of the Hopetoun Trust who opened the door to more discoveries regarding this same artist; Helen Smailes, Assistant Keeper, National Galleries of Scotland, who made useful comment about some teasing queries regarding that same artist; Patrick Simpson, who alerted me to the diary jottings of his late uncle; John Scott, for allowing me the use of some old nursery accounts; Ann Hope, who produced from her bag on a Cockburn Society walk round the gardens some early printed matter relating to the Moray estate; the Earl of Moray for allowing me access to family papers connected with the Moray Bank Gardens; Dr Richard Fawcett for rescuing items relating to the Moray Gardens which were nearly lost in a skip and found a safer home in the National Archives of Scotland; Virginia Holt, who generously allowed me access to some old family photograph albums; Mrs Ann Munro and Mrs Winnie Wilson, who first tamed my writings in my pre-literate computer days; my friends in the Scottish Garden History Society for encouragement, and likewise to those past and present in the Royal Caledonian Horticultural Society. To the 'girls' of coffee evening fame who over many years have given cheerful support: Margaret Veitch, Rosemary Flemming, Maureen McLennan, Alison Calder, Alison Williams, Helen Cook, Celia Foley and Caroline Bryce. And when the chips were really down I have to thank most sincerely David Flemming and Jim Goodfellow who helped avert various Apple Mac crises.

I must also mention the many groups and organisations who over the years have invited me to talk to them on the subject of the Edinburgh New Town gardens. Although sometimes requiring fortitude to bestir myself on a cold miserable winter's evening, the effort has always proved worthwhile, helping to keep the topic alive and even on occasion producing fresh snippets of information. The audiences' delight and interest at discovering unknown facets about Edinburgh's history provided the impetus to see the material through to publication.

And to John Tuckwell, my publisher, I owe much. Long ago he saw the potential for a book, and although the vagaries of publishing caused delays and setbacks, along with my own snail's pace at converting a thesis into more readable book form, he never wavered in that belief. His wife, Val, has been equally supportive. But time moves on and now Tuckwell Press has been merged with Birlinn: for the final push I am indebted to the latter and to the very helpful Andrew Simmons. Last, but by no means least, I would like to thank my husband, John Byrom, for his several useful comments and ideas: the competitive edge has proved a driving force of benefit to us both! I would also like to acknowledge the grant received from the Social Science Research Council, which helped to finance the initial stages of the research and thereby set the ball rolling, and to Edinburgh World Heritage for help towards funding the indexing of the book. The quest to find out but about the Edinburgh New Town gardens has taken me on a long and exciting journey of discovery which would not have been possible without the help and support of a great number of people: thank you all very much.

Every effort has been taken to establish ownership of copyright material, but should any reader have knowledge of copyright not found or recorded this will be rectified in any subsequent editions.

Notes

1 *The Conservation of Georgian Edinburgh: the Proceedings and Outcome of a Conference organised by The Scottish Scottish Civic Trust in Association with The Edinburgh Architectural Association and in Conjunction with The Civic Trust, London*, edited by Sir Robert Matthew, John Reid and Maurice Lindsay (Edinburgh, 1972).

ABBREVIATIONS

AGM	Annual General Meeting
ATS	Auxiliary Transport Squadron
BOEC	Book of the Old Edinburgh Club
DNB	*Dictionary of National Biography*
ECA	Edinburgh City Archives
ECL	Edinburgh City Libraries
ENTCC	Edinburgh New Town Conservation Committee (now Edinburgh World Heritage)
EPL	Edinburgh Public Library
EUL	Edinburgh University Library
HHM	Heriot's Hospital Minutes
NAS	National Archives of Scotland (formerly Scottish Record Office)
NLS	National Library of Scotland
NMRS	National Monuments Record of Scotland
RBG	Royal Botanic Garden Library, Edinburgh
RCAHMS	Royal Commission on the Ancient and Historical Monuments of Scotland
RHP	Register House Plan
RSA	Royal Scottish Academy
TCM	Town Council Minutes
WRH	West Register House
WS	Writer to the Signet; the principal and largest body of solicitors in Scotland

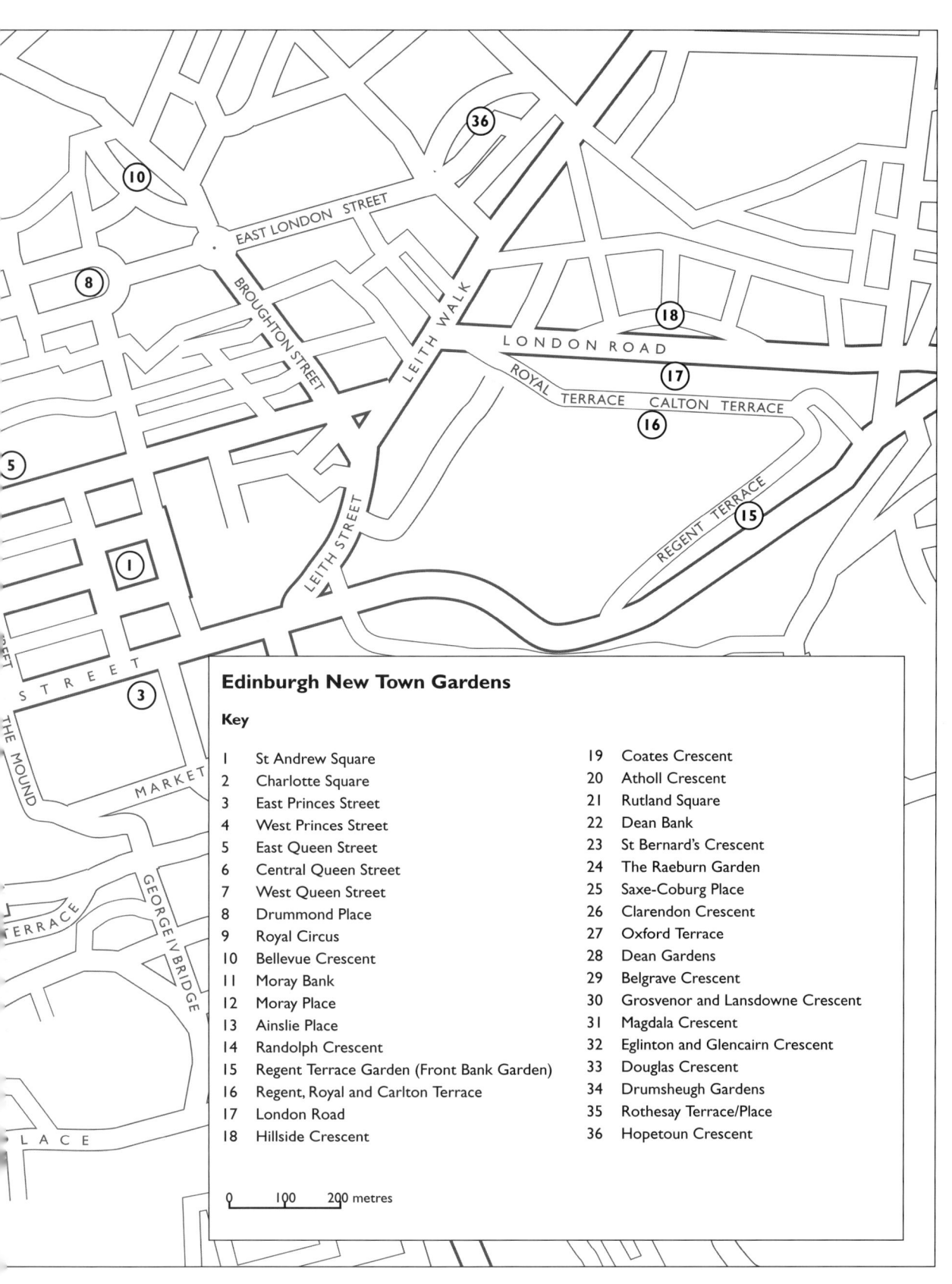

Edinburgh New Town Gardens

Key

1	St Andrew Square	19	Coates Crescent
2	Charlotte Square	20	Atholl Crescent
3	East Princes Street	21	Rutland Square
4	West Princes Street	22	Dean Bank
5	East Queen Street	23	St Bernard's Crescent
6	Central Queen Street	24	The Raeburn Garden
7	West Queen Street	25	Saxe-Coburg Place
8	Drummond Place	26	Clarendon Crescent
9	Royal Circus	27	Oxford Terrace
10	Bellevue Crescent	28	Dean Gardens
11	Moray Bank	29	Belgrave Crescent
12	Moray Place	30	Grosvenor and Lansdowne Crescent
13	Ainslie Place	31	Magdala Crescent
14	Randolph Crescent	32	Eglinton and Glencairn Crescent
15	Regent Terrace Garden (Front Bank Garden)	33	Douglas Crescent
16	Regent, Royal and Carlton Terrace	34	Drumsheugh Gardens
17	London Road	35	Rothesay Terrace/Place
18	Hillside Crescent	36	Hopetoun Crescent

0   100   200 metres

PART ONE

THE EDINBURGH NEW TOWN
PLEASURE GARDENS

CHAPTER 1

AN INTRODUCTION TO
THE NEW TOWN GARDENS

Leaving Queen Street behind, and passing northwards, we reach the second New Town, which is separated from the former by a series of beautiful gardens, extending nearly a mile in length. We cannot pass this great embellishment of the city, without some complimentary notice. The eastern division has been, for several years, laid out and planted with shrubberies, and has now attained considerable perfection; but the two divisions to the west are of comparatively recent date, and cannot be considered as seen at present to advantage. In the former, where, we understand, it is absolutely possible to lose one's self, evening fêtes are occasionally held; and as the gardens are only patent to the respectable inhabitants of the neighbourhood, a degree of harmony and freedom has hitherto characterised every such occasion. Scarcely any thing could exceed the brilliancy of such a scene – lights hung upon the trees amidst the flowers – festive groups of ladies passing lightly to and fro – and transient glimpses, occasionally caught, of the splendid houses around – the whole forcibly reminding the spectator of Moore's description of the gardens and palaces of Normahaul. All the gardens are laid out in the landscape style, with labyrinthian walks, which are the constant and favourite promenade of those privileged with a right of entry; and the whole is open to at least the sight of the public, on account of the inequalities of the ground, and the inclosures being of the kind called invisible. So large a space allotted to pleasure-grounds is certainly unusual in populous cities, and cannot fail to impress strangers with an high opinion of the very peculiar general character of Edinburgh. In this singular city – instead of what is common in all others, a dense unvaried assemblage of mere streets – we have, upon the one hand, projected into the midst of the traveled and crowded ways of men, mountainous places, never yet touched by human foot – and upon the other, we see, as it were, brought up to the very door of artificial existence, refreshing and unfailing supplies of the primitive commodities of nature.

Robert Chambers, 1825[1]

With only one of the three Queen Street Gardens approaching any semblance of maturity, the view across them nevertheless sparked an excited reaction from Robert Chambers when writing in 1825. They caused him to reflect on the very special qualities of Edinburgh. Here was a city not only rich with 'mountainous places' of wilderness character, but nature albeit in somewhat tamer form and by man's devising brought to the very doorstep of Georgian daily living: in Chambers' opinion a place without rivals and a veritable feast of *rus in urbe*. The balancing and harmonising of man with nature, so critical an element in the Scottish Enlightenment's philosophy, was here for all to see and marvel at. Nearly two hundred years on, Edinburgh's many pleasure grounds have become an established part of the landscape we associate with the Georgian New Town and its subsequent additions. Known by their individual names or more generally referred to as the New Town Gardens, they remain for the most part communally owned by the proprietors of houses surrounding or overlooking them.[2] But they are there for all to enjoy, either by surfing the eye over the canopies of green to the architecture beyond, or by savouring them more intimately by becoming a subscriber.

Their Uniqueness

Edinburgh's New Town Gardens are unrivalled. No other city or town in Britain or abroad has such a range or variety of comparable open space. True, the rapid growth of London during the seventeenth and eighteenth centuries yielded an abundance of town squares, each served with a central enclosed space. But very often these were poor dull affairs, slow to be exploited as green havens of retreat, and several over time fell victim to the incessant pressures for additional building land.[3] Other examples of contemporary Georgian developments in cities such as Dublin, Bristol and Norwich, and at fashionable resorts like Cheltenham, Bath, Buxton, Folkestone and Brighton very often included communal garden spaces linked with the surrounding housing; but not usually on the same lavish scale as occurred in Edinburgh. Even Edinburgh's near rival Glasgow, which was also growing rapidly in the eighteenth century with many elegant residences commissioned by its rich merchants, produced squares that were smaller and narrower; often with a church in the middle instead of gardens.[4] Nevertheless all these centres, and London and Bath in particular, provided an important impetus behind the Scottish capital's own expansion and improvement, once the confines of the Old Town had proved too restricting.

European Examples

The Continent, too, was rich in new schemes famed for their elegant plans which harmoniously united residential terraces with broad avenues, central open spaces, and magnificent vistas. Indeed, one writer has asserted that London's first real square – Covent Garden piazza – was modelled or at least influenced by the sixteenth-century Place des Vosges in Paris[5] (the former Place Royale), a view adopted with even greater conviction by Stuart in his book on Georgian Gardens.[6] He traces a direct lineage between all the various Georgian squares in this country and the French example. But in one respect the Place des Vosges differed significantly. Its central space was never intended as a semi-private garden area, but as a communal thoroughfare suitable for public gatherings and entertainments. Place Bellecour (formerly the Place Royale) in Lyon affords another comparable example. In a similar manner, the Italian piazza and German platz were fashioned as hard, formalised spaces, outwith the control of the surrounding residents who exercised no presumptive rights or responsibilities over them. The gentler British climate, coupled with the more cultivated taste for *rus in urbe*, helped to produce this distinctive variation; and nowhere was it adopted to finer advantage than in Edinburgh.

Place Bellecour, formerly the Place Royale, Lyon, is one of the largest squares in Europe: a hard-surfaced area open to pedestrians. A statue of Louis XIV stands at the centre. (C. Byrom)

Their Extent, Size and General Development

A little more than one-tenth of the area of the New Town consists of open space originally formed as private pleasure ground, ranging in size from the West Princes Street Gardens (32 acres (12.8 ha)) and Regent Gardens (12 acres (4.8 ha)) to the smaller strips and squares such as Saxe-Coburg Place (0.6 acres (0.24 ha)) and the diminutive Rutland Square (0.35 acres (0.12 ha)). Half in fact are under one acre (0.4 ha), with the rest divided almost equally between those from 1–3 acres (0.4–1.2 ha), and those over 3 acres (1.2 ha). Their creation, like that of the New Town itself, was greatly helped by being on land mostly owned by one body, namely the Heriot's Hospital (George Heriot Trust).[7] The Trust initially sold off a substantial portion to the Town Council with whom they were closely associated, but later themselves became involved in considerable land development. This made possible large-scale coordinated estate design, an advantage not shared by the southern capital whose own growth had been much more piecemeal.

The gardens were very much a product of eighteenth- and nineteenth-century neoclassical planning with its passion for order and symmetry characteristic of the age of reason and enlightenment. James Craig's (1739–95)* approved design for the first New Town reflected this influence. He produced a unified scheme on a grand scale, with long impressive vistas, broad streets and elegant squares; but in addition a considerable area was left free of all building, and devoted to garden ground intended for embellishment.

In this kind of grand design, individual private gardens attached to these Georgian town houses were usually by necessity very modest in size, quite frequently awkwardly shaped and often overshadowed. At best they provided a fairly restricted space, usually occupied with a central lawn, an outer footpath and with flower and shrub beds positioned against the boundary walls. Their use was mostly limited to clothes-drying and occasional children's play: the redoubtable Mrs Fletcher, for example, removed from 20 Queen Street to 51 North Castle Street in 1804, 'for the sake of additional house room and a larger back green as playground for the children'.[8] Even so the private gardens did allow a pleasant

* His date of birth of 1744 has now been established as incorrect; see *DNB*.

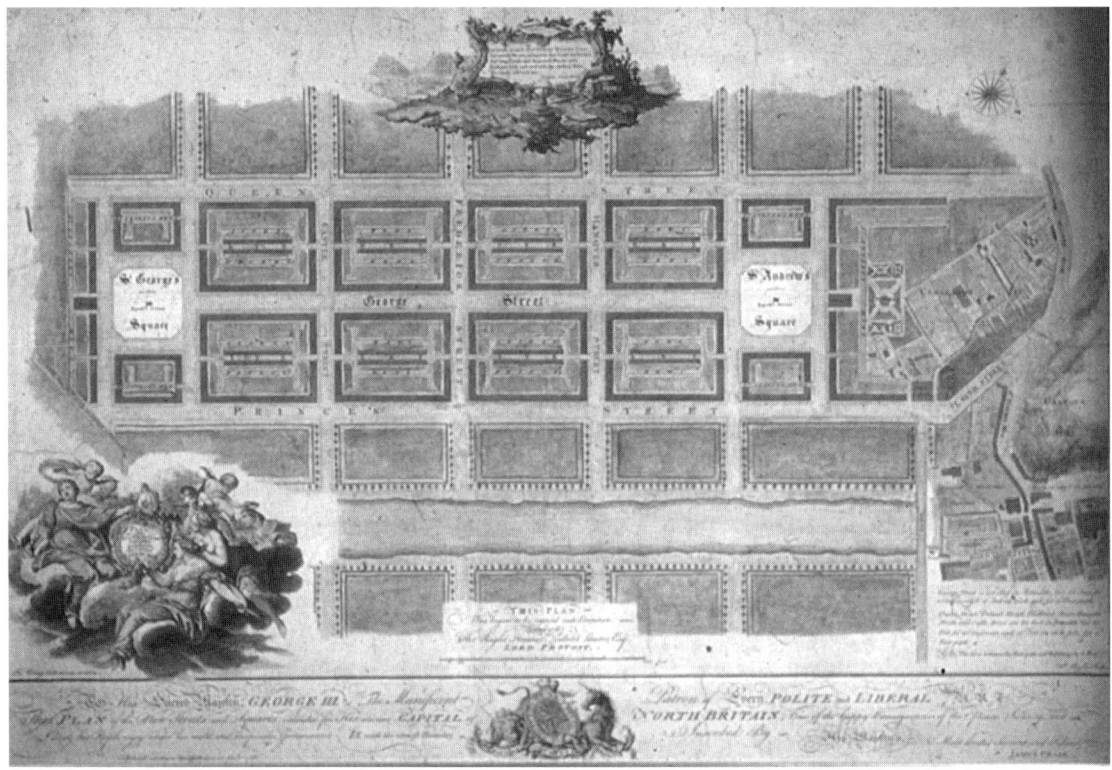

Plan of the New Town, Edinburgh, drawn by James Craig and engraved by P. Begbie, 1768. The two octagonal shaped squares at either end appear as bare spaces apart from a central equestrian statue. A wide band of formal parkland divided by tree-lined avenues is shown to the north and south: an early hint of the Princes Street and Queen Street Gardens although on land outwith the competition boundaries. (ECL)

and peaceful buffer to the more private rooms at the rear. In contrast the public rooms to the front of the house (the dining room usually situated on the ground floor with the drawing room above) were carefully positioned to face onto open squares, broad main streets and centrally placed gardens, thus providing a subtle balance between the bustle of street activities with refreshing glimpses of trees and greenery beyond. The surrounding open spaces were indeed seen as supplying the necessary light, ventilation and air, together with adequate opportunities for outdoor exercise and recreation: all supposedly essential safeguards for health and well-being, after the cramped living conditions of the Old Town. Such estates were perfectly acceptable to a population accustomed to a more communal way of life, and not yet seduced or conditioned by notions of villadom.

The Relationship Between Buildings and Open Spaces

As far as we can judge from the published plans (and we now know that they went through various stages of revision), Craig intended his two main octagonal shaped open spaces –

The Edinburgh New Town Gardens

St Andrew Square and Charlotte Square – to be in the form of an ornamental place or piazza; or of their London counterparts at Grosvenor Square, St James's Square, Cavendish Square and so on (before their later picturesque embellishment). That is, essentially a bare open space, hard-paved or grassed, each containing one or more sculptured figures in harmony with the grandeur of the surrounding architecture and main public buildings on the central axis.[9] Later architects involved with further developments in the New Town also tended to treat the smaller open spaces in a similar formal manner: for example, Thomas Bonnar's plan for a fountain in the middle of Atholl Crescent; and William Playfair's design for the land north of Calton Hill, where the small crescents and squares were all designed about statues and other ornamental detail. Unlike the London squares, however, Edinburgh's garden spaces often departed from the ideas shown in the set plans and developed instead into gardens of a much more relaxed character, having about them something at least of the Palladian rural retreat.

James Craig's plan also included a wide band of formal park land to the south of Princes Street and to the north of Queen Street, although both areas were outwith the boundaries of the competition brief. These eventually became the Princes Street and Queen Street Gardens, but while Craig's plan helped promote their use as such, this was not easily achieved. A near bankrupt Town Council was tempted on several occasions to allow building along the North Loch. Without a great deal of effort and financial commitment from the New Town residents themselves, the land might well have disappeared. The ground fronting Queen Street was indeed first sold and subdivided into many different plots, and put to all kinds of uses. Although the Heriot's Hospital had stipulated that this land should be used only as ornamental garden space,[10] even so part of the ground became a clothes-drying green, another pasturage for cows and pigs, a further portion was made into a coal yard, and much of the rest left wild. It took many years of patient negotiation by a few far-sighted and dedicated individuals, and with all kinds of daunting setbacks, before the three Queen Street Gardens were formed and safeguarded under a private Act of Parliament passed in 1822.

Plans for the second New Town to the north of Queen Street evolved much more slowly and involved a great many individuals including speculators, builders and architects. Details will be given in Chapter 7. Suffice it to say here that, as in the case of the first New Town, a public competition was held. Four entries were judged of equal merit and their authors, William Sibbald, John Baine, Robert Morrison and James Elliot – were given an equal share of the premium. Afterwards Robert Reid (1774–1856) was appointed to bring the several possibilities into one unified scheme. The plan finally adopted included two main spaces which were later formed into private amenity gardens, Royal Circus Gardens (originally intended as one circular space), and Drummond Place Gardens. Two gardens were subsequently added in front of Bellevue Crescent.

Further extensions to the New Town, including the ground to the north of Calton Hill, the Earl of Moray's Estate, several smaller developments and the Victorian additions on the west side, followed the earlier pattern of allowing generous areas of open space, for the purpose of being formed into communal gardens. Several of these later Victorian gardens occupied sites of great natural advantage, particularly those fronting the Water of Leith.

The Dean Gardens, Belgrave and Douglas Crescent Gardens were all carefully designed to exploit the character of the river valley and, by picturesque embellishment, formed into 'arcadian' woodland retreats.

The Age of the Gardens

The gardens were formed over a fairly long period covering about one hundred years, the first in the reign of George III and the last in the reign of Queen Victoria. Most followed the completion, or near completion, of the surrounding houses, but several were not set up until a few years later. Such an interval occurred, for example, in the case of the Queen Street and Princes Street Gardens. First of all the gardens was St Andrew Square which was levelled and enclosed in 1770. Charlotte Square followed, but although a substantial wall and a railing were erected in 1797, the interior was abandoned until seven years later. By

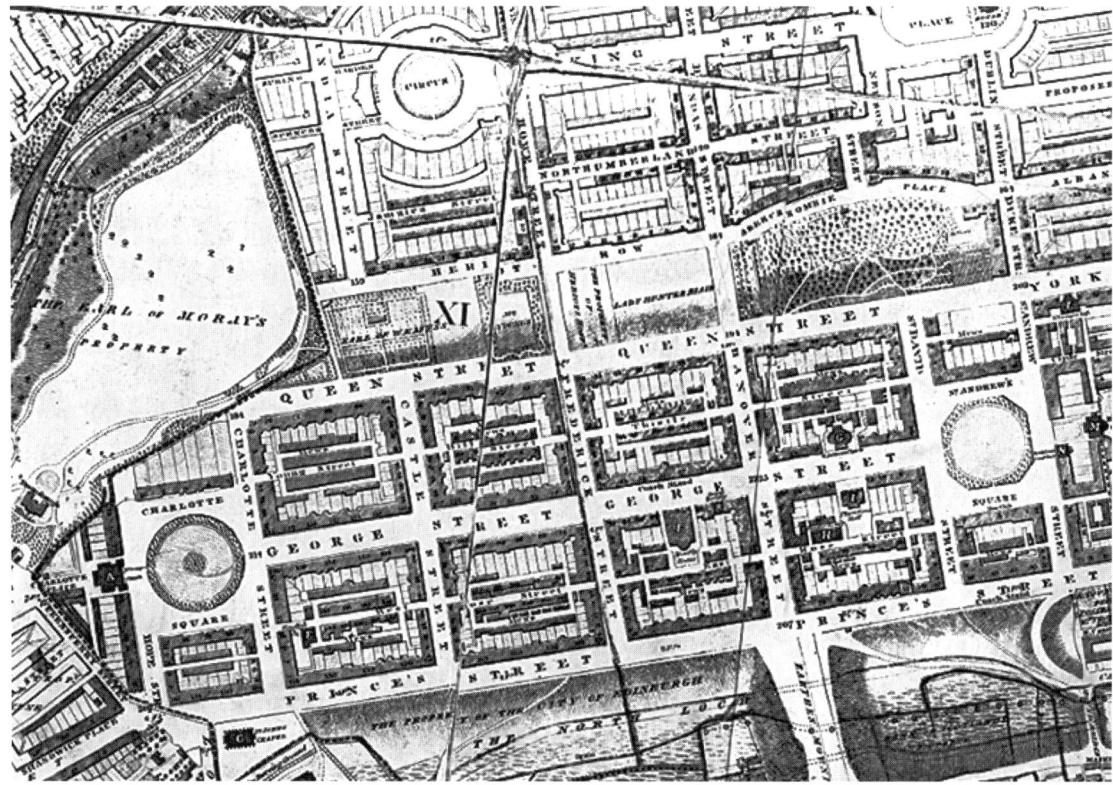

Kirkwood's plan of Edinburgh, dated 1817. Three pleasure gardens exist: St Andrew & Charlotte Square and the Queen Street Gardens (later extended and renamed the East Queen Street Gardens). The Earl of Moray's estate at Drumsheugh is in rural seclusion although the Raeburn property nearby at St Bernard's is up for development. Royal Circus and Drummond Place incorporate Reid and Sibbald's design for the second New Town.

then one of the residents, a military gentleman by the name of Colonel Dirom, had become so impatient that he summoned assistance from the Inverness-shire Regiment of Militia then stationed at the Castle, to have the ground levelled. Thereafter the garden remained without walks and planting until 1808 when a nurseryman, William Weir, began the work to an approved design produced by himself. Although the whole process had been slow and protracted it at least preceded the completion of the Square by several years. The continuing wars with France and fears of possible invasion concentrated minds on defensive matters rather than the niceties of environmental improvement. Ainslie's 1804 plan of Edinburgh indicates the minimal progress then achieved as far as the gardens were concerned.

Somewhat surprisingly perhaps, the East Queen Street Gardens (the first along Queen Street) were laid out as pleasure grounds before those of West Princes Street: the former in 1814, the latter not until the early 1820s when major drainage work to the North Loch enabled James Skene's tasteful plan to be carried into effect. Many of the other gardens were

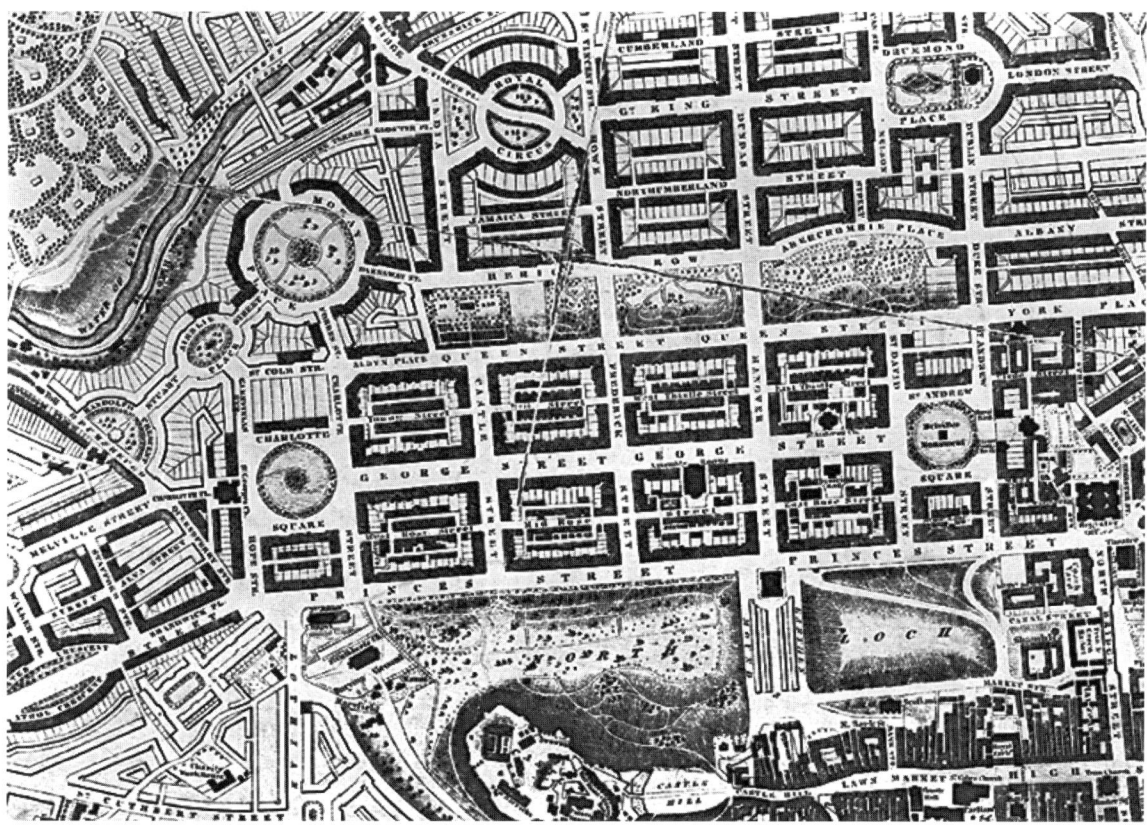

Lothian's plan of Edinburgh, dated 1825. Most of the central gardens are now complete with the exception of East Princes Street Gardens and the western end of the West Queen Street Gardens. Playfair's revised plan for Royal Circus is shown together with James Gillespie Graham's design for the Earl of Moray's land. To the south-west the Walker estate at Coates gets under way.

An Introduction to the New Town Gardens   9

formed during the development boom of the 1820s including the Central and West Queen Street Gardens, Drummond Place, Royal Circus Gardens, Moray Place Gardens, Rutland Square, St Bernard's Crescent, Saxe-Coburg Place Gardens and so on. Regent Gardens, adjoining Calton Hill, followed in 1830. By then the demand for new buildings had largely been met; if anything, there was a surplus of accommodation for the titled, professional and monied middle classes who had provided much of the original development impetus. Not until the 1860s and later was the New Town extended westwards, and several new gardens came into being. Amongst their number were the three already mentioned, bordering the Water of Leith. In addition several smaller ones were also created, notably the oval-shaped spaces at the centre of the two double-sided crescents (Eglinton & Glencairn, and Grosvenor & Lansdowne) and other gardens such as Magdala Crescent, Drumsheugh Gardens, Rothesay Gardens and Clarendon Crescent.

The Town Council's Involvement and the Role of the Builders

Although responsibility for setting up the gardens rested mostly with the surrounding residents, the Town Council on occasions provided useful encouragement in the form of financial help and other practical assistance. In the case of both Charlotte and St Andrew Squares, the Council contributed money for the unsold building plots in order to hasten progress; they also purchased a number of 'shares' in the East Queen Street Gardens at a time when pressure to raise money to buy the land was at its peak. Furthermore, the Council took an active role in promoting the extension of Drummond Place Gardens in the 1840s when the opportunity arose for the removal of the defunct Custom House. On a practical level, William Sibbald, Superintendent of Public Works to the Town, drew up plans for the layout of Charlotte Square Gardens, and designed the enclosing wall and railing. He it was who made the central area circular instead of octagonal as intended by James Craig. Similar professional help was also offered by another Superintendent, Thomas Brown, who in the early 1820s became involved with the design and detailing of the wall and railing attached to the Central, and West Queen Street Gardens, as well as Drummond Place.

In general, the relationship between the Council and residents was good; both sides were undoubtedly motivated by self-interest but also shared a positive desire to enhance the beauty and prestige of the New Town. But the Town Council's involvement with the East Princes Street Gardens was less laudable. This large and important area of open space had been declared the responsibility of the Council in 1776 for purposes of a pleasure ground. But acute financial difficulties made such a large undertaking virtually impossible, while the temptation to put the ground to more remunerative use became on occasions almost irresistible. In more recent times, and in the face of increasing pressure for city-centre car parking, the notion of tucking multi-storey car parks beneath several of the gardens has been mooted on several occasions; happily this is no longer seen as a viable option, and the gardens have fortunately been saved from mutilation.[11]

Rather like today's developers who provide landscaping around their schemes in order to encourage sales, several of the New Town builders adopted a similar approach in helping to promote the New Town garden areas. The builders in Drummond Place, for example, took a positive interest in having the central space established as a pleasure garden; likewise those involved with the Calton Hill scheme. Regent Gardens in particular owed a great deal to the efforts of one builder – William Henry – who for years was active on the garden management committee, yet never became a resident.

Ownership of the New Town Gardens

The more fortunate of the New Town residents had their garden ground made freely over to them by the developer, usually on condition that it was kept as open space, in good order and at their own expense. The first two, St Andrew and Charlotte Square Gardens, were both conveyed in this way; and the Town Council later transferred the central area of Drummond Place to the surrounding residents. Several other gardens, for example Rutland Square, Saxe-Coburg Place, the Moray Gardens, Royal Circus, Coates and Atholl Crescent, were held on a similar free basis. In comparison, the West Princes Street proprietors, in spite of committing themselves to considerable financial outlays for making their gardens, were never to own them, the land being mostly held on lease from the Town Council, although at a modest rent. When pressure mounted from the middle years of the nineteenth century for the gardens to become public, one of the most telling arguments was that by rights ownership of the land really belonged to the whole community. By the time the garden was re-acquired by the Town in 1876, Princes Street had long since ceased to be residential, and was almost wholly occupied by commercial, business and hotel premises; yet remarkably these gardens retained their popularity to the end. While the numbers of residents dwindled to practically nothing, outside subscribers eager to use the gardens had increased to well over four hundred.

The task of acquiring ownership was not always as simple or straightforward as the cases just described; the Queen Street proprietors, for example, experienced a long and protracted struggle to purchase the several plots of land which eventually were united to form the three Queen Street Gardens. They personally had to raise large sums of money to pay for the ground. But the impetus to improve and safeguard their property and surroundings never seems to have diminished. Four gardens – Drummond Place, Belgrave Crescent, Dean and Douglas Crescent Gardens – were all substantially enlarged during the course of their history by the purchase of additional ground

Apart from the West Princes Street Gardens, a few of the smaller ones have been taken over by the Town, for example, Gayfield Square (1887), Atholl and Coates Crescent (1951), and the southern portion of Bellevue Crescent (1965) under powers first granted by the Edinburgh Municipal and Police Act of 1879.[12] The Act allowed owners of any space set apart or used for ornamental or pleasure and garden ground, to enter into an agreement providing for custody and management by the Corporation. Frequently these gardens had presented difficulties in raising money for upkeep, and were dependent on too few subscribers. Most had fallen into a neglected state, and the remaining residents were happy to be relieved of responsibility for them. As all these gardens bordered major approaches into the city, the council had a vested interest in seeing that they were kept attractive and adequately maintained.

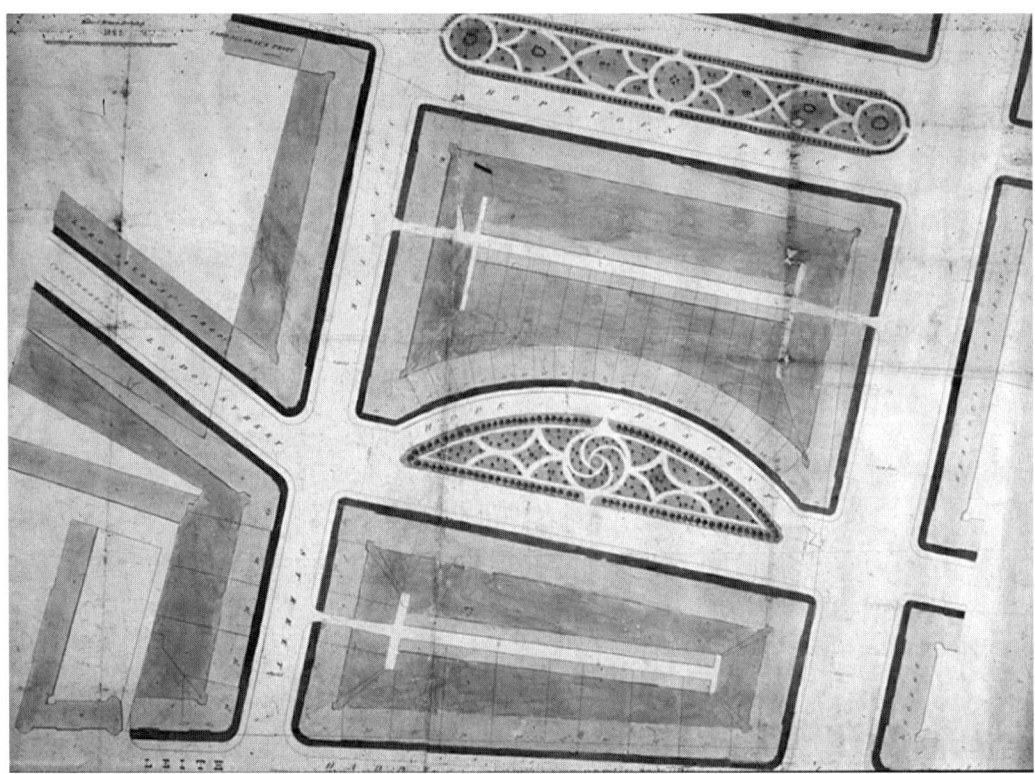

Robert Brown's feuing plan of 1825 for land belonging to the Hope family off Leith Walk, Edinburgh. Two pleasure grounds are shown, but only Hope Crescent (now Hopetoun Crescent) was formed, incorporating mature trees from the former Botanic garden down Leith Walk. (George Heriot Trust, Crown copyright © RCAHMS)

Some open spaces originally intended as private pleasure gardens never really became established as such, although they were formed into garden areas and used along similar lines. Their existence was generally precarious and they tended to limp from one crisis to another. East Princes Street, London Road and Hillside Crescent Gardens all fall within this category. Hopetoun Crescent Garden, off Annandale Street, is an even more curious case. Laid out as a pleasure garden in 1826 and enclosed by a wall and rail, it was formed on land which had previously been part of the Leith Walk Botanic Garden. When these gardens were moved to Inverleith Row, several rare old arboretum trees were found too large for transplanting. The Hope family, owners of the land, decided to form a crescent (Hope now Hopetoun Crescent), thereby safeguarding some of these unique trees. Other were added, winding walks were made and the rest grass seeded. But only a fraction of the crescent was ever built, and by 1865, with no one taking responsibility, it had become thickly overgrown. It remained that way until recently when, with the neighbouring area up for housing development, the ground was compulsorily purchased by the City. Now in the process of being upgraded and improved, while respecting the wildlife character the site has assumed, a wide range of tree species has been planted, partly to reflect its historic

Too far east of the main nucleus of the New Town, Hopetoun Crescent was never completed as originally planned. For most of its life the garden remained derelict. Acquired in the late 1990s by the City of Edinburgh, it has since been upgraded and improved as a wildlife reserve in conjunction with the recent redevelopment of the areas for residential use. (C. Byrom)

An Introduction to the New Town Gardens   13

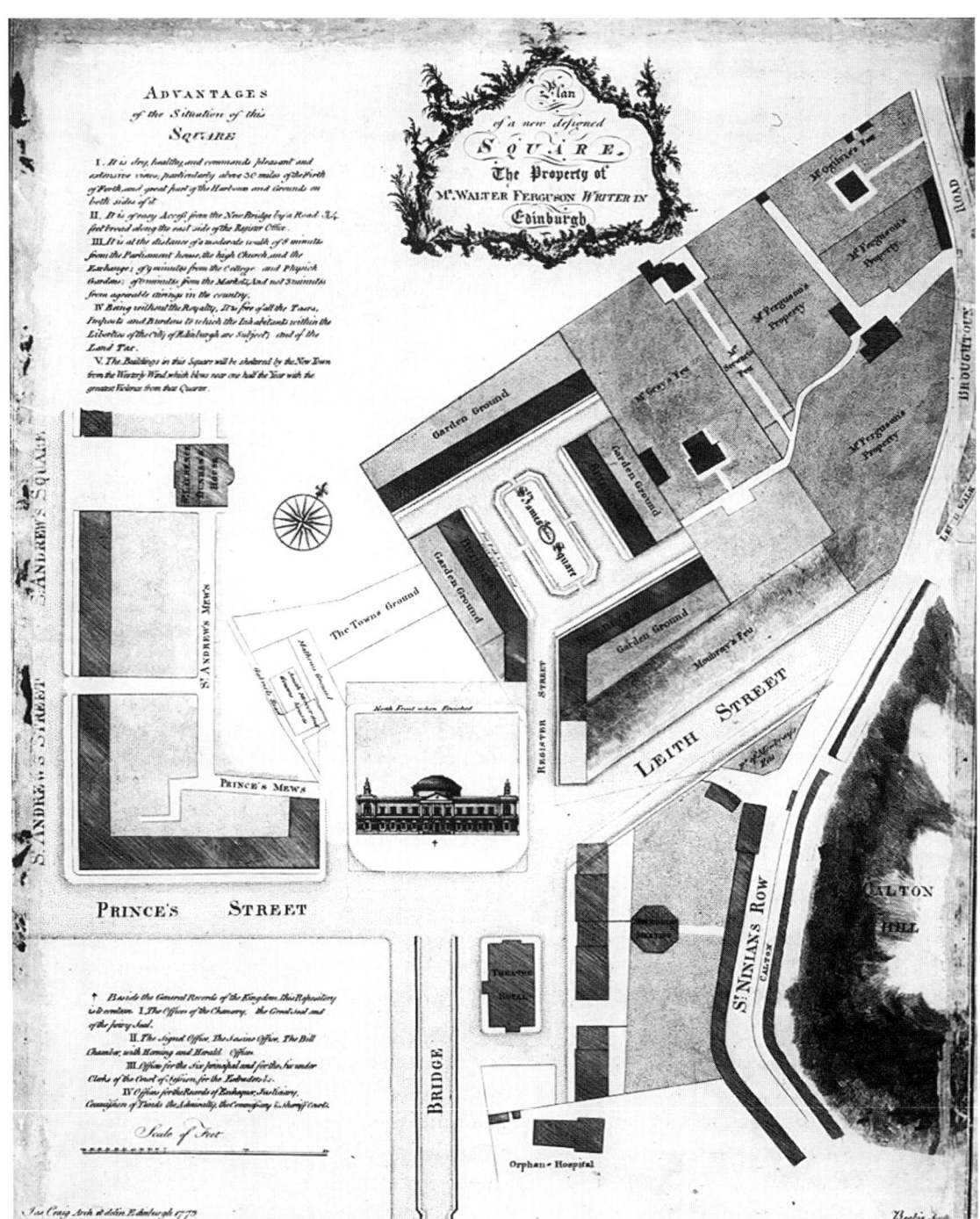

St James's Square, by James Craig 1773, and built between 1775 and 1790. (Crown copyright © RCAHMS)

Photograph of St James's Square before demolition. The central space boasts no planting apart from some care-worn turf. (*Scotsman* Publications Ltd)

connections.[13] Two gardens have disappeared altogether. St James's Square fell victim to redevelopment in 1965, and a circular plot formed at the centre of the Melville Street, Walker Street intersection in the 1820s vanished when the statue to the second Viscount Melville was placed there in 1857.

Availability of Nurseries and other Favourable Factors

Many of the New Town gardens were formed on ground previously cultivated as rich farmland producing such crops as wheat, barley, oats and rye; Lothian soil being reputedly as good as East Anglia's. If one adds to this a fairly equable climate, a low average rainfall and readily available soil and spoil as needed (Edinburgh's builders were only too happy to find convenient dumps for material accumulated during excavation), it can be seen that the gardens benefited from certain inherent advantages.

They were fortunate, too, in being created at a time when the number of nursery firms was rapidly expanding; and nursery grounds containing a wide selection of flowers, shrubs and trees were readily available. Only five seedsmen/seed merchants are listed in the Street Directory of 1773–74, but by the turn of the nineteenth century they had increased to nine; several by that time calling themselves both seedsmen and nurserymen. During the following years the numbers went on expanding with 37 firms listed in 1879–80, reaching a peak of the 85 names in 1909–10.

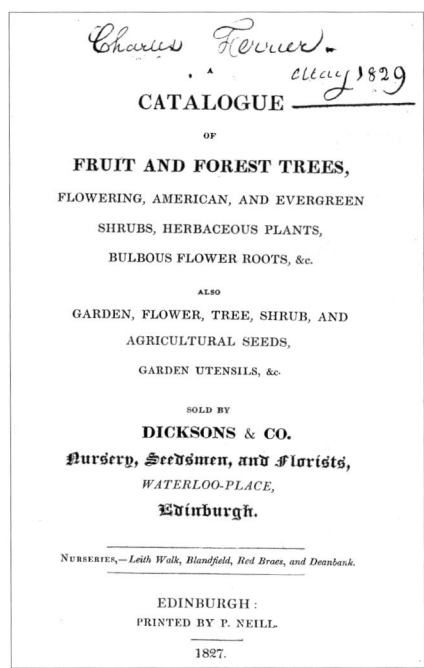

Title-page of Dickson & Co. catalogue, 1827. The largest and longest-surviving Edinburgh nursery firm who, for over one hundred years, occupied premises in Waterloo Place. (C. Byrom)

The largest and longest-surviving firm was Dicksons & Co., founded by James Dickson in 1782; they possessed extensive nursery ground in Leith Walk, at Blanfield, Redbraes, and at Deanbank and their shop was in Shakespeare Square before they moved over to Waterloo Place. Much of the New Town planting was supplied by this firm. Their closest rivals during the first half of the nineteenth century were James Dickson & Sons (not related), Eagle & Henderson, Thomas Cleghorn, John Hay, James Cunningham, Peter Lawson and Charles & John Peacock (rose specialists, Stanwell Lodge Nursery, Pilrig). All these names appear amongst the various garden minutes as suppliers of plants, equipment, gardening advice and labouring assistance. Names to appear later included Thomas Methven (Leith Walk & Stanwell Lodge), Downie & Laird (noted for their fine rhododendron collection), Daniel Mackay & Co. (Cameron & Echo Bank Nursery, Dalkeith Road), Ireland & Thomson (Craigleith Nurseries & Lynedoch Place), Cunningham, Fraser & Co. (Comely Bank), David King (Osbourne Nursery, Corstorphine Road) and J & A. Seth (Morningside Nurseries).

Nurseries had of course prospered with the introduction of many new plant species particularly after the Napoleonic Wars in 1804. Plants were brought home from every corner of the earth during the course of Britain's worldwide naval activity and seaborne trade: wisteria, peonies, roses and chrysanthemums from China; dahlias from Mexico; fuchsias from Central America and conifers from North America to name but some. Many of these were grown by Dicksons & Co. Their nursery, for example, propagated and sold more than 5,000 plant species,[14] including over 500 varieties of roses. The rarest and most tender of these plants required more sophisticated garden techniques for their nurture than

Henry Raeburn's portrait of Dr Andrew Duncan senior. Apart from his medical activities he was an enthusiastic horticulturalist and became known as 'the father' of the Caledonian Horticultural Society: several of whose members became involved with the New Town gardens. (Royal College of Physicians)

could be afforded by the pleasure grounds, and were in any case inappropriate for this type of garden. Nevertheless the attendant upsurge of interest in plants and gardens made this a propitious time for the creation of new open spaces.

Also of importance was the formation of the Caledonian Horticultural Society in 1809, following in the wake of its southern counterpart, the Horticultural Society of London (later the Royal Horticultural Society) and bringing together 'skilful professional gardeners and zealous amateurs'. The Society rapidly grew in size and influence under its enthusiastic Vice-President Dr Andrew Duncan the Elder (1744–1828), Professor of the Theory of Medicine at Edinburgh University. He was a significant force behind the setting-up of the Society's own Experimental Garden in the early 1820s next to the Botanical Gardens at Inverleith. Before then, some of their horticultural experiments had been carried out in the Earl of Wemyss's private garden in Queen Street, prior to them becoming the West Queen Street Gardens.[15] The Horticultural Society attracted a wide range of enthusiasts from many different backgrounds. William Playfair, Robert Reid, Sir Walter Scott, Henry Raeburn, Francis Jeffrey, Henry Cockburn, Rev John Thomson, Gilbert Innes of Stow, Alexander Henderson, Henry Jardine, Sir William Forbes and Robert Stevenson, for example, all became members. But the Society boasted many other eminent citizens on its lists, and several of the New Town proprietors connected with the gardens were also members including Wiliam Bell, first clerk to the Queen Street Gardens. Many of the office-bearers such as Patrick Neill, William and James McNab and John Hay went on to give advice on several of the New Town Gardens. Another to hold office was Walter Nicol (1769–1811) who was elected first joint secretary with Patrick Neill. Nicol had the reputation of being the best practical writer on Scottish gardening and his legacy of reference books covering kitchen, villa and town gardens remained popular and in demand for several years after his death.[16] The quarterly meetings of the Society held in the Physicians' Hall in George Street – the building designed by James Craig – provided a common forum for those interested in gardening and a useful means of becoming acquainted with key people in the horticultural world.

The Formation and Design of the Gardens

The layout of the smaller pleasure grounds tended to favour a formalised and symmetrical design of a rather stereotyped nature, not dissimilar, but on a larger scale, to the style adopted by many of the private gardens to the rear of the dwellings: that is, having an outer belt of trees and shrubs (to provide both privacy and shelter), a peripheral footpath, and the remaining area grassed. Usually the central space featured a group of specimen trees, a shrubbery or even ornamental flower plots and crossed by footpaths connecting with the various garden entrances. The gardens attached to St Andrew and Charlotte Square, Drummond and Saxe-Coburg Place, Bellevue, Atholl and Coates Crescent, Moray Place and the several smaller Victorian gardens all followed this pattern, and were well within the competence of the local nursery firms called upon to level, lay out and plant the garden spaces.

Divisions between gardeners, nurserymen and garden designers were vague at this time and frequently overlapped. As late as 1839 John Claudius Loudon was observing in the *Gardener's Magazine* that: 'both in England and Scotland it is customary for nurserymen to give in plans for the laying out of gardens, building structures etc'.[17] In Edinburgh, John Hay (1758–1836) was probably best known for combining these several roles. His skills are to be found catalogued in an advertisement appearing in the *Edinburgh Evening Courant* in 1812, and reveal a versatile and competent man of parts. Headed 'Garden Designing' (useful and ornamental) we are told that he plans 'all sorts of hot houses, greenhouses and conservatories, as well as designs for parks, plantations, shrubberies, approaches, ponds, icehouses'.[18] Hay, rather like his predecessor Walter Nicol, tended to be associated with the narrower range of flower

John Hay was a versatile garden and park designer-cum-nurseryman as this newspaper advert of 1812 indicates. He appears to have been responsible for the design of the greater part of East Princes Street Gardens.

GARDEN DESIGNING,
Useful and ornamental.
SEED-SHOP, &c

JOHN HAY, Planner, and Seedsman, begs leave to return thanks to the Nobility, Gentry, and the Public and to inform them, that he continues to give designs of Gardens, plans all sorts of Hot-Houses, Greenhouses and Conservatories (some of which he has lately executed on a new and improved principle, such as that at Milburn Tower and Oxenford Castle); he undertakes and executes the work on moderate terms, and on the best principles, in which those errors are avoided that so often cause disappointment, and to correct which much time is lost and expense incurred; also designs Parks, and lays out Plantatations, Shrubberies, Approaches, Ponds, Ice-houses, &c. &c.; and besides having had long experience as a practical gardener, both in England and Scotland, he has designed and executed plans of several of the principal places in both countries.

J. H. has also to intimate, that he has moved his shop from Bank Street to a more commodious one, No. 55 NICHOLSON STREET, opposite the Riding School where he keeps every article good in the Seed line, Garden Tool, Watering Engines, Garden Chairs, Bass Mats, and all articles necessary for gardens, and furnishing for hot-houses.

N.B–Noblemen and gentlemen supplied with experience Overseers and Gardeners. None but those of known abilities and character will be recommended.

Edinburgh Evening Courant, 22 August 1812.

---

gardens, kitchen gardens and hothouses rather than with larger estate plans. By the time the New Town gardens were being formed he was in any case approaching the end of his working life. However, he was certainly involved with the formation of George Square Gardens on the south side of the city and with a part of the Queen Street East Gardens.

A more imaginative approach was possible with the larger garden areas. Fortunately this was recognised by a number of garden committees who were sufficiently enlightened to apply what they considered to be the best professional, and artistic, skills to draw up plans and designs for their pleasure grounds. Edinburgh in the early years of the nineteenth century was still a relatively small, closely-knit society, rich with artistic, literary and scientific talent, all of which could be tapped for help or advice. Indeed, many of the distinguished names connected with the gardens were themselves proprietors, or friends or associates of proprietors, and therefore readily approachable. Certainly this was so for the West Princes Street and Queen Street Gardens. The first garden mentioned was designed by the gifted amateur painter James Skene (1775–1864), a highly cultured man of wide interests and a close friend of Sir Walter Scott.[19] Skene lived at the west end of Princes Street and was much involved in promoting art appreciation in Edinburgh. It is more than likely that through him, Andrew Wilson (1780–1848), a talented landscape artist, and Master of the Trustees Academy,[20] became involved with plans for the Central and West Queen Street Gardens. Neither Wilson nor Skene had previous experience of garden design but both were regarded as gentlemen of refinement and taste, and their proven artistic ability was considered recommendation enough. Much of Wilson's plan for the two Queen Street Gardens has survived, but Skene's design for the West Princes Street Gardens has largely been superseded by indifferent municipal improvements.

Their advice followed the picturesque tradition of landscape improvement in which the natural advantages of the site were sensitively assessed, and the layout designed to subtly enhance and extend the appearance in an informal if not romantic way. Associated with the picturesque movement in the eighteenth century had been the belief that not only had roughness and irregularity of form a special aesthetic value (for example rocks, ruins, wild landscape in general) but also that the art of garden design should be closely akin to that of landscape painting, composing the landscape according to classical precedents. The works of Claude, Poussin and Salvator Rosa were greatly admired in this respect.[21] Yet few painters either in the eighteenth or the early part of the nineteenth century became involved in garden design, although curiously enough Edinburgh appears to have produced more examples than most, making these gardens even more special. One does not expect to find a miniature classical landscape at the heart of the New Town, but this was certainly the effect Andrew Wilson aimed to achieve when designing the two Queen Street Gardens. What he sketched and painted in Italy found reflection here in Edinburgh: a special bonus, considering so much of his artistic output has since disappeared.[22]

In addition to Skene and Wilson, Alexander Nasmyth (1758–1840) must be mentioned in this context. As a teacher (Wilson for a short time studied under him) and practitioner, he more than anyone was responsible for the enormous interest and prestige of Scottish landscape painting during the first two decades of the nineteenth century. Nasmyth helped to shape 'the actual landscape of Scotland to bring it more into accord with the ideals of the picturesque movement'.[23] As far as we know, although commissioned to carry out several landscape projects in various parts of Scotland, he never became directly involved with any of the New Town gardens. Nasmyth was responsible, however, for creating a most ornamental and charming eye-catcher which ultimately did much to enhance two of the pleasure grounds, namely Moray Bank Garden and Dean Gardens. Both share magnificent views of St Bernard's Well, the graceful classical temple based on the one at Tivoli and designed for his friend Lord Gardenstone in 1789. This small Doric building on the banks of the Water of Leith close to Stockbridge, 'thoroughly in keeping with the beauty of the surrounding scenery',[24] marks the site of a mineral spring first discovered in 1760. It has considerably enhanced both gardens, and in particular the designer of Dean Gardens, the architect John Dick Peddie, took subtle advantage of it. By creating a series of carefully placed terraces with connecting footpaths and steps he allowed promenaders many varied and picturesque glimpses of the well from different heights and angles.

For the remaining larger gardens advice was sought from a number of individuals from various backgrounds including landscape gardeners, horticulturists, architects and others, all of whom with one exception were Edinburgh-based. The exception was William Sawry Gilpin (1762–1843), the English landscape gardener and nephew of the Rev William Gilpin, essayist and writer on the picturesque. For a brief spell he acted as consultant to the Town Council for the design of the East Princes Street Gardens at a time when controversy raged as to what the true intentions of the City were towards this land. Nothing is known of Gilpin's recommendations although he was paid 12 guineas for his advice. He was succeeded by Patrick Neill (1776–1851), then a member of the Town Council, and he was made responsible for directing improvements to this section of Princes Street.

Neill was head of a large and successful printing firm, Neill & Co, which he had inherited from his father. But business interests came second to his lifelong passion for botany, horticulture and natural history. He was in fact a founder member of the Caledonian Horticultural Society and its longest-serving secretary. Sadly the amazing energy expended in having the East Princes Street Gardens formed and planted was set at naught when the railway was extended through the grounds in the 1840s, causing havoc and destruction (a little later his own house and garden at Canonmills were under similar threat). The challenge of redesigning the gardens fell to David Cousin (1809–78), the first individual to be known under the title of City Architect. Neill's later advice on the planting of Regent Gardens adjoining Calton Hill happily suffered no such mishaps. On this occasion he was ably assisted by Dr Robert Graham (1786–1845) then Keeper of the Edinburgh Royal Botanic Garden and Professor of Medicine and Botany at the University, in cooperation with William Playfair. Now the largest of all the New Town Gardens still in private ownership, its main structure remains largely intact and still retains the flavour of a gentleman's country retreat.

But the man to have the greatest single influence on the gardens was undoubtedly James McNab (1810–79), particularly during the middle years of the nineteenth century. McNab started his working life as an apprentice gardener under his father, William McNab, Curator of the Botanic Garden. Twelve years later he was appointed Manager of the Caledonian Horticultural Society's Experimental Garden at Inverleith.[25] In 1849

Patrick Neill, printer, anti-quarian and keen horticulturalist who served for over 40 years as Secretary of the Caledonian Horticultural Society. He is associated with the East Princes Street Gardens and the Regent Gardens. (RBG)

McNab succeeded his deceased father at the Botanic Garden and during his curatorship much was achieved, including the garden's enlargement, a new rock garden and palm house. In spite of a demanding job McNab continued to practise his other skills as plants draughtsman and author of articles on gardening, landscaping and horticulture. During the 1860s McNab wrote a series of articles for the *Scottish Farmer* under the general title of 'Our Town Trees'.[26] Each one concentrated on a particular New Town Garden (twelve were covered), and included a frank critique of their condition and planting, together with suggestions for improvement. Many of the gardens were by then approaching maturity and in need of major renewal and reassessment not so unlike several of the gardens at the present time. McNab's timely comments sparked a wave of interest and stirred a number of lethargic committees into action; under his careful supervision major improvements were made to a number of gardens including Queen Street East, St Andrew Square and Charlotte Square.

At this time too McNab was also involved in the formation of some contemporary New Town gardens, such as the Dean Gardens (the major part of which was laid out in 1868). He also advised on the planting and alterations to Belgrave Crescent Gardens when they were greatly enlarged in 1878. In the Dean Gardens he worked closely with John Dick

James McNab, Manager of the Caledonian Horticultural Society's Experimental Garden at Inverleith and later Curator of the Royal Botanic Garden, Edinburgh. He advised most of the New Town garden committees and had the greatest influence of anyone on the New Town gardens in the nineteenth century, and his mark can still be seen today. (RBG)

Peddie, both men having liaised on the major improvements to St Andrew Square Gardens in 1866. McNab's preference for 'broad spaces of well kept grass, with fine trees standing upon it' very much in the gardenesque style advocated by Loudon – a man he knew and greatly admired[27] – saved many gardens from the spread of inappropriate rockeries and florid bedding schemes which were then in vogue.

Many of the gardens had also become choked and cluttered with trees originally planted for quick effect, such as poplars and willows. McNab did much to encourage their systematic removal, thereby encouraging the freer growth of trees intended for more permanent effect. Likewise his frequently stated belief that a garden's appearance from the outside was just as important as when seen from within, helped increase public awareness and challenged management committees to take a broader view of their responsibilities. In one respect McNab was less successful. He regularly stressed the importance of each garden having a 'definite plan', not only to act as a guide to the original planting but also 'to indicate minutely the course of after management'. Successful results depended on constant attention to such detail, 'for by allowing any of the gardeners who happen to be employed to follow their own fancy a deviation from the original plan may be the result, which will neutralise the labours of years, and probably prevent the garden ever again assuming that artistic appearance which the promoters had in view'.[28] Advice that has never been bettered, but only rarely, if ever achieved.

The Involvement of Architects

One or two architects' names have already appeared in connection with the design of, or later improvements to, the New Town gardens. It would be true to say that the majority of Edinburgh's architects were involved in one way or another with the pleasure grounds. In several instances their contribution was substantial. William Playfair, for example, was associated with several of the garden areas. His proposals for the East Princes Street Gardens in 1826 proved a useful basis for their subsequent development; he appears to have been much involved with the design of the Regent Gardens and certainly the laying out of the London Road ones. The redesign of the lower reaches of West Princes Street Gardens to reduce and disguise the passage of the railway was another of his achievements. Playfair was influenced by his mentor William Stark (1770–1813), who had emphasised the importance of keeping a balance between the natural and the man-made. Stark's comments on the need to treat the eastern flanks of Calton Hill with extreme care were largely responsible for their ultimate development as a garden area.

Two other architects to have close associations with certain New Town gardens were David Cousin (1809–78), City Architect from 1847, and John Dick Peddie (1824–91), who was in partnership with Charles Kinnear. Cousin became involved in the layout of many of Edinburgh's cemeteries and adopted a similar rather formal approach when redesigning the East Princes Street Gardens in 1849. Peddie worked closely with McNab in revitalising the St Andrew Square Gardens in the 1860s, and forming the first part of the Dean Gardens in 1868. But as the following chapters will reveal, many other well-known architects came to be associated with the gardens in one capacity or another, including serving on the garden management committees. If one also includes all the architects who provided communal pleasure gardens as an integral part of their plans, then the list becomes long indeed.

·

The Planting of the New Town Gardens

Early in 1803 John Claudius Loudon, then a young man of twenty, left Edinburgh for London where he began a successful career as a landscape gardener and a prolific writer on gardening horticulture and landscape. Almost immediately his attention seems to have been drawn to the parlous state of many of the London squares whose layout and planting appeared so 'miserably deficient' as to provoke him to write to the *Literary Journal*. This letter (his first-ever publication) was more in the form of an essay and was headed 'Hints respecting the manner of laying out the grounds of the public squares in London to the utmost picturesque advantage'.[29] In it he criticised the monotonous character of the gardens, the incongruous mixture and lack of harmony in the arrangement of the planting and the inappropriate choice of plants, selected for exotic rather than enduring qualities such as good growth, beauty and fragrance. Loudon also found the gardens lacking in evergreens and without a balance of form and colour throughout the year. When these hints were written, only one Edinburgh garden (St Andrew Square) had been completed, so his cautionary comments came at an opportune time.[30] Edinburgh's pleasure grounds were, however, saved from the worst excesses of inappropriate and extravagant forms of planting by cost-conscious management committees. Having already spent substantial sums on having the grounds enclosed and levelled (and in some cases for the actual purchase of the land), they were careful to spend what remained as frugally as possible. Hence gifts of plants were always warmly encouraged and a keen eye kept for other cheap, or free, sources of supply.

Evidence from early garden minute books shows that generally first planting concentrated on the provision of trees and shrubs, with flowers and smaller decorative planting being added later. Most trees selected were broadleaf hardwoods, with lime – because of its compact shape, fine foliage and promise of fragrant flowers in the years ahead – the most popular choice to border the edges and line the grander terrace walks.[31] Other trees such as elm, sycamore, oak, ash, horse-chestnut, whitebeam, hawthorn, plane, birch and beech were all freely used and still remain the predominant ones in the various gardens. Smaller ornamental trees, particularly those favoured for their blossom, such as lilacs, laburnums and cherries, did appear, but not in great numbers. Conifers, and trees with variegated foliage, were rarely if ever used. St Andrew Square Garden shows the most marked change in this respect for it is now dominated by smaller flowering trees: a tendency which Charlotte Square was in danger of emulating until recent policy exercised more careful restraint. Willows and poplars were commonly planted initially to provide quick growth and shelter until the slower forest trees became better established. Lizar's view of Royal Circus Gardens c. 1825 demonstrates how successful these were in adding depth and height to what were essentially young and very immature gardens. A few gardens inherited planting which was already well established; usually this was carefully absorbed within the new layout and added greater variety than would normally be expected. Thus for a number of years both Queen Street East and Queen Street West Gardens contained a number of apple and pear trees: remnants of a former kitchen garden.

The outer edges of the gardens were usually planted with shrubs to provide increased shelter and privacy. Laurel, aucubas, privet and holly subsequently attained tree-like proportions in the absence of any consistent pruning and management. It has been the shrub planting which has suffered most from long-term neglect and caused most offence to outside observers. McNab was certainly critical of the dismal condition of much of the shrub planting, a criticism still valid today.[32] Decorative shrubs such as rhododendrons[33], flowering currants, cotoneasters and roses tended to be reserved for inner display beds but could also occur in other areas of the garden; while box, yew, beech and privet were all used as hedging material.

While the summer season saw families disappearing to their country estates, sufficient must have remained behind to justify expenditure on the herbaceous and annual flowers reported in the minute books, and from soon after the gardens were first formed. Details are often lacking as the choice was frequently left to the gardener. Hence Alexander Henderson, the nurseryman responsible for planting West Princes Street Gardens, was instructed by the management committee in 1821 to plant annuals along the borders, the only proviso being 'that you will have a considerable proportion of mignonette'.[34] Mignonette, with its sweetly scented yellow-green flowers, was a firm favourite and was planted in most gardens. Otherwise a wide selection of flowers, of varied colours and fragrances, seem to have been grown: wallflowers, roses, sweet williams, sweet peas, phloxes, delphiniums, lupins, carnations, pansies, Canterbury bells, hollyhocks, columbines, campanula, verbenas, calceolarias, geraniums, night scented stock, chrysanthemums, dahlias, marigolds, clarkia, nigella, candytuft, alison and others, all are mentioned at some time or other. Some gardens such as Moray Place and the Central Queen Street Gardens had their own hot beds to aid propagation of the more tender seedlings.

As the nineteenth century progressed, the number of flower beds tended to multiply, although as the tree canopy increased, conditions for growing became less favourable. Several new beds, for example, were formed in Charlotte Square Gardens during the 1870s to decorate the pathway leading to the newly acquired Prince Albert memorial; his arrival marked, as one writer has observed, the completion of the 'Victorianisation of the Square'.[35] The advent of bedding-out would certainly have added to this flavour. The proliferation of flower plots and other Victorian excesses was, however, kept in check by the advent of lawn tennis: the demand for large continuous sweeps of grass took precedence over the desire for floral display. Increasing labour costs (particularly since the Second World War) have forced garden committees to simplify maintenance as much as possible. For this reason, when the gardens were reinstated afterwards greater areas than formerly were laid down in grass. Today the subtle balance of grass, trees and shrubs has become one of the hallmarks and most admired features of the gardens.

Without their walls, railings and locked gates the New Town gardens might well have found survival during the early years difficult. Respect for trees, shrubs and other planting was by no means assured, and indeed vandalism appears to have been rife, particularly at times of public celebrations. George III's birthday on 4th June was, for example, notorious for wild jinks and drunken excesses and said to be 'one of the greatest school boy events of the year'.[36] The persistent destruction and wanton damage to planting on these occasions reached such proportions that the Town Council found it necessary to advertise stern warnings and harsh punishments, seven years' transportation 'to any of His Majesty's plantations in America' being the ultimate sanction for those found guilty.[37] Gardens able to employ one or more full-time gardeners had their planting reasonably well protected from rampaging intruders. But best of all were the pleasure grounds with resident

Newspaper notice of 1791 warning of stern enforceable penalties should damage be done to planting during the King's birthday celebrations.

By order of the Right Hon.
THE LORD PROVOST AND MAGISTRATES
of the City of Edinburgh

Whereas, for some years past, it hath been the practice of boys and others, to pull down or cut Trees, particularly on the days previous to his Majesty's Birthday, which is not only a crime severely punishable by law, but much and justly complained of by the parties injured, THIS IS TO GIVE NOTICE, That every person in whose possession Young Planting of Branches of Trees shall be found within this City, Leith, or other liberties, will be apprehended, imprisoned, and punished as the law directs.

And in order to guard every person against the consequences of contravening this Proclamation, the Magistrates hereby intimate, That, by an act passed in the 6th year of his present Majesty, entitled,"an act for encouraging the cultivation, and for the better preservation of Trees, Plants and Shrubs,"—it is thereby declared, "That from and after the 2nd June 1766, all and every person or persons who shall in the night-time lop, top, cut down, break, throw down,bark, burn, or otherwise spoil or destroy, or carry away any oak, beech, ash, elm, fir, chestnut, or any timber tree, or other tree or trees standing for timber, &c. or shall pluck up, dig up, break, spoil, destroy, or carry away any root, shrub, &c growing, standing, or being in the garden ground, nursery ground, or other enclosed ground, of any person or persons. shall be deemed and construed to be *guilty of felony*. And the Court by and before whom such person or persons shall be tried, shall and hereby have authority to transport such person or persons for the space of *seven years* to any of his Majesty's plantations in America," &c.—Of which all concerned are hereby to take notice.
Given at Edinburgh, this 27 May 1791.

The Edinburgh Advertiser, 31 May 1791

gardeners; West Princes Street, East and West Queen Street were able originally to provide round-the-clock surveillance. When most of the railings were removed during the Second World War the gardens became vulnerable to misuse, and this was one of the prime reasons for their re-enclosure.[38]

The Management and Upkeep of the Gardens

In the majority of cases where an area of open space was clearly intended as a private pleasure ground, the houses surrounding and overlooking it had written into their individual charters several clauses referring to the open space (feuing conditions). Usually these described the different uses permitted, the obligations for enclosing and laying out the ground and the arrangements for upkeep. Thus, St Andrew Square and Charlotte Square shared the same condition; and similar ones applied to the garden areas at the centre of Royal Circus, Moray and Ainslie Place, Coates and Atholl Crescent and so on. This was the simplest and most straightforward method. In some instances, however, the ground itself was made over to the adjoining proprietors by a separate charter as in the case of Drummond Place and Regent Gardens. These charters tended to be more detailed, and were drawn up after the developer had been approached by the new residents to form the space as an ornamental garden. Some gardens were set up under a Private Act of Parliament, namely the West Princes Street Gardens in 1816, and the three Queen Street Gardens in 1822. Both of these large tracts of land were made into pleasure grounds some years after the neighbouring houses had been built. A Private Act became necessary as no earlier provision for such use had been made. While coming within the framework of the Act regulating the Queen Street Gardens, the Eastern section – established earlier in 1814 – retained its original and unique shareholding system. Even today anyone is entitled to 'buy' one of the 140 shares whenever advertised for sale, and thus its members are drawn from a wider area. Some gardens – mostly those coming as an afterthought – were set up without any predetermined rules or regulations, and these have as a result experienced greater problems, especially financial ones.

The raising and collecting of money to fund the costs of upkeep and improvements has always been one of the important functions of management committees. Annual assessments have been based on a variety of methods including the rateable value of property, feu-duty rates, the measured front width of a dwelling (foot frontage principle), and on a standard flat rate for all property irrespective of size or position. Garden committees and their clerks/ secretaries have provided valuable continuity in the management of the gardens. In several cases clerkships have spanned two if not three generations, passing from father to son to grandson, and on some occasions from uncles to nephews. Many eminent Edinburgh citizens have been associated with the gardens, perhaps the one best remembered now being Henry Cockburn.

The legal profession's preference for the New Town as a place in which to live and work has been reflected in the composition of these committees, and has proved invaluable when dealing with complex financial issues, in framing and enforcing rules and regulations, drawing up contracts for garden staff, and at all times when litigation or some other major issue threatened the wellbeing of the gardens. Had this professional expertise been lacking, the gardens would not have survived or prospered as well as they have. For much of their existence the committees remained an all-male preserve, but this has slowly changed as in other areas of life, and particularly since the Second World War. In many respects, garden management committees were early forerunners of amenity societies, and their interests have extended beyond the gardens, and still do. For the most part, however, proprietors have been content to leave the running of the gardens to the willing few unless some controversial issue or crisis has arisen. And although initially some exchange of ideas, experience and even personnel took place between a number of the gardens, they tended thereafter to go their own separate and independent ways. And the same spirit of independence still applies.

There is no doubt, however, that in terms of actual upkeep the New Town gardens have been indebted to the humble, lowly paid and ever abundant supply of gardeners. Many gave long years of faithful service for a low but assured wage, a degree of independence, and job satisfaction shared by few of their contemporaries. Much of their labour was physically very taxing as no mechanical aids were then available, and the tools in use were often clumsy and heavy. The formation of the larger gardens relied initially on large squads of men to form the drains, level and mound the grassed areas, shape the banks, cut and form the footpaths and so on. Afterwards the appointed gardener was allowed occasional unskilled or semi-skilled help at certain times of the year – usually during the summer and early autumn months – when the demands of the garden were at their peak.[39] The days of plentiful cheap labour have long since vanished, although three of the larger gardens manage to retain a full-time gardener. But the majority rely either on the services of a jobbing gardener or on a contract with a nursery firm.

The Uses of the Gardens

The gardens were intended partly as a visual amenity and partly to provide gentle, polite outdoor recreation, for walking and taking air, for small children's play, for sitting in and for passing the time of day. They were originally the preserve of the privileged, well off, and well connected members of society, and the early regulations carefully excluded those of inferior status although nursemaids in charge of children were permitted. The bounds of proper conduct were always prescribed in the set of rules issued to each proprietor and were occasionally updated as circumstances demanded. These varied little from one garden to another, and indeed this was one area where exchange of information did take place. Even the best-behaved Victorian child once exposed to fresh air and the free delights of an open space was unlikely to 'carefully keep upon the gravel walks' as directed in some of the regulations; usually committees were sanguine enough to adopt a lenient approach by not enforcing the rules too strictly, and a lot was left to the discretion of the gardener in charge. It would appear that even the gardens of more limited size have had to cope with a similar range of demands as the larger ones. Saxe-Coburg Place at 0.6 acres (.24 ha) has, in its time, gallantly accommodated croquet, tennis, cricket and football. Rutland Square – little more than half its size – found sufficient room for badminton and tennis in the late 1870s. But for these smaller spaces such activities could only be sustained by closing the garden completely for certain periods of the year to allow time for recovery.

Some semi-organised forms of games such as bowls (West and East Princes Street, and St Andrew Square Gardens all had greens), pitch and putt, and more popular still, croquet were all played in the gardens. But the game to out-rival them all was lawn tennis, first introduced in the 1870s when a rubber ball, able to bounce on grass, and a mower which

EXCERPT from Minute of the COMMITTEE of PROPRIETORS of DRUMMOND PLACE GARDEN,
31st March 1823

There was read to the Meeting certain Regulations which are proposed to be observed by the Proprietors of the Garden. The meeting approve thereof, and appoint the same to be printed, and a copy to be given to each Proprietor; and they request that these Regulations may be strictly complied with

REGULATIONS

In order that the objects for which the great expense has been incurred, in laying out this Garden, may be secured, the following Regulations shall be observed:-

. *1st,* Each proprietor or his tenant shall have access to the Garden at all times; unless where the house is let as a hotel, or lodging house, such hotel or lodging house, and all other houses of a similar description, and shops, being expressly excluded from access to said Garden, so long as they are possessed as such. Boarding schools for young ladies are not considered as lodging houses, and are not excluded.

2d, Each proprietor shall be furnished with a key, having Drummond Place, and the number of his house, engraved upon it.

3d, No person shall lend or transfer his key upon any account; and when the house is let to a tenant, the proprietor or the tenant may have access to the Garden, but the proprietor and tenant shall not both have access thereto.

4th, No proprietor shall be entitled to transfer his key upon any account, nor lend it though he and his family are out of town.

5th, No servant shall upon any account be allowed to enter the Garden, except female servants having the charge of, and bringing with them the children of persons entitled to have access to the Garden, or children residing in the families of such persons

6th, Proprietors or members of their families may occasionally introduce into the Garden, but only alongst with themselves, persons who are not proprietors.

7th, Boys shall not be permitted to introduce into the Garden any of their companions who are not sons of proprietors.

8th, No person shall cut or injure any of the trees, shrubs, or flowers in the Garden; and all children shall carefully keep upon the gravel walks and grass. No clothes shall be permitted to be washed or dried. No carpets beaten. Nor shall any game be allowed, such as cricket, golf, football, bows and arrows, and the like. Birds nests not to be robbed, or birds in any other way disturbed or annoyed.

. *9th,* The Committee of Management shall have power to impose fines, not exceeding ten shillings, for the infringement of any of the Regulations, which shall be recovered by the Gardener, and paid over to the Treasurer, to be applied either towards the expense of the management, or otherwise, as the Committee shall appoint. And the Committee shall further be entitled to insist for payment of damages for repairing injuries done to the Garden.

10th, The heads of families shall be responsible for offences committed by their children or servants, and shall be bound to make good all damages done by them, and pay all fines imposed on them; and in the event of any children being convicted of a second offence, it shall be in the power of the Committee to exclude them from the Garden for a given time

11th, All persons labouring under, or lately recovered from infectious diseases, shall be excluded from the Garden until the risk of infection shall have ceased. The attention of parents is particularly requested to this rule, which, it is evident, must be strictly enforced.

Besides observing and assisting in enforcing the foregoing Regulations, heads of families are requested to attend to the absolute necessity of abstaining themselves at all times from cutting a single flower or shrub, or even asking the Gardener to do so, as the practice would immediately become general, and would counteract all the pains and expense which gave been bestowed upon the Garden, and would destroy every regulation for the ornament and management of it. The Gardener is strictly prohibited from complying with all such requests; and he is entrusted with the carrying of all these Regulations into effect. The heads of each family must consider the key to the Garden as under their own charge, and must not allow it to go out of their keeping in any way that may admit of a breach of any of these Regulations. It is requested of all the parties connected with this Garden, if they shall at any time witness any breach of these Regulations, that they will give immediate notice thereof to the Gardener.

It is expected that every person on going into the Garden, will clean their shoes
on the scrapers at the doors.

Dummond Place Gardens: an early set of rules and regulations, dated 1825. Most gardens tended to copy each other in respect of these, so there is a common similarity between them all. (Belgrove Crescent Garden papers)

could keep the grass short enough for the new ball to bounce on, were both developed. Tennis was an ideal game for the Victorian leisured classes to play at summer parties. It was also the first active game in which women could play in the company of men. Courts were marked out wherever sufficient space could be found. Queen Street East, for example, had four at one time, and Charlotte Square three. Clubs were formed with their own separate rules, and some of these were amongst the first private tennis clubs to be formed in Edinburgh.[40] Tennis continued to be a popular pastime up until the Second World War, but afterwards the cost of reinstating and maintaining the courts was usually beyond the resources of most committees.

Other forms of garden entertainment have included garden fêtes, and fireworks displays, usually to mark special events such as Queen Victoria's birthday and the occasion of a royal marriage. Also popular were musical parties, when military bands were invited to perform,[41] while residents and their friends gathered to listen or promenade. Nothing created such an air of excitement as the sight and sound of smartly uniformed officers assembled with their musical instruments. The West Princes Street Gardens were the scene of most performances and usually drew large crowds. Although none begrudged 'persons of respectability' gaining entry, this was not always easily determined in the heat of the moment. While policemen were usually commandeered to guard the gates and railings, there were sometimes outbursts of rowdyism and drunken behaviour. But the majority came to enjoy the music as the adjutant of the King's Own Regiment reminded the West Princes Street Garden Committee in 1853. He wrote suggesting that while his band played, 'nursemaids and children shall not attend as the former occupy all the seats and the latter by their gambols interrupt the harmony and annoy those who really wish to attend the music'.[42] Military bands also performed in St Andrew and Charlotte Square Gardens, Queen Street Gardens and Regent and Belgrave Crescent Gardens.

A number of gardens continue to provide successful venues for garden parties, fêtes, celebrations and exhibitions, often for charitable and worthwhile causes, and are open to the public. Garden committees have generally been kindly disposed to requests by outsiders for any appropriate activity requiring outdoor space not otherwise available. Thus innumerable children from local schools within the New Town have enjoyed fresh air within the gardens during mid-morning or afternoon breaks, under the watchful eye of a master or mistress. In more recent times Brownies, Guides, Clubs and Scouts have all on occasion been allowed access for summer meetings. And during the war years Home Guard Battalions, Cadet Corps and Auxiliaries made good use of the central gardens for training and drilling. Certain gardens are now taking part in the Scotland's Garden Scheme and the annual Doors Open Day, allowing access to residents and visitors wishing to look round them. And most gardens are only too happy for non-proprietors to enjoy the gardens by becoming annual subscribers.

Sources of Friction

The two most common sources of friction have never changed, namely older children indulging in over-boisterous and rough play, and nuisance from dogs. Minute books tell of occasional contretemps, with unruly boys running wild and causing damage to flower beds, trees and garden equipment. But for the most part willful harm has been kept under control. Evidence from diaries and reminiscences have, on the other hand, pointed to the scores of children who over the years have enjoyed the freedom for imaginative play and adventure afforded by these spaces. And all within the safety of a railed enclosure and the watchful eye of the gardener.

Dogs, however, have generated more debate amongst management committees than the antics of mischievous children, for the gardens have always been well used by dog walkers. Early regulations tended to exclude dogs but gradually these were relaxed to allow dogs on a leash, or at certain times of the day: all in the interest of controlling damage and dirt. Dogs remain a contentious issue, but most gardens operate bag-and-shovel facilities, hopeful that with increasing environmental awareness dog owners will take their responsibilities seriously.

But it would be wrong to end this chapter on such a mundane note. Edinburgh's New Town gardens have provided so much delight and so many havens of green, whether from within or without, that their value can never be adequately assessed or indeed fully appreciated. They are an integral and essential part of Georgian Edinburgh, requiring the same thoughtful care and protection as the surrounding buildings. The concept of a private outdoor space accessible to key-holders paying an annual subscription or key-rental is still valid, particularly when so much of the surrounding property has become converted to flatted residential use. Their future looks promising, with official recognition now being given to their historic and landscape importance.[43] The designation in 1996 of the New Town together with the Old Town as a World Heritage Site also brings prestige and fresh opportunities for a dynamic future to these parts of Edinburgh. Local involvement, however, must continue to be the bedrock for the gardens' survival and well-being. But as maintenance costs escalate (particularly in matters such as tree removal and renewal), financial support and professional advice will soon become increasingly necessary.[44]

Notes

1. Robert Chambers, *Walks in Edinburgh*, (Edinburgh, 1825) pp. 201–03.
2. This chapter is based on an article by the author, 'The Pleasure Grounds of Edinburgh New Town', first published in *Garden History: The Journal of the Garden History Society* (Summer 1995), Vol. 23: No.1, pp. 67–90.
3. E. Beresford Chancellor, *The History of the Squares of London*, (London, 1907).
4. See Charles McKean, 'Provincial Style', *The Sunday Mail Story of Scotland* Vol. 3, part 20 (1984), p. 828.
5. Steen Eiler Rasmussen, *London* (London, 1937), p. 166.
6. David C. Stuart, *Georgian Gardens* (London, 1979), p. 175.
7. George Heriot, jeweller and goldsmith; banker and jeweller to James VI, 1601.
8. *Autobiography of Mrs Fletcher* (Edinburgh, 1876), 3rd edn, p. 85.
9. The revised and finally approved design of July 1767 (now on display at Huntly House Museum, Edinburgh) shows two squares each with an obelisk in the centre, together with two statues facing along the axis of the central street.

10. The Town, and new proprietors along Queen Street, were in the first place given a servitude or right over the ground in front of their houses by a clause in their charters limiting the use of the land for garden or park purposes.

11. James Crumley, 'Parking the twist in the tail', *Evening News*, 4 February 1986.

12. *Edinburgh Municipal and Police Act 1879*: 42 and 43,Vict c132.

13. For recent information on Hopetoun Crescent Garden I am indebted to Richard Barclay, City of Edinburgh Development Department.

14. David C. Stuart, 'The gardens of the New Town', *The Cockburn Association (Edinburgh Civic Trust) Newsletter* No. 3, October 1972.

15. Byrom, C. 'Dr Andrew Duncan, Senior (1755–1828): Father of the Caledonian Horticultural Society', *Caledonian Gardener, Journal of the Royal Horticultural Society* (1999), pp. 9–14.

16. Walter Nicol's books were both well written and organised and gave practical advice based on his own experience as head gardener at Wemyss Castle, Fife. His publications include: *The Scotch Forcing Gardener* (1797), *The Practical Planter* (1799), *The Villa Garden Directory* (1809), *The Gardener's Kalendar* (1810) and *The Planter's Kalendar* (1812).

17. *Gardener's Magazine, XV* (1839) p. 215.

18. *Edinburgh Evening Courant*, 22 August 1812.

19. Two volumes of the Waverley novels were illustrated by Skene, and Scott and Skene together planned to publish a volume of drawings and descriptions based on the Old Town – Reekiana, but this was never completed.

20. Established in 1760 the Trustees Academy provided instruction for pupils who followed or intended to follow a trade.

21. For one of the best accounts of the Picturesque movement, see Christopher Hussey, *The Picturesque: Studies in a Point of View*, (London & New York, 1927).

22. In comparison, only one London square is known to have been designed by a landscape artist – Edward's Square, Kensington – by Aiglio in 1819.

23. David and Francina Irwin, *Scottish Painters at Home and Abroad, 1700–1900*, (London, 1975), p. 138.

24. Samuel Smiles (ed.), *James Nasmyth, Engineer; an autobiography* (London, 1883), p. 44.

25. Established in 1825 on a 10-acre plot (4.0 ha) adjoining the south side of the Botanic Garden, to which it was later joined in 1867.

26. A valuable and comprehensive record of the state of the various gardens during the middle years of the nineteenth century; for a full account of James McNab and his many achievements, see Connie Byrom, 'James McNab (1810–1879): one of the foremost scientific gardeners of the century', *Caledonian Gardener, Royal Caledonian Horticultural Society* (1997), pp. 44–52.

27. When visiting London, McNab nearly always tried to visit Loudon.

28. James McNab, 'Hints on the planting and after management of the Trees etc in Town Squares and Suburban Villas', *The Scottish Gardener*, 1864.

29. *Literary Journal* 11, No. 2 (31 Dec. 1803).

30. In subsequent writings, Loudon gave further advice on layout and planting of public squares.

31. Sarah M. Couch, 'The Practice of Avenue Planting in the Seventeenth and Eighteenth Centuries', *Garden History*, Autumn 1992,Vol. 20, No. 2, pp. 179–81.

32. See for example, an article written by David Stuart: 'Outdated ideas put terraces into the shade', *The Scotsman*, 17 February 1990.

33. Rhododendrons became a popular addition to the gardens as more new species were discovered.

34. Princes Street Garden, Minute Book 2, Minute 10, April 1821.

35. Quoted from Ian Gow, 'Charlotte Square Beautified', *The Architecture of Scottish Cities*, ed. Deborah Mays (East Linton, 1997), p. 87.

36. *James Nasmyth, Engineer* (op. cit.).

37. Powers of enforcement were obtained by an Act of Parliament passed in 1766 'for encouraging cultivation and for the better preservation of Trees, Plants and Shrubs'.

38. 'Edinburgh's Private Gardens: ownership and refencing problems', *The Scotsman,* 2 January 1946.

39. In general the rate of pay and living conditions for gardeners in the nineteenth century compared poorly with other workers. See Martin Hoyle, *The Story of Gardening* (London & Concord, Mass, 1991), pp. 48–9.

40. G.H.P. Alexander, *Histories of the Edinburgh Lawn Tennis Club*s (Edinburgh, 1933).

41. The bands mostly came from regiments stationed at the Castle, but also on a few occasions from Piershill Barracks.

42. West Princes Street Gardens, Minute Book, 6 September 1853, letter from Lt. Col. Trevor, ECA.

43. *An Inventory of Gardens and Designed Landscapes in Scotland* (A report to the Countryside Commission for Scotland and the Historic Buildings and Monument Directorate, Scottish Development Department, July 1987). The Edinburgh New Town Gardens are now included (1998) in an updated issue. A design and maintenance manual for the use of garden committees is pending under the authorship of Dr John Byrom.

44. Douglas Crescent gardens secured a grant from Scottish Natural Heritage in 1992–3 towards the cost of felling and replanting its woodland area and restoration of pathways.

PART TWO

THE TWO OLDEST GARDENS

CHAPTER 2

ST ANDREW SQUARE
2.60 acres (1.05 ha)

> For Louis and me the St Andrew Square Gardens, spacious green lawned, their privacy ensured by elegant iron railings, were bare of interest, for no child ever played in them. In the centre the fluted columns of the Melville monument seemed in our eyes to rise to endless heights.
>
> Eleanor Sillar, *c.* 1880s.[1]

St Andrew Square Garden, dating from 1770, has the distinction of being the oldest of the New Town pleasure gardens. Most of the earliest building took place in St Andrew Square, and by 1781 the Square was complete. It became a fashionable place of residence, rivalled only by George Square to the south of the Old Town.[2] Gradually, however, its character began to change. Many well connected families continued to live there, but by the 1790s the New Town had progressed as far west as Castle Street. Besides greater choice, there was increasing demand for facilities to match an expanding population – shops, hotels, banks and so on – which the Old Town no longer conveniently supplied. From 1800 onwards St Andrew Square became less residential and by the 1820s the change was quite marked. One citizen, for example, noted in his diary in 1825 how 'the great folks' were migrating westwards, 'leaving Princes Street, St Andrew Square etc. to be occupied by public offices, hotels, shops, lodging houses and the like'. This was the year when the Douglas Hotel opened at 1 St Andrew Square, later moving to Nos. 34 & 35; it became one of the most fashionable in the city and the place where proprietors usually met for their garden meetings. Three years later the Royal Bank bought No. 36, formerly the Excise Office and originally the home of Sir Laurence Dundas.[3] This signalled the way for other banks, insurance and accountancy businesses to follow. By the end of the century the square was almost wholly commercial and has remained that way. Not surprisingly the garden's fortunes have been influenced by these changes, and the function of the central space more open to debate. No early garden minute books have survived but, due to the public nature of the square, material from other sources is available.[4]

Terms under which set up

Both St Andrew and Charlotte Square Gardens were established under the same regulations specified by the Town Council, owners of the land, and included within each house charter. It was stated that the central area was to become 'a common property for the accommodation, pleasure and convenience of the several feuars around the Square', and to be 'levelled, and enclosed by parapet wall and iron raill'. Two conditions were made: first, that the space was not to be converted into a common thoroughfare or used for any other purpose; second, that once formed it was to be maintained by all the feuars paying 'annually or oftener as may be required a proportion of the expense which the majority of feuars with consent of a committee of the Town Council found necessary'.[5] These conditions still apply and have provided a flexible management framework over time.

First Attempts to Form a Garden

The first meeting of residents relative to the centre space took place on 29 March 1769.[6] It was chaired by Sir Robert Murray whose death two years later was marked by a special funeral concert by the Edinburgh Musical Society, of which he had been a Director. Several 'conversations' had already taken place with the Lord Provost and Magistrates, and this gathering was to authorise a formal proposal being made to the Town 'for Beautifying the said square'. Their submission was introduced with the comment that: 'It must be obvious to the council that the forming of streets and laying out of ground in the middle of the square will be of manifest advantage to the Good Town as well as to the feuars, as nothing can contribute more to the speedy feuing of what remains in the Towns hands'. An estimate had already been procured 'for inclosing the middle of the square with a parapet wall and Iron Raill, and Levelling of the Ground', following Craig's octagonal shape. The overall cost amounted to £750, which 'shall be more than sufficient' to carry out the work; any surplus to be used for 'further beautifying the ground'.

What the residents wanted was for the Council to advance money as and when needed, in lieu of plots not yet feued – about half the square – and for the rest to be contributed by the residents, allowing the work to begin 'on or before the 1st day of January next'. In April 1769 the Lord Provost and his sub-committee 'unanimously' approved of this arrangement, recommending its acceptance by the full Council. Co-operation was of the essence and the Council had nothing to lose. The railings were to be of plain design, four feet (1.22 m) in height and set on a parapet two feet (61 cm) above street level and with four gates; the whole painted 'a fine green'. Having the ground levelled was no problem as plenty of spare earth was available locally. Ainslie's plan of 1804 shows the interior with an inner pathway round the perimeter and the rest grass-sown. In 1778 the Council agreed to add 16 lamps round the rails 'to be directly lighted at the public expense' as 'it will much promote feuing in the New Town'.[7]

For some time afterwards the Town contributed towards the cost of 'dressing' the garden. Thus in 1773 the City Chamberlain was authorised to subscribe a sum not exceeding £4. Again in 1775 a little over £3 was paid to Robert Gullon, as the City's share of 'dressing, cutting and rolling'.[8] Previously Gullon had worked as gardener at Drummond Lodge, the former residence of George Drummond, ex-Lord Provost.[9] After their efforts to make the garden the residents could be forgiven for being critical of the Council's dilatoriness in completing the roadways.[10] The north side was not in fact causewayed until 1782, making access to the centre awkward. Nevertheless the garden provided a welcome escape for James

Boswell when visiting his father in the Square. Family matters were more readily discussed 'on the gravel walk' away from the rather fraught atmosphere inside the house.[11]

The Arrival of the Melville Monument

By the time of Kirkwood's 1819 plan the outer border had been tree-planted, the footpath made circular and the rest left grassed. This rather simple layout was soon to be enhanced by a massive ornament, which still remains its most distinctive feature – the Melville monument. Henry Dundas (1742–1811), 1st Viscount Melville, had been Lord Advocate from 1775 to 1783. He had also filled some important positions during William Pitt's administration, becoming one of the most powerful and manipulative politicians of his day: a man deeply opposed to reform and radicalism and therefore not without detractors. But the memorial had been promoted by a committee of naval officers set up in 1817 in appreciation of his considerable services rendered to the navy when First Lord of the Admiralty. William Burn (1789–1879), although 'the premier architect' of Greek revivalism,[12] was in this instance commissioned to design a Roman pillar, based on a fluted version of Emperor Trajan's monument in Rome. As with many public memorials born in a fit of enthusiasm, problems quickly emerged, including where the column should be put.

Various positions were suggested including the north-east shoulder of Calton Hill, Coates Crescent Garden and the central intersection of Melville Street (already suitably named) with Walker Street. Sir Patrick Walker, who had recently succeeded to his father's estate of East Coates, had been a staunch admirer of Dundas, and was particularly keen to honour his hero by offering a site on his land. Of the possibilities mentioned the most favoured was Melville Street, and the foundations were dug in readiness. But negotiations collapsed when Sir Patrick Walker insisted that he and his heirs should retain the legal title to the ground as well as to the monument. Such conditions were unacceptable for a public monument. After much bitterness and legal wrangling, the memorial committee decided instead to accept the unanimous and unconditional offer by the St Andrew Square proprietors for the central portion of their garden.[13]

Securing the Foundations

Many residents were concerned, however, about the safety of accommodating a pillar of such considerable height (136 feet (41.8 m)) and colossal weight. To allay anxieties, Robert Stevenson (1771–1850), Civil Engineer, was asked to advise on securing adequate foundations. Stevenson's main employment was with the Northern Lighthouse Commissioners and he is best remembered now as engineer for the Bell Rock lighthouse, and as Robert Louis Stevenson's grandfather. But he acted as consultant on several Edinburgh projects involving the New Town Gardens, for example, West Princes Street, the Moray Bank Gardens and the lands east of Calton Hill. Described as a man with a 'love of the picturesque', and an interest in horticulture (he was a close friend of Dr Patrick Neill) and member of the Caledonian Horticultural Society,[14] his association with the gardens must have afforded a pleasurable diversion. Stevenson made no charge for his advice, but his recommendations[15]

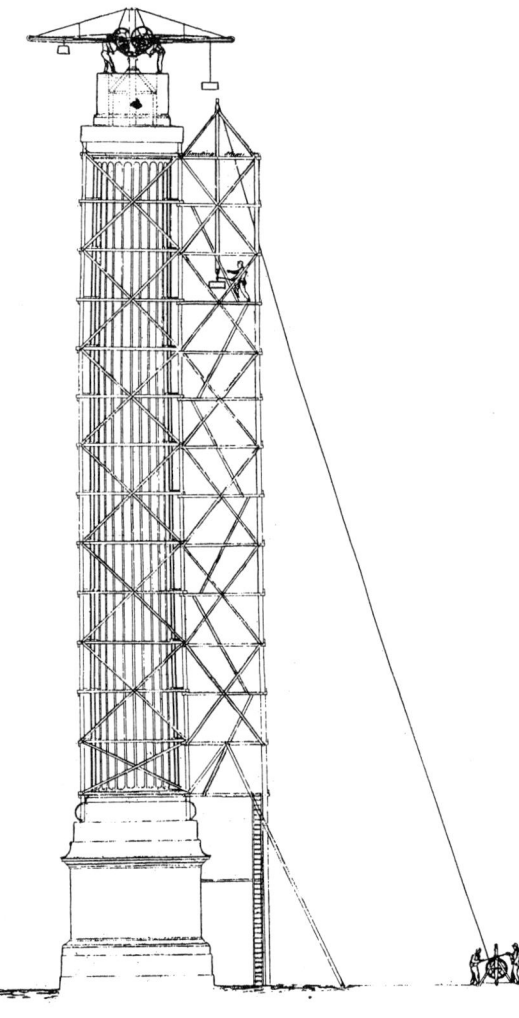

Not only did Robert Stevenson advise on the foundations for the Melville Monument but he also provided the model for the scaffolding and machinery required to raise the stone and statue to the top of the pillar. (Reproduced from the book *Bright Lights* by kind permission of Roland Patton and based on a drawing by Robert Stevenson in NLS. MS.Acc. 10706.356)

nevertheless proved costly, adding to the organising committee's increasing financial worries. Nothing daunted, however, they braved a further challenge in 1822 when it was decided to top the column with a statue of Melville; this increased the overall height by 14 feet (4.37 m). Modelled by the sculptor, Francis Chantrey (1781–1841), the figure was cut by Robert Forrest, (*c.* 1789–1852) a Lanarkshire stonemason. Forrest enjoyed modest fame through his popular exhibits of statuary on Calton Hill during the 1820s and 1830s, and a few of these pieces still survive and now command very high prices.[16]

Between 1821 and 1823 the garden was invaded by labourers assembling the column.[17] Further upheaval was experienced in 1827 when twelve horse-drawn cartloads set off from Nethan Foot quarry in Lanarkshire, pulling the 16 tons of statuary to St Andrew Square. On arrival the 15 separate pieces were lifted onto the grass, the lightest being the head at half a ton! Gradually by means of scaffolding and machinery 'constructed on new and improved principle, by J & J Rutherford from a model furnished by Robert Stevenson esq', the statue was safely raised to the top. While opinion on Dundas as a political figure remained divided,[18] most agreed that St Andrew Square had acquired a 'splendid', 'beautiful' and 'elegant' monument, to be ranked among the principal ornaments of the city.[19] The four large stone lions intended to guard the base were never executed for lack of money.

Improvements After a Slow Decline

It was as well that sightseers gazed upwards, for the rest of the garden was gradually deteriorating. We learn of this through a printed report produced in 1834 by the special committee elected to stem its further decline.[20] Since 1825 the garden had been looked after by Robert Turnbull, but he was now 'from old age and infirmity, quite incapable of any active exertion'. His services were dispensed with, but 'in parting with him' the committee felt obliged 'to administer in some degree to his relief', making him an allowance of 3s. 6d. (18p) a week; the report told that he had since become 'even more infirm and helpless than when he left the Square'. Charles Lyon was subsequently appointed gardener full-time on a weekly basis, at 12 shillings (60p). Financial matters had reached a parlous state: money was owed to two nursery firms, Messrs Dickson & Co (£110), and Eagle & Henderson (£20), and there were many residents with outstanding arrears: all indicative of lapsed management. Other matters needing attention were the 'ruinous state' of the parapet wall whose cope stones had become badly chipped, railings 'deficient in many places' and in need of paint and locks requiring renewal.

Apart from these priorities the committee were concerned to 'devise measures for the improvement and embellishment of the interior' and after 'many meetings, and mature deliberation upon plans and estimates' had, in the spring of 1833, carried out the following improvements: additional shrubbery (eight new plots were formed around the outer edges), the planting of 'several hundred young trees of various kinds' together with 'walks of a serpentine form laid down and gravelled' and a handsome cast-iron railing placed round the base of the column. Putting 'the new plan' into effect cost £140, with an additional £14 spent on trees, plants and shrubs. In the absence of any stated names one must presume that the work was carried out by a nursery firm – probably Dickson & Co – with whom the committee had already had substantial dealings. With so much new planting, a reliable water supply was now essential and a 24 foot (7.32 m) well was sunk in the north-east corner with pump attachment. A wooden tool house was also built, forms were constructed, outstanding repairs completed, the necessary painting done (still green for the railing), new locks and keys provided for the gates and tools purchased. The total outlay, including paying off old debts, came to £468. Stabilising the garden's finances was also one of the committee's priorities. To achieve this a better and fairer system of levying assessments was introduced, based on the measured width of each property fronting the Square (the foot frontage principle). Formerly the valuation lists, compiled for local taxation purposes, had been used. This system still applies, and was adopted by other New Town gardens such as Rutland Square and Clarendon Crescent. Finally a new set of regulations was printed and distributed.

View of St Andrew Square Garden from a painting by Ebsworth, 1845. The improvements of 1834 can be seen, including the rail at the base of the monument, the serpentine walks, peripheral planting and inner shrub beds. (City Art Centre, City of Edinburgh Museums and Galleries)

After long 'in a very neglected state', the garden's improvement was welcomed by the press, who congratulated the proprietors for their public spiritedness whereby 'St Andrew Square will equal in beauty and elegance any of the more fashionable gardens in town'.[21] One year later, however, the new planting had made little impact, and became the target of some scathing criticism by a young London journalist. His name was Charles Dickens, and he had been sent by the *Morning Chronicle* to cover Earl Grey's visit to receive the Freedom of the City. One of Dickens's duties was to attend a fund-raising promenade in St Andrew Square Garden organised on behalf of the Blind Asylum, the Deaf and Dumb Institution and the House of Refuge. It was held on a hot September afternoon and was, according to the young reporter, 'a most respectably attended, but a lamentably dull affair'; a military band played under a marquee 'erected in the centre of a parched bit of ground, without a tree or shrub to intercept the rays of a burning sun'. The *Courant* was more generous, describing the grand promenade as 'by far the most splendid for beauty and fashion that ever took place in Edinburgh, there being upwards of 2000 present'.[22]

1851: Proposals for a Place

In 1851 the garden sprang into the limelight on the issue of 'the propriety and practicability of converting the Area of the Square into a *Place*': that is, into a large open hard-paved

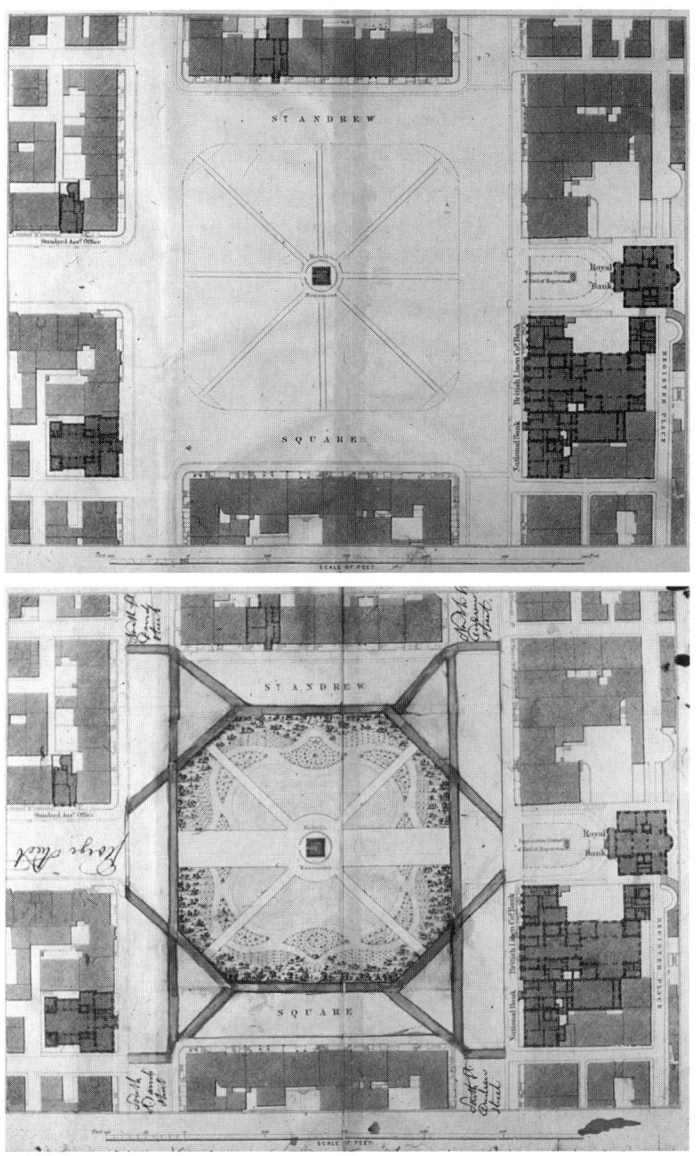

Proposals dating from 1851 to open up St Andrew Square and turn it into a *Place*. (McNab cuttings book, RBG)

space as found on the Continent. The notion had apparently been simmering for some time. Henry Cockburn, for instance, claimed that 'I did all I could to recommend it above 20 years ago', but it was now launched more vigorously by the business community within the square. When proprietors gathered for their February Annual General Meeting, two possibilities were presented:[23] one was to retain something of the garden's character, but with provision for a broad east-to-west pavement, accessible to the public during daytime;

the other for a completely open paved area. It was argued that as the Square had become a place of business, better public access was required Opening up the central space would not only be more convenient, but would allow 'the many handsome public offices' to be better displayed, and would thereby more than compensate for the 'by no means thriving shrubbery'. Those observations were contained in a circular produced by Robert Chambers (1802–71), chairman of the special committee set up to investigate. Chambers, a writer and bookseller, and known for his love of Edinburgh, favoured the change.[24] The committee, however, were anxious to glean the opinions 'of competent persons' on two points: the likely effect on property values, and the aesthetic and amenity implications of such a move. An early exercise in public participation was under way.

Thirteen architects, twelve artists, three builders, three civil engineers and fourteen 'others' replied to the circular;[25] two negative responses did little to dampen what was otherwise overwhelming approval.[26] It was generally felt that property values would not be adversely effected; the concept of a Place triggered undisguised enthusiasm amongst architects and artists, excited by a feature long denied them, and only available when on trips abroad. Imaginations were quickly fired with visions of a great open paved Place, filled with statues (it was suggested that George IV and Mr Pitt might be moved from George Street), monuments and fine fountains, all 'with a liberal supply of water'. With luck Edinburgh would have a Place to equal, if not surpass, the finest in Europe. The change in level between the north and south sides, which the circular had referred to, was not thought a particular hindrance. William Playfair's rather cautious note of approval, 'provided it was properly and completely done', was, in truth, echoed by several others;[27] and a few had reservations that, lacking constant blue skies and brilliant sunshine, a Place in Edinburgh might not be appropriate. Lord Cockburn, however, was staunchly in favour, noting that 'at present St Andrew Square is in its building, the most ambitiously ornamented square in Edinburgh while in its associated ground it is the meanest'.

The *Scotsman* noted that 'so large and respectable a mass of testimony is all but irresistible', but it was resisted in time-honoured David and Goliath style by a tiny group of long-established residents, fiercely opposed to any such change.[28] They shared The *Scotsman*'s reservations as to how far 'the elevated situation of the square, with openings on all sides may not render the proposed Place subject to frequent clouds and whirlwinds of dust'.[29] Meantime, in more peaceful mode, the garden hosted the first exhibition of the North British Professional Gardeners' Society in mid-May 1851, the press reporting that 'a more varied beautiful display of the varieties of horticultural produce has rarely if ever been witnessed in Edinburgh'. But the weather, alas, proved abysmal, and the anticipated 'numerous and fashionable attendance' failed to materialize.[30]

Later Attempts at Change

The garden survived intact, and 'the excellent keeping of its walks and grass lawns' was praised by James McNab when writing about the Square in 1865; he also commented on the fine mixture of well-formed trees both of forest growth and smaller ornamental varieties,[31] thirty years' growth now making an impact. But the outer appearance was spoilt in McNab's opinion by the decayed state of the wall and railing 'mean in appearance and a great blemish'.[32] Moreover, while in the 1850s 'the interior . . . during the summer months was a sealed letter to outside pedestrians', ten years later the border planting had degenerated to such an extent that 'it is now impossible to conceal from view those individuals privileged to walk in them'.

An opportunity to reconsider the garden presented itself in 1865, following a Police Notice requiring the outside rough causewayed footpath to be replaced by a proper pavement.[33] Once again a special committee was formed, this time under the chairmanship of ex-Lord Provost Sir William Johnston, founder of the firm W. & A.K. Johnston, geographical engravers, with premises at No. 4 St Andrew Square. As a member of the 1851 committee he was alert to past sensibilities. On this occasion the committee supported the complete replacement of the original old wall and railing, and making two wider footpaths to run from north to south, and east to west, open to the public during daytime. These proposals, with sketch plans, were circulated to proprietors in November 1865.[34] The previous suggestion of transforming the Square into a hard-paved Place was no longer on the agenda, for as the pamphlet explained, such an idea would be unacceptable to 'some of the most influential proprietors', and 'the doing away with a green spot in the heart of a city' was contrary to what the public wanted. Nevertheless it was clear that the committee hoped to introduce a more palatable version and at least push for limited opening.

In January 1866 the architect John Dick Peddie (1824–91) was appointed to design new railings, an outside footpath and a central east-to-west pathway 45–50 feet (14–15 m) wide. Maybe it was Dick Peddie's involvement with improvements to the Royal Bank

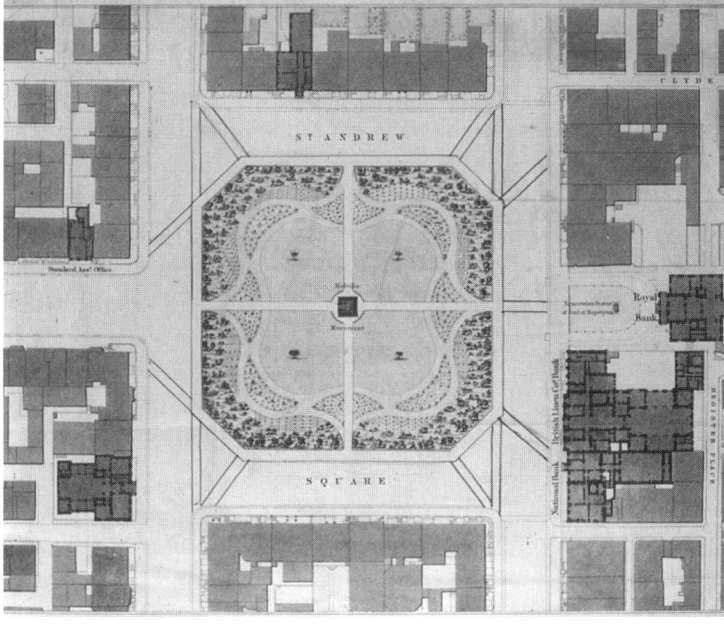

Modified proposals of 1865 to improve and partly open up St Andrew Square. (McNab cuttings book, RBG)

in 1857 which brought him to the notice of the committee; earlier he had come out in favour of converting the Square into a Place. Whatever the reason, this marked his first professional engagement with a New Town garden although his partner, Charles Kinnear, had long been active on West Princes Street Garden committee.[35] His association with St Andrew Square brought Dick Peddie into contact with James McNab who had been asked to advise on the interior planting. This partnership (and one of the few instances where an architect and horticulturalist worked closely together) was repeated the following year when Eton Terrace (Dean Gardens) were set up; and also for George Square Gardens (where Sir William Johnston resided).

When the draft plans were exhibited at a general meeting three months later, showing a wide thoroughfare from west to east in continuation of George Street,[36] they were greeted with an outburst by John Dundas, WS (1803–73). Many years before he had served on the 1831 Improvement Committee, and now shared with his near neighbour, Lady Boswell,[37] deep misgivings about the new proposals just as he had with the 1851 ones. He preferred that 'matters should remain as they are'.[38] Attempts to open up the Square were strongly resisted, not because of any loss of privacy but rather on the grounds that the garden 'acted as a great stopper for the dust and other horrors that blew down George Street'. Dundas complained that as the Water Company never watered the streets, such a change would leave him 'exposed to all the dust of the summer'. The architect's idea of introducing groups of statuary, of creating a large gravel space around the Melville Monument, and a more open promenade where other public memorials might be displayed, only served to fuel his displeasure and add to his fears. Such a reaction was not unexpected. The matter was deferred, however, until an appeal was launched to raise money for the outside path and new railings, estimated to cost well over £1,000.

The money in fact was collected with astonishing speed. Within forty-eight hours of the launch, the banking and commercial fraternity had guaranteed funds. This was no comfort, however, to either Mr Dundas or Lady Boswell, and they, together with another resident, James Finlay, began to take legal action should the old railings be so much as touched. They reminded the committee of the clause in their charters reserving the central area for residents, and forbidding any common thoroughfare whatsoever. Only after much diplomacy, and assurances from the chairman that no change would be made to the garden's character, was litigation abandoned. David had finally triumphed over Goliath.[39]

New Railings and Further Improvements

By the end of 1866 new cope stones and railings were in place and a Caithness stone pavement laid around the outside. It produced a remarkable change in appearance, 'the wanton funereal aspect of the place having given way to one of airiness and beauty'.[40] Dick Peddie had given much thought to the design of the railings, aiming to make the enclosure 'as slight and unobtrusive as is consistent with strength', to provide a feeling of openness so that 'persons walking on the pavements and roadways of the square should have the advantage of all the charms which the grass and foliage can give to it'.[41] Hence the cope stone was raised only some 6 inches (15 cm) above the pavement, and the iron railing was

View of the St Andrew Square Gardens, Edinburgh, around 1880. Not too dissimilar from today's appearance with its emphasis on smaller-growing trees. (Grant, *Old and New Edinburgh*, 1880–3)

designed to be much lighter than the previous one, with handsome lamp pillars provided at each of the angles and flanking the pathway, the whole being delicately touched with gilding. These attractive railings were removed during the Second World War, although ones to a similar design by the same architect can still be seen round George Square Gardens.

Improvements to the interior were carried out during the spring of 1867. Again the aim was to make the garden more visible from the outside by removing the old shrubbery and grassing over the vacant plots. Several ill-formed trees were also removed. Again the press responded enthusiastically, the *Scotsman* remarking that 'foremost in fairness as being newly redressed, is the enclosure of St Andrew Square; which the skill of Mr McNab, aided by the architectural taste of Mr J Dick Peddie has converted from a tangled wilderness of scrubby underwood into a truly ornamental bit of park or pleasure ground'.[42] The levelling and grass-sowing of the borders was thought especially successful, and a strategy many other gardens could usefully follow: 'very slow are our town gardeners to acknowledge particularly that grass is our finest evergreen.' The rejuvenation of St Andrew Square Garden stimulated a whole wave of improvements to other New Town gardens.

Two World Wars and After

Nothing further disturbed the garden's tranquillity until the First World War. In 1918 the proprietors gave permission for the American YMCA to erect accommodation for the use

St Andrew Square   45

A rare photographic image of a gardener at work in St Andrew Square Gardens *c*. 1870, using one of the early grass-cutters. Gardening items can be seen round the base of the column which provided internal storage space. In the background to the right are the offices of the British Linen Bank (now the Bank of Scotland) and on the left the house originally built for Sir Lawrence Dundas (now the headquarters of the Royal Bank of Scotland). (Calotype by Adamson & Hill, ECL)

of American soldiers and sailors while on furlough in the city.[43] A postcard view taken at this time shows the interior almost totally covered with wood huts.[44] The Second World War witnessed similar upheavals; the removal of Dick Peddie's fine railings was unfortunate enough, but the garden was requisitioned to provide space for air-raid shelters and a static water tank.

Not until 1947 was the ground reinstated and new railings erected, to a design by the architect Grahame Thomson. At this time a hard-paved footpath was formed across the centre from west to east and lined with cherry trees; other tree and shrub planting was also carried out. By then the circular rail at the base of the monument was dilapidated and was removed. Kate Hawkins (1897–1989), a garden designer with work both in Scotland and England, was responsible for the new planting, and in 1973 added a herbaceous border on the north side with other island beds.[45] In 1951 a semi-sunk store and brick toolshed was built to the south of the column. Today there are about 85 trees spread throughout the garden, mostly between 40 and 100 years old; these range from forest varieties such as elm, sycamore, plane and oak (mostly around the edges) to several smaller, ornamental species such as cherry, hawthorn and laburnum.

Although St Andrew Square Garden is well over 200 years old, only for a relatively

Postcard showing a grimy looking Edinburgh with the huts erected in St Andrew Square during the First World War to accommodate American soldiers and sailors on leave in the City. St James's Square can be made out as well as the Waverley Market with its roof-top garden. Although built as the main fruit and vegetable market it also served as a popular exhibition venue including, amongst others, horticultural shows. (NAS GD1/533/251)

short spell did it function as a recreational space for the benefit of surrounding households. Yet it remains a private garden run on the same principles as when it was first established, well maintained and cared for.[46] Periodically the space comes under scrutiny for other use. In 1890, for example, the Lord Provost's Committee considered moving the large bronze statue by Steell of Alexander and Bucephalus (then sited on the west side of the Square) into the garden, and forming a public pathway to it.[47] During the 1960s the Council discussed acquiring both St Andrew and Charlotte Square Gardens, 'so as to make them available to the public throughout the year and for use at the Festival'.[48] Reports from the Chief Constable, Director of Parks & Recreation, City Engineer and Town Planning Officer supported this use although access across a busy road was cited as a problem. The City Engineer, in line with contemporary thinking, noted the advantage of public ownership 'if consideration was later given to the provision of underground car parks'.

St Andrew Square has experienced many waves of improvements during its lifetime as well as moves to radically alter its character. The twenty-first century is witnessing another significant peroid of change to the square and its surroundings with the advent of new shops and an improved bus station. This has prompted a re-examination of the purpose and design of the central garden made under the aegis of the Edinburgh City Centre Management Company with the support of the St Andrew Square Garden Committee. The days of cherry trees (more appropriate to suburban gardens than a town square) may well be numbered in the proposals to revitalise the garden and to provide for more daytime access by members of the public. St Andrew Square Garden has always been a welcome green oasis at the eastern end of New Town and the present plans aim to uphold this historic role while maintaining high standards of upkeep and care. Its future looks promising.

Notes

1. Eleanor Sillar, *Edinburgh Child: some memories of 90 years*, (Edinburgh & London, 1961), p. 3.
2. And outwith its boundary: George Square was built form 1766 onwards and designed by James Brown, architect.
3. Extracts from an Edinburgh Journal 1823–1833, part 1, *Book of the Old Edinburgh Club (BOEC)*, Vol. 29, (Edinburgh, 1956); entry for 12 October 1825. See also a notice in *The Scotsman* (7 February 1824) advertising No. 1 St Andrew Square for sale.
4. A newspaper article written in 1949 entitled 'Lord Melville has no one to cherish him', *Scottish Daily Express*, (5 August) refers to the secretary, Mr F.G. More, as having been through the records up until 1850 to try and establish ownership of the monument.
5. Feu Charter, 5 St Andrew Square, John Adam, 7 May 1777, Chartulary Vol. 1, Edinburgh City Archives (ECA).
6. Town Council Minutes (TCM), 5 April 1769.
7. TCM, 4 November 1778.
8. TCM, 21 April 1773; TCM, 22 November 1775.
9. *Edinburgh Advertiser*, 13 January 1769, advertisement for sale of Drummond Lodge, 'Robert Gullen gardener at the lodge will show the policy'.
10. TCM, 1 September 1773.
11. *Boswell, Laird of Auchineck 1778–1782*, edited Joseph Reed & Frederick Pottle (McGraw Hill, 1977), p. 472, diary entry for 19 August 1782: Boswell was a frequent visitor to the Square and also became friendly with Sir Laurence Dundas and his wife.
12. David Walker, 'William Burn, and the influence of Sir Robert Smirke and William Wilkins on Scottish Greek Revival Design, 1810–40', The Scottish Georgian Society; *Scottish Pioneers of the Greek Revival* (1984), p. 14.
13. TCM, 17 January 1821. See also, W. Forbes Gray, *BOEC*, (March 1927), Vol. 15, pp. 207–13 for a detailed account of the history of the Monument.
14. Robert Louis Stevenson, *Records of a Family of Engineers*, (London, 1912), p. 89.
15. Stevenson recommended extending and strengthening the foundation, and the use of stones large enough to fill up the entire thickness of the walls instead of rubble as proposed by Burn.
16. One of his exhibitions in 1832 consisted of 30 groups of statuary under the patronage of the Royal Association of Contributors to the National Monument, using stone from Craigleith Quarry.
17. William Armstrong, builder, was awarded the contract for the job.
18. Not everyone was impressed however; Henry Cockburn, for example, on seeing the column after the scaffolding had been removed (in time for George IV's visit in August 1822) remarked that while the site was good, and the design 'not very bad', it nevertheless lacked a 'very correct grace in the proportion' which a plain column required. See *Some Letters of Lord Cockburn,* ed. H.A. Cockburn, (Edinburgh, 1932), p. 105.

19. *The Scotsman*, 4 August 1827.

20. *Report of the committee elected by a general meeting of proprietors, 21 March 1833* (and prepared for a meeting in 1834), printed copy, Edinburgh University Library (EUL).

21. *Edinburgh Evening Courant*, 27 April 1833.

22. *Morning Chronicle,* 20 September 1834; paragraph by 'our own correspondent', and quoted in E.F. Catford, *The story of a City* (London, 1975), p. 183.

23. *Report of the Committee of St Andrew Square proprietors, appointed at the Annual Meeting, February 4, 1851*, copy EPL; McNab manuscripts, Royal Botanic Garden Library; Clerk to St Andrew Square garden.

24. Robert Chambers lived at 1 Doune Terrace on the Moray estate, and is well known as the author of *Traditions of Edinburgh* and other works.

25. Many of Edinburgh's best-known architects replied to the circular. A résumé of the main comments by each was appended in the report (FN 24) and circulated to all the proprietors in the Square.

26. John Henderson, architect, and Peter Ramsay, Manager of Edinburgh branch of the Western Bank of Scotland, St Andrew Square, both supported keeping the garden.

27. Those specifically referred to included Place Vêndome, Paris; Place Royale, Brussels; Piazza del Populo, Piazza Navona, Piazza Vecchia and Piazza di san Marco in Rome.

28. The Town Council did not voice any initial objections. The Lord Provost at this time was William Johnston who business was based in the Square and he was favourably disposed to the idea.

29. *The Scotsman*, 31 May 1851, 'Proposed alteration of St Andrew Square'.

30. *The Scotsman*, 21 May 1851: 'Horticultural Show and Promenade'.

31. James McNab, 'Our town Trees, St Andrew Square gardens', *Scottish Farmer*, 12 July 1865.

32. Quoted in a pamphlet: *Improvement of St Andrew Square*, 27 November 1865; copy Clerk to garden; RBG library (McNab folder) and EPL.

33. *Edinburgh Police Act, 11 and 12, Vict. Cap113*, Sect, 270.

34. See note 32; information is also based on a small minute book entitled 'Improvement of St Andrew Square', in the possession of the Clerk to the Garden.

35. John Dick Peddie started as a pupil of David Rhind.

36. Meetings took place in the Douglas Hotel on the north side of the Royal Bank of Scotland. This hotel was frequented by the famous and well-off, including Empress Eugenie and Sir Walter Scott on his return from Italy shortly before his death.

37. Lady Boswell was probably the wife of Sir James Boswell, grandson of James Boswell.

38. A full account of the meeting was given in *The Scotsman*, 27 March 1866. John Dundas (1803–73) was the 5th son of James Dundas, WS.

39. *The Edinburgh & Leith Post Office Directory, 1865–6* indicates how few private citizens still lived in the Square. Only seven names are found listed for solely residential purposes.

40. *The Scotsman*, 30 November 1866.

41. *The Scotsman*, 18 March 1866, giving details of the letter written by J. Dick Peddie to the Chairman of the Improvement Committee.

42. *The Scotsman,* 1 July 1867, 'Our Town Trees'.

43. TCM, 17 September 1918 & 8 October, 1918.

44. Valentine's postcard, 'Calton Hill and the east end from the air', Register House GD1/533 No.251.

45. Obituary, Kate Hawkins, *Garden History Society Newsletter* (Autumn 1989) by Iris Strachan.

46. Care of the garden is sub-contracted out to Capability Scotland, who also take care of the Queen Street East Garden and some other New Town gardens.
47. TCM, 3 March 1890; the statue was by John Steell and had been presented to the City in 1884.
48. TCM, 20 February 1969; the following quotations are taken from this minute, which is a report of an earlier meeting of the Lord Provost's Committee held on 5 February 1969.

CHAPTER 3

CHARLOTTE SQUARE
2.70 acres (1.09 ha)

> In May we removed to Charlotte Square, a house I found the most agreeable of any we have ever lived in in Edinburgh; the shrubbery in front, and the peep from the upper windows at the back of the Firth of Forth with its wooded shores and distant hills made the look out so cheerful.
>
> Elizabeth Grant, *c.* 1817
> (the family were living at No. 5)[1]

St Andrew Square Garden had been in existence for nearly 30 years before its counterpart at the western end began to take shape. Charlotte Square took a long time to complete,[2] interrupted by the Napoleonic Wars and the consequent scarcity of money. Its beginning, however, was auspicious. Partly in response to criticism that much of the New Town was dull and lacking distinction, the Town Council commissioned Robert Adam (1728–92) in 1791 to produce a unified scheme of frontages. One year later Adam was dead and only the north side, the first to be built, kept faithfully to his design; nevertheless the Square is still a great *tour de force*. In its early years several nobility and gentry lived there, and later it became popular amongst the legal and medical professions. Business and commercial interests were slower to intrude,[3] and even by the end of the nineteenth century the Square remained mostly residential.

But the twentieth century has witnessed major changes. The middle years saw many law and financial companies establishing offices there; but these in turn departed for

Robert Adam's design for the east side of Charlotte Square, Edinburgh, 1791. (City of Edinburgh Council, City Development Dept.)

purpose-built premises better fitted for the computer age. Charlotte Square during the early 1990s took on a shabby and run-down appearance as many premises became empty. It was therefore a shot in the arm when in spring 1996 the National Trust for Scotland, with financial help from Historic Scotland, the Heritage Lottery Fund and Lothian and Edinburgh Enterprise Ltd, purchased six adjoining houses on the south side, in a move 'to stimulate a renaissance of the whole Square by encouraging the restoration of other building, the reoccupation of vacant buildings, and the restoration of Charlotte Square Gardens'.[4] The future now holds greater promise. Since Edinburgh was named the first UNESCO City of Literature in 2004, this number will continue to rise.

William Sibbald's Role

Charlotte Square Garden departed from Craig's octagonal shape and became instead smaller and circular.[5] It remained that way for the first 70 years of its life. The change

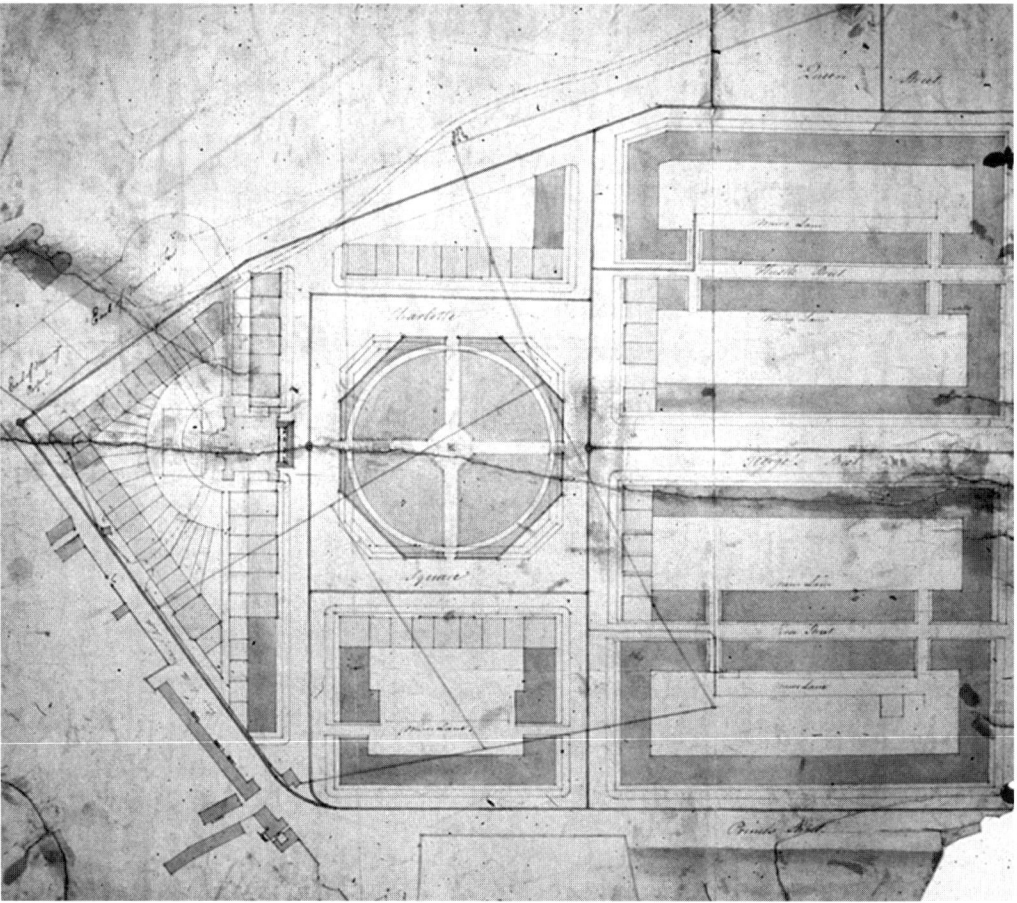

These three plans show the evolution of the central space, Charlotte Square Garden, Edinburgh. Robert Adam's 1791 drawing showing various possible alternatives. (ECL)

William Sibbald's 1795 plan echoing Adam's earlier proposals. (ECA)

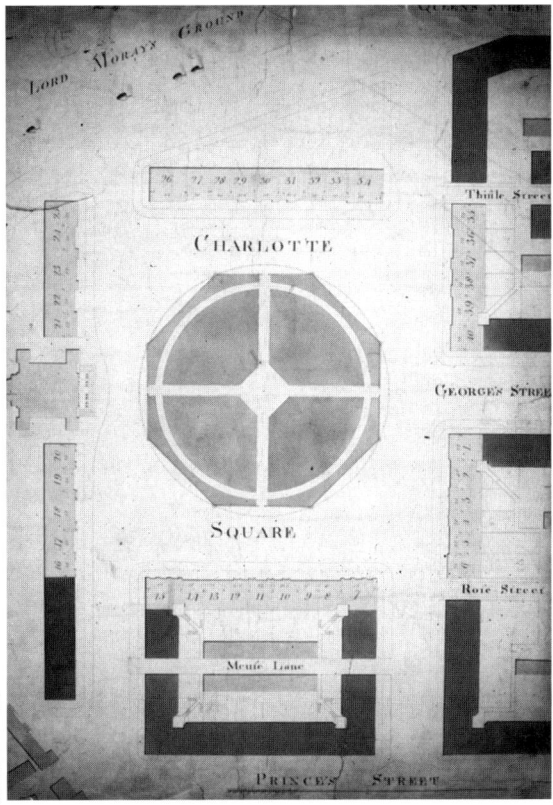

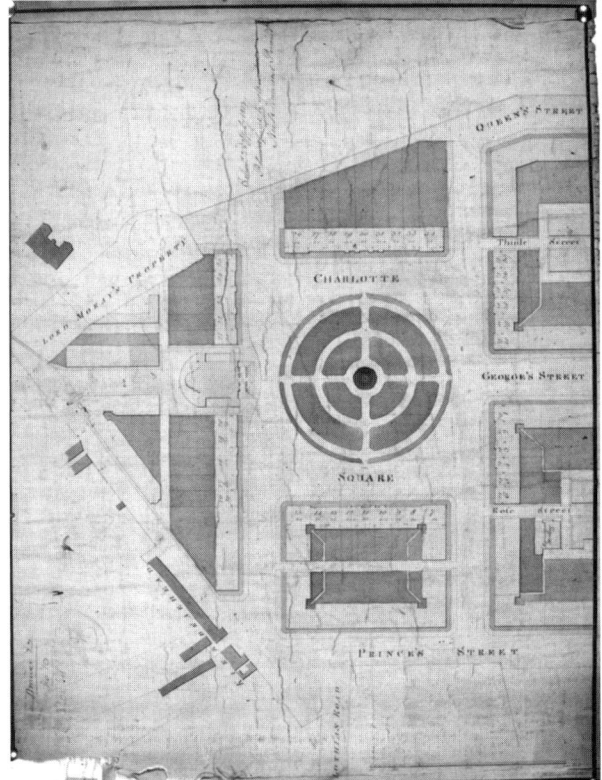

Sibbald's plan of 1803 showing preference for a circular garden. (ECA)

seems to have evolved from a series of sketch plans, the first prepared by Robert Adam in 1791 and the rest by William Sibbald, Superintendent of Works to the City (from 1790 to 1809). Sibbald's involvement highlights another difference between the two squares. St Andrew Square Garden had been set up by the residents. But Charlotte Square, designed to contain 46 residences, had for a long time only a handful of proprietors. It required the Town Council to assume greater responsibility for setting up the garden in the hope of encouraging sales of house plots. As early as May 1795 the Council had remitted to a sub-committee 'everything relating to completing the inner square of Charlotte Square', and several weeks later were informed by this committee that:

> they had directed Mr Sibbald to proceed to bringing it to a proper level, that they had procured a plan and estimate from Mr Sibbald and that they had got from Mr Chalmers [blacksmith in Potterow] different designs for a rail, but they had not yet met with the feuars on the north side of the square to settle the mode to be adopted when advertisements for estimates will be published.[6]

This was a busy period for Sibbald; apart from monitoring new building to see that contract specifications were being met, feuing plots had to be accurately measured and staked out, and boundaries checked. This in addition to day-to-day maintenance of other buildings within the city's care. But Sibbald also acted as Superintendent to the Heriot's Hospital besides being in practice as an architect-cum-builder, with a man called William Lumley. Although he held a fairly key position at this important period of Edinburgh's development, not a great deal is known about him. Originating from Inverness (and responsible for the Town's Burgh steeple, designed in 1791), he moved to Edinburgh and during his lifetime carried out various commissions including a new manse for St Cuthbert's Church (since demolished), the spire of St Andrew's Church, George Street (1789)[7], Lady Yester's Church (1803), Portobello Old and Windsor Place Church (1809), and plans for Edinburgh's Second New Town.[8] Competent and well respected, Sibbald was elected Dean of Masons from 1807 to 1808, and his death one year later was 'much and justly regretted'.[9]

Preparatory Steps

Nearly two years went by before the feuars met in March 1797 to discuss Sibbald's plans. During the intervening months efforts continued to sell off further house plots, the upset price being reduced in a bid to tempt purchasers.[10] Attention now focused on having the central area enclosed, and the meeting agreed 'in terms similar to what was adopted respecting St Andrew Square . . . to finish the inner space of Charlotte Square by building a circular parapet to be two and a half feet [85 cm] high above the level of the street'.[11] Also approved were details of the construction: full length balusters of cast iron to be five feet [1.52 m] in height, (one foot [30 cm] for the intermediate ones), with sixteen lamp posts and four ornamental gates. A circular garden was in the making. Was this solution favoured on grounds of economy (less stonework and railing required) or simply Sibbald's own preference? Adam's notion for an equal-sided octagon seems to have been considered by Sibbald, but later discarded.

Whatever the explanation, the departure from Craig's layout seems to have been accepted without query. In June 1797 another meeting was held when minor changes to the specification were discussed; these included increasing the height of the wall by 4 inches [10 cm]. Already six estimates had been obtained for digging and constructing the foundations, and Sibbald was asked to calculate the amount of rubble and ashlar work, besides the amount of digging, in order to judge 'which of the estimates is the cheapest'. It was also agreed that the 'Number 1' style of railing be adopted and Sibbald was asked to supply schedules and drawings of the new rail to allow revision of earlier estimates.

Progress now quickened. By July 1797, four tenders for the railings had been received and 'Mr Chalmers estimate found to be the cheapest, and George Winton formerly found the cheapest for mason work'; both men were appointed. Several years later Winton's name resurfaces in connection with another New Town garden for he became part owner of land which eventually became the East Queen Street Gardens. Both contracts survive in the City Archives and provide some interesting information.[12] The deadline for completing the parapet wall was set at 15 November 1797 'at the sight and to the satisfaction of William Sibbald'. No overall price was given for the mason's work but different rates applied to different parts; for example, rubble work of 16 inches [40 cm] thick was paid at '£5 per rood of surface measure', and the broached ashlar at '6½ penny per foot superficial'. Once that was built, the blacksmith was required to add the 1150 feet [351 m] of railings within three weeks for the sum of £509.[13]

Ideas for a Water Feature

For nearly six years this substantial railed enclosure merely served to protect a piece of derelict wasteland. Then in July 1803 the Lord Provost received a joint letter from Colonel Alexander Dirom (resident in Queen Street) and several builders with property erecting on the west side of the Square. Ostensibly it was to seek permission for small changes to their elevations as prepared by William Sibbald, chiefly by adding an extra foot to the window heights.[14] But the greater part of the communication was about the central area, and read as follows:

> With regard to the improvement of the interior or garden part of Charlotte Square it is extremely desirable that it should be done without delay – we find however, that there is not any hope of it being done by the proprietors themselves as it would be difficult not only to unite their opinion on the subject but also to raise the money for that purpose, as a great part of the lots are not yet sold – we therefore beg leave to submit to your Lordship and the Town Council whether it would not be most advisable to have the square laid out and finished under your own direction by Mr Sibbald and charge this further expense which cannot be considerable upon the different lots in the square in addition to the expense for enclosing it, which has been already incurred. In laying out the square it may deserve consideration whether it would not be desirable to have a piece of water in the middle of it, which may be easily obtained by bringing in a spring in the Lothian Road, as the distance is only a few hundred yards, the level of which has already been ascertained by Mr Sibbald. Such a reservoir which would command the whole of the New Town, might be extremely useful in cases of fire, might be occasionally employed to sprinkle

or wash the street, and in winter would be a safe and convenient place for the inhabitants to enjoy the recreation of skating. The additional expense of that improvement might be defrayed to the town by levying a small contribution, if they should think it an object, from the skaters not belonging to the square; as the proprietors of the square and their families would have a just right to it from giving up a part of the ground to be applied to that purpose.[15]

Alexander Dirom (1757–1830) of Mount Annan, chief instigator or the letter, was a military gentleman with experience of service in India, and was later appointed Quartermaster General for Scotland.[16] While consulting Sibbald about his new house (No. 18) Dirom obviously grasped the opportunity to discuss possibilities for the central space. The notion for 'a piece of water' corresponds exactly to Sibbald's previous ideas for a basin of water contained within a circus proposed for the western end of the Second New Town, a proposal made by him both in 1793 and 1802. And it would seem too much of a coincidence that the ideas for the one did not rub off on the other. Whether this suggestion was ever taken seriously is questionable, for the control and use of such a water feature would not have been without its problems. Such a centrepiece, for example, had once been considered for Finsbury Square, London (completed in 1791) but abandoned on sanitary grounds and a garden substituted instead. The experience of St James Square was also not very

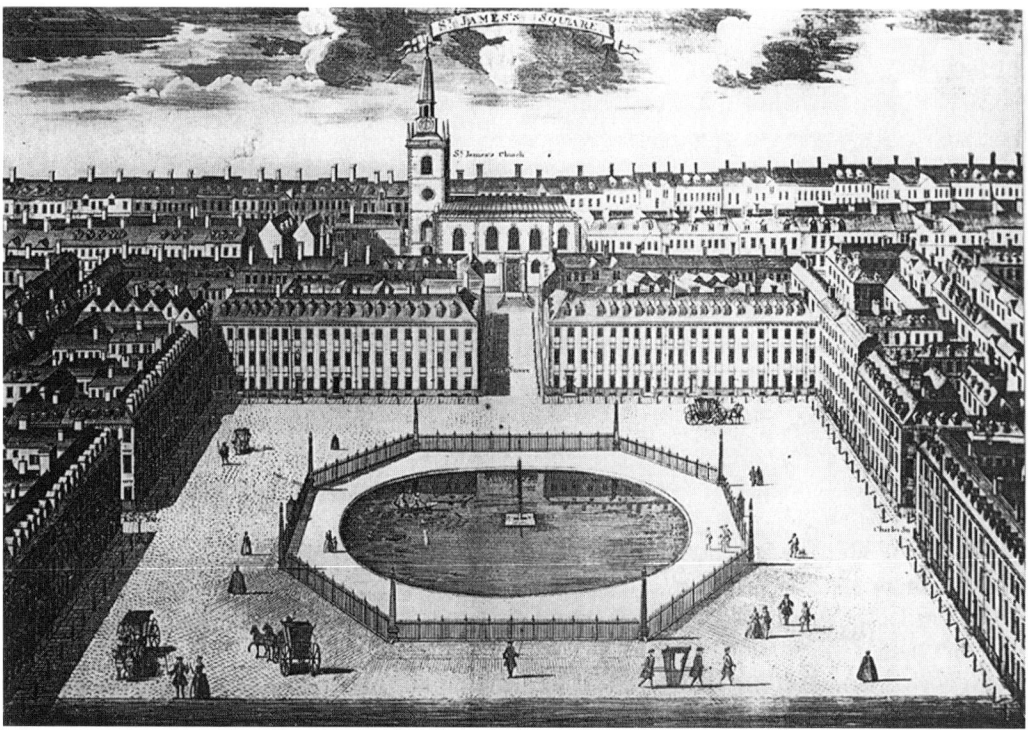

Engraving by Sutton Nicholls of St James's Square, Westminster, 1754. The Square had been laid out by Charles Bridgeman in 1727–8. The view shows a fountain set within a circular basin of water.

encouraging. Improved in the 1720s with the addition of a circular basin of water, fountain, and decorative boats, its upkeep proved troublesome and eventually fountain, water and basin all disappeared.[17]

Dirom, however, was a man of action and not easily deflected. A further letter from him to the Lord Provost, dated March 1804, reveals that during the intervening months he had begun to take steps for having the ground levelled and laid out, and in fact had come up with rather a novel solution which promised to be both quick and cheap. The letter ran as follows:

> My Lord, I beg leave to acquaint your Lordship that the Quartermaster of the Inverness-shire Regiment of Militia has represented to me that he cannot direct the working parties of the Regiment to level the Circus in Charlotte Square, or to carry the stones to where the walks are to be made until the levels are ascertained and the walks laid out according to the plan fixed upon by the Town Council. I beg leave to submit to your Lordship the expediency of giving instructions to Mr Sibbald to take the necessary levels and to mark out the walks according to the plan signed by your Lordship, bearing date 23 February 1803, in order that the work which may be done by the troops to level the Circus for their own purpose, may also be useful in forwarding the plan for the final improvement of it.[18]

The Inverness-shire Regiment of Militia

The Inverness-shire Regiment of Militia formed part of the Edinburgh's Castle garrison between December 1803 and January 1806.[19] During the period 1802 to 1815 this garrison was manned almost entirely by Militia and veteran battalions as most of the regular battalions of the line were involved in the Napoleonic Wars. The Militia were not regular soldiers but part of a reserve force which every town and county had to provide under the Militia Acts of 1798 and 1802.[20] They were never very popular and tended to be regarded as 'the scum of the earth'. As this Militia formed part of the Castle garrison, they were available in Edinburgh as 'labour' if the right strings could be pulled (such work would have been regarded as being beneath regular soldiers). It would simply

The Hon. Francis William Grant of Grant, Colonel of the Invernesshire Militia. Men from this regiment and under his direction were responsible for levelling Charlotte Square in 1803. (Kay's *Portraits*, 1877)

have been a matter of getting men available without disturbing their first responsibility of maintaining guards and providing sentries. Dirom was of sufficient importance in the hierarchy to authorise the use of the Militia (in agreement with the Commanding Officer, the Hon. Francis William Grant of Grant) for such non-military purposes. Hence the Inverness-shire Regiment provided a free source of labour for the back-breaking task of levelling the central area, justified no doubt as being a useful training exercise and time filler.

After the Militia

Once the area was levelled, a circular walk was formed around the perimeter. Sibbald's ideas for a more elaborate series of concentric pathways divided by ones running across the centre from north to south, and east to west, seems to have been abandoned; it was probably beyond the scope of men with limited time. With some progress made, the layout was still fairly rudimentary and devoid of planting. And so it remained for a further four years until the proprietors – now of increased number – called a meeting in December 1807 for those 'interested in the improvement of the Square'.[21] Colonel Dirom's energies were now directed onto a committee which also included Sir John Sinclair (initiator of the Statistical Account of Scotland), Sir William Fettes (founder of Fettes College), Thomas Allan (banker) and Walter Watson. The several resolutions passed on this occasion were later presented in a petition to the Town Council:

> 1st, that it is highly expedient, for the inhabitants of Charlotte Square and for the credit and ornament of the City of Edinburgh that the centre of the said Square shall be completed and laid out in a neat and elegant manner with gravel walks and shrubbery; 2nd, that the plan drawn up by William Weir of Greenside Place, Edinburgh . . . seemed to be well calculated for the object in view and that if a sum adequate to the expense thereof can be raised the said plan should be adopted with such alterations as may be judged necessary by the committee; 3rd, that for raising the sum required every feuar should subscribe the sum of £6 and a sum not exceeding £1 per annum for 3 years as the Committee shall judge necessary, in consequence of which each feuar shall be entitled to a key to the central area, and the liberty of walking therein for himself and family, and that the said privilege shall remain annexed to the house belonging to him subject to such regulations as the majority of feuars shall from time to time think expedient; 4th, that the Lord Provost and Magistrates be applied to . . . to subscribe for those stances of houses in the Square which have not yet been feued. That it be represented to them, in strongest terms, that it will greatly tend to improve the appearance of the City if this Square is elegantly fitted up; that in consequence thereof the feus still vacant will be more readily taken, that it can be no loss to the City, as any sum they advance will be repaid when the feus are taken, and that without this it is impossible for the existing feuars to take upon themselves the burden of said improvement.

Early in the New Year the proprietors' request for financial help was approved and the City Chamberlain authorised to subscribe for the unfeued stances. Judging from figures quoted in the feu charters on the proportional sum payable to the City for enclosing and laying out the central area, it would appear that the overall cost of forming the garden was in the region of £1,000.[22] Next to nothing is known about William Weir whose plan was 'well calculated' to achieve the 'neat and elegant' layout desired by the residents. A man of the same name had been employed by the Town Council in 1801 and 1804 for digging in Albany and Duke Streets[23], and a James Weir, merchant (father or brother?) at 6 Greenside Place (a continuation of Leith Walk), appears in the Street Directories and Stent Rolls for this period. Leith Walk was a popular area for nursery and seed shops, being close to the Botanic Gardens (then sited on the same road further towards Leith), and the several market and nursery gardens in the vicinity.[24] Sibbald, too, was then living in this district and may well have recommended Weir as a suitable man for the job. In the absence of evidence to the contrary, one has to assume that he was probably a small nursery contractor, capable of turning his hand to many different tasks.

William Weir's Plan; and Arrangements for Upkeep

Weir's plan, carried into effect in the spring of 1808, was relatively simple, but successfully transformed a dull empty space into a recognisable garden. A thick border of evergreen shrubs and trees, (consisting of thorns, laburnums, sycamores, limes, birches and elms,[25] was planted next to the railing; and two curved footpaths[26] were made from east to west leading to a circular walk around a central clump of trees and shrubs. The rest was grassed and planted with a scatter of specimen trees.

The new garden required looking after, but with only one-third of the Square built, raising the required funds seems to have been done on a fairly *ad hoc* basis.[27] A petition presented to the Town Council in 1817 by the management committee supports this view.[28] By then the Square was nearing completion and the committee had become concerned 'to settle upon an effective financial arrangement for maintaining the gardens', and to get the matter 'put upon a proper footing'. It was signed by the Convener, Henry Cockburn (1779–1854), who had moved to No. 14 in 1813.[29] Cockburn was then a successful advocate (later becoming Solicitor General for Scotland and, later still, a judge with the title Lord Cockburn) and is remembered now as a spry commentator on matters politic and legal. He was also a staunch defender of Edinburgh's open spaces. It was his spirited campaign, for example, that helped safeguard East Princes Street Gardens as open space. In all, an excellent man to have at the helm.

Most feuars had agreed to having the assessment fixed at the time of their January annual general meeting; with a set upper limit of two guineas per house to continue 'without any renewal' until no longer appropriate. The Town's response was to appoint a committee to confer with the proprietors, one of whom was Baillie Henderson, later Lord Provost. Alexander Henderson was a popular and experienced businessman, and head of the nursery firm Eagle & Henderson, a man likely to be sympathetic to the proprietors' cause. He was very much committed to Edinburgh's improvement, and had acted as the Council's representative on matters to do with the setting up of the East Queen Street Gardens; later he became involved with the planting of West Princes Street Gardens. As nothing further is heard on this subject, the arrangements for raising money must have proved satisfactory. The flat rate system of payment then adopted still applies.

Views of Charlotte Square, Edinburgh. View to the west side showing one of the pillared entrances to the garden. (J. & H.S. Storer, *Views of Edinburgh and its vicinity*, 1820)

View across to St George's Church showing a railed circular garden with boundary planting becoming established. (J. Ewbank, *Picturesque Views of Edinburgh*, 1825)

North-east corner with a peep of the West Queen Street Gardens and the Firth of Forth. (J. & H.S. Storer, *Views of Edinburgh and its vicinity*, 1820)

View of the gardens from George Street. (T. Shepherd, *Views of Edinburgh*, 1825)

Growing Maturity and Major Changes Ahead

By the late 1860s much of the planting was in decline and needing attention. In 1867 St Andrew Square had savoured enthusiastic press coverage following the refurbishment of their garden area, but Charlotte Square in comparison was described as 'particularly offensive in style' and dismissed as having 'little either within or without'.[30] Significant changes were, however, imminent, prompted by the acquisition of an important and prestigious statue: the Scottish National Memorial to Prince Albert. Earlier in the 1820s the garden had come close to acquiring two memorials: one 'a colossal statue' of Lord Hopetoun[31] and the other of the younger Pitt, based on a replica of the Column of Antoninus.[32] But Prince Albert was in a class apart, and the project kept a hard-working committee and numerous others busy for nearly fifteen years. Speculation as to what form the memorial should take and where it should be put was rife throughout.

The Prince Albert Memorial

Shortly after Prince Albert's death in 1861, a Memorial Committee was formed, chaired by the Duke of Buccleuch[33] and with William Walker of Bowland as Secretary.[34] Its aim was to raise subscriptions from as wide a range of Scottish people as possible including 'the industrial classes', and after much effort £13,000 was raised.[35] A competition was held in 1864 for design ideas; fifty entries were received including ones from several established artists and architects including David Bryce, David Cousin, John Steell (Her Majesty's Sculptor for Scotland since 1838), David Rhind, Robert Matheson, William Calder Marshall and J. Noel Paton.[36] No site had been decided upon, but in line with the democratic nature of the project an appeal for suggestions was advertised in various newspapers. Many sensible, and some outlandish, proposals were made.[37] The four short-listed as most promising were: West Princes Street Gardens, the east side of Charlotte Square, a knoll on the north-east spur of Arthur's Seat and another site in Holyrood Park. Queen Victoria, however, strongly favoured John Steell's (1804–91) equestrian statue being placed in Holyrood Park close to where she had inspected the Volunteers in 1861; the last occasion when the Queen and Albert had both visited Edinburgh.[38]

As time went by the Memorial Committee became increasingly nervous of supporting the Queen's preference due to the review ground being in 'the vicinity of the lowest and worst of the population of the City and it would therefore be almost impossible to protect the memorial from being injured'.[39] Far safer was the Palace forecourt but this, alas, would have required removal of the fountain whose position had been carefully selected by Prince Albert. An impatient public continued to favour Charlotte Square as well as a late contender – Chambers Street, opposite the new museum whose foundation stone had been laid by the Prince. But Chambers Street was pinched on space, and Charlotte Square remained a private garden.

Frustrated with this continuing stalemate, some of the Charlotte Square proprietors, 'feeling that it would be a very graceful and becoming act if the Square were to be placed at the disposal of Her Majesty, and the Memorial Committee', began to take action,[40] canvassing other residents, and seeking advice from Robert Matheson, architect, about possible changes to the garden should the Memorial be placed there.[41] Amongst those involved in the initiative were the Duke of Argyll, the Dowager Duchess of Atholl and Lord Ardmillan. At a meeting of proprietors held in July 1871 all but one of the forty-four present or represented voted in favour; full agreement was reached soon after[42] and the garden placed forthwith 'at the disposal' of the Memorial Committee. Relieved to have found a solution, the Committee recommended the Queen accept 'this fine position'.[43] It was also agreed that any alterations to the garden's layout would be undertaken by David Bryce, designer of the pedestal.[44] Plans already drawn up by Robert Matheson were forwarded to him. Matheson had favoured a square-shaped garden with rounded corners but Bryce changed this to one of octagonal shape, identical to St Andrew Square. Incorporated into the new layout was a wide gravel footpath twenty feet [7 m] from the centre of the east side, railed off from the rest of the garden but allowing full public access to and around the monument.

Consequent Alterations

Reshaping the central space, which also required a new cope stone and railing, was carried out between 1871 and 1873, and everything was completed by 1874. Costs were met by the Memorial Committee, although by now their funds were practically exhausted. Interior planting was based on James McNab's recommendations. He adopted a similar strategy to

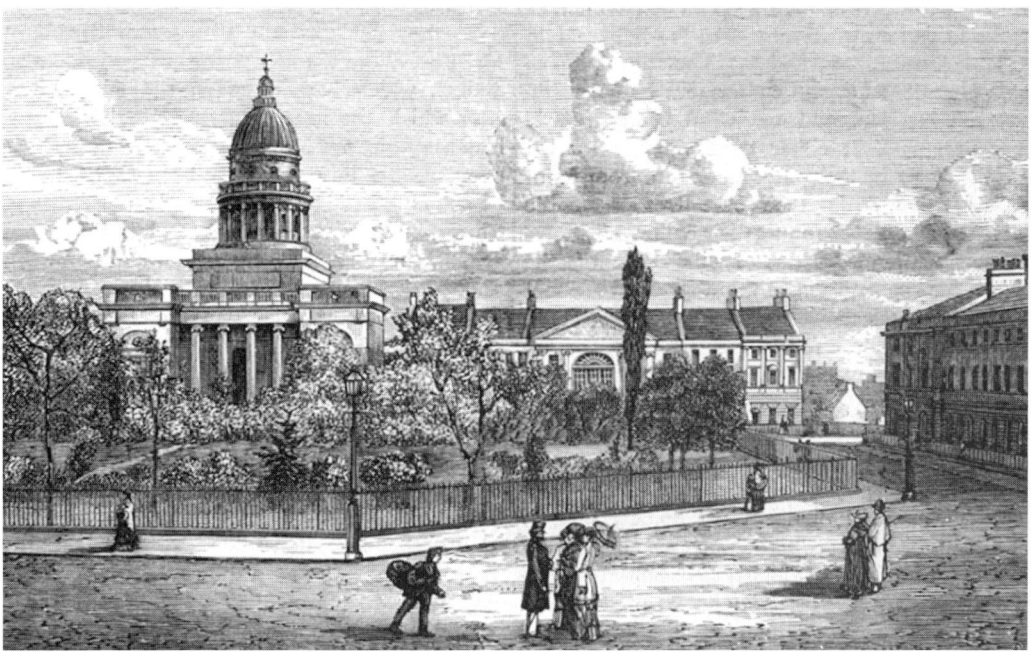

Charlotte Square mid-1870s. Now octagonal in shape, with new railings and an outer pavement but still minus Prince Albert. The garden appears rather bare after the removal of much of the old shrubbery.

St Andrew Square, aiming to open up views of the garden from the outside – particularly of the Memorial from George Street. Over half the perimeter planting was removed and some of the better-shaped trees were retained and left free-standing. Likewise the best of the evergreen shrubs (aucuba, variegated and green holly, boxwood, lawn cypress and bay laurel) were transplanted to 'regular shaped belts' close to the circular walk.[45] At each of the newly created corners McNab recommended planting five trees: four English Elm, and one

Holyrood Park, one of the earlier sites considered: a montage by Robert Matheson.

A rare photograph of the inauguration of the Prince Albert Memorial by Queen Victoria, 17 August 1876. Dense crowds, a fine show of flags and bunting and the raised platform for the Queen and dignitaries can be made out, if somewhat faintly.

Corstorphine Plane (*Acer pseudo Corstoptinum*). He also suggested the addition of statuary, suggesting Dean Ramsay (1793–1872) for the south-west corner; Thomas Chalmers (1780–1847) for the north-west corner; David Livingstone (1813–73) for the south-east corner and Dr James Young Simpson (1811–70) for the north-east, all 'of uniform height on pedestal'.[46] Three of these gentlemen eventually found sanctuary in Princes Street Gardens, and the fourth in George Street. Prince Albert, however, was left to reign supreme over the garden whose appearance he had helped fashion. The proprietors had the interior returfed in 1875, using supplies from the Braid Hills. Not only was Charlotte Square altered in size and shape but it was now much barer, and with a portion allocated to public access up to and around the Memorial.

Prince Albert's arrival was, however, delayed due to an accident to the bronze casting at the Grove Street foundry and Steell's continuing ill health. To the embarrassment of the Memorial Committee and consternation of the proprietors the only ornament to grace the newly-laid-out space was a solitary pedestal. Finally, with all the parts assembled, the day of the unveiling arrived, and on 17 August 1876 at 4 pm Queen Victoria performed the task 'most successfully, without hitch'. The Square was packed with onlookers.[47] A contemporary photograph shows a patch bereft of planting but covered with enormous

The National Memorial to Prince Albert in Charlotte Square, Edinburgh, *c.* 1880. The railed pathway with entry from the George Street end can be seen leading up to and around the Memorial allowing full public access. (Crown copyright © RCAHMS)

crowds. For some considerable time the Memorial attracted many sightseers. And there was much to see. Apart from the Prince on horseback in 'calm quiescent repose', there were detailed bas-reliefs illustrating his career and character. At each corner were groups of statuary 'representing the people of all classes from peer to peasant', all looking upwards 'with reverence and affection'.[48] Three of the groups had been sculpted by different artists: William Brodie RSA, Mr Clark Stanton and George McCallum (succeeded by David Stevenson on McCallum's death in 1868).

Soon afterwards the care and custody of the Memorial were entrusted to the Town Council,[49] and they appointed John Fraser, the Charlotte Square gardener, to look after the adjacent ground.[50] Flower plots were formed within the garden to ornament the pathway leading to the monument. For a number of years plants were supplied by the City's Parks Department. When this source ceased the proprietors bought their own, favouring dahlias, wallflowers and polyanthums.

The Second World War and After

By the 1930s the planting had matured to such an extent that Prince Albert was beginning to disappear from view. Some tree thinning was done and one of the shrubberies removed. But the garden's peaceful existence was soon to be disrupted by the Second World War. In

Removal of the garden railings from Charlotte Square during the Seond World War. Note the paving setts which survived until the road was realigned in the late 1950s. (George Scott Moncrieff, *Edinburgh*, 1947)

June 1941 the Council took possession,[51] air-raid shelters were erected, a gas decontamination hut was added, a 5,000 gallon static water tank built and one year later most of the railings were removed. The garden was not de-requisitioned until July 1946.

Now an ill-used space,[52] open to all and with few families remaining to enjoy it, some felt the time had arrived to make the garden over for public use.[53] The Management Committee were given authority to confer with the Town Council to see if, with certain safeguards, they would be willing to take over custody. The initial response, however, was hesitant. The proprietors meantime pondered on whether to replace the railings; an observation survey carried out over several weeks confirmed that the central area was being used mostly for short-cuts, and was vulnerable to wilful damage. If the garden was to be converted from an 'ill kempt wilderness into a tidy ornamental space',[54] some degree of protection appeared necessary and seemed best achieved by renewing the railings.

Leslie Grahame Thomson (1896–1974) was commissioned to design suitable railings and gates, and to advise on new footpaths to provide 'dignity, harmony and appearance of space'.[55] His draft proposals failed to match these simple objectives, for he suggested

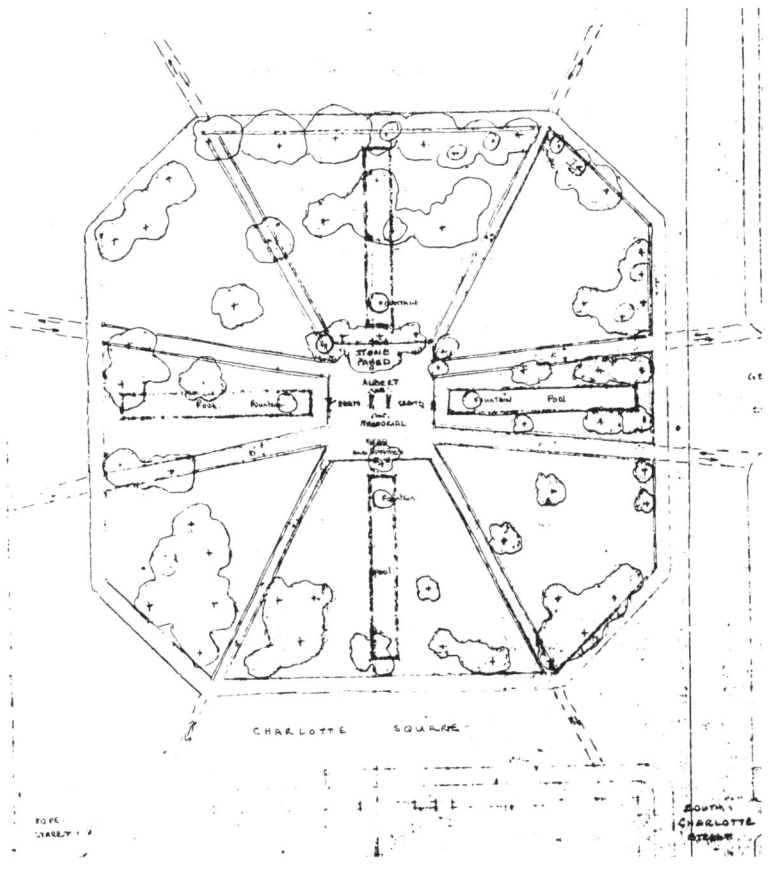

Leslie Graham-Thomson's sketch plan, 1946, for the redesign of the Charlotte Square Garden. It aimed to reduce short-cutting between the footpaths in the event of the gardens being made public. (Clerk's miscellaneous records)

providing no fewer than eight pathways cutting across the grassed area, further sub-divided by four concrete channels of water. The design was rejected on cost grounds and a simpler layout substituted, reducing the pathways to six and omitting the ornamental pools. This revised plan was submitted to the Council, the proprietors proposing to reinstate the railings and gates, with responsibility for the rest being undertaken by the Town prior to its becoming a public garden. But a counter-proposal to construct an underground car park beneath the garden halted negotiations. Frustrated by these setbacks, and faced with continuing deterioration, the proprietors had little choice but to press ahead with re-enclosure.

Permission for new railings was granted despite some hostility from the Council and public. Designed by Grahame Thomson, they were erected in 1947 at a cost of £2,500, each dwelling contributing £50.[56] Railings to a similar design by the same architect were also adopted for St Andrew and Rutland Square Gardens. Thereafter the ground was levelled and grass-seeded. The pathway leading to the Memorial was allowed to become overgrown, and the outer circular walk, the last remnant of Sibbald's 1804 plan, became obliterated. No longer a public attraction, the Prince Consort was left marooned in a sea of green, occasionally prompting the odd enquiry as to who the gentleman on horseback might be!

Uses Made of the Garden

It is hard now to imagine all the demands once placed on the garden which are hinted at in the gardener's contract during the nineteenth century. John Fraser, when appointed in 1875, was required, for example, to attend at all times whether there be work to do or not from 6 o'clock in the morning to sunset, Sundays of course excepted, in order to keep off all intruders, and to prevent children, servants, and others from doing injury to the trees and shrubs.

And to better fulfil these duties, 'shall reside as near the Square as possible';[57] all for the princely wage of £55 a year. From the 1850s pupils of 'The Young Ladies' Institution', 33 Charlotte Square, were allowed to exercise at midday in the garden supervised by a governess. This arrangement continued until the 1880s by which time the owner, a Mr Oliphant, had acquired another girls' school at 23 Charlotte Square. Increased numbers using the garden 'as a playground' provoked criticism both from the gardener and from other proprietors, and permission was eventually withdrawn.[58] One of the pupils at No. 23 between 1876 and 1883 was Elsie Inglis (1864–1917) later to achieve eminence during the First World War as instigator of the Scottish Womens' Hospital Movement abroad, with units in France, Serbia and Russia. A story is told of how she approached the school directors to see if the girls might again use the garden; and was told that the consent of all the proprietors would first be necessary. To someone of resolute spirit this proved no obstacle, and she immediately sallied forth with another girl to knock on all the doors. Her efforts were rewarded, with limited access once more being granted 'at certain hours'.[59]

In its heyday the garden accommodated three tennis courts, a popular sport introduced in the 1880s and played until the 1930s. Such was the pressure for courts that special rules were drawn up establishing the correct procedure for booking them and for operating time

Use of the gardens *c.* 1918. Small boy plays on the swing supervised by nanny. (Courtesy of the late Peggy Bowden)

Later, with his mother, he picks a flower. The original outer circular path can be seen quite clearly. This was obliterated after the First World War. (Courtesy of the late Peggy Bowden)

limits when demand was at its peak. Croquet was also played but a request for a putting green was refused in 1890.[60] Today the garden is used mostly by office-workers during their lunch-time break, and for occasional public events such as charity fêtes, exhibitions and concerts. In recent times the garden has attracted thousands of visitors to the Book Festival, held as part of the Edinburgh Festival.

A Useful Watchdog

Responsibilities concerning the well-being of the Square and Garden have always tended to overlap, with the garden management committee (small and informal) proving an effective vigilante group, quick to take action whenever a crisis threatened. One such instance occurred in 1890–91 when the Edinburgh & Leith Junction Railway Bill was presented before Parliament;[61] one clause contained a proposal to construct a tunnel through Charlotte

Rules for Lawn Tennis, 1882. At the height of its popularity three tennis courts were available in Charlotte Square Gardens.

Square, 40 feet (12.20 m) below the garden, running beneath the Albert Memorial and then along George Street. After being advised by A.W. Belfrage, C.E., the proprietors lodged a petition against the Bill and this, combined with other strong opposition, caused it to be withdrawn.[62] Another achievement was the granting of the Edinburgh Town Planning (Charlotte Square) Scheme Order 1930,[63] set up to preserve and protect existing features of the Square including the garden. Charlotte Square was unique in Scotland in having such a Town Planning order of its own.[64] The garden committee also spearheaded a move in the 1960s to encourage replacement of missing astragals and fanlights, together with improved lighting.

Less successful was the proprietors' acceptance in 1958 of a plan to introduce a one-way traffic system and removal of the stone setts. Extensive excavation work on the north side to alter the level and camber of the road aroused alarm, and it was rightly felt that the full implications of the changes had never been clearly explained. Although their subsequent protest received extensive support, plans had advanced beyond recall.[65] The increased and faster traffic flow created a greater barrier to the Garden than any wall or rail.

Once more traffic in the Square is under review and the latest plan concentrates traffic on the south side. Charlotte Square is promised a 'renaissance' and there is nothing to doubt that the goals set by the National Trust for Scotland will not be realised. This is a fine opportunity for buildings and garden to be revitalised in a sympathetic and comprehensive way. One day maybe the setts will be replaced, the Square calmed and Prince Albert given the appropriate attention he deserves as befitting a National Memorial.

Notes

1. *Memoirs of a Highland lady; the autobiography of Elizabeth Grant of Rothiemurchus, afterwards Mrs Smith of Baltiboys* 1797–1830 (London, 1911), p. 316.
2. Building started in 1792 and continued until 1820. Almost one-third of the Square was finished by 1808, but most buildings were completed from 1811 onwards.
3. One or two changes had taken place at an early date. For example, Oman's Hotel had taken over Nos. 4 & 6 on the north side in the 1820s, and in the 1850s No. 33 was occupied by The Young Ladies' Institution.
4. Douglas Dow, *Heritage Scotland*, Vol. 13, No. 2, Summer, 1996; *The Scotsman,* 3 April, 1996.
5. Some delicate negotiations were however, required with the adjoining owner, the Earl of Moray, regarding boundaries and servitudes relating to the north-west corner of Charlotte Square.
6. TCM, 9 September 1795.
7. Sibbald was the first Superintendent of Works employed on a regular basis.
8. Sibbald was probably responsible for the design and building of several houses in the New Town and at least was involved with working on the elevations on the west side of Charlotte Square.
9. *Edinburgh Evening Courant*, 8 April 1809.
10. TCM, 24 February 1796.
11. TCM, 19 July 1797.
12. Contract between the City of Edinburgh and the Heritors of Charlotte Square and Thomas Chalmers/George Winton, 1797, ECA.
13. The cost of the railings appears to have increased, as the final settlement was for £549; see TCM, 20 June 1798.
14. Leave to do this had already been granted to feuars of houses on the north side.
15. TCM, 10 August 1803.
16. *Grant, Old and New Edinburgh*, Vol. 2, p. 124.
17. E. Beresford Chancellor, *The History of the Squares of London; topographical and historical*, (London, 1907), pp. 103 & 383.
18. TCM, 21 March 1804.
19. And also from 1808 to 1809.
20. Under these Acts all men aged between 18 and 50 years had to be registered, and so many were 'called up' by ballot.
21. TCM, 6 January 1808.
22. Calculated on the basis of £21 specified in the later feu charters although this varied slightly according to the width of the frontages.
23. Town Council Accounts, 1800–09, ECA.
24. Dickson & Co. for example, had premises in Waterloo Place; Eagle & Henderson and James

Alexander in Leith Walk; and John Hay, landscape planner and nurseryman, had offices in Catherine Street (opposite Greenside Place). William Sibbald lived in Catherine Street.

25. James McNab, Report on the Charlotte Square Garden, 10 January 1874: Charlotte Square Minute Book 2, 1869–94, WRH, GD 282/ box 326/1.
26. The pathway on the west side had a downward curve, and on the east side an upward curve; many maps however, show the curves reversed.
27. The second Charlotte Square Minute book refers to an earlier one dating from 1807, but has not survived. Two Minute Books from 1869–94 and 1895–1906 are now deposited in WRH.
28. TCM, 22 January 1817.
29. Cockburn retained his house until 1848 although for many years his main residence was at Bonaly, at the edge of the Pentlands.
30. *The Scotsman,* 1 July 1867, 'Our Town Trees'.
31. *The Scotsman,* 1 September 1824; advertisement inviting people to contract for the erection of the statue.
32. W. Forbes Gray, *The Melville Monument,* op. cit.; the idea of a column was later abandoned in favour of a statue of Pitt placed in George Street in 1833.
33. Material relating to the Prince Albert Memorial is based on the Buccleuch Papers, RH, GD 224 666/3.
34. Walker lived at 26 Moray Place, and was also the 'indefatigable' Secretary of the Board of Supervision for the Relief of the Poor in Scotland. Cockburn described him as an 'honest, poor and a gentleman'.
35. Aberdeenshire and Glasgow decided to have their own memorial and therefore did not contribute.
36. *Catalogue of designs for the Scottish National Memorial to his Royal Highness,* the Prince Consort, December 1864, EPL.
37. For example, the top of Arthur's Seat, Craiglockhart & Corstorphine Hill.
38. John Steell was the son of a well-known wood carver who moved from Aberdeen to Edinburgh in 1805. Steell, who spent several years in Rome, became one of Scotland's most successful sculptors, designing almost one-quarter of the statues in Edinburgh.
39. Minute of Executive Committee, 2 July 1870, Buccleuch papers, op. cit.
40. Charlotte Square Minute Book, (1869–94), 30 June 1871.
41. Robert Matheson (1808–77), architect to Her Majesty's Board of Works.
42. Two residents had initially objected to the original proposal to form a public right of way across the middle of the garden from east to west; this idea was dropped in favour of limited access by a single gate in the centre of the east side, the gate being kept locked at night.
43. Minute of Executive Committee, 12 June 1871, op. cit.
44. David Bryce (1803–76); he had one of the largest and most successful practices in Victorian Britain.
45. James McNab, *Report on the Charlotte Square Gardens,* 10 January 1874, op. cit.
46. *The Scotsman,* 27 April 1874, letter by McNab.
47. *More leaves from the Journal of a life in the Highlands: Queen Victoria's notebook* (London, 1885).
48. *The Scotsman,* 11 March 1865, quoted by Steell in his letter to the Memorial Committee describing his submission.
49. TCM, 5 September 1876.
50. TCM, 20 August 1878. Fraser was paid £5 a year for keeping the pathway tidy.

51. Under the emergency powers conferred upon the Secretary of State for Scotland by the Defence (General) Regulations 1939.

52. *Edinburgh Evening News*, 28 February 1945, signed FGS, re the dilapidated state of the garden.

53. This and the following information are taken from miscellaneous papers in possession of the Clerk to the Management Committee.

54. Particularly in an east to west direction from George Street to the former St George's Church.

55. Leslie Grahame Thomson is best remembered as architect of Reid Memorial Church, Blackford Avenue, 1933, and Fairmilehead Church, 1937. He also designed the Clock Tower at Canonmills in Art Deco style, 1947.

56. Six gateways were made to allow for the diagonal footpaths if and when they were ever made. See also Gifford, McWilliam & Walker, *The Buildings of Scotland: Edinburgh*, p. 292.

57. Charlotte Square Garden Minute Book (1869–94)

58. Charlotte Square Garden Minute Book (1869–94), Minute 4 February 1885.

59. Lady Francis Balfour, *Dr Elsie Inglis* (London, 1918), p. 31.

60. Charlotte Square Garden Minute Book (1869–94), Minute 11 February 1890.

61. *Edinburgh & Leith Junction Railway Bill* was intended to set up a company of the same name with powers to construct railways connecting portions of the North British and the Caledonian Railway Companies' undertakings in Edinburgh and Leith, and other works in Midlothian, and for other purposes.

62. Charlotte Square Garden Minute Book (1869–94); minutes between 19 December 1890 and 13 March 1891.

63. This gave powers under the *Town Planning (Scotland) Act, 1925*.

64. The Town Planning Order had been prompted by pressure form proprietors anxious for stricter control over hotel and business signs and alterations to the frontages.

65. Charlotte Square Press Statement, 24 June 1960, issued by David Birrell, WS, Clerk to the proprietors; miscellaneous papers in possession of the Clerk.

PART THREE

THE GARDENS OF THE NORTH LOCH

CHAPTER 4

INTRODUCTION TO
THE NORTH LOCH

The North Loch, now that it is drained, and all miasma destroyed, is one of the lungs of the city. It is of immense consequence to the health of the citizens that it should be kept open; nor is this of less consequence to the picturesque effect of the city, the skyline of the Old Town, from Princes Street, being one of its finest, most important, and even sublime features.

The Scotsman, 1826[1]

As we hasten along Princes Street intent on our shopping, it is hard to imagine that some of the most respectable and well-connected members of society once lived here. A long row of family houses formed an early part of Edinburgh's fashionable New Town, the traces of which can still be seen in the storeys above the shop frontages. All the houses enjoyed a fine open outlook across the North Loch to the Old Town, the eastern end punctuated by the Castle. That outlook has remained an integral and valued feature of Edinburgh's landscape, secured by the making of the East and West Princes Street Gardens. It is to those early residents that we owe a debt of gratitude because the Town Council were tempted on several occasions to use the North Loch for building purposes. Preserving it as an open, decorative space was due to the efforts of many public-spirited citizens motivated not simply by self-interest, but also by an overriding concern for Edinburgh's well-being. The story behind this achievement is both fascinating and complex and begins with the North Loch itself.

The North Loch prior to the New Town

In the reign of David I (1124–53), this land may have been within the gardens of the Castle; and certainly the kitchen and orchard-cum-pleasure grounds extended a considerable distance to the south and west.[2] But cultivation was probably minimal, and until the Middle Ages the valley remained a marsh watered by two springs rising from the castle rock. In 1450 the streams were deliberately dammed for defence purposes. This catchment remained for three centuries and was known as the Nor' Loch. It became the focus of many legends and traditions, even the place for the punishment of certain offences.[3] At this period it was a reasonably pleasant stretch of water ornamented with swans and ducks provided by the magistrates, a favourite place for boating and skating.[4] In 1715, the year of the first Jacobite rebellion, the city dammed the sluice to increase the depth of water.

The North Loch belonged to the Town and in 1717 they extended their interest by purchasing 30 acres (12 ha) of adjoining land, known as Lochbank or Bearfords (Barefoots) Park. This was ostensibly to rid themselves of a troublesome neighbour,[5] but was also done with an eye to future expansion. By then the Loch, particularly the western end, had degenerated into 'a nearly impassable fetid marsh, a stinking swamp open on all sides, the receptacle of many sewers, and seemingly of all the worried cats, drowned dogs, and blackguardism of the city'.[6] Tanneries and slaughterhouses lined the south bank at the eastern end, causing pollution and unpleasant smells and there were quarry workings on the bank opposite. But there was an attractive 'green broad walk' along the north side linking those living in the eastern district of Multrees Hill (later the site of Register House) and St Ninian's Row to the West Kirk (St Cuthbert's).[7]

With the additional land, and the North Loch clearly proving 'rather a nuisance as a convenience', the Town Council decided to drain it and by 'opening an easier communication' with Lochbank to encourage residential development.[8] In 1720 instructions were sent to the Lord Provost, then visiting London to have these improvements included in an Act of Parliament; but the move proved premature. One year later the Edinburgh College of Physicians pointed to the Loch as a health hazard, recommending immediate action to drain and form it into a canal.[9] Money for this was authorised as part of an Act of Parliament obtained in 1723,[10] but again action failed to materialise.

Ideas to Ornament the North Loch

Ideas to transform the North Loch into an ornamental space had been suggested in 1726 by the exiled Jacobite sympathizer, John Erskine (1675–1732), 11th Earl of Mar. His enthusiasm for architecture and landscape improvement had already found outlet in his ambitious and rather fanciful designs for friends in Britain, but his ideas for Edinburgh were essentially practical, far-sighted and influential. As far as the North loch was concerned he suggested diverting one of the small tributaries of the Water of Leith into it, thereby ridding the valley of stagnant water, while providing 'a fine opportunity for gardens down to the North Loch' to complement the long street projected to the north – roughly in line with George Street. These were the first stirrings of the Princes Street Gardens.[11]

A canal 'with walks and terraces on each side' was later adopted as one of the improvements for Edinburgh proposed by the Royal Convention of Scottish Burghs when they met in 1752.[12] By then plans to expand the city had become more realistic; the 1707 Act of Union had brought greater prosperity, and increased political stability followed the crushing of the 1745 rebellion. But still progress was slow and spasmodic. Nevertheless when the time came for determining a layout for the New Town, James Craig, winner of the design competition, adopted these earlier ideas for the North Loch. His engraved plan of 1768 shows, for example, an ornamental sheet of water occupying the lowest part of the valley, bordered by formal tree-lined walks and grassed plots. Although the North Loch was not included in the competition brief, Craig's depiction of it as a decorative space proved critical; the public took it as proof that this was intended although the Council had made no formal commitment.

Building Developments on the South Side of Princes Street

In 1769, shortly after house building had started at the eastern end of Princes Street, the Town Council feued out land on the opposite side to John Home, coach-maker.[13] This adjoined the North Bridge and Home commissioned David Henderson (?–1787) mason-cum-architect, to draw up plans for housing and work premises.[14] Further land was added and by summer 1770 Home owned a 162-foot (49 m) frontage along Princes Street. Part of this area he sub-feued to Young & Trotter, upholsterers, and they successfully applied for additional land alongside for workshop and warehouse accommodation. Only one stipulation was made: that none of the new buildings were to rise above the level of Princes Street,[15] a ruling which in theory still applies.

Strong objections were made to these developments by, amongst others, David Hume, the philosopher and historian; Sir William Forbes, banker and Andrew Crosbie and Alexander Wight, both advocates.[16] A vigorous protest was mounted before legal action was resorted to. In October 1771 a Bill of Suspension and Interdict was presented by the New Town feuars to stop Young & Trotter's building. It was stated in the Bill that one of the attractions in choosing to live in the New Town had been the understanding that 'no

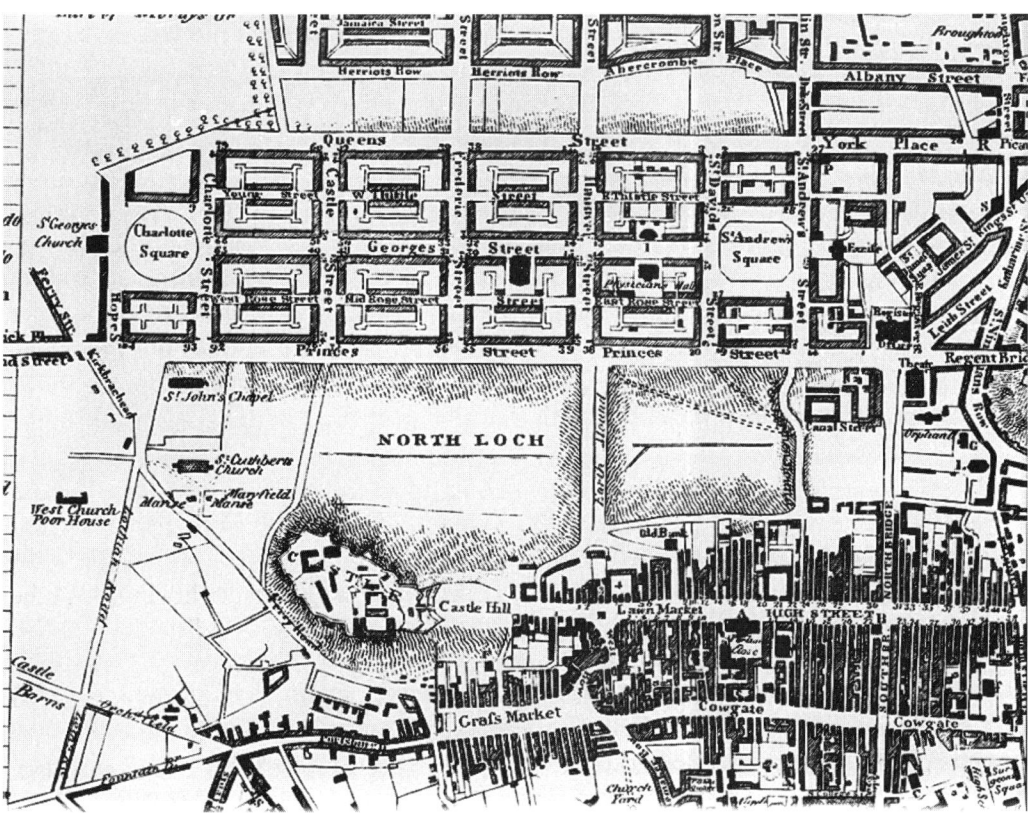

Brown's plan of Edinburgh, 1831 (based on an earlier engraving) showing the area of the North Loch divided by the Earth Mound and the disputed building development in the far eastern corner. (ECL)

buildings were to be erected on the south side of Princes Street', thereby allowing residents 'advantages which they considered as of the greatest value, viz., free air, and an agreeable prospect'.[17] No buildings had been shown on the published plan, hence the claim that the Council were in breach of faith. They in turn maintained that Craig's plan was not binding in its details, and that in any case one of the clauses in the Princes Street house charters referred to possible building along the south side at some time.

Arbitration and the Ruling for a Pleasure Ground

Eventually under the arbitration of David Rae (afterwards Lord Justice Clerk, and better known by his title Lord Eskgrove), the long, complicated and bitter legal battle[18] was finally resolved by way of a compromise. His decree-arbitral of 1776[19] allowed completion of the offending buildings,[20] with the height restriction upheld. Of greater importance, however, was his ruling that the rest of the land to a point just east of Hanover Street was to be 'kept and preserved in perpetuity as pleasure ground' and that it should be formed as such as soon as possible.

The initial costs of draining and preparing the area (including refilling the quarry ground with earth from the foundation of the new buildings) were made the responsibility of the Town Council.[21] Thereafter their liabilities for 'the dressing of the ground' ceased, apart from 'what may necessarily arise from humoring the natural lying and situation' (presumably drainage matters). This suggests that the intention was for the East Princes Street proprietors to take over responsibility for upkeep and care. Rae recommended forming a walk alongside the edge of the Loch, with temporary fencing next to Princes Street until such time as the Town could provide a parapet wall and rail, 'with proper gates and entrances to the pleasure ground'. The area formerly occupied by the Loch, 'shall be dressed up by forming a canal and making up the banks in a decent manner'; and 'as soon as the season will permit', the Council were to 'cast a ditch of sufficient breadth for the purpose of draining the loch'. Recognising that 'the Town's funds may not soon be in so favourable a situation as to admit of works attended with considerable expense' to be undertaken, the question of the canal was left in abeyance.[22]

Division of the North Loch into Two Sections

Princes Street by this time was slowly advancing towards Hanover Street. Already a crude pathway of stones and planks had appeared across the North Loch, providing a short-cut between the Old and New Town leading from James Court to Hanover Street.[23] From 1781 to1830 'The Mound', as it became known, mushroomed in breadth and height as rubble from house foundations was systematically dumped and spread.[24] Its growth not only blocked the natural flow of water in the Loch but also effectively divided the area into two separate parts – the east and west sections.

The east portion now enjoyed some legal protection as designated pleasure ground, but the west end had no such safeguards. Indeed, one of the clauses in Rae's ruling upheld the Town Council's right to feu out land for building on the south side of Princes Street

Donaldson's view of the North Loch, 1777. The crude path crossing the marshy ground can just be made out, the beginnings of the Mound. (ECL)

westwards of Hanover Street.[25] Mar's vision of ornamental gardens, while some steps nearer, was by no means guaranteed and many pitfalls and hurdles lay ahead. The history of the East Princes Street Gardens which now follows demonstrates just how perilous their survival as decorative open space really was.

Notes

1. *The Scotsman*, 8 November 1826.
2. C.A. Malcolm, 'The gardens of the Castle', *BOEC*, Vol. XIV, 1925, pp. 101–20.
3. In 1562 for example, the Town Council ruled that all persons of 'loose life' should be ducked in a certain part of the loch, and between 1589 and 1670 many witches were ducked there before being burned on Castle Hill. See D. Robertson and M. Wood, *Castle and Town*, (Edinburgh & London, 1928) pp. 10 & 14.
4. Robert Chambers, *Traditions of Edinburgh*, (London & Edinburgh, 1869) (new edn), p. 29.
5. Later corrupted to Barefoots Parks; Robert Hepburn of Bearford, the previous owner, had been in frequent dispute with the Town.
6. Henry Cockburn, *Memorials of his time*, op. cit., p. 371.
7. TCM, 24 April 1706.
8. TCM, 11 January 1720.
9. Alexander Wood, 'The Condition of the dwellings of the operative classes in Edinburgh', part of a report on: *The condition of the poorer classes of Edinburgh, and of their dwellings, neighbourhoods and families* (Edinburgh 1868).
10. An Act for enlarging the term granted by an Act made in the 3rd year of his Majesty's reign (for continuing the duty of 2 pennies Scots upon every pint of ale and beer sold in the City of Edinburgh) for the purpose therein mentioned and for discontinuing the payment of the

petty port customs there) and for making the said Act more effectual: passed on 9 October 1722 and printed in 1723.

11. Details of the Earl of Mar's suggestions for the improvement of Edinburgh (his paper being variously dated 1726 or 1728) are quoted in the *Statistical Account of Scotland*, vol. VIII (1793), pp. 647–9.

12. These proposals were subsequently published as a pamphlet entitled: 'Proposals for carrying on certain public works in the City of Edinburgh', reproduced in the *Scots Magazine* in August 1752 under the authorship of Gilbert Elliot, Lord of Justiciary.

13. John Home had originally bought land on the north side of Princes Street at the east end; the land in question on the south side had first been offered to Graham, a plumber, in exchange for his ground on Multrees Hill – the site intended for Register House.

14. Ann Street was built parallel to the bridge and consisted of tenements five storeys high, dipping steeply into the valley until joining Canal Street. This street was demolished in 1817 as part of the *Edinburgh Improvement Act, 1816*.

15. TCM, 8 August 1770.

16. *Princes Street Edinburgh: An Illustrated Account of its Origins and Development*, issued by The Life Association of Scotland (Edinburgh, 1938), p. 28.

17. Quoted in Youngson's *The Making of Classical Edinburgh*, op. cit., p. 86; which provides a useful background to this episode.

18. William Cowan, 'The buildings at the East end of Princes Street', op. cit., pp. 145–9.

19. Rae's Decree-arbitral was published on 19 March 1776.

20. The buildings on Home's feu remained almost unaltered until they were demolished in 1896 when the new North Bridge was under construction.

21. TCM, 16 August 1780, which gives details of the decree-arbitral.

22. To be settled and directed by the Lord President of the Court of Session, and the Lord Chief Baron of the Court of Exchequer when the occasion arose; John Stodart, then Lord Provost, was named as overseer for the other improvement work to be carried out.

23. The origins of this route seem to have been partly accidental. George Boyd, a clothier in Gosford's Close, is said to have made the first steps across the marshy valley which others then added to; for a long time it was named 'Geordie Boyd's Brig'.

24 See William Creech, *Letters to Sir John Sinclair*, first published 1793, and J.F. Birrell, *An Edinburgh Alphabet* (Edinburgh, 1980), p. 152.

25. And under the same stipulations as previously; viz., that any houses built were not to be less than 96 feet (29 m) from those on the north side, or extend more than 160 feet (49 m) in depth to the south.

CHAPTER 5

EAST PRINCES STREET GARDENS

That part of the North Loch which lies to the east of the Mound is just now enclosed for the purpose of being planted with trees. Hitherto, we may say since the days of Noah probably it has been open ground and a public thoroughfare.

Anon., Journal entry, November 1829

The eastern part of the North Loch has for some time been planted with trees along the sloping banks. It is now let to a nurseryman so as that the lower part may be converted into pleasure grounds and walks, the citizens to be subjected to a small yearly payment for the liberty of walking thro' it. This may do something for the embellishment of the city but there is an outcry against it as depriving the town folks of a right they have of bleaching their clothes, when it was formerly an open green.

Anon., Journal entry, May 1832

Within days of Rae's judgement the Council hired labourers 'to work at the banks of the intended canal between the Old and New Town';[2] and a ditch was cut to improve drainage.[3] A little later the quarry began to be filled, and the bank along Princes Street grass-seeded. But good intentions were short-lived and soon fell victim to shortage of cash and a suitable workforce. Unenclosed, still poorly drained, with open sewers running through it, criss-

Valley of the North Loch, east end, Edinburgh, 1807. Animals are being grazed and in the foreground is the new North Bridge. The Bank of Scotland stands aloft on the south bank, its rear still awaiting improvement. (ECL)

East North Loch, 1814. Various short-cuts wind down the steeply sloping banks including the Mound – now increased in height and width. The wall and railing alongside Princes Street can be seen. (ECL)

crossed by pathways shared by carts and cattle, and with the strip along Princes Street used for saw pits and carpenters' yards, 'what has already so properly begun has been greatly torn and defaced'.[4] The complainant was Alexander Wight, one of the stalwarts of the previous campaign to safeguard the East North Loch. In 1780 he presented a memorial to the Council on behalf of himself and others, expressing concern that while one quarry had been filled, the mason William Jamieson had been allowed to open another;[5] also of concern was the damage caused by grazing cattle 'gorging up' the ground in winter, leaving it wet and swampy.

Assurances were given that improvements would be made, including the covering of the common sewer, deep cuts on either side of the loch to allow better drainage, grass-seeding of the central area and a parapet and rail along Princes Street.[6] But the feuars' bid to prod the Council's conscience produced only one result – a railing erected 15 feet (4.58 m) north of the upper edge of the bank, allowing room for 'a commodious walk or terrace within the rail'.[7] Work began in 1781, and at Wight's request an extra gateway opposite St Andrew / St David's Street was provided for those living in the vicinity.[8] But the pattern of use hardly changed at all. Sheep and cattle were still grazed, and short-cutting to the Little Mound and the busy fish, meat, fruit and vegetable markets continued. In addition part of the south side was used for growing vegetables.

Continued Decline

Once more deterioration set in. In 1788, for example, George Sandy, a 16-year-old apprentice WS, noted in his diary that for several days in May the East North Loch was 'a good deal overflowed'.[9] And to such an extent that men were at work cutting trenches, laying broad drains and repairing the culverts below the Mound. According to Sandy, 'we hear that a canal is to be made in the North Loch', and he talks about taking a walk to survey it. But what he saw is uncertain and from this time on the idea for a canal seems to have lapsed.[10]

By 1800 Princes Street was practically complete and already many of the early residents had moved westwards, their former houses acquired for use as shops and offices. Not surprisingly the incoming business proprietors felt less concerned about the open space opposite them, while those moving concentrated their energies on the land at the western end. In spite of a 40-year start, the East North Loch began to lag behind. Indeed, the Improvement Act of 1816, under which the West Princes Street Gardens were established, allowed a new road to be made from the top bank opposite St Andrew's Street to the west end of Canal Street (using unemployed workers); thus the East North Loch became even more of a thoroughfare. By now the route to the markets, which cut almost diagonally across the site, had become wider. Old Town housewives used parts of the south bank for

Serpentine road made under the 1816 Improvement Act, leading from Princes Street to the north-west corner of Canal Street and the Edinburgh markets. (J. Ewbank, *Picturesque Views of Edinburgh*, 1825)

East Princes Street Gardens 85

East North Loch, Edinburgh, as a drying green. (T. Shepherd, *Views of Edinburgh*, 1825)

clothes washing and drying. Kirkwood's plan of 1819, for example, shows twenty clothes poles stretching across the ground in one long wavy line, and two water pumps. Washing was also laid out to dry or 'bleach' on any spare patch of grass, in competition with roving cats, dogs, and impromptu bonfires.

Plans to build on the East North Loch

From around 1812 the Town Council entertained various ideas for building on the land. And there was no shortage of establishments eager for a central position. Possible candidates included a gaol and Court of Justiciary, a church, a theatre, the Royal High School and a stable and riding establishment for the Midlothian Yeomanry. This last possibility was scathingly attacked by *The Scotsman* in 1822. While acknowledging William Burn, the project architect, as a man of ' taste and ability', the newspaper described these particular plans as nothing but a 'specimen of the abominable', a crude intrusive 'lump' and a blot on the landscape. Even worse was the intended use:

> a troop of horses implies a troop of horsemen; and these a troop of grooms; and these a troop of stable boys, with a due proportion of ostlers, farriers, dealers, breakers, jockeys and dogs:-to say nothing of the members of other troops – the sonorous trumpeter – the gallant pay sergeant – the everlasting rough rider – the lounging friends and the mob of vulgar gazers. The very dung itself is objection enough.[11]

Although none of these proposals gained public support, the Council seemed oblivious to the discontents they were helping to fuel.[12]

The Edinburgh New Town Gardens

Further Attempts at Improvement

West Princes Street Pleasure Grounds, newly formed and planted, opened their gates to proprietors in 1821, serving to highlight the miserable plight of the neighbouring space, and several East End proprietors felt impelled to present another petition to the Lord Provost. This was in April 1822.[13] Reference was again made to Craig's plan showing 'the whole grounds situated between the Old City of Edinburgh and Princes Street as Garden or Pleasure Grounds', and the Council was reminded of Rae's ruling that the East North Loch be laid down 'in Pleasure Grounds for the Beauty of the Town and accommodation of the Proprietors'. This was after all the age of improvement, and 'while taste requires and Justice demands, the Will cannot be wanting to an enlightened Magistracy to grant what they are bound to perform and what no-one can doubt must add much to the beauty of both the Old and New Town of Edinburgh'. Baillie Alexander Henderson (contractor for West Princes Street Gardens) was named as someone competent to aid progress. But as usual the plea fell on deaf ears; the City simply had no money for such improvements.

A more forceful public outburst came four years later, provoked on this occasion by the dumping of large quantities of earth between the Mound and the North Bridge during the summer of 1825. The Council had incurred 'great expense' in employing labourers 'to spread the earth laid down in the hollow ground east of the Mound and in constructing the drains necessary for adapting the ground for the purpose'.[14] Fears were rife that this was being done in preparation for building. Leading the protest was Henry Cockburn; a man deeply committed to Edinburgh's well-being and whose name lives on in the Cockburn Association, the Edinburgh Civic Trust.

Cockburn's Campaign

A powerful voice in the Faculty of Advocates, Cockburn had already liaised with the Town over a new Improvement Bill designed to provide much-needed south and west approaches to the City (one of the prime movers behind this was Alexander Henderson, now Lord Provost).[15] Not everyone supported these projected improvements; several New Town residents felt the costs unjustified at a time of economic depression, and better communications with the south side and Old Town were considered hardly worthwhile, particularly as the latter was in decline. Who in fact would choose to visit the 'cheerless Meadows' when more attractive walks and pleasure grounds were closer to hand?[16] The support of the Faculty was therefore crucial. Cockburn exploited this by insisting that the Bill should

Henry Cockburn, one of the chief protagonists for safeguarding the East North Loch as an open space. (Crombie, *Modern Athenians, 1837–1847*, ECL)

contain a clause prohibiting any building on the south side of Princes Street east of the Mound. Having already faced one defeat in Parliament (in 1824), the Council agreed. But the redrafted Bill fared no better.

By now, several New Town residents united to support Cockburn's campaign. Early in 1826 the following notice appeared in all the Edinburgh newspapers:

> As the rapid accumulation of Earth between the Mound and the North Bridge cannot fail soon to prove destructive of the picturesque effects of this City, and as very serious alarms have been for some time entertained that there is a design to erect Buildings along the south side of Princes Street east of the Mound, in consequence of the filling up of the valley, other circumstances give probability every day that these alarms are well founded we request a meeting of proprietors in the New Town to be held within the Waterloo Hotel on Monday the 6th instant (February), at 2 o'clock, and we earnestly entreat all such proprietors who feel any interest in preserving the beauty of Edinburgh to attend on this occasion.[17]

Fourteen signatures were appended, several belonging to West Princes Street proprietors including four of their garden committee.[18] Sir James Ferguson of Kilkerran chaired the 'highly respectable gathering'[19] which focused on the Lord Provost's written response to their queries. It was not thought 'a very satisfactory answer', lacking any firm assurances that the land in question was to be kept as open space.[20] Cockburn outlined all the previous attempts to erect buildings, and how their present anxieties arose from the Magistrates having 'in their possession at that very moment under lock and key a plan for building east of the Mound'.

Was such a plan surreptitiously tucked away? We simply do not know, but it is perhaps unlikely. At best the Council may simply have been providing a convenient central dump for builders, with no more sinister motive than raising the level of ground in readiness for later embellishment. The Improvement Bill was still not passed, and the Town would not have wished to jeopardise this by antagonising any of its influential citizens.

William Playfair's Involvement

Any lingering doubts about the Council's good intentions were dispelled by the appointment of a special committee in 1826 'to direct and superintend the arranging and dressing of the ground east of the Mound it having been brought to the intended level'.[21] More than this, the committee sought advice from the architect, William Playfair (1789–1851),[22] who for some time had been working in the Mound area, on plans for the Royal Institution (Royal Scottish Academy), approved in 1822, and completed early in 1826.[23] This was a sound tactical move. Playfair was already acquainted with several West Princes Street proprietors and was well regarded by Henry Cockburn. In addition Playfair had already demonstrated his abilities as a sensitive designer committed to the ideals of picturesque improvement in his plans for laying out the grounds north of Calton Hill.[24]

Playfair's report, submitted in June 1826, concentrated on an overall strategy rather than on planting details.[25] Funds in any case were limited. He singled out, as first priority, the formation of a broad terrace parallel to Princes Street. This was to be bordered by trees and shrubs, with a central gravel footpath. Surrounding banks, particularly the southern one, needed to be more gently sloped, with more soil added and trees planted. The central area (after removal of the diagonal road: the Serpentine one to remain but with improvements) was to be levelled and grass sown, with possible use for clothes drying and bleaching. The four wells, 'so judiciously provided' in the lower portion, could serve for irrigation or bleaching purposes. Thus the space would be transformed from a 'melancholy and neglected appearance' to becoming 'the greatest ornament to the City'.

Enter William Sawrey Gilpin

In addition to Playfair, William Sawrey Gilpin (1762–1843), an 'eminent landscape gardener', was also consulted. This was one of the rare occasions when an 'outsider' was approached for advice and was surely an act calculated to help restore public confidence.[26] Gilpin was the son of Sawrey Gilpin, the celebrated animal painter, and nephew of the better-known Reverend William Gilpin, influential writer on the Picturesque.[27] According to press reports he was employed for some time making plans for 'beautifying' the ground,[28] and in October 1826 was paid 12 guineas 'for attendance on account of the projected improvement of the North Loch'.[29] Gilpin, an accomplished watercolour artist and military landscape draughtsman, did not begin to practise landscaping until 1820 when he was in his late fifties (encouraged by Uvedale Price, a rich dilettante with literary aspirations and opinionated views on the theory of the Picturesque). With no close rivals (Repton having died two years before) and possessing a certain design flair, he went on to establish a very successful practice. Such a picturesque site would have immediately appealed to Gilpin, and he seems to have produced not only a plan but a model as well.[30] Sadly neither has survived, so his design recommendations remain a mystery. Soon afterwards he departed for Ireland to work on several commissions there,[31] and all connections with Edinburgh ceased.[32]

Cockburn remained sceptical, but the involvement of such eminent professionals reassured the press of the Council's 'good faith', amply demonstrated 'by their being, at this very moment, occupied in carrying into effect a highly ornamental plan for laying out the North Loch'.[33] The time had come to call a truce. More important still was the passing of the Improvement Bill in 1827, which amongst other things guaranteed the East North Loch as 'one of the lungs of the city' along with the Meadows and Bruntsfield Links.[34]

Slow Progress

Victory yielded few immediate results, and indeed further alarm was triggered when rumours began to spread that the central area was destined to be 'a vast exposé of the laid-out washings of the lowest classes' – possibly alluding to Playfair's report which had included provision for a washing green. This was anathema to one newspaper correspondent who shuddered at the thought of Playfair's Doric colonnade being set against 'six acres of squalid rags – on shirts and stockings, and duck trousers, and sheets ineffable, and patchwork quilts, and binding-blankets, in all their grades of service, treatment, and purification'. The Scottish practice of bleaching and drying clothes was dismissed as both

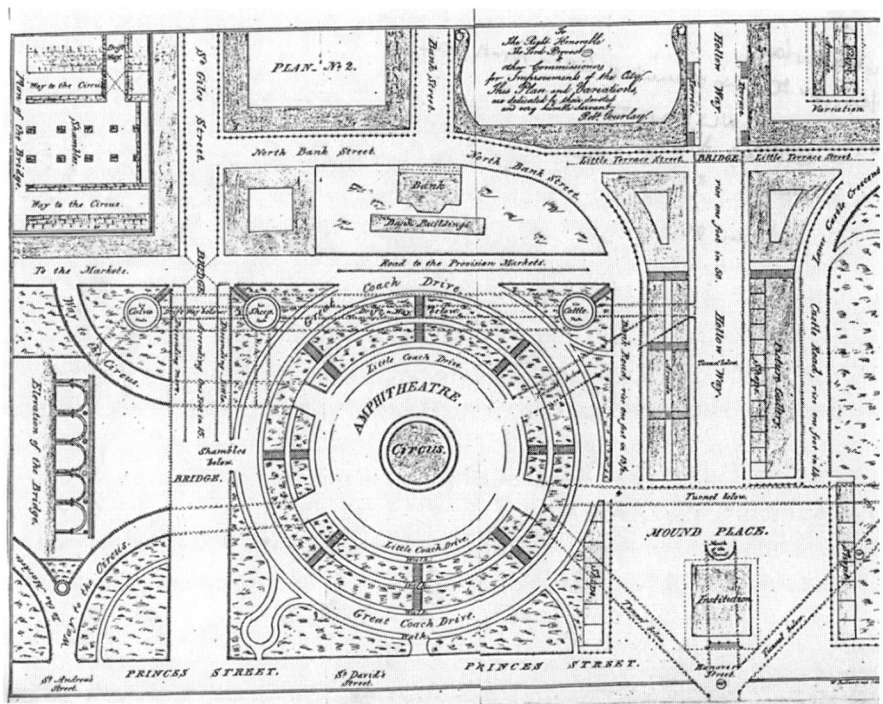

Robert Gourlay's plan for the improvement of the East North Loch, 1829. (ECA)

inefficient and extravagant of space; why, oh why, the writer asked, did housewives not boil their linen?[35] The editor sharply reminded the writer that there was now 'a great deal of ground laid out for ornament', and that it was not unreasonable to allow the poorer classes some central space for what was essentially a clean and wholesome activity.

Steps to improve the ground did, however, begin to get under way. Within the next two years Thomas Brown, the Town's Superintendent, supervised the shaping of the banks and filling the hollows (using earth and debris from 'restoration' work at St Giles' Cathedral under William Burn) together with some grass-seeding.[36] But still it appeared 'waste ground', prompting Robert Gourlay, 'a scientist' with a fertile imagination, to draw up a scheme for filling the void with a huge amphitheatre, flat-roofed, and ornamented with a tall fountain; and with exhibition space for equestrian displays, games, gymnastics, races and other large events. Recreation with classical overtones to match a city with similar pretensions![37]

Patrick Neill takes Control

Progress quickened once the Council appointed a committee to implement an ornamental terrace along Princes Street together with other improvements. The two key members were Baillie Robert Johnson (1765–1838) and Dr Patrick Neill, 'both individuals with eyes alive to the picturesque', and remembered many years later by James McNab for their significant contribution to the making of these gardens.[38] It was a productive partnership, but of the two, Patrick Neill, the committee's chairman, probably contributed more. Edinburgh was extraordinarily fortunate to have him on the Council. A modest and rather retiring bachelor, he was keenly committed to Edinburgh's well-being, and possessed both a practical and scholarly knowledge of horticultural.[39] Diligent in his printing business, then in Fishmarket Close (just beyond the Serpentine road)[40], his overriding passion was for natural history and in particular botany and horticulture.[41] Neill served as secretary of the Wernerian Natural History Society (founded 1808), and of the Caledonian Horticultural Society (founded 1809), holding the latter post for a record forty years. He was, in Cockburn's eyes, 'a useful citizen, a most intelligent florist, and one of the few defenders of our architectural relics',[42] an opinion equally shared by John Claudius Loudon who spoke of Neill as 'a most benevolent and intelligent man and a skilful horticultural connoisseur':[43] altogether, 'a man of great worth and public spirit'.[44] Under his guidance the East Princes Street Gardens finally became established. Later his advice was sought in connection with the Regent Terrace and Calton Hill Pleasure Grounds and the George Square Gardens in the 1830s. Neill's 'excellent' report written in the latter part of 1829, on which he had 'bestowed so much care and attention', met with the Council's approval as well as 'the approbation of Mr Henry Cockburn and other gentlemen of taste, who take an interest in the grounds in question'.[45] The terrace, complete with gravel walk, was to be rather broader than Playfair suggested, but narrower than the present-day one, planted with a row of lime trees parallel to the railings, and with a further row of English elm and sycamore; the gaps to be filled with privet, holly and laurel. To enhance the terrace bank, swells or hollows were to be formed and planted with common hardy forest trees. Further clumps of trees were also suggested. Likely costs were put at around £70, the biggest expense being the large amount of larch paling required to protect the new planting. The Town's own carpenters and labourers, 'among whom it is understood there is at least one experienced gardener and planter', were to do the work.

By the end of October 1829, forming and dressing the north bank was practically complete, Neill and Thomas Brown having liaised closely together.[46] Two months later the committee decided to enclose all the surrounding banks, these to be, 'more or less covered in trees'.[47] Negotiations had already taken place with the Bank of Scotland, part-

Dr Patrick Neill, whose contribution towards transforming the East North Loch from wasteland into a decorative space was outstanding. (Crombie, *Modern Athenians, 1837–1847*, ECL)

owners of the south bank. It was agreed that this portion be thickly covered with trees towards which the Bank would contribute £50. Subsequently this portion was leased to the City.[48]

Donation of Plants

By spring 1831 the work was complete. Something of the magnitude of the undertaking can be judged by Neill's final report.[49] Over five acres (2.0 ha) had been planted with nearly 27,000 trees and shrubs,[50] an over-generous number to compensate for variable soil conditions and the exposed nature of the site. Apart from the top terrace walk, several footpaths had been formed to sweep gently down the banks 'so as to render every part readily accessible'. The central 'meadow' had been limed and grass-sown;[51] and the 'offensive place of retreat', the public privy in the north-west corner, had been demolished. To ward off further nuisance should old habits persist,[52] the cleared ground was planted with wild brambles, briars and sloe thorns and sown with furze and whin seeds!

But the most amazing part of Neill's report was the description of his quest for plants, to which the response was overwhelming: a sure indication of his own high standing and the project's merit. He had initially approached individuals whose support could be depended on; hence James Skene, designer of West Princes Street Gardens and member of their management committee, donated 300 sycamores and poplars from the western garden; Dr Graham, Professor of Botany, to whom the request was made for 'suitable young forest trees and evergreens', gifted 1,500 plants, 'some hundreds of large size'. Neill's own Royal Caledonian Horticultural Society supplied about 500 plants from their experimental gardens at Inverleith, including 250 bay laurels and 50 common lilacs. With yet 'still many thorns and plants' required, Neill began to canvas local nurseries to see 'what kind of large plants suitable for the purpose could be procured at reasonable rates'. To his surprise he was met with a flood of free offers. Messrs Dickson & Co, of Waterloo Place, 'led the way' and donated over 1,200 plants including most varieties of forest trees, as well as willows, poplars, and 5,000 larch, spruce, fir and Scotch pine. After requesting Neill to list anything else required, they added over 2,500 ornamental and rare trees such as Turkey oak, striped gold leaf plane, fern leaved chestnut, purple beech, double scarlet thorn, guelder rose, Siberian lilac, evergreen privet and Balm of Gilead firs. The lime tree avenue was supplied by James Dickson & Son, Inverleith Nurseries, who also gave over 1,000 Turkey oaks, mountain ash, walnuts, hazel and bud cherry trees. Eagle & Henderson provided 200 Portugal laurels, 'trained in the tree style'. Three other nurserymen contributed: Alexander Wight, Thomas Cleghorn and Charles Lawson; while private donations were also made. John Bonar Esq. of Kimmerghame, Berwickshire, for example, gave 8,500 forest trees. The only sum spent on planting by the Town Council came to less than £5.[52]

Newly Resplendent, but What Next?

Although the Gardens had been developed into a well planted and potentially highly ornamented pleasure ground, the Council nevertheless lacked any clear vision for their

Edinburgh's Old Town from Princes Street, 1841. Clothes washing has now removed to the little mound, while Neill's planting on the eastern bank of what is now the East Princes Street Gardens looks to be thriving. (*Black's Guide Through Edinburgh*, 1841)

future. At first the area was fenced off to allow the planting to become established, and notices were erected warning against trespass. Various options were considered: for example, allowing public access by means of a rented key system (similar to other New Town pleasure gardens), using the central area as a bleaching green (an idea guaranteed to raise hackles), and finally, leasing the site for nursery purposes (Thomas Cleghorn, nurseryman and florist in Princes Street, had already made approaches).[53] One newspaper suggested setting aside part of the ground 'for the manly and athletic games of Scotland', and in winter curling and skating on a suitably formed pond of ice.[54]

Most feasible was the nursery proposition, and in May 1832 Cleghorn successfully bid at public auction for a 28-year lease.[55] Cleghorn's original intentions were to combine his nursery business with a scaled-down version of a pleasure ground, 'with pleasure walks, and ornamental shrubbery, to which respectable citizens will have access for a small sum annually'. This required the central area to be ploughed preparatory to forming an 'artificial rock work', from which radiated eight shaded walks hedged with holly and laurel. A moss house (a rustic structure with slated interior walls sealed with mosses) was to occupy the north-west corner, its coloured glass panes adding a touch of magic by transforming passers-by on the Little Mound or North Bridge into the shape, 'of green fairies, swart savages, or blue devils, as his fancy inclines him'.[56] To what extent these ideas were implemented is

East Princes Street Gardens   93

not known, but Cleghorn's business seems to have thrived, for he went on to add a keeper's cottage, greenhouse and conservatory.[57] In 1841 Cleghorn sub-leased the ground to Eagle & Henderson, who needed more space since their West Princes Street nursery ground had been reduced by half.[58] By then the trees on the banks were in need of thinning, and the fencing on the south side had become dilapidated due to assaults from boys.[59] A view painted by Charles Halkerston in 1843 from the Mound, looking towards Princes Street, includes the west side of the garden and shows neatly laid out paths and flower beds and well-established trees.

The Coming of the Railway and the Scott Monument

Soon after acquiring the sub-lease, Eagle & Henderson were faced with renewed attempts by the Edinburgh & Glasgow Railway Company to extend their line from the Haymarket terminus to the east end of Princes Street. Strong opposition by the West Princes Street proprietors had defeated their previous attempt in 1836. But public enthusiasm for railways

The Scott Monument under construction, 1843–4. Its arrival resulted in the top terrace being doubled in width with extra earth supplied from the railway excavation work. Neill's planting unfortunately suffered. (Calotype by Adamson & Hall, ECL)

was now overwhelming, and pressure for other lines from the north and east increased the need for a more central terminus. Permission for the extension was granted by Parliament in July 1844. Although it was a bitter disappointment to the West Princes Street proprietors, their fight at least guaranteed safeguards to minimise the intrusive effects of the railway, which applied to both gardens. Besides its proper enclosure, the Act required embankments to be formed to screen the trains and reduce noise.

But the consequences for East Princes Street Gardens were particularly devastating. Apart from the garden being cut in two, a large chunk was removed, reducing the overall size by more than a quarter. Worse still, much of Neill's dedicated work was completely ruined and the planting, so generously gifted, destroyed. For three years workmen occupied the garden, making tunnels and laying tracks. Debris was indiscriminately dumped and sufficient havoc caused to force the Council in 1845 to take legal action to prevent further abuse.[60] By 1847 the gardens were in 'a most dilapidated state' and could 'no longer be called a garden'.[61]

Compounding the misery was the arrival of further work squads to erect the monument to Sir Walter Scott, sited on the north side at the eastern end, and later to enclose a marble statue of the writer, sculpted by John Steell.[62] A vast and intricate Gothic pile slowly emerged, rising some 200 feet (61 m) in height, and designed by George Meikle Kemp (1745–1844),

Joseph Ebsworth's drawing from the Scott Monument looking west along Princes Street, 1847. The top terrace appears to have been tidied up. (Edinburgh World Heritage Trust)

an Edinburgh joiner and talented draughtsman. Playfair was not alone, however, when he criticised the monument as, 'too large for its position', and others likened it to a 'spire of a Gothic church taken off and stuck in the ground'.[63] Its arrival was to determine significantly the future character of the garden. As a first step towards integration permission was granted in 1845 to more than double the width of the top terrace, earth being supplied by the Railway Company from their excavations further below in the valley.[64]

All Neill's efforts at planting the top bank – the product of so much goodwill amongst Edinburgh's nursery fraternity – vanished forever, the trees cut down, 'without a murmur'.[65] With funds completely exhausted, the Monument's Committee were able to do only the barest minimum to enhance the immediate surroundings before the inauguration ceremony on 15 August 1846. The weather was so appalling, and the crowds so great, that probably no-one noticed or cared. In 1849 trains started to run through the garden; and after months of negotiation the Railway Company finally agreed to pay £4,000 to the Town Council in compensation.[66] A reversal in fortune for this long-suffering space was certainly overdue.

New Layout by David Cousin

David Cousin (1809–78), one-time assistant to William Playfair,[67] was responsible for redesigning the gardens. Appointed City Superintendent in 1847, he was the first to be known under the title of 'City Architect'. To this day the structure of East Princes Street Gardens remains largely as he planned it. Not only a competent architect, he also had experience of landscape work, having been responsible for four Edinburgh cemeteries (Warriston, 1843; Newington, Rosebank and Dalry, all in 1846), as well as improvements to Calton Hill and the Meadows. He also designed a housing development in Newington which, like the New Town, had housing formed round areas of communal pleasure ground.[68]

Cousin's aim with the East Princes Street Gardens was to create a bold effect as seen from the surrounding streets, and to incorporate the Scott Monument as an integral part of it. The width of the top terrace was further increased, and a central gravel walk was formed, bordered by grass and trees. To complement the Monument, Cousin designed a four-foot (1.2 m) high wall 'of gothic character', complete with handsome stairways at either end leading to a lower terrace walk.[69] The rest of the bank was laid with 'smooth turf' and planted with clumps of evergreens. Forest trees were reserved for the lower slopes. Gentle curving walks intersected the grassed areas on either side of the railway, with further clumps of evergreen shrubs. The south and west banks were to remain unchanged apart from some thinning and pruning, and making good existing pathways and slopes. The railway itself was to be enclosed by a wall, with the embankment formed on the garden side grassed, shrub-planted and surmounted with thorn hedging.

Cousin had wanted to create an open-air sculpture gallery along the 'Great Terrace', and allowed space for six pedestals along the wall. Like many Victorians, he believed in the ennobling and enriching value of the Arts as a means of improving and uplifting the minds and behaviour of the working class. His intention was for six 'colossal' statues but money was not forthcoming. Later, in the 1860s, John Dick Peddie promoted similar ideas for West Princes Street Gardens.

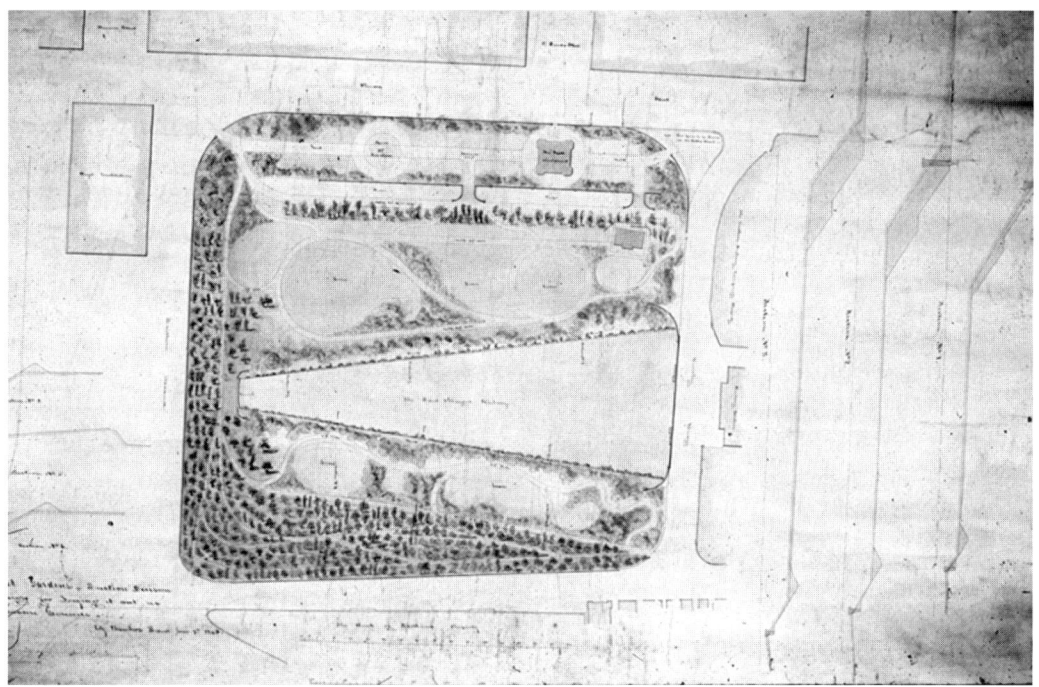

David Cousin's plan for redesigning the East Princes Street Gardens, Edinburgh, 1849. A site for a fountain is shown along the top terrace. (Crown copyright © RCAHMS)

The rest of Cousin's proposals were, however, realised. Earth and rubble from the Mound (the National Gallery site under preparation for building), and cart-loads supplied by John Alexander (excavating for the Castle Hill reservoir) were used to enlarge the top terrace and form the railway embankment.[70] By 1849 estimates for the terrace wall, stairs and a new parapet and iron railing along Princes Street (to Cousin's design) had been obtained; three different firms were involved at an overall cost of £1,218.[71] Because of 'great and irreparable damage from idle boys who overrun the grounds', particularly to the trees on the west and south slopes, Cousin suggested appointing a full-time watchman. It proved a fortunate move as the man employed turned out to be a 'practical gardener', and was soon applying his skills to the grounds.[72] During the winter of 1849 Mr William Langdon, 'proprietor of the Chinese Collection', was allowed to rent the central area for three months to accommodate his temporary exhibition sheds.[73]

Open to the Public

Most of 1850 was spent on forming the Great Terrace, and ancillary work such as realigning old walks, making new ones, demolishing and clearing Cleghorn's gardener's cottage and working on the railway embankments.[74] In May of that year Peter Thomson (the watchman) was appointed as the first full-time gardener, and made responsible for selecting much of the new planting.[75] On the anniversary of Sir Walter Scott's birthday, 15 August 1851, and with appropriate pomp and ceremony, the East Princes Street Gardens were officially opened. Adding to the festivities was the band of the 6th Dragoons of the 33rd Regiment, who provided musical accompaniment for the promenading public. Thus, after a very chequered history, the East North Loch became a public pleasure ground, making it one of the first municipal parks in the country. It was to be regulated by rules similar to, if not stricter than, those adopted by many of the private pleasure gardens.[76] Edinburgh citizens were now on trial.

Management, and Subsequent Additions

Peter Thomson went on to become Keeper of the Gardens, with charge also of the Meadows, Bruntsfield Links and Calton Hill. He was therefore Edinburgh's first Head Park Keeper, although at this stage no Parks Department as such existed. It was his duty to organise the workforce between the different open spaces, and to employ additional help when needed.[77] His responsibilities were considerable; in return he earned a modest £1.25p a week.

A very bare-looking East Princes Street Gardens, *c.* 1860. The effect of building up the terraces by depositing earth can clearly be seen. (Crown copyright © RCAHMS)

An engraving from the *Gardeners' Chronicle*, 1875, reveals a better clothed garden with an additional small fountain in the lower portion. The south bank (then leased from the Bank of Scotland) contains the most dense tree planting. (RBG)

Ornamental flower plots soon appeared along the outer margins of the Great Terrace, and to stimulate interest plants nearest the walks were provided with tags stating their botanical and common names.[78] At this time, as the contemporary photograph shows, the garden looked very bare with little visible planting to soften the rather formal layout. Nevertheless its novelty was sufficient to attract the public, particularly when musical entertainment was on offer. Saturday afternoons witnessed musical promenades organised by the Saturday Half Holiday Association, and by 1855 three bowling greens had been added.[79] In 1877 the wooden fencing along the south boundary (from the Mound to Waverley Bridge) was replaced by a cope stone and railing, stipulated by the Bank of Scotland when renewing the lease for the south bank.

Sir Walter Scott did not remain solitary for long. In 1865 he was joined by John Wilson ('Christopher North') (1785–1854), author and editor, his statue sculpted by Steel, and placed at the western end of the terrace. In 1876 Dr David Livingstone (1813–73), missionary and explorer, arrived at the eastern end. Amelia Hill, the sculptress wife of David Octavius Hill, would have preferred a more intimate space for her rather small scale-monument. At the centre, Adam Black (1784–1874), Lord Provost, Liberal MP and book publisher, who reappears in connection with Drummond Place Gardens, was added in 1877, the work of John Hutchison. All three stand on a broad strip of grass, ornamented with flower plots which have replaced the former gravel walk.

Thomas Begbie's photograph, 1890s, showing work on the new tunnel to Edinburgh's Waverley Station. Cousin's 'gothic character' wall along the upper terrace with pedestals for statues and the handsome stairway to the lower terrace can be clearly seen. (City Art Centre, City of Edinburgh Museums & Galleries)

Two views of the top terrace at the start of the twentieth century. Top: Shows and ornate parterre. (*Gardener's Chronicle*, 15 Nov. 1902, RBG). Bottom: A much simpler layout, mostly of grass. (Postcard dated and stamped 1903, C. Byrom)

In 1892 Waverley Station was rebuilt in its present form, with two additional tracks laid through the gardens and extra tunnels at the Mound. Prior to this Henry E. Milner (*c.* 1845–1906), partner in the firm of Milner & White, landscape gardeners, worked on plans to minimise the effect on the gardens.[80] At this time John W. McHattie was the Superintendent of Edinburgh Parks and Gardens and he took particular pride in the creation of an ornamental parterre along the whole length of the top terrace. Fifty-five individual beds were formed, stocked with over 100,000 plants, mostly of a low-growing kind 'to serve as a carpet, upon which flowering and foliage plants are sparingly disposed'. The effect was spectactular and was featured in all its glory in the November issue of *The Gardeners' Chronicle* of 1902.[81] In 1947 Professor Patrick Abercromby in his Plan for Edinburgh expressed regret at the intrusive effect of the railway, noting in his report that the railway development had 'blotted Edinburgh's copy book badly in bringing the railway uncovered through this magnificent gift of nature'. He recommended the entire station

A Second World War air-raid shelter in East Princes Street Garden. Many of the Edinburgh New Town gardens provided space for shelters, static water tanks and decontamination huts, as well as for training and exercise of the various defence units stationed within the New Town. (*Scotsman* Publications Ltd)

and railway route be covered 'beneath a roof of lawns and terraced gardens'.[82] During the Second World War more holes had been dug, this time for air-raid shelters beneath the top terrace. Bigger holes threatened in the 1950s for underground car parking, an idea strongly opposed by the Cockburn Association.[83]

Cousin's basic structure has survived although some of the details have changed; the looping system of central pathways has, for example, been superseded by larger grassed areas better suited to today's needs. An extensive long-term improvement programme has been under way since 1989, one of the aims being 'to emphasise the valley and to create flowing promenades',[84] another to combat ageing shrub and tree planting, and losses due to Dutch elm disease. The area south of the railway has been remodelled, with new tree, shrub and ground-cover planting added to the banks and other areas to provide all-year-round colour, interest and greater diversity. A serpentine footpath edged with whin setts has been formed and provides a more inviting view into the garden from the Cockburn Street entrance. Many of the old elms bordering Princes Street have been replaced by semi-mature lime trees, together with new railings (based on the previous ones). New trees have been added on the north terrace banks together with extensive bulb planting.

East Princes Street Gardens, fresh from their recent refurbishment, are probably better treasured today as one of Edinburgh's 'jewels' than at any other time. It is hard to appreciate now how miserable their existence was for so long, yet their rather inauspicious beginnings acted as a spur to the West Princes Street proprietors who made sure that such a fate would not befall their end. The story now continues with the West Princes Street Gardens.

General view of the lower terrace walk and central lawn in East Princes Street Gardens. (C. Byrom)

Notes

1. 'Extracts from an Edinburgh Journal, 1823–33', *BOEC*, Vol. xxx (1959); entries for 12 November 1829 and 30 May 1832.
2. *Edinburgh Weekly Magazine*, 28 March 1776.
3. Some previous drainage work had been carried out as early as 1763 prior to the building of the North Bridge.
4. TCM, 16 August 1780; Memorial subscribed by Alexander Wight Esq., Advocate, for himself and in the name of other feuars of Extended Royalty, dated 28 June 1780, and listing all their grievances.
5. William Jamieson was one of the most important of the first New Town builders. He was employed in the building of Register House, Sir Lawrence Dundas's house in St Andrew Square, and other New Town houses.
6. The Dean of Guild Grieve was at this time a Princes Street resident with a house on the corner of Hanover Street.
7. *Edinburgh Evening Courant*, 12 May 1781.
8. TCM, 29 August 1781; the proprietors volunteered to pay for the cost of the additional gate which the Town Council agreed to on condition it could be freely used by everyone, and the proprietors to accept responsibility for its upkeep.
9. *Diary of George Sandy: Apprentice WS 1788*; edited by C.A. Malcome (Edinburgh, 1943), pp. 29, 36, and 40.
10. At one period the idea for a simple, ornamental sheet of water had grown to a more ambitious notion of a North Loch canal forming part of an inland waterway connecting with Glasgow to the west, and with Leith (via an immense harbour at Greenside) to the east. References to this project appear in Grant, *Old and New Edinburgh*, Vol. 2, p. 99.
11. *The Scotsman,* 16 February 1822, article entitled, 'New attempt to build in front of Princes Street'.
12. The east side of the Earthen Mound (area unspecified), had in fact been advertised for sale by the Town Council in 1823 along with other building stances in Fettes Row, Royal Crescent, Duncan Street, Scotland Street, the east end of London Street and Bellevue Crescent; *Edinburgh Evening Advertiser*, 24 June 1823.
13. Memorial of the Proprietors of Princes Street to the Right Honourable the Lord Provost, Magistrates, and Council of the City of Edinburgh, 2 April 1822, signed by Robert Paterson, President.
14. TCM, 17 August 1825; 26 August 1825; details of 'the purpose' are not given, the business of the day being rather to recoup some of the money spent by levying a charge of 1 penny per cart.
15. Ideas for improved south and west approaches had first been suggested in 1823 and during the intervening years several different plans had been drawn up.
16. Opposition to the Bill was led by William Drysdale, WS.
17. *The Scotsman,* 4 February 1826; see also, *BOEC* Vol. xxix (1956), p. 169.
18. The fourteen names were: Robert Dundas, Lord Chief Baron of the Court of Exchequer; *H. Home Drummond* of Blair Drummond; Sir William Forbes, Banker; Henry Cockburn, Advocate; *Sir Henry Jardine*, King's Remembrancer in the Exchequer; *James Skene* of Rubislaw; Thomas Allan, Banker; John Cay, Advocate; A Alison, Advocate; John Russell, WS; John Kinnear, Banker, and *Alexander Douglas*, WS. The italicised names were all members of the West Princes Street Gardens Management Committee. At the end of the meeting seven

were elected to a committee to confer with the Town Council. These included: Sir William Forbes (convener), Henry Cockburn, James Moncrieff, Robert Graham (Professor of Botany), James Skene, Sir Henry Jardine and Alexander Douglas.

19. *The Scotsman*, 8 February 1826; *Edinburgh Advertiser*, 7 February 1826.
20. William Trotter was Lord Provost at this time. He was head of the firm of cabinetmakers and upholsterers who had their premises on the south side of Princes Street close to the North Bridge.
21. TCM, 1 March 1826.
22. TCM, 28 June 1826.
23. Playfair's best-known Edinburgh buildings include the Royal Scottish Academy, the National Gallery, Surgeons Hall, New College, the New Observatory (Calton Hill), St Stephen's Church and Donaldson's Hospital.
24. Most of Playfair's library consisted of architectural books, but there were also a number of influential publications on the principles of landscaping. The most practical landscape book in his collection was J.C. Loudon's *Encyclopaedia of Gardening* (1826). A copy of the sale catalogue is in NLS: Catalogue of the valuable library of the late W.H. Playfair Esq. (to be sold by auction by Mr T Nisbet in his great room, 11 Hanover Street, Friday and Saturday, 27th & 28th November, 1857).
25. TCM, 5 July 1826; also reported in *Edinburgh Advertiser*, 30 June 1826.
26. This step may have been prompted by Alexander Henderson, former Lord Provost and still active on the Council.
27. William Sawrey Gilpin illustrated his uncle's celebrated *Tours in Search of Picturesque Beauty – on the Wye*.
28. *The Scotsman*, 8 November 1826.
29. *The Scotsman*, 4 October 1826.
30. *The Scotsman*, 17 January 1827.
31. Gilpin advised on landscape improvements for Crum Castle, Enniskillen Castle, and Castle Blayney.
32. Gilpin's several Scottish commissions are listed in A.A. Tait's, *The Landscape Garden in Scotland 1735–1835*, op. cit., p. 255.
33. *The Scotsman*, 8 November 1826.
34. Act of 7th & 8th year of King George IV, Cap 76, An Act for carrying into effect certain improvements within the City of Edinburgh, and adjacent to the same.
35. *The Scotsman*, 17 November 1827.
36. TCM, 4 April 1827; 19 August 1829.
37. Robert Gourlay, *Plans for the Improvement of Edinburgh, No. 1*, printed by W. Burness, 1829.
38. James McNab, *The Scottish Farmer*, 28 June 1865, 'Our Town trees; East Princes Street gardens'.
39. TCM, 24 June 1829; 2 September 1829, which contains Neill's report on the improvements to be made to the East Princes Street area.
40. The business was inherited from his father, Adam Neill, and continued in existence until the 1970s, finally occupying extensive premises in Newington.
41. For further information about Neill see J.B. Barclay, 'Patrick Neill, M.A., LL.D., F.R.S.E.', *Royal Caledonian Horticultural Society Journal*, 1989; and Connie Byrom and George Dalgleish, 'A Massive and handsome silver vase; a testimonial to Dr Neill', *Royal Caledonian Horticultural Society Journal*, 1991.

42. Henry Cockburn, *Memorials of his time* (1971 edition) p. 215.

43. J.C. Loudon, *Encyclopaedia of Gardening*, 2nd edn, (London, 1824), p. 115.

44. *Edinburgh Evening Courant*, 4 September 1851.

45. See Report to the Commissioners for the City Improvements, Edinburgh 1830, EUL pamphlet 81; and TCM, 16 December 1829.

46. TCM, 21 October 1829; 13 April 1831; see also Thomas Brown's Letter Book, ECA, letter 30 July 1829, 7 September 1829 and 31 December 1829.

47. TCM, 16 December 1829; at this stage the Chairmanship of the committee had temporarily been taken over by Dr William Wood.

48. TCM, 16 December 1829. This gives a full account of all the transactions with the Bank.

49. TCM, 13 April 1831.

50. Crombie's *Modern Athenians, 1837–1847* (Edinburgh, reprinted 1881), p. 31; a printing error quotes 77,000 trees planted in the wrong garden! Neill was not consulted about the West Princes Street gardens until 1831, when asked to give some minor planting advice. Although an error, it has been quoted as fact ever since.

51. TCM, 2 March 1831, when Neill's request for a quantity of bag lime was agreed to.

52. TCM, 20 July 1831.

53. TCM, 7 March 1832; 21 March 1832; 4 April 1832.

54. *The North Briton newspaper*, 3 May 1832.

55. TCM, 25 April 1832; 30 May 1832.

56. *The Scotsman*, 30 May, 1832; also reported, but not in such detail, in *Edinburgh Evening Courant*, 31 May 1832.

57. When the buildings started to appear, a number of Princes Street proprietors protested, but were given assurances of the temporary nature of their use.

58. TCM, 10 August, 1841.

59. TCM, 10 July 1843; 23 August, 1843; 11 June, 1844; 8 April, 1845.

60. TCM, 6 May 1845.

61. TCM, 24 August 1847.

62. A fund-raising committee had been set up shortly after Scott's death, James Skene, a close friend and the designer of West Princes Street gardens acting as secretary. Sir Thomas Dick Lauder was chairman.

63. Quoted in a letter from Playfair to his friend Rutherlord, 28 April 1843, NLS Manuscript 9704.

64. TCM, 22 April 1845.

65. James McNab, 'East Princes Street Gardens', op. cit.

66. TCM, 13 March 1849, draft agreement discussed and approved; the Railway Company thereafter declined further liability.

67. While working for Playfair, Cousin was involved with both Donaldson's hospital and the National Gallery projects. He later acted as consultant architect to the Free Church of Scotland, and worked on a number of ecclesiastical buildings such as St Catherine's Convent, Lauriston gardens; St George's, Deanhaugh Street; and the reconstruction of Greyfriars Church.

68. The Waverley Park development, Newington, was on behalf of Lord Provost Duncan McLaren.

69. TCM, 12 June 1849; report by David Cousin to the Council of his design aims for East Princes Street Gardens.

70. *The Builder*, 30 November 1850, Vol. 8, p. 565.
71. TCM, 17 July 1849; 9 October 1849; 30 October 1849.
72. TCM, 11 September 1849; 19 March 1850; his first task was in firming and dressing the embankment on either side of the railway, and was soon needing additional help.
73. TCM, 23 October 1849; the rent charged was £10 per month.
74. TCM, 2 April 1850; 14 May 1850; 18 June 1850; 30 July 1850, which include progress reports by Cousin.
75. TCM, 22 October 1850; Cousin had obtained several lists of plants and prices from nurseries which he passed on to Thomson.
76. TCM, 9 September 1851.
77. TCM, 3 September 1861.
78. TCM, 6 July 1852; 400 tallies were purchased at a cost of £10.
79. TCM, 18 July 1854; 13 March 1855; 2 June 1857; the Council contributed 10 guineas towards the cost of the band.
80. Harriet Jordan, 'Public Parks, 1885–1914', *Journal of the Garden History Society*, (Summer 1994), vol. 22, No. 1, p. 99. No details of his plan are given but it is presumed that Milner was employed by the Railway Company to make good the damage cause by increasing the size of Waverley Station and the additional lines.
81. *The Gardeners' Chronicle*, 15 November 1902, p. 358.
82. Patrick Abercrombie & Derek Plumstead, *A Civic Survey and Plan for Edinburgh* (Edinburgh & London, 1949), p. 55.
83. George Bruce, *Some Practical Good* (The Cockburn Association, 1975), p. 35. The proposals were withdrawn on 16 December 1955.
84. J.C. Mackay, 'East Princes Street gardens; the gardens renovated', *Royal Caledonian Horticultural Society Journal* (1994), pp. 43–9.

CHAPTER 6

WEST PRINCES STREET GARDENS

Everyone must be gratified to see the improvements now commenced, and about to be carried into effect, on the western part of the North Loch. The promenade, along the south side of Princes Street, which we recommended for adoption in 1817, may be said to be already formed; and looking at the capabilities of the ground, and the picturesque objects which surround it, we cannot be too sanguine in our expectations.

The Scotsman, 1820.[1]

. . . We were kept late at the Court and when I came out I bethought me, like Christian in the Castle of Giant Despair, "Wherefore should I walk along the broiling and stifling streets when I have a little key in my bosom which can open any lock in Princes Street Walks, and be thus on the Castle banks, rocks, and trees in a few minutes?" I made use of my key accordingly, and walked from the Castle Hill down to Wallace's Tower [Later renamed Wellhouse Tower] and thence to the west end of Princes Street, through a scene of grandeur and beauty perhaps unequalled, whether the foreground or distant view is considered – all downhill, too. Foolish never to think of this before.

The Journal of Sir Walter Scott, 8 July 1828.

Whether *The Scotsman* intended to echo sentiments usually associated with the landscape designer Lancelot Brown (1716–83), the newspaper was certainly alive to the special qualities of the site soon to become West Princes Street Gardens. Most notably they had as their backdrop the Castle, about the only Edinburgh feature to excite the Reverend William Gilpin while touring Scotland in 1776 in search of the picturesque. These gardens became the largest (just over 32 acres (12.8 ha), and most popular of all the Edinburgh private pleasure grounds, attracting subscribers from every part of the New Town. Transformed from a stinking wasteland[2] to a highly ornamental space, this achievement was entirely due to the efforts of the West Princes Street proprietors.

Families of High Respectability

By 1800 Princes Street was completely built, the property west of Hanover Street wholly residential, and occupied by families of high respectability: lawyers, members of the nobility and a few affluent merchants. The Town Council's controversial legal skirmishes over the area east of the Mound made them anxious to avoid further confrontation. Nothing has emerged to suggest that any plans existed for building on this part of the North Loch, apart from proposals for a chapel on Peter Lawson's nursery ground at the west end[3] (for Bishop

Western section of the North Loch looking across to the old church of St Cuthbert's, Edinburgh. A swan skims the water and cattle graze: at the base of the Castle Rock is the Well House Tower. (Grant, *Old and New Edinburgh*, 1880–3)

Sandford's congregation, later named St John's Episcopal Church) and for the Mound itself. Nevertheless the threat remained.[4]

Not surprisingly, therefore, the new residents lost little time in conferring together, and in December 1801 submitted their view to the Lord Provost that no buildings could lawfully be erected on the south side; an opinion upheld ten years later on legal advice.[5] Reassured but still apprehensive, the proprietors decided to strengthen their position by exploring the possibility of having the loch drained and improved. Approaches were made both to the Town and the Commanding Officer of the Royal Engineers in Scotland to negotiate leases for the western portion and the adjoining Castle slope. A committee was formed, but was soon frustrated by lack of funds. With the task ahead of Herculean proportions, it was little wonder that some residents were hesitant to become financially committed. The Council on the other hand (now burdened with the eastern section) were only too happy to encourage improvements which would cost the Town nothing and indeed would generate some income. In 1813 they agreed to a fifty-year lease to allow the land to be 'laid out in an embellished form'.[6]

1816 Act of Parliament

No contract was, however, signed and nothing more happened for over two years. Then in 1816, prompted by the increasing pressure for a chapel,[7] the proprietors gathered at Oman's Tavern to review matters. More meetings followed, resulting in the decision to withhold support for this project unless the Council agreed to renew their previous offer. Already ahead of West Princes Street were the East Queen Street Gardens, the larger part of which had been open to subscribers since 1814. But their administrative problems were well known and something which the Princes Street proprietors were eager to avoid. Hence their request that a management framework be included as part of the Act of Parliament being applied for in connection with the chapel and other City improvements. No objections were raised and in May 1816 the Act was passed.[8]

Under the Act no building was allowed on the south side of Princes Street west of the Mound, apart from the above, and those necessary for a pleasure ground (for example, gardener's lodge, hothouses or conservatories). It authorised the West Princes Street proprietors (those living between Hanover and Hope Street, with one or more windows facing onto Princes Street) to erect a parapet wall and railing alongside the street, and to contract with the Council for a lease of the ground for the 'the purpose of laying out the same in whole or in part in a garden, nursery for trees, or pleasure ground, or under grass, or otherwise embellishing and enclosing the same'.[9]

Soon afterwards a five-strong management committee was elected[10] which, apart from minor changes, survived for many years under the attentive eye of the clerk and treasurer, Alexander Douglas, WS (1780–1851). Douglas, described as a 'strong and upright character', was himself a proprietor with a successful law practice at 137 Princes Street.

He also had the unfortunate nickname of 'Dirty Douglas', due to his scruffy, untidy appearance. Nevertheless he was extremely hard-working, and carefully piloted the gardens through many demanding periods and controversial issues. Douglas gave 35 years' continuous service before being succeeded by his son Christopher who continued the family tradition until the gardens became public.[11] Three of the committee had been concerned in earlier negotiations – James Clerk Rattray (Baron of the Court of Exchequer, Commissioner on the Regent Road project and also involved with the development of the lands north of Calton Hill), Henry Home Drummond (advocate), and Henry Jardine, WS (depute King's Remembrancer, and 'long conspicuous as a public spirited citizen').[12]) The other two members were Andrew Murray (advocate), and Alexander Munro.

Alexander Douglas, WS, Clerk to the West Princes Street Garden Proprietors for 35 years and nick-named 'Dirty Douglas' on account of his scruffy appearance. (Crombie, *Modern Athenians, 1837–1847*, ECL)

First Steps

The first and most laborious task was to obtain legal titles to the various parts making up the western section.[13] Next was the erection of a parapet wall and railing along Princes Street. Completed in 1818 at a cost of nearly £1,500, it was to a plain design by Richard Crichton (c.1771–1817) executed shortly before the architect's death.[14] Two arched gateways facing onto Castle Street and Frederick Street were provided and lit with overhead lamps. Extra earth was added to the top bank along Princes Street in preparation for a tree-lined walk. Meantime the ground was let as pasturage. No ornamental space could successfully be created, however, without the land being properly drained, and the central drain laid towards the latter half of the eighteenth century was no longer adequate. Robert Stevenson (1772–1850), civil engineer, was approached first, but his estimate of £2,900 was considered disconcertingly high.[15] It caused the committee to think about leasing the ground for nursery use, and placing the onus for improvement on the sub-tenant. But although favourable terms were advertised, no-one was tempted.[16] The committee therefore had no option but to tackle what they now knew to be an expensive enterprise.

A general meeting of proprietors in July 1818 authorised the committee to borrow up to £3,000, and a loan of £2,000 was subsequently negotiated with William Forbes & Co., financiers of many New Town enterprises.[17] Another and more modest estimate was obtained from Richard Stephens, 'land drainer, surveyor and engineer', and his 'plan number 1' costing £1,775 was the one accepted. He was paid £42 for his trouble and further asked to 'make out a sketch of a design for laying out the grounds'.[18] Meantime John Ormiston, a mason, strongly recommended by the architect William Burn, and submitting the lowest estimate, carried out the work, which was completed by the summer of 1820. Before then representatives of the Garden Committee had attended a consultative meeting with the Town, over plans to build the Royal Institution (Royal Scottish Academy) on the Mound. Prior to the meeting Stephen's brief had been extended to include, 'building on the Mound and embellishing the North Loch and grounds on both sides'. When his plan was shown, however, it was rejected as 'not suited to the views of the Magistrates or the Public'. By now William Playfair's design was favoured in preference to another by Archibald Elliot.[19] Stephen exits at this point, but his plan (about which next to nothing is known) was relayed to Mr Skene to be 'duly considered', and Mr Skene promptly produced another of his own!

James Skene's Advice Sought

But who was Mr Skene and how did he come to be involved? James Skene (1775–1864) of Rubislaw near Aberdeen (an estate inherited when his elder brother died in 1791) is now remembered for his artistic talents (with its legacy of paintings and sketches of Edinburgh and abroad[20]), and close friendship with Sir Walter Scott. He was clever and articulate, with a wide range of interests and enthusiasms encompassing science, history, literature and the arts; the last he ably demonstrated during his term as Secretary to the Board of Trustees and Manufactures from 1830 to 1838.[21] James was eight when his widowed mother

James Skene of Rublislaw, designer of the West Princes Street Gardens and close friend of Sir Walter Scott. (ECL)

and six siblings moved to Edinburgh, first to the Old Town, then George Street. The North Loch was familiar territory and the scene of many boyhood escapades, a natural adventure playground which he shared with other High School friends, skating and sliding in winter, kite flying in summer and perilous rock ascents whenever daredevil mood prevailed.[22] Although called to the Scottish Bar, he rarely practised, and early manhood saw wanderings abroad until his marriage in 1806 to Jane Forbes (the youngest daughter of Sir William Forbes).

After a spell in Kincardineshire the family returned to Edinburgh in 1816 for the children's schooling. Skene soon became active in several societies including the Royal Society and the Society of Antiquaries. This was why he attended the consultative meeting just mentioned, as both societies were due to be accommodated within the new building. Skene was not only closely involved in the Edinburgh scene, but was also a West Princes Street proprietor, living not many doors away from his brother-in-law, Henry Jardine, a stalwart member of the garden committee. But connections apart, his artistic flair, refined taste and helpful nature would have singled him out as someone capable of giving useful and sensitive advice on design, as the East Queen Street Commissioners were also to discover. Walter Scott himself was very trusting of Skene's opinion and freely consulted him about the grounds at Abbotsford (although Scott's own whims usually prevailed). Skene's commitment to West Princes Street Gardens was assured by his election to the management committee in 1821.[23]

Plan of the City of Edinburgh, 1823, showing James Skene's design. (Plan of the City of Edinburgh published 1820 by Thomas Brown, altered to 1823 by J. Wood)

James Skene and Alexander Henderson

James Skene's elegant design can be seen in contemporary plans; it combined ornament with utility, for the committee in order to defray costs decided to sub-lease the central portion as nursery ground. The plan included a tree-lined avenue adjacent to Princes Street, with paths from the gateways leading to a lower walk encompassing the whole garden, and merging at the western end into a somewhat elaborate circular arrangement of interlinked paths which was later simplified. Further picturesque serpentine walks were shown threading along the Castle slopes, and finally extending round the Castle onto its southern flank. All this required considerable tree and shrub planting along the borders and slopes, together with selective clumps in the centre.

Alexander Henderson (1769–1827), whose firm Eagle & Henderson had nurseries at Meadowbank and at Mignonette Bank on the west side of Leith Walk, was awarded the contract for making the gardens. His firm became involved with most of the New Town pleasure gardens, and as a member of the Town Council he frequently acted on committees when garden matters arose. Henderson was of humble origins (a herd boy from Peebles), yet became not only a highly successful businessman but also a popular and respected Lord Provost, and one much concerned with improving the City's amenities.[24]

The upper and lower walks along Princes Street were completed in March 1821, the top avenue being planted with a double row of lime and elm. Poplar and willow were added

Raeburn's portrait of Alexander Henderson, Lord Provost. His firm, Eagle & Henderson, contracted for the laying out of the West Princes Street gardens and later rented out a portion as nursery ground. The firm became involved with most of the New Town gardens. Henderson's connection with the Town Council brought him into contact with several of the New Town gardens on civic matters. (Courtesy of the Royal Bank of Scotland Art Collection)

to the Mound bank, and beech and fir on the west slopes of the Castle wherever there was sufficient soil. Thirty-four thousand trees were planted as well as a large stock of shrubs. Extra planting was donated from Lord Moray's estate at Drumsheugh which was then being cleared prior to development; and some young oaks and horse chestnuts were gifted by Mr Erskine of Mar (presumably a descendant of John, 11th Earl of Mar).

Henderson's connection with the gardens was further strengthened when he accepted the committee's offer to lease nine acres (3.60 ha) in the middle as nursery ground. The lease was for 19 years at a yearly rental of £63, one of the conditions being that he would allow 'a certain number of trees to grow up and remain permanently upon the ground as an ornament to the premises'.[25] In 1827 his son succeeded to the lease, and the firm continued there until 1843.[26] It must have given Henderson considerable satisfaction to be involved with such an important venture, but the experience was far from trouble-free. His 'much good sense, great experience of the world and knowledge of human character'[27] were sorely tested when the committee challenged his final account, describing it as 'highly exorbitant and highly objectionable'.[28] This was in March 1823 when a bill for nearly £850 was submitted. Practically every detail was queried, and a reduction demanded based on independent arbitration.[29] Kind and conciliatory by nature, Henderson found the tone hurtful. Believing his account to be honourable and fair, he declined arbitration. There the matter rested for two uneasy years until, having at last yielded to an independent assessor, he was completely exonerated.[30]

In the early days of forming the garden Skene was there to supervise. He took the opportunity, while digging was under way, to indulge in some archaeological explorations, surveying the area around the Wellhouse Tower (built in 1362 as a combined defence for the well and gatehouse), for ancient remains and artifacts. The results, while a little disappointing, were communicated in a paper to the Society of Antiquaries.[31] The workmen had discovered some adult skeletons[32] and even the uncoffined bones of a young infant, news of which had encouraged Skene's subsequent investigations. He was to observe ruefully in his paper that 'when the frequency of child murder was quite appalling . . . the miry state of the North Loch, sequestered, and at the same time adjacent to the city, rendered it the usual scene of these atrocities'. Child abuse, it seems, is as old as time. On a lighter note, the excavations revealed no signs of the North Loch having been used as a Royal garden or ornamented as such.

In the autumn of 1820 Skene left for France and was away with his family for one year, leaving Henderson in charge. During that time the old public right of way from Kirkbraehead Road (King's Stables Road) to Princes Street was closed. To prevent boys gaining access via the Castle rock a high wall was built from St Cuthbert's church manse to the back of the Castle as far as the old city wall. Completed in 1821, at a cost of between £400 and £500, it caused some misgivings. *The Scotsman,* for example expressed hopes that the promenades and shrubbery would be 'open to all the respectable part of the public on reasonable terms', but at the same time feared 'that the narrow and exclusive club spirit which disgraces the society of Edinburgh' would prevail, in which case 'there will be few reasons for boasting at what is in progress'.[33]

Open to the Public

By spring 1821 the garden was sufficiently advanced to open to proprietors and anyone else willing to pay four guineas annually. Amongst the first subscribers were: Lord Justice Clerk (the Rt Hon. David Boyle), William Burn, architect, David Hume, advocate, and Carlyle Bell, WS, City Clerk. As the summer advanced, all the walks were completed apart from those on the north-east slopes of the Castle. In Skene's absence, Robert Brown (1802–60), architect, was consulted on matters such as a linking stepway in the Wellhouse Tower area, and forming a bowling green 'in the hollow ground in the division west of Castle Street'.[34] A palisade was erected alongside the Mound, and 'by way of experiment' Mr Henderson provided some iron seats. Earlier in the season borders had been stocked with annuals, including 'a considerable proportion of mignonette', together with roses. Robert Murray was appointed as the first full-time gardener at fifteen shillings (75p) a week supplemented by any extras he could raise by selling grass from the bleaching and bowling greens.[35] A conscientious worker, he remained in charge until his death 25 years later. At Skene's suggestion (and based on a sketch made out by him) a gardener's house was built sometime during 1823, quite close to the present-day lodge.[36]

Improvements had still to be made on the Castle hill, and in the autumn of 1821 Skene (recently returned from a trip abroad) was asked to prepare a sketch showing 'what ought to be done'. Further planting was also required on the western boundary and elsewhere,

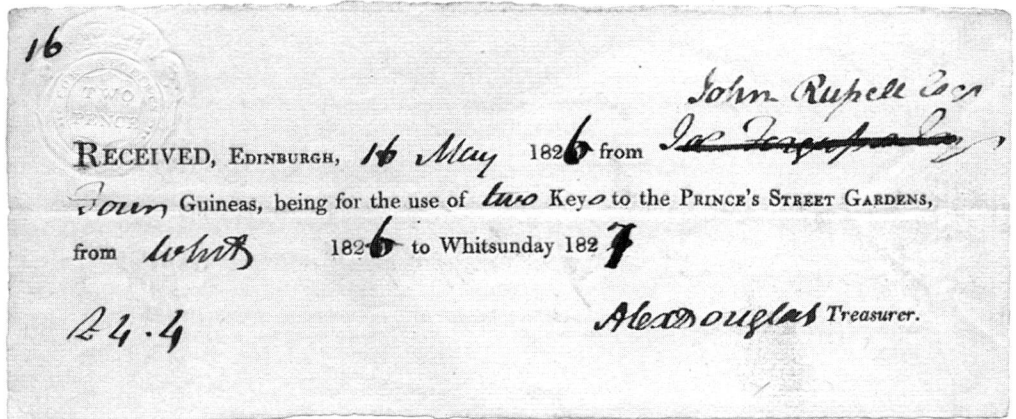

Top: Receipt for the annual subscription to the West Princes Street Gardens, dated 1826 and signed by Alexander Douglas. Right: One of the keys to the gardens. (Both: Museum of Edinburgh)

as much of the original stock had failed. It was at this time that Skene acquired a two-ton runic stone from the Society of Antiquaries (he was after all their Secretary and Curator!) which with difficulty was hauled up the Castle slope and remains there to this day.[37] But progress on the Castle hill was generally slow, delayed partly by lengthy negotiations with General Ramsay for a lease of the field behind Ramsay Lodge, and Skene's further absences. Not until 1829 was work resumed in earnest when the gardener acquired stones from houses being demolished behind the Castle, prior to building Johnstone Terrace. These were used to secure the embankments and for making steps.[38] Extra help was needed for making the pathways and the Treasurer applied to 'the Subscribers for the Relief of the Labouring Poor'. They provided fourteen men at one shilling each (5p) per day. Once completed, a crop of potatoes was grown for a couple of years to improve the soil, and their sale more than paid for outgoings on the bank. In addition the Castle banks had been let since 1825 to Principal Baird, tenant of Ramsay Garden, 'for sheep and lambs only', producing a yearly income of £24.[39]

One Fox and Many Cats

As the gardens grew in maturity, the thickening growth offered protection to all kinds of wild life. A fox had taken up residence on the south-west quarter of the rock (failure to detect him aided by the rule forbidding dogs), and the bird population had multiplied. The latter, however, had not gone unnoticed by the 'Society of Princes Street cats', who according to James Skene were prone to holding nocturnal hunting parties. Many were shot dead by the gardener, but even so they multiplied. It was their love of musical parties and serenades 'in the usual melodious style' which caused their downfall, alerting the 'ears of the terriers and other curs of Princes Street'. With both sides plunged into combat 'the slaughter of cats which were strewn in the garden in the morning showed that the contest would soon terminate'.[40]

Succeeding years saw even greater maturity, enough to surprise landscape designer and writer John Claudius Loudon (1783–1843), when visiting Edinburgh in 1841. He noted in his diary that 'nothing struck us more forcibly than the appearance of the Nor Loch, covered with trees that were not even planted when we left Edinburgh'.[41] The delights of the garden at this time prompted similar reaction from another infrequent visitor, Elizabeth Grant of Rothiemurchus, now married to an Irish landowner. During a short stay in September 1842 she took a walk through the gardens: 'which are really beautiful, laid out as far as the Castle walls including the rocks and the green hill side as a pleasure ground. There are shrubbery walks, and wild paths, and a long, long avenue of fine young trees, fields, flower gardens, kitchen garden; such a piece of beauty in a town must be unrivalled in Europe.'[42]

Although the appearance of the gardens owed much to Skene, we learn from Sir Walter Scott that his friend's efforts were not always appreciated. In the bleak days following the bankruptcy of Scott's publisher, Archibald Constable & Co., and of his printer James Ballantyne & Co., Skene was in the habit of 'unkenneling' his friend from his home in Castle Street to take a walk in the gardens and talk 'with a degree of subdued cheerfulness which seemed to soothe him very much'. After one of these perambulations with 'the good Samaritan Skene', Scott wrote in his journal that 'the walks have been conducted on the whole with much taste, though Skene has undergone much criticism, the usual reward of public exertions, on account of his plan'.[43]

The Coming of the Railway

In 1840 a new three-year lease was negotiated with Eagle Henderson (as it had now become) reducing their area by one half and allowing the western end to be taken over by the proprietors. A plan for this was made out by David Cousin.[44] Besides being urged into allowing more trees to grow up, the firm were also told to remove the dunghill and pigsty at the toolhouse, near the Wellhouse Tower. Was this a sign of declining standards, or a useful source of garden manure? Whatever the reason, the clerk was not amused; and even less so when, one year later, while walking in the grounds, he chanced upon 'the grunting of pigs' and on investigating discovered to his astonishment 'not only several pigsties but several pigs'.

Transforming the North Loch 'from a filthy and offensive bog' into 'one of the most beautiful and attractive objects of which this city can boast' had cost time, effort and money: over £7,000 for making the garden, together with annual maintenance costs of £300 and ground rents of £150. These facts provided part of the armoury in the proprietors' case to Parliament against the Edinburgh & Glasgow Railway Company. In 1836 the Company had applied for powers to extend their line through the 'low damp ground' of West Princes Street Gardens, under the Mound, through East Princes Street Gardens to a terminus close to the North Bridge. A circular addressed to the proprietors, signed by the Company's Chairman, ex-Lord Provost John Learmonth, claimed this to be 'the commencement of a great national work', good for the public (improved communications and a boost to an ailing property market), good for Edinburgh and Scotland, and with careful handling by no means a likely eyesore. Indeed, far from being a blemish, the circular asserted that damage would be minimal: ornamental arches would be thrown over the railway to connect the divided garden (or the gardens would even be reached by underground passageway) and trains and track contained and concealed by a walled embankment. Learmonth, a wealthy retired businessman with property interests, and active on many committees, was someone not lacking sensitivity to environmental issues. His appeal for judgment to be made with 'calm' and 'dispassionate consideration' was, however, almost impossible for those faced with the prospect of seeing their treasured garden destroyed.

James Skene was the first to react publicly, and his reply to the circular became the basis of the proprietors' case. His bid to save the gardens marks his last real connection with them. He had by this time moved to Moray Place (where Learmonth also lived), and within five years was to depart for Greece. The proprietors' petition that 'it had always been understood that Parliament would never sanction any attempt to carry Railroads or Canals through Gentlemen's Pleasure Grounds', and that 'Pleasure Grounds in the very centre of a City' should be treated on equal terms did, on this occasion, triumph. Haymarket, instead, became the terminus for the railway from Glasgow, and the gardens were left untouched.[45]

But victory was short-lived. In July 1844 Parliament, after further applications from the Railway Company, sanctioned continuation of the line to a new terminus by the North Bridge. Bowing to the inevitable, the proprietors on this occasion fought less vigorously. The battle was not entirely lost, for strict safeguards were added to minimise the intrusive effects of the railway and William Playfair was nominated to take charge of the remedial work. His strategy was to screen the line by an embankment running the length of the enclosing wall, thickly planted with evergreens and trees; his other approach was to plant trees, evergreens and ivy generously 'whenever the works of the railway occur'.[46]

Early in 1845 the Railway Company took possession of the lower portion of ground. The labourers were told to set aside carefully the earth collected during excavation for re-use when forming the embankments. Alexander Brown was appointed to superintend the garden work, and on Murray's death was made head gardener. Playfair prepared planting lists[47] and went on to design three wooden bridges over the lines.[48] Two years later the workers departed, leaving the whole 'in a most insufficient state'. Part of the problem had been irregular supervision due to Playfair's chronic ill health. Pressurising the Company to fulfil their obligations fell to the now elderly but still resolute clerk, Mr Douglas. Finally, in May 1848, Playfair was able to report that everything had been satisfactorily completed. Not only had the 'very considerable' costs of the landscaping been met by the Railway Company, but they also paid £1,745 by way of compensation. The money removed all the outstanding debts on the gardens, and for the first time ever there was a healthy cash balance of £271.[49] The cloud was not without its silver lining.

After the Railway

Although ground had been lost, this was partly compensated by taking over the rest of Henderson's nursery. With Skene abroad, the committee consulted James McNab on how best to unite the two portions. McNab at this time was working as manager of the Inverleith Experimental Garden belonging to the Royal Caledonian Horticultural Society. He was soon to succeed his father as Curator at the Edinburgh Royal Botanic Garden. By now his reputation as a skilful horticulturalist, capable of offering good practical advice, was becoming established. His plan included increasing the width of the nursery's central footpath, and linking this by gently looping pathways to the lower terrace and Playfair's new footbridges.[50] Intersections were to be generously planted with trees and shrubs, new

The Ross Fountain, acquired for the West Princes Street Gardens in 1869 by Daniel Ross, an Edinburgh gunsmith. This photograph was taken after the gardens became open to the public in 1876; the bandstand, seen further to the east, designed by Peddie and Kinnear, was donated to the City by the former proprietors out of surplus funds. (George Washington Wilson Collection, Aberdeen University Library)

The Edinburgh New Town Gardens

flower borders created and the remaining area grassed. By the summer of 1849 the work was complete.

McNab gave advice on two further occasions. In the mid-1850s he recommended removal of some of the decayed lime trees along the top terrace, providing opportunities to open up views of the Castle and the Old Town. The felling triggered uproar amongst the public: 'a more outrageous act of vandalism and impertinence never was perpetrated against a community than this'. The committee were accused of being 'assassin like', carrying out the deed in the early hours 'when nobody was stirring to cry shame upon them'.[51] Subsequent thinning and pruning under McNab in 1868 passed without incident.

During the 1860s the gardens acquired two large artifacts.[52] One was a statue to the poet Allan Ramsay, sculpted by John Steell and placed in the north-east corner.[53] The other was a fountain gifted by Daniel Ross, an Edinburgh gunmaker, of Rockville in Napier Road, and named after him. This elaborate iron structure, designed and founded in France by A. Durenne and cast for the International Exhibition of 1862, was modelled on a similar one in Paris. Its position at the west end of the central walk was chosen by James McNab and John Dick Peddie, both then engaged on carrying out improvements to St Andrew Square Garden. Dick Peddie's partner, Charles Kinnear (1830–94), was active on the garden committee from 1861 to 1876, and may have suggested their involvement. Any architectural matter was always referred to Kinnear; new seats, for example, were designed by him, and he vetted the railway company's plans for new bridges.[54]

It was perhaps this involvement with the gardens that inspired Dick Peddie to produce a large watercolour painting showing various projected 'improvements' including a large winter garden (a possibility later considered by the Town Council[55]) and an enlarged

Watercolour painting by John Dick Peddie, 1866, of West Princes Street Gardens, showing proposals for improvements. They included a winter garden and an enlarged upper terrace along Princes Street to accommodate an open-air sculpture gallery. (Crown copyright © RCAHMS)

upper terrace fashioned as an outdoor sculpture gallery. This painting, along with a companion piece featuring East Princes Street, was regularly exhibited at the Royal Scottish Academy.[56]

Uses and Abuses

West Princes Street Gardens were always a popular and fashionable place of resort, attracting subscribers from all parts of the New Town.[57] By the latter part of the 1820s there were more outside subscribers than proprietors. Prior to the railway's construction their number had risen to one hundred, and they simply went on increasing so that by the 1870s the Clerk had over four hundred names on his books. Such was the income from this source (key rental varied from between two and three guineas) that in 1853 the committee dispensed with the proprietors' annual dues, and from then on they paid nothing.[58]

Being of generous size, there was little danger of the gardens becoming overcrowded. Only occasional incidents of rough play, illicit cricket practice and maltreatment are recorded. The real problem with so many users was keeping control over the numerous keys in circulation. As more keys became lost, lent and unauthorised copies made, it became something of a management nightmare, leading ultimately to over half the rules being about keys and access. Another rule which became increasingly difficult to enforce was the ban on smoking. It was too strongly challenged by the cigar- and tobacco-smoking fraternity of the New Club, an all-male stronghold which had removed from St Andrew Square to Princes Street in 1834.

Musical entertainment featured from an early date, the gardens being well placed to tap the resources of whatever regiments were garrisoned at the Castle. Thus in March 1826 the *Edinburgh Advertiser* noted that 'the promenaders have lately had their walks enlivened during the fine weather, by the alternative attendance of the fine bands of the Carabineers and the 17th Foot'.[59] To the belles of Edinburgh the military bands added sparkle, the young officers proving dashing escorts with 'their military headgear and clanking swords quite cutting out the more sober accoutrements of the youthful advocates and writers to the signet, who were usually the only other representatives of the male sex to be found there'.[60]

But what had started as a pleasant afternoon's entertainment gradually became more fraught. Nothing attracts like a band, yet the humour of the crowds, denied access, quickly soured. Thus, in 1853, the King's Own Regiment agreed to play on Wednesday and Saturday afternoons during summer on the assumption that 'all respectable members of the public' would have free access. In the event many 'of all denominations' surged through the gates, overwhelming the gardens and causing damage. The committee's subsequent attempts to separate 'the respectable' from 'the rabble' by employing policemen at each gate proved only partially successful, and band performances were discontinued.[61] When they were resumed later the same problems recurred. All passions finally broke loose in 1875, triggered by the First Royal Scots band's decision to play on Saturday afternoons rather than weekdays. It was not a change welcomed by the committee. After various skirmishes, performances were once again abandoned, but this time not without provoking retaliation from the press. A bitter attack was mounted on 'the committee of shopkeepers' for converting what was essentially 'a municipal possession, nay, even a national glory and inheritance into a private demesne', simply because the users paid a few 'miserable' pounds a year for its upkeep.[62] Adding to the committee's embarrassment was the Town Council's request for the band to play in East Princes Street Gardens where they performed each Saturday to a delighted and well-behaved audience, shortage of seats being the only cause for complaint. The credibility of the garden committee was badly shaken.

Pressure to Open the Gardens

It was no coincidence that these wrangles over bands occurred most overtly from the 1850s when pressure to open up the gardens became more pronounced. The move was prompted partly by changes in the Princes Street population, and also by the opening of the neighbouring East Princes Street Gardens as a public park. It was a move in sympathy with the times. Many believed that the creation of public parks could provide opportunities for healthy, wholesome exercise; a panacea for the ills of cramped urban living and industrialised society. Not surprisingly, therefore, the justification for keeping West Princes Street Gardens an exclusive locked area came under scrutiny. One of the

Edinburgh's West Princes Street Gardens in 1875, shortly before becoming public. The railway tracks are well hidden and the simple landscape of grass and trees is restful to the eye. Only the Ross fountain appears unnaturally vigorous, although after many years of inactivity water once more flows through its pipes. (Grant, *Old and New Edinburgh*, 1880–3)

West Princes Street Gardens   123

Seated woman in the West Princes Street Gardens. Pen-and-wash drawing by William Yule, *c.* 1900. One of the most popular uses of all the New Town gardens has been for gentle recreation – sitting, observing, reading, talking, promenading and lying in the sun. (City Art Centre, City of Edinburgh Museums and Galleries)

Floral Clock, north-east corner, West Princes Street Gardens, *c.* 1927. First established in 1902 by the Superintendent of Parks, John McHattie, it has become a firm favourite with the public. (Valentines postcard, C. Byrom)

Proposed plan of 1893 for a winter garden at the western end of Princes Street Gardens, Edinburgh. The idea had been under discussion since 1880 with various designs drawn up. (ECA and Crown copyright © RCAHMS)

keenest champions of open access was the Reverend James Begg (1808–83), a prominent worker for the Free Church, and tireless campaigner for improving the housing and social conditions of the working and poorer classes.[63] When Henry Cockburn complained about lack of interest and inertia in matters affecting Edinburgh's appearance, Begg was quick to retaliate.[64] Public involvement, he declared, was dependent on public rights, and 'the shutting out of them from public parks and gardens has gone far to destroy their public spirit'. West Princes Street Gardens were a blatant example of something that rightfully belonged to the citizens, but from which they were most 'unjustly' excluded.

Although occasionally small concessions had been granted – for example, in the 1850s, the Scottish Association for the Suppression of Drunkenness succeeded in having the gardens open on Christmas and New Year's Day 'with a view of keeping parties out of the dram shop' – it was but snail's progress. Even these efforts could not have been achieved without the support of the Lord Provost, Duncan McLaren (1800–86), a man of liberal persuasion, sympathetic towards the working classes and a key-holder himself.[65] The Council's attempts to negotiate limited opening generated unease amongst the management committee, convinced that 'no respectable female would dare show her face on such occasions'. Once more they sought legal advice.[66]

Not until 1875 was the issue pursued with vigour when, compared to previous attempts, a lot was achieved remarkably swiftly. There was good reason for this. The first half of the 1870s was significant in the history of Edinburgh's open spaces. A wave of expansion on the west side and rapid development in areas such as the Grange united many citizens worried by the 'building out of nature'.[67] This led to the establishment in June 1875 of

Large crowds gathered round the Peddie and Kinnear bandstand, West Princes Street Gardens, Edinburgh, 1905. Band performances were popular and took place in several of the New Town gardens. (ECL)

the Cockburn Association (Edinburgh Civic Trust).[68] At its inauguration the Cockburn put forward seven suggestions for Edinburgh's improvement, all to do with open space. Heading the list was the opening of West Princes Street Gardens together with associated changes to alleviate congestion in Princes Street. Next was the acquisition of grounds at Inverleith, to serve as an arboretum and public park for the north of Edinburgh.[69]

The City Takes Over

Both the Gardens and Inverleith took priority on the Town Council's agenda, and the newly formed Cockburn Association promised their support. The City had at its helm a strong Lord Provost – James Falshaw (1810–89) – a blunt Yorkshireman and himself a West End resident (and an active supporter of Belgrave Crescent Gardens). His term in office was marked by 'getting needful things done'.[70] The Council applied directly to Parliament for powers to acquire the Gardens, together with the lands of Inverleith. With public support so firmly evident, the garden committee had to bow to the inevitable. The terms and conditions of transfer (including arrangements for widening Princes Street) were agreed in a series of meetings between the Town, the garden committee and the City Road Trust.[71] On 13 July 1876 the Act of Parliament was passed allowing the Council to take over the gardens, and before the end of the year they had assumed full responsibility.[72]

Two contemporary general views of Edinburgh's West Princes Street Gardens. Top: The Ross bandstand. Bottom: When the sun shines in West Princes Street Gardens. (Both: C. Byrom)

The affairs of the West Princes Street proprietors were slowly wound up. At their final meeting in January 1879 concern was voiced at the poor level of maintenance and 'the very offensive manner in which some individuals conducted themselves' since takeover; but acceptable norms of behaviour gradually became established and the worst fears of the former garden committee were not realised.

Changes After Takeover

Changes were inevitable. The top terrace disappeared once Princes Street was widened[73] and in its place a broad level walk was made about 20 feet (6.10 m) below street level, running from east to west (and criticised by some as too wide, too long and too dull). A unified design was created by the city architect Robert Morham (1839–1912) who was also responsible for the red sandstone cottage at the east end. Under the direction of John McHattie (*c.* 1859–1923), Superintendent of Edinburgh Parks, the gardens became more ornate, acquiring all the hallmarks of late-Victorian municipal planting including extensive borders of spring and summer bedding.[74] McHattie's floral clock, designed for the north-east corner in 1902, has become one of the garden's most famous icons, a rare survivor of this particular art form.[75]

Plans at various times to site the Usher Hall (south of the railway line), a winter garden and large covered rock garden (to the east end of the central area) were all seriously considered but then abandoned.[76] But a handsome bandstand (designed by Peddie & Kinnear) was added in 1880, gifted by the West Princes Street proprietors from surplus funds. It replaced a smaller, less ornamental one built in 1872, and was itself superseded in the 1930s by a more substantial structure known as the Ross bandstand, which still survives.[77] The number of statues, monuments and other artifacts have mushroomed since the gardens became public.[78] Other changes reflect greater and more varied use by the public: hard-paved surfaces in place of gravel walks, lavatories, shelters, memorial benches, a children's playground, open air café and piazza, ice-cream vans and so on; and the gardens are a venue for mass gatherings which would have made the West Princes Street proprietors tremble: the Festival fireworks concert, Hogmanay celebrations, even the odd film premiere and other Festival events.[79] The possibilities will go on multiplying.

Notes

1. *The Scotsman,* September 30, 1820.
2. Henry Cockburn, *Memorials of his Time,* op. cit., p. 317.
3. A letter survives by Peter Lawson, dated September 1815, to Mr MacRitchie, WS, about compensation for 'premature' removal from the nursery ground, held in lease from a Mrs Elder. Manuscript collection, EUL.
4. Rae's award of 1766 for example, upheld the Town's rights to feu out the south side, west of the Mound, provided the houses were not less than 96 feet (29 m) from those on the north side of Princes Street, nor extended more than 160 feet (49 m) southwards; and as stated in original house charters.

5. The Counsel consulted by the proprietors were David Monypenny (afterwards Lord Pitmilly), Mr Cathcart (Lord Alloway), and Mr Ferguson.

6. TCM, 3 August 1813.

7. The nearest Episcopal church at that time was St George's at the eastern end of York Place. The new chapel, later to become St John's Church, was erected in 1817 to a design by William Burn.

8. Act of Parliament, 56th George III c.41. *'An Act to enable the Lord Provost, Magistrates and Council of the City of Edinburgh to carry into effect certain purposes in regard to the erection of a chapel, at the West end of Princes Street and for effecting certain improvements in the neighbourhood thereof, and in other parts of the Extended Royalty of the said city.'* 1816, published by Spottiswoode and Robertson.

9. On management matters, the proprietors were empowered to hold meeting after due advertisement, to appoint a committee of not more than five persons to carry the Act into effect, to fix and levy assessments (the amount for the parapet and railing was not to exceed 10 per cent of the rents of the premises in any one year, a ceiling fixed for all other assessments) and to borrow money of up to £5,000 for carrying out all the improvements.

10. Minute Book 1, 10 June 1816; notice of the meeting was advertised in the *Edinburgh Evening Courant* and the *Edinburgh Correspondent*, and billed to take place at 12 noon on Monday, 24 June 1816, in the City Chambers.

11. He was the son of Dr Douglas, a leading practitioner in Kelso.

12. Henry Jardine became King's Remembrancer (Court of Exchequer) in 1820, being depute before, and was knighted by George IV in 1825.

13. Minute Book 1, 3 July 1816–25 May 1818, provides details of the various transactions.

14. Richard Crichton had been appointed architect for the St Anne's Street improvements.

15. Minute Book 1, 6 July 1818, Report of the Committee of the General Meeting of Proprietors of Princes Street west of the Mound.

16. Minute Book 1, 25 May 1818, the advertisement was placed in the *Edinburgh Courant*, once a week, for four weeks.

17. Minute Book 2, 20 November 1819; £2,000 was borrowed from Sir William Forbes & Co.

18. Minute Book 2, 19 February 1820. Little is known about Richard Stevens. He is recorded as having worked on several Scottish estates including Balnoon (Balnanoon) Angus (1812); Kimmerghame, Berwickshire (1812); and Lees, Berwickshire (1816); see A.A. Tait, *The Landscape Garden in Scotland,* op. cit., p. 258.

19. Minute Book 2, 8 June 1820. The Royal Institution at the foot of the Mound, facing Hanover Street, was completed to a design by Playfair in 1826, and later enlarged by him in 1833–6.

20. Many of Skene's drawings and watercolours (including those for Reekiana – see Note 22) are in the Fine Art Department, EPL; the National Galleries of Scotland have two large folios of pen and watercolour drawings made during a tour of France 1820–21, and others of Germany and France.

21. Information on James Skene has been taken from many sources including: Sidney Lee, ed. *Dictionary of National Biography*, Vol. 52 (London 1897), p. 335; William Forbes Skene, ed. *Memorials of the family of Skene*, The New Spalding Club (Aberdeen, 1887), pp. 139–45; Peter J.M. McEwan, *Dictionary of Scottish Art & Architecture*, Antique Collectors' Cub (1994), p. 531; James Skene, 'Reminiscences of Scott', NLS, MS 1909; James Skene, *Memories of Sir Walter Scott*, (London, 1909); Robert Buchart, *Skene's drawings of Old Edinburgh, BOEC*, Vol. xxv, pp. 128–39; together with miscellaneous notes on Skene lent by Mrs Meta Viles.

22. *Reekiana*, unpublished manuscript, descriptive notes by James Skene on the North Loch, EPL, 1836.

23. Minute Book 2, 19 January 1821; Skene was elected in place of Andrew Murray who had moved from Princes Street.

24. After Henderson retired from being Lord Provost (1823–5) he became Master of the Merchant Company. He was a man of considerable business capacity, and largely responsible for the formation of the National Bank of Scotland, of which he was first President.

25. Minute Book 2, 13 February 1821: tack between the proprietors and Alexander Henderson.

26. The rental provided a useful contribution towards the proprietors' own outlay for leasing the various parts of the ground.

27. *Edinburgh Advertiser*, 7 February 1827; report of an address by Lord Provost Trotter on his predecessor.

28. Minute Book 2, 19 March 1823; 30 April 1823; 2 May 1823. Minute Book 3, 17 May 1823; 18 July 1825; 24 December 1825.

29. Minute Book 2, 19 March 1823; this minute provides a useful account of work carried out by Henderson, and lists the various complaints about the final account submitted by him.

30. Minute Book 3, 13 November 1826; and 23 November 1826; Gibson Craig, WS, was appointed assessor, and he consulted with Mr Willet, factor on the Barnton estate.

31. James Skene, *Remarks on the Well House tower*, Antiquarian Society Transactions, Vol. 2 (Edinburgh, 1828).

32. Before Skene had become involved with the gardens, the workmen had discovered a coffin with three skeletons inside, one male and two female, which they then reburied close by.

33. *The Scotsman*, 30 September 1820.

34. Minute Book 2, 9 April 1821.

35. The bleaching green (for use of Princes Street Proprietors), formed part of the Glebe land belonging to St Cuthbert's church and leased from them until 1831; it was then repossessed by the Kirk Session as an extension to their burial ground.

36. Minute Book 2, 13 July 1821; 26 January 1822; 3 October 1822; 4 October 1822; Minute Book 3, 24 March 1824. The gardener's house was demolished in 1885 when it was judged 'insanitary'. It was replaced by a new lodge designed by Robert Moreham (1839–1912), City Architect.

37. Minute Book 2, 26 December 1821; 19 January 1822.

38. Minute Book 3, 11 February 1829. Mr Douglas, the clerk, wrote a letter to Thomas Hamilton, architect for the Johnson Terrace improvement project, requesting use of the stones.

39. Minute Book 3, 24 January 1825; some of this money would have helped offset the rent paid by the committee to General Ramsay for leasing the ground; this had been set up for three periods of 19 years; £12 for the first nine, and £17 thereafter. The ground was let for garden, nursery or pleasure ground use.

40. James Skene, *Reekiana*, op. cit.

41. Priscilla Boniface (ed.), *In search of English Gardens: The travels of John Claudius Loudon and his wife Jane* (Lennard Publishing, Herts, 1987), p. 223.

42. Elizabeth Grant of Rothiemurchus, *The Highland Lady in Ireland*, diary entry, 13 September 1842 (Edinburgh, reprinted 1997), p. 137.

43. James Skene, 'Reminiscences of Scott', op. cit.; Sir Walter Scott's Journal, January 1826, quoted in Grant, *Old and New Edinburgh*, Vol. 2, p. 98.

44. Minute Book 5, 25 March 1840; and the accounts for 1840/41; David Cousin was paid 2 guineas for his plan but no details are given.

45. The information has been taken from the following sources: Minute Book 5, Circular: To the proprietors and Tenants in Princes Street, west of the mound. Edinburgh & Glasgow Railway Company, signed John Learmonth, Chairman, 11 October 1836; Minute Book 5, letter James Skene, Esq., to John Learmonth Esq., Moray Place, 22 October, 1836; Minute Book 5: Case for the proprietors of Princes Street, west of Hanover Street, Edinburgh to the Bill brought into Parliament for a Railroad between the Cities of Edinburgh and Glasgow. More details about the proprietors' fight against the railway can be found in David Robertson, *The Princes Street Proprietors and other Chapters in the History of the Royal Burgh of Edinburgh* (Edinburgh 1935), pp. 37–46.

46. Minute Book 5, 30 September 1844, letter from Playfair to Mr Douglas, Clerk, outlining his proposals.

47. Minute Book 6, 21 February 1846; the list was made out with the help of various nursery catalogues in Playfair's possession.

48. Minute Book 6; letter to Playfair from the Clerk.

49. Minute Book 6, 1 August 1849; 11 September 1851.

50. Minute Book 6, Accounts, 1847–48; McNab was paid 10 guineas 'for a plan for laying out the ground'.

51. James McNab's manuscript file, RBG library, untitled article; see also *The Courant*, 6 September 1855, reporting the Town Council's proceedings relating to this matter.

52. Two large vases with pedestals gifted by George Mackay, of Grangemouth, had already been added to the garden during 1851, and placed on the central walk. The remnants of the vases now stand within the grounds of the gardener's house.

53. The statue to Alan Ramsay was unveiled in 1865, and financed by Lord Murray, a descendant of Ramsay.

54. Minute Book 8, 3 June 1868; 24 November 1869. Two dozen garden seats were ordered from a firm in Glasgow.

55. Mrs Ross, 9 Magdala Crescent, had left a legacy of £1,500 for a covered ornamental rock garden in West Princes Street gardens, and in 1879 Mr McLeod, Head Gardener, was given permission to visit Blackpool and Brighton to look at examples there.

56. The painting of West Princes Street Gardens by John Dick Peddie was first exhibited in 1866 under the title 'A Suggestion for the Improvement of Edinburgh', and thereafter in 1867, 1869, 1870 and 1880. In 1867 it was joined by a companion piece of East Princes Street.

57. Minute Book 5; Accounts 1844/5.

58. Their numbers were in any case dwindling as property became subdivided for non-residential use; and the rules of the committee did not generally recognise tenants as having rights to the gardens.

59. *Edinburgh Advertiser*, 17 March 1826; 24 March 1826.

60. *Mrs Storey's Early Reminiscences*, (Glasgow, 1911), p. 122.

61. Minute Book 6, 14 June 1853; 7 September 1853.

62. *Edinburgh Evening Courant*, 10 May 1875; 11 May 1875; 13 May 1875; and 9 June 1875; adding to the difficulties was the fact that staff left early on a Saturday.

63. Thomas Smith, *Memoirs of James Begg DD*, vol. 2 (Edinburgh, 1888), pp. 128–43.

64. Lord Cockburn, *A letter to the Lord Provost on the best ways of spoiling the beauty of Edinburgh*, (Edinburgh, 1849); James Begg DD, *How to promote and preserve the true beauty of Edinburgh: being a few hints to the Hon. Lord Cockburn on his late letter to the Lord Provost* (Edinburgh, 1849).

65. Minute Book 6, 16 December 1851; 15 December 1852; 21 December 1853. Minute Book 7, 7

November 1854; 26 December 1855. Duncan M. McLaren went on to become Liberal MP for the City.

66. Minute Book 6, 20 October 1852; 29 October 1852; 8 July 1853; 20 July 1854; 7 August 1854. Minute Book 7, 7 November; 27 March 1855.

67. *The Edinburgh Courant,* 23 April 1875.

68. *The Edinburgh Courant,* 16 June 1875, which contains a detailed account of the meeting. A briefer note appeared in *The Scotsman* of the same date. See also Vol. 1, *Cockburn Association Reports, 1875 to 1894.*

69. Other suggestions included: formation of a suitable public park to the north and south of Queensferry Road; provision of a suitable band of music to perform regularly; assisting the local authority to improve the Meadows; improvement of the walks in immediate neighbourhood of Edinburgh; preservation and planting of ornamental trees in and around the City.

70. George Andrew Hobson, *The life of Sir James Falshaw bart.,* (Chiswick, 1905). p. 204.

71. Minute Book 9, 26 April 1876: Agreement between the Lord Provost, Magistrates and Council, the City road Trust, and the Proprietors of West Princes Street Gardens.

72. 39 & 40 Victoria, The Edinburgh Improvement Act, 1876, Ch. xxx, 'An Act for the acquisition by the Lord Provost, Magistrates and Council of the City of Edinburgh of the West-Princes-Street-Gardens there, for the purpose of the same being laid open to the public; and for the acquisition of lands of Inverleith for the formation of an Arboretum and Public Park and Pleasure Ground; and for other purposes,' 13 July 1876.

73. This length of Princes Street lacked a footpath along the south side, and was having to cope not only with carriages but also horse-drawn trams, which had been introduced in 1871.

74. See Christopher Taylor: *Parks and Gardens of Britain; A Landscape History from the Air* (Edinburgh 1998), p. 178.

75. Installed as a floral tribute to Edward VII. John M'Hattie had formerly been the Duke of Wellington's gardener at Streatfiled Saye, Oxfordshire. Mr J. Ritchie, an Edinburgh clockmaker, supplied the mechanism.

76. After Andrew Usher donated £100,000 in 1896 for a hall, various sites were considered.

77. In 1872 and in 1893 the Sutherland Highlanders had offered to fund a bandstand, but the committee, on the advice of Mr Kinnear, agreed to contribute £50 to secure one 'of more ornamental and massive design'.

78. Statues and memorials not already described include: *Sir James Young Simpson,* sculpted by William Brodie; *Woman & Two Children,* sculpted by William Brodie; *The Royal Scots Greys Memorial,* sculpted by W. Birnie Rhind; *Dr Thomas Guthrie,* sculpted by F.W. Pomeroy; *The Scottish American War Memorial,* sculpted by Professor R. Tait Mackenzie, unveiled 1927; *The Falklands' Memorial,* replica of the garden planted on the same day in the Falkland Islands, in memory of those killed in 1982 conflict; *The Royal Scots Memorial,* designed by Sir Frank Mears, sculpted by C. Pilkington Jackson; *The Norwegian Memorial Stone,* large ancient boulder set on three smaller stones on flagstone base, erected 1978 by Norwegian Government; *Robert Louis Stevenson Memorial, 1987,* small grove of weeping birch trees, designed by the artist Ian Hamilton Findlay.

79. A useful account of what is being done in the gardens today, together with planting details and policy can be found in an article by James C. McKay, 'The Gardens Today', *The Caledonian Gardener,* 1996 (Royal Caledonian Horticultural Society), pp. 37–40. The former gardener's house is destined to become an interpretative centre.

PART FOUR

THE SECOND NEW TOWN

CHAPTER 7

EDINBURGH'S SECOND NEW TOWN
AND ITS OPEN SPACES

A few years ago the Magistrates of Edinburgh, finding that the New Town, extensive as it is, was inadequate to the increasing opulence and population of the city, purchased the house and grounds of Bellevue, and some extensive fields reaching nearly to Drumsheugh; and have begun to lay down another New Town that bids fair to eclipse the former in extent and beauty of the architecture.

The Stranger's Guide to Edinburgh, 1817.[1]

The development of Edinburgh's second New Town has until recently only been incompletely documented, yet it is helpful to know something about its origins in order to appreciate and make sense of the next group of pleasure gardens.[2] While the first New Town was being built, the ground to the north beyond Queen Street remained the scene of peaceful rural pursuits. The land formed part of the extensive and ancient Barony of Broughton which had belonged to the Heriot's Hospital since 1636.[3] Most of it was leased for grazing and arable purposes and the three principal tenants were farmers by the names of Thomas Wood, Henry Anderson and Robert Robertson. A portion on the eastern side, amounting to about 13 Scots acres (6.6 hectares),[4] later to be known as the lands of Bellevue, had been sold by the Hospital in the eighteenth century to Peter Blair, a skinner. More will be said about this portion shortly.

The Queen Street Garden Area

Unlike the first New Town, which from the start had been promoted by the Town Council, the development of the second was far more protracted and involved many more people. In all the proposals, however, it seems to have been accepted that the area now known as the Queen Street Gardens should be kept as open space. Indeed, the very first charter granted in 1769 by the Governors of Heriot's Hospital for a portion of this ground – long before designs for any overall scheme had been drawn up – stated quite clearly that it was feued 'for the purpose of a garden only'. In this particular case, the ground was to serve as garden for the first house built on Queen Street, Number 8, designed by Robert Adam for Robert Ord, Chief Baron of the Scottish Exchequer. The feu charter stipulated that in all time coming 'no dwelling house shall be erected . . . and no other building whatever excepting proper offices for the use of the house to be built upon said street . . . hot houses, gardener's house, or such other buildings as may be necessary for said garden'.[5] These conditions were repeated in the eight subsequent charters made out between 1781 and 1791 for land within this strip. Each one affirmed that the restrictions and servitude were made out in favour of the Lord Provost, Magistrates and Council 'as representing the community', the proprietors of houses in Queen Street, and the proprietors of houses to be built on Thomas Wood's or Robert Robertson's farm ground – that is, the land to the north of Queen Street.

Why the Governors took this course of action is nowhere stated. But they were probably influenced by James Craig's plan for the first New Town, with its residential layout shown flanked by a wide band of formal parkland to the south (the valley of the North Loch), and a similar one to the north (the Queen Street Gardens). The parkland in each instance stretched the complete length of the New Town itself. Compared to Craig's design the Queen Street garden area became considerably foreshortened; the land at the extreme western end was no longer owned by the Hospital and therefore outwith their control, while that on the far eastern end was eventually developed by the Hospital as York Place.[6] An attractive strip of open space, providing a buffer between the two New Town developments, could only enhance future feuing prospects; in addition the Governors no doubt wished to avoid any controversy and to be guided by existing plans.

David Steuart and Plans for Development

Although these basic safeguards existed from an early date, several years went by before more definite proposals for a second New Town began to emerge. The first scheme, however, was not instigated by the Heriot's Hospital but by David Steuart (1747–1824), Lord Provost from 1780 to 1782. Steuart was from a well-connected family in Perthshire, the fifth and youngest son of John Steuart of Dalguise, and his merchant business led him eventually to set up a private banking firm in partnership with his friend Robert Allan.[7] Described as a handsome man 'of excellent taste', passionately fond of literature and an avid book collector (the Advocates' Library, now the National Library of Scotland, became owners of some of his early printed book collection), he was enterprising and energetic, and possessed more than a moderate interest in the improvement of Edinburgh.[8] He was also European in outlook, his early working life having involved periods in France and Spain; just the man to become interested in

David Steuart, Lord Provost, merchant banker, land speculator and bibliophile. He provided the initial impetus behind the development of Edinburgh's second New Town. (City Art Centre, City of Edinburgh Museums & Galleries)

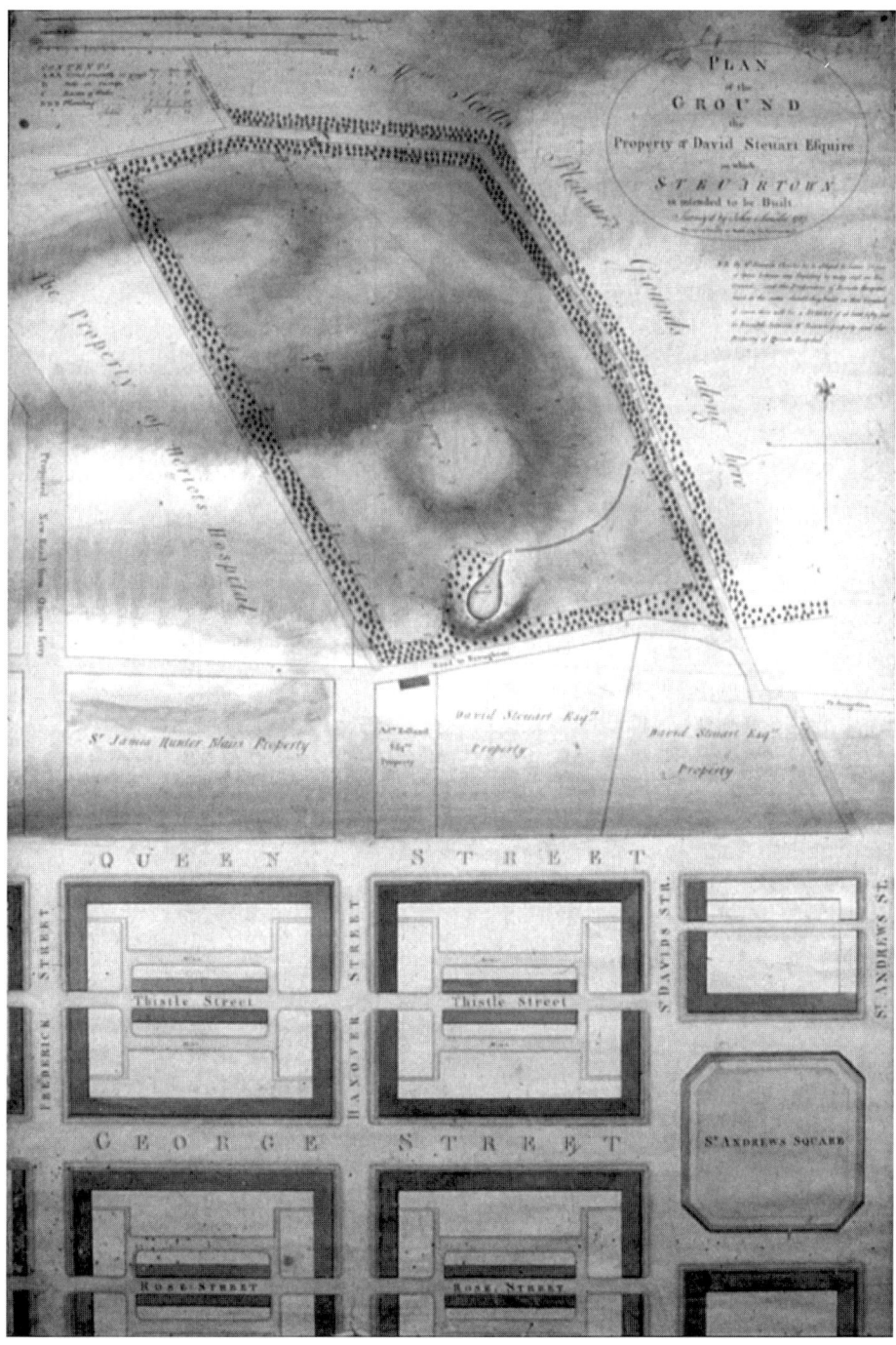

Survey by John Ainslie, 1787, of David Steuart's land to the north of Queen Street, Edinburgh, on which 'Steuartown' is intended to be built. (Crown copyright © RCAHMS)

land speculation and development.[9] Steuart's involvement with the second New Town dated from around 1780 when he moved to 5 Queen Street. In 1781 he purchased over two Scots acres of land (1 ha) from Heriot's Hospital opposite his house and adjacent to Ord's feu; as the next chapter will explain he made this into a private garden for himself and his family.[10]

Steuart's energies, however, were not contained here and he began to acquire other land in the vicinity on a purely speculative basis. The main and largest portion was 13 Scots acres (6.6 ha) lying to the north of his garden in the region of Abercromby Place and beyond. This land had been advertised for letting as 'garden ground' as far back as 1774 when Alexander Ramadge took over the tenancy, and in 1782 sub-tacked it to Steuart.[11] Three years later Steuart offered to buy it from Heriot's Hospital, and the conditions under which this was granted indicate that the Governors were alert to his motives.[12] In readiness for the likely changes ahead, the Heriot's Hospital did in fact in 1785 commission the surveyor, John Laurie, to produce 'a proper plan of the ground to the north of Queen Street . . . in the view of the same becoming building ground'.[13]

Meantime, the remaining land alongside Queen Street was feued off as private garden space. In 1786 Steuart acquired Ord's former garden, and in 1791 he bought another portion at the western end, adjacent to the one owned by his friend Robert Allan.[14] By then the banking partnership had been dissolved and Steuart was running his own general merchant's business in Leith. In 1787 he employed John Ainslie, land surveyor, to make out a detailed plan of his main and largest plot of land;[15] it was entitled 'Plan of the Ground – on which STEUARTOWN is intended to be Built'.[16]

Conflict with Heriot's Hospital and the Queen Street Proprietors

Shortly after Ainslie had completed this plan, Steuart applied to Heriot's Hospital for a small triangle of ground (about 3/4 of an acre (.3 ha)) which had been 'waste for sometime', immediately adjacent to the south-west corner of his feu, in order to 'square marches' (boundaries). In October 1789 the Governors agreed, but on certain conditions, which included the production of a plan, a bond for payment and restricting any building to one house and offices for his own use, not to be closer than 20 feet (6 m) from the mutual boundary. A plan was subsequently submitted to the Hospital's Treasurer and, according to Steuart's later account, an informal agreement was reached (to minimise costs, as the area of land was so small) to postpone payment for the new charter until the one for his larger 13-acre plot was due for renewal.

Steuart's next move proved hapless and inept. It is not clear what prompted him to give permission to 'two industrious young men – cabinet makers' to build a workshop on the triangular site. Was he anxious to establish claim to the ground or simply 'endeavouring to add a little to my own income'? Certainly his intentions would not have been to deliberately antagonise the Governors, nor for that matter his close neighbours. Sightings of the workshop under construction did, however, alarm the Queen Street proprietors. Captain Patrick Hunter, resident at 12 Queen Street, was, for one, greatly disturbed, and a letter of complaint was hastily dispatched to the Heriot's Hospital. Investigation revealed that none of the Governors had seen Steuart's plan, and that far from squaring of marches it 'misshapes the hospital grounds to the west'. As Steuart had not fulfilled the terms of the agreement, the Governors decided he had no rights to the land. Steuart's reply, delayed by 'a painful and tedious illness' (he was the victim of gout), denied any nuisance value either from the nature of the business or the building itself; he argued that he had proceeded in good faith and that possession of the land had been sanctioned. All things considered, he felt that the Governors should be sympathetically inclined, particularly as several had acquired their fortunes by application to similar tasks, and that 'if I can accomplish my intentions with respect to the ground I have feued from Heriot's Hospital I hope to plant as many buildings upon it as will bring the charity nearly £2,000 a year revenue, without any exertion on their part.'[17]

The Hospital Governors responded by asking Steuart to submit a revised drawing and informing him of the pressure they were now under from the 'Gentlemen of Queen Street . . . to effectuate taking down the house . . . which in every view is down on a place where you have no right to build'. Rumours and counter-rumours abounded. With mounting concern that long-cherished views over farmland and woodland to the Firth of Forth and the Fife hills beyond were now in jeopardy, the Queen Street proprietors made a second approach to the Hospital. Their proposal on this occasion was to purchase a servitude upon two fields to the north of Queen Street 'as may be necessary to preserve the present view of their house northward that no buildings be erected thereon'.[18] These events served to remind the Governors that decisions would soon have to be made about the land in question; and indeed, within the space of a few months Steuart had started negotiations with them for a joint feuing plan. As discussions and plans became further advanced the Hospital realised that it was not in their interest to come to any private arrangement with the Queen Street proprietors, and that instead the ground should be advertised on the open market as building land.[19]

Plans for the Second New Town

The first mention of a building plan appears in the Heriot's Hospital minutes of 4 June 1792,[20] which refer to a letter from David Steuart stating that 'in consequence of what passed between the Committee of the Governors of George Heriot's Hospital and me I have with the assistance of Mr William Sibbald Your Surveyor made out a plan for building on the ground lying to the north of Queen Street the property of the Hospital and myself.'

William Sibbald, it will be remembered, was also Superintendent of Works to the City, a post he held from 1790 until his death in 1809,[21] During the few months following production of this first plan, Sibbald prepared further sketch plans (none of which have survived) both on behalf of the Hospital, which was concerned to establish the land's feuing value,[22] and for Steuart, who wanted to resolve the boundary between his own and the Hospital's property.[23] By mid-1793 details of a mutual building plan finally became settled. Boundaries between the Hospital's and Steuart's land were readjusted on the understanding that the workshop would be removed, and agreement was reached that

Development plan by William Sibbald, 1793, for the lands belonging to David Steuart and the Heriot's Hospital. (George Heriot Trust and Crown copyright © RCAHMS)

'the area in the middle of the Square is to be common property to the houses fronting the same'.[24]

This plan, which shows the square to be a prominent feature, is dated 18 October 1793 – the date when the Governors and David Steuart formally contracted to conform to it.[25] Nothing is known about the plan's evolution except that Steuart and Sibbald, between them, seem to have come up with the ideas for it.[26] As well as a large square at the eastern end (three-quarters of which was contained within Steuart's feu) the other distinctive feature was an open space on the western side in the form of a circus, containing at its centre a water feature (the 'bason') not unlike a proposal later made by Sibbald for Charlotte Square. It should also be remembered that Steuart had at one time tried to promote a circus at the centre of George Street. These open spaces were connected by a central road, with cross streets linking with Queen Street, and with two crescents on the northern boundary. This was certainly a plan to complement that of the first New Town, and provided a similar balance of open and built space.

The plan, however, was not implemented, although it was to influence later thinking. Steuart, now increasingly beset with financial problems, met with frustration in his attempts to prod the Hospital into further action. In 1796 the Governors did agree – after being approached by him – to meet half the costs of having the plan engraved, with 'a thousand copies to be cast off . . . for the inspection of such persons as may intend to feu'.[27] One year later Thomas Wood, tenant farmer of much of the ground for upwards of 60 years, died – thus removing one obstacle in the way of the land's development.[28] This encouraged Steuart to renew contact with the Hospital Governors, and in 1798 he informed them of his intention to have printed 200 copies 'of my agreement with the Hospital relative to the building on my feu for the use of persons intending to feu as reference to it will be made in the feu charters'.[29] Without the Governors' co-operation, however, progress was unlikely; and at this time they were preoccupied with their ground further eastwards, and the building of Duke Street (later to be absorbed within the southern end of Dublin Street), Elder Street and York Place.

Steuart's Financial Collapse

Although initially Steuart's mercantile enterprises had prospered, from 1788 onwards his luck had started to plummet following the spate of bankruptcies amongst some of the biggest distillers of malt spirits in Scotland. As suppliers of barley he and Allan had been one of the largest creditors to these companies. His one-time boast that 'it will neither bend nor break me', proved sadly wrong.[30] His own trading company, established in 1790, survived for less than three years in the face of accumulating losses. Plans to revive fortunes by concentrating solely on the wine trade fared no better. As his financial situation worsened (and with the Hospital dragging their feet over the joint plan), Steuart decided to change tactics in the hope of raising some immediate cash. In February 1799 he again approached the Governors with the suggestion that the line of buildings in York Place, 'which so far from being of any publick injury are agreed ornamental to the city', should be extended westwards over his private garden, and that if they withdrew the servitude over this ground he would divide the money raised from the feus between himself and the Hospital.[31] Happily, the Governors stood firm and refused permission for any houses to be built in the Queen Street garden area.[32]

By the end of the year Steuart, in spite of help from friends and relatives, was bankrupt. Early in 1800 his land was put up for sale, being advertised first on 11 January in the *Edinburgh Evening Courant* as 'well adapted and will bring a considerable price for building stances'. His private garden in Queen Street (since 1793 the family had lived at Kirkbraehouse opposite St Cuthbert's Church on Lothian Road) was listed for sale as a separate lot, and had been rented out for some time to various nurserymen.[33] Agents for the sale were Maxwell Gordon and John Morison, WS (Morison had been appointed trustee for the creditors following Steuart's bankruptcy), 'who had in their hands the plan for building on the grounds', namely, Sibbald's plan of 1793. Whether Steuart's failure had branded such an enterprise as risky we do not know, but the land remained unsold although regularly advertised throughout the first half of the year, 'upset price reduced'. It was not in fact sold until 1802, and three years later changed hands again, when curiously enough the original agents for the sale in 1800 became part-owners.[34] By then, however, prospects for the land's development had considerably brightened.

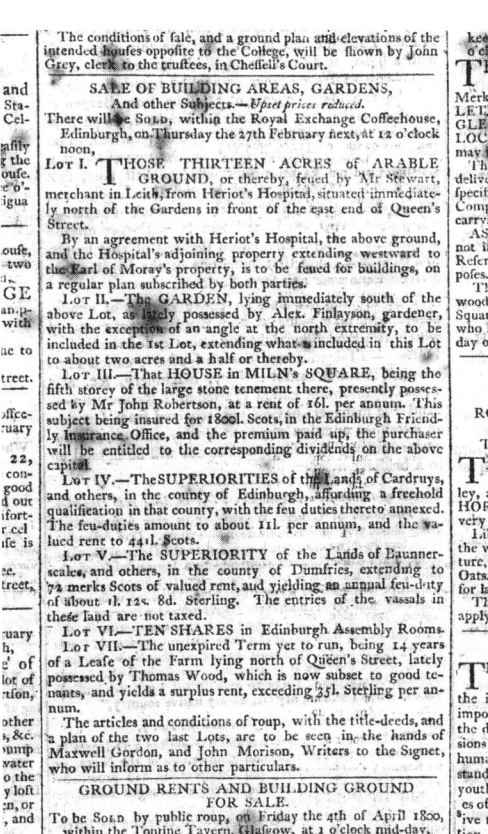

Edinburgh Evening Courant, 10 February 1800: advertisement for the sale of Steuart's property following his bankruptcy. Note reference to 'a regular plan' being available. (Trustees of NLS)

The Town Council's Involvement: Purchase of the Bellevue Estate

Without Steuart's enterprising spirit plans for the second New Town might well have foundered. No-one, it seemed, was prepared to buy his land and to take on a commitment which to some extent was dependent on the goodwill and co-operation of Heriot's Hospital. But the gap left by Steuart's withdrawal was almost immediately filled by the Town Council. Early in 1800 the Council purchased 'the whole property at Bellevue', including the mansion house, garden and adjoining land, 'for behoof of the City of Edinburgh'.[35] This piece of land had changed hands several times since first being sold by Heriot's Hospital to Peter Blair, eventually coming into the ownership of ex-Lord Provost George Drummond, instigator of the first New Town.

By then a modest mansion had been built on the site which he treated as his rural retreat, calling it Drummond Lodge. Drummond went on to purchase further areas of adjoining land, thereby increasing his holding to over 30 acres (about 15 ha).[36] Following his death, the whole property was eventually sold (in 1774) to Major General John Scott of Balcomie, Fife, a man of immense wealth, mainly derived from success at the gambling table.[37] He desired more lavish accommodation, so the former dwelling was demolished and in its place was built Bellevue House, sited a little further to the north, and based on a design by Robert Adam.[38] Scott died before the house was finished, but his wife and three

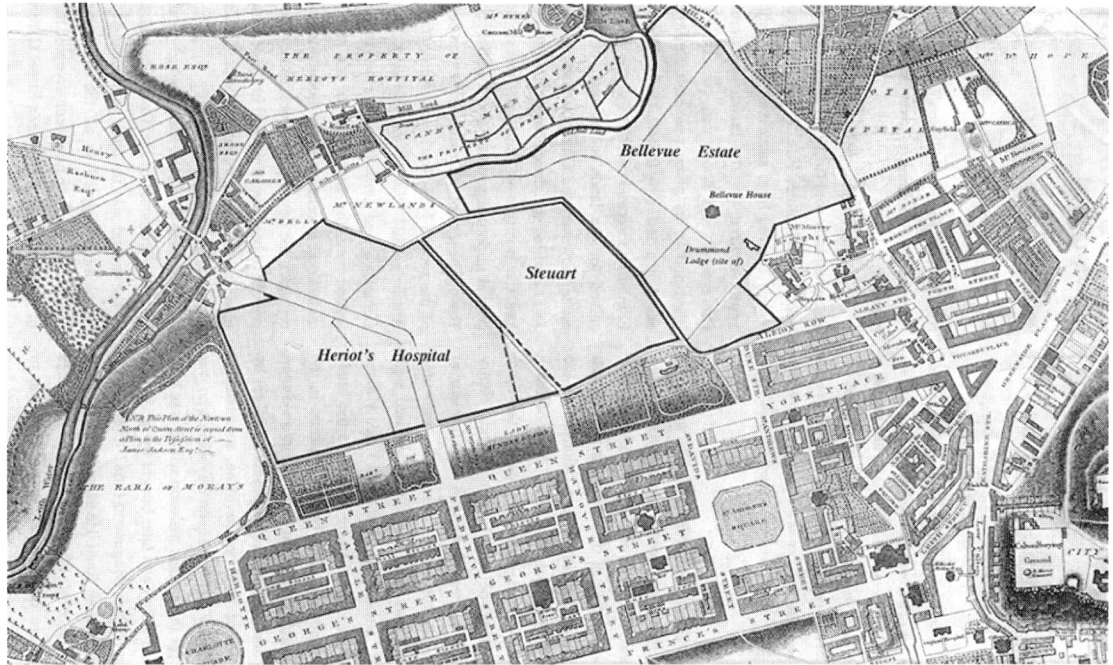

The lands on which the second New Town of Edinburgh were built, shown as they would have been in about 1800. (Allen Simpson, from various sources and superimposed on John Ainslie's published plan of 1804)

daughters lived there for many years.[39] The title to the estate passed to Henrietta, the eldest daughter, described as 'the greatest heiress in the country'. She married the Marquis of Tichfield, eldest son of the Duke of Portland; and it was from the Marquis that the Town Council purchased the property.

The Bellevue estate lay to the north-east of the Hospital's and Steuart's feus and formed a potentially useful addition. This purchase was not simply a fortuitous move but one calculated to give the Town Council a controlling influence in the next major development after the first New Town. As subsequent events indicate, the Council knew what they wanted to achieve, and considered themselves in the best position to take the initiative. That they grasped this opportunity at a time of widespread social unrest due to severe food shortages makes their action seem even more courageous.[40]

Once Bellevue had been acquired, the land was surveyed and cleared; vines and other garden and hothouse plants were sold by public auction, and the trees cut down and removed. Some plants were donated to the Royal Botanic Garden at the request of Daniel Rutherford, Professor of Botany.[41] No more were there the delightful views of 'the sea of the Bellevue foliage gilded by the evening sun', which had long given pleasure to strollers along Queen Street. Taken so completely by surprise, Edinburgh citizens apparently reacted passively, although 'shuddering when they heard the axes busy in the woods of Bellevue'. Henry Cockburn stood by and watched, and was forced to conclude that all that art and nature had done to prepare the place for foliaged compartments of town architecture, if being built upon should prove inevitable, was carefully obliterated; so that at last the whole spot was made as bare and as dull as if the designer of the New Town himself had presided over the operation.[42]

Competition for the Design of the Second New Town

The Town Council did not share Cockburn's sensibilities. As in the case of the first New Town, they decided to hold a public competition[43] for laying out in streets, squares, etc. for buildings, the Grounds of Bellevue belonging to the City of Edinburgh, also the grounds westwards, and north of the Gardens north of Queen Street, belonging to David Steuart, Esq., and to Heriot's Hospital, as far west as the grounds belonging to the Earl of Moray.

In October 1800 an advertisement appeared twice in the *Edinburgh Evening Courant* offering a prize of 100 guineas for the best, and 50 guineas for the second best, plan submitted – a considerable advance on Craig's premium for the first New Town plan in 1766.[44] Two months were allowed for submission (again a more generous time-scale than previously allowed); and Bellevue House (later to be sold to the Board of Customs) was required to be made part of the design. As most of the purchase price had in fact been tied up with the value of the house rather than the land, the City felt a responsibility to put it to some viable use.[45] Response was good and a 'great many' plans were received and judged 'by gentlemen of taste'. Four designs were singled out as being of equal merit and accordingly the prize money was divided

Announcement in the *Edinburgh Evening Courant*, 25 October 1800, of the competition for the design of the second New Town. (Trustees of the NLS)

between them. However, as each plan 'contained qualities which the others wanted', a further 50 guineas was set aside 'upon them producing a plan made up by them from the four plans to contain what shall be thought best in each of them'.[46] No names are mentioned in the minutes but Council accounts for this period reveal that payments were made to James Elliot, Robert Morison, John Baine and William Sibbald.[47]

The Prizewinners

All four prizewinners were experienced designers although now rather forgotten names. James Elliot (1770–1810) was in practice with his elder brother Archibald, who had an office in London; James remained in Scotland to supervise the firm's work there. Together they worked on a number of Scottish country houses including Dreghorn Castle, Midlothian; Stobo Castle, Peeblesshire; and Auchmore House and Taymouth Castle, both in Perthshire.

Had James lived longer his reputation would no doubt have matched that of his better-known brother.[48] John Baine and Robert Morison are both mentioned in a book published in the early part of the nineteenth century as examples of the many 'excellent architects' produced in Scotland, along with such other names as Adam, Craig, Henderson, Gillespie, Burn, Crichton, Baxter and Stark.[49]

John Baine, 'engineer', 'draughtsman' and 'surveyor', had been a student at the Trustees' Academy (Edinburgh School of Design) where he was an outstanding designer, regularly winning prizes for his damask patterns.[50] In 1785 he was a candidate for the Mastership of the School, Alexander Nasmyth also being a contender: neither was successful.[51] Shortly afterwards Baine established himself as a teacher of mathematics and scientific drawing, advertising in 1788 that he gave 'private lessons particularly to the gentlemen of the Army and Navy and to Engineers in Mathematics and those branches of the art of drawing dependent upon them as Perspective Fortification, the drawing of Machinery, Maps etc'.[52] Baine, the advertisement also informs us, was about to extend his classes to other members of the public, to be held 'at his lodgings at Mr Nasmyth's, No 11 South Bridge Street'. The two men were obviously on friendly terms and Baine was later to sponsor Nasmyth for membership of the Cape Club.[53] It has also been recently established that during 1793 Baine was employed by the British Fisheries Society (founded in 1786 to create new communities in remote areas) to do surveys at Skye and Ullapool. He was apparently regarded as something of 'an odd genius' of 'rather a peculiar temper' but good at his job.[54] But apart from these snatches of information little else has been discovered about him, and what happened to him subsequently remains a mystery.

Of the four, Robert Morison (d. 1825) was probably the most experienced draughtsman, having been a pupil of Robert and James Adam for several years, later becoming assistant to Sir John Soane. In 1794 he published *Designs in Perspective for Villas in the Ancient Castle and Grecian Styles..*[55] Morrison practised in Edinburgh from around the turn of the century until his death.[56] He was involved in the design of several houses in the New Town, and also submitted plans for completing the University buildings in 1815, having drawn up earlier designs in 1789.[57]

But William Sibbald's knowledge of, and familiarity with, the site out-rivalled that of the other prizewinners and placed him at a distinct advantage. A competent designer himself, he understandably had a vested interest in entering the competition, which he was able to do anonymously. He might even have been quietly encouraged to do so by the City.

The Competition Designs

None of the winning designs survived but two related items have been preserved which together tell us a great deal about what the competition achieved. First, and most important, is a drawing captioned 'PLAN FOR LAYING OF IN BUILDINGS THE LANDS OF BELLEVUE, AND THE ADJACENT LANDS WESTWARD', dated 25 April 1801, and signed by Robert Morison, William Sibbald Senior and James Elliot.[58] This is clearly the combined drawing produced at the request of the Town Council, which was to contain 'the best of each' winning entry. The absence of Baine's signature indicates that for one reason or another he withdrew at

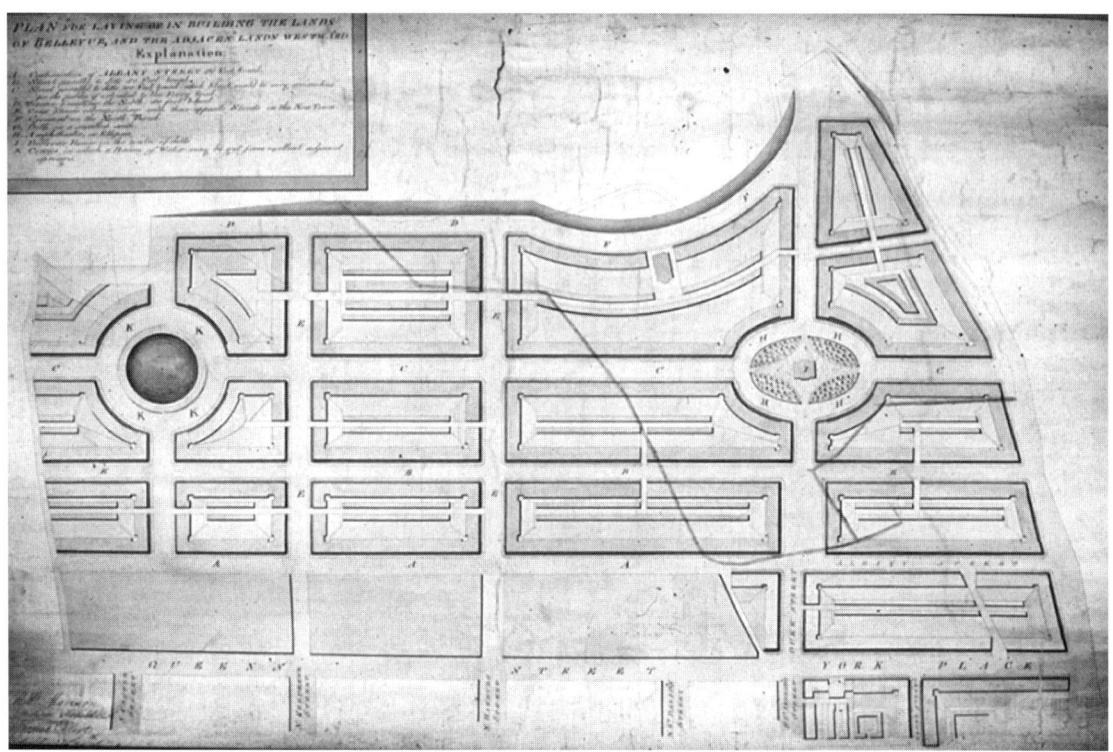

Combined plan of the proposed second New Town of Edinburgh by Robert Morison, William Sibbald and James Elliot, April 1801, incorporating the 'best of each' winning entry. (ECA)

this later stage. Perhaps he feared being compromised, a notion supported by the second item, an 'Explanatory Memoir' written by him to accompany his submission.[59] The Memoir reveals a man not only familiar with town-planning principles and knowledgeable about continental examples, but also someone possessing rather idiosyncratic and grand ideas. We learn from Baine's description that he intended to create two large enclosures. One at the east end was of octagonal shape, 'a figure new in this Country', and named Drummond Place in memory of George Drummond. The other at the west end was in the form of an amphitheatre, the centre of which was to contain a 'Monument to illustrious Scotch-men'. Baine dismissed the use of a circus as not suited to the ground, and too extravagant of space. Three broad streets were to link the open spaces: he carefully avoided any narrow streets or thoroughfares, the usual accommodation for 'common people', for he believed that 'good air, light and sunshine, the greatest Blessings of Bounteous Heaven . . . ought not to be withheld from the poorest of mankind'.[60]

Like Baine's lost plan, the combined competition design of 1801 also had, as its chief characteristic, an open space at either end. Sibbald's earlier circus reappears on the west side although moved further northwards, and to the east is an oval-shaped space having at its centre Bellevue House. A broad street connects the two open spaces, with other roads running parallel, together with several cross streets, three of which linked with Queen

Street. Two other features of Sibbald's first plan remain – a crescent on the eastern part of the north side, and a straight line of buildings facing Queen Street and parallel to it, across the intervening garden area. Had this straight frontage materialised it would have encroached upon part of the eastern garden area.

Events Following the Competition

In all these events, the Governors of Heriot's Hospital apparently acquiesced, and indeed no mention is made of them in the Hospital's minutes until well after the competition. Then in June 1801 the Treasurer reported to a meeting of the Governors that, consequent on the Town Council's purchase of Bellevue, several building plans had been made out of the ground north of Queen Street, and that 'it would be for the interests of the hospital and the ornament of the city to adopt some one of these plans, in place of the plan that had been already fixed upon'.[61] A joint meeting of all the interested parties was therefore agreed. Further work on the designs was, however, deemed necessary and it fell to Major James Stratton, Commanding Royal Engineer to North Britain, to 'revise and improve plans given in for a new town to be erected on the lands of Bellevue'. His professional training ensured his competence, as a surveyor and draughtsman, to handle the technical changes required. But Stratton did not live long enough to complete his work, although it was far enough advanced for his widow to be paid 25 guineas.[62] Instead, the task passed to Robert Reid, surveyor and architect.

Robert Reid (1774–1856) was then 27 years old. This commission helped launch him as a successful architect, although during the rest of his long career his work involved buildings of an institutional nature rather than residential development.[63] How or why he came to be approached is a matter for conjecture, but his background was certainly helpful. His father, Alexander Reid, was an established mason and builder who feued various areas in the New Town between 1785 and 1797 and also served on the Town Council as Deacon of the Masons from 1789 to 1791. To begin with, Robert Reid appears to have practised as a land surveyor in Trunk Close,[64] but by 1800 he was describing himself as an architect, occupying the same address as his father at 18 South Castle Street. Soon afterwards he began working with Richard Crichton on designs for the Bank of Scotland on the Mound.[65] Reid had therefore the advantage of his father's business connections, some useful work experience and the confidence of youth.[66]

Reid's remit would have been to bring together all the previous plans with their various amendments and modifications into one 'improved' design. Little time was lost and by the end of 1801 the joint Committee, made up of representatives of Heriot's Hospital and the Town Council, reported that they were unanimously of the opinion 'that the plan produced by Robert Reid ought to be adopted, except as to the north east part of Bellevue ground'.[67] Heriot's Hospital went on to give further instructions that 'a plan on a large scale should be made out with all possible dispatch by Messrs Sibbald and Reid from the sketch or plan now presented to the Governors'. This enlarged plan was approved at a meeting of the Hospital Governors held on 15 February 1802.[68] A few days later the Governors agreed that their lands to the north of Queen Street should be included within the new extension to

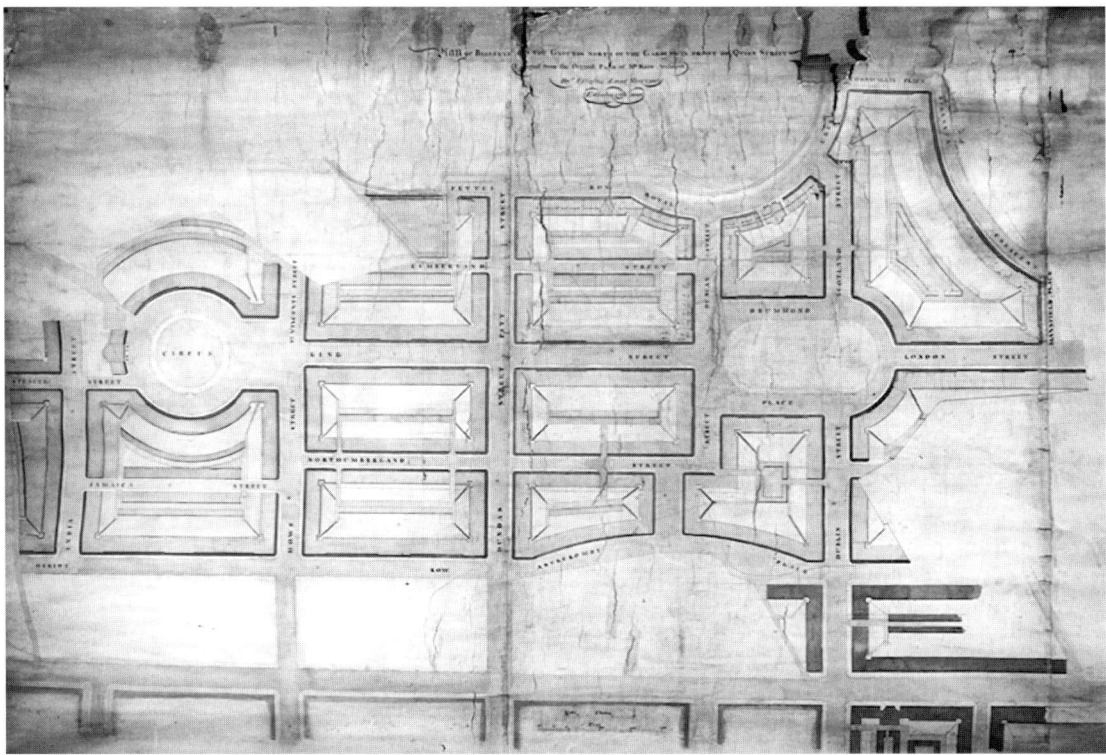

Robert Reid's 1802 plan for the development of the second Edinburgh New Town, shown in an enlarged and more legible copy by John Stirton, 1809. (ECA)

the Royalty of Edinburgh.[69] From this time on the plan was always referred to as the one made out by Messrs Robert Reid and William Sibbald, Architects in Edinburgh.

Changes Made by Robert Reid

The revised plan drawn up by Reid in 1802, and later used as the basis of a contractual agreement between the three parties involved, still survives, although in a frail state (the illustration is of a copy made in 1809).[70] Reid's layout was modelled on the previous plans, particularly the combined competition drawing, and with Sibbald's influence clearly visible. The two most distinctive features remain: an open space at either end connected by a broad street (named King Street, later to be Great King Street) with other main streets running parallel. The open space to the west is still in the form of a circus, but now the buildings form a continuous curve to the north and south. A wide entrance at the eastern end allows full view of a church positioned directly opposite. This circus, soon to be called Royal Circus, was the only part later to experience significant changes to its layout. Reid made a more radical change at the eastern end, with the open space (Drummond Place) enlarged into a square on three sides with a semi-circular crescent at the east end, mainly to integrate Bellevue House more sympathetically with the surrounding streets. The crescent on the

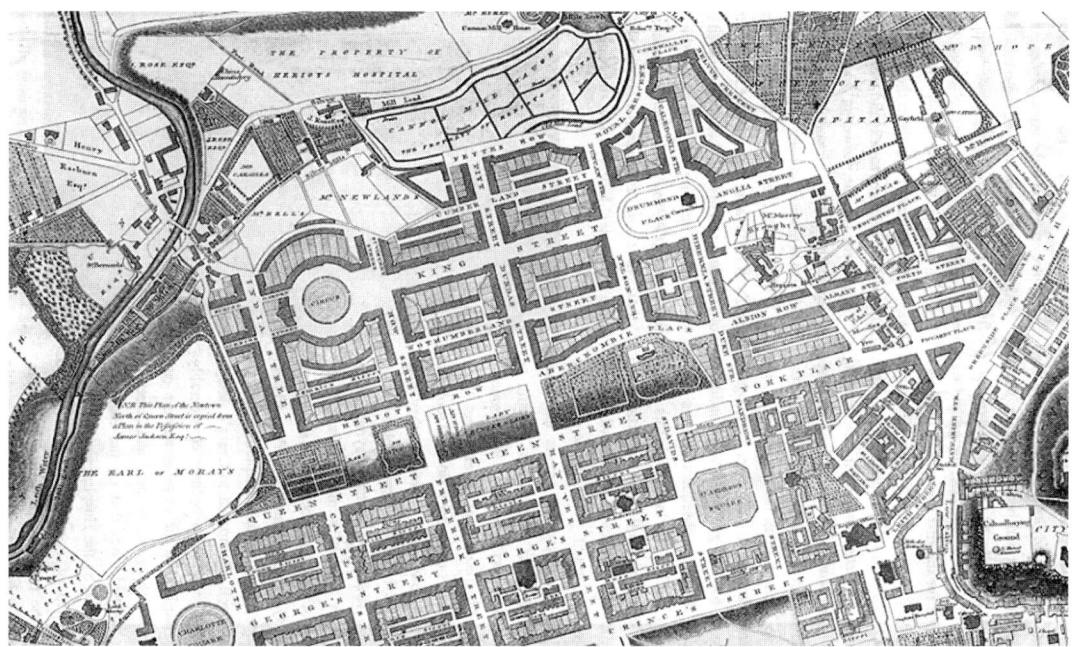

Part of John Ainslie's Plan of the Old and New Town of Edinburgh and Leith, published in June 1804, incorporating the proposed layout of the second New Town based on Robert Reid's 1802 development plan. This came to be known as 'Reid and Sibbald's Plan'. (David C. Simpson)

east side of the north boundary of the site (Royal Crescent) was retained – there was little opportunity for alteration here because of the slope of the ground – but Reid introduced two new crescents. One on the eastern side (Bellevue Crescent) provided a more attractive solution than the line previously adopted; and the other was Abercromby Place to the south, facing the gardens. Abercromby Place was the first curved street façade to be built in Edinburgh and because of its novelty it attracted widespread attention.[71] It was chosen, however, not so much on aesthetic grounds but rather to avoid encroachment on the Queen Street garden area, the whole of which was protected from building development. Earlier plans had all ignored this restriction.[72]

Reid therefore made few substantial changes, but successfully incorporated a number of improvements and refinements, and his plan became the blueprint for the Second New Town. He was further commissioned, between 1802 and 1806, to draw up elevations for the main streets – Heriot Row (east and west sections), Abercromby Place, Great King Street, Drummond Place and London Street.[73] These were all carried out, with certain modifications. The remaining streets, apart from Royal Circus (Playfair), Bellevue Crescent and neighbouring streets (Thomas Bonnar) involved several different architects and builders. But all were regulated by the detailed conditions, laid down when plots were sold for building and clearly stated in the individual house charters.[74] Some delay was experienced in finalising the contract – requiring all three owners of the land to abide by

Elevation by Robert Reid for the west side of Drummond Place, with a view along (Great) King Street towards the church proposed for the west end of Royal Circus, 1804. (Crown copyright © RCAHMS)

the common ground plan and regulations. This in fact was not achieved until March 1806, four years after building had commenced, and was caused by complications arising from David Steuart's ground having changed hands twice.[75] It was finally bought by a building consortium consisting of George Winton, James Nisbet and Thomas Morrison (architect builders who were already building in the Dublin Street area), together with Maxwell Gordon and John Morison, both Writers to the Signet. The last two gentlemen had been the original agents for the land when first put up for sale by Steuart in 1800.[76]

Implementation of the Plan

From 1802 onwards the land was gradually feued out. While Heriot Row and Dublin Street were largely completed by 1808, building went on well into the 1820s, particularly in the Royal Circus and Drummond Place areas. Work slowed down after the bankruptcy of the City in the 1830s, and parts of the eastern section of Royal Crescent and the northern half of Bellevue Crescent were not finished until the 1880s. This was also partly due to the surfeit of accommodation available and the popularity of such developments as the Earl of Moray's estate at the West End.

Nevertheless, not only was the second New Town 'by far the largest single scheme in the development of Georgian Edinburgh'[77] but it was also the largest joint residential development of a uniform character ever to be carried out in the city. That three separate parties should have agreed to come together and undertake such a venture, and so successfully, is remarkable. That the seeds for this co-operate enterprise were first sown by a private individual – David Steuart – is also important. Although Steuart was not particularly successful in worldly terms, his ideas and initiative were the springboard for everything else that followed. And in all the proposals for the second New Town the provision of open space formed an important element, providing a visual relief and balance to what was otherwise an intensive development.

Plans, however, can be beguilingly deceptive, conveying as they do a sense of order and agreement not necessarily existing in practice. The formation of the pleasure grounds which came to occupy these various spaces was far more haphazard, followed no set course, and as in the case of the gardens of the first New Town, depended a great deal on the persistence and initiative of local people. This is why there is so much variation in the ways the gardens were set up and run, and why their evolution was so long, complicated and piecemeal. The story begins with the Queen Street Gardens, the green corridor separating the first from the second New Town.

Notes

1. *The Stranger's Guide to Edinburgh*, 6th edn (Edinburgh, 1817), p. 47.
2. This chapter is an abbreviated version of an article which first appeared as: Connie Byrom, 'The Development of Edinburgh's Second New Town', *BOEC*, New Series, Vol. 3 (1994) op. cit.
3. The 34 Scots acres (17.3 ha) sold by the Heriot's Hospital to the Town Council in 1766, on which the first New Town was built, had been part of the same Barony. See Ian D. Grant, 'Edinburgh's Expansion: the Background to the New Town', in Kitty Cruft and Andrew Fraser (eds), *James Craig, 1744–1795, The Ingenious Architect of the New Town of Edinburgh*, op. cit., pp. 12– 24.
4. At this time land measurement was often quoted in Scots measure.
5. Heriot's Hospital Chartulary, Vol. 3, p. 259: Feu Charter granted to Robert Ord, Lord Chief Baron, 5 June 1769.
6. The 12 Scots acres (6.1 ha) estate of Meldrumsheugh had had several owners before coming into the possession of Francis, 9th Earl of Moray, in 1782. It was later developed by his eldest son, Francis, 10th Earl of Moray, from 1822 onwards; see Chapter 14.
7. Allan and Steuart (sometimes spelt Stewart) were both involved in trading in a wide range of primary products including tea.
8. While Lord Provost, he tried, for example, to remove the slaughter-houses from the North Loch (TCM, 20 June 1781).
9. *The Lord Provosts of Edinburgh 1292–1932* (Edinburgh, 1932), p. 80; see also *Kay's Portraits*, op. cit., Vol. 1, pp. 42–3; and Brian Hillyard, *David Steuart Esquire: An Edinburgh Collector* (Edinburgh, 1993).
10. HHM, 8 October 1781, Vol. 12, p. 156; Chartulary 4, p. 208.
11. Ramadge was granted a sub-tack by Agnes Steven, widow of Henry Anderson (farmer); HHM, 18 April 1785, vol. 12, p. 363.
12. One of the clauses stated that if the land was to be feued or leased for building purposes (other than for one family house) then an extra feu would be payable for each additional property: HHM, 18 May 1785, Vol. 12, p. 363.
13. HHM, 4 August 1785, vol. 13, p. 9.
14. Steuart seems to have had a house built next door to Allan's, at 28 Queen Street, but there is no record in the street directories of him having lived there.
15. Steuart would have known Ainslie through earlier survey work carried out during his term as Lord Provost.
16. The plan was in private hands when recorded by the Royal Commission on the Ancient and Historical Monuments of Scotland in 1995 but is now unlocated.

17. HHM, 24 January 1791, vol. 14, pp. 83–93.
18. HHM, 18 April 1791, vol. 14, p. 107.
19. HHM, 13 December 1792, vol. 14, p. 196.
20. HHM, 4 June 1792, vol. 14, p. 175.
21. This dual appointment system continued up until 1819, and demonstrates the close ties between the Hospital and the City.
22. HHM, 13 December 1792, vol. 14, p. 196: the minute reports that on the basis of the sketch 'upwards of £15,000 sterling would be expected if the land was feued out for building purposes'.
23. HHM, 8 October 1792, vol. 14, pp. 187–9.
24. HHM, 23 July 1793, vol. 14, pp. 228–30.
25. The plan is at the *National Monuments Record of Scotland*, RCAHMS, Inv. *GHT* (George Heriot Trust) p. 22.
26 Sibbald was an apt choice for Steuart to have made because the Heriot's Hospital was likely to be more receptive to a plan produced by their own Superintendent of Works.
27. HHM, 22 August 1796, vol. 15, p. 94.
28. Wood was a descendant of Johnston of Wariston, Midlothian (not to be confused with the lands of Warriston, Edinburgh).
29. HHM, 10 December 1798, vol. 15, p. 161.
30. A useful account of Steuart's trading and financial position is given in Brian Hillyard's, *David Steuart Esquire; An Edinburgh Collector*.
31. HHM, 25 February 1799, vol. 15, pp. 184–5: in his letter Steuart drew attention to the fact that the servitude had already been departed from in Sibbald's plan, where the street and buildings shown were to extend over the north-east of his garden.
32. A small portion of Steuart's former private garden area at the eastern edge of the protected Queen Street Gardens strip was, however, sold in 1807 in five separate lots to proprietors of houses on the west side of Duke Street (now Dublin Street) who wished to improve the shape and size of their back gardens.
33. A small triangle of garden on the north-eastern boundary was, however, included as part of the other area of land which was up for sale.
34. Heriot's Hospital Chartulary, vol. 7, p. 447: Charter of Confirmation, 20 April 1807.
35. TCM, 30 April 1800.
36. William Baird, 'George Drummond: An Eighteenth Century Lord Provost', *BOEC*, Vol. 4 (1911), pp. 46–7.
37. Scott was one of the most noted gamblers of his time, both at home and abroad: James Grant, *Cassell's Old and New Edinburgh*, 3 vols. (London 1880–83), vol. 2, p. 191.
38. For Adam's plans for Bellevue see David King, *The Complete Works of Robert and James Adam* (Oxford, 1991), pp. 127–9.
39. The Scotts also had their London residence in Piccadilly, as well as their country estate in Fife.
40. Due to an abysmal oat harvest at home and abroad.
41. The pasturage of the Parks of Bellevue was let by public roup (auction) to George Willoughby, flesher, for one year at £142: TCM, 19 November 1800. The sale of the timber, plants and vines was also by auction: TCM, 3 December 1800 and 28 January 1801. Rutherford's request for plants is recorded: TCM, 4 February 1801.
42. Henry Cockburn, *Memorials of His Time* (Edinburgh, 1856), pp. 171–3.

43. TCM, 22 October 1800.

44. *Edinburgh Evening Courant*, 25 and 27 October 1800.

45. The advertisements for the property had put all the emphasis on the house and offices, with no mention made of its potential as building ground.

46. TCM, 11 February 1801.

47. ECA, Accounts for the Proper Revenue of the City of Edinburgh, from Martimas 1802 to Martimas 1804.

48. Howard Colvin, *Biographical Dictionary of British Architects 1600–1840* (London, 1978), p. 287.

49. *A New Picture of Edinburgh being an accurate Guide to the City's Environs;* printed for William Whyte & Co. (Edinburgh, *c.* 1823), pp. 159–60.

50. Scottish Record Office (SRO), NG1/1 vol. 24, Board of Trustees, see entries for 11 February 1784, 10 March 1784, 7 March 1785, 23 January 1786, 6 March 1786.

51. Ibid., 14 June 1786. There were seven candidates for the post left vacant by Alexander Runciman's death, and the engraver David Allan was selected for it. See also, John Mason, 'The Edinburgh School of Design', *BOEC*, Vol. 27 (1949), pp. 70, 72.

52. *Edinburgh Advertiser*, 28 October 1788.

53. The Cape Club was a social nucleus for arts-minded Edinburgh tradesmen.

54. I am indebted to Michael Robson, Isle of Lewis, for drawing my attention to the material relating to Skye. He came across a Journal by Baine in Edinburgh University Library relating to two months of his expedition to Skye in the 1790s on behalf of the British Fisheries Board, an incomplete copy of which also exists in the Royal Scottish Museum.

55. Colvin, op. cit., p. 557.

56. Listed in the *1806 Post Office Directory* as Robert Morison, architect, 28 North Castle Street.

57. Nos. 24–30 Howe Street have been definitely ascribed to him: Colvin, op. cit., p. 557.

58. City of Edinburgh Council, Technical Services Department. Map Collection, No. TS 3, now held at the National Library of Scotland (NLS) Map Library, Edinburgh.

59. John Baine, 'An explanatory Memoir to accompany the Plan proposed for the Buildings intended to be raised on the Grounds of Bellevue belonging to the City of Edinburgh; and on those to the west, belonging Heriot's Hospital and to David Steuart Esq.', undated manuscript (before 10 October 1801) EUL, special collections, Laing Collection, Div. II, No. 415.

60. Baine instead relegated the 'common people' to the wynds and closes of the Old Town – hardly conducive to good living!

61. HHM, 1 June 1801, vol. 16, pp. 36–7.

62. TCM, 16 December 1801.

63. In 1803 Reid was appointed by the Trustees of Public Buildings to design the new Law Courts in Parliament Square and this marked the start of his life as a public architect.

64. Robert Reid was recorded as a land-surveyor in T. Aitchison, *Edinburgh Directory; 1797–98* (Edinburgh, 1797).

65. Once described by Henry Cockburn as a 'prominent deformity', the Bank building was extensively altered and added to between 1864 and 1871 by David Bryce, architect.

66. It is also of interest to note that Robert Reid's father had feued three building stances in York Place from Heriot's Hospital in 1799, and Robert Reid 'builder' another three in 1801.

67. TCM, 30 December 1801; HHM, 31 December 1801, vol. 16, p. 61. The north-east part would have included the Bellevue Crescent area, and as two possibilities were put forward,

the committee wanted to find which offered the better feuing prospects.

68. HHM, 31 December 1801, vol. 16, p. 61, and 15 February 1802, vol. 16, p. 70.

69. HHM, 18 February 1802, vol. 16, p. 71.

70. Edinburgh City Architect's map Collection No. 4, c.1, held at NLS Map Library, Edinburgh.

71. Cockburn, op. cit., p. 287; Robert Chambers, *Walks in Edinburgh* (Edinburgh, 1825), p. 203.

72. David Steuart had drawn attention to this as far back as 1797.

73. HHM, 23 January 1804, vol. 16, p. 239; TCM, 20 June 1804, and 19 March 1806. Reid's 1803 elevation for Heriot Row is reproduced in Youngson, op. cit., pp. 210–11. For elevations for Abercromby Place, Great King Street and Drummond Place see the *National Monuments Record of Scotland*, (NMRS) EDD/9/1, EDD/100/1, EDD/79/2, and DC 7745 & 7747.

74. The mutual contract contained items already specified in the articles of roup (sale).

75. Details about the subsequent owners of David Steuart's land and delay over the contract can be found in Connie Byrom, 'The Development of Edinburgh's Second New Town', *BOEC*, New Series Vol. 3 (1994), pp. 52–3.

76. The last we hear of Steuart in connection with his ground was in February 1802 when he approached the Heriot's Hospital, no doubt with pecuniary motives in mind, with the suggestion that their terrace (along Heriot Row and including his ground as well) be increased from two to three storeys.

77. Youngson, op. cit., p. 204.

PART FIVE

THE QUEEN STREET GARDENS

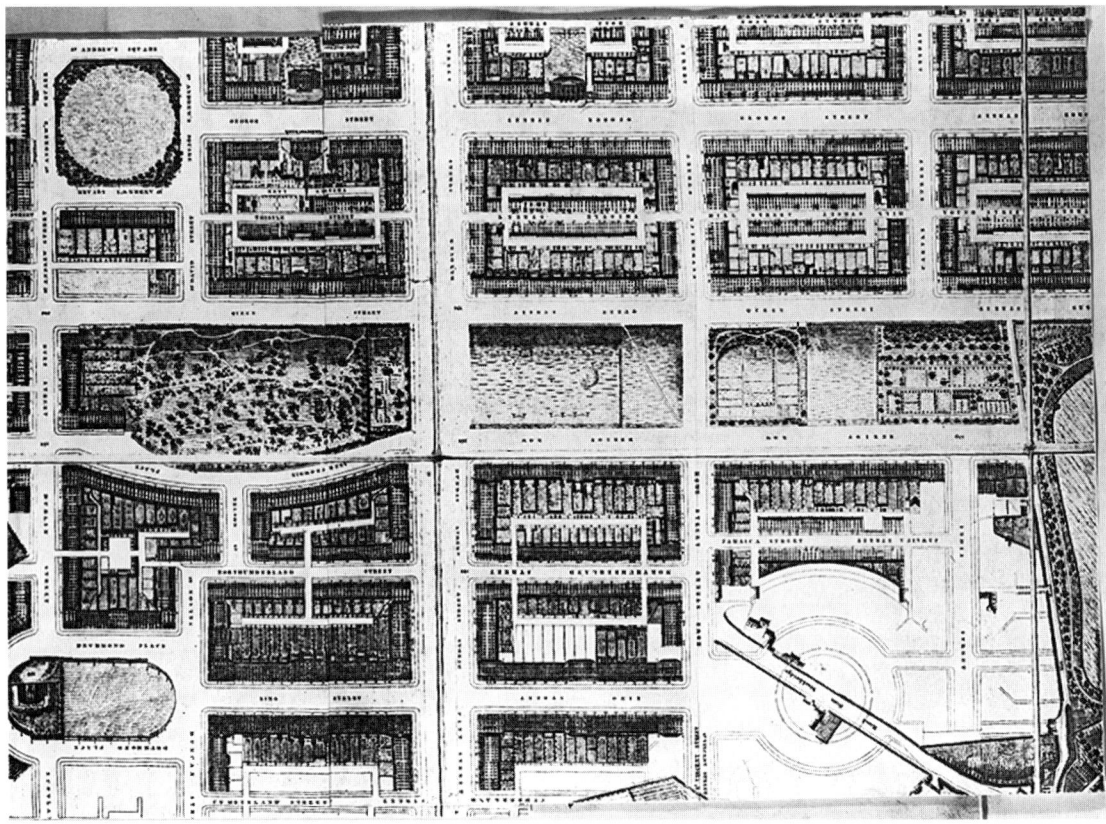

Kirkwood's plan, 1819, showing all three Queen Street Gardens, Edinburgh. Only the east section (minus the west strip) has been formed into a pleasure garden. The central portion is uncultivated and used to accommodate washing lines, a pump well and Farmer Wood's former cattle pond: a footpath cuts through the adjoining waste ground. The garden areas which later became the West Queen Street Gardens were then owned by the Wemyss Family, and apart from the rough pasturage at the centre the rest was well cared for.

CHAPTER 8

EAST QUEEN STREET
6.90 acres (2.76 ha)

Who would not regret if the gardens below Queen Street were to be swept away, and their place occupied by an insipid and monotonous pile of buildings.

W.H. Playfair, 1819[1]

In the summer we played in the Queen Street Gardens, to us an immense country where the shrubberies of rhododendrons had the half fearful charm of unexplored forests, and the lawns seemed endless stretches of grass and daisies.

Elizabeth Sillar, *c.* 1870s[2]

Playfair's observation was made to reassure those responsible for developing the area to the north of Calton Hill that to provide generous areas for pleasure ground was not an extravagance, but essential to the success of the whole. Most people now would assume that he was referring to all three gardens along Queen Street, but in fact only one such garden then existed. It was known as the 'Queen Street Gardens' and was situated at the eastern end. The land owned by Heriot's Hospital which eventually became East, Centre and West Queen Street Gardens was bounded on the south by Queen Street, on the north by the road leading from Broughton to Thomas Wood's farm, on the west by the track from Stockbridge to St Cuthbert's Church and by Gabriel's road on the east – the ancient route from Silvermills to the Old Town. As the New Town progressed (and by 1780 nearly three-quarters of Queen Street was built), the land became further divided by two cross streets – Frederick Street and Hanover Street. Besides linking the first and second New Towns, these streets cut the ground into three unequal portions. Each portion then became further subdivided when sold to local people for private gardens. These next three chapters unravel the somewhat complex process by which these several private plots eventually became united to form the East, Central and West Queen Street Pleasure Gardens. The story begins at the eastern end which pioneered the way.

Robert Ord and His Garden

Elizabeth Sillar's childhood memories of East Queen Street Gardens conjured up enormous areas of space but she was probably unaware that this magical world of forest, thickets and daisy-flecked lawns started life as three quite separate gardens. The first to be purchased was by Baron Ord, one of the earliest residents in Queen Street.

Bartholomew's Map of Edinburgh and Leith, 1891. The structure of the three Queen Street Gardens has changed very little from when they were first laid out under the direction of John Hay and James Skene in the case of the East Queen Street Gardens, and Andrew Wilson for the Centre and West Queen Street Gardens.

Robert Ord was Lord Chief Baron of the Court of Exchequer from 1755 to 1778, and in 1769 he acquired a large piece of ground, around 2.5 acres (1 ha), directly opposite his house. His important position as a senior judge was reflected in his elegant house at 8 Queen Street, designed by Robert Adam, and now occupied by the Royal College of Physicians. There he lived 'magnificently', entertaining in style his wide circle of friends, amongst whom were Henry Mackenzie and David Hume, who met to play whist and piquet. Ord's musical and accomplished daughters added sparkle to such gatherings.[3]

Ord had a keen interest in gardening and horticulture. At Dean House, his former residence, he had been amongst the first, if not the very first, in Scotland to successfully cultivate a pineapple.[4] These enthusiasms were not catered for by the limited space to the rear of his new dwelling, and well before moving he had negotiated a subtack (lease) with the farmer, Henry Anderson, for a piece of land in Queen Street. Later he successfully applied to Heriot's Hospital to buy it for £120 together with an annual feu (ground rent) equivalent to the price of '2 firlots of wheat and 7 bolls of barley according to the highest fiars of Midlothian'.[5] The conditions of sale have already been referred to; suffice it to say that the Hospital stipulated in Ord's charter, and in all subsequent ones made out for land along this stretch of Queen Street, that the ground was feued solely as garden ground, with a ban on all buildings apart from those necessary for a garden.[6] There seems to have been an overall commitment to keep the whole strip as open space, but with no clear idea how this should be achieved. Individuals making requests for private gardens therefore presented a neat solution.

Ord treated his garden very much as an extension to his house and went so far as to have a tunnel constructed beneath Queen Street to link his basement with the garden area. The garden was put to good use for clothes drying, fruit cultivation (apples and pears) and vegetable growing, besides more leisurely activities. James Boswell's wife, for example, a lady of delicate health, enjoyed having an evening stroll there.[7] After Ord's death his son John, a barrister and long-serving MP for various constituencies in the south of England, inherited the house and garden. By 1786 the Ord family had moved to George Street and their Queen Street property had been sold.[8]

David Steuart ups his Stake

The garden was purchased by David Steuart, who since 1781 had owned the adjacent and similar-sized plot on the east side – the second strip to have been sold by Heriot's Hospital.[9] His house at 5 Queen Street faced directly onto both.[10] Steuart, by his own account, had spent a lot of money having his garden laid out – around £500.[11] Ainslie's plan indicates a rather more ambitious design, featuring on the north side a serpentine pool with adjacent summer-house or similar building, and the rest formed into compartments 'in the modern taste'. It also included a gardener's house in the north-east corner.

Steuart's motive for buying Ord's garden may simply have been to extend and improve his own, but may also have been linked to his speculative interests, he having by then become owner of 13 acres of land immediately to the north. We know that Steuart was constantly juggling money and business matters, and treading a fine line between financial success and failure. As the latter became more common, he was forced to sell Ord's ground. He held on to his own piece, although by 1788 he was no longer living in Queen Street. By then his garden was rented to an enterprising nurseryman, A. Finlayson, who opened it 'for the reception of Ladies and Gentlemen to eat fruits through the season . . . amongst the best the country can produce', an added attraction – by popular demand – being 'music every Wednesday evening if the weather is dry, if otherwise the night following. To begin at seven and continue till nine o'clock'. Attendance at the musical evenings cost one shilling (5p), otherwise entry was 'gratis'.[12] In 1800 the lease was taken over by another gardener – John Richmond – who had a nursery down Leith Walk and a shop at the foot of the West Bow.[13]

Enter Major Roger Aytoun: Further Changes

Steuart sold Ord's garden to a former neighbour, Major Roger Aytoun of Inchdarnie in Fife, 'a man of remarkable stature being upwards of six feet four inches in height' and soon to become a Lieutenant-Colonel in the Royal Edinburgh Volunteers; his height, girth and easy manner proving useful assets when drilling the motley band which made up the Corps.[14] When Aytoun died in 1808, Ord's garden came into the hands of the Cunynghame family who had moved from George Square to Ord's old house. Although by then Sir William Cunynghame was nearing the end of his public life (for many years he was MP for Linlithgowshire and holder of other public offices), second marriage in 1785 had produced a fresh crop of children; and now that he had a teenage family of four boys and a girl, the garden was once more pressed into service. In 1810 he had a range of hot-houses, 'Forcing Houses for Fruit', built along the north side.[15]

Major-General Roger Aytoun of Inchdarnie in Fife, who bought Ord's former garden from David Steuart in 1793. He was an enormously tall gentleman. (Kay's *Portraits*)

Final Portion of Land

The last portion to the west of Ord's feu was smaller, about one-third the size of the other two.[16] It was bought in 1786 by Adam Rolland of Gask (1734–1819) whose house stood practically opposite. A timid, retiring bachelor, he was described by Cockburn as 'a learned and sound lawyer, and a good man, much respected by his few friends'. One of these was Henry Mackenzie. When Lockhart (Sir Walter Scott's son-in-law) once met him at Mackenzie's house he made a lasting impression on the young visitor, who later observed that he had 'never seen a finer specimen both in appearance and manner of the true gentleman of the last age'. Rolland's careful and old-fashioned style of dress (his favourite colours were black and mulberry) prompted the rather gleeful comment from Cockburn that 'when all got up, no artificial rose could be brighter, or stiffer. He was like one of the creatures come to life again in a collection of dried butterflies'.[17] Rolland's garden must surely have matched its owner, being meticulously dressed, with not a weed in sight. After his death the land stayed in the possession of his trustees until taken over as pleasure ground under the 1822 Act of Parliament.

Changes Ahead

By the end of the eighteenth century all three gardens had become well established. Various hothouses had been added along the north side and stone walls divided one garden from another. Changes, however, were imminent that would affect all the gardens along Queen

Adam Rolland's portrait by Henry Raeburn in his role as Deputy Director of the Bank of Scotland. He was the sole owner of the garden strip to the west of Baron Ord's feu. (Courtesy of the Governors and Company of the Bank of Scotland)

Street, and were connected with David Steuart and his plummeting fortunes. After a prolonged attempt to stave off financial disaster, Steuart was finally declared bankrupt in 1799, and his property put up for sale. Although his garden was advertised separately, it was eventually sold with his thirteen other acres. Purchased in 1802 by a group of individuals with no apparent interest in developing the land, it was sold within three years to the building consortium referred to in the previous chapter. This group were keen to co-operate with the Town and Heriot's Hospital in their plans for the second New Town. Steuart's former garden was only of marginal interest, although not without possible use. One idea, for example, was to make a roadway through the eastern side of the garden to allow better access from Queen Street to property in the neighbourhood of the Custom House.[18] And in 1807 a small part of the eastern side of Steuart's garden was sold to residents in Duke (Dublin) Street to improve the shape and size of their rear gardens.[19] During the interval, part of Steuart's former garden had become the 'Queen Street coal-yard', whose selling line was 'to supply the city of Edinburgh with the best coal at the lowest prices'; the best Scot's coal was advertised at 18 shillings a ton (90p), and Newcastle coal at 24 shillings (120p).[20] Whatever the coal's quality such change of use must have given some cause for alarm.

Move to Form a Pleasure Garden

First signs of action to form a communal pleasure garden appeared in June 1812 when a circular was distributed to houses in Abercromby Place, and the portion of Queen Street

Sir,   Edinburgh, 25th June 1812.

Lady Cunningham having sold her Garden to the north of Queen-street to the Subscribers, upon condition that the Street of Abercromby-Place shall be completed immediately, conform to a Plan, we have resolved to communicate the benefit of our purchase to all the Proprietors of Houses in Abercromby Place, and also to all the Proprietors of Houses in that part of Queen-street, which extends from the East side of St David's-street, to the East side of Hanover-street, upon the following Conditions :

1st, That the Garden shall be Common Property, and shall for ever remain Garden-ground, and not divisible among the Proprietors, unless the consent of two-thirds of them in value shall be previously obtained.

2d, That the price of the Garden shall be 3000 Guineas, which is the price we have agreed ourselves to pay to Lady Cunningham, bearing interest from Whitsunday last, and to be payable by three instalments, at Martinmas 1812, 1813, and 1814.

3d, That a Committee shall be appointed by a Majority of the Proprietors for managing the Property, and establishing such Regulations as they think fit concerning it ; and all profit and loss upon the Garden shall be borne by the Proprietors in proportion to their respective Shares.

Upon the above conditions we propose, that the Garden shall be divided into 20 shares of 150 Guineas each. If the requisite number of Subscribers at that sum do not appear, we have no objection that the amount of each Subscription should be increased.

But various proposals having been made for converting this Property into other uses than a Garden ; and having reason to think that the supposed servitude does not limit us in the free use and disposal of our Property, it becomes necessary to bring the present offer to an immediate conclusion. A Subscription-Paper is therefore to lye at No. 29, Abercromby Place, open for 14 days only from this date, for the Subscription of such of the adjoining Proprietors as choose to accede to the scheme. Your Subscription thereto, or your acquiescence in the terms now proposed, by Letter addressed to Roger Aytoun, Writer to the Signet, will bind us for 14 days, provided the requisite number of Subscribers appear within that time to take the Garden at the aforesaid price ; but we

hereby certify all concerned ; that if that period is allowed to elapse without the Subscription being filled up, we will no longer be bound to abide by this offer, but will proceed to dispose of the Property as we see most for our own advantage.

We are further authorised, on the part of the Proprietors of the adjoining Garden to the Eastward, to say, that if it appears to be the general wish of the Public, to throw both Gardens into one Common Property, they are willing to sell the same at the price of £ 2100 Sterling, payable at the foresaid terms, and bearing interest from Whitsunday last, provided the requisite number of Subscribers come forward within 14 days ; but with like certification to all concerned, that if the Subscription is not filled up by that time, the Proprietors will no longer be bound by the present offer, but will dispose of their Property to the best advantage.

We are, Sir,

your most obedient humble servants,

[signatures]

Circular dated June 1812. The first attempt to interest residents living at the eastern end of Queen Street and Abercromby Place in forming a communal garden. (Queen Street Centre Garden records)

Roger Aytoun, WS, grandson of Major-General Aytoun and one of the instigators behind the move to form a common pleasure garden. (Crombie's *Modern Athenians, 1837–1847*, ECL)

between the east sides of St David Street and Hanover Street. It was signed by William Cunyinghame, John Morison (on behalf of himself and other members of the consortium – Winton, Morison & Co.) and Roger Aytoun, WS; an abbreviated version also appeared in the Edinburgh newspapers.[21] The circular stated that Lady Cunyinghame had sold her garden ground to the signatories 'upon condition that the street of Abercromby Place shall be completed immediately'; and that they 'were resolved to communicate the benefit of our purchase' to all nearby proprietors. They offered to sell the garden for 3,000 guineas (the price agreed on with Lady Cunyinghame) as a 'Common Property and shall forever remain Garden ground'. In addition David Steuart's former garden was also offered for sale at £2,100 sterling.

Abercromby Place had been under construction since 1810, but the circular's reference was probably connected with the 'very handsome' parapet and rail intended for the south side of the street, 'leaving the gardens to view', which required certain adjustments to be made to the boundaries.[22] While this was being sorted out, the future of the two gardens seems also to have been discussed; and the decision was reached that the best option was to try and establish a communal pleasure garden for the benefit of local residents. Robert Aytoun (1769–1843) was already resident in Abercromby Place. He ran a 'steady going business' in Frederick Street, and was later to become a 'blazing Radical', but for the moment his energies were channelled into administering the subscription papers.[23]

The offer was open for fourteen days and the circular proposed creating 20 shares at 150 guineas each. This was a common method of raising money, used in a variety of projects such as the setting up of the Caledonian Horticultural Society's Experimental Gardens, Seafield Baths, the Gas Company, Assembly Rooms, Waterloo Bridge and the Regent Road development and so on. But the time set was unrealistic for such a major and novel enterprise; the idea, however, of raising money by a shareholding system took root, and became the basis of all future negotiations. Some months later another attempt was made to refloat the scheme, only this time more was done to make the purchase terms easier.

Fresh Attempts

In March 1813 John Morison, on behalf of the garden of the other two garden owners, contacted William Bell, WS (1783–1849) at 9 Queen Street. An offer was made to sell the gardens for £5,250, one half to be paid as an annual feu duty (ground rent), and the remainder in two equal instalments payable during that year.[24] William Bell was the third son of the noted Edinburgh surgeon, Benjamin Bell, and had been at the forefront of the previous attempt to raise money;[25] he now concentrated wholeheartedly on steering the project to a successful conclusion. Another circular was distributed and a small committee formed.[26] The appeal was widened to include any proprietor in the neighbourhood, and a choice was offered of either making a lump-sum payment for one or more shares, or else buying a cheaper 'annual' share, which carried with it the obligation to pay a yearly due (intended to cover the ground rent).

Approaches were made to the Town Council (owners of some unfeued plots at the eastern end of Abercromby Place), telling of the opportunity to purchase the land for the purpose of it being held a joint property and laid out in pleasure grounds, in order to prevent any use being made of them that might be disagreeable to the neighbourhood and offensive to the town in general; and also with the view not only of benefiting their own properties but of securing a very great increase of beauty to that part of the City of Edinburgh.

Contributions were invited, as 'a great public benefit must unquestionably result'. The Council responded by appointing Baillies Robert Johnstone and Alexander Henderson as a sub-committee to meet with the promoters, the outcome of which was the recommendation

PROPOSAL

Addressed to the PROPRIETORS of the Houses in the neighbourhood of the two Gardens situated between Queen Street and Abercromby Place, consisting of about five acres, for the purpose of purchasing them as the Joint Property of such Persons as shall subscribe to the scheme ; and for laying them out in Pleasure Grounds for the Accommodation of the Subscribers and their Families.

An opportunity having offered for purchasing these Gardens for the above desirable object on reasonable terms, it is proposed that the Sums required for the purchase, and for the other immediate purposes of the scheme, should be raised by subscriptions, either for Shares of L.30 each, in present money, or of Annual Payments of L.2 each, and an additional L.2 at the end of every Nineteen Years. Upon which data it is expected that less than 200 Shares, (at least 100 of which being in present money, the remainder in Annual Payments), may be sufficient.

A regular and binding obligation, with the conditions and detail of the scheme, to be drawn up by a Committee, to be named by the Subscribers at a General Meeting, to be held for that purpose, will be afterwards tendered for the signatures of the subscribers, in case there shall appear a sufficient concurrence to the measure. But, for ascertaining this essential part, in the meantime, this paper is circulated in order that Gentlemen may put down their names for such number of Shares, either in present money, or annual payments, as they shall choose. But declaring that, if a fund sufficient for the purchase of the Gardens shall not be raised, the Subscribers to this paper shall not be bound to pay the Sums subscribed for by them ; it being understood that after 175 Shares have been subscribed, a General Meeting of the Subscribers shall be called, to appoint a Committee to treat with the Proprietors of the Gardens, and to give such other instructions relative to the business, as shall be agreed to.

April 1813. Revised and approved by

JAMES HUNTER, JOHN CONNELL, JAMES KERR, JOHN WAUCHOPE,
ALEX ANDERSON, RICHARD HOTCHIS, JAMES JOLLIE, J. F. GORDON, WILLIAM BELL.

Proposal circulated in April 1813. By now the appeal had widened to all local residents and the proposed shareholding system was explained a little better. (ECA, Miscellaneous papers 1818–1822, Queen Street Gardens SL12 287 (50))

Gardens North of Queen Street.

In April 1813 proposals were published and circulated for raising Subscriptions to purchase these GARDENS for PLEASURE GROUNDS.

The price at which the Proprietors agreed to sell to the Public was L. 5250.

Which sum it was proposed to raise by Subscriptions of L. 30, for each share, in money, or L. 2, in yearly payments.

Previous to the 30th September many Subscriptions were procured, but not enough to accomplish the purchase, when, at a Meeting of the Subscribers of that date, it was proposed to raise the Subscription for each share to L. 40, and the Annual Payment to L. 2, 13s. 4d.

About 110 shares have been Subscribed for, which, at the increased rate of L. 40, would produce - - - - - - - - - - - L. 4400
Leaving a deficiency to be provided for of about - - - - 850

In this situation the Subscribers feel themselves called upon again to appeal to the public. The transaction must be closed with the Proprietors on or before the 15th of January 1814. If the Gardens are not then purchased for pleasure-grounds, the Proprietors have received offers for different lots of them, which they seem determined to accept of; and in that event this fine opening will be lost to the Public, who are certainly interested in getting it converted into pleasure-grounds, as well as the proprietors of the adjoining houses.

For the purposes of Public Walks, so much wanted in Edinburgh, and for safety and amusement of Children, such a space is nowhere else to be found.

Subscriptions, either in one sum, or in annual payments, will continue to be received by William Bell, W. S. Queen Street, till the 4th of January next.

December 1813.

LIST of Subscribers to the Proposal for Purchasing the Gardens in Queen Street, by Subscriptions for Shares of L. 30, or for Annual Payments of L. 2 each, and a duplication each 19th year.

	Shares.	Annual Payments.	Sums Subscribed.		Shares.	Annual Payments.	Sums Subscribed.
1 James Hunter,	5		L.150	Claud Russell,	1		30
William Bell,	5		150	25 Lady A. Clavering,	1	1	
John Wauchope,	5		150	John Campbell,	1		30
Alexander Anderson,	4		120	Colonel Ferguson,	1		30
5 James Ker,	3		90	James Moncreiff,	1	1	
Richard Hotchkis,	2		60	Robert Morison,	2	2	
James Farquhar Gordon,	3		90	40 J. Renton,	1		30
W. A. Cunyngham,	7		210	Mrs Riddell,	1		30
John Connell,	3		90	James Jollie,	1	1	
10 L. H. Ferrier,	1		30	A. Campbell,	1		30
Roger Ayton,	3		90	G. S. Monteath,	3		90
Winton & Morison,	4		120	35 James Hamilton,	2		60
Winton & Morison,	4		120	Joseph Bell,	1		30
Winton & Morison,	4		120	Mrs Beveridge,	1		30
Winton & Morison,	3		90	Walter Dickson,	1		30
James Gibson,	1		30	James Mackay,	1		30
John Forman,	1		30	40 Lady Anne Stewart,	1	1	
15 John Brown,	1		30	Charles Ross,	3	3	
John Watson,	1		30	John Manderston,	1		30
William Henry,	1		30	W. Trotter,	1		30
Charles Hay,	1		30	James Nairne,	1		30
Mrs M'Gregor,	1		30	45 C. K. Robison,	5	3	60
20 Mrs Morison,	1		30	Robert Hill,	1	1	
H. Moncreiff,	1	1		George Bell,	1	1	
George Watson,	1		30	Robert Bell,	1	1	
J. M'Farquhar,	1		30		102		

NOTA.—The Town of Edinburgh have agreed to take Ten Shares. The Shares have subsequently been raised to L. 40, or L. 2, 13s. 4d. annually, and a duplication each 19th year; and to this the above Subscribers generally have agreed.

Circular dated December 1813 telling of progress to raise money and listing the names of subscribers, with the number of shares purchased by each. (Queen Street Centre Garden records) that the Council should support the project 'as a measure intimately connected with the beauty and elegance and respectability of the City'. Alexander Henderson's involvement was a good omen. Interested in environmental improvement and a nurseryman to trade, his name frequently crops up in connection with other New Town pleasure gardens. The Council agreed to purchase two shares for each of their unsold plots – ten altogether.[27]

The outlook now looked brighter. By the September deadline, 102 lump-sum subscriptions had been promised, together with 16 annual shares. But this was still not enough. Publicity was stepped up, the deadline extended to 15 January 1814 and another circular launched.[28] The matter now had some urgency, for 'if the gardens are not then purchased for pleasure grounds, the proprietors have received offers for different lots of them which they seem determined to accept of; and in that event this fine opportunity will be lost to the public, who are certainly interested in getting it converted into pleasure grounds, as well as the proprietors of the adjoining houses.'

In addition, the public were gently reminded that 'for the purpose of public walks so much wanted in Edinburgh, and for the safety and amusement of children, such a space is nowhere else to be found'. Princes Street had no such gardens, and although Queen Street had once been a popular boulevard, its rural charm was fast disappearing in the wake of new building and an expanding population.[29] A generous-sized pleasure garden open to subscribers was therefore an exciting possibility, to be grasped with enthusiasm.

Success was close to hand. By the closing date, William Bell (himself the buyer of five shares) purchased 'on behalf of a number of individuals' the two private garden areas. Altogether 140 shares were bought: 92 as lump-sum payments of £40 each, and 48 as annual shares at £3 each (with further yearly payments of £3). This number has remained constant throughout the garden's history. Just over one-quarter of shareholders bought more than one share, and the former owners purchased one-fifth of the number (Sir William Cunyingame, for example, bought seven), indicating their commitment to secure the garden for communal use. Sales advertisements lost no time in capitalising on this splendid new amenity, and indeed have gone on doing so.[30]

A New Pleasure Garden

Two gardens of rather different character now needed to be united. Kirkwood's plan of 1817 (see p. 156) shows the new layout, distinguished by its network of pathways radiating from the centre in a star-like pattern, and connected to a serpentine walk around the perimeter. A number of mature trees were retained and new ones added, the areas between being grass-sown. A parapet and iron railing had already been added to the north side, and in 1816 a similar one was placed along Queen Street and 'the old dead wall' removed. John Hay (1758–1836) was probably the man responsible for the design. He was then involved with forming George Square pleasure ground on the south side, and was later consulted when Adam Rolland's garden was added – suggesting an earlier connection. Hay was a versatile and experienced nurseryman who worked both within and outside Edinburgh. He variously described himself as a 'seeds man', 'surveyor' 'landscape gardener', 'garden architect', 'ground planner', and 'hot house builder', his main speciality was with flower and kitchen gardens, and hothouses (he may well have contracted for the ones built for Sir William Cunyinghame in 1810): someone in fact competent to handle jobs of diverse range and size. Hay was also a stalwart member of the Caledonian Horticultural Society, and his draft plan for their Experimental Garden in 1816 earned him a gold medal.[31] The gardener's house on the north side was retained; it not only accommodated the gardener and his family, but also provided space for garden meetings.

Administrative Problems

Newly designed and planted, the garden itself posed few demands in the early years apart from routine maintenance. But administrative difficulties relating to the shareholding system quickly began to surface. Shares soon started to change hands, for example, on death, removal from the district, or a desire to be rid of surplus ones. Problems arose despite a whole battery of specially concocted rules and regulations to try and overcome them. The procedure for the sale and transfer of share nevertheless remained ambiguous and complex; and the recovery of arrears proved virtually impossible. In addition, problems were compounded by difficulties in convening meetings of proprietors and confusion over voting procedures.[32] It caused William Bell, now appointed Clerk to the Gardens, to produce a Memorandum (dated 1st March 1820) outlining these various problems and stating his belief that 'these various evils can be remedied only by the intervention of the authority of Parliament'. The case of the newly created West Princes Street Gardens was cited in support, and a copy of their 1816 Act of Parliament appended.[33]

   After lengthy debate, Bell and a small steering committee were given responsibility to draft details for a similar Act. In addition, provision was to be made for the proprietors

Drawing of Queen Street, Edinburgh, in the early 1820s. The trees bordering the south side of the East gardens provide the only foliage along Queen Street prior to the formation of the other two gardens. (*New Picture of Edinburgh*, printed William Whyte, London n.d., ECL)

further westwards, with property facing onto Queen Street and Heriot Row, 'to acquire, enclose, layout, and embellish the remainder of the ground between the two streets' and for their long-term management and care. The birth of the Central and West Queen Street Gardens was imminent. These other portions of private gardens, as we shall see, had not all prospered, and attempts to make them over as communal pleasure gardens had failed on several occasions. It was no coincidence that two members of the committee, John Cay, Advocate (11 Heriot Row), and Donald Horne, WS (17 Heriot Row), had both been closely involved in trying to achieve this end, and therefore welcomed the opportunity to promote and extend the Bill in this way. It was an apt and popular move.[34] The Act, which remains effective to this day, was passed on 15 May 1822, after notices had been displayed on the parish church doors, and the Court of Session notified.[35]

The 1822 Act of Parliament

Three major pleasure grounds were established under the Act: East Queen Street Gardens (already three-quarters formed as 'Queen Street Gardens'), and Central and West Queen Street Gardens. The Act carefully specified how the gardens were to be set up and managed, and in the case of the eastern garden procedures relating to its share-holding system were clearly stated.[37] One of the first requirements was that all the shareholders, together with the other proprietors westwards, with property facing onto Queen Street and Heriot Row (even if their entrance was from another street), were to meet and elect 24 General Commissioners: 12 for the eastern section and six for each of the other two.

Once appointed, it was the General Commissioners' duty to divide the ground 'into such number of districts as they shall see expedient', and to elect from their own number 'certain persons to act as Commissioners within each district'. It was with the District Commissioners (these titles still apply) that the responsibility for forming and managing the gardens rested. The Act gave them power to purchase the ground (although not without prior approval of the proprietors), to levy special assessments for this purpose,[38] and to borrow money. All matters relating to upkeep and running costs became their responsibility, with the help of a clerk or cashier. Should legal action become necessary the District Commissioners (or their clerks) were given rights to sue or be sued (one of the early shareholders to lapse from grace was the architect James Gillespie Graham).[39] Proprietors' rights were also stated; their wishes were to be upheld in such matters as key rental, and the framing of rules and regulations, and all within the context of how and when to call meetings and voting procedure.[40]

The first general meeting and election took place in June 1822 at the new Waterloo Hotel. It was held in a spirit of camaraderie and optimism when there was talk of uniting all three gardens by underground tunnel. The idea persisted for a number of years, but with dwindling support.[36]

The Gardens Completed

Negotiations to purchase Adam Rolland's garden from his trustees were already under way before the Act was passed. The ground was bought for £1,045 and the money raised either by a levy of £2 per share over four successive years, or a lump-sum payment of £7.50; the interim gap was met by a loan from Ramsay, Bonar & Co. bankers, and finally paid off in 1831.

Once the stone dividing wall was removed[41] the District Commissioners (as they were now called)[42] 'proceeded in the first instance with the aid of Mr Hay, planner, and latterly with that of James Skene Esq of Rubislaw, to incorporate the property so purchased with the garden'.[43] By spring 1823 the work was nearing completion; Hay was paid £3.70 for his plan and James Skene was gifted a free key 'for the use of himself and his family during their residence in Edinburgh'. Having Skene's name associated with the gardens, however slightly, was a matter of some prestige following his successful contribution to the West Princes Street Gardens. The task of uniting the two parts was relatively straightforward and mostly involved extending the existing network of footpaths. Even so, the improvements cost around £250. A large proportion of this was spent on removing the high stone wall on the north side and erecting a parapet and rail in its place to allow the whole ground to be 'laid open to view from Abercromby Place'.[44] A thick belt of shrubs was planted to screen the remaining crude stone wall along the west boundary; once established, the wall was removed (in 1828) and replaced by a cope stone and elegant railing. At this time a pump was fitted to the old well on the north side, west of the gardener's house, and an existing greenhouse was improved.

The new pleasure grounds were soon to witness a colourful ceremony presided over by Sir Walter Scott. It was associated with George IV's state visit to Scotland in August 1822, an event largely stage-managed by Scott. While the King slumbered, Sir Walter, bright and early at 6am, was up and about: arrayed in the Garb of old Gaul (which he had of the Campbell tartan in memory of one of his great grandmothers) [he] was attending a muster of these gallant Celts in the Queen Street Gardens, where he had the honour of presenting them with a set of colours, and delivered a suitable exhortation, crowned with their rapturous applause.

The Celtic Society, 'a flourishing and respectable institution', took part in various processions connected with the visit and their new colours were soon out and being paraded.[45]

Besides being used by shareholders and their families, the Garden attracted others prepared to pay an annual key rental. They too were drawn from further afield and included those living in Charlotte Square, Royal Circus, Northumberland Street, Albany Street and so forth.[46] These early days saw some efforts at flower growing – China roses were planted against the Dublin Street boundary walls and dahlias, pansies and wallflowers are all mentioned in the minutes. Flower seeds were regularly purchased and a flower-bed was formed at the centre. But once the tree canopy thickened, flower cultivation became more difficult. Grass was cut by scythe and the cuttings were sold as cattle feed. The fruit trees continued to be productive, and accounts for 1826 showed that fruit sales had raised £11; for many years the sale of grass and fruit yielded a modest income. Gradually the old fruit trees were removed, but one pear tree survived until the 1940s. Over time the radiating system of pathways became less well defined and developed into a looser collection of interconnecting paths.

REGULATIONS

To be Observed by the PROPRIETORS *of Queen Street Gardens.*

I. Shares may be let on lease for a period not less than one year, and at a rent not less than L. 3, the lessee paying the annual assessment for the repairs, &c. of the Gardens, and agreeing to conform to the other Regulations, and entering the lease in the transfer-book. The term of entry must be at Whitsunday in every case.

II. Each Proprietor, or his Tenant, shall have access to the Gardens at all times of the day, until one hour after sunset, when the Gardens shall be shut up by the Gardener.

III. Each Proprietor shall be furnished with two Keys, having his name engraved upon them. Tenants of shares shall also be furnished with two Keys.

IV. In case of a Key being lost, application for another (if required) must be made to the Cashier. Those procured in any other way will be considered as forgeries. The price of Keys is 3s. each.

V. Private Doors, which now communicate with these Gardens, may continue to be used by the Proprietors, upon condition of a Lock, which can be made fast by the Gardener with his Master-Key, being put upon each door.

VI. No Person shall lend or transfer his Keys to Non-Subscribers upon any account, nor shall any one be entitled to lend them even to a Subscriber, though he himself shall be out of the Town.

VII. Access to the Gardens shall not be given to the inmate of any hotel or other lodging-house, or to the members of any club, upon or in respect of any share belonging to the hotel or lodging-house-keeper, club-master, or any other person, or to the proprietors of any house occupied in such way.

VIII. No Servant shall on any account be allowed to enter the Gardens, except Female Servants having the charge of, and bringing with them children of persons entitled to access to the Gardens.

IX. Proprietors, and Members of their families, may occasionally introduce, but only when along with themselves, Non-Subscribers into the Gardens.

X. Boys shall not be permitted to introduce into the Gardens any of their Companions who are not Sons of Proprietors.

XI. No person shall cut, pull, or injure any of the trees, shrubs, or flowers in the Gardens. All children shall carefully keep upon the gravel walks and grass. No clothes shall be permitted to be washed or dried,—no carpets beaten ;—nor shall any games, such as slinging or throwing stones, or any hard substance, cricket, golf, foot-ball, bows and arrows, and the like, be allowed. No person shall bring in dogs. Birds' nests not to be robbed.

XII. The Commissioners have power to impose Fines, not exceeding L. 1, for the infringement of any of the Regulations. These fines shall be recovered by the Gardener, and applied either towards the expence of the management, or be given to the Gardener, as the Commissioners shall appoint ; and the Commissioners shall further be entitled to insist for payment of damages, for repairing the injury done to the Gardens.

XIII. The heads of families shall be responsible for offences committed by their children or servants, and shall be bound to make good all damages done by them, and pay all Fines imposed on them ; and in the event of any children being convicted of a second offence, it shall be in the power of the Commissioners to exclude them from the Gardens for a given time.

XIV. All Persons labouring under, or lately recovered from, infectious diseases, shall be excluded from the Gardens until the risk of infection shall be certified by a medical gentleman to have ceased. The attention of parents is particularly requested to this rule, which will be strictly enforced by the Gardener.

Besides observing and assisting in enforcing the foregoing Regulations, heads of families are requested to attend to the absolute necessity of abstaining themselves at all times from pulling or cutting a single flower or shrub, as the practice would immediately become general, and destroy every regulation for the management of the place. The younger members of families will take notice, that confidential Serjeants of Police have been furnished with keys to the Gardens, who are entrusted with carrying all the Regulations into effect. The heads of each family must consider the family key to the Gardens as under their own charge, and must not allow it to go out of their keeping in any way that may admit of a breach of any of the Regulations. Particular care ought also to be taken to prevent keys from being lost, and thus passing into the hands of persons not entitled to access to the Gardens.

By order of the Commissioners,

WILLIAM BELL, *Clerk.*

10, QUEEN STREET, EDINBURGH,
24th July 1827.

Queen Street Gardens' set of Regulations, 1827. The gardens are still referred to by their original title. (Queen Street Centre Garden records)

James McNab

After being established for many years, James McNab, Curator of the Botanic Garden, was consulted in 1859 about possible improvements. True to his belief that 'a well balanced landscape picture' was best achieved by 'broad spaces of well kept grass, with fine shaped trees standing upon it',[46] his initial response after having surveyed the grounds was that they had become too cluttered. He advised removal of a number of trees including several poplars (originally planted for quick effect), together with some elms, thorns and other trees in the central area. The elm and plane trees around the periphery (planted at the suggestion of Dr Robert Graham, Professor of Botany and Regius Keeper of the Royal Botanic Garden (1820–45)[47] were requiring attention and in danger of becoming 'a mass of confusion', destroying both themselves and the shrubs beneath. McNab also suggested reducing the number of shrub-beds, making the remaining ones smaller and abandoning further attempts at flower growing.

In addition he had some other rather more radical suggestion to make. One was to improve access from Abercromby Place by forming a limited terrace practically level with the outside footpath, with access via two gently sloping pathways (in place of the steep flight of steps). This would allow the gardener's house, 'an eyesore and very inconveniently situated' and occupying valuable space, to be demolished.[48] Opposite, on the south side, he advised increasing the embankment along Queen Street to allow an upper terrace walk and a more gentle descent into the garden. Such operations were feasible during a period of renewed house-building activity, when surplus rubble and earth for mounding were readily available.

First priority, however, was to salvage a basically overgrown garden, the necessary cutting, thinning and replanting all being supervised by McNab.[49] When asked to report on progress, he took the opportunity to repeat his earlier suggestions.[50] By now other matters requiring attention had cropped up. The gardener's house was soon to be vacated but was thought 'unlettable' because of its poor condition; the cope and rails along Queen Street and Abercromby Place were in urgent need of repair; there were problems with drainage in the lower parts of the garden; and a new tool house was required. The time for more radical action had arrived.[51] To aid progress an Improvement Committee was formed, and rather astutely the services of the architect Robert Matheson (1808–77), living at 25 Abercromby Place, were commandeered. He rapidly moved from being a non-shareholder, to shareholder, to District Commissioner, to convener of the committee, and his technical skill was to prove invaluable.[52] Matheson worked as Surveyor to Her Majesty's Board of Works, and was a versatile architect, his projects ranging from the recently designed Post Office in Waterloo Place to the lodge houses in Holyrood Park, but perhaps most important in this context was the Palm House at the Botanic Garden planned in close collaboration with James McNab. Matheson, it should also be noted, had around this time purchased land at Wester Coates and was responsible for the layout of Grosvenor/Lansdowne Crescent which included a central area of pleasure garden.

By the end of 1867 estimates had been obtained for the new railings, and the removal of the gardener's house; and James McDonald, a builder in Dalry Road, had offered to supply

Four general views of East Queen Street Gardens. (C. Byrom)
Beating of the Retreat, Royal Scots Territorial Regiment
(perhaps not unlike Sir Walter Scott's gathering of the Celts in 1822).

Temple of Pluto, built in 1984 as a gas governor sation.

A former Nissen hut in use as a tool-shed.

Portion of railing: note the additional lower rail to deter cats and dogs.

free quantities of earth and rubble for enlarging the banks. There was some debate whether to extend the terrace along the whole length of the north side, but McNab preferred to keep the several fine trees and shrubs, 'some of them exceedingly beautiful', rather than see them sacrificed.[53] Matheson had calculated that these various improvements would cost around £900–£1,000, but appeals for money mostly went unheeded.[54] Determined, however, not to let such an opportunity slip by, Matheson placed his confidence on careful budgeting. Thomas Tait (Smith & Ironmonger, 30 St Andrew Square) provided the new railings at a cost of just over £550,[55] and also removed the gardener's house. When the upper terrace was formed along Queen Street, Ord's old tunnel was extended by building a double arch under the mound, thus providing space for a tool shed. By the spring of 1869 the work was complete.[56] Matheson's young assistant, Hippolyte Blanc (1844–1917), prepared a plan of the changes which was presented to the committee; some years later Blanc himself advised on improvements to the drainage of some of the steep walks.[57]

McNab's final advice was given in 1869 when he recommended the removal of certain trees and the planting of new ones. He also recommended the acquisition of a shelter, which appeared two years later complete with verandah and lock-up space for tools and croquet equipment. This rather handsome structure, situated in the north-west corner, survived until 1997. Little further remedial work was necessary until 1887 when Mr Mackenzie of Methven & Son was approached; on this occasion the thorn and laburnum were selected for removal, as well as several lime trees in a 'back going condition'. Scotch elm, sycamore, oriental plane and white birch were suggested as replacements.[58]

During the Second World War the garden was pressed into use for air-raid shelters, vegetable plots (at the eastern end), Home Guard practice space and storage of army

A small boy astride his fairy tricycle: these were tolerated in the larger gardens, but not bikes. (From a 1930s family photograph)

ammunition.[59] A Nissen hut is the only reminder of these fraught times: bought for £5 in 1946, it stands on what was once a tennis green on the south side of the garden in rather a prominent position. McNab would most certainly have labelled it 'a great deformity', although in a curious way it has assumed some historic interest. There are now about 170 mature trees in the garden, including most forest species, together with some ornamental trees, shrubs and hedges. Maintenance in recent years has been carried out by an outside contractor.

The Temple of Pluto

No one could have imagined that this *grande dame* of the New Town pleasure gardens would have acquired in its maturity something that appears to be a whimsical folly. In fact the so-called 'Temple of Pluto' in the south-west corner cleverly disguises a gas governor station, installed in 1984 to regulate the pressure of town gas within the city centre. The Gas Board's initial design was for a structure 'resembling a half buried lock-up garage',[60] but after criticism by the Cockburn Association this ingenious and attractive solution was born. Not only ornamental, the presence of the gods has brought other riches in the form of a useful annual ground rent.

Management, Maintenance and Use

Management has tended to devolve on a few dedicated Commissioners supported by their clerk.[61] There were only three changes of clerkships during the first hundred years: William Bell, WS (1814–43), John Rutherford, WS (1843–65), followed by his son John Rutherford, WS (1865–1913). Because of the complexities of the share-holding system their duties were more demanding than for most gardens, although time has brought simplification. There

A new sister has arrived. (Family photograph, 1930s)

is no longer any distinction, for example, between 'annual' and 'money' shares. All 140 shares are now of equal standing.[62]

For a long time the garden was cared for by a full-time gardener living within the grounds and working long hours. From March until October he was obliged to unlock the gates at 6 am (8 am in winter) not securing them again until 'a reasonable hour after sunset' after warning of closure by ringing a bell. His pay changed little over the century; the first gardener earned about £40 a year and by 1900 this had risen to just over £60. Not all gardeners proved satisfactory, but relationships between management and the workforce were usually benign. Roderick Robertson, for example, a man with experience of working at Scone Palace and Kew, joined the garden in 1847 and remained till his death in 1860; burdened with a 'numerous family', he constantly struggled to fend off debt. On one occasion the Commissioners advanced him money which they later discharged in place of his Christmas bonus. On another occasion when the Commissioners learned that he had been forced to surrender an insurance policy, it was revived on his behalf and a further year's premium paid.[63]

Life was never easy, but the reminiscences of one of Robertson's large brood – his son William (1847–1936) who later became a Doctor of Divinity and a church minister – indicate a happy childhood spent within the gardens. They were, he wrote, 'a real joy' to the youngsters of the neighbourhood, with a relaxed atmosphere – 'nowhere had people to obey the usual notice 'please keep off the grass'. Adventurous games included 'French and English' which involved forfeits, enemy territory and 'no-man's-land'. Trees were climbed, primitive shelters built; and the 'venerable elm with wide stretching arms' on the west side became a viewing platform for watching soldiers marching from the Castle to Leith en route for the Crimea. The ingredients of play remain curiously constant. Thus a more recent description of boyhood escapades in the gardens during the early 1940s conjured up

Brother and sister sit with nanny on the grass bank; these gardens soon became the scene of much adventurous childhood play shared with other children in the locality. (From a 1930s photograph)

Commandos and Jerries, Mudders (slinging earth from newly-dug borders), fights on the green slopes, hiding in shelters and dug-outs under trees and bushes, throwing sticks and stones at the ripening fruit of an old pear tree and sledging down great snow hills.[64] The garden experienced its own mini-invasion during the 1870s when tennis took hold. At its peak there were four courts and, for a time, space to swing a racket took precedence over space to plant trees.[65]

Miscellanea

Reference to wanton damage appears only rarely in the garden minutes. One incident of 'undesirable mischief' in the 1820s arose when boys brought in friends from 'outside', resulting in one offender being expelled for one whole month. To reassert order a 'Captain Brown late of the Police' was taken on to keep watch.[66] Cats and dogs, however, have probably given more cause for concern than naughty boys. Did the Princes Street cat fraternity find sanctuary in the Queen Street Gardens? James Pillans (1779–1864), the Professor of Humanity, probably thought so. He lived at 22 Abercromby Place, and was known as a fine teacher and promoter of educational reform. A conscientious shareholder who bothered to attend annual meetings, Pillans suggested in 1829 that in order to protect the bird population, the gardener should 'be furnished with a terrier or two in order to exclude cats, or that cats should be killed by some other method'. Later in 1831 he proposed that one of the gardener's children be sent round each morning 'to pick up the rubbish thrown over such as pieces of paper, stones, tin canisters etc'.[69] Litter is by no means a new phenomenon.

But a far greater threat to the Gardens arose more recently, making boys, cats and dogs seem positively harmless. In 1970 proposals were made to solve Edinburgh's parking problems by forming large underground car parks beneath the Queen Street Gardens. The idea was promoted by a councillor, and supported by others who claimed that 'lifting' the gardens to a level with Queen Street was 'a simple engineering feat'. It caused an instant outcry, the public protesting that the gardens were 'irreplaceable' and 'sacrosanct' and not to be meddled with. As one person commented, 'only when outrageous suggestions are submitted do Edinburgh citizens react in a positive manner'.[70]

Notes

1. W.H. Playfair, *Report to the Right Honourable the Lord Provost, Magistrates and Council of the City of Edinburgh, the Governors of Heriot's Hospital, etc, on the plan for laying out the new town between Edinburgh and Leith*, 12th April 1819.

2. Eleanor Sillar, *Edinburgh's Child: some memories of 90 years* (Edinburgh & London, 1961), p. 2.

3. Robert Ord was the son of John Ord, solicitor and Under-Sheriff of Newcastle from 1685 to 1703.

4. Thomas Sommerville, *My life and times 1741–1814*, excerpts of which are to be found in *Diaries of Eminent Scotsmen, Scottish Diaries and Memoirs 1746–1843*, ed. J.G. Fyfe (Stirling, 1942), p. 227.

5. The annual feu on all the subsequent private garden areas was based on a grain feu; this method of calculation continued until 1924 when it was converted into a money stipend under the Conveyancing (Scotland) Act of the same year.

6. Heriot's Hospital Chartulary, vol. 3, p. 259; HHM, 10 April 1769, vol. 10. p. 55; the 2.5 acres (1 ha) did not, however, lie 'in a proper manner fronting the area where the house was to be built but off at the east side thereof', so that it became necessary to exchange part of it for the ground on the west which the Town Council had a right to, see TCM, 26 April 1769.

7. J.W. Reed and F.A. Pottle (eds), *Boswell, Laird of Auchinleck 1778–1782* (London, 1963), diary entry 21 July 1782, p. 462.

8. *Williamson's Street Directory 1786–1788*; *Edinburgh Advertiser*, 15 November 1785; the house and garden were advertised for sale together, but in the end were sold separately.

9. HHM, 8 October 1781, vol. 12, p. 156.

10. No. 5 Queen Street had been built by ex Lord Provost Dalrymple and was advertised for sale in the *Edinburgh Advertiser*, 8 November 1781.

11. HHM, 25 February, vol. 15.

12. *Edinburgh Evening Courant*, 7 July 1794.

13. *Edinburgh Evening Courant*, 6 January 1800, 10 February 1800, 8 May 1800.

14. *Kay's Portraits*, vol. 1, p. 236.

15. William Playfair, *British family Antiquity: illustrative of the origins and progress of the Rank, Honours and Personal merit* (London, 1811), vol. 8.

16. Heriot's Hospital Chartulary, vol. 5, p. 143, Charter dated 17 April 1786.

17. John Gibson Lockhart (ed. William Ruddock), *Peter's Letters to his Kinsfolk* (Edinburgh, 1977), p. 26.

18. TCM, 17 January 1810: Report by Thomas Bonnar about 'easier' access than Duke Street; TCM, 11 March 1812; HHM, 3 June 1805, vol. 17, HHM, 28 February 1812, vol. 19.

19. See Chapter 7, n.32.

20. Reference to part of the garden being used as a coal-yard can be found in: Memorial for the Commissioners of the Eastern District of the Queen Street gardens, East Queen Street gardens, Minute Book 2, 10 February 1858; see also the *Edinburgh Evening Courant*, 28 December 1812.

21. Circular to Proprietors, 25 June 1812, Miscellaneous papers in the Queen Street Centre garden records; see also *Edinburgh Evening Courant*, 27 June 1812.

22. TCM, 20 January 1813.

23. B.W. Crombie, *Modern Athenians 1837–1847* (Edinburgh, 1882), p. 70.

24. The information which follows is taken from various subscription papers in possession of the Clerk to the East Queen Street Gardens.

25. William Bell ran a busy legal practice and was later appointed Crown Agent from 1840 to 1841; see The *History of the Society of Writers to His Majesty's Signet*, p. 76.

26. The Committee consisted of William Bell, WS; Richard Hotchkis, WS, 18 Duke Street; James Gordon, Advocate, 13 Heriot Row; James Jollie, WS, Clerk to the Merchant Company, 26 Abercromby Place; Alexander Anderson and James Kerr.

27. TCM, 11 August 1813; see also Miscellaneous paper relating to Queen Street Gardens 1813–1822, SL. 12. 287[50], ECA.

28. Circular, dated December 1813, Queen Street Central Garden records.

29. Sir John Carr, an English traveller who visited Edinburgh in 1809, remarked about Queen Street that 'it is truly delightful to join the evening promenade in this street when the sun is

shedding his last light upon this exquisite prospect, and also shining upon a number of well dressed and beautiful females, who add not a little to the witchery of the whole'.

30. *Edinburgh Evening Courant*, 19 March 1814; 13 June 1814.

31. John Hay started life as a seedsman, and became a burgess in 1807. He had premises in Bank Street, off the Mound, but later moved to Catherine Street (part of Leith Walk), a popular area for nursery firms; later still he moved to 35 Nicolson Square.

32. An account of the early history of the gardens relative to administrative matters is to be found in 'Memorial for William Bell WS on behalf of the Eastern District of Queen Street gardens in cause Lady Ashburton – to prepare condescendence 1833' (in connection with Lady Ashburton's 10 years' arrears on her share), miscellaneous documents, East Queen Street gardens.

33. William Bell, 'Memorandum, Proposition respecting Queen Street gardens', 1 March 1820, miscellaneous documents, East Queen Street Gardens.

34. It helped in any case to spread the cost of obtaining the Act which came to around £500.

35. 1822 Act of Parliament, III George IV, Cap. 28.

36. Queen Street Garden Minute Book, General Proprietors 1820–1920, (records of East Queen Street Gardens).

37. The transfer of shares was placed on a similar footing as a formal conveyance. The clerk was required to keep a book listing all the holders, and a set procedure followed whenever shares changed hands.

38. For the East Queen Street Gardens this was to be an annual payment of £3 per share: in the case of the other districts the amount was to be based on the property rentals or according to the width of the house frontages.

39. Gillespie Graham had become an annual shareholder while living at 34 Albany Street; he moved to Duke (Dublin) Street in the late 1830s, even closer to the gardens.

40. A general meeting of all proprietors in each district could be called at any time by the District Commissioners (apart from 15th July–15th November – when many legal people were absent), or by requisition of seven proprietors, provided they stated the reason for calling a meeting (to be advertised in three Edinburgh newspapers ten days beforehand).

41. Sederunt Book of General Meetings of Queen Street Gardens or the Eastern District (1822–1836), Accounts, 12 March 1823.

42. The first East District Commissioners appointed were: Sir John Connell (convener), Sir Henry Moncrieff, Edward Earl, John Wauchope, Richard Hotchkis, John Morison, John Campbell, Lewis Ferrier, James Hunter, Roger Aytoun, Richard McKenzie and William Trotter.

43. Sederunt Book of General Meetings of Queen Street gardens of the Eastern District (1822–1836), Minute, 19 May 1823.

44. Ibid., Account 12 March 1823, 12 March 1824.

45. James Lockhart, *Life of Scott* (1842 edition), p. 482. *Edinburgh Advertiser*, 13 August 1822.

46. Sederunt Book of the District Commissioners, Queen Street East, (1857–1893); James McNab, (1 June 1859), Report on the Abercromby Place Gardens; James McNab, 'Our Town Trees: The Queen Street Gardens', (31 May 1865), *The Scottish Gardener*.

47. Dr Robert Graham (1786–1845), Regius Keeper of the Botanic garden and Professor of Medicine and Botany at the University, had suggested to the General Commissioners in 1837 that all three Queen Street gardens should plant a row of matching trees around their boundaries, either limes or elms.

48. McNab suggested the possibility of building a new house on the south side, or else increasing the gardener's wages to cover the cost of renting a house elsewhere.

49. Sederunt Book of the District Commissioners, Queen Street East, (1857–93), Minute 26 July 1859; 2 April 1860: McNab advised on the replanting but no details are given.

50. James McNab, Report on the East Queen Street Gardens, (21 March 1867), Sederunt Book of District Commissioners, Queen Street East (1857–93).

51. In spite of considerable improvement to the house in 1860, carried out under Charles McGibbon, architect.

52. Sederunt Book of the District Commissioners Queen Street East, (1857–93). Minute, 1 April 1868; a vacancy had occurred with the retirement of Dr Lyon Playfair, Professor of Chemistry.

53. Sederunt Book of the District Commissioners Queen Street East, (1857–93). Minute 11 December 1867; and James McNab, Report submitted to the Improvement Committee, 18 December 1867.

54. Statement on behalf of the Commissioners, 23 January 1868 (note 51). Sederunt Book of the District Commissioners, Queen Street East, (1857–93), Minute, 15 June 1868.

55. The bars of the new railings were placed 5 inches (12.5 cm) apart – sufficient to allow thin stray dogs to squeeze through.

56. Sederunt Book of the District Commissioners, Queen Street East, (1857–93), Minutes 13 August 1869; 12 October 1868; 16 February 1869; 26 February 1869.

57. Hippolyte Blanc later had his own architect's practice in Rutland Square. He became involved in a number of restoration projects.

58. Sederunt Book of the District Commissioners, Queen Street East (1857–93); Minute 30 December 1886, Report by Alexander Mackenzie.

59. Sederunt Book, Eastern District Commissioners (1894–1970), Minutes: October 1941; 4 April 1946; 7 April 1952; 20 March 1953; 18 March 1954; 27 May 1954; 22 December 1966; 20 April 1967.

60. *The Cockburn Association Newsletter*, (Edinburgh Civic Trust), 27 April 1984, p. 11.

61. Provision was made in the 1822 Act for four new Commissioners to be elected each year – allowing the opportunity for 'new blood' to be added from time to time.

62. The holding of an 'annual share' with the additional burden of £3 per year was never a very attractive proposition; particularly as non-shareholders could make use of the garden by renting a key at lesser cost.

63. Sederunt Book of District Commissioners, Queen Street East (1857–93), Minutes 3 April 1857; 17 April 1858.

64. Reverend William Robertson, DD, *The Scotsman*, 5 April 1939; Hamish Coghill, 'Childhood Summers: At war in the gardens of the New Town', *The Edinburgh Evening News*, 30 June 1976.

65. Sederunt Book of District Commissioners, Queen Street East (1857–93), Minute, 20 December 1883: thirty-three shareholders signed the petition asking for removal of some of the newly planted trees. Tennis continued in the gardens up until the Second World War.

66. Sederunt Book of General Meeting of the Queen Street Gardens, Eastern District (1822–36), Minute 19 May 1828.

67. Ibid., Minute, 18 May 1829.

68. James Pillans was Rector of the Royal High School before taking up his appointment at Edinburgh University.

69. Sederunt Book of General Meetings of Queen Street Gardens, the Eastern District (1822–36), Minute 16 May 1831.

70. *Edinburgh Evening News,* 19 February 1971, 'Park Plan dropped'. Councillor Hugh Macpherson who put forward the idea in Council, did not pursue his motion after an overwhelming vote in his own progressive group against the plan.

CHAPTER 9

CENTRAL QUEEN STREET
4.25 acres (1.26 ha)

Wood's Farm, whose cattle pond now ornaments Queen Street Gardens was then in its pure integrity as a Scotch farm steading and the fine spring well which bubbled forth close to the court is now hid in a cellar in Heriot Row. I well recollect the venerable figure of the old farmer, father to Dr. Alex Wood of celebrated memory, stepping about his fields and chiding us boys in our amusement of navigating his pond on an old door, of which shipwreck was the invariable result accompanied with a ducking in the pond. Escaping from one of these disasters with my companions General Ainslie and his brother, we had repaired to the shelter of a saw pit to scrub off the mud from our clothes, and have a leaping match among the logs of wood where I had the misfortune to break my arm.

James Skene, *c.* 1780s[1]

It was a short walk from Skene's home in George Street to Farmer Wood's fields, the scene of many of his boyhood adventures. And while trespassing on the farmer's land and enjoying muddy play around the cattle pond, he could not have foreseen that many years later this same ground would become pleasure gardens, nor that he would be approached to design them. In 1769 the Town Council sub-tacked (leased) a portion from Heriot's Hospital in order to provide space for the masons and carpenters working in this part of the New Town to lay down their materials; rather as happened on the south side of East Princes Street, and later in Drummond Place, hence Skene's reference to saw pits.[2]

But by 1785 the land was no longer required, and the Council, in agreement with the Heriot's Hospital, made over the ground to anyone wanting to form a private garden. For the portion lying between Hanover Street and Frederick Street (the future Central Queen Street Gardens), two sub-tacks were granted in 1786, one to Sir James Hunter Blair (descended from the ancient family of Hunter of Hunterstone in Ayrshire) and the other to John Brough.[3] Hunter Blair's portion was about twice the size of Brough's. Shortly afterwards Heriot's Hospital as feu superiors granted charters to both individuals, containing the same restrictions as had been placed on Ord's and Steuart's land to the east. In essence use was limited to garden, nursery or park purposes.[4] As subsequent events will show, this central area fared the least well, and the restrictions were flouted on numerous occasions. The extent of malpractice was sufficient to spur local residents to take action; but it was not until efforts became concentrated on obtaining a private Act of Parliament to safeguard all the open space along Queen Street as communal pleasure gardens that success was guaranteed.

Sir James Hunter Blair, owner of the largest private garden plot within central Queen Street. (Kay's *Portraits*, 1877, ECL)

Sir James Hunter Blair's Plot

When Sir James Hunter Blair (1741–87) acquired his garden ground he was on the verge of moving his large household from George Street to Queen Street. By then he had become joint head of one of the most important private banking firms in Scotland: Forbes, Hunter & Co.; his partner, Sir William Forbes, was a close friend and long-time working colleague.[5] His life was marked by public distinction and success, yet he was eminently approachable, open-minded, wise and good-humoured. James Hunter Blair had succeeded David Steuart as Lord Provost in 1784, and prior to this served as Member of Parliament for Edinburgh. While Provost, he promoted many worthwhile projects including the rebuilding of the University, and the construction of the South Bridge.[6] He was also an agricultural improver, carrying out extensive work to his wife's family estate in Wigtownshire, and practically rebuilding the village of Portpatrick.[7] His newly acquired plot would not have escaped such zest for improvement had not ill health, then death, intervened. With a family of twelve (eight sons and four daughters), and a household noted for its hospitality, the garden would certainly have been put to good use.

The bereaved family took up residence in Queen Street, but changed addresses several times before finally moving to No. 34 in 1796, practically opposite their garden space. But apart from enclosing the ground with a crude stone wall (later damaged when the new roadways were under construction[8]), little else was done. By 1804 the family had left Queen Street although they held onto the garden ground. It was now in the name of the eldest son, Sir John, who, having acquired the mansion and estate of Powderhall in 1795, lived there until his early death in 1800. The Queen Street ground then passed to the second son, David Hunter Blair of Brownshill, who was in partnership with John Bruce, being printers and stationers to George IV, with offices in Blair Street.[9] Sir David was then 22 years old but already the owner of Blairquhan, a large estate near Maybole in Ayrshire. Gradually, as finances permitted, his attention turned to his country estate, and in 1820 he commissioned William Burn to draw up designs for a new residence there. Sir David, it should be noted, was an enthusiastic amateur landscape architect and went on to create a delightful and picturesque approach to his house at Blairquhan.[10]

Clothes Washing and Drying Green

These talents, however, were not expended on the Queen Street plot. Instead, the ground was rented out, and then in 1814 advertised for sale by auction. It was described as a field which 'from its very central situation is applicable for a great variety of useful purposes'.[11] There were no takers, and once again the land was let out. What 'useful purposes' was it being used for? The answer seems to have been for clothes washing and drying, in similar fashion to the southern slopes of the East North Loch and parts of Calton Hill. The famous or infamous habit of 'Scotch washing' was duly taking place right there, for all to

Washerwomen at work. These ones are busy on Calton Hill, but similar scenes took place in the centre of Queen Street, the East North Loch, Holyrood Park and elsewhere in Edinburgh. (M. Egerton, *Airy Nothings*, 1825, ECL)

```
                TO BE SOLD
By Auction, on Wednesday the 6th April 1814, at two
o'clock afternoon, within the Royal Exchange
Coffeehouse, if not previously disposed of by private
bargain.
THAT FIELD, bounded by QUEEN STREET on the
south, and HERIOT ROW on the north, lying between
Hanover Street and Frederick Street.
    The Field consists of two acres, one rood, and thirty
falls; and from its very centrical situation is applicable
to a variety of useful purposes. Being out of lease at
Whit Sunday, possession may be had at that term.
    For further particulars apply to John Bell, WS
32 Heriot Row
```

Sale of Blair's unimproved garden plot advertised in the *Edinburgh Evening Courant*, 17 March 1814.

behold. An activity which went on regardless of the weather or time of year, and in time-honoured fashion, required the stamping of feet in wooden tubs, with skirts held aloft. The end results were then draped over washing lines, or scattered on the grass. Kirkwood's Plan of 1819 shows the range of lines and posts, the pump wells and the farm pond (was this, too, pressed into use?). For those whose houses faced onto the space, the sight was hardly inspirational.[12] In 1814 the Grants of Rothiemurchus rented a 'warm and cheerful' house at 4 Heriot Row, but as their daughter Elizabeth ruefully noted in her journal:

> There were no prettily laid out gardens then between Heriot Row and Queen Street, only a long strip of unsightly grass, a green, fenced by an untidy wall and abandoned to the use of the washer-women. It was an ugly prospect, and we were daily indulged with it, the cleanliness of the inhabitants being so excessive that, except on Sundays and 'Saturdays at e'en', squares of bleaching linens and lines of drying were ever before our eyes.[13]

Pigs and Cows

Matters did not improve. In 1820 Sir David sold his Queen Street land for £1,450 to James Webster, a builder and 'late plasterer in Edinburgh'. Very likely he was the former tenant,[14] for only two years previously he had approached Heriot's Hospital offering to rent the adjoining waste ground for 5 guineas a year.[15] His motive for buying the land can only have been speculative, providing him with a useful income in the short term. He leased the ground to Robert Winter for £100 a year. Winter was a flesher (butcher) by trade, having premises in Jamaica Street. Although still bound by the original conditions, Webster stipulated in the lease that his tenant 'shall not plough or dig upon the turf . . . but shall keep the ground in good order . . . and likewise keep the posts at present placed in said ground for the purpose of drying clothes and the fences and gates . . . in perfect good order and condition'.[16] In addition to clothes-washing part of the ground was pressed into use for accommodating the butcher's livestock.[17] A piggery, cow byre and a small house were added. Washerwomen now had cows and pigs for company, complete with all the accompanying noise and odours. Elizabeth Grant would certainly not have approved of this latest development. Were those secure behind their elegant façades doing anything to improve matters? For clues we need to turn to the adjacent piece of land.

First Attempts at Pleasure Gardens

John Brough, it will be remembered, had bought the adjoining plot in 1782. He is variously described as a builder-cum-architect, with an interest in an upholstery and cabinetmaking business. Brough had taken several feus in the New Town, including ones in Princes Street, George Street, Rose and Thistle Street and also Queen Street; he probably acquired the Queen Street site for use as a builder's yard. His business, however, did not prosper and by 1788 he was bankrupt.[18] Part of the sequestered estate was advertised for sale and included his ground in Queen Street with an upset price of £40.[19] It was sold in two portions, one to Alexander Sheriff, a wine merchant in Leith, and the other to Alexander Wight, WS, who lived at 23 South Hanover Street. Maybe the latter had intended to form a private garden but in all events both plots remained rough ground.

In 1803, when Sheriff's portion (on the west side) was advertised for sale, it came to the notice of Heriot's Hospital. They decided that if the ground 'could be obtained for a reasonable price', it would allow the roadway between Queen Street and Heriot Row to be made 'of a proper breadth'. The deal was successful and the land was bought for £200; the Hospital went on to add Wight's strip which he sold for £150.[20] Thus after an interval of 18 years this piece was re-acquired by the Hospital but continued as before as rough ground.

By 1809 East Heriot Row was mostly built, and the last thing the new residents wanted was a scruffy bit of ground opposite their new property. Several residents therefore made approaches to the Hospital to see if the land could be acquired for pleasure-garden purposes. This marked the very first attempt to establish such a garden along Queen Street. The Governors' response was encouraging. In January 1810 they agreed to sell the land for £427, and on condition that the feuars took responsibility for erecting 'a sufficient retaining and parapet wall on the west side for the security of the road and safety of the public'.[21] A draft charter was prepared in favour of 'John Ferrier WS and others'. John Ferrier (1771–1852) lived at 15 East Heriot Row and was acting as spokesman for the group: he was the brother of Susan Ferrier, the authoress of three popular satirical novels.[22] But the move proved premature: there was insufficient financial backing. Pleasure gardens were still a new phenomenon, for only St Andrew Square and Charlotte Square then existed, and the latter was known to have had a slow and troublesome birth. The reluctance of some residents to become involved was, under the circumstances, not surprising.

Three years later another attempt was made. In 1813 the Hospital received two separate proposals: one from James Horne, WS, resident in Heriot Row, offering to lease for ten years 'the ground lying waste . . . at a reasonable rate';[23] the other from John Mowbray, WS, (in succession to Ferrier who had now moved to York Place). Mowbray's letter, dated December 1813, spoke of the impossibility of getting 'all the parties concerned in the western area, between Queen Street and Heriot Row to advance their proportion of the sum necessary for the purchase of that area', but observed that if the amount could be converted into an annual payment of £25, together with the yearly feu, 'I have little doubt, that the transaction will be immediately closed'. Mowbray pointed out that the costs to themselves of making 'a proper enclosing wall and railing and retaining wall on the west side' would be considerable – around £2,000 – added to which was the expense 'of levelling and ornamenting this piece of ground which forms, on one side of the main entry to all the ground belonging to the Hospital, which is as yet to be feued'.[24] Permission for a small gardener's house was also sought. Neither proposal suited the immediate interests of the Hospital. By now attention was focused on the eastern end of Queen Street, where efforts to convert the ground there into communal gardens was gathering pace. Under the circumstances the Governors rightly preferred to keep their options open.

Limbo Land

Several residents of East Heriot Row were also involved in the campaign to establish the east 'Queen Street Gardens', requiring as they did substantial fund-raising. It was not surprising, therefore, that the Centre Queen Street Gardens project came to a standstill. Once the 'Queen Street Gardens' were secured, however, interest in the central area slowly revived. In 1819 three fresh approaches were made to Heriot's Hospital: two from builders, and one from Charles Cunningham, WS.[25] Robert Watson, one of the builders, wanted the ground 'for the purpose of a garden';[26] the other, James Webster, builder, offered no reason, but we know from his record that he was more interested in hiring washing lines than ornamental gardening. The third applicant, Charles Cunningham (1775–1856), had recently moved to 14 East Heriot Row, directly overlooking the space. Described as 'a very good natured, kindly man, generally very indifferent about business' (although perfectly efficient when circumstance demanded), his family connections had secured him the post of City Clerk in 1807 and helped establish his legal business.[27] A comfortably well-off citizen, he seems to have acted as much for the public good as for his own ends.

The Hospital decided initially to sell the land by public auction,[28] but this was subsequently cancelled when Watson and Cunningham both submitted firm offers. But before reaching any decision the Governors instructed their Superintendent of Works, Thomas Bonnar, to design a gardener's house 'suited to the ground', a sensible safeguard in view of the apparent desire for such a structure.[29] His plan, dated 6 August 1819, shows a single-storeyed building in classical style, similar to the later one built in the London Road Gardens. Finally, in February

Portrait of Charles Cunningham, City Clerk, and the last individual to buy a private garden plot along Queen Street. (Crombie, *Modern Athenians, 1837–1847,* ECL)

Advertisement for the sale of John Bough's former garden ground. It was bought by Cunningham. (*Edinburgh Evening Courant*, 1 July 1819)

Proposed plan by Thomas Bonnar, 1819, for a gardener's house 'suited to the ground', then being advertised for sale in Edinburgh. (George Heriot Trust and Crown copyright © RCAHMS)

1820, 'after deliberating at considerable lengths on the subject', the Governors decided to accept Cuningham's offer of £427, and on the same terms as the draft charter of 1810.[30]

On this occasion Cuningham moved swiftly. Within two weeks of purchase he had circulated proprietors living in East Heriot Row, and Queen Street (between Hanover Street and Frederick Street), informing them of his initiative to further 'any general plan for improving the whole ground between Heriot Row and Queen Street which the proprietors interested may deem it advisable to carry forward'.[31] He offered to make over the ground without profit at any time during the following twelve months, provided he was reimbursed for his expenses. Failing this, the space would be enclosed and turned to 'some beneficial purpose on my own account'. It is not hard to imagine Cunningham's disappointment when a few weeks later Hunter Blair's adjoining field was sold to Webster, and hopes of pleasure gardens were once more crushed. He had little choice but to enclose his ground and put an end to a popular short-cut.[32]

Nearly There

It was now apparent that without some legal backing to allow the ground to be formally taken over and maintained on a common basis, success was never likely. By this time certain proprietors in East Heriot Row had become shareholders in the 'Queen Street Gardens', familiar with their increasing administrative problems. The remedy decided upon, as already described, was to apply for a private Act of Parliament to establish a proper legal structure; and this provided the opportunity to extend provision to all the other areas of open space along Queen Street, allowing them to be constituted as communal pleasure grounds. Two residents from East Heriot Row, John Cay, advocate, (1790–1865), and Donald Horne, WS (1787–1870) were members of the committee appointed to draft a suitable parliamentary bill. Once the Act was passed in May 1822 progress was rapid. The Middle or Central District was set up in June when six District Commissioners – the first management committee – were elected.[33] Five were legal gentlemen and two were already familiar names – James Cay and Charles Cuningham.[34] Cay was appointed convener and remained involved until he left the area in 1846, his outstanding contribution acknowledged by the presentation of an honorary key.[35] Donald Horne became the first clerk and freely gave his services for 14 years before moving to his new residence in Royal Terrace.

Purchase of the Ground

Cuningham's western portion was acquired without difficulty; all he wanted was enough to cover his out-of-pocket expenses which amounted to £736.[36] James Webster proved a tougher proposition. He had bought the land two years before for £1,450 but now considered it worth £3,000, and was very dismissive of the Commissioners' offer of £1,750. A shrewd opportunist and prepared to fight his corner, he was met by an equally hard front from the Commissioners. They decided to call his bluff, threatening legal action if their offer was refused, on the basis of misuse in terms of the feu charter. Webster reduced his price to £2,500, then to £2,100, and after further bargaining eventually accepted £2,000. He was not pleased, as his agent made clear: 'he thinks it very hard that so wealthy a body as your constituents, and to whom £100 can be of little consequence should after he had reduced his demands seek still further to reduce them to £2,000'. Nevertheless Webster made a handsome profit and had little to gain by prevaricating. The deal concluded, Mr Horne was asked to order the removal of the piggery, and to come to some arrangement with Webster's tenant 'to prevent any clothes from being hung up during his Majesty's visit to this city'.[37]

Before departing for the summer recess, the Commissioners had agreed on the method of funding the gardens (an annual assessment based on the police rating list,[38] and had been in touch with Eagle & Henderson to 'furnish a plan and estimate of the manner in which the grounds should be levelled and embellished'; the nursery firm were asked to keep in mind that 'at some future period it may, if practicable be resolved on to communicate the whole gardens by tunnels under the streets leading from Hanover and Frederick Streets'. Thomas Brown (Bonnar's successor as Superintendent of Works), who had recently designed railings for Drummond Place Gardens, was asked to supply similar plans and costings for enclosing the grounds.

First Moves

The Commissioners next met in November when a 'bargain' was struck with Robert Winter, the tenant. He was allowed to stay until May 1823 provided access was given for 'the inclosing, levelling and trenching going on during the winter'. Clothes drying was permitted to continue 'on such part of the whole grounds (including the field purchased from Mr Cuningham) as may not be cut up in carrying on the improvements'. It was also agreed that Winter could 'occupy the house and byre as at present but that he shall not allow the cows or other animals to go at large on the grounds'; and that he should guard against trespassers.

As Brown's estimate for enclosing the whole area was rather high – £900 – the Commissioners decided to concentrate on the Queen Street and Heriot Row sides; but not before three of their number were sent off 'to examine different enclosures of that kind about town and report back'. Alexander Henderson had already told the Commissioners that it was 'premature or even impossible to give in such a plan' until the ground was properly secured. Not to be forestalled, however, the Commissioner's forged ahead, and being aware of the good taste of Mr Skene of Rubislaw in such matters, and of the great benefit derived by the Commissioners of the Princes Street grounds, and of the Eastern District of these gardens from Mr Skene's directions, they are extremely desirous of availing themselves of his superior judgment, and therefore resolve before going on with this part of the work to consult him thereon.

Economy in the face of burgeoning expense was paramount and, 'having observed that the evergreen shrubs, and trees are removing from Lord Moray's ground in consequence of the building going on there', the Commissioners directed their Clerk to apply to Lord Moray's 'man of business' for permission to remove some 'for transplanting into these grounds', and if successful to employ 'some skilful person' capable of carrying out the necessary preparations.[39]

By December eight estimates for enclosing the north and south sides 'according to the amended specification and plan made up by Mr Brown' had been received. Walter Stewart Dinn, builder (in 1822 he bought five plots in Royal Terrace but seems to have been made bankrupt some time after), submitted the cheapest at £597, and this was accepted subject to various conditions. The work was to be carried out under Brown's supervision, and completed by 1 April 1823 or by 20 April if the winter proved unfavourable. The footpath outside, and ground within, had 'to be brought to a proper level', and 'cut up' as little as possible. Did pressure to meet deadlines cause one of the masons – James Ding – to experience 'a distressing accident' when a curb stone fell upon him? It was sufficiently serious for the Commissioners to open a subscription on his behalf, and 'in the meantime to supply him therefrom with what is necessary for the support of himself and family'.[40]

The Design of the Garden

Reference to designs for the garden do not resurface until January 1823 when a new name enters the arena. The garden minutes report thus:

> Mr Wilson's plan of the grounds was submitted to the meeting and he explained to the Commissioners his ideas thereon. The Commissioners approved of the design generally and requested of Mr Wilson to superintend the execution and to suggest such alterations as may from time to time occur . . . In regard to the pond, as its being preserved or not, will make no material alteration, they delay deciding thereon until it can be seen whether a sufficient supply of water can be commanded, and they particularly wish it to be ascertained whether a service pipe can be got from the Water Co without much expense and in the meantime direct the clerk to make enquiries of that point.

It was a busy meeting. Not only was a design agreed to, but a contract made with George Ross 'for cutting and carrying away the bank opposite to Heriot Row' and a gardener by the name of Richard Walker appointed 'as superintendent, at two guineas a week during the time he is actually engaged'. He was given permission to buy plants, 'where they can be got cheapest and most suitable'.[41] But who was Mr Wilson, the man responsible for the design? Although his name keeps recurring, it is not until the appearance of a draft report in April 1823 that he becomes identified. Prepared for the benefit of proprietors who were soon to be asked for money, the report was framed to encourage and impress.[42] Thus the proprietors were informed that the Commissioners had obtained several plans for laying out the grounds 'but before adopting any one of them, we had recourse to the professional skill and admitted taste of Mr Andrew Wilson, landscape painter. The plan for the railing was not fixed on until after the most mature deliberations, and after much pains had been bestowed in examining the different works of a similar description in and around Edinburgh'.

Andrew Wilson

Andrew Wilson's association with the Central Queen Street Gardens, and subsequently with the Western ones, is an exciting discovery for several reasons. In the first place this is one of the rare examples of a professional artist becoming involved in garden design. Secondly, although Andrew Wilson was an active and talented artist whose paintings were regularly exhibited and sold, in 1826 he went to live in Italy; consequently only a small proportion of his extensive output remains in Scotland, the rest scattered abroad and probably unattributed. Over and above this, Wilson was a key figure in Scottish art, not only as a teacher but as a promoter of exhibitions and a collector of old masters both for private individuals and for the Royal Institution. He in fact laid the foundation of the collection now in the National Galleries of Scotland – one of the best-known works being by the great Van Dyck of the Lomellini family. In his lifetime he was described as 'one of the most eminent landscape painters of the Scottish school';[43] and shortly after his death as one whose name 'holds first place in the annals of Scottish art as a promoter of its progress and as an artist of high power',[44] one who united in his work 'a real and brilliant style of colouring, an admirable manner of representing light, and much elegance of composition'.[45] Wilson painted both in oils and watercolours and enjoyed particularly those landscapes which provided a balance of land and water. It is remarkable therefore that this hitherto unknown facet of his career – the design of the two Queen Street Gardens – should survive and with only minor changes to their structures, a fitting and living testament to one whose reputation was based on picturesque landscapes and Claudian effects. Described today as 'a grossly under-rated and unrecognised artist', this discovery may help re-establish his worth.[46] A brief outline of his career is therefore merited.

Andrew Wilson (1780–1848) came from an old Scottish family[47] but one of diminished wealth, hence his need to earn a living. He nevertheless had the opportunity to develop his artistic talents, first briefly, under Alexander Nasmyth, followed by two years at the Royal Academy Schools in London when he was seventeen; there he met and became friends with Turner. Afterwards he visited Italy, staying in Rome and Naples, sketching and painting (his work was later exhibited at the Royal Academy) and studying the Old Masters. It was the beginning of his love affair with Italy. In 1802 he returned there, having been commissioned by several wealthy individuals to acquire works of art: this was a favourable time as prices were depressed due to the unsettled state of Europe. Travel, however, was hazardous and Wilson experienced many hair-raising adventures;[48] but useful contacts were made and he gained access to several aristocratic families. It was a successful mission, and his taste for collecting was never to leave him.[49]

In 1808 he married Rachel Kerr, 'an amiable lady of great personal attraction' and for a time eked out a precarious living as an artist. As his family increased, so too did the need for greater financial stability, hence his move to become Professor of Drawing at Sandhurst Military Academy. It proved a pleasant interlude, allowing him to continue with his art as well as playing host to fellow exiled Scots. He still kept in touch with his native city; in 1813, for example, he held a private exhibition of his drawings, two of which were later engraved (views of Tivoli and Rome), and the prints were advertised for sale at an address in Broughton Street.[50]

The opportunity to return to Edinburgh came in 1817 when the Mastership of the Trustees' Academy fell vacant on John Graham's death. Established in 1760 (on Lord Kame's initiative), the school's original purpose was to provide instruction in drawing

THE COMMISSIONERS and TRUS-
TEES for MANUFACTURES, & c. in SCOT-
LAND, hereby give notice to Students of the Fine
Arts, and to those young men engaged in such
Manufactures and House-works as required to be
figured or ornamented, that they have appointed
Mr ANDREW WILSON, professor of painting, to be
the master and conductor of their Drawing Academy, in
the room of the late Mr Graham: That it will be opened
on Monday the 23d instant, at Six o' clock afternoon:
and that those desirous of being continued or admitted
as students, must lodge at this office written
applications, stating their ages, professions, and
parentage, with certificates of character from their
masters, of gentlemen who know them; nd the
masters must at the same time oblige themselves to
allow their apprentices to attend *regularly* four times a
week, from six to eight in the *evening*, for two years, in
case of their being admitted.
   To prevent unnecessary trouble, it is particularly to
be observed, that no young men are eligible, who
merely study drawing as a polite accomplishment.
                         TRUSTEES' OFFICE
                         Edinburgh, 4th Feb. 1818.

Notice of the appointment of Andrew Wilson as Master
of the Trustees' Academy, *Edinburgh Evening Courant*.

and design for pupils who intended to follow a trade.[51] As such it was one of the first
industrial design schools in Britain. The post was considered to be 'one of great importance
to the public at large', and although there were eight other applicants,[52] Wilson was the
undoubted favourite. His Italian and teaching experience combined with 'many respectable
testimonials of character and ability' all impressed; having supplied the Board with examples
of his work, received 'with much satisfaction', he was appointed in February 1818 at a salary
of £150 a year. Wilson was a caring and enthusiastic teacher; his pupils included Robert
Scott Lauder, William Simpson, Walter Geikie, David Scott, and David Octavius Hill.[53]
In addition, when the Institution for the Encouragement of Fine Arts was founded in 1819,
Wilson became its manager and was responsible for arranging two annual exhibitions
of Old Master paintings (gathered from private collections of noblemen and gentlemen)
followed by ones of living artists.[54] He quickly became a key figure in the Scottish art world,
using his knowledge to advise 'on all subjects connected with the collections of works of
art and the promotion of taste', while forming a circle of friends 'including the noblest and
most eminent men in Scotland'. When time permitted, he continued to paint and exhibit,
'his admirable pictures finding a ready sale'.[55] Wilson was one of the seven artists chosen by
George IV to exhibit privately at Holyrood House during the Royal visit in 1822.[56]

   Against this background Wilson's association with the Central Queen Street Gardens
appears less surprising. His immediate connection, however, must have been through James
Skene, who had first been singled out as a possible designer of the grounds. Skene, however,
was about to depart for a lengthy stay in France and in any case was still involved with the
West Princes Street Gardens. Both men were on friendly terms and their paths frequently
crossed. While Wilson was manager of the Institution for the Promotion of Fine Arts,
Skene was its secretary, and business, exhibition and other matters constantly overlapped.[57]
Skene would not have hesitated to recommend his colleague who, moreover, lived close by

From Farmer Wood's cattle pond to the making of a Claudian landscape in Central Queen Street Gardens, Edinburgh. (Tom Watson)

the gardens at 35 Howe Street. That he had no immediate experience in landscape design was of little consequence compared to his outstanding merits and reputation as an artist.

In contrast to the East Queen Street Gardens, Andrew Wilson inherited no cultivated space or established planting; the 4½ acres (1.8 ha) consisted of nothing but coarse grass, a steep bank sloping down from Queen Street and a pond. No drawing survives of Wilson's layout but the minutes suggest that his plan was considered flexible, depending on whether or not Farmer Wood's cattle pond was retained. Wilson frequently visited the ground with the clerk and became increasingly convinced of the merits of keeping the pond as a feature in the design: a means of composing the central main vistas to east and west in a distinctly Claudian manner. The Water Company's response that 'the supply from public pipes of water to the pond cannot be relied upon' was not too encouraging, but the Commissioners, 'being satisfied after consulting with Mr Wilson that it is an object of the first importance towards the embellishment of the grounds that there should be a pond', decided to see if 'sufficient command of water can be obtained by boring'.[58] The pond became the central focus of the garden, 'finished according to Mr Wilson's design' in a more subtle oval shape; a small rocky island was added to increase the sense of space.

The middle area of ground was kept open with three main sections of lawn crossed by gravelled paths. Other walks were made around the perimeters, with an upper and lower terrace walk along the south side. Tree and shrub planting were concentrated around the boundaries to provide privacy and shelter; some specimen trees were planted within the central area and a number of shrub beds formed between the outer walks. Most of the trees selected were deciduous hardwoods made up of sycamore, elm, ash, lime, beech, Spanish horse-chestnut, oak, whitebeam and birch, together with some hawthorn, holly, yew and rhododendron. The several weeping ash and elm trees were a later addition.

Plant Acquisition

Winter's tenancy soon proved a hindrance and he was asked to leave by the end of February 1823.[59] By then the railings on the north and south sides were well advanced, the rough bank along Heriot Row removed, and estimates had been obtained for extending the railings and draining the inner area. A busy period followed when a large squad of labourers were hired to work under the surveillance of Richard Walker. After Winter's various buildings had been removed, the ground was shaped and prepared for planting, and the pathways were marked out. Mr Dinn was instructed to erect 'in or near the present situation' two pump wells, 'of elegant pattern and with movable handles'.[60] Early in April Walker was told to visit Sang's nursery at Kirkcaldy and 'if suitable plants there at moderate prices to buy or order in addition to those obtained from Mr Ballantyne at Dalkeith'. He was, however, warned not to take plants 'of such an oversize as may endanger their thriving', besides the more dubious advice of avoiding 'the resinous tribe, as they never thrive in a smoky atmosphere'.[61] Some planting was donated. Alexander Henderson, for example, gifted 300 weeping birch plants; thanks are recorded in the garden minutes, with the note that 'Mr Henderson's nursery to provide plants still required if he has them'. Mrs Graham, 18 Heriot Row, supplied six weeping willows, presumably to edge the pond.[62]

By mid-May the Commissioners were complaining of tardy progress due to the poor standard of the workforce. Walker was told to dismiss 'some of the worst workmen and to reduce the number to about 24 good hands', it being observed that 'some have been employed quite untrustworthy of the wages stated for them and that the men have not been so industrious as the liberal wages allowed should have induced them to be'.[63] By August Walker and his gang had been sent packing. In their place Henry Bell was appointed as full-time gardener; he was paid 15 shillings (75 p) a week, and allowed occasional assistance.[64] During the first part of 1824 the footpaths were completed, using material from Trinity gravel pits; larger gravel was laid at the base of the pond ready for the addition of ornamental fish. Plans for a tool-house were also under way.[65] With the garden now virtually complete, it was agreed to boost funds by allowing non-proprietors to rent keys at 3 guineas a year.

It took well over twelve months to make the garden and Andrew Wilson was closely involved throughout, and his advice frequently sought. The decision to extend the railings on the east and west sides with 'rounded off' corners was based on Wilson's opinion that 'the operations carrying on would be incomplete unless the whole were enclosed';[66] likewise his firm views helped to save the pond. When it was agreed that a tool-house was 'indispensable', Wilson was again consulted and his ideas were adopted: 'It should be erected in the centre of the eastern bank, showing a front to the west as laid down on Mr. Wilson's sketch and sunk in the bank as far as possible'.[67] This building, dating from 1824,

Andrew Wilson's tool-house designed as a Doric pavilion and an important element in the overall picturesque effect. The metal doors have now been replaced by wrought iron ones through which can be seen a stone commemorating the late Lord Dunpark's long association with the garden. (Tom Watson)

An old pump well near the central gate, East Heriot Row: several of the larger gardens had the advantage of such wells and one existed on this site long before it became a pleasure garden. Spikes are intended to be added to the post-war railings seen in the background to help to deter vandals from gaining access. (Tom Watson)

Portrait of Charles Heath Wilson by Sir John Watson Gordon. The eldest son of Andrew Wilson with whom he shared much in common, Charles's career followed a not dissimilar course to that of his father. (Glasgow City Museums)

is quite unique and was erected according to Wilson's design by Walter Dinn, the builder responsible for enclosing the garden. It was a good deal more than just a tool-house,[68] serving also as a portico for any future tunnel connection to the eastern gardens. It takes the form of a small Doric pavilion and completes the composition of what is in effect a miniature Claudian landscape with tree-framed sward and water.

The artist's 'great trouble and unremitting attention' undertaken without 'pecuniary recompense in view' did not go unappreciated; just prior to completion the Commissioners decided to present Andrew Wilson with a key 'for his own use', together with 25 guineas 'for his plans etc'. Thomas Brown was given seven guineas for his work on the railings. Wilson enjoyed his key for less than two years; in 1826 his wife inherited money from her brother's estate and the family decided to move to Italy.[69] He remained in contact with Scotland, collecting works for the Royal Institution and the Trustees Academy, as well as for the 5th Earl of Hopetoun, and sending his paintings for exhibition. His two eldest sons, Charles and John, both stayed with the Skene household when they made return visits. His eldest son Charles (1809–82), whose own career followed a similar course to his father's, was instrumental in maintaining these links.[70] After an absence of over twenty years Andrew Wilson came back to visit Edinburgh in 1848 following a short stay in London. By then his health, already fragile, was beginning to deteriorate; we may hope that he enjoyed glimpses of the gardens he had helped create, but by then he was too weak to venture into them, or even to attend a public dinner planned in his honour by the Royal Scottish Academy. He died at 49 Great King Street, close to 'his' gardens, and was buried

Notice of the death of Andrew Wilson.

at Warriston Cemetry in the presence of his fellow Academicians. No headstone marks his plot – only a tree and rough grass.

The Gardens Since Formation

Unlike the majority of New Town gardens, these ones kept a careful check of their planting during the first few years. In 1829, for example, William McNab (1780–1848), curator of the Botanic Garden, supervised the thinning and pruning of certain trees and transplanting of others. New planting was added, including 20 'handsome' beech plants, 20 white and red arbutus, and 10 sweet bays.[71] Curiously enough, when McNab's son James was consulted in 1875, he was given rather short shrift, the minutes noting that the Commissioners were 'in the main condemnatory of any action being taken'. His advice no doubt focused on the need for a radical overhaul, for he had been openly critical of the wild state of the outer shrub and tree planting when writing in the 1860s.[72] Dr Robert Graham's suggestion that all three Queen Street Gardens should plant an outer border of elm or lime was implemented in 1837; he was Professor of Botany and Keeper of the Royal Botanic Garden.[73] The gardens benefited from having James Jardine (1776–1858), civil engineer, as one of their Commissioners. He lived at 12 Queen Street and after his election in 1831 continued as such for many more years. All maintenance matters connected with footpaths or railings were referred to him. Later he became professionally involved with the Moray Bank Gardens.

The Gardens' exemplary beginning was not, however, sustained and during the late 1830s and 1840s signs of neglect appeared. Part of the problem was the gardener's habit of taking outside work, contrary to the terms of his employment. His periodic absences encouraged misuse, and in 1847 an outbreak of vandalism was sufficiently serious to prompt a circular to all proprietors, telling of the damage caused by several young gentlemen: firing pistols at the doors of the summer-house, breaking the glass in the hot-bed frames, injuring the seats and railings and destroying plants, some of them rare and of slow growth. 'Stones have been thrown, and several hurts received by persons in the garden and passengers in the adjoining streets; the remonstrances of the gardener have been met with rudeness and incivility, and generally the conduct of many of the boys is unruly and riotous.'[74]

It had also become common practice for entry to be gained by scaling the railings which, 'being dangerous to the boys and injurious to the rails', the Commissioners were 'determined to put a stop to'. The police were asked to keep stricter watch. As a further deterrent the short intermediate balusters were replaced with full-length ones.[75]

Continuing deterioration, combined with growing complaints from proprietors, forced the gardener's dismissal in August 1848. James Dickson & Sons, suppliers of plants and seeds for many years, were asked to advise. Their opinion was that to return the garden 'into a proper state of keeping' would require 'a great deal of extra labour the first year', the trees in particular being in need of 'a great deal of attention'. They also recommended additional planting which would 'much ornament the place and make it like the other gardens'; their recommended list included 500 mixed dwarf roses, 50 standard roses, 100 dahlias and a collection of 'showy herbaceous plants such as hollyhocks, sweet williams, phlox's, verbinas, calceolareus, wallflowers etc'.[76] Minutes rarely disclose details of routine planting, for this was left to the discretion of individual gardeners. But floral display did form a part of most gardens as the firm's comments indicate, and the Central gardens were no exception. In 1829, for example, the gardener had been instructed to 'prepare suitable beds of mignonette, and to provide annuals, and a moderate collection of spring flowers but not to overload the border with them'.[77] And the cultivation of dahlias seems to have been particularly popular. More tender plants were nurtured with the aid of a hot-bed acquired in 1842.[78] James Dickson & Sons maintained the gardens from 1848 to 1853, after which a full-time gardener was reinstated.[79] Professional advice on the condition of the trees has always been readily taken.[80]

The Second World War saw removal of the railings along Heriot Row; a Nissen hut and Home Guard ammunition huts were erected and a static water tank was installed. But damage was contained by retaining the gardener.[81] An extensive programme of tree removal and renewal was carried out during the 1960s together with additional shrub, ground-cover and spring bulb planting in the early1980s.[82]

Treasure Island

It cost about £6,000 to form the Central Gardens; half that sum was spent on purchasing the land, the cope and rail costing over £1,000, and a similar amount went to forming and planting the interior. These large sums required money to be borrowed, and in 1829 the Clerk negotiated a loan of £2,000 with a Dr James Johnston of Kirkcaldy, repayable over a nine-year period.[83] Under the 1822 Act of Parliament, 53 residences are liable for assessment

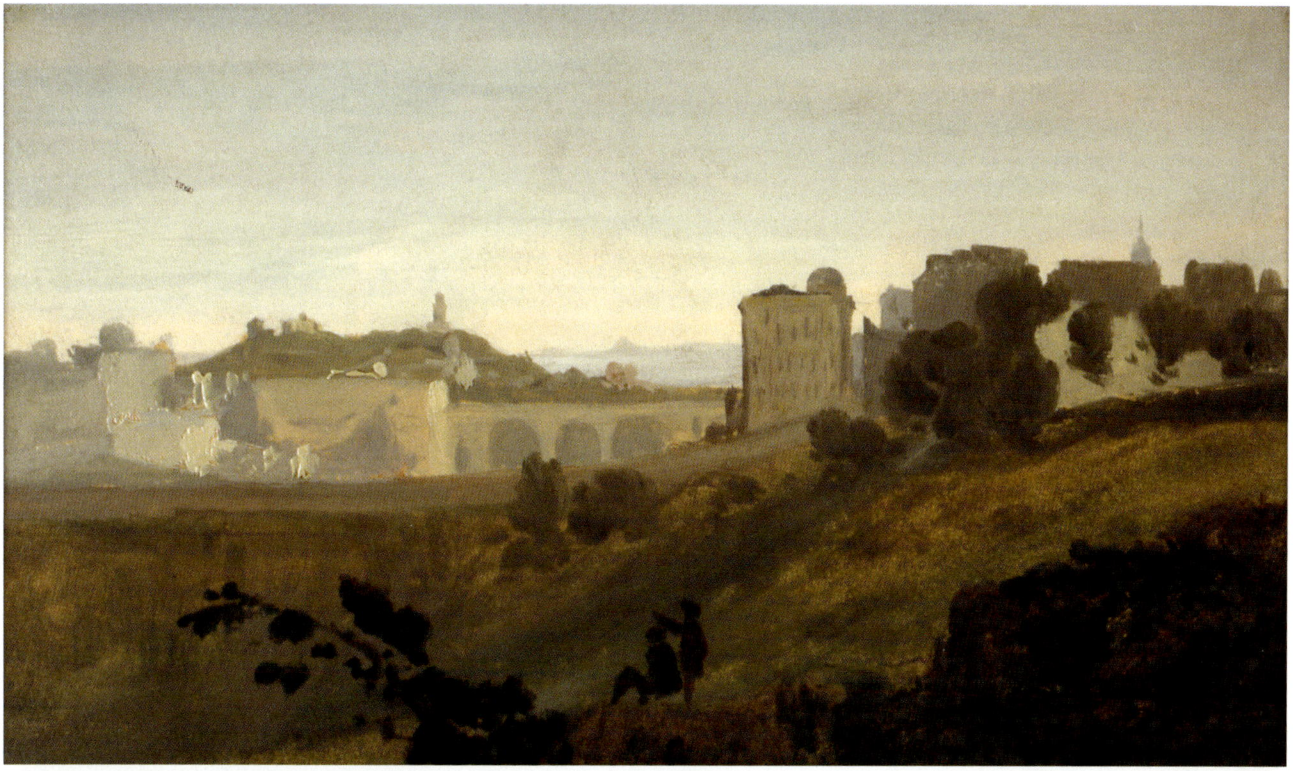

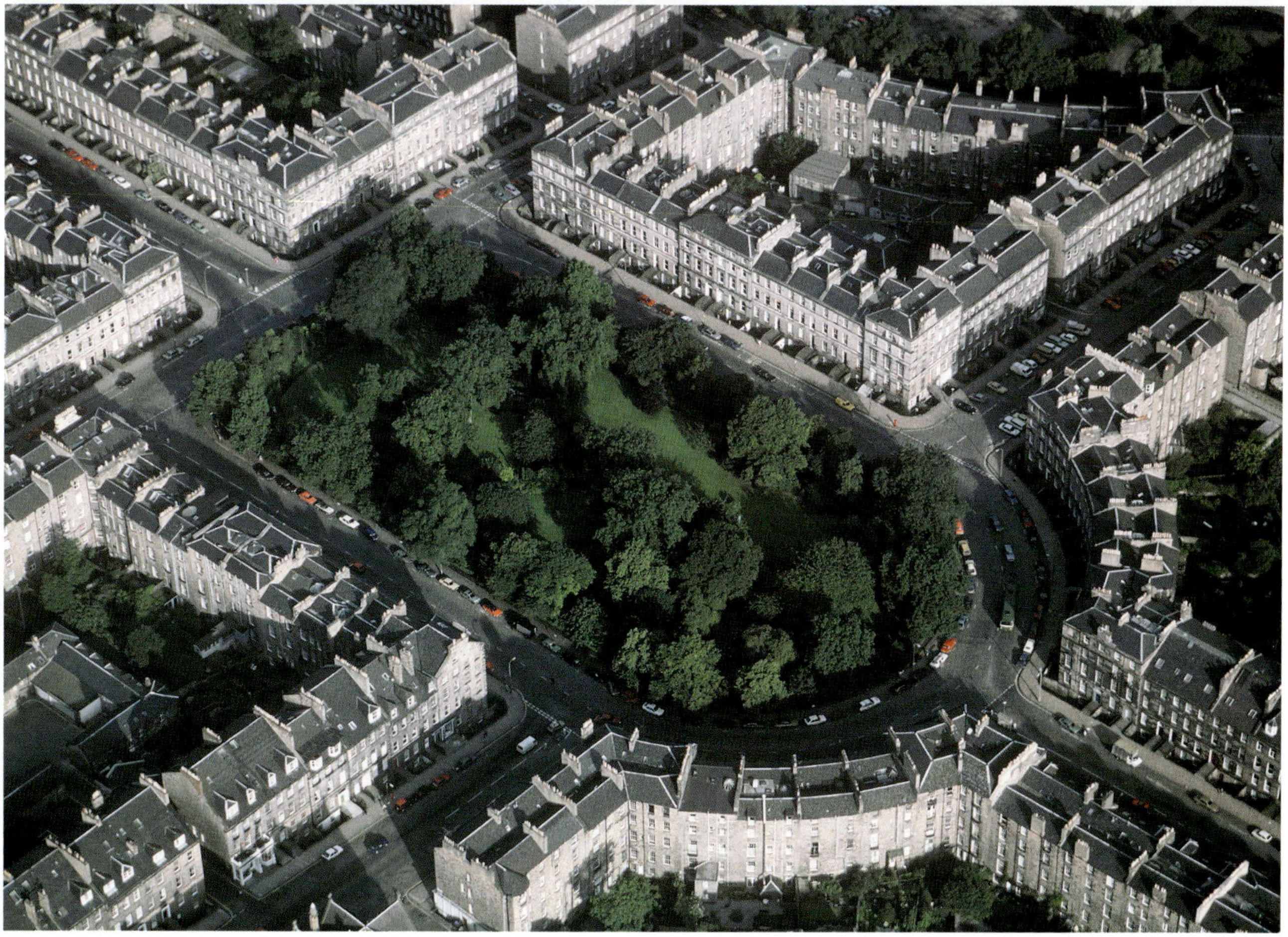

RIGHT.

The top terrace, Queen Street East. Completed in
1869, when the south bank was considerably
increased to allow an upper walk to be formed under
the direction of Robert Mathieson, architect.
(C. Byrom)

BELOW.

Queen Street Central. Andrew Wilson's design for
the Central Queen Street Gardens was very much
modelled on an idealised Classical landscape of a
kind he enjoyed painting when living in Italy. The
crude fencing marking off the children's play area
(far centre) would have caused him dismay.
(C. Byrom)

LEFT.
East Princes Street Gardens, the lower terrace walk, formed in 1850 to a design by David Cousin, Edinburgh's first named City Architect. The outline of the Scott Monument can be seen at the far eastern end of the upper terrrace. (C. Byrom)

BELOW.
A peep into Queen Street Central Gardens, with Heriot Row beyond. The garden, laid out by the architect Andrew Wilson, still retains several elements of his original design. (C. Byrom)

TOP.
Princes Street from the Mound, 1843, by Charles
Halkerston. This shows the panorama rotunda – a popular
entertainment – together with a travelling menagerie plus
elephant. Also in view is a corner of East Princes Street
Gardens, then rented out as nursery ground. The
beds of plants can be clearly seen, supervised by a gardener
with watering can at the ready and potential customers
looking around. By now the peripheral tree planting
has grown tall and thick.
(City of Edinburgh Museums and Galleries)

ABOVE.
A view from the north of the Castle Rock, c. 1860, by
David Octavius Hill, providing a bird's-eye view of West
Princes Street Gardens. A puff of smoke indicates the
passage of a train, boys play a shinty-type game on the
upper slopes, and in other parts men, women and children
perambulate or else gather to talk and pass the time of day.
The trees along Princes Street Gardens have become quite
dense, and apart from a central cluster the rest of the garden
consists of grass and pathways. Flower beds have long since
disappeared. (The Royal Bank of Scotland)

TOP.
Early spring, Charlotte Square Gardens, enlivened
with a colourful display of crocuses.
(The National Trust for Scotland)

BELOW.
Building of the Royal Institution, 1823, by Alexander
Nasmyth. This well illustrates the paraphernalia and mess
associated with building work throughout the New Town.
The East North Loch remains very unkempt but is soon to
undergo the deposition of large quantities of earth.
(National Galleries of Scotland)

TOP.
Aerial view taken from the west showing the New Town of
Edinburgh and the garden areas. (Patricia & Angus Macdonald)

RIGHT.
The Melville Monument, erected in St Andrew Square Gardens
and completed in 1827. (C. Byrom)

OPPOSITE TOP.
Oil painting by Andrew Wilson of the North Loch, *c.* 1820.
This picture dates from sometime after he became Master of
the Trustees' Academy in 1818, and prior to the laying out
of West Princes Street Gardens by his friend James Skene. It
reveals many of the subtle qualities of his work – his careful
composition and skilful use of colour finely balanced to
produce a work of serenity and tonal effect. The broad
horizontal line of the Mound can be made out as well as the
rocky outcrops along the southern bank of the North Loch.
Wilson's talents as a landscape artist were put to good effect
in his design for the Central and West Queen Street
Gardens. (In a private collection)

OPPOSITE BELOW.
Aerial view of Drummond Place Gardens.
(Patricia & Angus Macdonald)

ABOVE.
Springtime in Royal Circus Gardens. (S. Guthrie)

ABOVE.
Aerial view of Royal Circus Gardens showing the road snaking through the centre and the four divisions of garden ground. (Patricia & Angus Macdonald)

LEFT.
Moray Place Gardens has seen extensive thinning of its borders in recent years, allowing more light to penetrate and providing an opportunity to renew some of the plantings. (C. Byrom)

OPPOSITE TOP.
Aerial view showing the garden areas attached to Playfair's design for the lands east of Calton Hill. Regent Gardens looks jungle-like when compared to the barer, more exposed upper reaches of the hill. The strips of garden land opposite Regent Terrace and Carlton Terrace can be seen, as well as the broad band of London Road Gardens and the eastern tip of Hillside Crescent Gardens.
(Patricia & Angus Macdonald)

OPPOSITE BELOW.
Regent Gardens in winter with their dramatic views of Nelson's Monument and the unfinished National Monument. (J. Byrom)

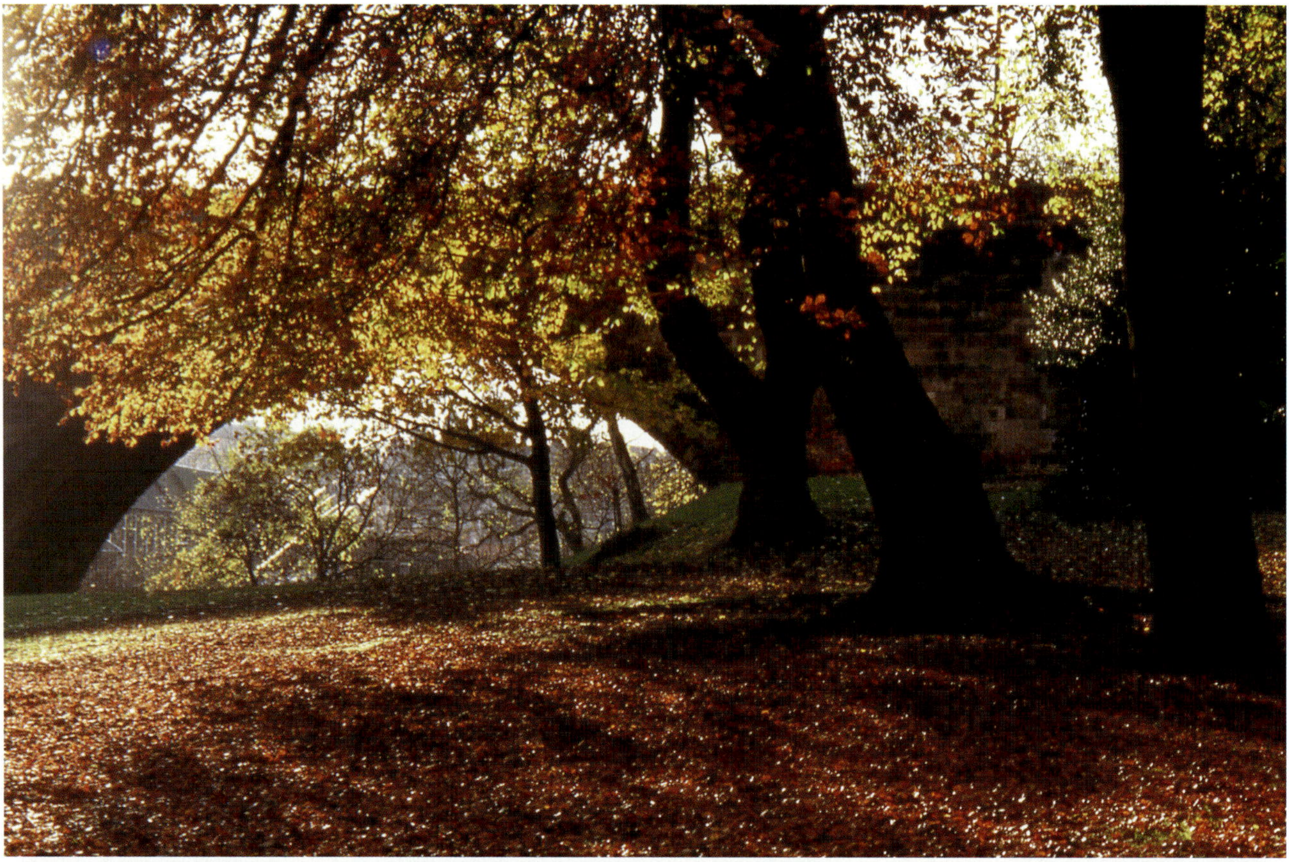

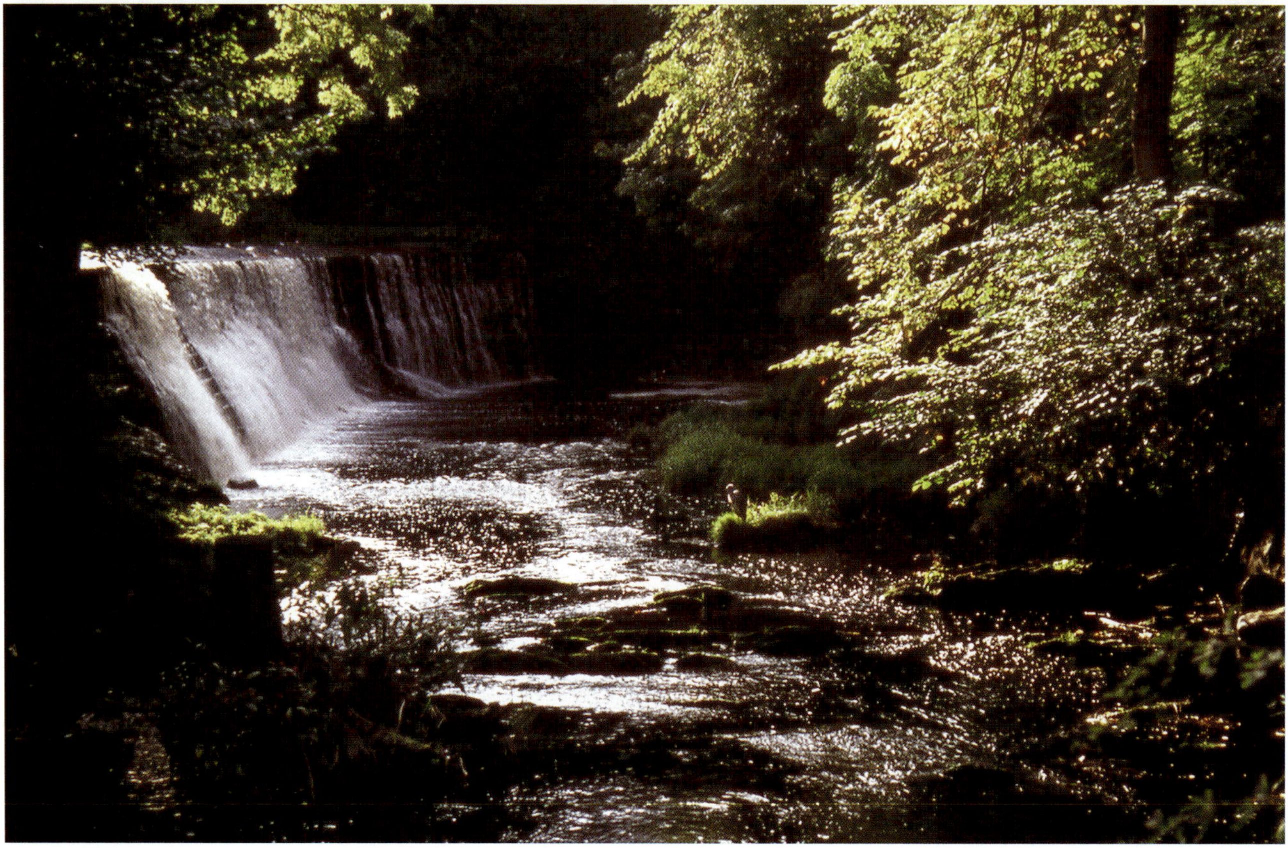

Dean Bridge from Moray Bank Gardens taken from the upper level walkway above the first portion of retaining arches. (M. Griffiths)

The lower portion of Dean Gardens with a view of 'the waterfall' together with heron. The New Town gardens provide a rich sanctuary for all kinds of wildlife. (M. Griffiths)

St Bernard's Well from Moray Bank Gardens (C. Byrom)

TOP LEFT.
Belgrave Crescent
Gardens. (C. Byrom)

TOP RIGHT.
View from the lower
reaches of Belgrave
Crescent Gardens
looking across to the
weir and the former
West Mill. (C. Byrom)

RIGHT.
Woodland pathway
at the west end of
Douglas Crescent
Gardens – a garden
rich in bird life.
(C. Byrom)

Photograph of Robert Louis Stevenson, one of the children to tread the gravel footpath of Central Queen Street Gardens and whose father Thomas was a Garden Commissioner. (City of Edinburgh Writers Museum)

(based on the former rating system); these originally were private family households, but much of the property in Queen Street has been converted to office use. Heriot Row retains its residential flavour although largely subdivided into flatted accommodation.

Rather smaller than its neighbours, the Central Gardens have tended to exercise rather stricter control over childrens' activities, hence the rule stipulating that they should 'carefully keep upon the gravel walks and grass', and the emphasis placed on good behaviour.[84] But tolerance and goodwill usually prevailed; for example, when James Dickson & Sons took charge, one of the requirements was that they took care to appoint a gardener 'of such disposition as to ensure kindness to the children'.[85] The best-known child to 'keep the gravel walk' was Robert Louis Stevenson whose family moved from Howard Place to 17 Heriot Row in 1857. His father followed family tradition to become a civil engineer; a well-respected man of deep religious conviction. He became a Garden Commissioner in 1860 and remained one for the following 22 years. Robert, a rather sickly child, was probably content to amuse himself in quiet imaginative play while pacing the garden and studying the pond life. *Treasure Island,* we know, took shape during a cold, wet summer holiday in Braemar[86] but who would wish to deny that its first glimmerings were drawn forth where farmer Wood's cattle pond had once been?[87]

Notes

1. James Skene of Rubislaw, *Reekieana*, (1836), typescript of manuscript. EPL, p. 10.
2. The Heriot's Hospital had previously tacked the land to Rachel Anderson, wife of Robert Robertson, a farmer in Broughton; the couple entered into a joint sub-tack with the Town on payment by the latter of £264 for 36 years.

3. TCM, 21 June 1786.

4. HHM, 17 April 1786, vol. 13, p. 36. See also, Heriot's Hospital Chartulary, vol. 5, pp. 122, 137.

5. Both men had been apprenticed to the banking firm of John Coutts & Co., founded in the 1730s. On the death of John Coutts, the principal partner in 1763, the two men were admitted to a share of the business. Sir James was then only 22 years old. A few years later they became partners and the name changed in 1773 to Sir William Forbes, J. Hunter & Co.

6. The foundation stone for the bridge was laid on 1 August 1785. Blair Street and Hunter Square, both off the South Bridge, were named in honour of Sir James Hunter Blair.

7. His wife was the eldest daughter of John Blair of Dunskey, Galloway; she succeeded to the estate in 1777 after the death of her several brothers. At this point, her husband, who was born the second son of Mr John Hunter, a merchant in Ayr, assumed the name of Blair. The Hunters were descended from a landed family in Ayrshire, a cadet branch of the Hunters of Hunterston, that had been established at Abbothill near Ayr since 1569 (information from James Hunter Blair). Portpatrick was once the chief port in Scotland for the Irish, exporting cattle and horses. Hostile weather conditions caused its demise and Stranraer took over in importance.

8. The roads were built between 1803 and 1805: several years later John Bell, WS, on behalf of Sir David Hunter Blair, wrote to the Heriot Hospital pointing out that although earlier complaints had been made, the Hospital had done nothing to make good the damage for which they were liable. HHM, 24 February 1817, vol. 21, pp. 100–101.

9. Colonel William Hunter of Brownhill, Sir James's elder brother, rallied to the family's support and made David his heir.

10. For useful information on the Hunter Blairs and Blairquhan see: Alistair Rowan, 'Blairquhan, Ayrshire, The home of Mr James Hunter Blair', Country Life, 19 April 1973.

11. Edinburgh Evening Courant, 17 March 1814.

12. Douglas M. Gunn, 'Scotch Washing', The Scots Magazine, vol. 146, No. 1 (January 1997), pp. 76–80.

13. Elizabeth Grant, Memoirs of a Highland Lady (Edinburgh, 1992), Vol. 2, p. 5.

14. Disposition Sir David Hunter Blair in favour of James Webster, 1 June 1820, Clerk's papers, Queen Street Central Gardens.

15. HHM, 9 February 1818, vol. 21, pp. 223–4; Webster also made a further offer in 1819; HHM, 15 April 1819, vol. 22, pp. 32–3.

16. Tack between James Webster and Robert Winter, 1821; Clerk's papers, Queen Street Central gardens. Winter took possession of the land from 19 December 1820.

17. Minute Book of the District Commissioners, Central District (1822–79); Minute, 30 July 1822.

18. Brough's office was at 4 St Andrew Street, while his home address was St Anne's Street – a five-storey tenement parallel to the North Bridge; so it would seem unlikely that he ever intended to use his land as private garden space.

19. Edinburgh Advertiser, 28 October 1788.

20. HHM, 22 February 1803, vol. 16, p. 175.

21. HHM, 27 February 1804, vol. 18, pp. 210–11; 25 January 1810, vol. 18, pp. 317–21.

22. John Ferrier's wife was the sister of Professor John Wilson, the Christopher North of Blackwood's Magazine; his sister wrote Marriage (1819), The Inheritance (1824) and Destiny

(1830). She was thought of as a Scottish Jane Austen, but not quite so good, though with a clever wit.

23. HHM, 7 June 1813, vol. 19, pp. 411–12.
24. HHM, 3 December 1813, vol. 20, pp. 91–4.
25. HHM, 15 April 1819, vol. 22, pp. 30–2.
26. Watson also requested the right to build a gardener's house; he offered to pay £300 for the land. See: HHM, 6 April 1819, vol. 22, p. 27.
27. John Laurie, 'Reminiscences of a Town Clerk' (ed. W. Forbes Gray), BOEC, vol. 14, 1925, p. 153.
28. Edinburgh Evening Courant, 1 July 1819; HHM, 19 April 1819, vol. 22, p. 40.
29. HHM, 27 July 1819, vol. 22, pp. 67–8.
30. HHM, 18 February 1820, vol. 22, pp. 153–6.
31. Charles Cuningham, 'Circular to proprietors of East Heriot Row and Queen Street between Hanover Street and Frederick Street', 29 February 1820, EPL.
32. HHM, 5 June 1820, vol. 22, pp. 226–7.
33. Minute Book, District Commissioners, Central District (1822–79), Minute 24 June 1822.
34. The other Commissioners were James Gordon, Advocate, 13 Heriot Row; John Borthwick, Advocate, 16 Queen Street; William Innes, WS, 13 Queen Street; and Thomas Corrie, 33 Queen Street. Donald Horne, WS, (clerk) lived at 17 Heriot Row.
35. Minute Book, District Commissioners, Central District (1822–79), Minute 26 April 1846. Cay was Sheriff of Linlithgow from 1822 to 1865.
36. Ibid., Minute 28 June, 1822.
37. Ibid., Minutes, 3 July 1822; 4 July 1822; 5 July 1822; 8 July 1822; 9 July 1822; 9 July 1822; 10 July 1822; 30 July 1822, 3 October 1822.
38. The Commissioners had first consulted with the Western District Commissioners to see what method they were adopting, and as a result fixed on the police rating list as the simplest and fairest.
39. Minute Book, District Commissioners, Central District (1822–79), Minute 22 November 1822.
40. Ibid., Minutes, 23 December 1822; 2 April 1823.
41. Ibid., Minutes, 11 January 1823.
42. Ibid., Minute, 28 April 1823; which contains a draft printed copy of the Report to the Proprietors, which was approved at the meeting.
43. Rev. Thomas Thomson (ed.), A Biographical Dictionary of Eminent Scotsmen, new edition, vol. 3, (London, 1870), pp. 536–7; this provides the most detailed and accurate account of Wilson's life so far found.
44. Obituary, Mr Wilson ARSA, The Art Journal, vol. 3, published by George Virtue, (London 1851), p. 85. This obituary 'by one who knew him intimately', (David Octavius Hill?) provides useful comment about Wilson and is likely to be reasonably accurate, having been written not long after his death.
45. The Scotsman, 24 March 1821.
46. Peter J.M. Mc Ewan, Dictionary of Scottish Art and Architecture (Woodbridge, 1994), p. 609.
47. Usually described as an old Scottish family, they did in fact originate from Cumberland.
48. Andrew Wilson's adventures have all the ingredients of some extravagant thriller. He was, for example, arrested by the French at Turin, sent to Verdun as a prisoner-of-war, made an

escape, was later pushed off a cliff side by his guide, had his fall broken by a fig tree and was then rescued and cared for by some monks from a nearby convent.

49. NLS, Manuscript 3836, which contains a list of accounts kept by Andrew Wilson between 1803 and 1805.

50. *Edinburgh Evening Courant,* 1 January 1814.

51. Lord Kames was also closely involved with the early stages in setting up Edinburgh's first New Town.

52. The other applicants were Alexander Nasmyth (who had also tried for the post in 1796 on the death of David Allan), William Allan (who was Wilson's successor in 1826), John Watson, James Howe, Donald McLeod (all from Edinburgh); Alexander Carse (then in England), and Robert Munro (from Montrose). See John Mason, 'The Edinburgh School of Design', *BOEC* vol. 27 (1949), pp. 67–96; and SRO, WRH, NG1/1/34, Minute Book of the Board of Manufacturers, 16 December 1817; 20 January 1818; 3 February 1818.

53. James Caw, the art historian, held a somewhat jaundiced view about Wilson, claiming that he had no marked success as a teacher, and that his painting of Scottish scenery was 'wanting in virility and artificial in effect'.

54. The Institution had 24 directors, headed by the Duke of Argyll.

55. *The Art Journal,* 1851, op. cit.

56. The King, it appeared, wished to 'judge the state of Art in this country'.

57. Another matter brought Skene and Wilson together at this period, namely, the proposal to build at the foot of the Mound a building capable of accommodating the Trustees' Academy, the Royal Society, the Institution of Fine Arts and the Society of Antiquaries.

58. Minute Book, District Commissioners, Central District (1822–79), Minute, 2 April 1823.

59. Ibid., Minute, 20 February 1823.

60. Ibid., Minute, 7 March 1823; one pump well (no longer in use) still stands close to the eastern entrance on the Heriot Row side.

61. Ibid., Minute, 2 April 1823.

62. Ibid., Minute, 17 May 1823.

63. Ibid., Minute, 17 May 1823; eight shillings (40 p) a week had been paid to the most experienced labourers.

64. Ibid., Minute, 21 July 1823; 8 December 1823.

65. Ibid., Minute, 30 March 1824.

66. Ibid., Minute, 7 March 1823.

67. Ibid., Minute, 30 March 1824, on which the following information is based.

68. Wilson's tool-house (which proved to be a rather damp space) is now secured by an iron gate and shelters a memorial stone to Lord Dunpark, one of the Commissioners in the 1970s and 1980s who did a great deal for the garden's improvement during his term of office.

69. Wilson's brother-in-law had been one of the judges of the Supreme Court in Calcutta, and left a large fortune. In Italy the family lived for periods at Rome, Florence and Genoa – their final destination.

70. Charles Heath Wilson trained as an artist by his father; he was also involved with the Institution for the Encouragement of Fine Art, and later become a teacher at the Trustees' Academy. In 1849 he was made head of the new Glasgow School of Design. He spent his last years in Italy.

71. Minute Book of District Commissioners, Central District (1822–79), Minute, 23 February 1829.

72. Ibid., Minute, 17 February 1875. See also, James McNab, 'Our Town Trees: The Queen Street Gardens', *The Scottish Farmer*, May 1865.

73. Ibid., Minute, 27 February 1837; 2 March 1837.

74. Ibid., Circular, dated 1 May 1847.

75. Ibid., Minute, 26 April 1846.

76. Ibid., Letter from James Dickson & Sons, 32 Hanover Street, 5 August 1848.

77. Ibid., Minute, 23 February 1829.

78. Ibid., Accounts, 31 March 1842.

79. Ibid., Minute of General Meeting of Proprietors, 7 November 1854.

80. City Superintendent of Parks – A.A. Macleod, in 1881 and 1882; and Mr Jeffreys in 1885. In 1930 Mr Imrie, forester, was consulted. More recently the Royal Botanic Garden has given advice and the Scottish Woodland Owners' Association Ltd.

81. Minute Book of District Commissioners, Central District (1880–1953), Minute, 26 November 1947; 7 December 1948.

82. Dr John Byrom acted as landscape consultant, and the work owed much to the energy of the late Lord Dunpark. Another Commissioner to give long and useful service was the Hon. Lord Sands who died in 1934, having played an active part for 30 years.

83. Minute Book of District Commissioners, Central District (1822–79).

84. Sports and games of a more organised nature were rather discouraged during the last century due to one of the Commissioners, Alexander Stevenson.

85. Minute Book of District Commissioners, Central District (1822–79), letter from James Dickson & Sons, 12 August 1848.

86. See article: 'Under a wide and starry sky', *Daily Telegraph Colour Supplement*, No. 519 (November 8, 1974); and based on extracts from James Pope-Hennessy, *Robert Louis Stevenson* (London, 1974).

87. The pond is still a distinctive and attractive feature of the gardens but has caused some minor problems over the years.

The Allen family in their Edinburgh Queen Street drawing room, sketched by John Harden, husband of daughter Jessy. The family were the first to buy a garden plot within the western section, although they failed to make much use of it. (Harden Drawings, Trustees of NLS)

CHAPTER 10

WEST QUEEN STREET
5.70 acres (2.28 ha)

After drawing a sketch from our window I went this morning to Nasmyth's to ask his opinion of it. He said it was very well done and advised me to try and finish it on canvas.

Journal of Janet 'Jessy' Allan, 1802[1]

When Jessy Allan (1776–1836) sketched the view from the upper window of her father's house at 28 Queen Street, before her lay the rough unkempt space of what was later to become the Central Queen Street Garden, with a row of nearly completed houses beyond 'just under Lady Blair's field so that our situation is still very open for a town'. One year later the western half of Heriot Row was advertised for feuing[2] but it too was kept at arm's length, separated by a similar strip of land which eventually became the West Queen Street Garden. This portion, like the others along Queen Street, first became established as private gardens, the Allans buying the first plot.

The Land becomes Divided

Sometime during the late 1780s the Allan family had moved from George Street to Queen Street. Robert Allan (1745–1818), Jessy's father, was a banker (at one time in partnership with David Steuart) and a newspaper proprietor, a well-off and respected citizen who served on the Town Council as well as being active in the Chamber of Commerce.[3] In 1789 Allan approached Heriot's Hospital, 'craving a feu of 1 and a half or 2 acres [0.6 ha or 0.8 ha] of ground for a garden to the west adjoining Frederick Street'.[4] Soon afterwards the Hospital received two further requests for land within this section. One was from the Honourable Alexander Gordon of Rockville (1739–1792), third son of the second Earl of Aberdeen and then a Senator of the College of Justice. Lord Rockville, a tall, handsome man was affectionately nicknamed 'Lang Sandy Gordon';[5] he wanted two acres [0.8 ha] or so 'nearly opposite' the house he was having built at 64 Queen Street. The other was from Robert Brown, WS, of Kirklands (1758–1812) for 'a small piece' of about half an acre [0.2 ha] facing his Queen Street residence.[6] The Hospital agreed to sell one acre [0.4 ha] to Robert Allan for £32; an adjoining half-acre [0.2 ha] to Robert Brown for £18; and two acres [0.8 ha] 'eastwards of the old road leading to Stockbridge' to Lord Rockville for £72, and under the same conditions as set out in Baron Ord's charter of 1769. Thomas Wood, the long-standing tenant whose farmhouse stood within Lord Rockville's feu, was allowed to 'possess the house and offices during his life'.[7]

One acre remained to the east of Rockville's feu. By June 1790 three applications had been made for it: one from Alexander Wallace, a banker living at 29 North Frederick Street; another from Alexander Young, WS (1759–1842), 48 Queen Street (only son of the Reverend William Young, Minister of Hutton); and the last from Dr Deans. Rather than favour anyone, the Hospital decided to sell by auction. When the sale took place on 2 March 1791 in the Exchange Coffee House, the successful bidder at £72 (double the upset price) was no less than ex-Lord Provost David Steuart.[8] As we already know, he owned two other gardens at the east end of Queen Street, besides land to the north. Was he being driven by greed, speculative over-drive, or was he simply cherishing a dream to move closer to his old friend Robert Allan? We shall never know.[9] These various transactions produced three feu charters, each dated 17 April 1791, and made out to: Alexander Gordon (Lord Rockville), David Steuart and Robert Allan. Allan's portion was increased by half an acre [0.2 ha] on Robert Brown's withdrawal following his removal to North Hanover Street.[10] They were the last ones to be granted for open space along Queen Street and preceded by several months the first tentative plans for developing a second New Town.

In spite of this competition for garden plots, nothing either ornamental or functional was immediately forthcoming. Indeed little happened during the next five years apart from a complete change in ownership. David Steuart, already beset with financial worries, quickly sold his middle portion to Alexander Young who had earlier registered an interest. Farmer Wood had used this section for grazing cattle and horses and it contained a stable, cow byre and pump well.[11] Its rough state probably explains why the ground remained as pasturage. In 1796 Young had the chance to buy Robert Allan's adjacent and rather larger plot, and one better related to his own dwelling. Allan had enclosed the area with a stone wall but had done little else, his brief ownership, perhaps indicative of the novelty of possession, having worn off rather quickly, although the family remained in Queen Street. Young suffered no such misgivings, and soon set about having the ground laid out. Ainslie's plan of 1804 shows a neatly formed garden, with a serpentine path around the perimeter, planted borders and the interior grassed. A gardener's house was built in the north-west corner. By the time of Kirkwood's plan of 1819, the central area had become divided into vegetable, fruit and flower beds and the gardener's corner had been extended to include space for clothes' drying and hot-house accommodation.

Portrait of the Hon. Alexander Gordon of Rockville, owner of the two-acre plot 'nearly opposite' the house he was having built at 64 Queen Street, Edinburgh. (Kay's *Portraits*, 1877, ECL)

Left: Sale of the remaining plot of land in Queen Street West (*Edinburgh Advertiser*, 25 February 1791). Right: Lord Rockville's house and garden advertised for sale (*Edinburgh Advertiser*, 15 May 1795).

Young sold his surplus ground to Sir James Grant (1738–1811), who had become owner of Lord Rockville's house at 64 Queen Street together with the two-acre [0.8 ha] plot. The latter had been advertised for sale either separately or with the house and was described as containing 'a large hot-house'.[12] From now on the two portions remained under the one ownership. Rockville's move to Queen Street had been brief; barely had he sampled his fine house and garden when a tumble during wintry weather caused a broken bone and consequent fever from which he never recovered.[13] His widow Anne, Countess of Dumfries, sold the property in 1796 to Sir James Grant whose town house had been at the foot of the Canongate. Grant's loyalties really lay with his Highland estate, he being Chief of Clan Grant and Lord Lieutenant of Inverness-shire. His Speyside tenantry referred to him as 'the good Sir James', for although promoting agricultural improvement he remained committed to his tenants' welfare, inspiring universal support when raising a regiment of Fencibles on declaration of war with France in 1793.[14] Sir James, however, was soon to apply his improving zeal to his Edinburgh property. One of his first tasks was to remove the high stone wall along Queen Street (similar ones remained on the south and west sides[15]) to be replaced with a cope stone and elegant railing. The improved appearance was remarkable. When, for example, 50 Queen Street was advertised for sale in 1800, pride of place was given to this new local amenity:

> The advantages these premises enjoy from the situation are too well known and too much prized to require any aid from an advertisement; but it may be just mentioned in general, that the street at this place is finished off to the north with a handsome iron rail which is not only a great ornament but preserves the full view even to the parlour windows.[16]

Sir James Grant of Grant with his Regiment, the Strathspey or Grant Fencibles, and new owner of Rockville's house and garden (his brother had been involved with arrangements for the levelling of Charlotte Square Gardens in 1803). (Kay's *Portraits*, 1877, ECL)

The middle strip continued as rough pasturage, a useful facility for a household keeping several horses,[17] while the western end was laid out in a practical, well-ordered way. A hot-house had been added in Rockville's time. This survived until 1825 and stood close to the centre, forming the focal point around which the rest of the garden was organised. Grant seems to have added further buildings. The layout was similar to a kitchen-cum-walled garden, a place to take leisurely exercise but at the same time productive of fruits and vegetables; and with a gardener's house in the north-west corner. Farmer Wood's orchard was retained on the south side. Several rows of apple trees were later incorporated into the pleasure ground and provided fruit up until the 1850s.[18] Of Wood's farmhouse nothing more is heard.

Both Young and Grant carefully tended their gardens. There was one occasion for alarm, however, in 1803 when building plots along West Heriot Row were advertised for feuing. The two garden owners feared that access from this side might become denied once the new roadway was made level with East Heriot Row. Meetings with Heriot's Hospital did nothing to allay anxieties. On the day of the sale Young and Grant both lodged a formal protest, and the auction was hurriedly cancelled. Court proceedings went in favour of the Hospital although liability for any damage was made their responsibility.[19] Two years later Sir James retired to his Speyside castle and the family subsequently offered to sell their Edinburgh property to Heriot's Hospital; £5,000 was asked for the Queen Street house, and £3,000 for the garden and park, but the Hospital expressed no interest.[20] Eventually in 1810 the house and ground were sold together, to Francis Charteris (1772–1853), 8th Earl of Wemyss and March, who a few years before had moved from the Old Town to larger accommodation at West Lauriston.

A wealthy man of refined tastes,[21] he also owned two country estates, Amisfield House outside Haddington and Gosford House close to Longniddry. The Queen Street house remained the family's town house up until 1888.[22] It has been discovered that in 1816 the Earl of Wemyss invited the Caledonian Horticultural Society, of which he was President, 'to perform at his expense, in his excellent garden situated nearly in the centre of the New Town of Edinburgh, any experiments which . . . can be there properly accomplished'. The Society at this time were eager to set up their own 'experimental garden' but lacked the necessary finance. As an interim measure they relied on the generousity of some of their members to provide space for such activites. One of the 'experiments' carried out in the Earl's Queen Street Garden was the trial of some mountain rice from Nepal received from Dr Nathaniel Wallich (1786–1854), botanist to the East India Company in Bengal and later to become director of the Calcutta Botanical Garden; this type of rice could be grown without irrigation and 'might with advantage be cultivated in many of the hills of Scotland'. Other trials followed and later in the same year the Society's minutes record that the Fruit Committee having received, 'a basket of uncommonly fine Morella cherries . . . produced from a branch of a tree reflected from a north to a south wall in the Earl of Wemyss's garden, at Queen Street, Edinburgh', recommended that 'a medal should be awarded to Mr Thomas Dewar, gardener to his Lordship, on the ground not only of the excellence of the fruit, but for his great attention in conducting experiments suggested by the Society.'

The Earl's involvement with the Horticultural Society and his willingness for them to make use of his ground probably explains why he later appeared reluctant to part with his garden for pleasure-ground purposes.[23]

From Private Plots to Pleasure Gardens

Had all the private garden areas along Queen Street fared as well as this particular group, the impetus to form communal pleasure grounds might never have occurred. The residents at the western end nevertheless supported the idea once it began to develop momentum. One in particular – the Right Honourable James Wedderburn, Solicitor General for Scotland – made a significant contribution by helping to shape the legal framework behind the 1822 Act of Parliament.[24] The 'Western District', created as a result, included the whole of West Heriot Row, and the section of Queen Street from the corner of Frederick Street up to and including 64 Queen Street, the land between becoming known as the 'West Queen Street Gardens' or the West District. Owners of property whose windows fronted these two streets were deemed proprietors and made responsible for the costs of forming and maintaining the gardens. In 1827 the Act was extended to include property in Wemyss Place.

Nearly all the newly elected Commissioners were from legal backgrounds although James Scott, the first convener, was an accountant – a useful qualification, bearing in mind all the financial transactions ahead.[25] William Bell, WS, the long-serving clerk to the East

Queen Street Gardens and well versed in local affairs, was appointed clerk and cashier. Informal discussions had already taken place with Alexander Young about acquiring his ground, so negotiations began with him. Young was now over 60 and obviously finding his garden too large for his requirements; in a letter to Bell he observed that should his offer be rejected, 'it is my purpose to carry into effect a plan of my own during the ensuing spring by curtailing the size of my garden'.[26] He wanted £3,000 for the land with entry by Martinmas (November) 1822, although 'reserving the crop in the garden and the young nursery to be removed in the spring'. This suggests that some nursery firm or gardener was already making use of the ground. Thirty years before the land had fetched £54, so not surprisingly the Commissioners considered the price 'much too high'. Bell suggested offering £2,300 to match the rate paid for Rolland's garden at the east end.[27] Young, however, remained adamant; and 'in order to prevent any further dispute' the proprietors, when they met at the Waterloo Hotel in December 1822, sanctioned payment of the full amount.[28]

Bell appeared more apprehensive in his approach to Lord Weymss, knowing that the Commissioners were not inclined to be over-generous, yet appreciating that the ground was of considerable size and still in use by the family.[29] A delicate situation was approached by emphasising the worthiness of the cause, rather verbosely expressed in a letter sent to Lord Weymss in May 1823. It ran as follows:

> Holding however that the elegant embellishment of Lord Wemyss's garden may save expense in the adoption of our general plan we shall take the liberty of offering for it a sum of £4,000, and for the park which is little more than an acre on which no improvement has taken place the sum of £1,000. We do so both on account of the importance of this great object to the unrivalled elegance that this general plan will produce if carried fully into effect and that we are particularly called upon to follow this mode in treating with Lord Wemyss who we are convinced will only dispose of this property from a desire to adorn the city not from the amount of any price whatever, but still in suggesting so great a sacrifice to family comfort, we are bound to offer the highest sum that our Trust will allow.

It yielded a very curt response. Mr Bell was informed through the agent that Lord Wemyss 'was not inclined to part with his garden or field opposite to Queen Street'.[30] Matters were temporarily put on hold while the Commissioners concentrated their energies on transforming Mr Young's garden into the first section of pleasure ground

The neighbouring Central Queen Street Gardens, already a step ahead, were tapped for advice. Little, however, could be done until the removal of Young's nursery plants, which was delayed until March 1823 owing to the season being 'so far backward'.[31] First priority was to have the ground enclosed with cope stone and rail. Design details had been supplied by the Central District and the Commissioners hoped that this, combined with recycling material from the old walls, would reduce costs. It was a shock therefore when Mr Dinn, builder, put in a comparatively higher estimate for enclosing the north and south sides. Other estimates produce a wide range of prices, the lowest being by Ralph Buchan at £217. The Clerk was asked to 'enquire into his character ' and, if satisfactory, to accept his offer, the work 'to be begun instantly and completed with the least possible delay'. Apart from a few minor changes the railings were to be 'of the same dimensions, pattern, quality and workmanship as those in front of Hillside Crescent ' (by Playfair) and finished with 'three coats of oil or lead paint, green in colour'. A little later Thomas Brown, City Superintendent, was consulted about adjustments to the wall along Heriot Row. With the erection of the new railings, the high stone wall on the east side looked out of place, and therefore it was decided to extend the railings at an extra cost of £150.

The next step was to have an embankment formed on the north and east sides running the same height as street level and tapering gradually inwards. Time was opportune for 'it is understood that earth and rubbish can at present be obtained from the Royal Circus for nothing'; and therefore 'no delay should take place in arranging for Mr Young as to breaking open the wall for this purpose'. Soon a skilled gardener would be needed, and the Clerk was asked to be on the look out 'for a proper person to act as gardener who must be well qualified to attend to and give his assistance in making the necessary alterations and improvements'. Once more the experience of the Central Gardens was tapped, and their contractor, Richard Walker, invited to meet with the Commissioners. Walker's ability to handle several projects concurrently must have impressed, for Royal Circus and Drummond Place Gardens were also under his charge. His skill at juggling these several commitments was certainly aided by his system of commandeering other family members. Without further ado Walker was appointed at one guinea a week to undertake the superintendence of the operations in this district, of employing labourers, and removing the good soil along the north side and part of the east and receiving earth to complete the bank along these two sides and replacing the good soil again. There was no point, however, in organising a team of labourers without an overall design to work to. The Clerk was therefore instructed to request Mr Wilson to furnish them with a plan for laying out the grounds calculated so as to admit of its extension in the event of the ground to the westward being acquired, and to request him at the same time to give them a slight sketch of such a bridge as might suffice for enabling the two districts to communicate underneath the street.

Andrew Wilson's Involvement

Mr Wilson, as we now know, was Andrew Wilson, the landscape artist and Manager of the Trustees' Academy. His 'professional skill and good taste' were already transforming the Central Queen Street Gardens from wasteland into a carefully composed layout, drawing inspiration from the classical landscapes he so much admired and enjoyed painting. What was his contribution to the West Queen Street Gardens? The ground was in a fairly sorry state, most of the planting had been removed, the ground trampled by workmen busy with the railings and, apart from some trees around the edges, there was little of note. The challenge was not only to design a new garden but one capable of later extension if and when the Earl of Wemyss's land was added.

Within two weeks of being approached, Andrew Wilson had visited the site and produced a plan. On 22 March 1823 he presented his design to the Commissioners who 'approved generally of it, with these exceptions. That the principal walks shall be 10 feet [3 m] broad, that the walks in the south east corner shall be done away, and the space planted up, and the south west walk also planted up'. Spring was imminent and it was with a sense of urgency that the Commissioners agreed to direct Walker under Mr Wilson's superintendence to plant all the banks, as soon as possible, with such forest trees and shrubs especially evergreens as are most suitable to the situation, and to execute with the utmost dispatch such portions of the walks, and alterations of the surface as must be done before the trees are planted, and to plant trees and shrubs throughout the grounds under Mr Wilson's directions.

No other details are given, and no sketches or drawings have survived; but the adopted design was indicated in Knox's plan of Edinburgh published in 1824. This is the only known plan showing the layout prior to extension in 1825. It shows an outer border of trees and shrubs with abutting footpath, and the inner area crossed with walks (carefully placed to allow for later extension), with clumps of trees and shrubs. All matters connected with the design were now referred to Wilson. There was, for example, quite a lot of discussion about the position of the main gates on the north and south sides, the Commissioners finally agreeing to place them in the centre of the rail, 'or as nearly so as Mr Wilson shall find to be conformable to his plans and to the general plans for the garden'.

Before the end of May 1823 work on the footpaths was under way, with gravel being supplied by Henry's pit at Bellevue. Before the Commissioners disappeared for the summer Walker was 'urged the necessity of dispatch in finishing the work and seeing that the men are attentive in their work'. They returned to find the garden practically finished. Garden seats had been bought, together with a garden roller, and rope for securing the trees. And the workforce had been paid off. Accounts for September 1823 show that £237 had been spent on Walker and his labourers, which on a rough calculation would indicate that around 20 men had been employed over a six-month period. Payments for earth, gravel, turf, trees, plants and manure amounted to £134.[32]

All too conscious of a shrinking workload, Walker applied to the Commissioners offering to continue superintendence of the garden: 'I would esteem it a particular favour should the proprietors be pleased to entrust me with the keeping of it in good order', he wrote, and 'as to the yearly allowance of keeping the same I refer to the proprietors what they may deem adequate for the purpose'.[33] The Commissioners recognised the advantage of having an experienced gardener to hand, but felt this might be better combined 'with the benefit of an operative person being constantly engaged'. Another possibility was to combine operations with the Central District, until it was discovered that they had already engaged a full-time gardener. In the event Richard Walker was given 'the entire charge of keeping the gardens in most proper prefect order' for £35 a year on condition that he supplied 'a decent steady civil person as gardener', in constant attendance and performing 'all the duties of a garden keeper'. These responsibilities included locking and unlocking the gates, excluding strangers and preventing damage 'to plants or otherwise'; he was, however, allowed to do occasional work on the back greens of local houses. Walker's margin of profit must have been slim and nepotism was probably his means of survival. His brother Archibald was put in charge and on his death in 1834 was succeeded by another brother, James.[34]

After a demanding twelve months, requiring the Commissioners to meet on nineteen separate occasions, procedures for opening the gardens were well advanced; keys were available for distribution, and a set of rules and regulations was drafted early in 1824.

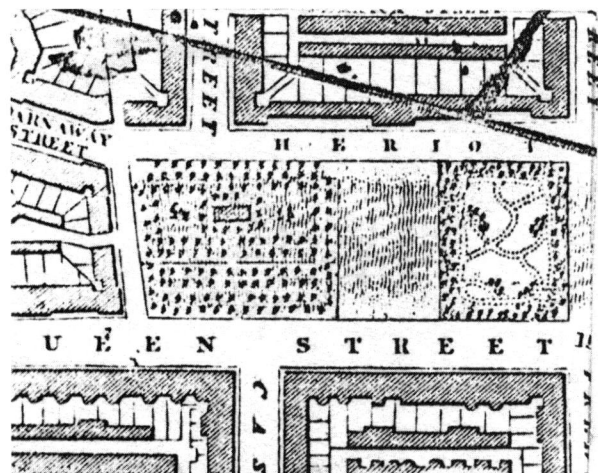

Knox's Plan, 1824, showing the newly made section of pleasure garden as designed by Andrew Wilson.

Soon the proprietors were able to sample the new garden. This was a testing time for the gardener, mindful of the new planting; by mid-April he had 'judged it necessary to prevent the children from running on the walks and grass till these acquire firmness'.[35] The next year in comparison was relatively uneventful; the Commissioners met only six times, and Mr Bell was mostly taken up sorting out administrative matters including payment of outstanding accounts. One of these was to Andrew Wilson who had been asked to forward his bill 'for laying out the ground': a source of mild embarrassment, as he explained in his reply:

> He wished rather to be considered as wishing to forward so laudable a public improvement than as making professional charge. That unasked he would not have rendered an account, and now would wish it to stand on this footing. That as he had acted on the same principle with the centre district and had accepted 25 guineas from them, and as the ground was about one half the size the sum should probably be fixed at the corresponding amount of £12. 12s.[36]

Purchase of Lord Wemyss's Land

Towards the end of 1824 a fresh attempt was made to acquire the Earl of Wemyss's land, and on this occasion the response was more encouraging.[37] By then the Caledonian Horticultural Society were engaged in setting up their Experimental Garden at Herd's Hill, Inverleith, adjacent to the Botanical Garden and no longer needing space in the Earl's Queen Street Garden. The Commissioners were informed that Lord Wemyss 'had received two several liberal offers for the purchase of his whole property in Queen Street', but that he wished 'to give the Commissioners first chance of securing the garden and park for the public'. The threat of competition sharpened resolve, and an immediate offer of £6,080 was made – 'the same rate paid for Mr Young's garden', and well over the previous bid. Early in 1825 the Commissioners heard that their offer had been accepted, but on condition that should the ground cease to be a public garden, his Lordship would have the right to re-purchase and at the same price. The Commissioners would have preferred an independent valuation under these circumstances, but Lord Wemyss claimed that 'the turning of the small pasture field into pleasure garden will no doubt cost some expense, but in the very improbable event of the clause of pre-emption coming into operation . . . it will cost Lord Wemyss and his successors a great deal more to convert his garden into a private and productive one than every expense now to be conveyed on the small field'. Rather than take issue over what was basically a trivial matter the Commissioners accepted without more ado.

Soon afterwards the proprietors gave their official blessing. Altogether the ground making up the West Queen Street Gardens cost the proprietors £9,000, making them the most expensive of the New Town gardens. Reassurance was offered on this occasion by explaining to proprietors that the recent acquisition was 'favourably situated and will cost comparatively little in laying it out . . . and the value of the materials on the property much more considerable than those of Mr Young's'. In addition the Earl of Wemyss had agreed to the inclusion of his house within the Act of Parliament, and the Commissioners 'entertained expectations' that proprietors from other streets might follow suit. It was also hoped to raise money by selling a strip on the west side to complete the new roadway (Wemyss Place).

Preparations to Unite the Ground

The first and most expensive task was to have the railings extended along Queen Street and West Heriot Row; Mr Buchan undertook the work at a cost of £700.[38] Next, the ground had to be cleared of 'stones, iron and other items' – materials from the former old railings (dating back to Sir James Grant's time), stone walls along West Heriot Row and the demolished hot-house. A public sale of the materials raised a useful £200. The gardener's house remained, and was occupied by Archibald Walker and his family. Richard Walker was no longer involved, his contract having terminated in November 1824.

Once the ground was cleared, attention turned to the interior; and the minutes record the following item of information: 'resolve to employ a person to superintend the operations and having considered Mr Neill's letter, approve of Mr Niven and direct the Secretary to see him and learn what are his terms, and if he has been in the habit of making out plans to desire him to furnish one.'[39]

Mr Neill was most certainly Patrick Neill, the printer and publisher, well known for his scientific and horticultural interests, and a stalwart member of the Caledonian Horticultural Society. He later became involved with East Princes Street, and the Regent, Carlton and Royal Terrace Gardens. Richard Niven, Neill's protégé, was a gardener based at Allanfield on the Ferry Road. But this tantalising piece of information leads no further. The rest of the minutes for 1825 remain silent on the subject of the laying out of this section. It is tempting to think that the cost and effort of having such an extensive area enclosed sapped energy for anything else. But this is quite erroneous, as a later financial inventory shows. In the first nine months of 1825 payments amounting to £1,268 were made for 'levelling, enclosing and laying out'. If we deduct the £700 spent on the railings, this leaves a sizable £568 for the two other items. The money, as before, would have been spent on employing a superintendent (Niven perhaps), labourers, and on items such as earth, gravel, turf, trees, shrubs and other planting. Other substantial sums were spent the following year (£368), and even the year after (£189). So a lot was going on even if for the most part it went unrecorded.

There is no specific reference to the garden until March 1826, when the minutes note that the Commissioners met and 'approve of proceedings in laying out the ground'. Again details are frustratingly absent although arrangements for key rental are referred to, indicating that by then the garden was practically complete.[40] Not until near the end of 1826 is light shed on what 'proceedings' consisted of, when it is minuted that the Commissioners considered 'Mr Wilson's charge', and authorised the cashier 'to settle the amount claimed by Mr Wilson for behoof of his brother Mr A. Wilson'.[41] In a later financial review there is listed against September 1833: 'Account to Mr Wilson for making a plan of the garden and superintending the laying out – £31. 10.' (i.e. 30 guineas, a seemingly delayed payment). So while details elude us, the evidence is firm that Andrew Wilson completed the design for the whole of the West Queen Street Gardens. Wilson had been absent from Edinburgh during the middle of 1825, having been granted one month's leave of absence to visit public and private exhibitions in London and Paris.[42] This probably explains why Neill's advice had been sought in the interim, although not apparently acted upon. The Commissioners in the end remained loyal to their original designer.

Andrew Wilson's Enlarged Design

As before, no sketch or drawing survives, but Wilson's plan can be identified in contemporary plans. A comparison between these and present-day ones reveals how little the original structure has altered. This portion had no distinctive feature such as Farmer Wood's cattle pond, but it did possess a variety of mature trees and was the most level of the three gardens along Queen Street. Andrew Wilson, in a simple but extremely subtle manner, exploited these assets and created one of the most successful and delightfully laid-out gardens in the New Town.

The greater part was formed into two large oval-shaped areas of lawn which carefully linked with the existing grassed area and walks. From the western end the central lawn appears continuous, but by sudden dips contrives a number of cross paths undisclosed from a distance, leaving the vista of sward undisturbed. Along the base of the Queen Street embankment a terrace walk was formed with linking footpaths to the gates at street level. In February 1826 Wilson resigned from the Trustees' Academy, and soon after the family left Edinburgh for Italy. Not everything had been completed before his departure. The December minutes of 1826 note that the central bank next to Queen Street had still to be laid in grass, and the walks to be gravelled; while instructions were issued to the gardener for the 'large trees to be uplifted and planted where the Convener and Cashier direct'. But the gardener and Commissioners at least had a design to work to, and the result was to produce a green Arcadian retreat in the best classical manner. These special qualities were soon to be noticed. An article written in 1858 on 'Trees for Towns', while criticising the paucity of fine trees and planting in Edinburgh's open spaces, cited the West Queen

Two views of West Queen Street Gardens, Edinburgh: in winter (C. Byrom) and spring (J. Byrom).

Street Gardens, despite their 'present immature state', as the only example 'of really artistic and scientific treatment of trees and shrubs, and turf'.[43] Ten years on, and once more the gardens were praised as being among the most pleasing in Edinburgh, their 'park like style' successfully combining 'a certain feeling of interior privacy with fine peeps of grassy slopes from outside the railings'.[44]

Rights to the Garden Extended

In 1816 David Scott, WS (1791–1839) bought land between Albyn Place and Wemyss Place from Lord Alva and almost immediately commissioned plans for its development.[45] Several West Queen Street residents initially opposed the idea, seeing it as a threat 'to the beauty and uniformity of the New Town', and a loss of their open views. But they were unsuccessful, and building slowly began from 1821 onwards.[46] But what had first been viewed with dismay was soon to be regarded as a possible asset, and as a means of raising money and reducing the garden's debts. It came about like this.

In 1825 the Commissioners approached James Gillespie Graham (Lord Moray's architect) and David Scott to see if they were interested in having the 1822 Act extended to their property. Scott's response was positive, and two years later a settlement was made to extend full rights and obligations of the West Queen Street Gardens to property in Wemyss Place.[47] In return a strip of garden ground was made over to Scott for road-widening purposes. He agreed to assume responsibility for constructing a new garden wall with railing along the west side, although the cost was to be met by the Commissioners. Early in 1829 the high stone wall was removed together with the gardener's house, and Scott paid the Commissioners £30 for the materials. His account for the new wall and railing, amounting to £501, was not submitted until 1835, when it was considered 'too much'; but tactful bargaining reduced the price to £428.[48] The benefits of increasing the number of subscribers, however, proved financially worthwhile and more than offset the small loss of ground.

Subsequent Care

For the next ten years Archibald Walker remained in charge, his earnings being increased from £32 to £42 per annum to reflect the increased area. It was no more than a breadline existence, and when he died just before Christmas 1834 the minutes record that 'he left a young family mainly destitute'. When brother James, 'a gardener at Brunstain', applied for the vacancy, he was favourably considered, having said that he was willing to take 'some charge of the deceased's family' and to employ one of them, 'a lad of fourteen', for occasional help, the boy having previously assisted his father. Walker's contract provides a useful résumé of the duties required of the gardener, which also applied to most of the larger gardens. It assumed total commitment (with no leeway this time for extra earnings from outside work) and the skills of a seasoned diplomat. It ran as follows:

> I shall cut the grass from 9 to 10 times a year and shall always have it as it ought to be in well kept lawn and shrubbery ground, and pull the fruit before it is ripe. I shall keep the gardens in the best style and shall attend to the rules of the gardens as these have been in use to be observed,

and in particular as to the time of opening and shutting the gardens, and shall always be there myself. I shall give my whole and undivided time to the gardens and shall not engage myself in any other occupation whatever. I am to be allowed the assistance of a labourer for about four months in the year whose wages the commissioners are to pay. I shall be constantly civil and attentive to all persons entitled to access to the gardens, and at the same time firm in repressing any breach of the rules.

James lasted only three years when some 'accident' befell him, leaving him unable to do active work. Confronted with a deteriorating garden, the Commissioners had little option but to 'part with Walker at Martinmas' when his contract expired. He left with a lump sum of £5, intent on launching himself on a new career selling fruit and vegetables. And that is the last we hear of the beleaguered Walkers.

To bring the garden back to standard the Commissioners opted to employ a nursery firm; both Peter Lawson's (at Hunter Square), and Thomas Cleghorn (Princes Street – with nursery ground in East Princes Street Gardens) were approached and Cleghorn won the contract. Later the gardens reverted to former methods, when the Commissioners struck gold, or rather George Dickson 'residing at Hillhousefield'. Dickson, then a young man, devoted the next 40 years or so to the gardens, until 'age and infirmity' forced his semi-retirement in 1878. During that long period of service his wage never varied; he received £60 a year, out of which he provided his own tools, paid for any labouring help and supplied the annual bedding plants.[49]

During Dickson's régime the gardens prospered and reached maturity. Even by the 1850s much of the 'new' planting was requiring attention and James McNab of the Royal Botanic Garden was called in to advise. His first report, dated January 1855, warned of the damage caused by haphazard and careless pruning, and reminded the Commissioners that 'in the management of Town gardens . . . their beauty does not depend upon the number of trees so much as upon a fine outline of foliage'; consequently 'everything should be freely sacrificed for those trees selected for permanent effect'. It was McNab's constant theme. Most of the poplars, and rows of old apple trees at the western end, were recommended for removal, with thinning and pruning of the planting on the south and east sides. Suggestions were also made for replacing the many deciduous shrubs with evergreens such as hollies, aucubas, Portugal laurels and box. McNab was given a free hand to carry out the work within a £10 budget, but was told not to touch the central willows. Two years later his advice was sought again. Although McNab became involved with most New Town gardens, he developed the closest relationship with this one. Over a twenty-year period he submitted no fewer than five detailed reports, and was consulted on other occasions. The garden still exhibits the benefits of this extensive period of planned care.[50]

The Gardens During Wartime

The habit of such consistent care must have augured well for subsequent years, but the absence of any minute books covering the late nineteenth and early twentieth centuries does create a gap. When they resume in the late 1920s, we return to the rhythm of routine care with more radical work undertaken at intervals. For example, Mr W.S. Imrie, a forester, supervised a fairly extensive tree-removal and pruning programme in 1931 (and was employed as gardener during the war years). When the Commissioners met, it was usually to discuss such niceties as the merits of providing bird boxes, replanting the central bed and whether or not to employ a summer ranger.[51] But all this changed with the Second World War. Although all the Queen Street Gardens were affected, the greatest demands were placed on the western one simply because many army detachments were stationed at this end of the New Town. First to use the Garden were the 1st and 2nd line Lothian Border Armoured Car Company, who in 1939 were allowed to drill for two hours during the summer evenings; numbers were limited to 60 men, wheeled vehicles were banned and the Commanding Officer was asked not to use the ground when wet. The tread of army boots was less damaging, however, than over-reaction by the Company to an air-raid warning, when the troops made a dash for the gardens and frantically started to dig trenches 'for their own protection'. It took much longer for the holes to be refilled, and then so crudely that bumps and hollows persisted for years. Not until 1951 was the ground properly reinstated.

At other times during the war years the Garden was made available to the Womens' Auxiliary Air Force (for drilling); local battalions of the Home Guard (bayonet practice); ATS Detachment Division (basketball); the Anti Aircraft Defence Group (football); and the 1st City of Edinburgh Battalion Army Cadet Corp (training). In addition, the Garden provided space for three air-raid shelters (one for the Royal Engineers, and two for pupils and staff of Mary Erskine School, then situated at the West end of Queen Street) and two ammunition stores.[52] The railings along west Heriot Row and most of Wemyss Place were removed in 1942, allowing children from Jamaica Street (demolished as sub-standard housing in 1960) to enter and cause 'mischief'. But a degree of control was exercised by keeping on a full-time gardener, and sharing a ranger with the East Garden during the summer months.[53]

In 1946 the huts and shelters were removed, and two years later new railings were erected at a cost of just over £700, the work being carried out by Alexander & Sons.[54] In the early 1970s a garden-management plan produced by the late Professor David Skinner, landscape consultant, was adopted; it aimed at a phased removal of some of the older trees and shrubs, to be replaced by planting of a similar character and balance. The work continues under the guidance of Peter McGovern, landscape architect. The Garden continues to enjoy the benefits of a full-time gardener supplied under contract with a nursery firm.

On a Financial Note

Eight of the New Town pleasure gardens were either wholly or partly bought by the would-be users; but the West Queen Street one proved by far the most expensive. The land cost £9,080, over £3,000 more than the considerably larger East Queen Street Garden. It made the Central District seem positively cheap at £2,736. Even the later gardens fronting Eton Terrace (Dean Gardens) and Belgrave Crescent were acquired for significantly less. The greater cost was partly due to the ground being in better condition, and Lord Wemyss, for example, was not looking to sell. But it meant that from the start the Commissioners were preoccupied with money matters. Strict economy, combined with a sharp check on those falling into arrears, were the hallmarks of the early years.

Most proprietors opted to pay their contribution towards purchase and forming the gardens over a ten-year period. The Commissioners therefore had little option but to borrow the shortfall. They were fortunate to have Sir Robert Dundas as a Commissioner, for he was a Governor of the Bank of Scotland, with whom a loan was successfully negotiated: £2,100 in 1823, and a further sum of £6,000 on the purchase of Lord Wemyss's land.[55] From the figures available it would appear that the cost of buying the land and turning it into a pleasure garden approached £12,250, making it the most expensive garden in the New Town.[56] It is little wonder that one of the early minutes records with an air of despondency, 'needing money badly'. As a result the use of the gardens by non-proprietors was positively welcomed although the numbers renting keys were never very significant and amounted to no more than three or four non-proprietors annually.

Despite strict economy, and from 1837 the benefit of increased revenue from those living in Wemyss Place, the debt on the garden remained a considerable burden. The two neighbouring ones became solvent relatively early (the East by 1831, and the Centre in 1839); but the West continued to struggle. Indeed, the minutes of May 1838 record a comment by Dr Craigie that 'there was at present a feeling amongst proprietors and Commissioners that every exertion should be used to reduce the amount of debt'. It was therefore 'solely with a view of saving expense' that when Thomas Gray Scott (1811–56), one of the Commissioners' sons, volunteered his services as Clerk free of charge, the offer was warmly accepted. After nearly 16 years of service, William Bell was accorded a vote of thanks and dispatched. The manner of his departure proved hurtful. Never claiming all his rightful dues, Bell now reacted with bitterness and put in a string of claims. A series of legal wrangles followed which were not finally resolved until 1841, and then only by arbitration.[57]

On a happier note the Scott family went on to contribute almost 100 years in their role as clerks. Thomas Scott was succeeded by his brother Archibald, who in turn was succeeded by his son, Andrew Scott, WS (1851–1931); Andrew was appointed in 1887 and resigned shortly before his death, making him one of the longest, if not the longest, serving garden clerk on record.[58] The size of debt, however, continued to haunt the Commissioners and in 1842 they appointed Patrick Brodie, accountant, to examine the financial state of the Garden. His report contained both good and bad news. On the positive side he discovered that the cost of the land had already been paid off, but 'considerable debt still existed for levelling and laying out the gardens'. It took thirteen more years before the bank's overdraft was finally cleared. On 23 February 1855 the formal discharge was registered; it was a day none of the original Commissioners lived to see.[59] Since then finances have remained stable, and from 1867 money for the upkeep of the Gardens has been based on rateable values, the same method used by the Central District.

Uses and Amusements

The early regulations were designed to limit acts likely to cause injury, damage or annoyance. During the first 'green' years no dogs were permitted and smoking was banned (probably because John Hope, the anti-smoking campaigner, then lived in Queen Street). Likewise carpet beating, clothes drying and play with a hard ball were all forbidden, and stone throwing, fireworks and 'discharging guns, canons' absolutely vetoed. Few wanton acts of mischief were severe enough to be recorded in the minute books. There was some trouble in 1836 when 'lads' broke tops off the railings and threw stones into the garden, and other 'depredations' including striking the gardener. The trouble stemmed from a gang of local boys who were generally proving troublesome, hence 'the East District is in the same scrape'. A team of young cricketers posed another early threat and were noted in the minutes of 1839 as 'destroying everything in the neighbourhood of the place where they play'. The worst offenders on this occasion were said to be not the proprietors' sons but their friends, whom the gardener found 'very unruly and mischievous, running through the borders and the like'; 'friends' generally tended to bear more than their fair share of blame.[60]

Genteel activities such as croquet never posed problems but there were some misgivings about inviting military bands to play. Mrs Sandford in 1829, for example, repeatedly requested such performances, but was refused on the grounds that 'broils and misunderstandings occurred in other districts where this practice was followed'. Undeterred, however, she rallied her supporters and tried again. On this occasion her plea was carefully tailored to meet all possible objections:

> The Lieutenant of the 12th Royal Lancers having politely offered his band to play occasionally in the Western division of the Queen Street and Heriot Row Gardens between the hours of 3 and 5 o'clock, and having at the same time expressed his willingness to send dismounted troopers to guard the gates and railings, we the undersigned, request the Commissioners to take these circumstances into consideration, and allow a trial to be made, which need not be repeated if injury is done to the garden or anything unpleasant occurs.

Persistence paid off, and the Commissioners cautiously agreed 'to allow a trial to be made for a short period'.[61] The next reference is not until 1868 when Professor Maclagan suggested that the band of the Queen's Edinburgh Rifle Volunteer Brigade be invited to play during the autumn evenings. So successful was this event that a subscription was raised as a mark of appreciation, and the band was asked to return the following year.[62]

Attempts to clutter the garden with artifacts have always been resisted, although ideas have never been lacking. One of the first requests was by John Leslie (1766–1832), Professor of Mathematics, who wished to have a telescope purchased for the garden.[63] Two years later came a proposal for a *jet d'eau*, and on another occasion a memorial bird-bath. Gifts of plants and trees have on the other hand always been welcome. The earliest recorded donation was in 1838 when the minutes note that Miss Cockburn 'had presented a handsome collection of flowers to the garden' and that the lady 'was in delicate health and will soon request permission to take her chair into the garden as before'. This was Jane Cockburn (?–1876), invalid daughter of Henry Cockburn, who along with two or three other ladies, was allowed to bring 'light carriages' or wheel-chairs into the grounds.[64] Would she recognise the Gardens today? Possibly. The basic structure has changed little since her time, and she would have welcomed the hard-surfaced path on the south side, making her carriage ride easier. But the size and maturity of the planting would no doubt have pleasantly surprised her, accustomed as she had been to a more sparsely clothed garden, still in the first flush of its youth.

Notes

1. 'Extracts from the journal of Jessy Allan, wife of John Harden, 1801–1811', *BOEC*, Vol. 30 (1959), entry for 27 July 1802. Alexander Nasmyth was a friend of the family and lived not far away in York Place. A delightful account of life in Queen Street, with drawings produced by Jessy's husband John Harden, can be found in: Iain Gordon Brown, *Elegance and Entertainment in the New Town of Edinburgh; The Harden Drawings* (Edinburgh, 1995).
2. *Edinburgh Evening Courant*, 27 July 1803.
3. Allan was proprietor of the *Caledonian Mercury*, published between 1736 and 1816.
4. HHM, 19 April 1790, vol. 14, pp. 16–19.
5. Alexander Rockville, advocate, became Sheriff Depute of Kirkcudbright in 1764. Twenty years later he was raised to the Bench under the title of Lord Rockville, named from an estate he had bought in the County of Haddington.
6. HHM, 1 March 1790, vol. 14, p. 6.
7. HHM, 19 April 1790, vol. 14, pp. 16–19. The farmer seems to have left his farmhouse soon after, and died in 1797.
8. HHM, 7 June 1790, vol. 14, p. 48; 18 April 1791, vol. 14, p. 113.
9. Allan & Steuart & Co.; founded in the late 1780s combining Allan's banking experience with Steuart's merchant background. See also Chapter 7.
10. Heriot's Hospital Chartulary 5, pp. 360, 365, 369.
11. Sederunt Book of the District Commissioners of the Western District (1822–37), Minute, 21 December 1835.
12. *Edinburgh Advertiser*, 15 May 1795; Heriot's Hospital Chartulary 5, p. 360; feu disposition dated 28 April 1796.
13. Rockville's accident appears in different versions. One holds that he slipped and fell outside his door in St Andrew Square and broke his leg (*Kay's Portraits* (1877) Vol. 1, p. 72); the other that he fell and broke an arm when walking down the High Street, and on being conveyed back to Queen Street, the sedan overturned causing further injury to his arm (James Grant, *Old and New Edinburgh* (Edinburgh, 1882), vol. 2, p. 194).
14. Another corps known as the 97th or Strathspey Regiment was raised almost immediately afterwards for more extended service, Grant being Colonel of both regiments.
15. The wall on the south side, said to have 'long disfigured' the street, was removed in the 1820s when acquired as communal gardens. (Grant, op. cit., vol. 2. p. 194).
16. *Edinburgh Evening Courant*, 21 November 1800.
17. The 1795 advertisement for the sale of 64 Queen Street (FN12) refers for example, to stabling accommodation for six horses.
18. Sederunt Book of the District Commissioners, Western District (1838–79), Minute, 24 January 1856; Report by James McNab recommending removal of several rows of apple trees.
19. HHM, 22 February 1803, vol. 16, pp. 170–3, & 18 April 1803, p. 189. No compensation was ever claimed.
20. HHM, 23 August 1805, vol. 17, p. 125.

21. Lord Wemyss was, for example, President of the Society of Arts for Scotland, and President of the Caledonian Horticultural Society, set up in 1809.

22. Since then it has been used as office accommodation by various commercial concerns, but has recently been carefully refurbished by the present occupants, Tods Murray, WS.

23. *Caledonian Horticultural Society Memoirs*, Vol. 2, 1818, (Library, Royal College of Physicians) and a discourse read at the annual election meeting of the Caledonian Horticultural Society 7 December 1820, by Andrew Duncan (Volume of miscellaneous papers, Royal College of Physicians). Royal Caledonia Horticultural Society Minute Book, vol. 1 (1809–24) RBG.

24. Sederunt Book (1822–37), Minute, 21 December 1835.

25. The first Commissioners were Solicitor General Wedderburn, 31 Heriot Row (replaced on his death a few months later by Andrew Murray, advocate, and former member of West Princes Street garden committee); Sir Robert Dundas (1761–1835) of Beechwood, 30 Heriot Row, a principal Clerk of the Court of Session and a loyal member of the committee until his death; Lieutenant General Martin Hunter, 54 Queen Street; Alexander Irving, Advocate, 27 Heriot Row (raised to the bench in 1826 as Lord Newton); William Inglis, WS, 49 Queen Street, Deputy Secretary to the Prince of Wales in Scotland; and James Scott, Accountant, 50 Queen Street.

26. Sederunt Book (1822–37), Minutes, 24 June 1822 & 1 July 1822.

27. Ibid., Minute, 16 November 1822.

28. Ibid., Minutes, 2 December 1822; 10 December 1822.

29. Ibid., Minute, 2 May 1823.

30. Ibid., Minute, 17 May 1823.

31. Ibid., Minutes, 10 March 1823; 22 March 1823; 23 April 1823; 25 April 1823; 29 May 1823; 20 June 1823; 10 September 1823; on which this and the following information is based.

32. Sederunt Book (1838–79), Report of 1843 by Patrick Brodie, Accountant.

33. Sederunt Book (1822–37), Minute, 10 September 1823.

34. Ibid., Minute, 23 December 1823.

35. Ibid., Minutes, 16 January 1824; 15 April 1824.

36. Ibid., Minute, 19 November 1824.

37. Ibid., Minutes, 19 November 1824; 15 December 1824; 8 January 1825; 25 January 1825; 11 February 1825.

38. Ibid., Minutes, 19 February 1825; 23 February 1825; 1 April 1825; 21 April 1825.

39. Ibid., Minute, 9 July 1825.

40. Ibid., Minute 6 March 1826. Sixty keys were ordered; the cost of renting one was put at 4 guineas, the letter R to be stamped on each, and to be available via application to the Clerk.

41. Ibid., Minute, 26 December 1826.

42. SRO, WRH, NG1 2/7, Trustees' Academy Minute Book, Minute 15 April 1825. Wilson's resignation is noted in the Minute, 21 February 1826.

43. 'Trees for Towns', 24 November 1858; James McNab's collection, RBGL; origin of article not traced, but presumably by McNab.

44. *The Scotsman*, 1 July 1867, 'Our Town Gardens and Trees'.

45. RHP 211, dated 1818; this plan was not carried out.

46. The Earl of Wemyss, James Hope, WS (later to move to Moray Place), and Francis Walker led the opposition, and after placing an advertisement in the newspapers arranged a joint meeting with the Town Council in August 1818.

47. Sederunt Book of District Commissioners, Western District (1822–37); Notice of Settlement, dated 10 July 1827.

48. Ibid., Minutes, 17 April 1824; 21 December 1835; 18 January 1836; and Report by Patrick Brodie, 1843, with note of payment recorded 12 September 1837.

49. Ibid., Minutes, 26 December 1826; 8 December 1834; 17 March 1835; and Sederunt Book of District Commissioners, Western District (1838–79), Minutes, 6 February 1838; 11 July 1838; 31 October 1838; 7 November 1838 (Minute of Agreement).

50. The dates of James McNab's Reports are as follows: January 1856; November 1858; August 1861; January 1866; and February 1872.

51. Sederunt Book of the District Commissioners. Western District (1927–71); Minutes, 16 May 1939; 4 October 1939; 18 December 1939; 5 February 1940; 1 April 1940; 29 January 1951.

52. Ibid., Minutes, 24 January 1941; 21 March 1941; 18 May 1943; 9 October 1944; 26 March 1945; 1 February 1942; 27 August 1943.

53. Ibid., Minutes, 6 October 1942;1 February 1943; 9 October 1944. A privet hedge was planted along the Heriot Row side.

54. Ibid., Minutes, 14 May 1945; 18 February 1946; 1 April 1946; 31 January 1947; 23 February 1948; 3 May 1948; 28 June 1948.

55. Ibid. (Minute Book 1822–37), Minutes 22 March 1823; 17 May 1823; 9 July 1825.

56. The Central gardens cost £6,000 in total. Figures for the East gardens are incomplete, and there is no information on the cost of laying out the first section.

57. Sederunt Book of District Commissioners, Western District (1838–79); Minutes, 4 June 1838; 11 July 1838; 13 December 1838; 21 December 1838; 2 May 1839; 21 June 1839; 13 December 1841; 21 December 1841.

58. Ibid. (1927–1971), Minute, 26 January 1931.

59. Ibid. (1838–79), Minutes, 26 December 1843; 22 February 1855.

60. Ibid. (1822–37; 1838–79); letter by William Bell, clerk to A. Murray, 8 March 1836; Minute, 14 June 1839.

61. Ibid. (1822–37), Minutes, 3 July 1829; 10 August 1829.

62. Ibid. (1838–79), Minute, 24 December 1868.

63. Ibid. (1822–37; 1927–71), Minutes, 23 February 1825; 19 November 1827; 24 October 1935. Leslie lived in Lord Jeffrey's former residence at 62 Queen Street.

64. Ibid. (1822–37), Minutes, 23 April 1831; 19 April 1832.

PART SIX

GARDENS WITHIN THE SECOND NEW TOWN

Bellevue House, 1796, erected in the grounds of Drummond Lodge in the vicinity of present-day Drummond Place, Edinburgh, as the residence of Major-General Scott. (*The Edinburgh Magazine: or Literary Miscellany*, vol. 13–14, 1799)

CAPITAL VILLA
AND GROUNDS NEAR EDINBURGH.
To be Sold, and entered to at Whitsunday next
THE HOUSE of BELLEVUE, with the Grounds, Garden, Coach-houses, Stables, Poultry Houses, Gardener's House, Shrubbery, Pleasure Grounds, Ice-house and whole appurtenances belonging thereto, all as presently possessed by the Duke of Argyll.

The House is finished in the most complete manner; and the situation is remarkably pleasant, possessing the beauty of the country, and all the convenience of a town's residence, being within a few minutes walk of the New Town of Edinburgh. The house commands a delightful prospect of the Frith of Forth and country adjacent. The hot-houses, green-house, and garden, are well stocked with fruit trees and shrubs of the best kinds. The grounds are divided into small fields, are well inclosed, and ornamented with thriving plantations. In short, the whole premises are finished up in a style that is seldom to be seen in this country.

Tickets for viewing the house, &c. can only be delivered to those who intend to purchase the premises, by applying at the office of James Walker, W.S. The house will be shewn by the housekeeper at Bellevue and the gardens and grounds by Thomas Henderson gardener.

Any person who may incline to purchase the premises may apply to Mr Walker.

Bellevue House and grounds advertised for sale, *Edinburgh Evening Courant*, 17 August 1799.

CHAPTER 11

DRUMMOND PLACE
2.70 acres (1.88 ha)

No part of the home scenery of Edinburgh was more beautiful than Bellevue, the villa of General Scott. It seemed to consist of nearly all the land between York Place and Canonmills – a space now wholly covered by streets and houses. The mansion house stood near the eastern side of the central enclosure of what is now Drummond Place; and a luxurious house it was. The whole place waved with wood, and was diversified by undulations of surface, and adorned by seats and bowers and summer houses.

Henry Cockburn[1]

George Drummond, Edinburgh's visionary Lord Provost, had, even if somewhat circumstantially, almost as important a connection with the second New Town as with the first. Drummond Place is so named not merely to honour an eminent citizen but to mark his close association with the district as the owner of Drummond Lodge and adjacent land – an estate which became an integral part of the second New Town. That this land would be swallowed up by the very success of his dream would have both surprised and delighted him.

Bellevue House

The history and fortunes of Drummond Place Gardens were closely related to Bellevue House, the substantial villa built by the Scott family to replace Drummond's more modest villa. Bellevue estate had, however, been purchased by the Town primarily to allow them to become involved with plans for a second New Town. The mansion, although extremely fine, was really only of secondary interest. Nevertheless it accounted for a high proportion of the cost, and therefore the building had to be put to some use. One of the challenges posed by the 1800 competition had been how to integrate Bellevue house as part of the overall design without making it appear an oddity. John Baine, one of the competition prizewinners, had rightly observed that it 'should not be placed in an obscure corner, otherwise it would lose all its value'.[2] This building therefore influenced the shape of Drummond Place, and the solution finally determined by Robert Reid was for a square with an oval or crescent-shaped eastern end, at the centre of which stood the former mansion.

Stripped of its furnishings and marooned within a diminished landscape, the number of its potential users was, however, likely to be limited. Having identified the Board of

The New Custom House (Bellevue House with an additional storey) and enclosed garden *c*. 1820. (J. & H.S. Storer, *Views of Edinburgh and its vicinity*, 1820)

Customs as a possibility, the Council wasted no time in making overtures, offering the house 'on reasonable terms' and spelling out the advantages this would bring. A detached property would be less of a fire hazard, and the premises were conveniently placed for the port of Leith and the Excise Office in St Andrew Square:[3] far superior in fact to the cramped accommodation then occupied by the Board at the rear of the Exchange building in the High Street. The Board, however, queried whether there was sufficient space, and to allay anxieties the Council offered to add another storey, and to enclose the surrounding one-acre plot (0.4 ha) with a parapet wall and rail. In return the Board agreed to pay £8,000 on completion.[4] As part of the bargain the Commissioners 'and those having authority from them' were also given rights to walk 'in the remainder of the plot of ground or area to be enclosed' i.e. the future Drummond Place pleasure gardens, with gated access specially provided on the west side.[5] Work began in 1803[6] and by 1805 the Board of Customs had moved in. The surrounding plot was soon 'tastefully laid out in walks and shrubberies', a small green oasis amidst the slowly advancing tide of builders and labourers.[7]

House plots in Drummond Place began to be sold from 1817 onwards, following the feuing of most of Great King Street, and the filling and levelling of the quarry in the north-west corner (close to Nelson Street).[8] A number of builders bought several plots: for example William Henry, Thomas Pringle and Thomas Caldwell purchased frontages on the south side; Charles Alison, John Neill and William Wallace & Son the north and eastern ends; and Charles Watson the west side.[9] By 1823 Drummond Place was built and largely occupied; and with the central space cleared of saw pits and other building paraphernalia[10] the time had arrived to consider making the garden.

Elevations of Drummond Place, by Robert Reid, 1804. Top: West side with view down (Great) King Street. Bottom: North and South sides. (ECA and Crown copyright © RCAHMS)

Setting up the Garden

It is puzzling that the Town Council did not adopt the same method for regulating Drummond Square Gardens as they had for St Andrew and Charlotte Square. But they did not, probably because the matter was simply overlooked. Only one feu charter granted in 1821 makes any reference to the garden area. This was for a corner plot on the north-west side. After it had twice changed hands James Greig, WS, became owner and he had built for himself a main-door house (entered from Drummond Place), with five flats above entered from Great King Street. In the terms of Greig's charter the whole of this corner stance was given the right 'in common with the several feuars around Drummond Place to the area of the Square within the lines of the street ways thereof', which was to become 'a Common property for the accommodation, pleasure and health' of the surrounding feuars. The remaining conditions repeated almost word for word the ones included in the St Andrew and Charlotte Square charters, a seemingly belated attempt to rectify what was otherwise an embarrassing omission.[11]

The Council now found itself in rather an ambiguous position. They had never intended to become involved with forming the gardens, yet they had failed to clearly set up a mechanism for doing so. Under the circumstances they felt obliged to make the first move. In March 1822, Thomas Brown, their Superintendent, drew up designs and specifications for a wall and railing to enclose the central area, similar to those around the Custom House. Tenders were obtained and the lowest submitted, at £540, was by

Thomas Ponton, 5 London Street, one of the builders with property in Drummond Place.[12] It was put to the proprietors that half the cost of 'enclosing the area in a very handsome stile by a cast iron railing' would be met by the Council, provided the Drummond Place proprietors assumed responsibility for 'inclosing the same and receiving and maintaining it as a common property'. If the offer was rejected, the Council would 'proceed to do the work in as economical a manner as possible'.[13]

The proprietors, together with some of the builders, met to discuss the offer. William Dallas, WS (1759–1852) took the chair. He had recently moved from York Place to 7 Drummond Place and this occasion marked the beginning of his long association with the gardens.[14] Yet little has been discovered about him apart from the fact that his father was a wright (carpenter or joiner).[15] It was put to the meeting that 'if an arrangement is not made with the Town Council . . . the area may be enclosed by them at a much smaller expense than the estimate, and of course it would be done in such a way, as would not improve the appearance of Drummond Place'. A sobering thought to concentrate minds! In addition to enclosing the garden the proprietors reflected on other expected outlays. Levelling, planting and forming the walks were estimated to cost around £260, making them liable to a total bill of £800. As a counter-proposal therefore (and believing the Town in any case to be wholly responsible for the central area) Mr Dallas suggested that the Town be asked to increase its offer to £400 in return for the proprietors assuming full responsibility. Dallas, along with David Munro Binning, advocate (24 Drummond Place), was appointed to negotiate.

Something of a cat-and-mouse game followed. The Town agreed to increase their offer to £300 (without admitting any liability) but refused to budge further. The proprietors continued to push for more, even threatening to withhold payment of their feu duties; but such heavy-handed tactics were counter-productive and brought negotiations perilously close to collapse.[16] Happily all contentious issues were finally resolved at a joint meeting held on 4 June 1822. The long-awaited Royal visit was fast approaching and no-one in Drummond Place wished to disgrace the Town by the scruffy appearance of their central plot. There was every reason for speedy resolution. The Town's improved offer and willingness to grant feu rights to the land were now formally accepted; in return the feuars agreed to give up further claims and become responsible for the garden. William Dallas, David Munro Binning and John Greig were chosen to draft a charter vesting rights and responsibilities in the surrounding residents, and including management details.

The Feu Charter

Drummond Place was the first pleasure ground to be set up under a special charter granted by the feu superior. A similar practice was later adopted for the Calton Hill Pleasure Grounds, and when extra land was later added to Dean and Belgrave Crescent Gardens. Once the draft charter was available, it was scrutinised by the Council and some small adjustments were made;[17] on 26 April 1823 it was formally recorded in the Register of Sasines. At this time most of Drummond Place consisted of single houses with just a small number of flats; because of the retrospective nature of the charter, proprietors had the right to say whether or not they wanted to be included within its terms. Three feuars (Nos. 10, 36 and 42 Drummond Place) opted out and their property was (and still is) excluded from the rights and privileges of the garden.[18] Those who agreed are all listed in the charter; several were builders, for at least one quarter of the property was still in their hands. They had always been supporters of the move to form a garden, no doubt seeing it as a useful boost for sales.

The charter was drawn up against the background of administrative problems experienced by the neighbouring East Queen Street Gardens, with the result that the committee took special care to avoid any such flaws. Theirs was a most meticulously crafted document, setting out a comprehensive set of regulations. Briefly, they covered three main areas: who had rights to the garden, general administration and financial matters. Under the first item, all hotels, lodging-houses and shops were to be excluded, although the owners retained rights to the garden as well as responsibility for upkeep; 'boarding schools for young ladies' were granted special dispensation.[19] Where property was let to a private household they were allowed use of the central area provided the landlord relinquished his right. Strict control was to be exercised over keys by limiting their issue to one per family[20] (and stamped with the house number). Non-proprietors were allowed to rent a key under certain safeguards. Administrative matters were kept fairly simple. Initially all the proprietors (following the practice adopted by the Queen Street Gardens) were to meet to elect a management committee (five plus secretary), with provision for an Annual General Meeting each May. On financial issues, it was specified that annual assessments were to be based on the width of each property (the foot-frontage principle), with corner blocks (including the main door and flat above) paying a three-fifths' part. Drummond Place was the first to use this method which was later adopted by St Andrew Square, Rutland Square and some of the Victorian gardens. Exact measurements of all the individual properties were included in the charter.[21] Since 1949, and after much heated debate, the annual assessments have been switched to a flat-rate system, considered more appropriate following the widespread division of property into flats. The only other significant change was in 1952 when the AGM was moved to March to coincide with the financial tax year.

Design and Layout

By September 1822, the parapet and railing were practically complete and the Town paid their share to the contractor.[22] A section of these railings, topped with the fleur-de-lys design, together with the ornamental gateway, still survive at the western end. Once enclosed, the garden was laid out and provided with a pump well and a small tool-house.[23] No garden minutes survive for this early period (1822–56) but we do know from the West Queen Street minutes that the gardener in charge was Richard Walker, the contractor for both the Central and West Queen Street Gardens. It would seem highly likely that he was responsible for laying out the interior of Drummond Place and for the planting. At just over one acre (0.4 ha) of reasonably level ground, it presented no particular physical challenge to an experienced gardening contractor and Walker was well used to taking instructions from management committees.

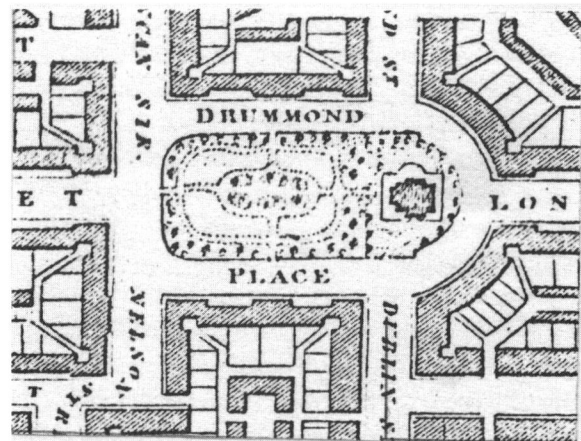

Knox's Plan of 1824 showing the newly-laid-out garden and its relationship to the Custom House, Drummond Place, Edinburgh.

At this time the area of ground was rectangular in shape and in design was not dissimilar to George Square Gardens on the south side (formed in 1814 by John Hay, nurseryman and landscape planner). There is of course a possibility that Hay may have been involved, for he was certainly being consulted by the Queen Street East garden commissioners in 1823; and professional expertise had a habit of being exchanged from garden to garden. A wide border of shrubs and trees was planted around the periphery with a footpath alongside which connected at each of the gated entrances to a central oval-shaped walk, inside which were several ornamental shrub and flower plots. To protect the young and immature garden, regulations were drawn up and circulated, 'in order that the objects for which the great expense has been incurred in laying out this garden may be secured' and the gates were opened to the proprietors later in 1823. Curiously enough, while the regulations were similar to those of other gardens, they also bear the hallmark of the same individuals who had so painstakingly assembled the garden charter with their eyes still alert to possible loopholes, and ready to pounce if necessary. To have cleaned one's shoes even before entering certainly outstripped the standards set by other gardens.

Attempts to buy the Custom House

The garden had barely been in existence for two years when William Dallas was making overtures to the Town Council and Heriot's Hospital about the possible purchase of the Custom House; rumour had it that 'if £5000 was offered for the Custom House . . . the Lords of the Treasury would accept of it and erect a new building at Leith'.[24] What had formerly been considered an 'elegant mansion' was now described as 'a very great deformity to one of the finest streets in the City'. A blot on the landscape and a suitable candidate for demolition! Time was opportune as the Parliamentary Commissioners were then visiting Edinburgh. According to Dallas's calculations the sale of materials (should the building be removed) would produce £200. He now wished to know what financial support might be forthcoming from the Council and the Hospital before 'instantly' calling a meeting 'of the inhabitants of the adjoining streets to endeavour to raise the balance'. The Town

The Custom House, Edinburgh, 1829, surrounded by new buildings, its bulk providing shelter for the immature Drummond Place Gardens. The steeple of the recently built St Mary's Church, Bellevue Crescent, can be readily identified. (Grant, *Old and New Edinburgh*, based on a drawing by Shepherd)

volunteered 100 guineas 'as for a general improvement', and the Hospital (who still had some building land to sell) a more liberal £300. But the sums promised were insufficient to encourage further action. Soon after, the Excise Office moved from St Andrew Square to Drummond Place following the merger of the two boards; from 1841 the building became the property of the commissioners of Excise and became known as the Excise Office. Whether a blemish or not its presence at least sheltered the as yet immature garden.

The Demise of Bellevue House

While the railway through Princes Street Gardens had been seen as catastrophic by the garden proprietors' proposals to build a line beneath the Excise Office in Drummond Place met with cautious approval. It would be hidden from sight, and the only likely damage would be to the foundations of the old mansion – providing a golden opportunity and excuse for its removal and the extension of the garden. The Drummond Place proprietors were lucky to have at this time a new resident – Adam Black (1784–1874), who in 1843 was elected Lord Provost.[25] A keen Whig who later became MP for the City when in his 70th year, he was an able, energetic and 'noble' man, respected as the founder of the publishing firm A. & C. Black. His drive in 'procuring the removal of the Excise Office . . . and so effecting a great improvement in the amenity of the neighbourhood' was one of his many achievements noted in his obituary.[26]

The railway line in question was the final section of the Edinburgh, Leith & Granton Railway which connected Canonmills Station (later Scotland Street) to Canal Street (now absorbed within Waverley Station). It opened on 17 May 1847 and formed part of a larger network linking Canonmills to Trinity. Set up in 1835 as the Edinburgh, Leith & Newhaven Company (the last local railway company in the City), it experienced various setbacks and never reaped the profits forecast. Particularly difficult was this underground section requiring at least half a mile to be excavated beneath Scotland Street, Drummond Place, Duke Street, St Andrew Square and Princes Street, described as 'the most arduous feature hitherto connected with any Scottish railway or other public undertaking'.[27] No locomotive was then capable of hauling trains up the steep incline towards the City (a 1 in 27 gradient), so instead they were drawn by a cable rope operated by a stationary engine, and in the final stage horses pulled the trains to and from the station entrance. Such a cumbersome system was doomed to early obsolescence and the line closed in 1868.[28]

Under Adam Black's leadership the Council adopted a positive approach to these railway developments. Briefly, events were as follows.[29] Towards the end of June 1844 the Railway Company offered to buy the Excise Office for £5,000. Almost immediately the Town stepped in and made a successful rival bid, noting in their letter of acceptance that 'we purchase the property for the purpose of preventing nuisance or the disfigurement of that part of the City'.

By February 1845 the contract was finalised and some time later the Excise Office moved to 12 Picardy Place.[30] Various discussions followed between the Council and the Railway Company about the tunnel and the future of the defunct Excise Office. As time went by it became increasingly obvious that the building was unlikely to survive underground workings without damage to its structure. In any case none of the interested parties – the Town, the Railway Company, the Drummond Place residents – wanted to keep the building provided the money spent on buying it could be satisfactorily reapportioned.

A Council minute of 18 November 1845 marked the culmination of several informal meetings between the interested parties and the strategy finally agreed 'relative to the removal

Adam Black, Lord Provost, who helped secure the demolition of the Custom House and the consequent enlargement of the garden in 1846. (Crombies *Modern Athenians, 1837–1847*, ECL)

of Bellevue House'. In attendance were Adam Black, Mr Thomson (City Treasurer), Mr Alexander Douglas, WS (Clerk and on behalf of the City Creditors), Mr E.D. Sandford (Chairman and on behalf of the Edinburgh, Leith and Granton Railway Company) and Mr John Stodart (for the Drummond Place proprietors). Three of the five were Drummond Place residents, including Alexander Douglas – the long-standing Clerk to the West Princes Street Gardens, and likely to be supportive. The meeting's recommendations, which later received formal approval, sanctioned the demolition of Bellevue house, allowing the Railway Company to carry the tunnel beneath the site. Once the site was cleared, the Company were required to 'put it in a condition to be taken into the pleasure ground' and for it to be handed over 'to the Proprietors of Drummond Place to form part of their pleasure ground under an express obligation that the same shall never be built upon'. Costs were to be met by a contribution of £600 from the Town, £1,200 from the Drummond Place proprietors and £3,200 from the Railway Company, to be paid on or before the first of January 1846.[31]

The Newly Extended Garden

In March 1846 a feu charter was made out in favour of all the subscribing proprietors in Drummond Place; as five proprietors had declined to become involved, the overall contribution per household came to around £30.[32] The mansion was demolished in April 1846 and by July the Drummond Place proprietors were in possession of their new plot, thereby increasing the garden by nearly one third, to an overall size of 2.70 acres (1.08 ha).

Not surprisingly the treatment of the extended area was largely determined by the existing garden, just as the layout of this had been influenced by the presence of the mansion house. Nothing changed a great deal; the outer border was continued right round the garden and likewise the footpath. The former pathway at the east end now served to link the north and south sides. Perhaps the most significant effect was to throw the existing central focus out of balance; to compensate for this a small railed rhododendron plot was formed at the 'new' eastern end with a linking central footpath. As time was to prove, the garden really became over-supplied with paths, resulting in too many rather fussy small compartments.

From the middle years of the last century the garden minutes reveal a garden growing in maturity, without any signs of setbacks or damaging incidents.[33] Maturity, however, did result in

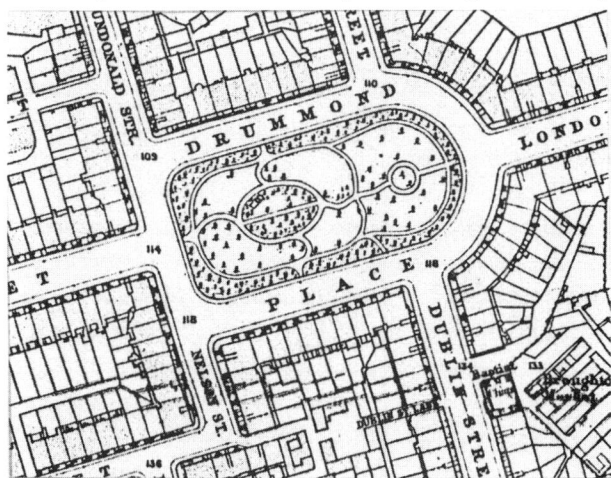

Bartholomew's Plan, 1891, showing the layout of the expanded garden. Since the Second World War the central network of paths has been grassed over.

certain problems being revealed, particularly easterly drafts, as border planting became increasingly spindly and less effective. Mr McHattie, Head Gardener to the Council, was called upon to advise in 1912 when he recommended having the borders widened on the east and west ends and stocking them with wind-resistant shrubs; also heightening the beds in the 'central' area to improve shelter. But victory over easterly winds has never been entirely won. Over time the central raised beds have gradually shrunk to become herbaceous plots stocked with a variety of small shrubs, roses and other decorative planting.[34]

The only connection James McNab had with these gardens was his recommendation of Thomas Finlay as gardener in 1856. Finlay's appointment lasted twenty-three years, during which time his wages showed a modest increase from £40 to £52 per annum. He was succeeded by John Orr from Princes Street Gardens, who was followed by William, his brother. After a run of successful gardeners, William proved a disappointment and was dismissed in 1895 on account of his 'intemperate habits, persistent inattentions and idleness'. To some extent these had been matched by equal apathy amongst the proprietors, as for several years no AGMs had been held because of poor attendance. But the appointment of William Wilson, an 'active and capable' gardener, rejuvenated the fortunes of the gardens and helped revive interest. Wilson devoted the rest of his working life (an amazing 55 years and surely a New Town record) to the gardens, and became known as 'Gaddy', the man under whose kindly but watchful eye generations of children played.

This and That

During Wilson's time croquet was overtaken by tennis as the most popular summer pastime. Grace Milne Rae, a minister's daughter whose family moved to Drummond Place in 1892, recounted to the writer how former times had seen the gardens alive with young ladies at play, and how demand had led to a second, then a third tennis court.[35] She spoke of days when children and babies were taken to the grounds by their nannies (although few wore uniform), mothers rarely being seen there except perhaps at weekends. Most vivid of all were her memories of play with neighbouring children – the Henderson and White families. The Whites were daredevils all, and particularly fond of climbing trees. Once the boys were caught singing from the top branches 'Drunk, drunk, drunk, I'm as drunk as a Lord', and on another occasion Freda White (author of several travel books), when forbidden to climb trees, organised a revolt amongst her girl friends, who then climbed all the trees in protest.

During the Second World War a static water tank was built at the western end and for safety reasons the railings along this portion were retained. Not until 1965 were new railings erected in place of the temporary mesh fencing. These cost the proprietors £1,800 and were designed by Christopher Fyfe, an architect living in Drummond Place. Around this time the ornamental wrought iron gates formerly belonging to West Warriston House (demolished 1966) were placed within the gardens and can still be seen inside the western entrance gate.[36] The drive to renew the railings provided an opportunity to rethink the garden's layout, and several footpaths were dispensed with, leaving larger areas of grass more suited to children's play. Further modifications have seen the removal of the rhododendron

Two general views of Drummond Place Gardens in Edinburgh. Top: View from the oval flower and shrub plot (originally at the centre of the garden) looking towards Great King Street. Bottom: The residents' annual summer party. (Both: C. Byrom)

plot and linking footpaths.[37] This simplified design combining continuous sweeps of grass and trees heightens the feeling of increased spaciousness. It is also easier to maintain and helps disguise the bumps at the eastern end due to subsidence caused by the tunnel. Today the garden contains over 80 trees including some of the finest ash in Edinburgh. Small numbers of beech, sycamore, gean, elm and other species make up the balance. As a number of these are now past their prime, a long-term replacement programme is underway.

Drummond Place retains its residential character although much of the property is now subdivided. Several distinguished residents have lived there, some of whom have served on the garden management committee, including John Henry Lorimer, RSA (1856–1936), artist and portrait painter and brother of Sir Robert Lorimer, architect; and Colonel F.M. Bailey who was responsible for introducing the blue poppy from Tibet.[38]

Notes

1. Henry Cockburn, *Memorials of his Time* (Edinburgh, 1971), p. 171.
2. John Baine, *An Exploratory Memoir* (1800).
3. TCM, 24 March 1802.
4. ECA, Chartulary 21, Disposition Bellevue House to Commissioners of Customs, dated 8 October 1808 (which contains details of the Minute of Sale, 2 October 1802 which is no longer traceable).
5. In a similar fashion the governor and officers at Edinburgh Castle were granted free access to the West Princes Street gardens as part of the 1818 contract.
6. TCM, 10 August 1803; payment made to James Thin, mason of £845 'for work done at the Custom House'; TCM 24 July 1805, payment of £ 300 to James Paterson, Edinburgh Foundry for surrounding iron railings and gates.
7. *Views of Edinburgh and its Vicinity*; drawn and engraved by J. & H.S. Storer Vol. 2 (Edinburgh, 1820). 'Notes on Bellevue now the Custom House'.
8. TCM, 13 October 1819; 27 October 1819; 17 November 1819; 1 December 1819; 15 December 1819; 29 December 1819; 5 January 1820; 12 January 1820; between these dates £272 was paid by the City Chamberlain 'for poor labourers employed at levelling the ground at Bellevue'.
9. TCM, 7 January 1818; 25 February 1818; 29 December 1819.
10. Mr Watson had applied for permission to 'lay down building materials on the quadrant of Drummond Place'. His request was granted (TCM, 31 March 1819) but was also extended to other builders who had taken up feus.
11. ECA, Chartulary 21, 28 March 1821, Feu Charter in favour of James Greig, WS.
12. TCM, 27 March 1822; a little later the Central Queen Street Garden commissioners asked Thomas Brown to supply them with a design and cost details for a similar wall and railings.
13. TCM, 17 April 1822.
14. TCM, 24 April 1822.
15. *The History of the Society of Writers to his Majesty's Signet,* op. cit., p. 127.
16. TCM, 15 May 1822; 29 May 1822; 5 June 1822; these several minutes record in some detail the various meetings of the proprietors, culminating in the joint meeting of 4 June 1822.
17. A draft copy of the conditions proposed for the Charter still exists in the Edinburgh City Archives.
18. Proprietors of these houses could apply to become annual key holders.

19. A school run by Miss Blackstone, 25 Drummond Place, made frequent use of this privilege during the early years of the present century.

20 The old ledger books of Alex Kirkwood & Son show them to have been responsible for the making and particularly the engraving of keys for several of the New Town gardens, including Drummond Place. This firm, still extant, was first set up in Meuse Lane, off St Andrew Square, before moving to larger premises in St James' Square in 1859, where they remained until their move to Albany Street in 1963.

21. The Charter contained one of the most detailed lists of management and financial requirements for any of the New Town gardens.

22. TCM, 4 September 1822.

23. The cast iron pump can still be seen in the south-west corner of the garden and still supplies water, although now supplied with pipe and tap; it is referred to in the Feu Charter.

24. TCM, 8 December 1824; HHM, 2 November 1824, and 18 July 1825.

25. A statue in honour of Adam Black was erected in East Princes Street gardens in 1877, sculpted by John Hutchison.

26. *The Scotsman,* 26 January 1874.

27. *The Scotsman*, 19 May 1847.

28. When an easier route opened from Abbeyhill to Leith and Granton. Since then the tunnel has had occasional use for wagon storage, mushroom growing (abandoned after the spread of parasitic fungus) and for air-raid shelters during the Second World War.

29. TCM, 25 June 1844; 2 July 1844; 25 February 1845; 6 May 1845; 18 November 1845.

30. In 1849 the Excise Office, together with Assessed Taxes & Stamp Offices were amalgamated to become the Inland Revenue, with offices in Waterloo Place.

31. TCM, 23 December 1845; payment by both parties to be made by mid-January 1846.

32. Feu Charter in favour of the proprietors of Drummond Place, 17 March 1846, Chartulary 38, ECA.

33. Drummond Place Garden Minute Book (1856–1936), from which this and the following material is taken.

34. Advice on greater shelter from east winds was first taken from Mr MacKenzie of Thomas Methven & Sons, but his suggestions, which included the removal of the rather ugly tool-shed, were thought too expensive.

35. Interview held with Miss Grace Milne Rae, 28 October 1971. See also: Lettice Milne Rae, *The Story of Drummond Place* (Edinburgh revised edition 1970), p. 34.

36. See Joyce Wallace, *Canonmills and Inverleith* (Edinburgh, 1994), p. 115.

37. A survey and plan was produced by Mrs Eleanor Morris, planner, and later modified by Frank H. Clark, landscape designer and member of the committee. The work was undertaken by E.M.P. Collet, nurseryman and landscape gardener, New Saughtonhall Gardens, Polton, Lasswade, for £235. More recent advice on planting improvement has been given by John Byrom, landscape consultant.

38. John Lorimer lived at 4 Drummond Place, and was a member of the garden committee from 1909 to 1910; his brother, Sir Robert Lorimer, architect, made some alterations to his house. It later became the home and studio of another distinguished artist – Sir William MacTaggart. Colonel Bailey was a member of the committee in 1909 and the plant *Meconopsis Baileyii* is named after him.

CHAPTER 12

ROYAL CIRCUS

Ann our nurse had led us by way of Queen Street Gardens and Heriot Row down to the, then to us unknown regions of Royal Circus. It was May and in the Circus Gardens, facing the crescent of tall grey houses, the trees fresh with the green of spring, lilacs scented the air, and laburnums gleamed.

Eleanor Stillar, *c.* 1878[1]

Eleanor Stillar's memories of Royal Circus centred on journeys to Madame Kunz's school at No. 19 and the associated fragrances, colour and freshness of the gardens in their spring awakenings. They appeared warm and inviting in contrast to the more sombre 'tall grey houses' around and beyond. Her recollections highlight, even if unwittingly, the importance of the gardens in helping to unite the two sections of crescent, masking the steep descent northwards. When Royal Circus was being built in 1821, the press was less than enthusiastic, claiming that the plan failed to compensate for the marked change in level, with the north side 'so much sunk and disjoined' from the southern half as to give the circus a 'distorted and disagreeable appearance'. It was, in the reporter's view, 'a most glaring defect' and a 'monstrous deformity'.[2] Most people today would be puzzled by these remarks, for Royal Circus is now described in more hallowed terms as 'this superb Craigleith stone development' exhibiting 'very refined and plain detailing'.[3] An example in fact of the skill and sensitivity of the architect William Henry Playfair. But without the gardens these criticisms might well have appeared more apparent.

Evolution of a Circus

Ever since the innovative Circus at Bath designed by John Wood and built by his son from 1767 onwards, Edinburgh aspired to something comparable. Bath's Circus was originally planned with a central hard-paved space; the plane trees (still magnificent but in slow decline) were a later addition. Ideas for an Edinburgh circus followed along similar lines; thus Craig's proposals of 1774 for a circus in George Street had at its centre a statue surrounded by grass or hard paving. The revived attempt for a similarly placed circus, promoted by Lord Provost David Steuart in 1781, also promised little in the way of soft landscaping. Over ten years later, however, a circus re-emerged as part of a plan for the second New Town, and again promoted by David Steuart. William Sibbald's design included a circus at the western end, divided into four quarters by cross streets and having at its centre an ornamental basin or pool of water. This layout, as we know, was superseded, but in all the subsequent plans right through to the final modifications by Robert Reid in 1802, the idea of a circus at the western end persisted, although moved further to the north-west. By then it had evolved into two continuous semicircular crescents with a broad opening on the east and west sides, the latter being reserved for a church. The inner space was shown as a circular enclosure but no longer filled with water.

The 1802 'Reid and Sibbald's plan' became the basis of the contractual agreement between the Town Council, Heriot Hospital and the new owners of David Steuart's feu. No change was permitted unless it could be considered an 'improvement'. The circus area owned by Heriot's Hospital was the last major part to be feued; it was also the only section to experience fairly substantial changes to the ground plan and to the arrangement of the open space. What were these changes, and why did they occur?

Changes to the Ground Plan

If we look carefully at the 1802 plan, it becomes clear that the road system between the western end of the Circus and surrounding areas, particularly Stockbridge, had not been satisfactorily resolved.[4] Sometime after the plan had been agreed, Heriot's Hospital acquired a small piece of adjoining land to the west known as Spring Gardens. When several builders approached the Hospital early in 1819 about purchasing land in the Circus, it prompted the Governors to consider how to link this additional property with the existing plan.[5] Thomas Bonnar, their Superintendent, submitted revised proposals to the Middle District Road Trustees, 'for liberty to alter the present line of road from Howe Street to Stockbridge to suit these ground plans'.[6] Neither the Road Trustees (nor their consultant engineer Robert Stevenson) were impressed, and the new line was criticised as being 'very objectionable'; the number of awkward turns and narrowness of the streets northwards were particularly disliked, likewise the eastern access, described as being 'dangerous' and 'unhandsome'. Revisions were called for, and suggestions made for improved realignment.[7] Heriot's Hospital responded by appointing a sub-committee with power 'to take the opinion of Mr Playfair or any other architect of eminence'.

That their Superintendent was side-tracked was partly political. Bonnar was under a cloud, having been dismissed from his City post following an embarrassing and riotous incident connected with a bungled public hanging, for which he became the unlucky scapegoat.[8] While the Hospital remained loyal to Bonnar, they no doubt thought it expedient to seek independent professional advice and Playfair was the obvious choice. He was already working as their consultant on the lands east of Calton Hill, where his first task had been a road matter – advising on the level for the new London Road. Technically competent, thorough and with design flair, Playfair was recognised by the Hospital as someone well able to solve the problem.

Two of Playfair's sketch proposals for Royal Circus survive, showing possibilities for resolving the roadway system and siting the church at the west end. Both matters were to influence significantly the extent and distribution of open space. The church was intended to face the centre of the Circus, forming a focal point along the east-west axis. Playfair

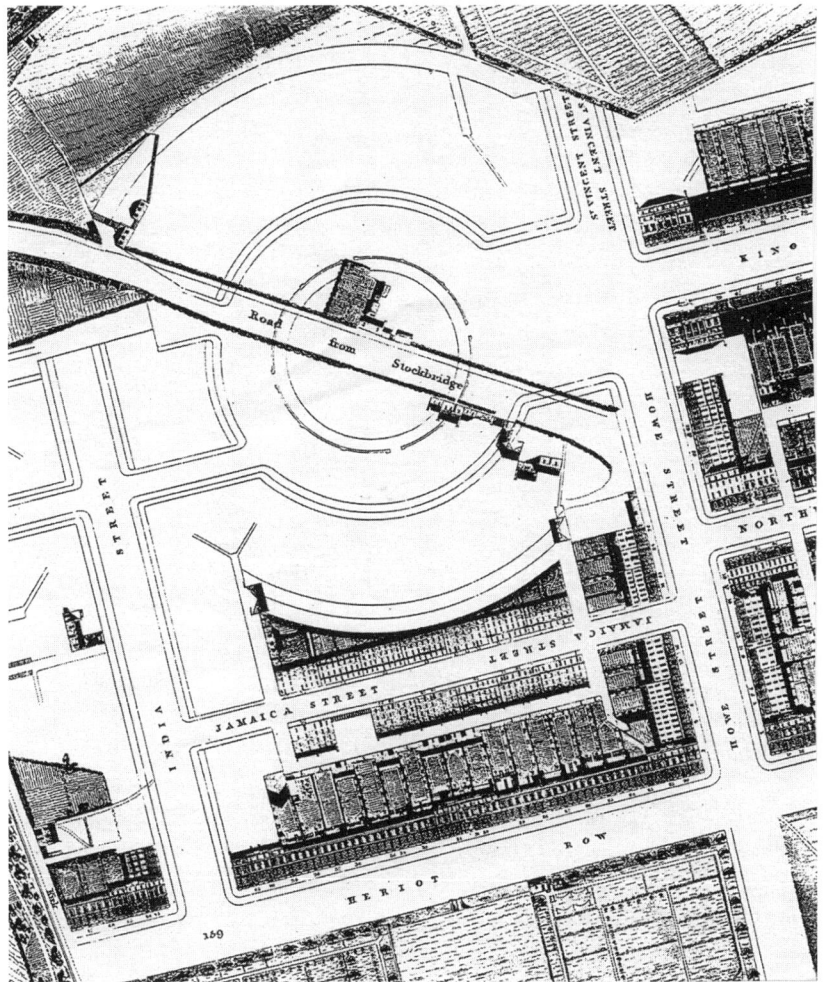

Kirkwood's Plan and Elevation, 1819, showing an outline of the intended layout for Royal Circus, in Edinburgh, but also the problems posed by the existing route to and from Stockbridge cutting through the centre.

extended this idea and suggested moving the church further west so that it could also become a feature at the head of India Street. To relate to the existing route to Stockbridge, while allowing improved access from the east, the new road was made to curve gently through the centre, with the ends of the crescents becoming oblique-angled rather than straight. As a result the inner circular space became divided into two complementary crescent-shaped garden areas. A sculptured monument or obelisk was indicated for the small residual area at the eastern end in line with the church.

Playfair's proposals, submitted in July 1819, 'showing how that part of the plan could be executed without interfering with the present road' (i.e. the route to Stockbridge), received prompt approval by the Road Trustees and other interested parties.[9] The Hospital were now at liberty to press ahead with feuing the land 'agreeably to said alteration and appoint Mr

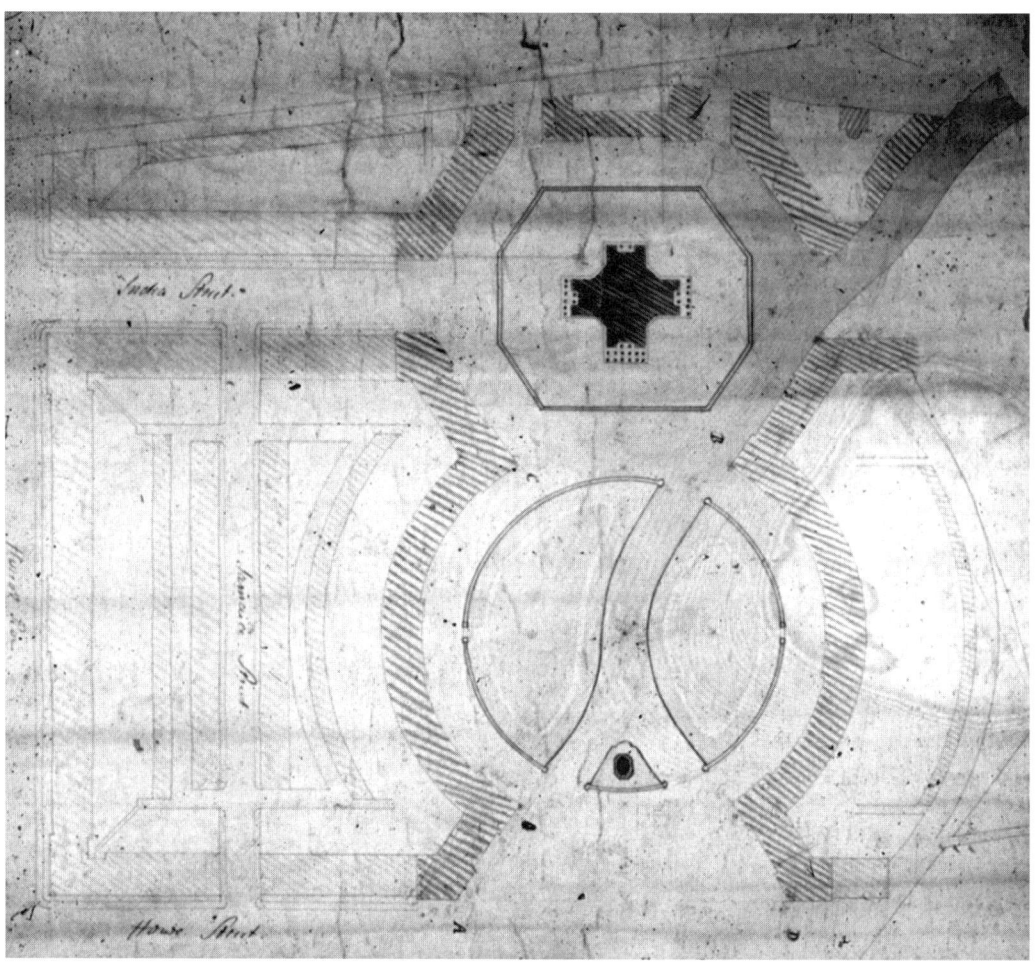

One variant by William Playfair (1819), attempting to resolve the road alignment through Royal Circus, and how this affected the allocation of open space. (George Heriot Trust and Crown copyright © RCAHMS)

Playfair architect, to make a clean copy . . . and directed him also to make out levels and elevations for the buildings'.[10] On the last day of 1819 Edinburgh newspapers advertised the forthcoming sale of building plots in the Circus and to an 'improved plan'.[11] Copies of the engraved feuing plan still exist, showing a central serpentine road sandwiched between two crescent-shaped gardens. The church has, however, disappeared, leaving an empty space, matched by a similar void at the east end. The plan provided no clues as to what these spaces were intended for, and this element of ambiguity caused problems later.[12]

Setting up the Central Gardens

One of the feuing conditions specified that owners 'upon the circular part of the plan' were bound to enclose the areas in the Circus 'with parapet and retaining walls and iron railings

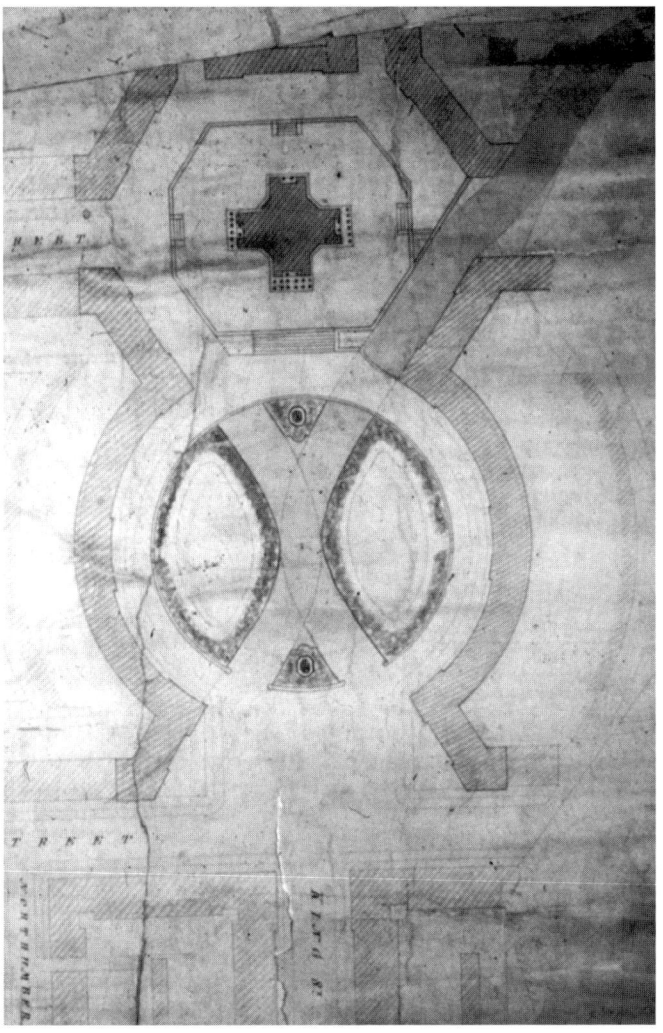

Playfair's alternative variant (1819) for road alignment through Royal Circus. (George Heriot Trust and Crown copyright © RCAHMS)

in a suitable and handsome manner according to drawings and directions to be given and furnished for executing the same by Mr Playfair . . . and the said proprietors shall have the exclusive privilege of using the same as ornamental pleasure grounds'. The cost of upkeep was also made the proprietors' responsibility. No other contemporary pleasure garden had conditions quite so brief. With no previous experience to guide them Heriot Hospital's main priority seems to have been to ensure that the space was properly enclosed, and all subsequent responsibility transferred to the proprietors. As only 26 houses were involved, the Governors perhaps felt justified in leaving administrative details as simple as possible. However, the uniform development of the two gardens (one acre (0.4 ha) each in size) was safeguarded by making them over as a single common area. Only since the

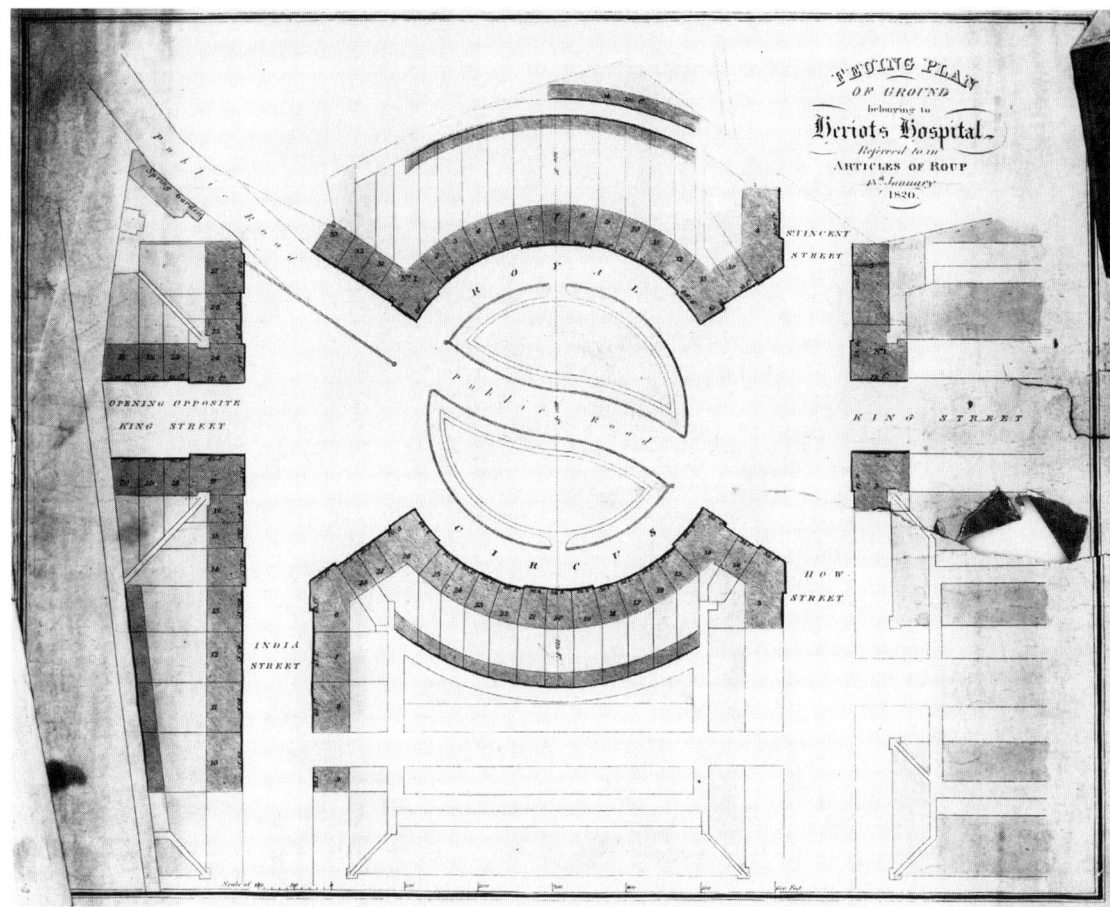

Feuing Plan for Royal Circus, by Playfair, dated 18 January 1820. The central space has now become two crescent-shaped gardens, and the two open spaces at either end remain unallocated. (George Heriot Trust and Crown copyright © RCAHMS)

Second World War have the two gardens become separated and managed as the 'North' and 'South' side gardens.

Most houses became occupied between 1821 and 1823, but 1821 plans of Edinburgh show the central space already laid out, placing them slightly ahead of the Central and West Queen Street and Drummond Place Gardens. What do we know about their makings? Unfortunately not a great deal. As with many of the smaller gardens, little recorded material survives; the only minute book traced – and that very incomplete – was one dating from 1893.[13] It appears, however, that much of the original impetus came from one of the new residents, Alexander Wood (1788–1864), an advocate by profession, who had moved from Charlotte Square to 1 Royal Circus. For several years he served as Sheriff of Kirkcudbright before becoming Dean of the Faculty in 1841, gaining the title of Lord Wood one year later.[14] He was the first chairman of the garden committee; and it was due to his initiative that the two empty spaces on the east and west sides were also formed into garden areas.

Two early views of Royal Circus Gardens. Top: Royal Circus from India Place, 1825, showing the gardens in their infancy. (Ewbank, *Picturesque Views of Edinburgh*, 1825). Bottom: The north section of the central garden, 1829. (Shepherd, *Views of Edinburgh*, 1825)

Both central spaces were laid out in a complementary manner; each had an outer belt of trees and shrubs with a gravel path running alongside. The interior was grassed and planted with specimen trees with an entrance at the centre of each crescent. It is likely that Richard Walker undertook the layout just as he did for the Central and West Queen Street Gardens. We know that he became responsible for the upkeep of Royal Circus Gardens as well as Drummond Place, and later the West Queen Street Gardens. He seems to have built up a useful garden contracting business, competently handling moderate-sized projects, supplying extra labourers when needed, besides having a useful network of relatives. Pictures of Royal Circus during the mid and late 1820s show a garden gaining maturity with the outer planting already well established, and several poplars or 'nurse' trees attaining respectable heights.

The Gardens Since Formation

By the middle years of the century both sides had became more ornate, with additional footpaths and shrub beds. But by 1868, when James McNab was writing about the gardens, standards had plummeted.[15] His forthright criticism was designed to provoke action. He wrote as follows:

> At the present time when so much is being done for the embellishment and general improvement of the town squares and gardens of Edinburgh, it is surprising to see that this taste for improving has not yet been taken up by the proprietors of Royal Circus grounds . . . the thinning of trees, as well as the general improvement of the surface of the ground in the two garden sections is much required. Both compartments contain many fine trees, but rather crowded together, and it is a pity to see that nothing is being done to relieve them.

Several trees were recommended for removal, including all the poplar (apart from the Lombardys), together with 'judicious' pruning of the rest. Not only would this improve the appearance of the gardens but additionally 'the houses would also be rendered decidedly more healthy than they can possibly be with such a mass of close vegetative matter in the vicinity, particularly during the autumnal months'. In 1868 the proprietors met and arranged for remedial work to be done, but management soon lapsed and for twenty-five years there were no further meetings.

When meetings resumed in 1893, it was due to the imminent resignation of Mr John Young, WS (1836–97), who had acted as clerk 'for upwards of 23 years' and was now nearing retirement and in declining health. For all that time Young had paid the gardener's wages out of his own pocket 'to the extent of upwards of £400'; he was not, however, seeking reimbursement, but simply to shed his responsibilities. As a well-off bachelor, he probably found that money counted for less than the bother of chasing up a host of annual dues.[16] It was a time for stocktaking, and the proprietors had to admit that 'the gardens are not at present being properly kept up' and indeed were suffering from the rough play of older boys. The following spring they were given a much needed overhaul, supervised by a specially constituted Improvement Committee. Some trees were removed, others pruned, repairs made to the railings and seats, pathways relaid with red ash and the area of turf extended. Mr W. Whitlaw carried out the work and continued as gardener.[17]

Inadequate Management

Lackadaisical practice soon reappeared. Financial matters were placed in the hands of an 'interim clerk' (on this occasion George McIntosh, SSC, of Waddell, McIntosh and Peddie) but drifted along on this basis for twenty-nine years, until his death in 1923. Only one meeting of proprietors was recorded during that period.[18] Garden dues had remained fixed at one guinea a year, and for the five years prior to the clerk's death nothing had been collected. Debts had accumulated and the garden had been neglected. When the next meeting was held, it was under the leadership of Sheriff Crole, the sole survivor of the 1894 Improvement Committee. During the 1920s and 1930s Lynedoch Place Nurseries were engaged to bring the gardens back to standard. Property by then was becoming increasingly subdivided, so a flat-rate system of contributions was introduced in place of the previous one based on feu duties.

The Two Sides Separate

The Second World War saw the removal of the railings, and the south side requisitioned to provide space for two air-raid shelters and a static water tank. Deprived of much of their garden, several proprietors decided not to pay their annual dues. Such changed circumstances also provoked debate on existing management arrangements. At a meeting of proprietors held in July 1942 it was 'amicably agreed' that the two sides should split and become independent.[19] From then on they became known as the North and South Gardens,

After the war the North side was brought back to standard relatively quickly, benefiting from the hard work and commitment of one of the residents, Colonel Charles Usher (1892–1981), former director of Physical Education at Edinburgh University. In 1975, with help from the Edinburgh New Town Conservation Committee, and to mark European Architectural Heritage Year, the proprietors were able to renew their railings to a design similar to Playfair's. At present there are about thirty mature trees in the garden, mainly elm, ash, lime, whitebeam, sycamore, hawthorn, holly and horse chestnut, with a variety of shrubs around the outer border and the central bed. Some new tree planting has been carried out during recent years.

The South garden suffered more from the war years. In 1950 the ground was bulldozed and levelled, and the interior grass-seeded. It accommodates a similar range of trees to the north side, but they are fewer in number; and with some 'alien' introductions such as Lawson cypresses. Play equipment and seats are provided, and new planting is labelled to encourage interest. New railings were added in 1992, again

One of the cast iron gateways added in the late 1990s to all four main garden entrances, modelled on the one at the west end of Drummond Place. (J. Clark)

with assistance from the New Town Conservation Committee: more recently the same body have funded the addition of a cast iron archway, over the main gateway into both the central gardens. These have been modelled on the one over the west gateway into Drummond Place Garden and similar to those in Claremont Crescent.[20]

East and West Gardens

At the time of feuing it had not been decided what to do with the residual spaces at either end, although a church was still intended for the west side. The 1821 newspaper article, already quoted, was critical of siting a church in this position, claiming that it would make 'that which is bad still worse'. Placing a church on a level platform would distort the circus still more, for it 'will have the effect of sinking apparently the north side still further from the surface level'. Did these decided opinions prejudice attitudes, and was this why Alexander Wood hastened to confer with Heriot's Hospital about enclosing the east and west ends 'agreeably to a plan produced'?[21] The Governors were happy to consent; it was simply left to Mr Wood 'and those who consider with him to obtain consent of all concerned' and to take on the whole responsibility and expense. Ownership, however, was to remain with the Hospital in case required for a church.[22] But the general mood seemed wholly against this idea, as Lord Provost William Trotter soon discovered when, 'after making every exertion . . . he found it impossible to induce the proprietors of the Circus to give up the stance looking eastwards towards Great King Street'. The garden had won the day. Instead, the church (St Stephen's, by Playfair) was consigned to the bottom end of St Vincent Street, a position where 'comparatively speaking, it would be much out of view'.[23]

These two gardens, formed on a voluntary basis, and in no way tied to the neighbouring property, lacked any legal sanctions regarding upkeep or assessments, making their survival more precarious. They continue to remain wholly dependent on the goodwill and commitment of those living nearby. Of the two, West Circus Place Garden (now renamed India Street Gardens) is slightly larger (0.60 acres (0.24 ha)) and enjoys greater privacy. It has experienced fewer crises and a more consistent standard of care. Enclosed sometime between 1822 and 1823 a portion of the original railing survives along the east and north sides where the garden sits high above the level of the main road; the rest were removed during the last war and have since been replaced by ones of plainer design. The garden consists of trees and shrubs planted around the outer border, the interior grassed and crossed by a central curved pathway from east to west. Of all the Royal Circus Gardens, this was the only one to merit praise from McNab. His sole criticism was reserved for the Lombardy poplars – 'rather unsuited for such a windy spot', and long since gone. Most of the 20–25 mature trees consist of lime, ash, elm, whitebeam and sycamore; a more recent addition is a weeping beech. A pleasant informal garden (committee meetings are held beneath a tree) it provides a safe haven for children and is well appreciated by those living nearby.

East Circus Place Garden (0.50 acres (0.20 ha), and now known as East Circus Garden, is situated at the busier, more exposed end of the Circus and has experienced a rather more chequered history. To improve privacy and shelter, embankments were formed around the sides and planted with trees and shrubs, and the interior levelled and grass sown. By McNab's time the garden was 'very neglected' with the grass high above the parapet wall, and the trees in a 'miserable state, and not above three of four of them capable of improvement and fit to be retained'. No-one, it appears, was taking much interest.

The garden continued to deteriorate and in the face of lapsed care Heriot's Hospital decided in 1883 to let it to a Mr Crichton for £1 a year, 'he keeping the ground in order and maintaining the railings'.[24] Mr Crichton, however, was only interested in providing recreation space for the boys attending his Circus Place School directly opposite. Such apparent 'abuse' produced action from neighbouring proprietors who contacted the Hospital to see if they might 'take the management of the ground in front of their feus and use it as a pleasure ground'.[25] The Governors agreed, but only on condition that it was kept 'in good and sufficient order'.[26]

Good intentions, however, were short-lived. Within sixteen years the garden had again deteriorated. On this occasion the Town Council stepped in to serve a notice under Section 148 of the Municipal and Police Act of 1879. This amongst other matters required owners of public spaces and squares held in common to keep them in good condition. Failure to comply could result in a fine, or the ultimate sanction of the Council assuming custody 'for the public benefit and advantage'; this had already happened in the case of Gayfield Square Garden.[27] From the Hospital's point of view this presented a simple solution to a tiresome issue, and they decided to grant the Town a twenty-year lease. It was not, however, to the liking of the residents. In December 1900 a deputation headed by Professor Sir Henry Littlejohn (1828–1914), Edinburgh's first Medical Officer of Health, Gerald Crole, advocate (both members of the Central Garden Committee) and William Smith, WS, 'on behalf of the feuars of Royal Circus and Circus Place' met with the Governors 'to arrange for the proper upkeep of the gardens'. Also present was the Convener of the Council's Parks Department.[28] This time a more formal arrangement was made. Littlejohn and Crole were appointed Trustees to act on behalf of the other feuars; they were made personally responsible for seeing that the Garden was looked after 'to the satisfaction of the Governors and the public authorities' during the term of the ten-year lease.[29]

The system of a renewable lease and appointed Trustees has continued ever since,[30] with subscribers being drawn from south-east and north-east Circus Place and other nearby streets. In recent years a careful programme of renewal work has been initiated largely under the direction of one long-serving Trustee, John Dewar, who during the 1970s and '80s devoted considerable time to the garden.[31] At present it contains some twenty or so mature trees, mainly elm, hawthorn, sycamore and ash. It is enclosed by a plain iron railing to the same design as the West Garden.

Notes

1. Eleanor Sillar, *Edinburgh's Child: some memoirs of 90 years*, p. 90.
2. *The Scotsman*, 10 November 1821.
3. *Walks in Edinburgh New Town,* published by the Edinburgh New Town Conservation Committee, (1989, 3rd edition) p. 17.
4. India Street appears destined to be continued as a main thoroughfare northwards, with access to the Circus being limited to two narrow streets positioned on either side of the proposed church.
5. HHM, 8 January 1819, vol. 21.
6. HHM, 22 January 1819, vol. 21.
7. HHM, 23 March 1819, vol. 22; details of the Road Trustees' criticisms are contained in these minutes.
8. The public hanging was of a young persistent robber by the name of Robert Johnston on 30 December 1818.
9. HHM, 27 July 1819, vol. 22.
10. HHM, 3 December 1819, vol. 22.
11. *Edinburgh Advertiser*, 31 December 1819.
12. A ground plan drawn to a larger scale shows both areas enclosed and coloured green; Playfair drawing collection, EUL, Portfolio 7.
13. Royal Circus Minute Book (1893–1947); now in possession of the Secretary to the South garden.
14. *The Faculty of Advocates in Scotland 1532–1943*, ed. Sir Francis J. Grant. Scottish Record Society (Edinburgh, 1944), p. 222. *The Scotsman,* 20 July 1864, carried a short obituary of Lord Wood.
15. James McNab, 'The Town Trees of Edinburgh, No. 12 The Royal Circus Gardens' (*The Farmer*, 26 March 1868).
16. Mr Young, 22 Royal Circus, the former clerk, was absolved from further payment towards upkeep.
17. Royal Circus Minute Book, Minute, 27 November 1893.
18. The meeting was held on 13 June 1907 when Sir Henry Littlejohn was listed as being on the committee.
19. Interview (1974) with Miss Irvine, 3 Royal Circus, one time secretary of the management committee, South Garden.
20. Claremont Crescent, by William Burn, on the far eastern limb of the New Town, was begun in 1823 but took many years to complete. No minute books for the garden area survive.
21. HHM, 11 January 1822, vol. 22.
22. HHM, 28 February 1822, vol. 22.
23. *Edinburgh Advertiser,* 26 January 1827; report of Town Council proceedings relative to the building of St Vincent Street Church.
24. HHM, 7 June 1883, vol. 47; he was probably the David Crichton listed in the Edinburgh and Leith directory of 1880–81 as resident at 6 North West Circus Place.
25. HHM, 3 April 1884, vol. 48; & 1 May 1884.
26. HHM, 18 August 1884, vol.48.
27. *Edinburgh Municipal and Police Act 1879* (42 & 43 Vict c 132); see also: TCM, 18 September 1900; 17 October 1900; and 14 December 1900.
28. HHM, 10 December 1900.

29. Such a leasing system has never operated for the West Garden (India Place Gardens) although technically the land is still owned by the George Heriot Trust. The leases have varied from between 5 and 15 years, with the overall responsibility resting with two or three Trustees.

30. There have been the occasional blips in the arrangement; for example, the proprietors allowed the lease to lapse in the 1920s, whereupon the Hospital agreed to convey the ground to the Council as a garden (TCM, 3 March 1927, and 7 April 1927).

31. In 1970 the East Circus Garden featured in a small exhibition associated with the conference on the Conservation of Georgian Edinburgh, to demonstrate how the gardens could be improved. It was put together by John Byrom, Architecture Research Unit, with the help of post-graduate students in Landscape Architecture, Edinburgh University. It was followed by a careful replanting and management programme.

CHAPTER 13

BELLEVUE CRESCENT

Bellevue Crescent Garden was formed about the year 1840, after lying for a long period as an open waste. The laying-out and arranging of this piece of ground was done chiefly under the direction of the late William Crawford, Esq. of Cartsburn, he being at the time one of the Crescent proprietors.

James McNab, 1865[1]

None of the proposals for this north-east corner of the second New Town had included pleasure ground. Preliminary ideas all favoured an oblique line of buildings following the angle of the road to Canonmills. Robert Reid's revised plan of 1802 put forward two possibilities, and the one favoured as having better feuing potential was for a continuous crescent lying practically adjacent to the old roadway.[2] The land continued to be let for pasture and also contained some profitable sand pits.[3]

Engraving of Bellevue Crescent, Edinburgh, 1827, prior to any gardens being added. (Courtesy of David Easton, photograph Crown copyright © RCAHMS)

One of Thomas Bonnar's last projects as City Superintendent was to design Bellevue Crescent. In July 1818 the first building plots were advertised for sale,[4] and by 1823 the southern half was complete and occupied. But not before a change had been made to the original plan, allowing for a new Burgh church to be placed at the centre. Sites in London Street and Albany Street had also been considered but rejected.[5] Unlike Royal Circus, the Bellevue Crescent proprietors welcomed the church, seeing its arrival as a means of improving their surroundings. Close by were the recently formed Drummond Place Gardens, and these perhaps inspired the Bellevue proprietors to think along similar lines. When they met with the Council in November 1822 to give their approval for the church, two ideas were raised: first that 'the ground marked as stable ground in the general feuing plan should be converted into pleasure ground', and second, that an enclosure should be formed in front of the crescent 'as might be considered suitable'.[6] The Council expressed interest, and declared 'their readiness to co-operate'.

Ideas of transforming the stable ground into pleasure gardens (the largest backland area of any in the New Town (1.5 acres (0.6 ha)) proved hopelessly unrealistic. Not only were there insufficient proprietors to shoulder such a burden, but the consent of all surrounding property owners would have been necessary. The notion persisted until the land became divided by a carriageway linking Scotland Street to the church.[7] Still owned by the City, this phantom pleasure ground serves a variety of uses from wilderness space to allotments, tennis courts, clothes drying and garaging.[8]

Bellevue Crescent – South Garden

St Mary's Church (now Broughton St Mary's, following unification in 1992 with Broughton McDonald – formerly Broughton Place Church) was designed by Bonnar's successor, Thomas Brown, who also drew up proposals for 'an enclosure' as desired by the proprietors. An oval-shaped garden was planned to front each wing and to frame the church whose foundation stone was laid by Lord Provost William Arbuthnot on 15th August 1823, the first anniversary of George IV's visit to Edinburgh.[9] The occasion was marked by pomp and pious speeches, but did little to change *The Scotsman*'s judgment that the church was a 'decent, orderly, old fashioned, poor sort of, indifferent thing'.[10]) Brown had already been associated with three pleasure grounds, having designed the railings enclosing Central and West Queen Street Gardens, as well as Drummond Place. But no garden area was possible until the old road to Canonmills was realigned. This was not accomplished until nearly twenty years later when Heriot's Hospital began to feu the land opposite for building Bellevue Terrace and Place.

In March 1841, the Town, Heriot's Hospital, the Middle District & Cramond Road Trustees, Mr Blackwood, Overseer to the Road Trustees and Bellevue Crescent proprietors met to discuss the road improvements proposed by Thomas Brown. His plan required the old road to be moved further eastwards, thereby allowing room for two small garden areas in front of the Crescent. The land gained, however, was at the expense of Heriot's Hospital, and by way of compensation it was agreed that not only should the proprietors in Bellevue Crescent 'enclose with a proper parapet wall and iron railing and lay out in shrubbery the

Photograph of Bellevue Crescent taken
shortly after the Second World War.
(Ian Lindsay, *Georgian Edinburgh*)

area shown in the plan opposite to the southern division of the Crescent' (the part built),
but that access should be granted 'to the feuars of Heriot's Hospital on the opposite side
of the road . . . in the same terms with the feuars of Bellevue Crescent'.[11] Further, the
creation of the garden should be carried out 'simultaneously' with the other work and to
the satisfaction of all the interested parties.

Laying Out the South Garden

Work started promptly. It soon became clear, however, that the proprietors were toiling to
fulfil their part of the bargain in the face of rapidly escalating costs. When they appealed
to Heriot's Hospital for extra time and financial help, they met with a frosty response;
the Governors simply reminded them of their agreement and disclaimed any liability
for financial support.[12] Months later everything ground to a halt as the money finally
ran out. Towards the end of October 1842, the proprietors appealed to the City, 'praying
that the Council in respect of St. Mary's Church would contribute liberally towards the
improvement'.[13] Each resident had already subscribed £25, but the enclosure was still 'not
two-thirds completed', and there were accumulated debts of just over £32. Somewhat

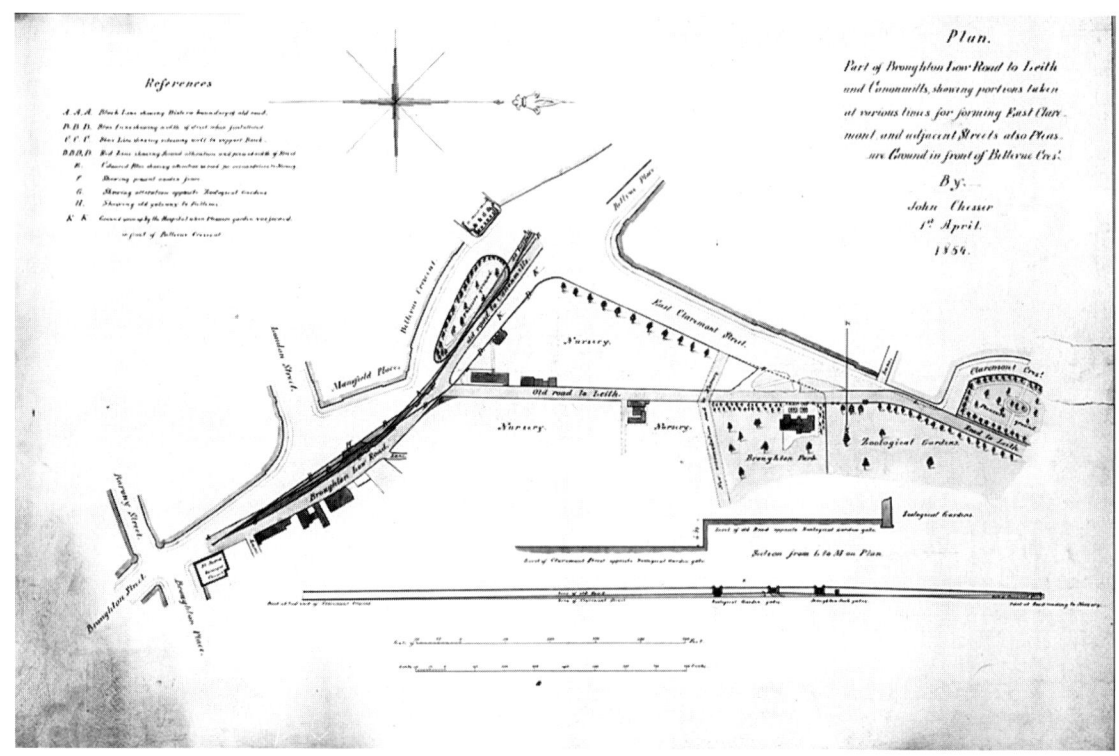

John Chesser's plan, 1854, showing the road realignments carried out at various times and the south section of pleasure garden. Note the neatly laied-out Claremont Crescent Garden to the west and the Zoological Gardens practically opposite them. (George Heriot Trust, Crown copyright © RCAHMS)

reluctantly the Town agreed to donate £125, the equivalent of five house spaces the church was deemed to occupy.

All the extra cash was swallowed up, completing the parapet and railing and leaving nothing for interior improvements. Eventually, in March 1844, some proprietors plucked up courage to approach the Hospital once more. On this occasion the reception was more sympathetic. On the strength that 'the completion of the work will be to the advantage of the Hospital feuars', they agreed to contribute £40 provided no further demands were made and the garden was 'fully and properly completed'.[14] Although modest in size (just under one-third of an acre (0.12 ha) and one of the smallest of the New Town gardens, it had proved a costly and protracted exercise.

Subsequent Fortunes

The Garden's subsequent history is somewhat elusive. No minute books have been found (like other smaller gardens it was probably run informally with little in the way of records); and with no legally stated rights or responsibilities there was little hold over residents unwilling to contribute towards upkeep. We do know, however, from a report by James

McNab, that the layout and planting were carried out under the direction of William Crawford, one of the original proprietors keen on a garden. A council member of the Royal Caledonian Horticultural Society, he was known to McNab and also to Patrick Neill – a near neighbour and an elder at the church. Crawford therefore not only had an interest in horticulture but also had ready access to friendly experts.

The choice of planting, according to McNab, was a little unusual insofar as it was limited to two varieties of trees: elms along the east side, and a row of limes around the west side, together with an outer border of evergreen shrubs. Mr Crawford had planned 'to attend carefully to the pruning and thinning' but his death halted this dedicated commitment. By the 1860s the Garden was described by McNab as a dense mass of trees and shrubs, obscuring views from all but the upper windows and tempting 'idle youths' to break off branches overhanging the road. The trees at the centre were 'dwarf stinted' and the grass in poor condition. McNab wanted two-thirds of the elms removed and every alternate lime tree, but such radical advice was probably ignored.

During the Second World War the railings were removed and the Garden used for shelters.[15] Restoration was carried out in the late 1940s, when a post and wire fence was erected inside the original cope stone, and a privet hedge was planted. Not long after, the proprietors approached the Council to see about taking the garden over as a public ornamental space. The offer was initially refused, but was eventually accepted in 1965.[16] There are thirty trees or so in the garden, made up of lime and elm, with some ash and hawthorn, but there is little in the way of shrub planting apart from privet hedging around the boundary. Firmly padlocked, the garden's main function is to provide some protection from the busy roadway and a welcome splash of green.

Bellevue Crescent – North Garden

The north side was not built until the early 1880s under John Lessels, the City architect, and was completed within two to three years. Only flatted accommodation was provided, and maybe for this reason the Town's Parks Department assumed responsibility for making the Garden in 1883, and for its subsequent care. Peter Sinclair, builder, was responsible for erecting the parapet wall, at a cost of £259, and Wilson & Dunnet provided the railings at £85.[17]

The interior was designed to complement its neighbour; lime and elm trees were planted around the perimeter, and the central area was grassed, with three or four specimen trees added and a footpath made around the outer edge. During the Second World War the railings were removed and later replaced by an inferior post and wire mesh fence.[18] The Garden contains about thirty or so trees made up mostly of lime and elm with some ash, whitebeam, sycamore and hawthorn; but lacking any boundary hedging, the Garden appears more bare and open. But open it is not, for the gate is chained and padlocked and a notice warns 'No ball games'. As with its companion, it provides a green approach to the City and a buffer between the crescent and the main road.

Notes

1. James McNab, 'Our Town Trees; Hope and Bellevue Crescent gardens', (*The Scottish Farmer*, 13 September 1865). Later information quoting McNab is taken from this source.

2. TCM, 30 December 1801; details of the two plans are not given, but presumably one followed the earlier proposals of an oblique line of terrace housing, and the other a crescent.

3. TCM, 13 March 1811; the lease of Bellevue Parks and sand pit was settled by public auction when the highest bid was made by John Kirkham, builder in Edinburgh, for £226 per annum.

4. *Edinburgh Evening Courant*, 9 July 1818; (incorrectly named as Melville Crescent, but rightly given as Bellevue Crescent in a subsequent advertisement: *Edinburgh Evening Courant*, 23 July 1818.

5. TCM, 11 September 1822, St Andrew's (George Street) and St George's (Charlotte Square) were the first two Burgh churches erected for the Town Council, followed by St Mary's, then St Stephen's (St Vincent Street) and finally Greenside Church (Royal Terrace).

6. TCM, 20 November 1822.

7. Thomas Brown, Superintendent, when writing to Carlyle Bell, WS, City Clerk, in 1833 about land still to be feued in the area, refers to the space behind Bellevue Crescent. Thomas Brown's Letter Book 3, dated 12 March 1833, ECA.

8. The tennis club (two hard courts) who lease the ground from the City was established before the First World War by former pupils of Mary Erskine's school, becoming known as Drummond Tennis Club in the 1930s.

9. *Edinburgh Evening Courant*, 18 August 1823. The church cost £13,000 to build, and provided room for a congregation of 1,800.

10. *The Scotsman*, 22 August 1824.

11. HHM, 18 March 1841, vol. 29; this and the following information is taken from this minute.

12. HHM, 2 July 1841, vol. 30, and 2 September 1841.

13. TCM, 8 November 1842.

14. HHM, 18 March 1844, vol. 31; 15 April 1844, vol. 31; 13 May 1844, vol. 31.

15. TCM, 5 January 1950; no details of usage are given.

16. TCM, 30 March 1965.

17. TCM, 22 May 1883; Report by Public Parks Committee recommending making the garden, which received approval.

18. TCM, 5 January 1950; the fencing cost £175, and work on the interior, £60.

PART SEVEN

THE EARL OF MORAY'S FEU

Two early nineteenth-century views of the Dean Valley and the Water of Leith. Top: St Bernard's Well and the Moray Bank Gardens, now formed and enclosed, but prior to the first landslip. Directly opposite is the rough bank which later became the Dean Gardens. (Ewbank, *Picturesque Views of Edinburgh*, 1825) Bottom: St Bernard's Well, designed by Alexander Nasmyth in 1789 on the site of a mineral spring. A delightful eye-catcher for both the Moray Bank and the Dean Gardens. (Shepherd, *Views of Edinburgh*, 1825)

CHAPTER 14

THE EARL OF MORAY'S GROUNDS

These grounds, which have a beautiful variety of surface, envelop the northern and western (which is the finest) part of Edinburgh. They lie on an eminence, and are washed by the Water of Leith, from which they are separated in part by a beautiful sloping bank, and partly by a perpendicular rock of great height and most picturesque character. The view embraces the greater part of the course of the river, – the whole line of the Forth from Largo-Law to Ben-Lomond, – and, more nearly, St Bernard's Well, the Mills, Stockbridge, and several other fine objects. But this is not all. Looking towards them, (and, in particular, viewing them from the opposite bank) we have St George's Church, the Castle, and the town, seen above the wooded park and river, which form a foreground worthy of the finest picture, and in character most strikingly Italian.

The Scotsman, 1821[1]

A site of such rare beauty as to prompt comparison with the finest classical landscapes: this was the Earl of Moray's estate at Drumsheugh. By 1821 the buildings of the first and second New Town were elbowing closer but the extent and character of these grounds kept them at a 'proper' distance, creating a feeling of *rus in urbe*[2] a sanctuary from city life, a healthsome retreat now that 'the grounds about the Castle have been made into *private* property' (West Princes Street Gardens), and the Meadows, King's Park and Calton Hill 'too far distant from the seat of fashion' for convenient perambulation. It was a sentiment shared by Henry Cockburn for whom the peace, glorious sunsets and sound of corncraiks' nesting happily in the dewy grass' held special charm.[3] Hopes that its magic might endure were little more than a pipedream. By highlighting its unique qualities, *The Scotsman* hoped, however, to encourage architecture of the highest quality to harmonise with the existing landscape. Lord Moray should therefore 'apply to the first architects in the island' and, failing this, 'to take competition plans from such as will give them'; for in thus regarding the public benefit, 'he best consults his own private interest'.

The Land's Development

The ground had formed part of the Barony of Broughton, known as Drumsheugh or Meldrumsheugh, and was bought by Heriot's Hospital in 1636. Thereafter it passed into the hands of various owners. One of them, Adam Drummond, a surgeon, built a house which stood near the junction of Great Stuart Street and Randolph Crescent[4] (slightly to the east of the axis adopted in the development plan). Eventually the land and house, extending to about 30 Scots acres,[5] came into the ownership of Francis, 9th Earl of Moray (1737–1810), who lived there until his death.[6] His son Francis, the 10th Earl (1771–1848), was responsible for developing the land.

James Gillespie Graham (1775–1855) is the architect associated with the Moray estate, but Robert Reid and William Burn were also involved in the preliminary stages when other professionals were invited to put forward plans.[7] These various submissions were scrutinised by individuals 'of the first eminence in the kingdom, as well as persons of acknowledged taste in such matters',[8] indicating more of a selection process than previously acknowledged. Details have not survived but we now know that Gillespie Graham also prepared 'a variety of designs . . . one of which was acted upon'.[9]

The successful architect was born James Gillespie[10] in Dunblane, Perthshire, the son of 'a writer' (i.e. solicitor) employed as sheriff substitute; he was therefore of middle-class background, and not of humble birth as once supposed.[11] His early training, however, remains uncertain. We know that from 1800 he was director of the 2nd Lord Macdonald's improvements in Skye and North Uist, afterwards establishing a successful practice on the mainland. Self-confident, energetic and something of an opportunist, Gillespie Graham's projects were wide-ranging and included public buildings, mansion houses (favouring the castellated style), churches (mostly Gothic in character)[12], and numerous residential layouts. And practically all confined to

Scotland.[13] The architect had already worked on this side of Edinburgh, being responsible in 1809 for Alva Street on behalf of the Erskine family.[14] In 1819 he designed a large villa development for the Nisbets' Dean estate, with a connecting bridge over the Water of Leith. Had this latter plan together with his 1825 layout for Wester Coates (on behalf of Heriot's Hospital and others) been fulfilled, his presence in these parts would have been considerable.[15] And Edinburgh (in the case of the Coates plan) would have been the richer by several more pleasure grounds. In all these schemes, however, the land abutting the Water of Leith was reserved as ornamental space – an idea eventually adopted, if on a rather reduced scale.

Gillespie Graham's Design

The design 'acted upon' followed the classical tradition of the New Town but with architecture

James Gillespie Graham, architect for the Moray feu and other (unrealised) projects at the west end of Edinburgh. (Crombie, *Modern Athenians, 1837–1847*, ECL)

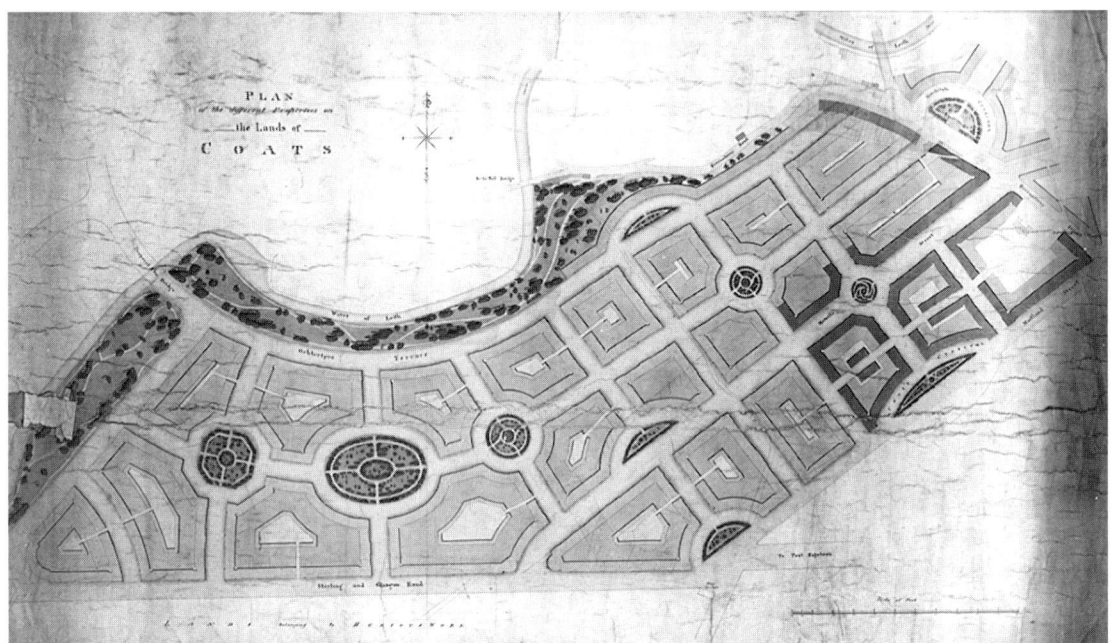

Gillespie Graham's plan for the lands of Wester Coates, 1825, instigated by the George Heriot Trust. If implemented it would have continued the character of the Moray development further south-westwards, creating many more pleasure gardens. (George Heriot Trust, Crown copyright © RCAHMS)

particularly robust and monumental in scale turning to advantage the site's distinctive shape by creating a strong, self-contained and unified scheme: one that balanced a fairly tight development with generous amounts of open space. Nowhere else in the New Town are architecture and landscape so well matched and happily married. The three central gardens have been compared to 'an emerald pendant' of crescent, oval and circus; the buildings curving along each side of the central chain, their palace-like frontages turned inwards 'as dancing partners' up and down their steep changes in level.[16] In contrast to these well-mannered central spaces is the garden area formed along the north flank of the estate. Contained within the steep and rugged southern bank of the Dean gorge, its feet 'washed by the Water of Leith', it represents the quintessence of the picturesque – a heady mix of the sublime and the beautiful. Later to become known as the Bank Garden, it was the first pleasure ground to be formed adjacent to the Water of Leith; and set a precedent for those that followed – Dean, Douglas and Belgrave Crescent Gardens.

In the summer of 1822 the first house plots were sold by public auction.[17] During the site's clearance several alert citizens seized the opportunity to rescue planting to add to their own recently formed pleasure gardens. Central Queen Street and West Princes Street Gardens both benefited in this way. By the late 1830s the estate was mostly built and occupied, its prime position and exclusive nature safeguarding it from the downturn in house sales which blighted other developments such as Playfair's Calton Hill scheme.[18]

The Earl of Moray's Grounds   267

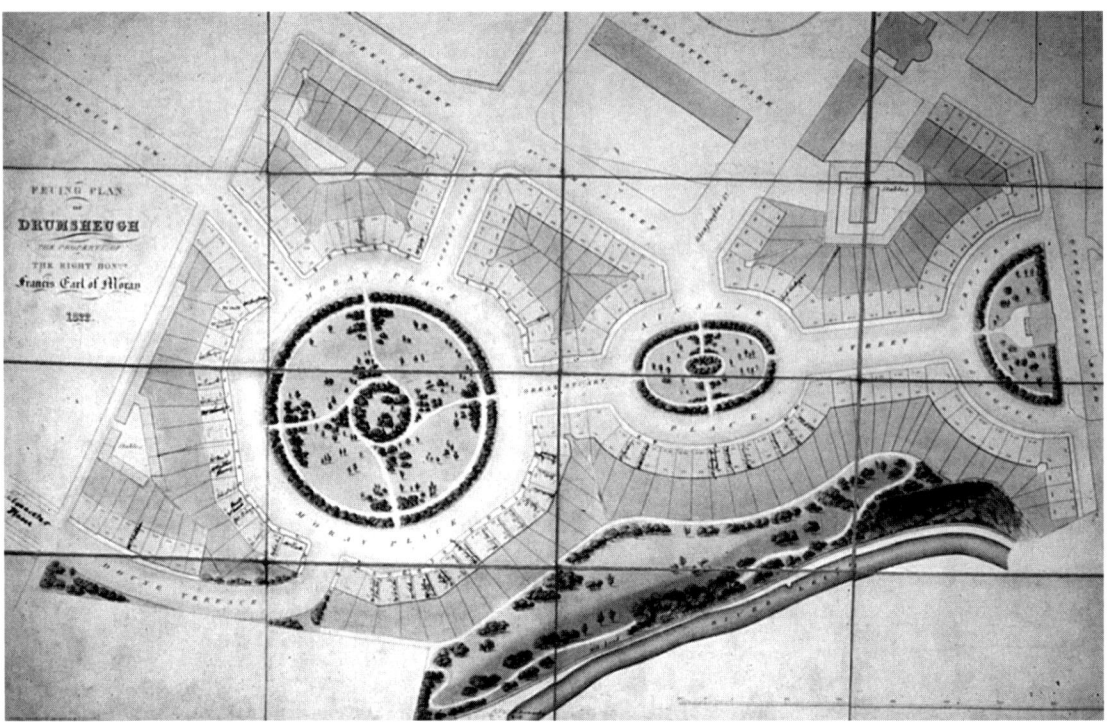

Gillespie Graham's 1822 Feuing Plan for the Moray estate, indicating the design for the centre and bank garden areas. (NAS, RHP 756)

New and fashionable the scheme may have been, but some critics dubbed the design 'beautifully monotonous, and magnificently dull', its introverted character being considered an 'incurable fault'.[19] The aristocracy were accused of having 'contemptuously turned their back on all their neighbours' in a bid to escape the advancing tide of shops and lodging-houses.[20] The Moray estate, however, has never failed to attract the aristocratic, well-off and professional members of society.[21] Although much of the property in now subdivided, with some invasion from office and business premises, it remains an attractive and desirable residential area.

Conditions of Sale

The claim that conditions of sale (Articles of Roup) for the Moray feu were the most detailed and stringent ever produced[22] is misleading for they were closely modelled on ones already operating for the second New Town.[23] As far as the pleasure grounds were concerned the clauses relating to rights and responsibilities contained ambiguities and inconsistencies which soon surfaced during the crises affecting the Bank Garden. The feuing conditions relating to the gardens are summarised below:

The Bank Garden

The wilderness area with its breathtaking views across the valley was a bounty to be cherished. Lord Moray had reserved a large plot on the south-west side for his town house (28 Moray Place, although never occupied by him) and understandably he wanted to exercise careful control over the use of the bank. The Articles of Roup (compiled by Gillespie Graham) stated the Earl's intention to 'preserve the beauty of the bank on the south side of the river . . . and to reserve the same as pleasure ground for the benefit of himself and his feuars'. It was specified that all feuars of houses within the Moray feu were to have 'access in common' to the Bank Garden provided they contributed towards the initial costs of laying out the ground, and agreed responsibility for its future upkeep. This implied that Lord Moray would be responsible for having the garden formed, with the feuars deciding individually whether or not to take advantage of it. Failure to make the Bank over unequivocally as common property was to have unfortunate financial repercussions for the Earl. In addition, those with property adjoining the Bank were not allowed to erect stables or similar buildings in their back ground, and the boundary walls were not to exceed three feet (92 cm), and were to be topped with a light iron rail to preserve the view.

Over time, 'by custom and habit', those with property abutting the Bank have come to be regarded as the main proprietors. They have overall responsibility for upkeep which is financed by a separate assessment (originally based on the feu duty but later changed to the rateable value system, which still applies). Other feuars and 'outsiders' can become subscribers.

Moray and Ainslie Place Gardens

Rights and obligations for Moray and Ainslie Place Gardens (front gardens) were more specific, although like the Bank Garden, they lacked detail on management matters. All the feuars were obliged to enclose the two areas with parapet, retaining walls and iron railings 'in a suitable and handsome manner', according to drawings made by Gillespie Graham. These were not to be 'more expensive than those adopted in Royal Circus' (recently erected to designs by William Playfair). They were also required 'to lay them down in shrubbery and walks, as shown by the plan', and in return were granted 'the exclusive privilege, along with the said Earl and his foresaids, of using the same as ornamental pleasure ground', with responsibility for their care and upkeep.

Proprietors of flatted accommodation were excluded from all the garden areas unless the Earl 'and his foresaids' granted permission, and then only on condition that they contributed towards the original costs, together with the annual dues. Corner stances had originally been allocated for flats, having their entry from the 'side' streets; they were meant to provide for a rather broader range of residents including a number of tradespeople.[24]

Randolph Crescent

The open space within Randolph Crescent was excluded from the conditions of sale; the area was retained by the Earl with the intention of completing Gillespie Graham's design for a building serving as a focal point.[25]

Notes

1. *The Scotsman,* 10 November 1821.
2. John Geddie, 'The sculptured stones of Edinburgh; the West end and Dalry group', *BOEC* Vol. 11 (1909), p. 133.
3. Henry Cockburn, *Memorials of his Time* (Edinburgh, 1971), p. 402; Cockburn's enjoyment was enhanced by the presence of his close legal friends – Jeffrey, Richardson and Rutherford.
4. For a detailed account of the various owners refer to: John Clerk Wilson, 'Lands and houses of Drumsheugh', *BOEC*, Vol. 25 (1945), pp. 71–89.
5. Some other small areas of neighbouring ground were later added, including two pieces of land behind Charlotte Square (in 1808), and a strip opposite Doune Terrace (1 February 1823; part of the lands of Stockbridge belonging to Raeburn family).
6. On acquiring Drumsheugh house the family left their old town house, Moray House in the Canongate.
7. See, for example, Gifford et al., *The Buildings of Scotland: Edinburgh*, p. 355.
8. *Edinburgh Evening Courant,* 17 June 1822, letter by 'an observer'.
9. Detail in the accounts submitted by Gillespie Graham to Lord Moray, which makes mention of the preliminary work which was costed at £300. See Earl of Moray's Archives, Tin box 26 (formerly wooden box No. VI), 16–18, Summons, Lord Moray and J. Gillespie Graham, March 1832.
10. In 1815 James Gillespie married Margaret Graham, heiress of the Orchill estate in Perthshire.
11. Although many biographical references persist in the claim that James Gillespie Graham was of humble birth, there seems to be no foundation for this: his maternal grandfather was a schoolmaster and his father, Malcolm, was a writer (lawyer).
12. Gillespie Graham's predilection for Gothic architecture found a happy partner in A.W. Pugin (1812–52).
13. Hamilton Square, centre of the proposed town at Birkenhead; and designs (prepared by Pugin) for the competition for the Houses of Parliament in 1836.
14. The land had been acquired in 1755 by Charles Erskine, a Lord of Session and one of the Erskines of Alva (and a branch of the Earls of Mar).
15. *HHM,* 18 July 1825.
16. John Byrom, landscape consultant: 'Outline management plan, Randolph Crescent, Ainslie Place, Moray Place' (November 1995); presented to the garden committee. This was a second report and followed an earlier management plan on 'The Moray Bank Garden' (1994).
17. *Edinburgh Advertiser,* 26 July 1822; notice of sale to be held at the Royal Exchange Coffee House, 7 August 1822.
18. The building trade, which had experienced such a boom in the early 1820s, was slowing down by the middle and latter part of the decade, and a number of builders were beginning to face financial hardship as house sales plummeted.
19. Grant, *Old and New Edinburgh,* Vol. 2, p. 202.
20. *The Scotsman,* 12 November 1825, letter headed 'The extension of the city'.
21. Some of the early residents whose names are still remembered today include: Lord Francis Jeffrey, editor of the Edinburgh Review and elevated to the bench in 1834 (town house, 24 Moray Place); Duguld Stewart, Professor of Moral Philosophy (5 Ainslie Place); Thomas Chalmers, DD, leader of the Free Church Movement (3 Forres Street); William Playfair, architect (17 Great Stuart Street), and Dean Ramsay, Minister of St John's Church (23 Ainslie

Place). Many other people eminent in their day had their residences there (both owning and renting) and it seems to have been particularly popular with the legal, medical and academic professions. James Skene also lived for a time in Moray Place. For a detailed account of the various residents over the nineteenth century refer to Ann Mitchell, *No More Corncraiks: Lord Moray's Feuars in Edinburgh's New Town*, (Edinburgh, 1998).

22. 'Articles and conditions of Roup and Sale of the grounds of Drumsheugh belonging to the Right Hon Francis Earl of Moray', copy, Edinburgh Room, Central Library, YDA 2294;1822.

23. Connie Byrom, 'The Development of Edinburgh's Second New Town', *BOEC*, New Series, Vol. 3 (1994), pp. 53–4.

24. Information kindly supplied by John Butters who has conducted extensive research on the various feu charters within the Moray feu.

25. It has been suggested that this was the site for the Earl of Moray's house (see Gifford et al., p. 355).

CHAPTER 15

THE MORAY BANK GARDEN
(5.2 acres, 2.0 ha)

> . . . the rear of Moray Place in particular, sustained on a series of Arches that gives its hanging gardens an altogether Babylonish aspect, whilst woods and shrubberies and sloping lawns thrown in everywhere the brilliant and grateful varieties of the tint termed green to relieve the perpetual rigidity of hugh precipitous crags, cliffs or buildings.
>
> *Imperial Gazetteer of Scotland, c.* 1865[1]

A narrow strip parallel to Doune Terrace was added to the Bank Garden in the early 1820s when the Earl acquired the land from the Raeburn estate. This provided a green frontage to those living in the terrace, besides allowing a woodland division between the Moray feu and the proposed housing development further southwards (India Place – part of the lands of Stockbridge).[2]

Gillespie Graham's design for the Bank was simple; it consisted of a continuous path, looping around the edges which were tree-planted, and with clumps of trees scattered within the grassed interior. A number of existing mature trees were retained. Looking at the feuing plan, it is hard to appreciate the severe fall in ground towards the river, so steep in places to equal a gradient of up to one in two. In its natural state, the bank was relatively stable. But it became a slippery, self-destructing mass when subjected to unaccustomed pressures from earth deposited by builders and others at the higher levels. Three major landslips occurred between 1825 and 1837, causing extensive damage and depriving proprietors of the full use of the garden for considerable periods. The remedial action taken was responsible for creating the 'Babylonish aspect', for along two-thirds of the southern boundary and in three places a massive retaining wall was built consisting of 46 arches. It was an unexpected and costly outlay which fell most heavily on Lord Moray's pocket. Because of the legal and financial implications for the several parties concerned (the Earl, his feuars, several builders and the proprietors of Greenland Mill), records survive which provide a useful catalogue of events.[3]

The First Slip, June 1825

The most dramatic slip – because totally unforeseen – occurred in June 1825. On the first occasion the mill proprietors (the Incorporation of Bakers) sought advice from George Buchanan, civil engineer; he also acted for the Moray feuars in 1837.[4] Built in the early years of the eighteenth century, Greenland Mill was one of the lowest on the Water of Leith, standing at the base of the bank, roughly midway below Randolph Crescent and Ainslie Place.[5] The main thrust of this slip occurred to the rear of the mill with devastating results. Most of the mature trees in its path were ripped out, and the mill lead was choked with debris. Not only were the safety and functioning of the mill threatened, but the builders at the top feared the imminent collapse of their houses – some of which had reached dining-floor level. Professional opinion unanimously agreed that the slippage had been caused by large quantities of earth being heaped onto the upper reaches during the preliminary stages of forming the pleasure grounds 'into a regular shape', together with the 'raising up' of the private gardens attached to the new houses.[6] The steepness and substructure of the bank, resting as it did on a stratum of slatey clay rock or shale, added to the problem. Blame was hard to apportion as many were inadvertently at fault. Immediate action was, however, crucial and the responsibility for this fell on Lord Moray, although his agents (Messrs Walker, Richardson & Melville, WS) were quick to disclaim any liability. Much was at stake, and the Earl could ill afford to lose the confidence of his feuars, potential feuars and the builders; the livelihood of the millers was also at risk.

Robert Stevenson, Civil Engineer, appointed Lord Moray's Consultant

Now best remembered for his role in lighthouse design and construction, Robert Stevenson was a versatile and extremely hard-working engineer. His association with several New Town Gardens (St Andrew Square; West Princes Street and the Calton Hill development) added perhaps a refreshing diversity to his exceedingly busy life. Known for his interest in horticulture (a member of the Royal Caledonian Horticultural Society and a good friend of Patrick Neill, its long-serving secretary), he showed a sensitivity to the environment that went far beyond the strict confines of engineering.[7] Stevenson made several recommendations. These included removing all the added earth from the top of the bank and other areas where slippage had made the bank too steep to hold; rebuilding the retaining walls of property in Great Stuart Street and Randolph Crescent (to be founded on solid rock and carried by a series of arches to form and retain the soil of the private garden areas); reducing the slope prior to planting with grass and shrubs; and repairs to the mill lead. In all this Lord Moray 'was a very heavy sufferer', for in order to set at rest 'all apprehensions' on the part of the builders he agreed to meet the whole expense of rebuilding the rear walls of the houses affected.[8]

The Feuars Meet

When the feuars first met in October 1825, Gillespie Graham was present to explain about the slip and the remedial action taken; they were told that, on completion, 'his Lordship would not be at any further expense in securing the ground from further slips, but would bear a rateable and proportional part of securing and laying out the ground'. This was round one in what was to become a long-running contest to determine who was responsible for what, and ultimately who should foot the bill. The slippages, not surprisingly, caused great anxiety amongst the feuars, and when they examined their feuing conditions the

Right: Part of the massive retaining wall and arches at the top of the Bank Gardens behind Moray Place and Ainslie Place, built to redress the problems caused by land slippages and now a distinctive feature of the gardens. Below: Another view of the wall with recently planted white Japanese cherry trees on the bank below. (Both: C. Byrom)

ambiguities and inconsistencies regarding the status of the Bank Garden became apparent. John Hope (1794–1858), Solicitor General for Scotland since 1822, and living at 12 Moray Place (his father was Charles Hope, later Lord Granton), offered his view that proprietors in general could not take responsibility for slips occasioned by individual feuars 'throwing out earth on the bank'. The meeting closed with the appointment of a committee 'for purposes of having plans prepared and taking estimates of the expense of enclosing, dressing up and laying out the Pleasure Grounds on the Banks of the river'; members included John Hope, Sir Patrick Murray (Baron of the Court of Exchequer, 24 Moray Place), Alex Moneypenny, WS (7 Moray Place), Mr Russell (possibly Claud Russell, accountant, who in 1827 was living at 13 Ainslie Place), Mr Forsyth and two builders – Mr Dods and Mr Dobson. Gillespie Graham was made convener.

When the committee met in February 1826 it was to try and establish who was responsible for the layout and upkeep of the bank. Gillespie Graham's attempt to clarify matters was not wholly convincing. He stated that although the clause relating to the Bank Garden differed from the other two pleasure grounds, it imposed a similar obligation on builders and feuars in general, 'and that it was his intention in preparing the Articles of Sale that all the grounds on the property shown on the plan as pleasure grounds should be dressed and kept in order according to one rule'. It was an opinion which did not satisfy the builders, now anxious about the effect of the slippages on their businesses; they had no wish to become burdened with a garden they would never use, and which was fraught with problems. The issue was held over for further debate.

In March 1826 Gillespie Graham was asked to call a general meeting to consider 'on whom the obligation to inclose, dress and take charge of the pleasure ground on the Bank of the River lies'. This meeting also failed to resolve matters. When the committee reconvened in May 1826, Gillespie Graham brought with him plans of a palisade for enclosing the grounds along the river bank, together with an estimate for making the pleasure garden. Once again the Articles of Roup were scrutinised, with the Solicitor General giving his opinion that the dressing and laying out of the bank were Lord Moray's concern, after which any proprietor agreeing to pay a share of the expense and accepting responsibility for upkeep would be granted right of use. All these contentious issues were, however, quite literally to become buried in the wake of a further slip.

The Second Slip, March 1827

The second slip occurred further to the west of the first one. On this occasion blame fell on the shoulders of Henderson & Currer, builders of four houses on the south-west side of Ainslie Place.[9] As part of the original agreement they had been granted £160 by the Earl towards the cost of under-building in order to bring their houses up to street level; subsequently they were accused of depositing 'a mass of rubbish' in the back garden areas, 'in order to make up their ground' prior to enclosure: a charge hotly denied. The slip swept away both walls and garden ground. Once more the mill owners suffered, the race being obliterated and large quantities of earth flung into the Water of Leith. A worried Thomas Brown, the Town's Superintendent, wrote to Gillespie Graham declaring that 'we have been thrown into considerable alarm', and requesting swift removal of all debris as it was feared that damage might be caused to Leith harbour.[10] To avoid legal disputes the Earl again took the initiative; damages were paid to the mill proprietors, the mill race was replaced, superfluous earth and rubbish were removed; and at a cost to himself of around £1,000–£1,200. Having so far 'occasioned much loss and uneasiness', Lord Moray decided 'to adopt measures to prevent any further slip from taking place'.

Stevenson was again consulted, together with James Jardine and George Buchanan. They advised extending the stone arched retaining walls eastwards, and removing the vast quantities of earth deposited by Henderson & Currer, to be dumped by agreement 'upon the lands of Dean'. This ground had been bought in 1825 by John Learmonth (1789–1858), a successful entrepreneur and last Lord Provost prior to the 1832 Reform Act. A man of considerable wealth, he was on the verge of retiring from business to devote more time to public affairs. As a Moray Place resident (although not adjoining the Bank area) he took a genuine interest in the gardens and later served on the management committee.[11]

At a meeting attended by Lord Moray, his agents, James Gillespie Graham, and Henderson & Currer, Lord Moray offered the builders 'a present' of £420 towards the costs of making the walls as specified by the engineers: a sum which the builders later complained was totally inadequate. Although they threatened legal action, the Earl's agents were adamant that responsibilities agreed to were mutually binding, and that no more concessions or payments would be forthcoming. Attitudes were beginning to harden in the face of escalating costs and fears of insolvency due to a stagnating housing market. It was basically a no-win situation with unwelcome financial repercussions for all sides.

Prior to extending the arches, Stevenson and Jardine wrote a formal report based on a thorough inspection of the bank in the presence of Gillespie Graham and John Steedman, a land surveyor. Dated 7 July 1828,[12] it refers to trial pits sunk by Steedman at predetermined points to establish the depths of artificial earth and natural clay. Their findings supported previous recommendations, but advice was also added on improving drainage and allowing the ground to be more gently graded by reducing the width of the proposed top walk. Likely costs were estimated at £2,318, the retaining walls accounting for about three-quarters of the total. All this upheaval appears to have delayed the garden's formation by about four years. The feuars, however, were not left idle, for their attention was soon to switch to the two front gardens.

Forming the Bank Garden

In March 1831 came news that Lord Moray had completed the layout of the Bank Garden, when a detailed note of 'the expense of dressing the Bank' was dispatched to the feuars. The work had been done by contract after having being advertised in three Edinburgh newspapers, and was supervised by Gillespie Graham. Costs amounted to £324, with the largest proportion (£129) being spent on shaping the slopes and making the footpaths – undertaken by John Wightman. The next biggest outlay at £90 was for 'dressing the bank' (trees and shrubs) by Peter Sinclair (probably of Sinclair & Son, seed merchants in West Bow). John White provided the paling for the base of the garden, which cost £86. Other incidentals included £17 to Thomas Page for building walls around the trees, and a few shillings on grass seed supplied by James Dickson. With the account came a note saying that keys would be delivered to each proprietor agreeable to paying a share of the cost and willing to take responsibility for future upkeep.

Management Matters and Additional Planting

The Bank Garden was initially considered 'a separate and distinct matter' for management purposes, to be run by the proprietors; this, however, was soon found unviable in view of the slow trickle of feuars taking up the option (by June 1832 some 64 feuars had done so). As a result the committee set up in 1831 to manage Moray and Ainslie Place Gardens soon found themselves becoming involved with the Bank Garden. Thus the first management report for the two front gardens of January 1832 recounts how, in the previous summer, it having been found

> that some parts of the Bank were so steep that the grass could not be cut without the men taking off their shoes, and even then with considerable risk, and that latterly they said it would be impossible to go on with it; it having also been found that the children run considerable risks in going on these places, whilst others were aggravating the evil by making slides on them; your Committee thought it not so much a matter of choice as one nearly of necessity, that these places should be planted, which has accordingly been done. They considered it their duty also to dress up the ground at the east end, and at the entrance, [Doune Terrace] which is now in course of progress.[13]

By the summer of 1832 the same committee expressed concern that 'in consequence of the steepness of the walks, the gravel is carried off by very heavy rain' and there was a need therefore to provide storm gutters 'such as they have in East Heriot Row [Central Queen Street Gardens], which look neat and are found to fully answer the purpose'. Such improvements cost money, hence the urgent need to formalise the management structure to allow assessments to be levied on the Bank users. The solution was to extend the powers of the existing committee to include the Bank Garden with a representative of the Bank feuars added to their number. The new member chosen was Charles Hope (1763–1841) who lived at 12 Moray Place; he held office as Lord President before his promotion in 1836 to the highest legal post in Scotland – Lord Justice General. A distinguished and able lawyer, and strongly patriotic, he is shown in Kay's portraits as a rather portly figure on horseback when acting as Lieutenant-Colonel of the Edinburgh Volunteers.[14] A new central walk formed during these early years and called 'The President's Walk' was presumably named in his honour.

David Smith

Credit for the efficient running of all the Moray feu gardens during these somewhat fraught and troublesome years was largely due to the efforts of one very committed individual, David Smith, WS, (1802–80), the first elected convener and, at other times, secretary and treasurer, 'a well known and much respected citizen'.[15] The son of Alexander Smith,

Charles Hope, Lord Justice General, first representative of the Bank Garden on the management committee. One of the garden walks was named after him. (Grant after Kay, *Old and New Edinburgh*, 1880–3)

banker, who had died in a freak accident[16] and grandson of Donald Smith, a former Lord Provost (1807 and 1808) he had been one of the first to move to Moray Place. At the time of his father's death David Smith was in partnership with James Kinnear as law agents for various public companies including a number of railway enterprises, and on marriage had moved to 3 Doune Terrace, which became the venue for garden committee meetings. He gave years of devoted service, until moving from the Moray scheme in 1857. He reappears later in connection with the Dean Gardens where he again played a pivotal role. During the difficult period of the Bank slippages he acted as the feuars' spokesman, ever vigilant and prepared to do battle with firmness, civility and tenacity. This commitment to worthy causes was to dominate his life, so it is not surprising to find him becoming a founder member of the Cockburn Association and the Edinburgh Civic Trust. He also played an active role during the somewhat long and complicated negotiations which resulted in the Caledonian Horticultural Society's Experimental Garden being added to the Botanical Garden in the 1860s.

New Planting

With the management of the Bank Gardens now established, a surge of activity followed. Three times the amount of money was spent on these gardens compared to the front ones during this period, with substantial outlays on plants, gravel and sand for footpaths, wall building, garden tools and garden furniture. Early nursery accounts rarely survive, but one

Eagle & Henderson's Nursery Invoice, 1833, provides useful detail of the planting and tools ordered for the Front and Bank Gardens. (John Scott)

from Eagle & Henderson's for 1833 does, telling us exactly how the money was spent. Their bill shows that plants and equipment were supplied every month of that year apart from two. The largest order was in February, when supplies of 152 'picked' limes are listed as well as 50 tall *syringo* (lilacs), 30 large *ponticum* (rhododendrons), 20 'picked' elms, 30 large Portuguese laurel, 25 guilderose (*Viburnum opulus*), 4 variegated hollies, 1 large *laurustinus* (now *Viburnum tinus*), and 1 *Rhododendron hirsutum*. Other months saw the addition of laurel shrubs (72 Portuguese laurel and 200 bay laurel), privet (150), box (3,200) and sweet briar (100). Sir Charles Bell (1774–1842), the eminent surgeon, noted for his work on the nervous system, wrote about the Bank Garden where 'the walks there among the sweet-briar hedges, made our home in Edinburgh very delightful'; they had moved from London to Ainslie Place in 1836.[17] Amongst the various items of equipment were 7 pruners, 4 grass

REGULATIONS

To be Observed by the PROPRIETORS of HOUSES Feued from the EARL of MORAY, relative to the inclosed Pleasure Grounds in MORAY PLACE and AINSLIE PLACE, and the Bank on the South side of the River.

I. EACH Proprietor shall be furnished with one Key gratis, and in case of one or two additional Keys being required, or in case of a Key being lost, application must be made to the Committee. Those procured in any other way will be considered as forgeries. Not more than two additional Keys will be allowed to any Proprietor.

II. All Keys shall have the number of the House and Street to which they belong stamped upon them, and the whole Keys belonging to any Proprietor may be given by him to the Tenant of his house; but the Proprietor is not to reserve one Key and give his Tenant another.

III. No Proprietor or Tenant shall lend or transfer his Keys to Non-Proprietors.

IV. No Servants to be entitled to have access to the Grounds, except when in charge of children and invalids.

V. Proprietors or Tenants entitled to access to the Grounds, and members of their Families, may introduce Non-Proprietors into the Grounds, but only when along with themselves.

VI. Boys shall not be permitted to introduce any of their companions who are not sons of those entitled to access to the Bank, which is not calculated for Play Ground.

VII. No person shall cut, pull, or injure any of the trees, shrubs, or flowers in the Grounds, nor climb the trees. All children shall carefully keep upon the gravel walks and grass. All games, such as slinging or throwing stones or any hard substance, cricket, golf, bows and arrows, and the like, are strictly prohibited. No person shall bring in dogs. Bird's nests not to be robbed.

VIII. The Committee resolve to impose Fines, not exceeding £1, for the infringement of any of the Regulations. These Fines shall be recovered by order of the Committee, and applied towards the expense of the management; and the Committee will farther insist for payment of damages for repairing the injury done to the Grounds.

IX. The heads of families shall be responsible for offences committed by their children or servants, and shall be bound to make good all damages done by them, and pay all fines imposed on them; and in the event of any children being convicted of a second offence, or in the event of the fines imposed not being paid, it shall be in the power of the Committee to exclude them all from the Grounds for a given time.

X. All persons labouring under, or lately recovered from, infectious diseases, shall be excluded from the Grounds until the risk of infection shall be certified by a medical gentleman to have ceased.

Heads of families will see the propriety of observing and assisting in enforcing the foregoing Regulations, particularly the last. The younger members of families will take notice, that, in case the Regulations are disregarded, confidential Sergeants of Police have been furnished with Keys to the Grounds, who will be intrusted with carrying them into effect. The heads of each family must consider the Key as under their own charge, and must not allow it to go out of their keeping in any way that may admit of a breach of any of the Regulations. Particular care ought also to be taken to prevent Keys from being lost, and thus passing into the hands of persons not entitled to access to the Grounds.

By order of the Committee,

Edinburgh, 5th July 1832.

Copy of the 1832 rules relating to all three Moray Gardens. Note the reference to the Bank Gardens as being unsuited for children's play. (Anne Hope)

INSTRUCTIONS

GIVEN TO

THE POLICE OFFICER.

THE first duty which the Policeman has to perform is generally to enforce the keeping of the Printed Regulations.

Should any Lady or Gentleman be in the Pleasure Grounds, who, the Policeman has reason to think, has no right to be there, he is to request their Names; and if they do not appear in the List, he is to report to Mr Smith.

Should any boys be there who have no right, or should any of the Regulations be infringed by them, they are to be immediately turned out, and their Names taken; and should they refuse to give their Names, their hats are to be retained.

Should any particular boys persist in the infringement of these Regulations, the Officer is instructed to report to Mr Smith.

In consequence of many serious accidents having happened already, by the throwing of stones—should any boys be found doing so, either at each other, or at others on the outside, or any other infringement of public Police, orders are given to the Officer to take them to the Police Office, in doing which the Gardeners have orders to render every assistance.

The Officer has orders also to take possession of all bows, arrows, or bats for cricket, in the event of boys playing with them in any of the Pleasure Grounds.

Instructions given to police officers for keeping order, 1832. (Anne Hope)

rakes (of varying sizes), 4 spades, a pair of hedge shears, 8 lb of rope yarn, 3 lb of garden twine, 48 yards 'Roonds' (circular plant supports?), and 1,400 wall nails.[18]

New gardens require regulating, and the first set of rules applying to all three of the Moray Feu Gardens was drafted in the summer of 1832; one clause referred specifically to the Bank Garden and stated that 'Boys shall not be permitted to introduce any of their companions who are not sons of those entitled to access to the Bank, which is not calculated for Play Ground'; steeply sloping banks might make excellent slides, but did nothing for the garden. Interlopers and illicit behaviour were to be kept in check by a policeman hired to patrol the gardens; as part of the job he was provided with a greatcoat.

Yet Another Slip

But the joy of a new garden was short-lived. Friday, 13 October 1837 – an appropriately ominous date – saw the feuars gathered at the Hopetoun Rooms, Queen Street, to consider a note received from the Earl's agents. It concerned 'the slip which is taking place in the north or Bank gardens', and told of Lord Moray's plan of action, 'the expense of which they allege must be bourn by the proprietors generally'.[19] The feuars had been alerted some months before, and had in fact lodged a legal directive with the Earl's agents in August

1836. In it they referred to the 'great tendency in the earth on the said Bank or Pleasure Grounds to make a slip so as to force the ground towards the Water of Leith and thus to injure and probably entirely destroy the beauty of the said gardens and Pleasure Grounds'. The directive also stated that if any slip threatened their garden the Earl would not only be responsible for making good any damage, but would be liable to pay compensation for loss and injury.[20] The game of apportioning blame and financial liability was again in play, and under David Smith's leadership the feuars' corner was ably defended.

This time the slip occurred in the angle of ground between Ainslie and Moray Place, and stretched downhill towards the river midway between St Bernard's and St George's mineral wells. By now Gillespie Graham was no longer acting as the Earl's architect, having been replaced by William Burn; their relationship had ended on rather a sour note.[21] James Jardine was again consulted. He had recently superintended Telford's design for the Dean Bridge which had opened in 1832, largely financed by John Learmonth. The routine was by now well established. Burn and Jardine inspected the ground and reported that 'a large quantity of earth must be taken away immediately – at least before winter'. Burn also considered the expediency of purchasing the old mill 'lately burnt' and thereby ridding Lord Moray 'of all questions and difficulties as to its preservation', but the Earl's agents decided otherwise.[22]

Surplus earth was once more to be dumped on Learmonth's land. By the end of October 1837 the contract had been awarded to a man described as 'respectable and active, and an Excavator to trade, and possesses all the necessary tools, scaffolding etc' and whose price was middle of the range of the five submitted.[23] When operations started, they triggered fresh falls of rock and further slippage. Rather alarmingly, the lower portion of one of the private gardens collapsed, with large wide cracks appearing in the boundary wall, and that of the adjacent property. The proprietor thus affected was James Hope, WS (1769–1842) who lived at 31 Moray Place.

Hope was a well respected gentleman, employed as Secretary and Law Agent for Highland Roads and Bridges,[24] another of Thomas Telford's great engineering projects in Scotland. By then the work was nearing completion but had involved Hope in resolving a mass of complicated legal and financial issues. Shortly after moving from Queen Street in 1824, to join his brother Charles Hope, the Professor of Chemistry and Chemical Pharmacy at Edinburgh University, he had written to a colleague about his new home perched eyrie-like 'on top of a bank above a ravine'.[25] It was now a worried Mr Hope who contracted the Earl's agents about 'the large fissure . . . in my garden within fifty feet of my house and within twenty feet of my offices'. While the cracks looked ominous, Jardine was not unduly alarmed, being satisfied that the house, built on solid rock, was not under threat. Further test bores were, however, carried out to allay anxieties.[26] Hope's neighbour, a Mrs Riddell, was equally concerned. In March 1838 she wrote an agitated letter to the garden convener declaring that

we are all very wrong in not bringing Lord Moray to an explanation of what his intentions are. In the meantime he is exposing all the houses immediately above his very injudicious operations to the most eminent danger. For some days he has had men cutting up the fine trees which certainly belonged to the feuars and for the beauty and shelter of which we pay this most enormous feu duty and if we do not instantly get an interdict to stop him he will cut the whole down for Pyles to drive in to support his Mill wall . . . I would willingly join in any reasonable expense to save our once Beautiful bank and trees.[27]

David Smith replied by speaking of his own vexation 'at the destruction of our Bank after all the trouble and expense which we have laid out upon it'; the last meeting of feuars had, however, instructed the committee 'not to interfere' as there was 'no certainty what the consequences of such interference might be'. Lord Moray had initiated the work and 'he is therefore responsible both for the expense of the operations and the damage they might occasion to the beauty of our pleasure grounds'.[28]

Communication between the two sides had therefore been suspended, but subsequent intelligence 'of some extensive alterations upon the Bank behind Moray Place' prompted Smith to renew contact towards the end of July 1838. The feuars were told by Lord Moray's agents that ' the works to be executed consist of a series of Arches like those behind Ainslie Place', plans and specification already being in the hands of the contractor – James Macpherson – a builder from Port Hopetoun. Both the specification (dated 28 June 1838) and contract (23 July 1838) survive in the Moray archives,[29] and the corresponding drawings in the National Archives of Scotland;[30] all bear the signature of James Jardine. The documents demonstrate a concern to maintain high standards and to contain disruption as much as possible.

The Last Section of Arches

A substantial wood paling was erected round the building operations, no carts were allowed entry and all materials had to be brought to Doune Terrace gateway and then by railway to the places where needed. Foundations for the seven new piers were required to rest on a bed of hard sandstone excavated without the use of gunpowder. Any trees, shrubs, plants, turf and soil (up to a depth of two feet) that had to be disturbed were to be carefully removed and laid aside, to be replaced once the masonry was complete. Private garden areas had to be re-formed and dressed off to suit the new access and parapet wall. The contractor was also required to supply any additional turf, soil and gravel, and was made responsible for reinstating the cast iron railing on the boundary walls of houses, and supplying new sections along the eastern terrace extension, together with additional steps and paving. Overall costs amounted to £1,549 and these, plus consultant's fees, were all paid by the Earl. His agents had intended to recoup some of the expense from the feuars, but it became such a fraught and emotive issue that claims were eventually abandoned. Maintaining the goodwill of proprietors in the face of extended disruptions and privations was rightly judged more important than engaging in acrimonious battle. At the end of the day the feuars' only out-of-pocket expense was £35 – the cost of engaging George Buchanan to report on the slip.

As work neared completion, a vigilant David Smith took up cudgels with Lord Moray's agents, complaining of the 'inadequacy of the plans' for reinstating the Bank. Need they be reminded, he asked in his letter of July 1839, 'of the beauty of the grounds before your operations commenced or of the utter destruction to the Pleasure Ground which has been for the last two years caused by them?' Concern was voiced at the lack of soil at the base of the Garden where screen planting was needed. The response was terse: the feuars were told to 'wait till they see the work completed before finding fault'.[31]

Back into Use

Towards the end of May 1840 the committee were able to report to a feuars' meeting 'that the operations which have been so long carried on in these gardens by Lord Moray have now been completed and the gardens are now again put in order and are ready for the occupation of the feuars'. Various grievances were aired – the slopes were too steep in places, and there was so little earth as 'to make it nearly impossible for the plants to grow' – but as these complaints had already been rebuffed, the committee felt it prudent to let matters rest. Similarily the quest for reimbursing costs of retaining a gardener during the disturbances was dropped. The meeting decided instead to authorise spending £35 on Kensington gravel to improve the walks.[32]

After such prolonged upheaval it seems remarkable that when James McNab was consulted twenty years later, the Bank Garden had assumed such a mature woodland park appearance that he was able to judge it 'one of the most romantic about Edinburgh', the glimpses of 'architectural objects' heightening the effect. It was through McNab that the feuars gained one of their best head gardeners; in 1864 he recommended James Bruce, his former foreman at the Horticultural Society's Experimental Garden at Inverleith. Bruce became one of the longest-serving employees, holding the post for 23 years. His pay remained a constant £70 per annum throughout that time (even by 1908 the sum had only crept up to £ 84 annually). Bruce was allowed two under-gardeners and was responsible for all the gardens within the Moray feu.[33] Ill health finally forced his resignation in 1887; he died soon afterwards, comforted maybe by the subscription raised on his behalf by a number of appreciative feuars.

McNab, however, was not without criticism. His report of 1865 highlighted 'the want of harmony existing throughout; or rather it is too much in compartments, suddenly approached from one division to another'.[34] He considered the garden over-provided with trees and shrubs which fragmented the overall appearance and caused the grass to wilt. Continuous sweeps of sward, with groups of specimen trees, had always appealed to McNab. Some modest shrub-thinning followed. His advice, however, was largely disregarded, having fallen victim to the uproar centring on his recommendations for the Front Gardens. When Angus McLeod, the City's Superintendent of Parks, was consulted in 1890 'in way of cutting trees and removing shrubbery and brightening the garden', his advice was similar to McNab's.[35]

More Recent Times

In 1880 James Balfour, secretary of the Dean Gardens, approached the Moray feuars to discuss the possibility of linking both gardens by footbridge. But the response to this imaginative idea was parochial to say the least; no advantages were seen and any financial commitment was hastily declined.[36]

During the Second World War the bottom railings were removed, allowing open access from the Water of Leith. When faced with substantial costs for re-enclosing all the gardens after the war, the committee debated two possibilities for the Bank: first that the feuars' rights might be 'merged' with the Royal Botanic Garden,[37] and second that the Town Council might assume part as a public park, with responsibility for new boundary railings falling to one or other party.[38] But neither body had funds available, and the committee had no choice but to raise the money themselves. As an interim measure two wardens (distinguished by their peaked caps and arm bands) were employed to patrol the gardens at weekends.[39] The Bank Garden was finally made secure in 1949, when Smith Fletcher & Co erected a wire mesh fence at a cost of over £361.[40] By June 1950 Lord Sorn, Chairman of the Committee, was able to report at the AGM that the Bank Garden was gradually 'being restored to its former state'.[41]

A long-term management and improvement plan has been under way since 1995. It aims to maintain the woodland character of the Garden, with its sequence of spaces ranging from the upper and more carefully kept formal areas, gradually descending through close-cut lawns to the lower, wilder, semi-natural woodland; and aims also to open up several vistas including views of Stockbridge, the Firth of Forth and St Bernard's Well. The Garden now contains about 150 large trees consisting mainly of lime and a number of sycamore, elm, ash, birch, beech, hawthorn and holly; together with some ornamental trees, shrubs and hedges. The handsome lime avenue at the westmost end, which probably dates from when the retaining arches were built, will need careful replacement in the years ahead.[42]

Notes

1. *Imperial Gazetteer of Scotland*, (London & Edinburgh, n.d. *c*. 1865) Vol. 1.
2. The charter for this land had been granted by Heriot's Hospital to Henry Raeburn on 5 June 1758 (part of the lands of Stockbridge).
3. Earl of Moray's archives, Tin box 26 (formerly wooden box No. VI) & box 27.
4. Garden Minute Book (1837–57). Report by George Buchanan dated 1 December 1837. The various garden minute books relating to the Moray Feu and other miscellaneous matters have now been deposited in the Edinburgh City Archives.
5. TCM, 23 December 1713, where Greenland Mill is referred to as 'new Mill'.
6. Report by George Buchanan, see n.29.
7. Robert Louis Stevenson, *Records of a Family of Engineers*, p. 89.
8. Earl of Moray's archives, Tin Box 26, item 18; letter from James Gillespie Graham to Wilkie & Dobson, builders, dated 6 April 1826, and other miscellaneous items.
9. This and the following information are based on a miscellaneous collection of papers in the Earl of Moray's archives, as noted above.
10. ECA, Thomas Brown's letter book, 10 March 1827.
11. John Learmonth lived at 6 Moray Place until his death in 1858, and was one of the first residents.
12. Earl of Moray's Archives, Report by Robert Stevenson and James Jardine, Civil Engineers, relative to the houses and grounds of Moray Place, 7 July 1828.

13. Information on the early days of the Bank garden is based on the following sources: 'Report by the Committee appointed by the Feuars of Moray Place &c. for taking charge of the Pleasure Grounds and Gardens of Moray Place, Ainslie Place &c.' dated 4 January 1832, with David Smith named as Convener (printed copy in RCAHM Scotland, and SRO (Moray feu unclassified); 'Regulations to be Observed by the Proprietors of Houses feued from the Earl of Moray, relative to the inclosed Pleasure Grounds in Moray Place and Ainslie Place, and the Bank on the south side of the River' (5 July 1832); and 'Report of the Committee of Management of Moray Place Gardens' (1 December 1833); these two latter items in the possession of Mrs Ann Hope, Edinburgh.

14. Kay, Vol. 2, pp. 246–55.

15. *The Scotsman,* 17 December 1880; see also *Edinburgh Evening Courant,* 17 December 1880; both contain long obituaries with contain a lot of useful detail about David Smith's life.

16. Alexander Smith had died when a floor collapsed during the sale held of the deceased Lord Eldin's effects at his home in Picardy Place.

17. Sir Gordon Gordon-Taylor, *Sir Charles Bell; his life and times* (Edinburgh & London, 1958), p. 155.

18. I am indebted to John Scott, London, for allowing me access to three nursery invoices relating to the Moray Feu Gardens as follows: Eagle & Henderson, 1833 (planting for Moray & Ainslie Place and the Bank Garden and equipment), Charles & John Peacock, 1833 (roses for Moray Place Garden) and Dickson & Co., 1869 (trees for Ainslie Place Garden).

19. Garden Minute Book (1837–45), minute, 13 October 1837.

20. Earl of Moray's Archives, Schedule of intimation and protest, the feuars of grounds within mentioned against the Right Hon Francis Earl of Moray, 7 August 1837 by John Galloway, WS, as procurator for, and on behalf of the committee named and appointed by the feuars of the grounds afore mentioned.

21. All the hassle associated with the slippages, and the upset caused by having the architect's accounts queried, must have proved very damaging to the relationship between the Earl and Gillespie Graham.

22. Attempts were made by some feuars to purchase Greenland Mill, and thereby remove what was then considered an eyesore.

23. Earl of Moray's Archives, Box 27, No. 17, letter dated 5 October 1837, from James Melville to P.B. Ainslie.

24. James Hope's role as Secretary and Law Agent to the Commissioners for Highland Roads and Bridges is described in R.B. Haldane, *New Ways through the Glen* (London, 1962), p. 42.

25. R.B. Haldane, op. cit. p. 202.

26. Earl of Moray's Archives, Letter from James Hope, WS, to Messrs Walker Richardson & Melville, WS, dated 6 January 1838.

27. Garden Minute Book (1837–45), letter dated 15 March 1838 from Mrs Riddell to David Smith.

28. Ibid., letter from David Smith to Mrs Riddell dated 16 March 1838.

29. Earl of Moray Archives, Specification of alterations proposed to be made on the ground behind Moray Place, Edinburgh 28 June 1838; contract between Messrs Walker Richardson & Melville on the part of the Earl of Moray, 25 July 1838, and Mr James Macpherson.

30. RHP 6793/1, Design of piers, arches and parapets etc proposed to be erected on the westward of Moray Place and Ainslie Place, 28 June 1838; plan of the pleasure ground behind Moray Place and Ainslie Place as altered, 1 June 1839.

31. Garden Minute Book (1837–45), letter dated 12 July 1839 from Messrs Smith & Kinnear to Messrs Walker & Melville.

32. Ibid., Minute, 2 May 1840; the complaint was also made at this meeting that 'a great many people were coming into the garden who had no right to it', on account of forged keys being used (the West Princes Street Gardens had similar problems); the locks and keys were ordered to be changed.

33. The position had previously been held by George Stirling who, after 18 years of service, was given notice due to the progressive neglect of the garden.

34. Garden Minute Book (1857–71), Report by Mr McNab, RBG Edinburgh, 6 October 1865.

35. Garden Minute Book (1881–92), Minutes 12 March 1890 and 15 November 1890.

36. Garden Minute Book (1871–80), Minute 27 April 1880.

37. Garden Minute Book (1944–53), Minutes 25 June 1945 and 8 May 1946.

38. Ibid., Minutes, 6 May 1948 and 11 June 1948.

39. Ibid., Minutes, 13 June 1947 and 4 November 1948.

40. Ibid., Minutes, 29 July 1948, 27 March 1949, 9 June 1949; the cost of the Bank garden railing was mostly met by the feuars who abutted the gardens.

41. Ibid., Minutes, 20 June 1950.

42. John Byrom, 'The Moray Bank Garden' (Management Plan, 1994).

CHAPTER 16

MORAY PLACE, AINSLIE PLACE
AND RANDOLPH CRESCENT
(the Front Gardens)

We still think that Murray Place has been injudiciously planned, and that the fine capabilities of the ground have been sacrificed. But the eye cannot resist the splendour and richness of the architecture. We cannot survey it without feeling that it deserves to be named emphatically, 'the place of palaces'.

The Scotsman, 1826[1]

Feuing conditions for Moray and Ainslie Place Gardens placed responsibility for enclosure, formation and upkeep squarely on the shoulders of the feuars in accordance with Gillespie Graham's plans. We know that during 1825 and 1826 the feuars met with the architect several times about issues to do with the Bank Gardens, and it is very likely that the Front Gardens were discussed at the same time. Information relative to these two gardens first appears in a report circulated to residents in January 1832. It had been prepared by the management committee established the previous year and was signed by the convener, David Smith. From this it is clear that the two front gardens had been enclosed and laid out by 1827 and that preparations may well have been under way from around 1826. The report was mostly about financial matters and reflected growing pressure for a more businesslike approach towards raising and administering money; hence the need to appoint an accountant.

By this time three groups of assessments had been levied. One labelled 'First Assessment' concerned 'the necessary expense of laying out and inclosing the Gardens of Moray Place, Ainslie Place' which amounted to £2,669, and covered the period up until Whitsuntide 1828. Most of this had already been met by a flat-rate contribution of £14 per house, but the circular reminded feuars that future levies would be based on the amount of feu duties paid. Most of this money would have been spent on the cope stone and railings for the two gardens. The 'Second Assessment' related to foot pavements which had been 'laid across each street' to increase 'the comfort of the inhabitants', financed by a levy of £1.10s (£1.50) per house, with an additional £1 'for Black Earth' (presumably for the gardens?). The 'Third Assessment,' amounting to just over £170, covered upkeep from 1828–30; one year later the sum had shrunk to £52, mostly spent on gardener's wages. This reduction 'which they trust will never now be exceeded' merited a note of congratulation from the committee. Moray Place feuars had also paid a small extra assessment 'for additional gas and more expensive lamp-posts', and some other trifling expenses.

North-west angle of Moray Place, 1829, showing a neat but rather immature garden.

Moray Place Garden
(2.6 acres; 1.44 ha)

Circular in shape and based on the layout shown in Gillespie Graham's feuing plan, this is the largest of the front gardens, intended as the main recreational space for children and adults alike. Four gated entrances were provided (two in line with the central axis along Great Stuart Street) with linking pathways to a grassed inner area, and thence to a circular tree and shrub plot. Around the perimeter a broad shrubbery and woodland belt was formed (planted with elms, poplars, willows and white thorn) flanked by a circular walk. The original plan indicated a greater concentration of planting at each of the four entrances and central junctions, possibly to emphasise the four compartmented areas; in practice, however, planting has tended to become more dispersed.

At this time the garden was less level, sloping downwards at the northern end. This was one of the reasons behind one resident's attempt in the summer of 1832 to have improvements made. The gentleman was James Hope (the same individual who later experienced alarming cracks to his back wall at 31 Moray Place), and his ideas were outlined in a pamphlet circulated to other proprietors.[2] Hope, it seems, was not impressed with the new garden, which he thought dull and inferior compared to other contemporary gardens such as West Princes Street and West Queen Street.

Proposals for Improvement

The Hope family's architect, Robert Brown, designed a new layout and also made a model showing what could be done. To make the space more useful and attractive, the suggestion was that the whole central area be levelled, and then united with the existing

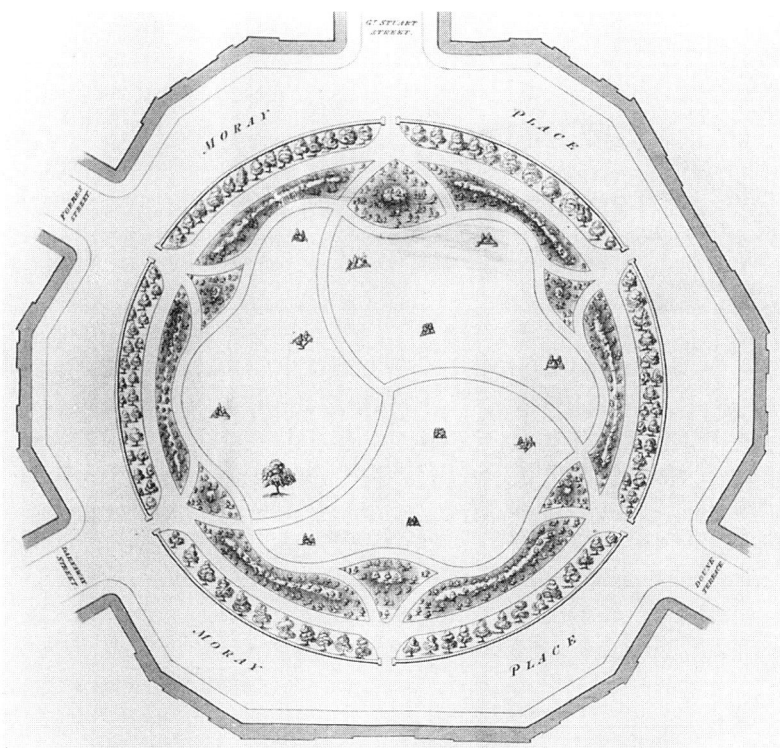

Robert Brown's plan for improving the Moray Place Gardens, 1832. (Anne Hope)

outer border by a series of mounds, thereby creating more variety and interest. This would allow a sheltered level walk to loop round the base of the mounds, with space for more generous flower borders; the rest to be left as a children's play area, easily viewed from the surrounding houses: 'The children must not only have playground, but they must have sufficiently extensive play-ground, else they will, to a certainty, as has been already experienced, trespass on the flower borders, and do much injury.'

Earth for levelling and mounding presented no problems; John Learmonth had already volunteered supplies from his Rutland Square development. There was also the possibility of reinforcements from road-widening works in Wemyss Place. Advice from 'another gentleman of first-rate authority in gardening' had also been taken – very likely James Dickson, nurseryman. Response was generally encouraging, including the support of two key residents, David Smith and the architect William Playfair. But attention soon became diverted to the recently adopted Bank Gardens which required substantial funding for plants and equipment.

The Hope Family

For any proprietor to go to such lengths to radically change a garden so soon after its creation, was unique. So why did James Hope become so involved? His action must surely have stemmed from his own experience of speculative development following the inheritance of land off Leith Walk. This ground had been bought in 1763 by his father, Dr John Hope (1725–86), Professor of Botany and Materia Medica at Edinburgh University, as a new Botanical Garden.[3] In 1825 (following the garden's removal to Inverleith) Robert Brown was employed to draw up development plans for the newly released land. Hope Crescent (now Hopetoun Crescent) was the first part advertised for feuing;[4] the adjacent 'handsome pleasure ground'[5] was fashioned to accommodate the trees too large to move from the former arboretum. Supervising the contractor, Charles McCall, was nurseryman James Dickson. Such practical experience, combined with easy access to skilled professionals, must have made the challenge of righting the inadequacies of Moray Place Gardens too tempting to resist.[6]

A further impetus probably came from James Hope's eldest son John (1807–93), also WS, then exhibiting enthusiastic leanings towards architecture, and a developing interest in the welfare of young people. Certainly the pamphlet's emphasis on play space reflects one of John Hope's lifelong passions. A bachelor and fitness fanatic, he was much involved with the young, and during his long spell as Town Councillor relentlessly campaigned for better recreational provision within the City as well as other humane causes.[7] Remembered now for his dedicated pursuit of total abstinence from liquor, smoking and taking snuff which sprang from strong protestant evangelical convictions, he established in 1847 the British League of Juvenile Abstainers, a temperance movement based mostly in Edinburgh. Ever vigilant against tobacco smoking in public places, his name appears regularly in New Town garden minute books, Moray Place being no exception.[8] A Green before his time and mildly eccentric, he was, however, no killjoy. In 1869 he was the first to suggest that bands should play in the gardens during the summer months.[9]

Flower Power

Although the Hopes' proposals fell by the wayside, they seem nevertheless to have triggered a wave of new planting. During 1833 many additions were made to the gardens with quantities of laburnum, lilac, laurel, rhododendrons, hollies, elm and limes planted in the outer border. Over one hundred assorted rose bushes were supplied by C. & J. Peacock to decorate the eight inner beds. But most impressive of all were the quantity and variety of annual and perennial flower seeds bought from Eagle & Henderson (the earliest detailed list yet discovered); it ran as follows:

> 1.5 lbs sweet peas, 1.5 lbs mignonette, 4 4 ozs larkspur, 4 ozs mist candytuft, 4 ozs blue lupine, 2 4 ozs minor convolvulus, 2 4 ozs major lupine, 4 ozs Indian cress (? Gillenia trifoliata), 2 4 ozs Prince's feather (Amaranthus hybridus), 1oz lychnis, 1oz dwarf lychnis, 4 ozs purple sweet peas, 4 ozs yellow lupine, 2 4 ozs Dutch blue sweet peas, 4 ozs sunflower, 4 ozs dwarf Dutch blue sweet peas, 1oz virginia stock, 1oz sweet Williams, 2 4 ozs purple clary, 2 4 ozs red hawkweed, 2 4 ozs tall larkspur, 1oz nigella romana, 1 oz sweet alyssum, 2 4 ozs adonis, 2 4 ozs red lavatera, 1oz love lies bleeding, 2 4 ozs perennial larkspur, 2 4 ozs perennial lupin, 2 4 ozs double rose hollyhocks, 1oz dwarf lupin, 2 4 ozs oenothera grandiflora (clarkia), 1oz monks hood, 2 4 ozs French honeysuckle, 2 4 ozs red foxgloves, 1oz garden viberion (? viburnum), ½ ozs scented

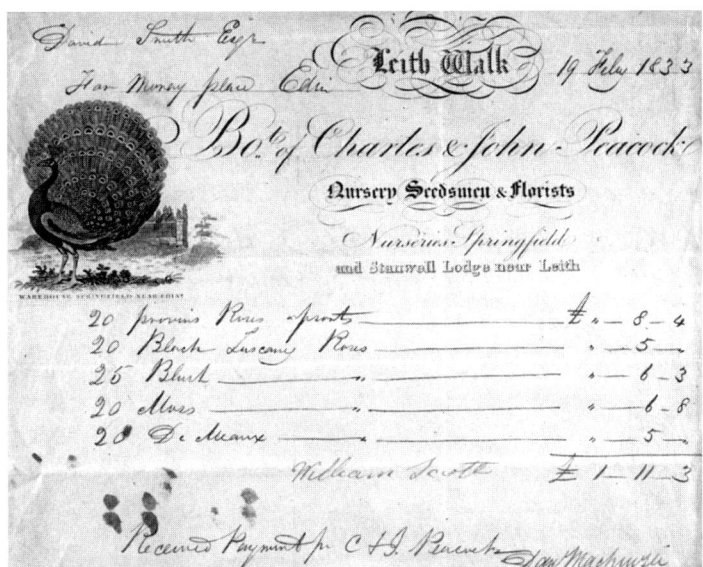

Peacock & Sons Nursery Invoice, 1833. The firm's speciality was roses. (John Scott)

Brompton stock (Matthiola incana), ½ oz purple viberion, ½ oz 10 week Brompton stock ½ oz cape viberion, ½ white queen stock, ½ oz, white wall leaved viberion, ½ oz polyanthus, ½ oz auricula forts, ½ oz campanula, ½ oz Canterbury bells, ½ oz double columbines, ½ oz thyme, ½ oz African marigolds, 2 4 ozs assorted carnations, 2 4 ozs mint china asters, 1oz marvel of Peru (mirabilis jalapa), 1oz Indian pink?, 1oz Prussian stock, 1oz guild marigold, 1oz dwarf marigold, 1oz striped marigold, 1oz rose larkspur, ½ oz Venus looking glass (legousia speculum – veneris).

A veritable frenzy of colour, scents and new varieties, and all possible at a time when the tree canopy was still more open. But the triumph of seasonal display became increasingly doomed as light sources gradually diminished. By the 1890s the committee had in fact decided to turf over all the flower beds, but in the event managed only one, in the face of protests. Today greater emphasis is placed on shade-tolerant shrubs and hardy perennials.

In the late 1830s a suggestion was made to 'increase the beauty of the surrounding scene' by accommodating at the centre Kemp's design for the Scott Monument; but happily a more appropriate home was found in East Princes Street Gardens.[10] Of lesser but equally bizarre proportions were the four *Araucaria araucana* (monkey puzzle trees) donated by Admiral Mitford in 1852;[11] their survival appears to have been brief. John Hope's idea to add the Ross Fountain as a central feature was not taken seriously either.

James McNab

McNab's involvement during the 1860s came at a time when the garden required extensive pruning and removal work: the outer border had become, for example, 'such a thicket of forest growth' that the surrounding architecture was obscured, views from upper windows being reduced and branches overhanging the street becoming a nuisance.[12] The Queen

Tennis play in the Moray Gardens, Edinburgh, early 1930s. (The late Peggy Brown)

Mary thorn originally planted 'for permanent effect' he was happy to keep, but McNab wanted to remove most of the ill-formed trees, and to achieve a 'park appearance' by concentrating on the better specimens set on extended areas of lawn. One of his proposals – a series of grassed earth mounds, sloping towards the boundary rail and connected by serpentine walks – echoed something of the Hope family's draft improvements of 1832. McNab also sharply criticised the abundance of street weeds, 'stronger than in any other part of the town', one of the consequences of horse-drawn traffic and wind-blown dirt. The 'beautifully verdant' causeways in Moray Place, Charlotte Square and other central areas had been remarked upon as far back as 1826 when another Edinburgh citizen noted that 'this urban crop of grass is reaped by rows of old men who, moving on their knees across the causeway . . . eradicate the plants with old forks and crooked bits of iron'.[13]

The committee arranged for some elm trees to be removed, pruning work to be done, new shrubs added to the central clump and a fairly recent, but in McNab's view totally inappropriate tool-house banished to the Bank Garden.[14] But further work was suspended after similar improvements to Ainslie Place provoked fierce controversy. Tree pruning and removal became a very vexed issue.[15] Even when Angus McLeod, the City's Superintendent of Parks, gave comparable advice in the 1880s it fared little better.[16] The ground, however, was made more level when cartloads of earth were added to the centre and northern ends.

Uses made of the Garden

Tennis was first introduced in the 1800s, and prior to the First World War four courts were marked out in the summer months; by 1947 these had shrunk to one, and now there are none.[17] Always a popular recreational space, the centre garden was particularly well used when a number of private schools operated in the area, and the children were allowed to use the garden at break times. Balancing use against misuse was always a delicate act, depending as it did on 'a question of degree'. A game of Tig or Prisoner's Base, as the garden clerk explained in a letter of complaint to one of the headmasters, 'would be a harmless pastime with young children of five of six attended possibly with nursemaids, while the same games would be decidedly objectionable with boys of fourteen or so'.[18] But the garden has always proved flexible, catering for a wide range of activities including drill practice during the war years,[19] meetings of a fencing club, children's gardening competitions, parties and other social gatherings and events.[20]

Today Moray Place Garden is well maintained and contains about a hundred forest trees, reasonably well balanced for age, distribution and species. In 1997 extensive thinning was carried out to the centre roundel and new planting added, and in 1998 similar work started on the outer border. As in McNab's time, this has aroused heated debate; on both occasions the intention was to revitalise the garden and not to destroy it. Hopefully the new level of interest generated by these changes will leave the garden in better and more vigorous health.[21]

Ainslie Place Garden
(0.9 acres, 0.36 ha)

Oval in shape with a fall of some three metres from west to east, Ainslie Place Garden is identical in size to the one in Randolph Crescent. It consists of a perimeter border of shrubs and trees with an outer and inner oval walk, and a central clump linked by a north–south footpath. The garden contains around fifty trees, consisting mostly of wych elm, hawthorn and sycamore; their ages range from over a hundred years (three wych elm) to some twenty years or so. The planting is presently under review, as it is feared that over-dependence on elm could leave gaps in the future. Only occasionally referred to in the minute books, it did leap into prominence in the 1860s when James McNab was asked to advise and to look at ways of overcoming the rather draughty nature of the garden. His recommendations unfortunately sparked off bitter controversy.[22]

A Storm in a Tea Cup

When McNab reported on Ainslie Place Garden in 1867, the outer border was in poor condition, stocked with elms and lilacs supplied by Eagle & Henderson in 1833. Both types of trees, he noted, had 'root robbing propensities' to the detriment of other planting. He recommended thorough pruning, and the removal of one or two ill-shaped elms and other planting in poor condition.[23] This would allow the grassed areas to be improved. Similar

Ainslie Place, Edinburgh, 1828, with the garden still in its infancy. (Shepherd, *Views of Edinburgh*, 1825)

treatment was advised for the central area with the removal of all the trees apart from 'two limes and two thorns, one being a small one standing near the well'. At the same time he suggested reducing the width of the pathways, and sprinkling them with yellow shell gravel, to provide 'a pleasing effect from all the neighbouring windows besides forming a better contrast with the grass than is now afforded by the dirty coloured gravel'.[24]

Once the basic work was completed, new trees were planted (including three 'extra large' limes, three lilacs, one laburnum and two single-scarlet thorn.[25] The garden's 'diminished state', however, took the residents by surprise. A letter of complaint was dispatched to the garden committee in December 1870 stating that 'too many trees have been removed' and requesting the addition of a 'few forest trees, lilacs and flowering shrubs to relieve the somewhat too open and bare aspect of the garden'. One of the signatories was the Reverend Edward B. Ramsay (1793–1872), Minister of St John's Episcopal Church, Princes Street, and Dean of the Diocese of Edinburgh. He lived at 23 Ainslie Place. An accomplished man, loved and respected, his voice carried some weight.[26] Rather sharper in tone was the letter sent by Mr William Forbes of Medwyn (advocate and Secretary to the Board of Lunacy) who lived at 17 Ainslie Place. He was distressed at 'the wholesale destruction of trees . . . which was carried out a great deal too far'; his only consolation was that 'the Moray Place people' had in consequence been saved from a similar 'act of vandalism'. He too appealed for more trees.[27]

The committee remained loyal to McNab who in a further report expressed satisfaction with the already 'enhanced' appearance of the garden. Ten additional trees were suggested,

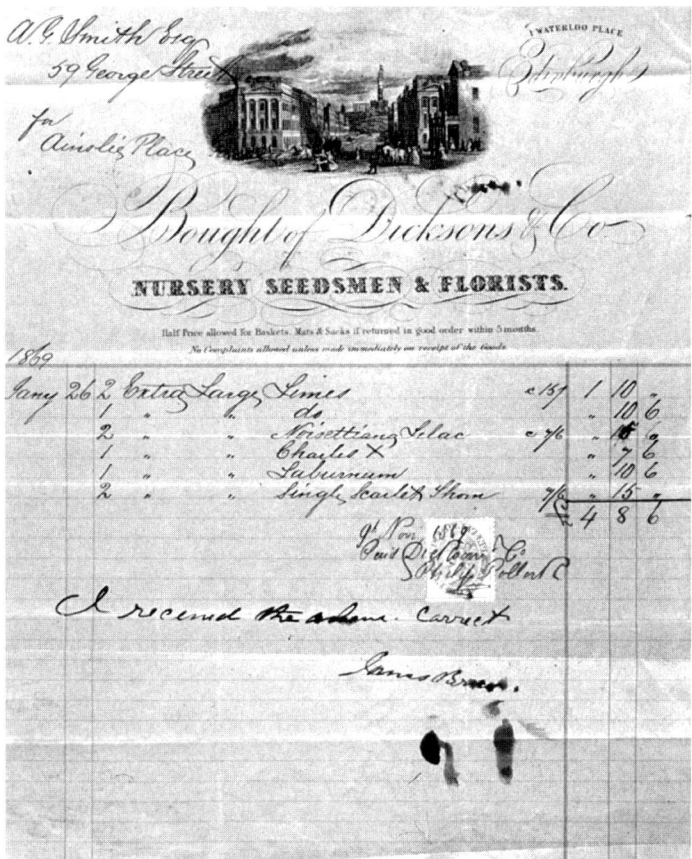

Dickson & Co. invoice dated 1869 for supplying new plants to Ainslie Place Gardens. The letterhead has an engraving of the firm's premises in Waterloo Place. (John Scott)

including two English elms (small-leaved varieties), one Turkey oak, one scarlet horse chestnut, one yellow horse chestnut, two Corstorphine planes, one Norway maple, one flowering ash and one weeping ash, as well as four hollies (two variegated and two-broad leaved) and two *Acuba japonica*.[28]

Mr Forbes, however, was still not satisfied. In March 1871 he visited the chairman armed with his own planting list. But the committee wisely deferred action 'to see the effect of simply carrying out Mr McNab's recommendations'. Discontent rumbled on. Not long before his death Dean Ramsay delivered a written request to the AGM, graciously noting that 'It would give me much pleasure if you would kindly direct that a few shrubs etc be planted in Ainslie Place gardens'. Mr Forbes and his next-door neighbour, Dr Cumming, on the other hand raised the motion for poplars to be added and 'other fast-growing trees'. To the credit of the chairman he held firm.[29]

McNab's final report in March 1872 was more assertive in tone and designed to curb well-meaning but misguided interference. The general appearance was now 'very satisfactory', and his only suggestion was for the grass to be 'dotted over with snowdrops'. McNab had won the day[30] but the battle lingered on. When the Council were discussing McNab's and Mr Morham's (City Architect) improvements for the Meadows, for example, Councillor John Hope scathingly referred to McNab's association with Ainslie and Moray Place Gardens. But someone calling himself 'Old Boy' sprang to McNab's defence, observing in the press that 'If anyone wishes to see what having Mr McNab means . . . let him look at Ainslie Place – tidy, green, and enjoyable thanks to our Botanic Gardener, and then let him contemplate the jungle in Moray Place'. To which Mr Hope replied that, while having great respect for Mr McNab, 'they all knew the way that gentleman manipulated the trees in Ainslie Place and it was as well that they put a check to his operations in regard to Moray Place'.[31]

While the long-term aim has always been to maintain a balance of trees and grass, some residents still yearn for a more colourful display, considering the garden 'quite like a desert'.[32] But flower-growing, apart from springtime bulbs, has never been a realistic option. The railings, removed during the Second World War, were replaced in 1950 by ones of simpler design.[33]

Randolph Crescent Garden
(0.9 acres, 0.36 ha)

Legend tells that an old plague pit once occupied the site of Randolph Crescent Garden together with an ancient rookery attached to Drumsheugh House. Some of the old trees appear to have been kept and made part of the small semicircular railed and walled enclosure.[34] Raised some three metres above street level and situated at the highest point of the Moray estate, it serves both as a terminal and entry feature at the western end.

Gillespie Graham's plan showed the garden with an outer woodland belt and a central access leading up steps to a porticoed building; the rest was grassed and studded with trees. What the building was intended for remains unclear, but its most obvious function was to serve as a focal point and a link between the Moray scheme and any further extension westwards. This is why Lord Moray retained ownership of the ground and took responsibility for its enclosure. When it became apparent that this part of the plan was unlikely to be implemented, the feuars seem to have informally assumed responsibility for its upkeep. This was probably around 1843.[35]

In January 1853, David Smith, convener of the garden committee, drew attention at one of the meetings to 'the state of the small garden in Randolph Crescent'; the committee were directed 'to take such measures as they might think right to put the garden in better order'.[36] It was not until 1866, however, that the owners of property in Randolph Crescent bought the land 'for the sole use as pleasure gardens only' from Lord Moray for £2,000; it was sold on condition 'that the trees thereon are to be preserved'.[37] News of the purchase was relayed to the next meeting of Moray feuars held in April 1867, when plans for its future were also discussed. By then the ground had been put into better order at the expense of the Randolph Crescent proprietors, in the hope that its subsequent maintenance could be included within the same management framework as the other two front gardens.

To promote its adoption the Crescent owners agreed to use the same locks as elsewhere and to pay an additional annual assessment. This arrangement was 'unanimously' accepted and still applies.[38]

Near Extinction

Like Ainslie Place, this garden too only occasionally features in the garden minutes, and usually in response to some urgent remedial work. In 1877, for example, two old lime trees required removal, another in 1884, and near the close of the century Angus McLeod (City's Superintendent of Parks) advised removal of several old trees. New additions are occasionally noted; for example, during Lord Curriehill's chairmanship in 1880 (he lived at 5 Randolph Crescent) four plane trees were added (one still survives), and in 1893 six *Acubas japonica*, four laburnum and two flowering thorn were planted. Later attempts to clothe the banks with periwinkle and ivy, as suggested by McLeod, failed, but his holly hedge alongside Queensferry Road proved more successful.[39]

During the Second World War air-raid shelters were added and these remained until 1946. The cost of reinstating the garden (estimated by Dickson's nursery at £135) was met by compensation from the Ministry of Works; but their award of £24 for the railings was wholly inadequate.[40]

It would be easy to dismiss this small and rather exposed garden as having little value, yet when it was threatened with extinction the public rose swiftly in its defence. In 1958 Edinburgh City Council sought approval to alter the Development Plan, to include a new roundabout at the junction of Randolph Crescent and Queensferry Street.[41] Officials claimed that the 'position and height of this mound' contributed to traffic delays and congestion. The garden and its seventy mature trees it seems, were doomed. Ainslie Place was also threatened, for a portion of the garden was to be sliced off, setts removed, and all to allow adjustments in road levels (similar to the 'improvements' made in Charlotte Square) and faster traffic flows. Several amenity groups supported Lord Moray's feuars in their protest[42]; the Cockburn Association, for example, declared that 'the removal of mature trees from the centre of any street is serious enough, but even more serious will be the architectural confusion which will follow on the removal of the gardens'.[43] After a public inquiry held in November 1960 the plans were rejected and Randolph Crescent and Ainslie Place Gardens lived to fight another day.[44]

Notes

1. *The Scotsman*, 25 February 1826.
2. *Suggestions for the improvement of the Pleasure Ground in the interior of Moray Place*, Edinburgh, 1832, copy EPL, Edinburgh Room, YDA 2290.
3. GHT, Charter of Confirmation, 26 February 1757.
4. *The Edinburgh Advertiser*, 11 January 1825, feuing plan for the grounds being advertised for inspection; ibid., 1 March 1825, ground being advertised for feuing.
5. *Edinburgh Advertiser*, 25 October 1825, 'the remaining part of the crescent now erecting upon the ground of the late Dr Hope, at the back of the Old Botanic Garden'.
6. When only seventeen John Hope was writing enthusiastically to his aunt that 'I have the character of a great architect and hardly a house in Moray Place can be built without being revised by me. I have also given in twelve good plans for our grounds in Leith Walk which is to be feued in the Spring'. Quoted in Rev. D. Jamie, *John Hope, philanthropist and reformer* (Hope Trust 1907), p. 6.
7. John Hope campaigned for shorter hours for shops, a Saturday half-day holiday for trades, compulsory education and parks suitable for sporting activities including a public park at Stockbridge.
8. Garden Minute Book (1845–58), Minute 4 June 1847, reference to a key having been withdrawn from a subscriber living at 14 Gloucester Place for smoking 'to the great annoyance of ladies walking in the garden', and refusing to desist when approached by the gardener.
9. Garden Minute Book (1857–71), Minute 8 February 1869.
10. *Edinburgh Evening Courant* 25 June 1838, letter to the Editor signed J.N.S.
11. Garden Minute Book (1845–58), Minute, 8 May 1852. The Admiral presented these trees to the garden committee, requesting that they be put in a sheltered position 'care to be taken to provide proper soil and sufficiently fenced to preserve them from injury'.
12. Garden Minute Book (1857–71), Report by Mr McNab, Royal Botanic Garden, Edinburgh, 6 October 1865; 'Moray Place Gardens', *The Farmer*, 21 August 1867; Garden Minute Book (1871–81), Mr James McNab, Report on the state of Gardens, 24 February 1877.
13. B.C. Skinner, 'The Royal Visit of 1842', *Edinburgh, A Symposium for Dr J.B. Barclay*, (University of Edinburgh. Department of Extra Mural Studies, 1975).
14. Garden Minute Book (1857–71), Minute, 6 February 1865; the tool-house was removed in 1869 on the advice of McNab and the materials used to build another in the Bank garden.
15. Garden Minute Book (1871–81), Minutes, 3 March 1877; 4 March 1878; 23 February 1880; 27 April 1880.
16. Garden Minute Book (1881–92), Minutes, 15 November 1890; 13 December 1890; 21 March 1891.
17. Garden Minute Book (1906–25), 31 March 1911; all those with rights to the garden were allowed to play provided they supplied their own nets, posts and balls.
18. Garden Minute Book (1871–81), Minute, 22 March 1875, includes copy of letter sent to Dr Bryce and Dr Ferguson, 30 March 1875.
19. As with the other central gardens the railings were removed during the Second World War. New ones, 'Thomas Hadden's No. 3' design were erected in May 1952 costing the feuars just under £2,000. In the first instance the committee had approached Basil Spence, architect, but his design was considered 'too easily climbed'; Garden Minute Book (1944–53), Minutes, 17 October 1950; 12 December 1950; 16 March 1951.

20. Garden Minute Book (1902–25), Minute, 11 November 1918, letter from Miss Cowan, principal WRVS Depot Hostel, 15 Royal Circus, seeking permission to use pathways for drill purposes during the winter months; Garden Minute Book (1944–53), Minute, 8 June 1948, application by Scottish Fencing Club and Scottish Association of Girls' Clubs to use garden; 28 March 1950, Colonel Hope to make arrangements for the children's' garden competition: he was chairman of the committee and an active supporter of the gardens for many years. In more recent times the garden has proved a useful venue for marquee receptions.

21. John Byrom, Moray Gardens, Outline Management Plan, 2 of 2, Randolph Crescent, Ainslie and Moray Place, November 1995; presented to the management committee. The project to upgrade Moray Place gardens has now been taken over by Belinda Hayter-Hames, landscape architect, who lives in Moray Place; her plans aim to provide interest, colour and focal points throughout the seasons in all parts of the garden and to renovate much of the old planting.

22. Garden Minute Book (1857–71), Report by Mr McNab on the Ainslie Place garden, 15 November 1867.

23. Eagle & Henderson's Account, 1833 op. cit; these accounts show that a large quantity of elms, limes and lilacs were supplied for both the Moray and Ainslie Place gardens.

24. McNab recommended reducing the footpaths from ten feet to six or seven feet. Twenty five tons of shell gravel were taken from the Cockle Burn, by Dalmeny beach, and removed by boat, and used for resurfacing the front garden areas. The gravel has been replaced in recent years by tarmacadam, bestowing 'a rather mean municipal character' to the surface of the footpaths (John Byrom, Moray Gardens, Outline Management Plan, op. cit.)

25. Garden Minute Book (1857–71). Accounts for 1868.

26. Dean Ramsay was also a musician, avid charity fund raiser and successful author; see *Collins Encyclopaedia of Scotland* (London, 1994) eds John Keay & Judith Keay, p. 804.

27. Garden Minute Book (1857–1871), Minute, 14 January 1871.

28. Garden Minute Book (1874–81), Report by James McNab, Royal Botanic Garden, dated 27 January 1871, recorded in Minute, 6 February 1871.

29. Garden Minute Book (1871–81), Minute, 5 February 1872.

30. Garden Minute Book (1871–81). Report by James McNab dated 27 January 1871.

31. The letter was signed 'An Old Boy', and came in response to a report in *The Scotsman* on 7 October 1874 about a special town council meeting relating to improvements to the Meadows; RBG, James McNab manuscripts.

32. Garden Minute Book (1892–1907), AGM, 12 April 1893, letter from Mr Fitzroy Bell.

33. The Ministry of Works made a settlement of £30; new railings were erected by the firm of Thomas Hadden.

34. Grant, *Old & New Edinburgh*, Vol. 2, p. 115; the description notes that the old rookery in Randolph Crescent was 'removed recently'.

35. Garden Minute Book (1845–1858), note of assessment rate fixed for the front gardens including Randolph Crescent, from November 1843 to Whitsuntide 1845.

36. Garden Minute Book (1845–1858), Minute, 26 January 1853.

37. Feu Disposition of James Melville, WS, and the Earl of Moray in favour of the Feuars of Randolph Crescent, dated 22/23 February 1866, and registered in *PRS* Edinburgh, 6 March 1866.

38. Garden Minute Book (1858–71), Minute, 15 April 1867.

39. Garden Minute Book (1871–81), Minutes, 7 January 1877, 12 February 1880; Garden Minute

Book (1881–92), Minutes, 15 November 1890; 28 March 1892; Garden Minute Book (1892–1907), Minutes, 3 May 1897, 9 November 1897, 31 March 1898.

40. Garden Minute Book (1944–53), Minutes, 25 May 1945; 10 October 1946; 6 February 1947; 5 February 1948; 18 October 1949; the new railings were probably erected in 1950, the same year as Ainslie and Moray Place ones were renewed.

41. TCM, 5 June 1958, the Council were acting on the recommendations of the Chief Planning Officer (Mr Hewitson), and the City Engineer (Mr Haldane).

42. Amongst the groups protesting were the Edinburgh Architectural Association, the Georgian Group (now the Architectural Heritage Society for Scotland), and the Cockburn Association (Edinburgh Civic Trust).

43. George Bruce, *Some Practical Good: the Cockburn Association's 100 years participation in planning, 1875–1975* (Edinburgh, 1975), p. 64 (quotation taken from the 1958 Annual Report).

44. Details about the controversy can be found in the collection of press cuttings available in the Edinburgh room, EPL, YHE 369. The public inquiry was held in June 1959 and conducted by Mr R.S. Johnston, QC.

PART EIGHT

THE THIRD NEW TOWN

CHAPTER 17

THE LANDS EAST OF CALTON HILL

A bridge will be thrown over the Calton, and a street formed from Shakespear Square, parallel to Princes Street, to join the Calton Hill nearly at the gate of the burying ground . . . The air and situation are excellent, and the whole will form a most picturesque and beautiful addition to this elegant city. A new road will be opened up by the Abbeyhill, and property of every kind in that quarter greatly ameliorated . . . The ground feued for building in the new streets will produce a large sum . . . If this plan be adopted, as we hope it will, the access to the most beautiful and healthful walk in Europe, the admiration of all strangers, will be facilitated, and there will be an easy and pleasant approach to the Astronomical Observatory, Nelson's monument etc. We understand the greatest care will be taken to have the buildings and the bridge executed with taste, combining at once elegance, accommodation and utility.

Edinburgh Evening Courant, 19 February 1814

Splendid as are the various views in and about our capital, the terraces and the crescents in the new plan will exceed anything we have as yet to boast of.

Edinburgh Evening Courant, 25 December 1819

When the Bridewell (House of Correction) opened in 1795 on the south side of Calton Hill, its only approach was 'the steep, narrow, stinking, spiral street' known as Leith Street.[1] This part of the hill including the summit had been purchased by the Town from Lord Balmerino in 1724. The eastern flank was owned by Heriot's Hospital, and their land extended northwards in the direction of Leith and occupied a wedge-shaped piece of ground between Leith Walk and Easter Road. Quite a lot of this land was let for grazing and nursery-garden purposes. When first considered for residential development there was no direct communication from Princes Street to the south-eastern side of the hill. Circumstances were to change, however, and the change brought a new road, Regent Road, which was to have significant consequences for the proposed development. Alongside these changes came a growing concern that the eastern flank of Calton Hill must be treated with great care and sensitivity. It was under these altered circumstances that the creation of what is now the largest private pleasure ground in Edinburgh began to take shape. How these changes came about, and the way they influenced the allocation of open space, is important to our understanding of this particular group of pleasure gardens, and the way they came into being.

As early as 1810, with the second New Town still under way, Heriot's Hospital began to think about developing their portion of land east of Calton Hill. They would have been aware that the intended new road to Haddington (the future London Road) which would run through their site connecting Leith Walk with the Eastern Road (Easter Road) was not so far off. John Bell, land surveyor, was commissioned to prepare a measured plan.[2] This promised to be a major venture, even bigger than the first and second New Towns combined and one which the Town Council was also eager to promote. It was the Lord Provost, William Calder, who first brought all the interested parties together, and in January 1811 appointed a committee to:

> draw up an advertisement for plans for feuing the Hospital lands of Quarry holes, in conjunction with the Governors of Trinity Hospital and any other adjacent proprietors that it may be judged proper to invite to come into the measure of a general plan, and to enter into a joint contract.[3]

The area now under consideration included Heriot's Hospital land as well as ground further north and east belonging to Trinity Hospital;[4] between them they owned the greater part and in almost equal portions. Alexander Allan of Hillside (d. 1825), the most significant 'adjacent proprietor', possessed around 5 per cent of the area, but an important part, because a portion of his Hillside estate overlapped the line of the new road.[5] As the governors of Trinity Hospital were drawn entirely from the Town Council, the bond between them was even stronger than that between the Council and Heriot's Hospital. The appointed committee was therefore strongly biased towards the City's interests.[6]

The site's importance in visual and landscape terms, dominated as it was by the heights of Calton Hill, should have merited careful appraisal. But the committee rushed headlong into organising a design competition.[7] The sequence of events is well known,[8] and our purpose here is simply to focus on open-space issues relevant to the future pleasure gardens. Suffice it to say that during July and August 1812 advertisements appeared in Edinburgh, Glasgow and London newspapers inviting submissions for a 'Building Plan or Design for laying out in Streets, Squares, etc for Buildings'.[9] Design guidance was minimal.[10] Six months later 35 entries (from 32 'artists' – mostly Edinburgh based) had been received (several of a fairly sketchy nature);[11] the results were long delayed.

The Competition

The notes added by several competitors, as well as the written comments by the architectural assessors (including John Paterson, William Burn, Robert Reid, William Stark and John Baxter junior) have rather remarkably survived.[12] William Stark died before completing his report, but this was thought of such merit as to justify being printed in 1814 for wider circulation.[13] All these items provide unrivalled insights into the various approaches to design issues, the treatment of Calton Hill and views about access.

As far as competitors were concerned, several of them placed emphasis on aspects conducive to healthy living, and open space tended to be linked with these ends. Hence a good street plan was one that admitted 'free currents of air'; and features such as squares, circuses, crescents, octagons etc were a means of achieving this, as well as producing the best 'effect'. Regularity of form (but not so regular as to become monotonous) also appeared important. Picturesque effect could be achieved by terminating vistas with public buildings, or monuments set in public spaces. Pleasure grounds as such were not specifically mentioned. As to the appropriate treatment for the east side of Calton Hill, contestants appeared more divided. Relatively few left it substantially untouched or gave it special consideration.

After being publicly exhibited, the plans circulated among the architectural assessors[14] whose overall response was extremely lukewarm. Many designs were found 'wholly inadmissible', being inappropriate to the site's physical features. Four viable solutions were requested, but Burn and Patterson struggled to place even two. Points of criticism centred on: the ground being over-developed; insufficient space at the rear of buildings; too many cross streets, and buildings positioned at awkward angles (layouts radiating from a central crescent in Leith Walk were faulted on this score); poor distribution and balance of open space; and insufficient variety in the accommodation provided. Burn and Patterson both highlighted the need for improved access from Princes Street to the south side of the hill,[15] and both were unequivocal about treating the upper reaches with restraint. Burn expressed dismay that anyone 'with taste' could think of peppering the hilltop with villas 'and that so grand a feature as it is to our metropolis should be ruined by so vile a piece of patchwork'.

William Stark in his observations avoided criticising any one plan, but concentrated instead on issues arising from his own detailed appraisal of the site. His comments have come to be seen as the core of good town-planning practice. The site's unique qualities, configuration and existing planting, each a 'vendible commodity', were not in his view to be compromised by any artificially regulated plan, 'the niceties of square and rule', but rather to be sensitively exploited. Great landscape artists, he declared, never wearied of painting nature in harmony with the built form, 'nor the world of admiring what they painted'. A similar symbiosis was needed here.

Three related ideas to which Stark had given much thought were added by 'a friend' to the printed report by way of a postscript. One was the need for access from Princes Street to the south side of Calton Hill (via an elegantly arcaded bridge); another was a grand terrace to sweep round the lower southern and eastern flanks of the hill (on a similar level to the new road); and the third was about forming the upper portion of the hill, 'too elevated for

Pages 308–311: Competition prizewinners (1813) for the layout of streets East of Calton Hill:

Page 308: William Reid, architect, Glasgow, first joint prizewinner. His plan, somewhat angular in style, included four large continental-style piazzas and kept most of Calton Hill free of buildings. (NLS)

Page 309: Alexander Nasmyth, landscape artist, Edinburgh, first joint prizewinner. Like several competitors he adopted a radial plan centred on Leith Walk. The eastern flank of Calton Hill is quite extensively developed and little common open space is provided. (NLS)

Page 310: Richard Crichton, architect, Edinburgh, first joint prizewinner. Similar to Nasmyth's design but with more generous provision of open space and more variety in the accommodation provided. (NLS)

Page 311: James Milne, architect, and Benjamin Bell, both of Edinburgh, second prizewinners. This design aroused interest because of its greater originality and mixture of accommodation but was criticised for its over-development of Calton Hill. (NLS)

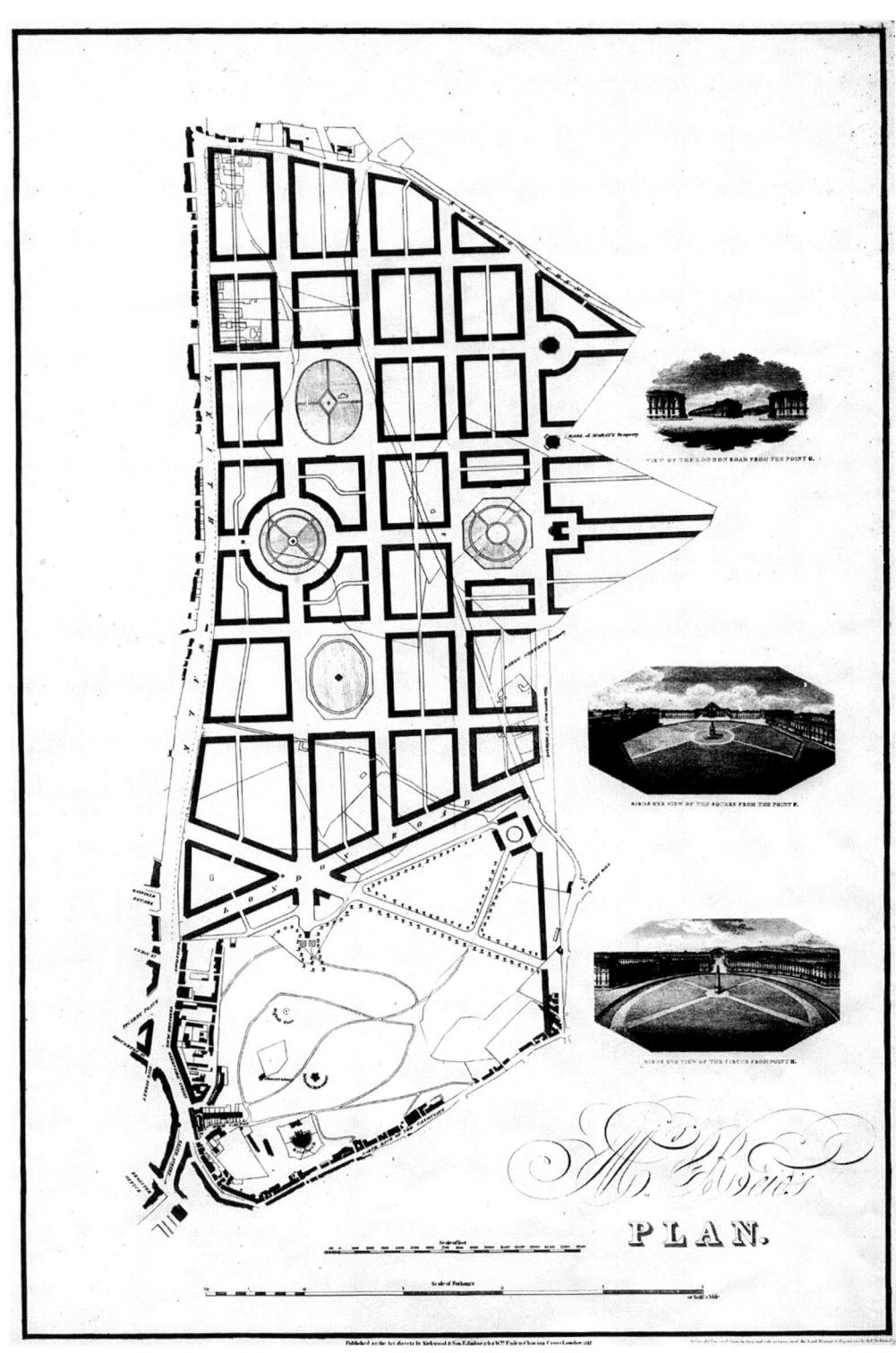

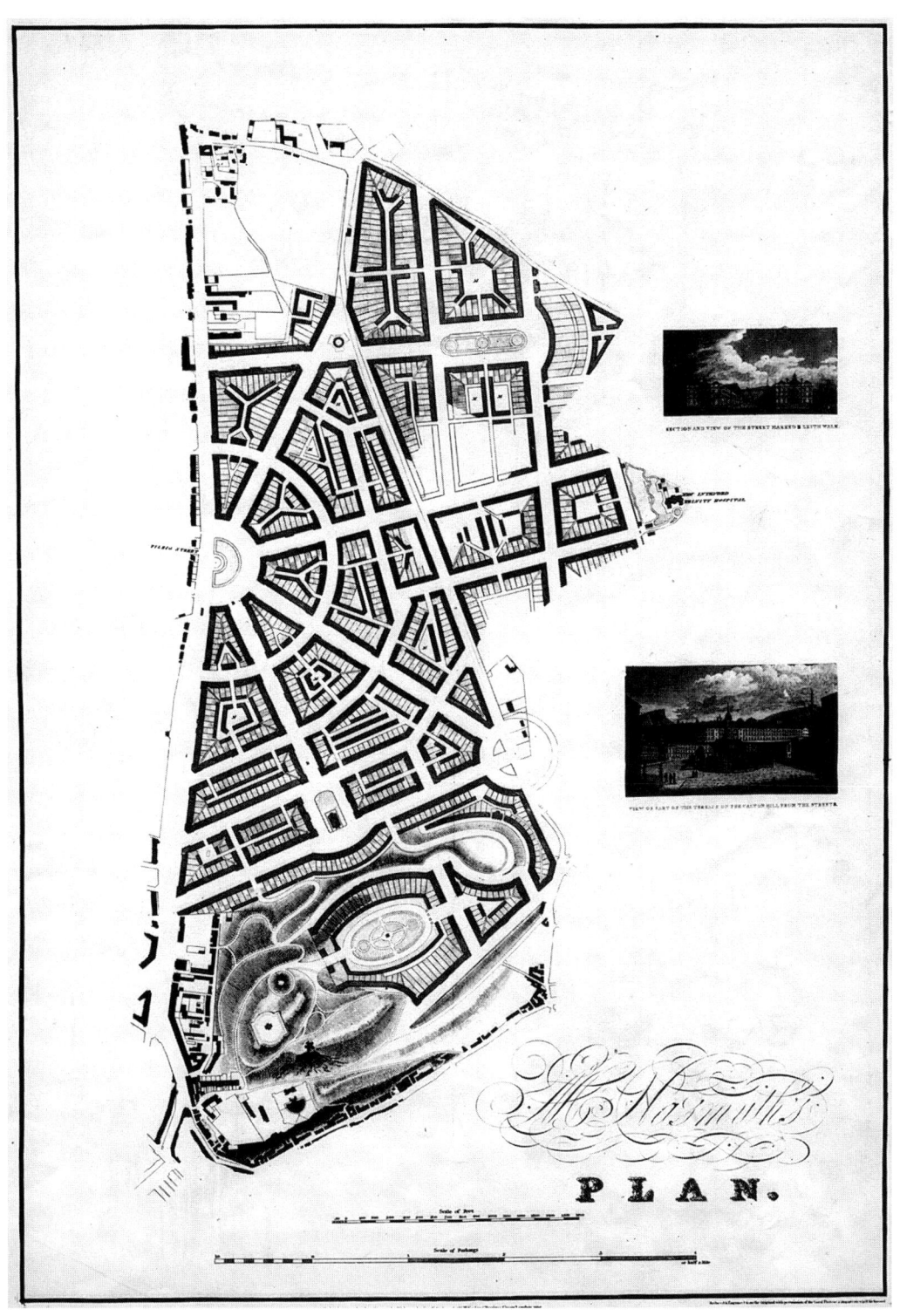

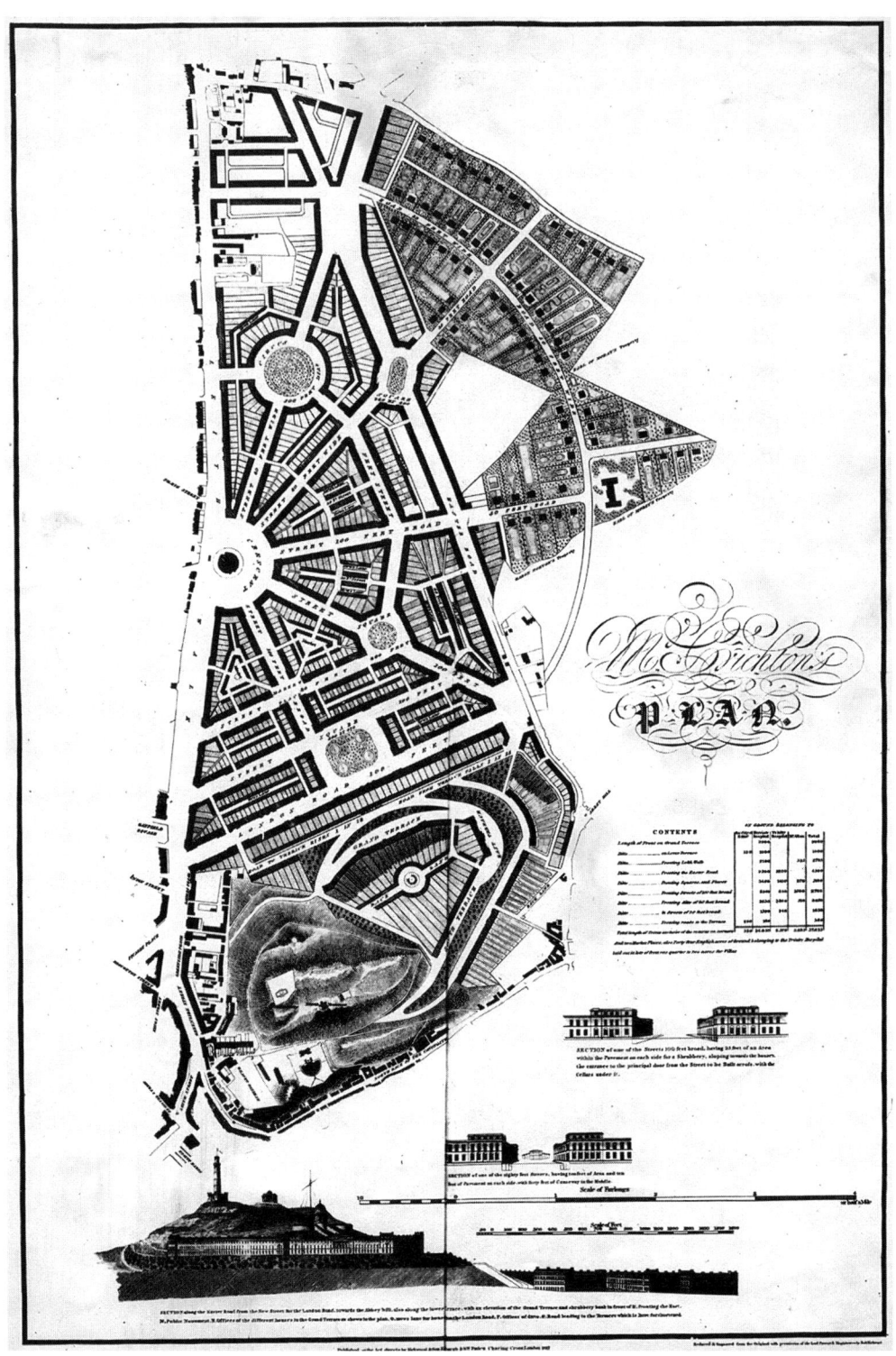

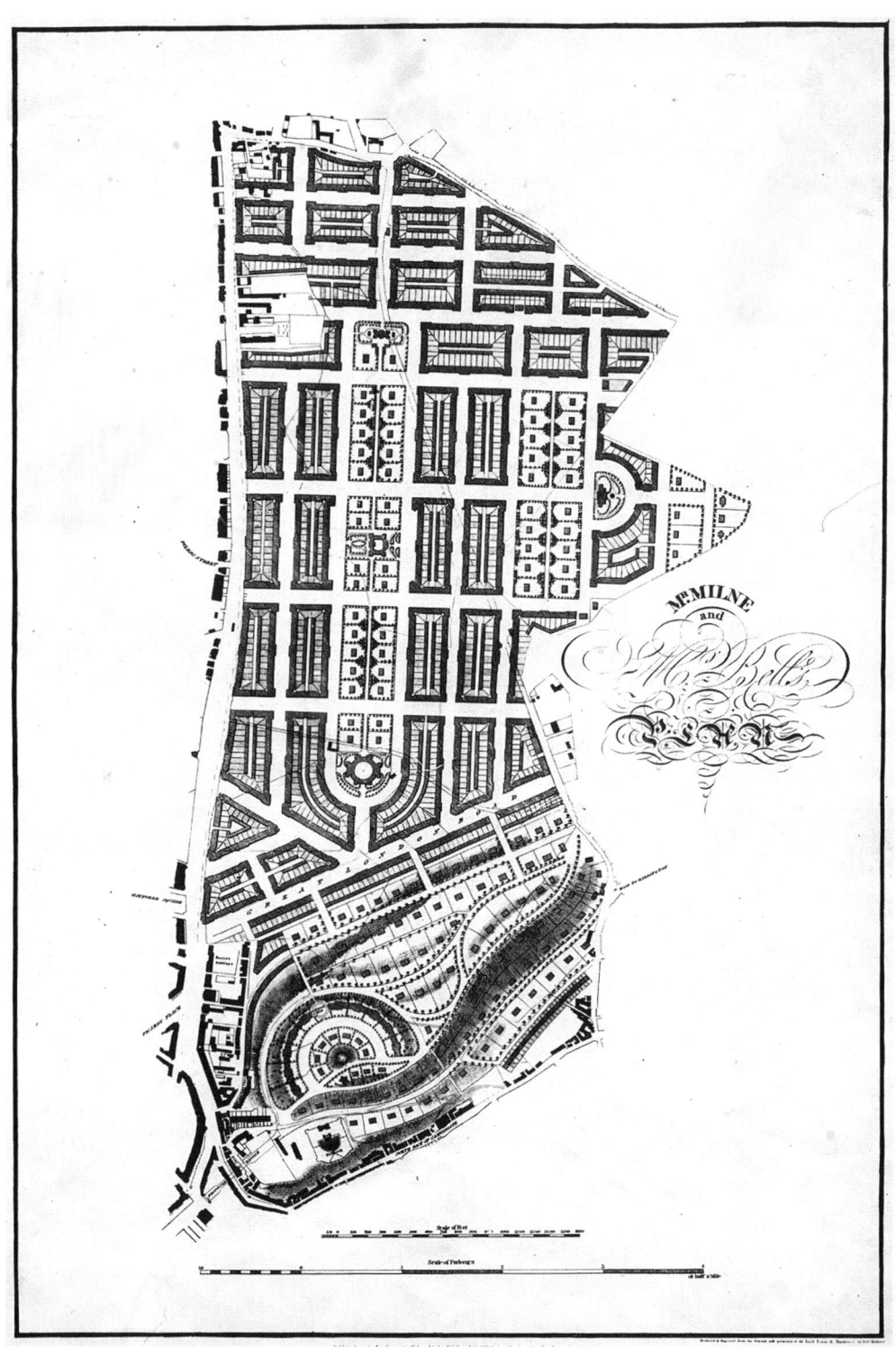

dwelling houses', as public open space, 'laid out in shrubbery, and enclosed with a parapet wall and rail'. Such an open space – a 'necessary appendage to a great city' – would add 'considerable attraction to the buildings in its vicinity', be ornamental, and a safe haven for young and old alike, and could be funded by the users. Life was being breathed into the idea of a major part of the hill being preserved and formed into pleasure ground as an essential ingredient of any new development.[16]

What the Competition Achieved

In March 1813 the plans, by now rather the worse for wear,[17] passed to a sub-committee with the recommendation that they 'advise with and take the opinion of Sir John Hay, Baronet, Baron Clerk, and Mr Innes of Stow'. All three were prominent citizens, with the necessary financial acumen to judge feuing potential.[18] Their report (two years in preparation) upheld the architects' conclusion that while 'several of the Designs evince much genius and skill in the artists', overall they displayed 'such defects, as to render it unwise to adopt them'.[19] Prize money, however, needed to be awarded and four entries were singled out as exhibiting 'superior merit'. Three were ranked equal first and the other was placed second, so in practice all received identical sums; the results were declared some weeks later.[20] William Reid from Glasgow; Alexander Nasmyth, portrait and landscape painter, Edinburgh and Richard Crichton, also from Edinburgh, won first prize. A joint entry by James Milne and Benjamin Bell[21] was placed second. The only non-architect was Alexander Nasmyth, a man whose creative energies spilt over in many directions.[22] Crichton and Milne both had New Town garden connections; Crichton designed the railings for West Princes Street shortly before his death in 1817, and Milne was responsible for designing St Bernard's Crescent and Saxe-Coburg Place in Stockbridge.[23]

Was the competition an expensive, long-drawn-out, ill-conceived flop? Superficially perhaps, but ideas were generated, public interest was aroused and a thoughtful and influential report produced. What must also be appreciated is that on the back of the competition rode another project that ultimately overtook it but worked to its advantage: the proposed new road between Princes Street and the south side of Calton Hill. Even before the competition results were announced, Heriot's Hospital was seeking professional advice on the feuing implications should such improved access become available.

Robert Stevenson's Involvement

The impetus for the new road was connected with the difficulty in finding a suitable site for the new national gaol. This had been sanctioned by Act of Parliament in 1813,[24] to replace the 'living grave' – the old Tolbooth – west of St Giles'. A space east of Libberton's Wynd in the Old Town had been allocated, but abandoned as too small; the sloping bank between the Mound and Canal Street – the future East Princes Street Gardens – was considered, but was already designated as pleasure ground, and any change would have caused public uproar. In any case it was felt that the 'exhalations arising from the North Loch' would prove detrimental to the prisoners' health.[25] Eventually a position on Calton

Robert Stevenson, Civil Engineer and consultant to the George Heriot Trust. (*Architect's and Builder's Journal*, 18 March 1914)

Hill, next to the Bridewell, was agreed, and in June 1814 a further Act was obtained naming this location and giving powers, 'for opening communications, Building a Bridge over the Calton and for other purposes relating thereto'.[26]

The timing of the Act corresponded with the circulation of Stark's report; and the competition's tardy progress must be measured against the accelerating pace of these other events. Nearly six months before the 1814 Act was passed, the Town had met with Heriot's Hospital to discuss plans for the new Regent Road 'made out by Mr Stevenson, Civil Engineer'; to establish if 'those likely to benefit from the road' would be, 'willing to contribute'.[27] At a time of increasing economic gloom any venture to provide work for the unemployed was welcome. But before becoming committed the Hospital asked their Superintendent, Thomas Bonnar, together with Robert Stevenson and other 'practical builders' for advice; a visit to the site had to be abandoned, however, due to 'the very inclement state of the weather, and the ground being deeply covered in snow'.[28]

Robert Stevenson's, 'love for the beautiful'[29] found fruition in his association with Calton Hill and was seen reflected both in his report to Heriot's Hospital, and later to the Road Commissioners.[30] This was home territory, for the Stevenson family had lived in Baxter's Land (property along Greenside Place) since the 1790s. Stevenson, now best remembered as engineer to the Northern Lighthouse Board, was involved with several Edinburgh projects including the New Town gardens; and he shared many of Stark's values. His report to the Hospital confirmed that the new road would provide a more direct

Stevenson's proposals for three semi-elliptical crescents on the east side of Calton Hill, 1814. (George Heriot Trust, Crown copyright © RCAHMS)

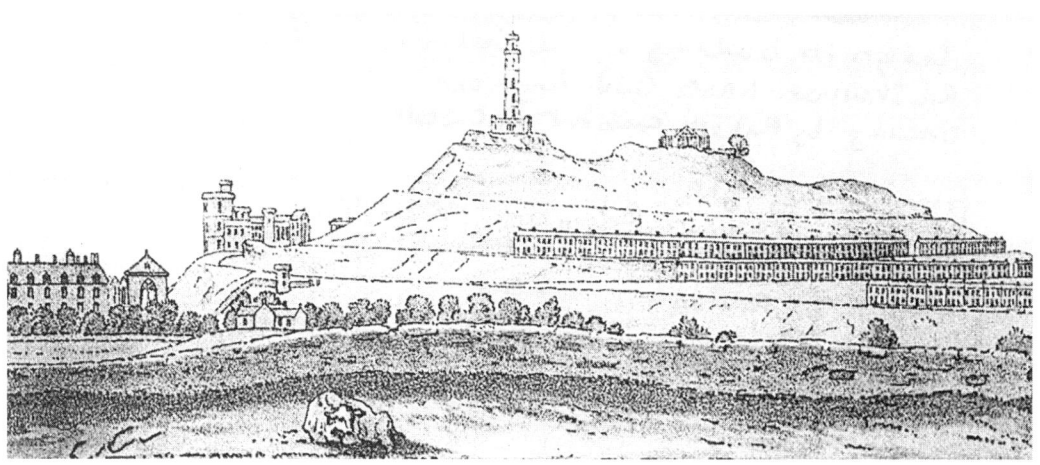

Drawing by Stevenson's assistant, G.C. Scott, showing the terraces as they would have appeared from Holyrood Park. (Roland Paxton)

and scenic route besides producing 'about 30 acres or thereby for building grounds which would otherwise remain as grass lands for a much longer period'. Study of the competition drawings had yielded little guidance in establishing monetary values but he was confident that the ground 'may be laid out agreeably to the taste and judgment of the artist in almost any form whatsoever'. Stevenson's own proposal was for three semi-elliptical crescents (high, mid and low terraces) divided by areas of pleasure ground, providing an outlook 'far excelling the views of Clifton or Bath or the Terrace at Ramsgate'.

The predicted increase of around £3,000 annually in the land's value was enough to persuade the Hospital to contribute £800 a year towards the new road. It was to be an expensive exercise, requiring as it did the removal of old buildings blocking the eastern end of Princes Street, bridging a fifty-foot-deep ravine,[31] blasting a passage through solid rock and relocating an old burial ground. Despite both Trinity and Heriot Hospitals' impatience to see the work finished,[32] much was achieved relatively quickly; the gaol was completed in 1817, the road and bridge in 1819 and all to a remarkably high standard of design and workmanship.[33]

Enter William Playfair

The joint feuing committee reconvened as the work neared an end; their first task to determine levels for the intended road between Leith Walk and Easter Road – the main entry point into the site. The Leith Walk Road Trustees had already agreed to accept whatever the committee's architect recommended.[34] In February 1818 it was 'unanimously' decided that 'an Architect of eminence and taste' should be appointed 'to prepare a general plan suited to the varied and picturesque state of the ground' (Stark's comments had not been in vain!).[35] Mr Allan communicated through his agent that the road should have

Portrait of William Playfair, architect. (National Galleries of Scotland)

priority, but those present believed that 'the general principles' of the plan required to be established in conjunction with the road level; and that 'Mr Playfair was the architect that ought to be employed'.[36]

Playfair, a former pupil of Stark (whom he had much admired),[37] was beginning to launch himself as a successful designer. His plans for an Observatory on Calton Hill had just received unanimous approval,[38] and not long before he had won first prize to complete Robert Adam's scheme for Edinburgh University. Probably absent when the Calton Hill competition was under way (reputedly working in the London offices of Wyatt & Smirke), Playfair would have monitored progress through family and friends.

Playfair's first report, dated April 1818, concentrated on the new road which he wanted kept as level as possible to protect views from the proposed upper terraces.[39] One year later, and received with 'high approbation', was Playfair's detailed layout and explanatory report. One thousand copies of the plan were printed, and 'noblemen and gentlemen of taste' were invited to comment.[40] Playfair's debt to Stark shines through this second report. All his mentor's ideals of harmonising building with existing landscape, respecting the special qualities of Calton Hill and creating a balance between architecture and open space find faithful translation in Playfair's hands.

In brief, the architect's plan contained two interconnecting parts; one to the south with

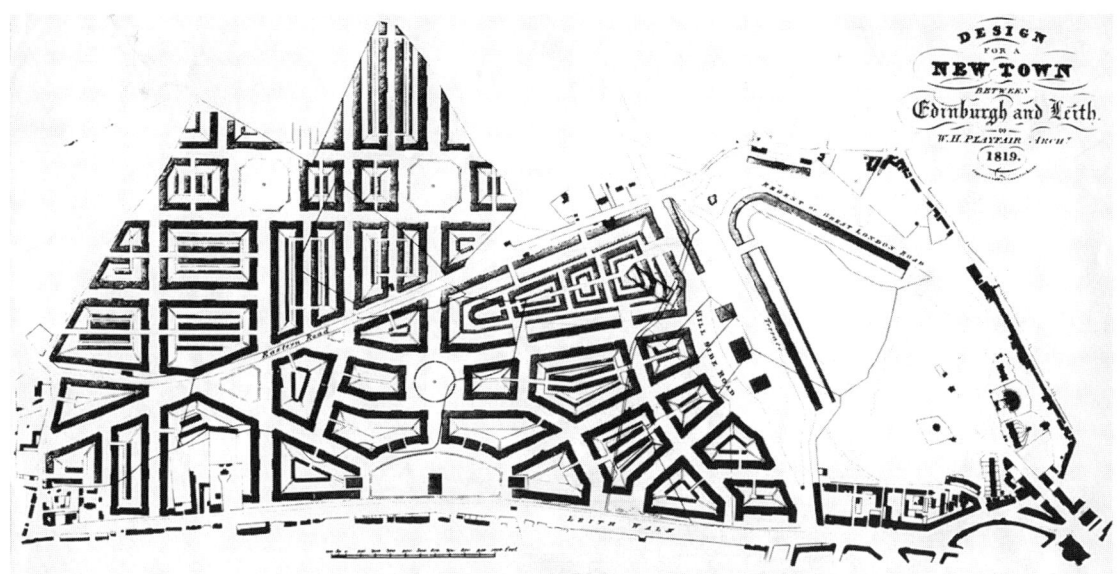

Playfair's plan, April 1819. Note the public buildings and other developments opposite the markets and Hillside Road (Crescent). (Crown copyright © RCAHMS)

a grand entry from Baxter's Place, and the other to the north radiating from a handsome crescent half-way down Leith Walk; this northern section was never built.[41] The building layout was set against views inwards and outwards of open spaces, foliage, public buildings and other monuments. The southern half – Hill Side Road (the future London Road) – contained a large crescent along its north side with three main streets radiating into the interior; the final eastern segment was reserved for a large market, with a short terrace immediately opposite. The rest of the south side (unlike the competition solutions) was left open, apart from suggested sites for three public buildings (never adopted, likewise the market area). Above these, 'rising from among the trees', was a handsome row or terrace, sufficiently elevated for 'an extensive view of the more distant country', these being the only buildings 'I would venture to place on Calton Hill'. This terrace, designed to sweep gently eastwards before curving westwards to continue parallel with Regent Road; was to enclose a large triangular piece of ground which 'I would convert into gardens, which, when properly arranged and planted, will become an agreeable and inviting retirement; and, at the same time, present a pleasing foreground to the enchanting landscape which is to be seen from the public walks above.'

No gardens existed at this time either in West Princes Street or in the greater part of Queen Street, so this was a bold and courageous proposition; but Stark had already helped prepare the way. Playfair's plans were well received by the noblemen and 'Gentlemen of taste' gathered at the City Chambers in April 1819 to review them. Amongst those invited were the Earl of Moray, the Earl of Wemyss and March, Lord Ashburton, Sir William Forbes, Sir William Fettes, Walter Scott, Professor Playfair (Playfair's uncle) and Henry

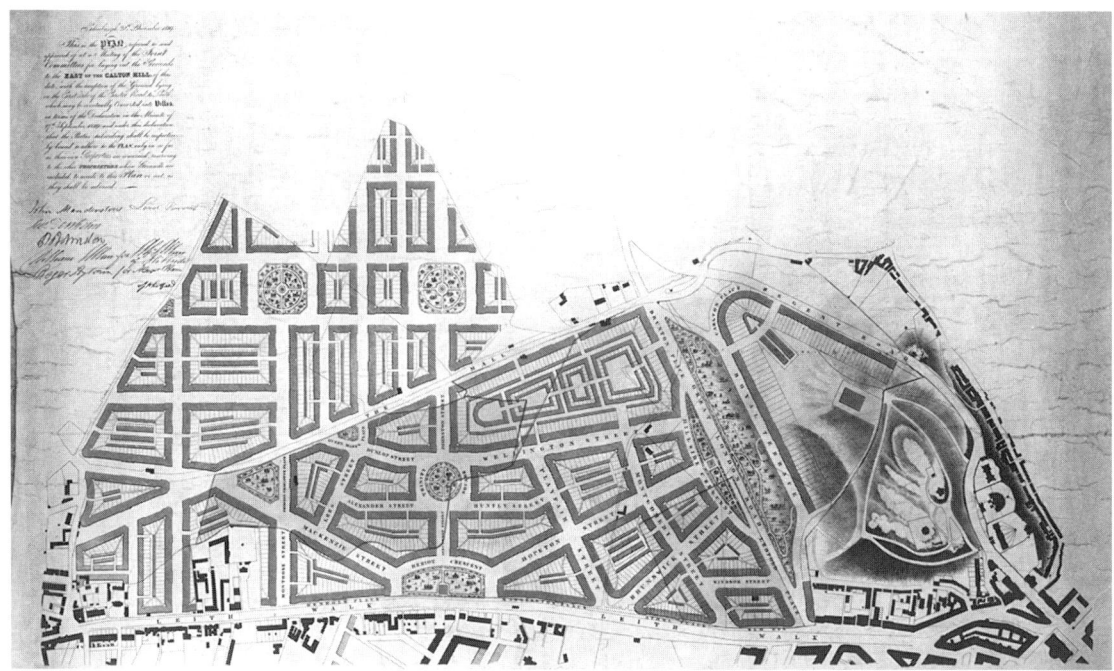

Playfair's engraved plan, December 1819. The garden spaces are drawn in detail and gardens have replaced the space previously occupied by public buildings along the Great London Road. (George Heriot Trust, Crown copyright © RCAHMS)

Mackenzie; also present were the three former assessors, Baron Clerk Rattray, Sir John Hay and Gilbert Innes.[42] The public also had the opportunity to view and comment.[43]

Playfair afterwards augmented his report with 'a few additional remarks' making comparison with the existing New Town and the competition entries, and demonstrating that his own design offered greater convenience and economic return.[44] He queried whether too much space had been allocated for pleasure ground on the Calton Hill, but went on to say that far from the space being wasted, it would produce 'a considerable revenue by the sums that will be paid for permission to walk there'; additionally, 'the Houses in the vicinity will be much more productive from the beauty of the situation in which they will be placed'. This had been the experience of East Queen Street Gardens where neighbouring property values had 'materially improved' following the gardens' formation. Nor was it to be forgotten that, 'in bringing this ground into the market there is a formidable Rival to contend with, in the Buildings which are now going forward at the western end of the present New Town' (was he referring to his own plans for Royal Circus, soon to be feued; or the Moray feu still some way off?)). To entice people eastwards a 'strong inducement' was required which 'I should hope will be obtained in the magnificent Gardens in question – this is the mainspring by which the whole may be set in motion'.

Playfair need not have worried. The committee fully supported his plans, determining that no building be placed on this part of the hill, 'except erections as may be necessary for two public gardens [the future Regent and Royal Terrace/ London Road Gardens]

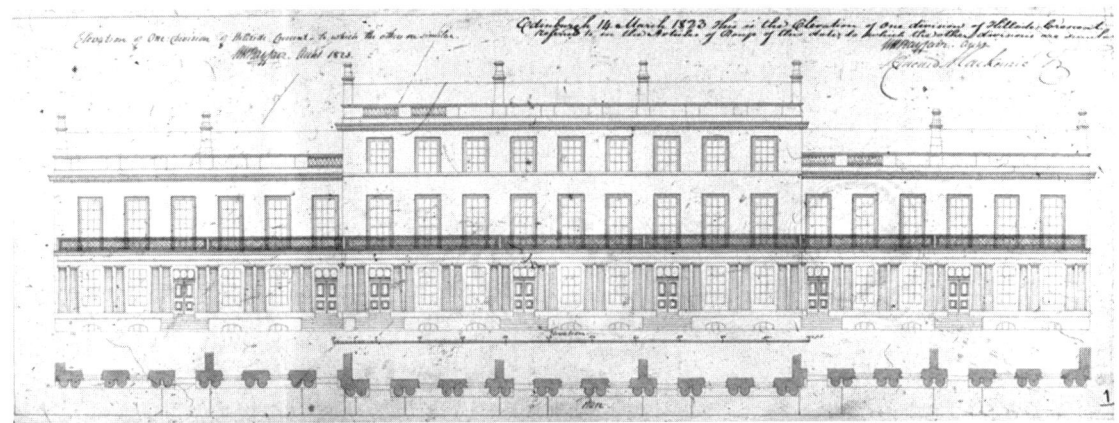

Elevation of Royal Terrace by Playfair, 1819. (EUL Special Collections)

and a church or other public buildings recommended by Mr Playfair'.[45] In December 1819 Playfair was made architect for the project and his plan engraved 'upon a reduced scale', for the benefit of potential feuars.[46]

Subsequent Progress

Between 1820 and 1821 elevations for Royal Terrace, Carlton Place (later renamed Carlton Terrace), the east end of Baxter's Place, Hillside Crescent, Elm Row and Leopold Place were completed.[47] Regent Terrace followed in 1825. Although building plots in Royal Terrace were advertised for sale in April 1820 (and the first house charter granted in June 1821), over 40 per cent of these dwellings were not completed until the 1850s and 1860s despite reducing plans in 1831, 'to a size which were likely to take the market . . . without destroying the effect of the original design of that street'.[48] Regent and Carlton Terraces fared rather better, with the majority of houses occupied by the end of the 1830s. Allan's estate at Hillside, which included Elm Row, Windsor Street, Brunswick Street and about one third of Hillside Crescent, was built in the early 1820s; the rest of the crescent – owned by Heriot's Hospital – not until the 1880s and 1890s – and then as flatted accommodation to plans by John Chesser. Playfair's plan for a third New Town was only partially realised, its ambitious scale out of step with a shrinking market and one already spoilt for choice. Somewhat isolated as it was from other parts of the New Town, the arrival of the railway in the 1860s killed any lingering hopes for the scheme's northward completion.[49]

But the portion to which Stark, Stevenson and Playfair had devoted so much attention – the eastern slope of Calton Hill – was finished, to the highest of picturesque principles and to the lasting benefit of Edinburgh. Failure to implement the whole did, however, have repercussions for the pleasure gardens. Five never materialised, and of four that did, two experienced a more chequered history as a result. The most important one, however, – Regent Gardens – has survived to become one of the finest and most intact of the pleasure grounds in Edinburgh.[50]

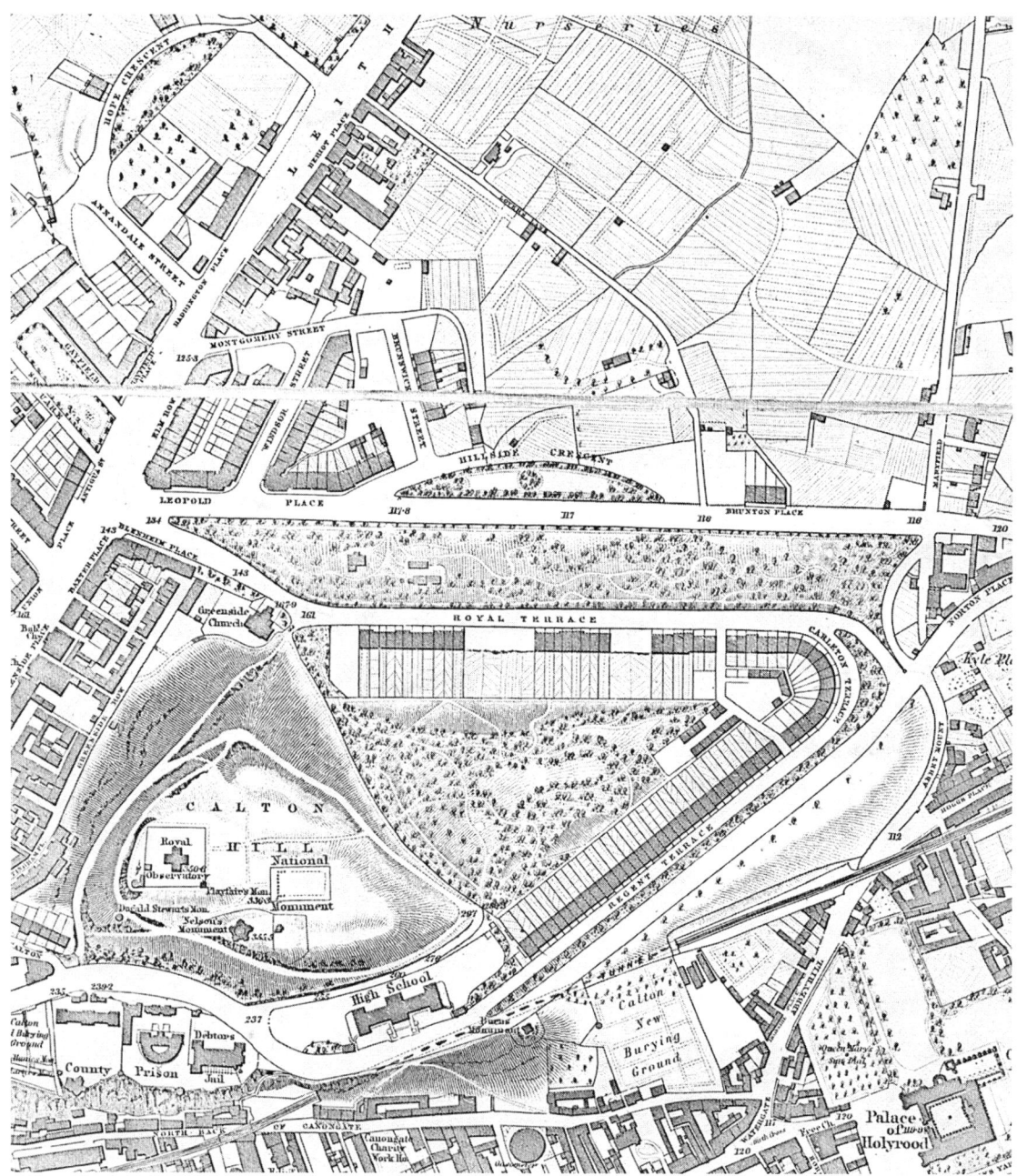

Johnston's map of Edinburgh, 1851, showing the garden areas. Quite a lot of Royal Terrace remains unbuilt; likewise for Hillside Crescent and Brunton Place. The line of prisons can be clearly seen at the head of Waterloo Place and the new Royal High School, which opened in 1829.

Notes

1. Henry Cockburn, *Memorials*, p. 241.

2. HHM, 9 July 1810; an Act of Parliament had been obtained authorising the new road and allowing the Leith Walk Road Trustees £3,000 for its construction.

3. HHM, 14 January 1811; and Minutes of the meetings of the Joint Committees of Heriot's Hospital and the Trinity Hospital and others, respecting the feuing of the lands called Quarryholes (to be referred to subsequently as Minutes of Calton Hill Grounds etc), Minute, 14 January 1811, ECA.

4. Some other smaller portions eastwards beyond Easter Road were also included; these belonged mostly to Trinity Hospital.

5. Allan would have been aware of the importance of his property relative to the proposed road.

6. Trinity Hospital, founded in 1461 by Mary of Gueldres, Consort to King James II, to provide accommodation (Trinity Hospital) for the maintenance of 'decayed burgesses' and their wives and families.

7. Minutes Calton Hill Grounds etc, 19 March 1811; 19 June 1812, and 27 June 1812. Mr Bell was paid £70 for his work which included sections, levels and four copies.

8. Peter Reed, 'Form and Context: A study of Georgian Edinburgh', in *Order in Space, Architectural Form and its Context in the Scottish Enlightenment*, ed. Thomas Markus (Edinburgh, 1982) pp. 135–44. See also J.C.B. Cooksey, *Alexander Nasmyth 1758–1840: A Man of the Scottish Renaissance* (Paul Harris, Whittingehame House Publishing, 1991), Chapter 9, p. 91.

9. Minutes Calton Hill Grounds etc, 27 June 1812; advertisements were placed in the *Courant*, *Mercury*, *Advertiser & Correspondent*, *London Courier*, *St James's Chronicle*, the *Times* and the *Glasgow Courier*.

10. Competitors were told that no alterations could be made to the Observatory, Monument, Flagstaff, and Bridewell and Bell's survey plan was made available.

11. Minutes Calton Hill Grounds etc, 4 January 1813; 11 January 1813.

12. GD 113 (SRO) Innes of Stow, V 322.

13. William Stark, *Report to the Right Hon the Lord Provost, Magistrates & Council of the City of Edinburgh, & the Governors of George Heriot's Hospital etc, of the plans for laying out the grounds for building between Edinburgh & Leith*, printed Alex Smellie, Edinburgh, June 1814 (EUL); see also Minutes of Calton Hill Grounds, 1 July 1815.

14. Minutes Calton Hill Grounds etc, 11 January 1813; 13 January 1813.

15. Patterson mentioned having been involved in surveying for such a road in 1789 and 1790. At that time (1789–93) he was working as Adam's Clerk of Works at the University. Sir James Hunter Blair, when Lord Provost in 1784–6, had promoted the idea for such a connection.

16. 'Civis', one of the entrants for the competition, had also conveyed similar ideas suggesting that the lower parts of the hill could 'afford an opportunity of making one of the most magnificent terraces in existence, where houses could be placed with shrubbery banks in front, ample private ground behind'.

17. Minutes of Calton Hill Grounds etc, 18 March 1813, refer to several plans being considerably 'injured and some torn from being transported from place to place', and direct the Agents to get the plans mounted on canvas before circulating amongst members of the sub-committee.

18. James Clerk of Craighall (later Clerk-Rattray, died 1831) advocate, Sheriff Depute of Edinburgh, Baron of Exchequer from 1809 and soon to become an active Commissioner for

the Regent Bridge project; also founder member of West Princes Street garden committee. Gilbert Innes of Stow, Deputy Governor of the Royal Bank of Scotland and celebrated millionaire; keen musician and founder of St Cecilia's Hall; in 1814 he was awarded freedom of the City for public services. Sir John Hay of Smithfield and Hayston was on several important committees including Trustee for Manufacturers & British White Herring Fishing, a Commissioner for Improvements 1827, and involved with the Royal Institution for the Encouragement of Fine Arts and the Society of Arts for Scotland.

19. Minutes Calton Hill Grounds etc, opinion of Baron Clerk and Gilbert Innes, Edinburgh, 22 March 1815.

20. Minute Calton Hill Grounds, 1 July 1815; the meeting also decided to apportion expenses incurred (£877) to each of the parties according to the extent of their building ground. See also *Edinburgh Evening Courant,* 22 July 1815 for a notice of the winners.

21. Benjamin Bell was a surgeon, a farmer and property developer and it must have been in this last context that he linked up with Milne. In 1806 he was involved in the development of Newington.

22. J.C.B. Cooksey, *Alexander Nasmyth 1758–1840; A man of the Scottish Renaissance*, Chapter 9 in particular concentrates on his architectural and landscaping projects.

23. Richard Crichton and James Milne both competed a little later in plans to complete the University.

24. 53 George III C77. An Act for erecting and maintaining a new gaol and other buildings for the County and City of Edinburgh, 21 May 1813.

25. Minute Book of the Trustees named by the Act of the 53 George III over the Low Calton 1814–1820, ECA (to be referred to as Minute Book, Calton Bridge Commissioners).

26. 54 George III C170. An Act to amend an Act passed in the last session of Parliament for erecting and maintaining a New Gaol, for opening communication.

27. HHM, 27 January 1814; Minute Book Calton Bridge Commissioners, Minutes, 30 January 1815 and 19 December 1816.

28. HHM, 22 February 1814.

29. Quoted in H. Bagenal, 'Robert Stevenson: A great Architect-Engineer', the *Architect's and Builder's Journal*, 18 March 1914, p. 188; see also Robert Louis Stevenson, *Records of a family of engineers* (London, 1912).

30. HHM 22 February 1814, Report to the Trust by Mr Stevenson, 12 February 1814; and Minute Book Calton Road Commissioners, Minute, 6 December 1815, with Report by Stevenson, 5 December 1815.

31. In addition to Elliot's design for Regent Bridge (refer above) the architect appears to have included plans for a free-standing monumental gateway (Triumphal Arch) to be sited north of the bridge and to the south of the new gaol.

32. Minute Book, Calton Road Commissioners, Minute 27 June 1816.

33. For example, their attention to detailing (including the bridge, steps to Calton Hill, retaining walls etc (all by Elliot), and the care taken to achieve good standards of design for the adjacent buildings in Waterloo Place (also by Elliot).

34. Minutes of Calton Hill Grounds etc, 24 June 1817.

35. Minutes of Calton Hill Grounds etc, 5 February 1818.

36. Minutes of Calton Hill Grounds etc, 13 February 1818.

37. NLS, 9704, Manuscript department, Collection of Playfair's letters to the Rutherford family; letter to Lady Elizabeth Rutherford, dated 1st September 1841.

38. *Edinburgh Evening Courant*, 12 February 1818. Notice by D. Brewster, Secretary of the Astronomical Institution, informing the public of the Council's approval of the plan commissioned by them from Mr William Playfair, architect; and their subsequent approbation by the Lord Provost, Magistrates and Town Council.

39. Minutes of Calton Hill Grounds etc, 8 May 1818 (containing Playfair's report as to the level for the London Road); and Minute Book, Calton Road Commissioners, Minute, 7 July 1818.

40. Minutes of Calton Hill Grounds etc, 12 April 1819; see also HHM, 15 April 1819.

41. This second area centring on a crescent 'of great size' off Leith Walk 'the management of which I consider of as much importance as the management of the buildings on Calton Hill', was to include four public buildings and three principal streets rather in the character of the Piazza del Popolo in Rome.

42. Minutes of Calton Hill Grounds etc., 12 April 1819.

43. *Edinburgh Evening Courant,* 22 April 1819, Notice of this 'very elegant design' now open to viewing.

44. Minutes of Calton Hill Grounds etc., 30 August 1819, Report by W.H. Playfair.

45. Minutes of Calton Hill Grounds etc., 27 September 1819. The several other spaces marked by Playfair for public buildings were to be left optional to the individual owners of land.

46. Minutes of Calton Hill Grounds etc., 20 December 1819.

47. Minutes of Calton Hill Grounds etc., 9 March 1821.

48. HHM, Vol. 25, 1 April 1831.

49. It has been suggested that building was delayed by difficulties over rating, arising where buildings were beyond the bounds of the barony of Calton.

50. For an account of the residents and other items relating to the social history of the Calton Hill area, see Ann Mitchell, *The People of Calton Hill* (Edinburgh, 1993).

CHAPTER 18

REGENT TERRACE GARDEN, REGENT, ROYAL AND CARLTON TERRACE GARDEN

Regent Terrace Garden
(Front Bank Garden)
1.3 acres (0.52 ha)

We begin with this long narrow woodland bank fronting Regent and Carlton Terraces, simply because this was the first to bring the feuars together. Under the conditions of sale proprietors in the two terraces were obliged to enclose the area 'with parapet and retaining walls and iron railings in a suitable and handsome manner', according to drawings and directions provided by William Playfair. They were given exclusive use of the space and made responsible for its upkeep. The same conditions applied to Hillside Crescent Gardens.[1]

It was the builders in the terraces who took the initiative to have the ground enclosed. In March 1825 the first recorded meeting of feuars took place, and it was predominately a gathering of builders anxious to resolve various practical matters, such as having the west end of Regent Terrace connected with Regent Road (requiring rock to be excavated), arranging pipes for sewage and water and enclosing the Front Bank Garden with retaining walls, parapet and railings. The committee appointed to take action were all builders apart from one. It was at their request that Playfair adjusted the line and level of Regent Terrace at the eastern end to allow the pleasure ground to be slightly widened.[2] Money to meet the cost of enclosure was raised by a special flat-rate contribution levied on all the proprietors in the two terraces.

Little is known about the garden's formation. A letter received from Mr Bayley, SSC (the first resident in Regent Terrace, and in whose legal chambers the feuars first met), was presented at a feuars' meeting in March 1827, 'on the subject of planting the sloping bank with shrubbery'. Action was thought premature until the railings were complete, but 'it might be proper to lay it down with grass meantime'.[3] The Carlton Terrace end remained without railings until September 1830, the year when the whole bank was planted with trees and shrubs according to advice most likely given by Patrick Neill and Dr Graham. Connecting footpaths were provided at the centre and eastern end to link the terrace with Regent Road. For the most part it is a long, steep and narrow strip, although the rather wider eastern end does allow some space for seating. Costs for making the garden were later quoted as over £3,000, but the large area of retaining walls and railings must have accounted for a substantial part of this.[4]

James McNab, when writing about the ground in 1865, suggested that periodic inspection of the Garden's 'picturesque condition' was best conducted from one of the upper terrace windows. But care rarely attained such lofty levels. Two years later he was complaining about the overcrowded shrubs and neglected trees which 'sadly mar the beauty of the bank'.[5] In 1895 the Council, then engaged in making a pavement and erecting lamp standards along the north side of Regent Road, issued an ultimatum that the bank be kept in better order, 'or hand this pleasure ground over for maintenance by the Magistrates and Council'. A 'groundless complaint', muttered some of the committee, but improvements were made in consultation with Mr Macleod, the City's Head gardener. In 1947 a number of proprietors proposed that as there was 'no benefit from the Front Bank Garden' it should be made over to the Council, but the notion was rejected.[6]

Over a hundred open-grown hardwood trees (mainly elm, sycamore, ash, horse chestnut, lime and laburnum), with sixty or so mixed ornamental trees and shrubs (holly, yew, rhododendrons) and some hedging, are grown in the bank although little of the original planting survives. The strip is cared for by the gardener responsible for the larger garden; proprietors pay a separate assessment and have their own small management committee. The terrace railings remain the most vulnerable part, with damage caused in former times by bolting horses (frightened by a doorstep scrubber, a stationary car and 'a carpet cleaning machine at work'), and today by errant cars. This was once a popular viewing platform for Royal and other ceremonial processions from Holyrood, with crowd control maintained by a ticket system supervised by the gardener and his assistants.[7] The Garden's main function has been and still is to serve as a visual and noise buffer between the houses and the main road, as well as providing a bold foil to the architecture.

Regent, Royal and Carlton Terrace Garden
Also known as the 'Carlton Hill Pleasure Ground', the
'Large Garden' and as 'Regent Gardens', 11.70 acres (4.6 ha)

> Much has been done recently for the beauty of the west end of the town, by laying out the North loch and the Queen Street Gardens, as shrubberies and ornamental pleasure grounds, and we are happy to state that the eastern part is soon to receive its share of this species of decoration. The large park on the east side of Calton Hill, extending from the public ground down the east road to Leith, has, we understand, been let on a long lease to the proprietors of the new buildings in Royal Terrace for conversion into Pleasure Ground. The park which is the property of Heriot's Hospital, and about 9 acres in extent (Scots acres), has been let for some years for feeding cows . . . By this arrangement all parties will be benefited. The hospital gets, we understand, a few pounds more than it got or could get for the park as a pasture ground. The occupiers of the building will secure, at a trifling expense (not exceeding, we believe, 20 or 30 shillings each house), the exclusive possession of one of the finest private promenades in Europe, and the privilege will be so much the more valuable, as from the position of the ground behind the plots attached to the houses, each family will have its own private entry. The public will gain too, first, by having the area kept perpetually free from building; secondly, by the addition which so great an improvement will make to the picturesque beauty of the town; and thirdly, by the new interest which the walks on the upper part of the hill will derive from such an adjunct. The shrubbery, and walks are to be formed at the expense of the proprietors

of the new buildings, and under the supervision and control of Mr Playfair on the part of the hospital.

The Scotsman, 15 September 1827

The prospect of another pleasure ground, this time on the east side of Edinburgh, was greeted with enthusiasm by *The Scotsman*, alive to the widespread benefits this would bring. It is triangular in shape and enclosed by Regent, Carlton and Royal Terraces, whose green canopy provides a petticoat – like frill to the barer and more windswept upper reaches of Calton Hill, sweeping the eye forward to views of the Forth and the Fife hills beyond. To be invited within this secret and magical space never fails to surprise, few being aware that such a large woodland park exists so close to the city centre. Playfair's belief that such an amenity would enhance property values has been more than vindicated, and the 'stunning views' into the 'famous Regent Terrace Gardens' receive almost as much sales emphasis as the properties themselves.[8]

There has been little change to the Garden's structure since it was first formed between 1830 and 1832. The design consists of an upland lawn planted with specimen trees in an early and uncluttered gardenesque style strongly reminiscent of the late Humphrey Repton (1752–1818). It has many of the attributes of a scaled-down country gentleman's seat, a miniature improved park of a kind then much in vogue in the lowlands. The lawn is traversed along its contours by a number of paths leading to a mount footpath at the top of the ha-ha, formed in two portions and connected by a rustic bridge erected in 1842. It cunningly conceals the high stone perimeter wall which separates the garden from the public ground and is lined with a double row of horse chestnuts. Flanking the lawn are hedged walks, with steep wooded slopes beyond, so that the building mass is set picturesquely after the manner approved by the Gilpins and as promoted by Stark and Playfair, and within a broad canopy of large trees – mainly elm, sycamore, lime, horse chestnut and ash.[9]

Setting up the Garden

Initially the ground was protected by a servitude forbidding any building apart from a site reserved for a church or similar public building at the centre of the west side; a similar restriction applied to the land fronting Royal Terrace which later became London Road Gardens. It was the same group of builders who had provided the impetus behind Regent Bank Gardens who were mostly responsible for establishing these much larger gardens. Of the five committee members elected in 1825 to oversee various practical matters, four were builders: William Henry, John Neill, John Thin and Lewis Wallace. The first two owned the largest number of plots, and Wallace and Neill both became residents. Three (Henry, Neill and Wallace) had previously worked in Drummond Place, and all three had supported the central garden there when it was set up under a separate feu charter granted by the Town Council. The only non-builder was Adam Ellis, WS, one of the first residents in Royal Terrace, whose legal skills were soon to prove useful. At this time the committee met at the Ship Tavern in East Register Street, moving up the hill to the Waterloo Hotel at the beginning of the 1840s.

Panorama as seen on a walk round Calton Hill, 1847. Over the wall we have a glimpse of the fairly newly-formed Regent Gardens, beyond which can be seen unbuilt plots in Royal Terrace. On Calton Hill people stroll and the washer-women keep busy. (Paul Harris Publishing)

The same procedure for setting up the gardens was adopted as for Drummond Place, only this time negotiations were with Heriot's Hospital. They began in November 1825 – well before the terraces were finished – and under William Henry's leadership.[10] Henry was one of the main builders in Regent Terrace, but never lived there, continuing to reside in Scotland Street. His contribution and commitment to these gardens is therefore all the more remarkable, for it extended well beyond any initial motives he may have had to promote house sales. Indeed he did far more than most other residents. Responsibility for organising and supervising all the practicalities associated with making the garden were assumed by Henry, no mean undertaking considering the scale of the enterprise. For many years he acted as chairman and treasurer to the committee, keeping a watchful eye over the garden's progress. He remained involved until 1844, the Minute Books paying tribute to his 'long, zealous and efficient services'. Earlier his contribution to setting up the Gardens was acknowledged by the presentation of a piece of silver plate.[11]

By October 1826 the framework of the charter had been agreed. The ground was to be enclosed 'in a tasteful manner and laid out as pleasure ground to the satisfaction of the Governors at the expense of the feuars'.[12] Various conditions were made. The land was to be used solely for pleasure ground, and no buildings were allowed apart from those necessary for a garden. Rights of access and responsibility for upkeep were to be vested in the owners of individual house plots within the three terraces (93 in total). Annual assessments to cover the costs of upkeep were not to exceed £10 per plot, and rules and regulations agreed by the majority were to be binding.[13] In addition, feuars were required to build a wall between the Garden and the public part of the hill (to be completed by Whitsuntide 1829) 'of neat coursed hammer dressed rubble, to the satisfaction of Mr Playfair'. The Hospital upheld their right to resume one acre (Scots) at any time (but have never done so), and to receive an annual feu duty of just over £93.[14] Compared to Drummond Place, the feuars were burdened with greater financial responsibilities and a less well defined management structure, but had acquired the use of an unrivalled and generously sized piece of land.

In November 1830 (the boundary wall being now complete), the proprietors met under the chairmanship of Adam Luke (Heriot's Hospital Treasurer) to form a committee 'for the purposes of carrying the plan of the pleasure ground into execution'. The builders' presence remained strong. Four were elected onto the new committee (Lewis Wallace, William Henry, Robert Dobson and John Neill) together with three residents: Dr John Easton, Adam Gibb Ellis and Isaac Bayley. Mr Henry was appointed convener. The committee was authorised 'to make an arrangement with any nurseryman for laying out and planting the ground', and to explore the possibility of renting out a portion as nursery ground. It was also suggested that advantage should be taken 'of the advice of Dr Graham and Mr Patrick Neill who have already very kindly given, and still offered to give their assistance'.[15] This would suggest that these two had already given advice in connection with the newly planted Regent Bank Gardens.

Few could equal Graham and Neill in terms of horticultural knowledge and practical experience. Dr Robert Graham (1786–1845) had master-minded the creation of Glasgow Botanic Garden, and shortly after being appointed Regius Keeper at Edinburgh in 1820, repeated a similar exercise when the Botanic Garden moved from Leith Walk to

Inverleith; he also had some connections with the Queen Street Gardens. Patrick Neill was then serving as a Town Councillor, and was closely involved with making the East Princes Street Gardens. Neill's council work brought him into contact with the property maintenance sub-committee of Heriot's Hospital; and on both scores, when gardening matters arose, they tended to be directed to him.[16] This link with the Hospital would have made his advisory role all the more pertinent. But additionally both Neill and Graham had close associations with one of the committee – Adam Gibb Ellis, WS. Ellis was Treasurer of the Wernerian Natural History Society (established in 1808 and surviving until 1857) of which Dr Graham was Vice President and Patrick Neill Secretary. Society meetings would have provided easy opportunities for conversation about the new gardens and what should be done.

The Garden in the Making

Nothing has emerged to substantiate the curious claim that these gardens were designed by Sir Joseph Paxton, or that he had anything to do with them at any time whatsoever.[17] But likewise no neat description exists which pinpoints exactly who was responsible, or what precisely was done. Nevertheless it is possible to construct a reasonably accurate picture from the sources available. Playfair as the appointed architect certainly had a key role in all matters practical and supervisory; this applied not only to the buildings themselves but also to the areas of adjacent space; and no critical change could be made without his prior agreement. Hence the detailed work of adjusting boundaries, providing plans for walls and railings and overseeing their construction fell to Playfair; he was also responsible for directing where earth dug from house foundation had to be deposited. The ha ha formed parallel to the western boundary wall, and designed to screen it, would most certainly have been masterminded by him: thrown up with spoil partly from some of the houses, and more likely from the foundations of the boundary wall itself. It was a most economic and successful solution to disposing of vast quantities of unwanted earth and waste, yet turning it to clever advantage.

We can be fairly confident that the main structure of the Garden, including the ha ha and network of footpaths, was determined by Playfair.[18] The houses in Royal Terrace had stated in their charters that a row of lime trees be planted at intervals alongside the rear boundary walls, a detail which Playfair would have been responsible for, and indicating a concern to relate buildings to the landscape. It is unlikely that the treatment of the central space would have progressed without his involvement and comment. The minutes tell nothing about relationships between William Henry, the Garden Chairman and Playfair, but one suspects that it was a useful and co-operative one, for there were many practical issues that brought them together and there are no hints of progress being halted due to disputes or misunderstandings. It must be appreciated, too, that Playfair had already advised on a layout for East Princes Street Gardens where his proposals later became the basis of Neill's planting plan. A similar partnership may well have operated here. And we certainly know that Playfair designed the layout of the London Road Gardens.

A complete silence descends for the next twelve months following the appointment of

Two general views of Regent Gardens, Edinburgh. (C. Byrom)
Top: The path at the top of the ha ha.
Bottom: The sweep of lawn leading up to the ha ha.

Tennis party, Regent Gardens, May 1887. The two families involved both lived in Regent Terrace. (James Bertram)

the Garden Committee. Lack of activity could not have been the reason. Maybe too much was happening to keep up with, as the ground must have been full of labourers digging, trenching, forming and shaping, doing all the preparatory work prior to planting. When information next surfaces it is about this very issue. In December 1831 the Committee considered various estimates (based on a list prepared by Patrick Neill, Graham's name having now disappeared), deciding to accept Alex Wright's offer, 'but upon condition that the committee shall only be bound to take and pay for such of the plants as they think proper'. Wright was a local man with business premises at 1 Greenside Place and a nursery in Pilrig Street. The Committee subsequently offered temporary employment (at 10 shillings (50p) a week) to Edwin Neilson 'to take charge of the pleasure ground, plant the same and do whatever work relating to the ground as the Committee may order'. Neilson remained in charge for the next sixteen years, during a demanding period when not only had the immature garden to be coaxed into life, but a sharp watch had to be kept for interlopers gaining access via unsecured building plots, as well as little boys trespassing from the newly-built Royal High School.

Mr Henry was authorised to employ additional help 'so as to have the planting put in without further delay'. He was also asked to supervise enclosing the eastern end 'according to the plan approved of by Mr Playfair', as well as the building of a tool-house 'behind Mr Dallas's stable'. In August 1833 the minutes refer (without detail) to Mr McCaul, 'the contractor having finished the whole operations on the hill'. Was this in connection

A fundraising garden party. (C. Byrom)

Open Door Day, spring 2000. (C. Byrom)

WRVS red alert: Open Door Day (inside the gardener's tool house, formerly a garage). (C. Byrom)

with the tool-house, sinking a 15-foot (4.57 m) well close to the centre, or more general labouring work connected with forming the garden? Charles McCaul had been the contractor for Hope (Hopetoun) Crescent Garden in 1826, and also appears in connection with Hillside Crescent Gardens; so with this experience he might well have contracted for Regent Gardens.[19]

All this work cost money, and by May 1832 the minutes report that over £1,100 had been spent on having the Gardens laid out, with a further expected outlay of £400. The latter was probably for the planting, and the rest for enclosing, earth shaping and path formation. Already 'a great many' proprietors were behind-hand with their payments and Mr Bayley was asked to chase these up. By 1834 management of the Gardens was becoming better regulated, with Isaac Bayley and Andrew Ellis acting as joint clerks without charge; by then the committee had added three feuars from each of the terraces, a practice that has continued.

Subsequent Fortunes

The Gardens opened for use in the spring of 1832, and one of the clerk's first tasks was to draw up regulations 'solely with a view to the comfort, safety and convenience of the whole inhabitants'. Early excesses were quickly clamped down upon. Thus in 1832 the committee resolved 'rigidly to enforce the regulations and to prevent by every possible means the using of fire arms and the playing of Quoits except upon the ground appointed by the committee for this latter purpose'. To provide greater authority the committee applied to the sheriff 'to have the gardener Edwin Neilson armed with the powers of a constable'; and a 'Watch Committee' was set up to keep an eye on things when the gardener was absent. Later, one of the assistant gardeners was provided with a livery suit when patrolling the Gardens during the summer evenings.[20]

An outbreak of 'improper behaviour' occurred in 1835, when rough play by boys caused damage to the planting. The committee perhaps overreacted, for circulars were delivered to every house warning that if miscreants were caught they would be 'placed in the hands of the police'; and notices to this effect were posted on billboards around the grounds. It was therefore rather foolhardy for any youngster to tamper with them, but tamper with them they did, and the resulting furore brought committee and parents close to litigation.[21] But for most of the time the presence of a full-time gardener kept wanton damage at bay.

Two tennis courts were levelled and marked out between 1882 and 1883 on the north-west side of the Garden. Until then the grass had been cut by scythe, but the advent of tennis heralded the purchase of a lawnmower. Between 1902 and 1906 the grass was cut by a mower drawn by a hired horse, which was fitted out with a set of boots to protect the turf from hoof marks. Not wholly successful, the machine and boots were later sold for just over £12.[22] In 1889 a rather more permanent brick-dust tennis court was made close to the gardener's tool-house in the northern angle of ground and still remains in use. Summer tournaments – both of tennis and putting – became a highlight of the summer calendar. Other entertainments have included military bands (from 1838 to 1843, supplied by the 7th Dragoon Guards, and Inverkeithing Dragoons), while Queen Victoria's birthday was traditionally marked with a fireworks display. Garden parties, fireworks and fund-raising events continue to take place from time to time.

Since the 1940s much of the surrounding property has become subdivided into flats, or converted into hotel and office use, and whole houses are increasingly rare. Ground-floor residences are counted as the main stance holders with full rights to the Gardens. Flat holders have no such rights, although they, along with other people living locally, are welcome to rent a key. In 1970 a private Act of Parliament became necessary to remove the original limit of £10 imposed on the annual assessments.[23]

Notes

1. Charter in favour of Dr John Easton & spouse for building stance (No. 17) in Regent Terrace, 28 July 1828, Chartulary Vol. 21, GHT archives; Articles & conditions of Roup and Sale, Royal Terrace, 25 April 1820 and 4 March 1825, GHT archives.
2. Garden Minute Book (1825–41); Minute, 28 March 1825. These minute book are now in the care of EPL.
3. Ibid., Minute, 23 March 1827.
4. Ibid., Minute, 3 February 1834; 9 February 1837; 12 November 1840.
5. James McNab, 'Our Town Trees, Royal & Regent Terrace gardens, etc', *Scottish Farmer*, 16 August 1865; 'Our Town Trees', 1 July 1867.

6. TCM, 4 June 1895; 9 July 1895; Garden Minute Book (1892–1912), June and October 1895. The privet hedge along Regent Road was gradually renewed; see also Minute Book (1936–1950), December 1947.

7. For example, in 1886 the public were granted access to view Queen Victoria's procession from Holyrood to the International Exhibition held in the Meadows; six watchmen having been hired from the Chief Constable to keep order.

8. *The Scotsman,* 17 July 1997; 27 Royal Terrace advertised for sale as flats with photographs showing pictures of Regent gardens alongside a view of the entrance lobby.

9. This description is by John Byrom and is taken from a Year 1 Landscape project on Regent Gardens, carried out by students in Landscape Architecture, Edinburgh University, in June 1972. This exercise proved useful to the garden committee, and follow-up advice has been given since.

10. HHM, Vol. 24, 11 November 1825.

11. Garden Minute Book (1825–41), Minutes, 22 May 1832; 18 February 1834; 27 January 1835; 29 January 1836; 23 January 1840 (thanked for 'long, zealous, and efficient services'); and 31 January 1844.

12. HHM, Vol. 24, 11 November 1825;18 May 1826; 15 June 1826; 16 June 1826; and Garden Minute Book (1825–41), 15 June 1826.

13. Contract of Feu between the Governors of George Heriot Hospital and the Feuars of the Royal Terrace, Carlton Place and Regent Terrace of Calton Hill Pleasure Ground, GHT archives.

14. The feuars had hoped that the Hospital might be willing to relinquish altogether their right to the piece of land intended for a church or whatever, but the Governors were not prepared to do so at this stage.

15. Garden Minute Book (1825–41), Minute, 8 November 1830.

16. Including, for example, the steep bank on the opposite side of Regent Road which was eventually formed into the Regent Road Gardens.

17. Two previous writers on Edinburgh refer to Joseph Paxton as having been responsible for the design: George Scott Moncrieff, *Edinburgh* (London, 1947), p. 89 and Ian G. Lindsay, *Georgian Edinburgh* (Edinburgh, 1948), p. 51, but without any source being given.

18. Garden Minute Book (1825–41), 19 April 1832, 22 May 1832.

19. Ibid., Minutes, 27 December 1831; 22 May 1832; 9 November 1832; 2 May 1833; 16 August 1833.

20. Ibid., Minutes, 25 June 1832; 29 June 1832; 27 January 1887.

21. Ibid., Minutes, 5 May 1835; 11 May 1835; 22 June 1835; 24 July 1835; 30 July 1835; 4 August 1835.

22. Garden Minute Book (1876–1920), 30 January 1902; 30 January 1908.

23. *Regent, Royal & Carlton Terrace Gardens, Edinburgh Order Confirmation Act 1970, Chapter ii; An Act to confirm a Provisional Order under the Private Legislation (Scotland) Act, 1936, relating to Regent, Royal & Carlton Terrace Gardens*, Edinburgh, 15 May 1970 (HMSO). The limit was raised from £10 to £20 with powers to increase further on consent of three-quarters of the individual stance owners.

CHAPTER 19

LONDON ROAD AND
HILLSIDE CRESCENT GARDENS

London Road Gardens
(Royal Terrace Gardens)
10.8 acres, (4.37 ha)

Originally known as Royal Terrace Gardens, this substantial woodland strip is now referred to as the London Road Gardens. Playfair deliberately kept the space free of buildings to preserve the views from the upper terraces and to enhance the main thoroughfare; ultimately he became responsible for its design. Like Calton Hill Pleasure Grounds, the space was protected by a servitude (restriction) forbidding any building apart from those necessary for a garden. No obligations were placed on any of the house purchasers because of uncertainties about who would make use of the ground, or how it would be set up. Apart from the Royal Terrace residents, the feuars of Allan's Hillside property as well as future Hospital proprietors in Hillside Crescent and adjoining streets were all potential users.

Certain factors, however, were to influence the site's development: first, the unexpectedly slow sales of house plots in Royal Terrace, and second, the presence of sandstone quarries within it, which had been worked by two builders – Mr Dinn and Mr Dickson.[1] In November 1823 Playfair was asked to report on the viability of extending the life of these quarries, and opening a third one. His favourable response was very much tempered by hopes that this might aid feuing prospects, and provide a convenient dump for surplus soil. His wrote as follows:

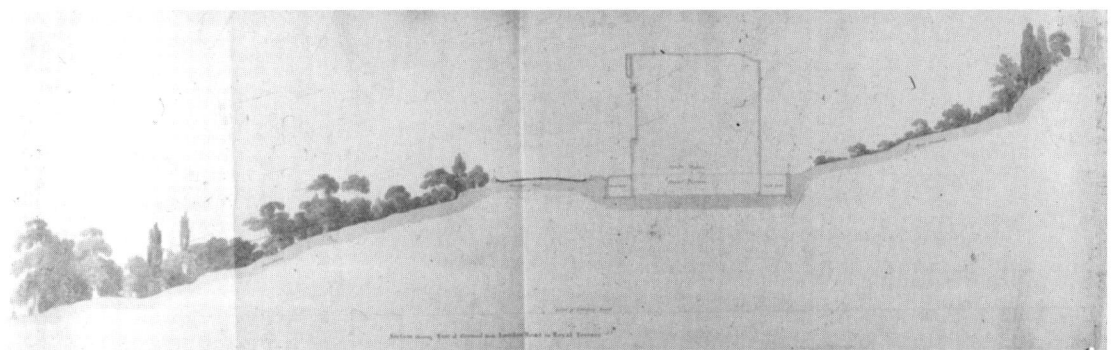

Cross-section London Road – Royal Terrace, showing the generous area allocated to garden use. (EUL Special Collections)

London Road Gardens' lower lime tree walk, along which the outline of the former quarries can be detected. (C. Byrom)

It will enable the Builders in that district to procure stone at a lower rate than when brought from the Hailes or Craigleith quarries. The great difficulty to be encountered is to create a neighbourhood in that part of the Town and almost any circumstance, which can facilitate the accomplishment of that most desirable object should be eagerly grasped at, whether the Buildings to be erected should happen to be on the grounds of Heriot's Hospital, or on those of Mr Allan. It is in vain to draw a line of distinction between the interests of these two properties . . . It is certainly nothing but the proximity of other buildings which has given so high a value to the stances lately offered to the Public on the western end of the Town. Besides it is of consequence that excavations should be made in that particular quarter as in forming the pleasure ground, and in cutting at the Royal Terrace places will be wanted for the deposition of soil. The Bank between the quarries of Mr Dickson and Mr Dinn must be partially cut away in all events, and the Governors by following this course will be receiving money instead of paying it away.[2]

In essence, the forming of the London Road Gardens was determined by the building process itself, with Playfair the master sculptor, shaping and moulding the humps and hollows into smooth-flowing landscape features. At one time there were many such quarries in Edinburgh, but few examples remain where signs can still be seen of former workings.[3] As a result Heriot's Hospital retained control of the land for longer than intended, and its metamorphosis into a private pleasure garden never quite took off. The land still belongs to the Hospital although for many year the City has held it on a lease and has been responsible for its upkeep.

Early in 1824, Henderson & Currer, owners of five building plots in Carlton Place (Terrace), made a successful bid at £180 annually to quarry stone for three years.[4] While there were not many people living in Royal Terrace, there was still concern about the safety aspects of reopening the quarries, and the Hospital was asked to have the excavations fenced. Rather than face such an expense, the Governors decided, in October 1826, 'that the time has come for the quarries to be filled up' largely because 'the present period is particularly favourable for having this work accomplished'. Unemployment was widespread and the Committee for Relief of Distressed Manufacturers offered to supply labour to fill the quarries 'with the earth now lying around them to the satisfaction of Mr Playfair for the sum of £100 sterling'; this did not, however, include 'either levelling or dressing, but merely filling up the quarries'.[5]

Laying Out the Ground

Apart from having the quarries filled, two years went by without anything else being done. Action was again triggered by complaints about 'the present state of the ground' from residents in Royal Terrace, and also 'proprietors of houses on the lands of Hillside'. The Governors were asked 'to get the same inclosed and laid out into ornamental pleasure grounds' as shown on the feuing plan. As the matter involved feuars of the Allan estate, the complaint was remitted to the Calton Hill Committee; and it was William Allan (son of the deceased Alexander Allan) who took the matter in hand. By March 1829 he had secured estimates from Kay in Annandale Street for enclosing the whole area with larch fencing; from James & Thomas Scott, carpenters, for its erection, and from Messrs Eagle & Henderson, 'to plant the Bank when so enclosed'. The Hospital minutes note that as far as costs were concerned, 'in the event of the Governors of the Hospital approving of the enclosing and planting the Banks in the manner which will be fully detailed by Mr Playfair, Mr Allan will endeavour to raise one third of the whole expense provided it does not exceed £300'.[6]

Later in 1829 the land was fenced, shaped and laid out under the supervision of William Playfair. The architect's plans had shown the bank planted with clumps of trees, a pathway running parallel to London Road, and serpentine walks at the east and west ends linking the foot of the gardens with the upper reaches, and with gated access to Royal Terrace and the London Road. Playfair staked out the footpaths for inspection by the Lord Provost, Dr Bruton and Mr Luke (the last two representing the Hospital), and some adjustments were consequently made. An additional footpath was formed at the request of the exiled ex-King of France, Charles X.[7] Resident in Holyrood Palace for the second time in October 1830, following the July revolution which brought Louis Philippe to the throne, his previous stay in 1796 had lasted for three years. The desired pathway probably provided a sheltered and convenient walk between the upper and lower part of the garden, a private short-cut between the palace and St Mary's Catholic Church, Broughton Street, where a Royal pew had been fitted out.[8]

Residents in the upper terraces were by now busy forming the Calton Hill Pleasure Grounds. Most of the expense and responsibility for the London Road Gardens had so far fallen on the Hospital, and with no immediate prospect of the feuars taking charge, they had little option but to continue with their care. The Governors employed a gardener who was allowed to rent out keys to local residents; in 1836 'the persons having keys to the pleasure ground in front of Royal Terrace' unsuccessfully petitioned Heriot's Hospital for a fish-pond.[9] The Hospital were soon to admit, however, that care of the ground 'without considerably more hands than have hitherto been employed – can never be done in a creditable manner'.[10]

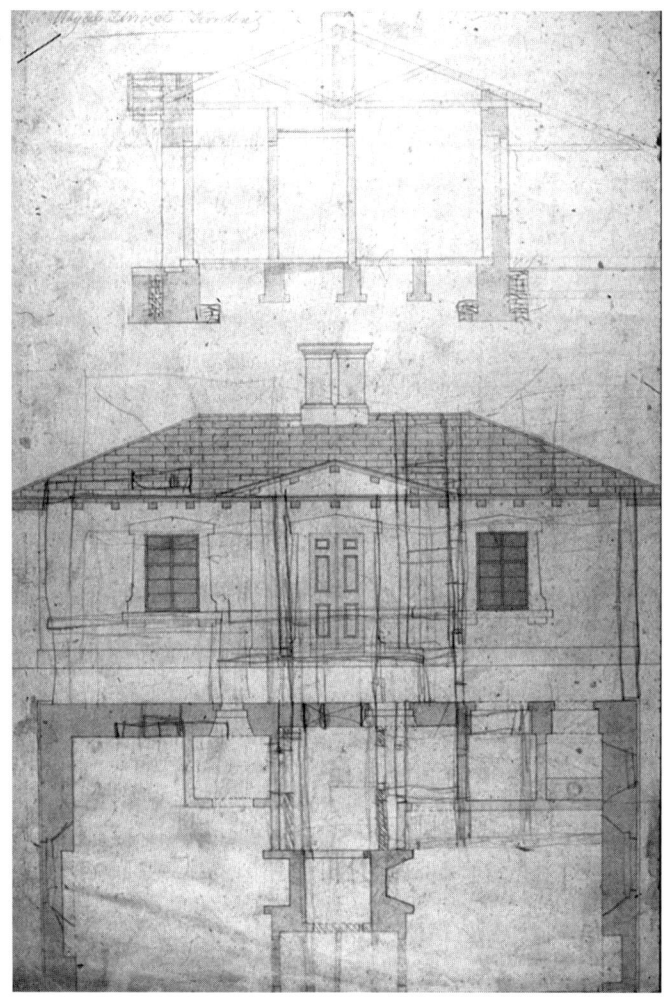

Design for a cottage, London Road Gardens, Edinburgh, 1836, by Alexander Black, Superintendent of Works, Heriot's Hospital, and bearing the signature of one of his assistants. (George Heriot Trust, Crown copyright © RCAHMS)

A Garden Committee, appointed in June 1834 to consider the problem,[11] came up with the idea of renting the space as nursery or garden ground, provided the tenant, 'keep and uphold the walks in a proper manner . . . and also such parts of the present planting as may be considered necessary for preserving the general appearance of ornamental pleasure ground'. The key letting system was to continue 'to the neighbouring proprietors and tenants of houses at a certain rate'. Thus a liability would hopefully be transformed into an asset. It was also agreed to improve renting prospects by building a house 'upon some part of the ground least likely to prove a deformity', the cost not to exceed £250. Alexander Black (1798–1858), the recently-appointed Superintendent of Works, promptly informed the Governors that in his opinion a cottage was essential because 'the greater part being merely shivers and rubbish', the land suitable for cultivation was less than he had anticipated.[12] Black drew up plans for the cottage and not long afterwards became involved with designing foundation schools for the Hospital when they expanded into education for the poorer families in Edinburgh.[13] The cottage was built by Robert Shillinglaw, whose tender at £212 was the lowest. Shilinglaw and his partner, Nicol Brotherston, owned four building plots in Regent Terrace. Although always careful with money, the Governors on this occasion reassured themselves that 'a plainer or less expensive plan of building would not be advisable' in such a prominent position.[14] The cottage was completed in the spring of 1837 and became known as Royal Terrace Gardens' House. Although modest in size, it has in its time accommodated families with six children, and more than one household. It still stands at the western end.

Finding a Suitable Tenant

John Niven, gardener at Dunnikeir (the 'new' Dunnikeir House, Kirkcaldy),[15] was the first to make an 'adequate offer' when, in March 1838, he negotiated a ten-year lease at 15 guineas a year. Quite stringent conditions were made; for example, no other buildings were allowed, the whole was to be kept in good order and the tenant 'or a servant' was required to live constantly within the grounds. He was given total charge of renting out keys, and the Governors accepted responsibility to maintain the fences until the hedging became established.[16]

As a goodwill gesture the Hospital also had Black design a greenhouse which cost nearly as much as the cottage, and was placed to the east of it. Its construction caused William Allan, now resident in Hillside Crescent, great consternation, for rumours abounded that a cow byre was intended; in alarm he took legal action. The case went before Lord Jeffrey, who found in favour of the Hospital, but not before criticising them for poor communication, 'as it appears that there really had been a suggestion as to keeping cows in the garden'. Mr Allan in consequence was excused paying legal costs. The delays, however, caused Mr Niven's plants to suffer from frost damage, and the losses assessed by Dr Neill and Mr McNab were put at £15 and deducted from the following year's rent. Niven in fact did keep cows, but at Quarryholes.[17]

Mr Allan's anxieties had not gone unnoticed by others in the community, and in August 1838 a letter was sent to the Hospital from a Mr William Alexander, WS, stating that 'a sufficient number of the feuars of the Hospital and Mr Allan would be quite disposed to accept of a perpetual feu-right of the ground between the Royal Terrace and Hillside Crescent, and oblige themselves, their heirs and successors to maintain and uphold it as ornamental pleasure ground at their own expense'. No mention was made of recompensing the Hospital for the substantial sums already spent, and the appeal was dismissed as a very poor bargain.[18]

The tenancy, however, proved troublesome. Mr Niven was accused of neglecting the grounds, leaving gates unlocked at night, allowing 'the whole ground to be used as play ground', keeping his horse pastured and generally flouting the rules. Finally, bowing to pressure, he agreed to surrender his lease at the beginning of 1841.[19]

Subsequent Tenants

James Turner, gardener at Heriot's Hospital, took over the lease, initially for eight years at 15 guineas annually. He was allowed £5 yearly to maintain the fences and gates. Regulations were revised and 'circulated among the families in the neighbourhood of the pleasure ground' as well as to the tenant. Any 'respectable family', the rules stated, could become key holders on payment of one guinea annually to the tenant for 'the privilege of *walking* in the grounds' (i.e. with due decorum!). Thereafter the rules were similar to those operating in other gardens covering such matters as arrangements for additional keys and visitors; not injuring the plants; the banning of dogs, firearms, stone throwing or 'play at games'; keeping gates closed and responsibilities regarding misdemeanours. Some clauses related specifically to the tenant and ruled 'no horses cattle sheep or other animal to be brought within the ground on any pretence' (a requirement that still obtains); doors to be double locked at sunset; and the right granted to inspect keys 'and retain such as have not been furnished by him'.[20] Key holders were soon to complain that 'the use of the grounds was being severely curtailed' due to the walks 'being laid with the coal ashes of the Gas Work in place of gravel'; but gravel, the Hospital declared, was costly and the income derived from the ground negligible.[21]

Turner's tenancy lasted 18 years until increasing age began to affect standards of care. The Hospital had occasionally carried out tree maintenance; for example, in 1843 thinnings had been made and surplus stock transplanted to ground beside Greenside Church and the Hospital's land on Regent Road (the future Regent Road Gardens). In 1852 Mr Smith had been consulted. Presumably this was Charles H.J. Smith (1818–95), landscape gardener, active in the Caledonian Horticultural Society and known to James McNab. Smith had just had his book published on *Park and Pleasure Grounds*.[22] The lime tree avenue which still survives along London Road probably dates from around this time.

The next incumbent was George Wood, a gardener from Catherine's Lodge, Inveresk, later described in the census as 'a florist'. His lease was longer-term but at double the price.[23] About this time the proprietors in Royal and Carlton Terrace canvassed for a parapet and iron rail to be placed along the upper length of the gardens from Blenheim Place to Regent Road. David Stevenson (1815–86) acted as co-ordinator; he had moved to 25 Royal Terrace in 1855, and was a member of the illustrious family of engineers – a lighthouse and beacon builder as well as a river engineer. His father Robert, it will be remembered, had been a consultant on the Regent Road project. Stevenson approached John Chesser (Black's successor) for plans and a specification, and the work was completed in 1860 at a cost of £600. Most of the funding came from the residents, with the Hospital contributing for the four unfeued stances in Royal Terrace.[24] The Second World War saw most of these railings removed and never replaced. Less successful was the key holders' application for a bowling green in 1861.[25] Tree maintenance over these years was supervised by James McNab.[26]

Wood's tenancy had its problems and he seems to have been bowed down by his large family and indifferent health; the standard of care under his tenancy left much to be desired. By 1867 the Governors had had enough and considered terminating his lease and using the ground for grazing sheep. Finally, in 1871 Wood gave up his lease, but on condition that any extra rent derived from a new tenancy would go to supporting his wife and family during the three years still left to run. It was a small price to pay to be rid of him.[27]

Was it the threat of sheep, or disenchantment with tenants, that drove one feuar, John Crabbie, 22 Royal Terrace (of green ginger-wine fame) to enquire in 1871 on behalf of himself and others, 'whether the Governors would be disposed to sell the Royal Terrace Gardens and if so on what terms and conditions'? But having once more spent money on having the ground refurbished, the Hospital decided to hold on. They were soon re-let to Alexander Donald for £60 a year, and he remained a tenant for the next twenty, mostly trouble-free, years.[28] The only cause for concern was at the start when certain residents in Windsor Street, and Leopold and Blenheim Place used the grounds for clothes bleaching and drying, a practice instigated by the former tenant and without permission. Mr Donald had assumed this to be a legitimate source of extra income. As a compromise Mr Chesser and the Dean of Guild were asked to 'make such arrangements for bleaching green purposes as shall be least objectionable'.[29]

The Town Council Take Over

In 1891 a public footpath was formed adjacent to London Road and alongside the Garden. The Governors agreed to the Council's request to add a cope stone and rail in place of the rickety wood fence, to match the one enclosing the upper part. The work was undertaken by Duncan McGregor at a cost of just over £760.[30] Soon afterwards the City began negotiations to acquire the Gardens for public use. Although happy to have found a solution to unsatisfactory tenants, the Hospital were reluctant to relinquish the ground outright, offering instead a 25-year lease at £40 annually. The first one was granted in June 1893 and the arrangement has continued ever since. Initially the residents in the upper terraces were concerned that standards and property values might plummet with the opening of the Garden to all members of the public. But protective clauses were added to smooth the way: it was stipulated, for example, that the grounds had to be kept in good order; used solely as ornamental pleasure grounds with walks ('to be thoroughly reformed and carefully gravelled'); the shrubbery, grass, flower plots and the lime-tree walk along London Road all to be preserved; no trees removed without consent; a caretaker or park officer to live in the cottage; and gated access along Royal and Carlton Terraces to be limited to terrace key holders only; and – shades of former days – no horses, cattle, sheep or other animal – to be tolerated.[31]

Upkeep is now more regular although, having lost its railings during the Second World War, street-blown litter is more abundant; and the walks still wait to be properly gravelled. Part of the eastern corner was acquired in 1955 for public conveniences, but attempts by the Parks Department to form a private car park in 1974 (east of the cottage where the greenhouses once stood) produced instant outcries from Edinburgh citizens, themselves having to contend with new parking restrictions. Finally the matter went to the Secretary of State, William Ross, and was overruled.[32] The victory would have pleased Playfair, relieved that despite mixed fortunes, the ground whose layout he had supervised had fully survived as an ornamental space.

Hilside Crescent Gardens
1.45 acres, (0.58 ha)

This crescent-shaped garden departed from the rather formal layout shown in the feuing plan to become a miniature woodland area. It is now in three sections, separated by hard

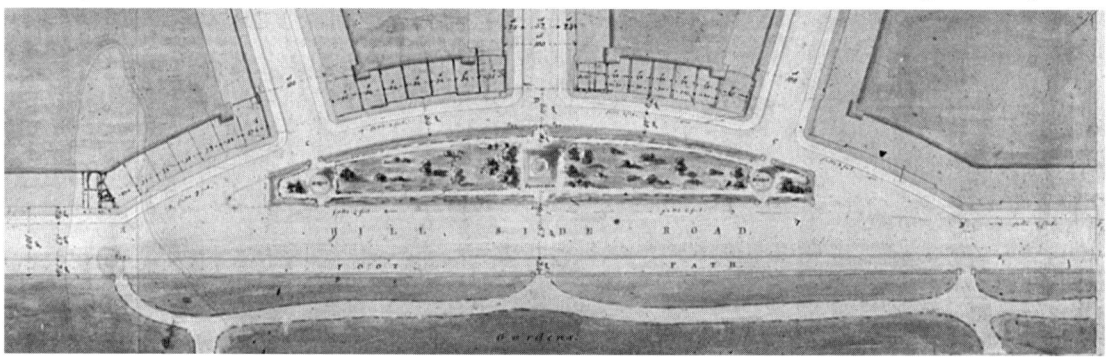

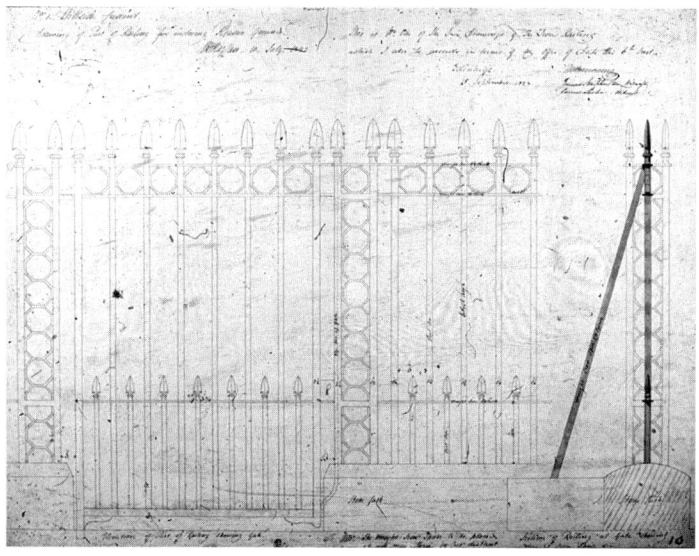

Two drawings by Playfair. Top: Plan for Hillside Crescent showing the garden area with central fountain. Right: Playfair's drawing for the railing in Hillside Crescent, 1822. A small portion of these railings still exist at either end. (Both: EUL Special Collections)

paths and surrounded by the original parapet and somewhat dilapidated mesh fencing (a small section of Playfair's railings survives at either end). The central section is grassed and planted with maple, elm and lime trees, while the east and west portions contain many fine horse chestnuts.

The 1823 Articles of Roup (sale) contained similar rights and responsibilities relating to this garden area as those for the Regent Terrace/Front Bank Gardens;[33] but the divided nature of ownership (about one third of the ground on the west side belonged to the Allan family; the rest to Heriot's Hospital) and slow feuing contributed to the Garden's precarious existence. The Allans began selling their plots fairly quickly, but the Hospital's portion did not get under way until the 1880s, when smaller flatted accommodation replaced whole houses. A crescent with mostly phantom residents did not augur well for its pleasure garden, and this explains why for most of its early life it simply limped from one crisis to the next.

Attempts to Form the Garden

In August 1821 William Allan, acting on behalf of his father, took steps to have the garden formed, making an offer of £200 towards the expense, 'as it will be a most prominent feature in the new city', and if not done as a whole 'it would create a deformity which time could never cure'. He wanted the work carried out 'according to Mr Playfair's plan' and to be completed within three years.[34] A parapet wall and railing was erected soon afterwards (a signed drawing by Playfair of the railings is dated July 1822)[35] and the cost divided proportionately between Allan and the Hospital. Nothing more happened until the Hospital began forming the London Road Gardens, and in 1836 they employed James Cross and Charles McCaul to supply earth for levelling the ground in Hillside Crescent. McCaul was an experienced contractor, having carried out similar work for Regent Gardens and Hope (Hopetoun) Crescent Gardens. Eagle & Henderson's nursery then top-dressed the ground before it was planted with trees and shrubs. Expenditure came to £265, of which £86 went to McCaul, and £44 to Eagle & Henderson. Collecting Mr Allan's share proved troublesome and time-consuming; he seemed more adept at criticising than meeting his financial obligations.[36]

The layout had much in common with other small crescent gardens, having an outer border of trees and shrubs flanked by a gravel pathway. Two circular beds were made at either end, and one in the middle; a gesture perhaps towards Playfair's drawings which had shown a central fountain and a statue at either end within a circular plot. Both parties agreed to keep up 'its present style of pleasure ground' and to organise a contract 'with some proper person for doing so'. As a means of generating funds the Hospital decided to 'let out keys thereto for the use of families in the neighbourhood corresponding to the number of lots of ground in said crescent belonging to them'; there is no evidence that this ever happened.[37]

The Garden Struggles On

The 'proper person' was usually the Hospital's tenant from the London Road Gardens opposite. By 1853 the planting had matured sufficiently for pruning and thinning to be

Hillside Crescent, Edinburgh, today. (C. Byrom)

required; and this was supervised by Charles Smith.[38] But care at best was cursory. In 1860 one of Allan's feuars, Mr Huge Rose, 3 Hillside Crescent, described the Garden as 'not only overgrown with weeds but open and exposed to visits from all sorts of vagrants who are stealing and destroying what they please'. As an experiment, George Wood, the Hospital's new London Road tenant, was allowed to use the space for growing flowers and shrubs in return for free upkeep. But the trial was short-lived, for Mr Allan decided to take over control.[39] Following Allan's death Mr Rose was again complaining of deterioration, forced entry and use for 'improper purposes'. A site visit verified Rose's grievances, the garden being found to be 'in a most disgraceful state, box and walks having disappeared, and nothing done to them for some years'.

While the Hospital were not unwilling to improve the grounds (and tree thinning under James McNab's supervision was considered first priority), with no residents to fund a gardener, 'it was out of the question' to maintain it as 'a regular pleasure ground with shrubbery and flowers'. Instead the Governors proposed renting their portion for grazing sheep, believing that 'under sheep it will look better'. But neither the Allan family nor Mr Rose warmed to this idea. As an alternative the Hospital decided to rent the ground to the Hillside Curling Club who had formed two curling ponds in 1867 slightly to the north of the Gardens, and were in the process of setting up a bowling green.[40]

Eventually the Allan Trustees assigned rights and obligations for their section to their own feuars. But by the time the Hospital began to develop their part of Hillside Crescent it was too late to impose the original garden conditions, as the nature of the property had changed from whole houses to flatted accommodation. In 1896 Heriot's Hospital employed Methven & Sons, nurserymen, to put the Garden into good order, preparatory to offering it to the City on a similar basis to the London Road Gardens. Negotiations progressed well until the divided nature of ownership became apparent.[41] Another attempt in 1936 also failed.

Finally, in the face of increasing deterioration and complaints, and after surrounding proprietors failed to comply with an order to put the grounds into good order, the Hillside Crescent Gardens were compulsorily acquired by the Town Council in 1952 as an ornamental pleasure garden for the benefit of the City.[42] Their struggle for survival had not been totally in vain, for the tree planting had survived to maturity and now contributes greatly to the pleasant green approach to the town centre.

Notes

1. Walter Stewart Dinn with Patrick Rose purchased five building plots in Royal Terrace but they were later made bankrupt.
2. HHM, Vol. 23. 26 December 1823.
3. I.T. Bennyan, J.A. Fairhurst, A. Mackie, & A.A. McMillan, *Building stones of Edinburgh* (Edinburgh, 1987). This provides an interesting account of the several quarries in Edinburgh.
4. HHM, Vol. 23, 14 May 1824.
5. HHM, Vol. 24, 6 January 1826, 31 October 1826 & 27 November 1826.
6. HHM, Vol. 25, 6 October 1828; 20 April 1829.
7. HHM, Vol. 25, 10 January 1831; W.H. Playfair's letter book, 1830–1833. Report to the Calton Hill Committee, 27 January 1831, EUL Manuscripts.
8. Charles-Philippe, the Comte d'Artois, was the youngest brother of the late King of France, Louis XVI. On the second occasion of seeking refuge at Holyrood, Artois, by then Charles X, the last Bourbon King of France and Navarre, stayed for two years, and his son, the Duc d'Angoulême, rented accommodation for a few months in Regent Terrace until their own apartments at Holyrood were ready for use. See A.J. Mackenzie-Stuart, *A French King at Holyrood* (Edinburgh, 1995), and Kay, Vol. 2, pp. 198–202. The footpath with gates at either end was made by Mr John Simpson at a cost of just under £9.
9. HHM, Vol. 27, 1 September 1836 & 3 October 1836.
10. HHM, Vol. 26, 31 October 1834; Report by Garden Committee on how the Pleasure Garden in front of Royal Terrace should be managed.
11. HHM, Vol. 26, 20 June 1834; six people were on the Committee including: Bailie Sawers, Councillors Graigner, Richardson and Robertson, Dr Brunton and the Reverend Wilkie.
12. HHM, Vol. 27, 26 October 1835 & Vol. 28, 1 September 1836. Some writers have claimed this cottage to have been designed by Playfair, but this is incorrect; see: Gifford et al., *The Buildings of Scotland*, p. 446.
13. Schools designed by Alexander Black included the one at the corner of the Pleasance and Cowgate (1840) now the Salvation Army hostel; west side of Old Assembly Close (1839–40); 32 Broughton Street (1858), which later became St Mary's Free Church hall. All the schools adopted a Jacobean style with some of the characteristics of the main George Heriot's school.

14. HHM, Vol. 27, 1 September 1836. Other builders to supply estimates were John Nicol (£235); John Robb (£270); and Young & French (£258).

15. Dunnikier House, off Dunnikier Way, Kirkcaldy was built in 1791–3 by James Townsend Oswald, formerly of Dunnikier House, Pathhead, Kirkcaldy. The architect was Alexander Laing of Edinburgh; see John Gifford, *The Buildings of Scotland, Fife* (London, 1988) pp. 294, 298.

16. HHM, Vol. 28, 15 March 1838, 7 June 1838, 29 June 1838, 5 July 1838.

17. HHM, Vol. 28, 5 July 1838, 6 September 1838, 8 October 1838, 21 March 1839; Vol. 29, 9 January 1840.

18. HHM, Vol. 28, 9 August 1838, 6 September 1838.

19. HHM, Vol. 29, 29 October 1840, 7 January 1841, 11 February 1841.

20. HHM, Vol. 29, 12 April 1841; Vol. 30, 2 July 1841.

21. HHM, Vol. 30, 18 August 1842.

22. Charles H.J. Smith, *Parks and Pleasure Grounds* (London, 1852). Smith was an active member of the Royal Caledonian Horticultural Society and was well known to James McNab. He was also asked to advise on the trees in Hillside Crescent Gardens; see also HHM, Vol. 30, 2 February 1843; Vol. 34, 8 November 1852, 6 January 1853.

23. HHM, Vol. 37, 6 October 1859.

24. HHM, Vol. 37, 6 October 1859, 7 November 1859, 1 December 1859, 5 January 1860, 5 July 1860.

25. HHM, Vol. 38, 4 April 1861, 19 August 1861.

26. HHM, Vol. 38, 18 August 1862; Vol. 39, 4 December 1862, 9 April 1863.

27. HHM, Vol. 41, 3 October 1867. See also HHM, Vol. 42, 21 August 1871; Vol. 43, 5 October 1871.

28. HHM, Vol. 43, 13 November 1871, 7 December 1871.

29. HHM, Vol. 43, 4 January 1872.

30. HHM, Vol. 3, 11 May 1891, 8 June 1891.

31. HHM, Vol. 4, 14 December 1891, 11 January 1892, 8 February 1892, 13 February 1893, 13 March 1893, 10 April 1893, 18 May 1893, 12 June 1893.

32. *Edinburgh Evening News*, 2 May 1974; 6 May 1974; 27 January 1975.

33. Articles of Roup of Hillside Crescent, etc. 14 March 1823, GHT archives.

34. HHM, Vol. 22, 17 August 1821.

35. EUL, Playfair drawing collection.

36. HHM, Vol. 27, 3 October 1836; this gives details of the work carried out, and the areas of dispute relating to the account. See also, HHM, Vol. 28, 9 January 1839, 7 March 1839; Vol. 29, 15 April 1839.

37. HHM, Vol. 27, 2 March 1837.

38. HHM, Vol. 28, 21 March 1839; Vol. 34, 8 November 1852, 6 January 1853.

39. HHM, Vol. 37, 7 June 1860.

40. HHM, Vol. 41, 3 October 1867, 9 July 1867.

41. TCM, 7 April 1897; HHM, 11 February 1895; 10 February 1896; 13 July 1896; 9 November 1896; the City was to have rented the ground for ten shillings (50p) per annum.

42. TCM, 6 November 1952; transferred to the City under Section 211 of the Edinburgh Corporation Order, 1933.

PART NINE

OTHER CONTEMPORARY GARDENS

Aerial view showing Coates Crescent and Atholl Crescent in Edinburgh's West End, with Rutland Square to the far right. (Edinburgh World Heritage)

CHAPTER 20

COATES AND ATHOLL CRESCENTS
AND RUTLAND SQUARE

One great improvement in our civil architecture has been the introduction of crescents. Till Abercromby Place was built (and it is very badly executed) the peculiar beauty and sweetness of the circular line in streets was not known, but it is now coming more and more into fashion. It has a material advantage, besides its beauty, in the opportunity it affords for withdrawing houses from the noise of carts and carriages when the road happens to be a great thoroughfare. Of this we have a fine example in Coates and Atholl Crescents, Maitland Street, which is part of the great Glasgow Road, and often thronged with noisy vehicles passes through the middle of the area, and forms the chord of the two circular segments. From the noise and from the clouds of dust that accompany it, the houses are well protected, by the segment of green sward on each side, and the screen of elms (on one side) growing in it.

The Scotsman, 1826[1]

Crescents became increasingly more common within the New Town, and this and the following chapter describe several such examples. The small garden areas thus created have always been amongst the most vulnerable, largely because responsibility for upkeep rested with so few residents. This, combined with changes in population and conversion of property into office and business use, has added to their insecurity. Two of the gardens described here have fallen victim to this kind of change; their gardens now under the care of the City. We also look at some other contemporary schemes which followed the character and style of the 'official' parts of the New Town but were developed independently; their pleasure grounds tended to be modest in size. This chapter also contains an example where an existing landscape feature was incorporated into the garden area and in fact was the reason for the garden's creation.

Coates Crescent Garden
0.03 acres, (0.012 ha)

In regard, however, to crescents, I think it objectionable to break the line of them by cross streets. The eye is thereby disturbed, and you do not grasp the effect at one glance, from the want of the continuance of the curve. We have examples of both kinds of crescents at the west end of the New Town. The effect produced by Atholl Crescent is much superior to that of Coates Crescent, notwithstanding the defective nature of the Architecture. These crescents, with the pleasure grounds intervening between them and the public road, have a fine effect in approaching the town from the west

Patrick Wilson, Architect, *c.* 1850[2]

This was the first crescent garden to be formed in Edinburgh and owes its existence to a row of elm trees which lined the old Glasgow road and which the owner wanted to preserve. The ground on which Coates Crescent was built formed part of the manor and lands of East Coates acquired in the 1780s by William Walker (1738–1816), Attorney in Exchequer, and descended from an old Aberdeenshire family who were staunch Episcopalians. As time went by Walker purchased other neighbouring property. Already wealthy by profession and marriage, he appears to have been motivated as much by the political advantage and privilege ownership bestowed, as by any gains from development.[3] Nevertheless he lost little time in setting about feuing his land. In May 1800, ahead of the competition for the second New Town, he was advertising a plan which included 'two new streets, 80 feet wide immediately west of Charlotte Square, Edinburgh between it and the intended Crescent proposed to be built on the lands of Coats': an embryonic Melville Street, Walker Street and Coates Crescent.[4]

Communications on this western side were, however, still undergoing improvement. Lothian Road for instance, had been formed in 1795, and the Glasgow Road was due for

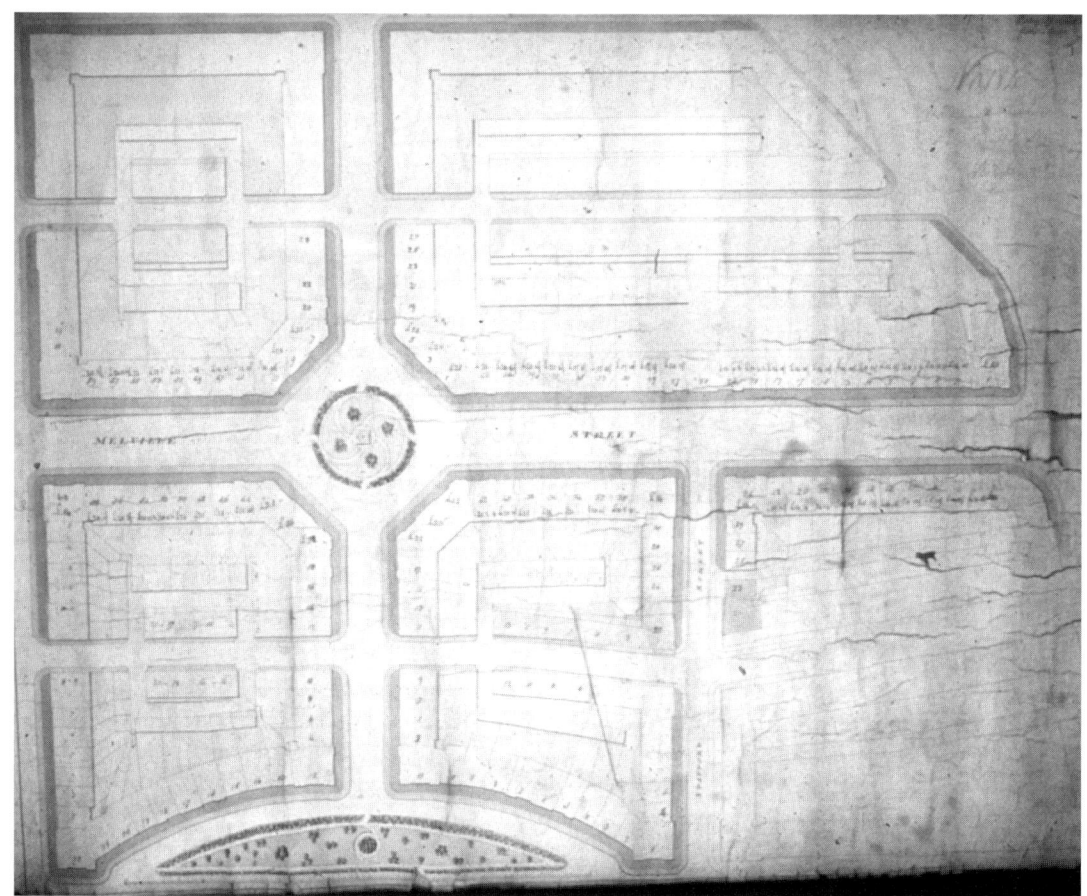

Robert Brown, arthitect: 1820 plan for Coates Crescent. (Walker Trust)

realignment. Uncertainties still hovered over the proposed Glasgow to Edinburgh canal. John Rennie's proposals of 1798 included a projected link between Kirkbraehead and Leith, running close to the south-east corner of Walker's grounds.[5] This was probably the reason why feuing was delayed, but it was certainly under way by 1810 when the first sales are recorded for Coates Crescent.[6] By then Robert Brown (d. 1834), surveyor and architect, was working for the Walker family. A man of practical skills (from *c*. 1809 he superintended Robert Reid's alterations to Parliament House), his name is associated with other parts of the New Town including Hopetoun Crescent off Leith Walk, and improvement proposals for Moray Place Gardens.[7] His plan included two small garden areas, Coates Crescent and a circular plot at the intersection of Melville Street with Walker Street. The latter disappeared when the monument to the 2nd Viscount Melville (1771–1851) was erected in 1857 (on the site once earmarked for his father!) Coates Crescent was completed by 1823, providing 18 spacious family houses with flatted accommodation at the ends; several stances in the 'bosom of the Crescent' were developed by the builders, Gordon & Tait.[8]

The Forming of Coates Crescent Garden

As part of the condition of purchase proprietors were granted the 'right of servitude and use of the pleasure ground lying betwixt the crescent street and the high road . . . with the trees growing therein . . . for the pleasure or other accommodation of the several feuars and families', but not to be used as a common thoroughfare. It was also stated that the ground 'with the parapet walls, railing, entries, gravel walks, trees, grass ground shall be made, preserved, and kept in order and repair at the common and rateable proportion of the whole feuars', paying annually or oftener as might be required 'a portion of the expense which the majority of feuars may find necessary'.[9]

The garden seems to have been enclosed ahead of the crescent's completion. By then William Walker had died, so too his eldest son George, a barrister in London. Sir Patrick Walker (1772–1837), the favourite son, therefore succeeded to the land. An advocate by training, his strong sense of patriotism had driven him to serve at Waterloo. His return to civilian life coincided with a peak in the feuing of the estate, and this, together with other public duties, occupied his time.[10] One of his immediate tasks was to negotiate ownership of the garden area, for in fact it still formed part of a small triangle of ground belonging to Heriot's Hospital. His father's application to buy the land in 1807 had never progressed because the original document had been lost. In 1820 a new submission was made. David Scott, architect, was appointed assessor, but following differences in opinion was replaced by William Playfair; he valued the land at £1,150, a figure satisfactory to both parties. In 1823 the Hospital granted a feu charter for 'the angle of ground in front of Coates Crescent, now enclosed with an iron railing and possessed for several years past by the said Sir Patrick Walker and his feuars as foreground to Coates Crescent'.[11]

The most noticeable feature of the new garden was the existing row of elms, the remainder being levelled and grass sown, with a gravel walk formed around the perimeter. As no garden records survive, information about its subsequent history remains patchy. We do know, however, from comments made by Henry Cockburn, that the new residents were less than enthusiastic about the trees so carefully preserved for their benefit. It was apparently 'with the greatest difficulty that Sir Patrick Walker . . . succeeded in rescuing the row in front of Coates Crescent from the unhallowed axes of the very vassals. It cost him years of what was called obstinacy'.[12] Did the proprietors feel overshadowed and too well screened from the road for comfort? Later the same trees and garden received liberal praise from John Lorimer, advocate. He wrote to the *Scotsman* in 1874 telling of a visit to London and how the simplicity of their park gardening had impressed him, with its emphasis on grass and tree planting. Edinburgh, he noted, had only one such example, and that was Coates Crescent. True, this garden did not escape the ever-present display of dying evergreens, but trees and grass predominated and 'their effect in beautifying what in itself is a very poor strip is such as to convert the most sceptical'. If only those, he reflected plaintively who planted and replanted Charlotte Square and St Andrew Square with evergreens, which profited nobody except the nurserymen who stuck them in and pulled them out, had had the sense to plant them with good honest forest trees. By this time they might have rivalled Berkeley Square, which they can never do now in our day. But they may do so in the days of our children's children, if we should become as wise as those who laid out Berkeley Square and Coates Crescent.[13]

Acquisition by the City

Nothing more is heard about the garden until 1926 when Mr H.M.D. Watson, CA, chairman of the garden committee, approached the Town Council offering to hand over the garden to the City.[14] Numbers of residents were by then dwindling as more office and business premises moved into the Crescent. On this occasion the proposal was declined. In 1930 the possibility was revived, when Councillor Mackie put forward a motion that the proprietors of both Atholl and Coates Crescent Gardens be approached to see 'if they would agree to the Town Council taking over upkeep and partially opening up same and laying out in the same way as Princes Street Gardens'. The matter was debated, but again no action was taken. This move may have been connected with the long-standing debate regarding the Gladstone Memorial.[15]

Official attitudes changed following the Second World War. Both Coates and Atholl Crescent Gardens were in poor condition, and their position bordering one of the main approaches to the centre made it 'desirable' to reinstate them as 'ornamental plots'. A preliminary costing by the Superintendent of Parks (J.T. Jeffrey) in September 1949 put a figure of £500 for reconditioning both gardens.[16] Soon afterwards the Council voted to take them over.[17] The formal agreement (dated May 1951) upheld the integrity of Coates and Atholl Crescent Gardens as ornamental pleasure ground, not to be built upon or used as a public playground, although appropriate statues or monuments were not excluded.[18]

The Gladstone Monument

This last provision was important. The search for a less dangerous position for the Gladstone Monument (then standing on the west side of St Andrew Square) was becoming urgent.

The Gladstone Memorial as first sited in St Andrew Square. (Crown copyright © RCAHMS)

The sculptor's preferred position in Coates Crescent. (C. Byrom)

Controversy had raged from the outset as to where to place the memorial to William Ewart Gladstone (1809–98), the former British Prime Minister with strong Edinburgh connections. Possibilities had included a variety of public and private spaces including the Mound, East Princes Street Gardens, Melville Crescent, Charlotte Square Gardens, Saughton Gardens, Taylor Gardens Leith (close to where Gladstone's family had once lived), the centre of the Meadows Walk, St Andrew Square Garden and Coates Crescent Garden. The Aberdonian sculptor James Pittendrigh Macgillivray (1856–1938) – later to become King's Sculptor for Scotland – had wanted all along to place it in Coates Crescent Gardens and had designed his statuary to take advantage of the southern aspect and backdrop of trees.[19] He was bitterly disappointed when the proprietors refused permission. The selection of St Andrew Square in 1903 caused the artist great dismay. Unveiled by the Earl of Rosebery in 1917 (and having occasioned Steell's Alexander and his horse Bucephalus to flee to the City Chambers), Gladstone never rested comfortably there, and soon became branded a traffic hazard. His removal in 1955, piece by piece, and re-erection in Coates Crescent Garden as the sculptor had wished was therefore a happy end to a rather miserable saga.[20]

In 1992 and 1993 both Coates and Atholl Crescent Gardens became the subject of landscape upgrading under a joint project funded by Lothian and Edinburgh Enterprise Limited (LEEL), and the Department of Recreation, City of Edinburgh District Council.[21] Three elm trees including a Wheatley elm at the western end were retained, but the rest, because of age and disease, required removal. A number of semi-mature trees (maple, birch, hornbeam, hazel, ash, gean, oak, rowan, lime and cherry) were added, with species selected to give a more vertical emphasis. Other improvements included new paving, returfing and other minor repairs.

Atholl Crescent Garden
0.05 acres, (0.02 ha)

This wedged-shaped piece of land opposite Coates Crescent was owned by Heriot's Hospital. It was being considered for development as early as 1811, but not as a crescent; this idea came later, on the appearance of Coates Crescent, resulting in Thomas Bonnar designing a complementary scheme. The small area of pleasure ground fronting the crescent is shown in Bonnar's plan thickly planted with trees and shrubs and having a large basin or fountain at its centre. House plots were advertised for sale in 1823 and most properties were completed within two years. One of the first residents was Sir David Brewster (1781–1868), physicist, whose house was said to have been built out of the profits from the kaleidoscope, a popular optical toy invented by him in 1816.[22]

As part of the feuing conditions proprietors were required 'to enclose the area or piece of ground in front of said Crescent betwixt it and the Glasgow Road with parapet walls and iron railings in suitable and handsome manner according to drawings and directions to be given and furnished by Thomas Bonnar'. In return they were granted the 'exclusive privilege of using the same as ornamental pleasure ground'. Nothing was specified about future management or financial liability; the residents were simply left to get on with it, rather like the proprietors in Royal Circus.[23] Proposals for a *jet d'eau* never materialised,

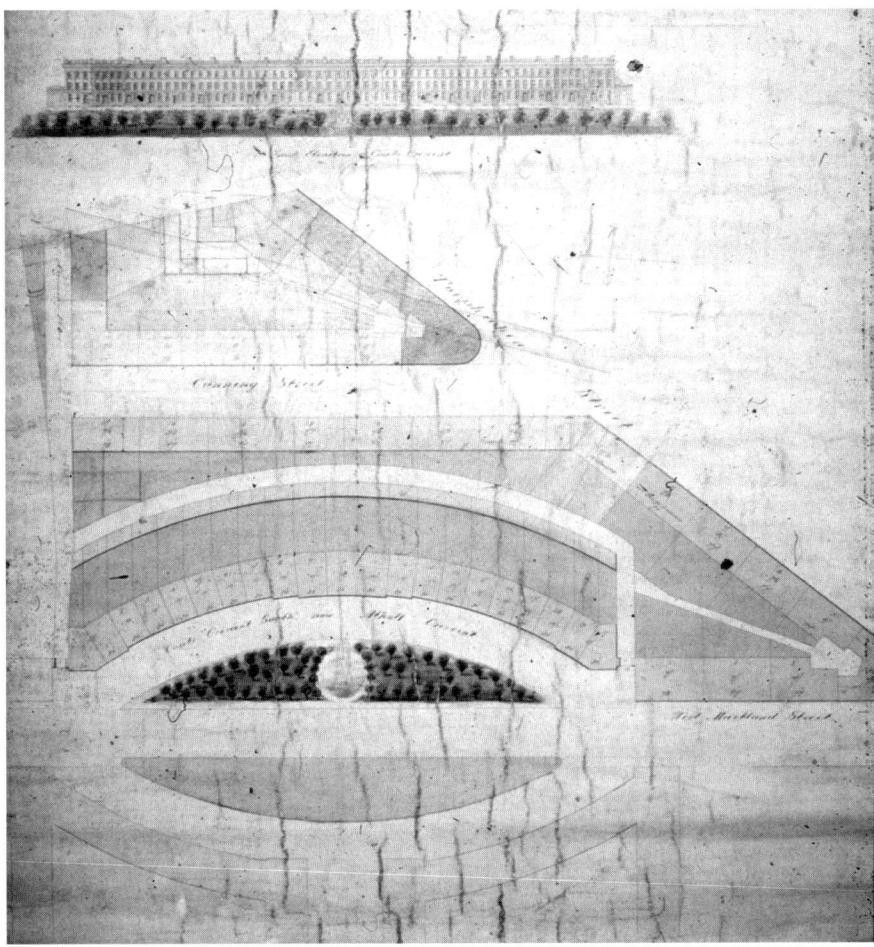

Thomas Bonnar's design for Atholl Crescent, 1823, showing an intended fountain placed at the centre of the garden. (George Heriot Trust, Crown copyright © RCAHMS)

and instead and more practically, the space was 'tastefully adorned with shrubbery'.[24] No garden records have survived[25] but by the end of the nineteenth century the outer edge was planted with trees with an inner footpath linked to a central plot.

From an apparently unremarkable existence, the garden leapt unexpectedly into prominence in 1896 following a gift of £100,000 made to the City by John Usher, the wealthy brewer. The money was for a new hall, and Usher could not have foreseen how troublesome finding a suitable site would prove. The north-west corner of the Meadows and West Princes Street Gardens (close to the foot of the castle) were both serious contenders. But by 1900, municipal opinion had switched to Atholl Crescent Garden, although controversy raged as to whether part of the Crescent should be included as well. In 1901 the Council (fiercely opposed by Heriot's Hospital and the Cockburn Association) promoted a parliamentary bill to acquire the Crescent and adjoining garden ground. Happily these plans were rejected, and the Usher Hall moved instead to a less contentious position in Lothian Road.[26]

Like its counterpart, Atholl Crescent gradually became less residential and was taken over for office use, and increasingly by the Edinburgh School of Cookery and Domestic Economy (College of Domestic Science), which first made its appearance in 1891, and from modest beginnings took over a large part of the Crescent until its removal in 1970.[27] During the Second World War the railings were removed and the ground used for air-raid shelters. Not long afterwards the Town acquired both Atholl and Coates Crescent Gardens as public pleasure grounds and the garden was remodelled in 1951 to complement Coates Crescent.

Twenty years on, and the garden was being described as 'the deserted and not over-attractive stretch of grass at Atholl Crescent' – a space that could be commandeered perhaps to help 'solve' Edinburgh's growing car-parking problems.[28] The garden was spared such an ignominious fate, and has survived to experience a further wave of upgrading along with Coates Crescent. When sites for statuary and monuments have always been at such a premium, it is surprising that the garden has never acquired a central feature of this kind. Bonnar suggested a fountain; maybe one day something of similar interest might appear to help keep Gladstone company.

Rutland Square
0.35 acres, (0.14 ha)

Originally part of the lands of Coates known as Kirkbraehead, Rutland Square and Street were a small development opposite the west end of Princes Street, but tucked out of sight. The erection of the Caledonian Hotel and Station in the 1860s caused more than half of Rutland Street to be demolished, overpowering the entry into this small but elegant scheme. On the site had once stood the house and pleasure grounds belonging to James Stuart of Dunearn (d. 1777), a prosperous merchant and art collector[29] who had succeeded George Drummond in his final term of office. He was twice Lord Provost during a troublesome period marked by food shortages, rioting and public uproar when the nearly completed North Bridge partially collapsed.

When Stuart's property was advertised for sale after his death, and later his widow's, it was described as being suitable for buildings 'either in streets, rows, or a small square', or for a 'large public building'.[30] There were no purchasers and the ground eventually passed to the grandson, James Stuart, WS (1775–1849), an ardent Whig, of gentle disposition. He had had contact with the architect Archibald Elliot in 1818 while actively campaigning – along with Henry Cockburn, Professor Playfair and Alexander Nasmyth – for a reduction in height of some buildings then erecting in St Ann's Street, adjoining the east side of the North Bridge. The hope was to preserve views of Calton Hill, newly opened up with the construction of Regent Road. Ellliot, the designer of the new gaol and governor's house, Regent Bridge and the buildings in Waterloo Place was asked to draft an alternative scheme for the part under dispute.[31] Soon after he was employed by Stuart to draw up plans for the ground at Kirkbraehead, the architect's only known venture into urban housing. His brother James, it will be remembered was one of the prizewinners for the design of the Second New Town.

Elliot's 'uniform simple and handsome' layout was intended to be approached through ornamental gateways secured by lodge keepers; it consisted of a street leading into a small square with a railed central garden enclosure.[32] Advertised for feuing in 1819,[33] progress was abruptly halted by a terrible event. In 1822 James Stuart became involved in a duel with Sir Alexander Boswell, the eldest son of James Boswell; a rumbustious character who, completely unprovoked, had written a vicious personal attack on Stuart in a disreputable political newspaper. By freak chance Boswell was killed, and although honourably acquitted of murder, Stuart for a time withdrew to France.[34] One year later Elliot too had died.

In 1825 John Learmonth, already a wealthy businessman, bought the land and later in the same year acquired the Dean estate[35] He was also the last Lord Provost before the Burgh Reform Act of 1833.[36] Learmonth commissioned John Tait (c. 1787–1856) to draw up revised plans adopting Elliot's initial concept of a street and square. Feuing began in the early 1830s and was completed by the end of the decade. The square kept its residential character until the end of the nineteenth century but has since accommodated various offices, a club and a hotel. Several well-known architects have lived in the Square including Hippolyte Blanc (1844–1917), 25 Rutland Square; Francis Deas (c. 1871–1951), 23 Rutland Square; and A.F. Balfour Paul (1875–1938), 16 Rutland Square; all three served on the garden committee. Sir Rowand Anderson (1834–1921) purchased No. 15 as an investment.[37]

Rutland Square Garden

Rights and obligations relating to the central garden area were briefly stated in the house charters; all the feuars living in the Street and Square were made responsible for enclosing the ground with a parapet and iron railing, laying out the space 'in an approved manner' and for its perpetual upkeep, the costs to be apportioned according to the extent of the individual house widths; the 'per foot in front' principle still applies. In return feuars were given 'the exclusive privilege of using the same as ornamental pleasure ground'.[38] Formed soon after the houses were built, the garden is one of the smallest, almost half the size of Saxe-Coburg Place, its nearest equivalent. It served more for visual relief than active use, and for a long time only the gardener was allowed access. Its design was simple: trees and shrubs planted around the perimeter (elm, plane, hawthorn and lime) and the interior grassed. Upkeep was mostly in the hands of a jobbing gardener. From 1858 until 1863, for example, John Brown (d. 1873), head gardener of the West Princes Street Gardens, took charge. He was an able man who was also Secretary of the Edinburgh Naturalists' Field Club and a keen collector of mosses. A fairly lightweight rail was originally erected but this proved insufficiently robust to withstand the constant batterings from schoolboys at Number 12. In 1872 it was replaced by a stronger railing which survived until the Second World War.[39]

Limited access by a key rental system was introduced for a trial period in 1864, but soon led to 'great disorder' due to over-use – the grass worn, shrubs damaged and the railings broken – all causing the Square to take on 'a disreputable appearance'. The experiment

View of Rutland Square Gardens, Edinburgh, in spring time. (Edinburgh World Heritage)

lapsed but was later revived when lawn tennis took hold. It is difficult to see how such a tiny space could cope with tennis and badminton, or how energetic returns could be contained within the garden enclosure. But the only practicalities recorded in the garden minutes relate to the establishment of a separate tennis club committee, responsible for preserving the grass and limiting access to club members. These arrangements continued up until the First World War. In 1881 the rules were relaxed to allow children under seven to use the garden between '10 a.m. to 2 o'clock it being a condition that they shall be in charge of a nurse'. They were not, however, allowed to play games, and the central area was reserved for the tennis club. Another experiment in 1899 opened the garden to all residents and tenants on payment of an additional subscription, dogs being excluded and no games allowed apart from tennis and croquet. This arrangement again was of short duration.

During the Second World War the garden was used for six air-raid shelters. Afterwards funds were raised for new railings similar to those surrounding Charlotte and St Andrew Square. Small though this garden is, it has nevertheless provided a green oasis in the midst of a rather tightly packed development. It remains a privately maintained garden, well looked after, with two of the original trees surviving, a plane and an elm.

Notes

1. *The Scotsman*, 25 February 1826.
2. Patrick Wilson, 'Remarks on the Architecture of Towns', *Transactions of the Architectural Institute of Scotland*, Session 1850–51, No. VIII; EAA library.
3. For example, William Walker bought his second son Patrick the Ushership of the White Rod in 1805. A curious office attached to which were certain ceremonial duties on Royal occasions, and dues when earldoms and dukedoms were created.
4. *Edinburgh Evening Courant*, 10 May 1800; this notice does not mention which architect is associated with the plan.
5. John Rennie, Civil Engineer, *Edinburgh Glasgow Canal Report*, 1798.
6. Chartulary, Vol. 1, 1807–24, Walker Trustees.
7. For details, see Howard Colvin, *Biographical Dictionary of British Architects*, p. 14. Robert Brown also designed the Queen's Hall (1823) the former Newington & St Leonard's church, South Clerk Street.
8. The Walker Trust, Chartulary, Vol. 1, 22 May 1813, Dame Mary Elliott, No. 3 Crescent; she had purchased the plot from these builders who also owned the five adjoining plots.
9. The Walker Trust, Chartulary Vol. 1, 22 May 1813.
10. Sir Patrick Walker was an accomplished scholar, a distinguished antiquarian, and a keen freemason.
11. HHM, 27 November 1820; 24 January 1823; & Charter in favour of Sir P Walker of angle of ground in front of Coates Crescent, 24 January 1823, Vol. 16, Heriot Trust Archives.
12. Henry Cockburn, *Memorials of his Time*, (Mercat Press, 1971), p. 293.
13. J. Lorimer, Newspaper cutting, dated June 10, 1874, James McNab folder, RBG Library.
14. *TCM*, 16 September 1926.
15. *TCM*, 3 July 1930.
16. *TCM*, 29 September 1949. This included removal of most of the trees and shrubs, the formation of flower beds, levelling and returfing.
17. *TCM*, 3 November 1949.
18. *TCM*, 17 May 1951. The Minute of Agreement between the City, the Walker Trust and proprietors of Coates Crescent, is dated 13 April 1951. The Minute of Agreement between the City and the George Heriot Trust, and the proprietors of Atholl Crescent, was not carried out at this time, but was done retrospectively in 1957.
19. Another Edinburgh statue by Macgillivray is John Knox, standing in New College courtyard. The sculptor was also a poet, a photographer and a nationalist who enjoyed a good fiery argument.
20. *TCM*, 28 April 1955; 3 November 1955; the cost of moving the statue was £2,950 and was carried out by William Arnott McLeod & Co, Russell Road, Edinburgh.
21. William Tucker Associates acted as landscape consultants.
22. According to Elizabeth Grant (*Memoirs of a Highland Lady*, p. 106) had he 'managed matters well' he would have made quite a fortune rather than a few thousand pounds from this particular invention. Brewster was responsible for many useful optical inventions and was a prominent academic and author.
23. Articles and conditions of Roup and Sale of that Park lying on the south side of the Glasgow road opposite to Coates crescent, 14 March 1823, George Heriot Trust Archives.
24. *Imperial Gazetteer of Scotland*, ed. Rev. John Wilson (London & Edinburgh, n.d. – probably around the 1860s), p. 520.

25 Detail is lacking as no minute books are known to have survived; they were however, kept and are referred to in the Rutland Square Minutes of 1858 when a connecting passageway between the Square and the Crescent was mutually agreed to.

26. David Robertson, *The Princes Street Proprietors and other Chapters in the History of the Royal Burgh of Edinburgh*, p. 174; and George Bruce, *Some Practical Good; the Cockburn Association 100 years participation in planning* (Edinburgh: The Cockburn Association, 1975), p. 59.

27. Many domestic science colleges were founded during the nineteenth century: the one in Edinburgh was amongst the first, and was certainly one of the best and most influential.

28. *The Scotsman*, 14 May 1970; letter by George Cunningham.

29. *Edinburgh Advertiser*, 24 July 1789; notice of sale of paintings, part of the collection of the late Mr Stewart (Stuart) of Dunearn. There were 'upwards of 40 pieces' still to be sold, including works by Guido, Corregio and Holbein. James Stuart was also a great grandson of the Earl of Moray.

30. *Edinburgh Advertiser*, 6 January 1778; *Edinburgh Evening Courant*, 3 January 1814.

31. One of the proprietors of the new St Anne's street development, William Trotter asked Elliot to draft out another proposal for reducing the scale of the building then under construction.

32. The elevation by Elliott of the gated entrance to Rutland Square, dated 1819, is in the archival drawing collection, Architect's Department, City of Edinburgh Council, YDA 2280.3; now under temporary safekeeping, National Library of Scotland.

33. *Edinburgh Evening Courant*, 4 February 1819.

34. For an account of the trial, see Henry Cockburn, *Memorials of his Time*, p. 396. According to Cockburn the trial caused a lot of interest.

35. Heriot Trust Chartulary, Vol. 19, 16 December 1825, p. 106; Charter of confirmation in favour of John Learmonth of the just and equal half of Kirkbraehead etc: this charter includes details of the previous owners.

36. John Learmonth came from a successful merchant background and was partner of a coach-making business at the east end of Princes Street; he also worked with his brother as an army contractor.

37. Sir Rowand Anderson's town house (No. 15) was gifted to the Institute of Scottish Architects for their headquarters (soon afterwards becoming the Royal Institute of Architects for Scotland).

38. Excerpt from Instrument of Sasine of John Learmonth of *inter alia* Lot 44 having frontage of 27 feet to Rutland Street on feu between him and James Paterson dated 1 November 1836, and Disposition and Assignation by James Paterson dated 8 November 1836; recorded P.R. Edinburgh 26 May 1837.

39. This and the following information is taken from the two minute books held by the Clerk to the garden, and covering the periods 1875–1923, and 1926–41; together with miscellaneous loose minutes from 1855–71.

CHAPTER 21

ST BERNARD'S STOCKBRIDGE
AND SAXE-COBURG PLACE

St Bernard's Stockbridge (Raeburnville)

The houses are of various sizes, substantially built and well finished, and possess every convenience. Almost all of them have good background, with the privilege of walking in a beautiful shrubbery in front, and some of the largest have ground for coach houses and stables. The architecture, particularly in St Bernard's Crescent, is perhaps superior to that of any houses in the city. The situation is in many respects very desirable; and the fine old Elm and Beech Trees, and young shrubbery interspersed through the grounds, give a novelty and beauty not to be met with elsewhere in this city

The Scotsman, 3 February 1827

Until the early years of the nineteenth century, Stockbridge – situated to the north-west of the New Town and beside the Water of Leith – was a hamlet sustained by its flour mills, tan pits and surrounded by farm land.[1] There were two large houses in the neighbourhood. The oldest, Deanhaugh House, was set in two acres (8 ha) of grounds. St Bernard's, the other, was surrounded by four acres (1.60 ha), 'laid out in shrubbery, strawberry banks, kitchen garden and grass grounds including a neat greenhouse, a fine mineral well and an elegant summerhouse decorated with paintings, prints, busts etc'.[2] Fine orchards covered what later became Danube Street; and close to where St Bernard's Crescent now stands were the kitchen gardens and hot-houses. The approach from Dean Road was along a fine avenue of stately elms, and along the banks of the Water of Leith stood a row of handsome beech trees.[3]

The name associated with the Deanhaugh and St Bernard Estates (which until 1726 had formed part of the lands of Dean) is that of Sir Henry Raeburn (1756–1823). A successful portrait painter, and son of a Stockbridge yarn boiler,[4] he is a rare example of an artist becoming involved in speculative housing. In 1778 Raeburn married Ann Edgar, a widow whose late husband John Leslie had bought Deanhaugh House.[5] For a time Raeburn lived and had his studio there, but later the family moved to St Bernard's House, renting it from the widow of Walter Ross, WS (1738–89), one-time Registrar of Distillery Licences in Scotland. Somewhat eccentric by nature, Ross had been known for his wit, humour and love of the fine arts. During his lifetime he amassed many ancient stones (including the derelict cross from the High Street) which he added to his house, garden and summerhouse – in

Self-portrait of Henry Raeburn, owner and developer of the St Bernard's estate. (National Galleries of Scotland)

the form of a tower – the last becoming known as 'Ross's Folly'. Cartloads of these stones were later removed under James Skene's direction to Abbotsford, Sir Walter Scott's border mansion; and some were gifted as ornaments to West Princes Street Gardens.[6]

On Mrs Ross's death in 1809, Raeburn purchased the property. Reputedly a keen gardener,[7] and much given to hospitality, he found the large rambling house and grounds suited him well, providing also sufficient space to accommodate his married son and family. Why the artist should have considered destroying such an idyllic rural retreat is therefore puzzling. The reason was probably the business failure of his son Henry in 1808, involving both himself and other family members.[8] Such was Raeburn's standing as a portrait painter that he quickly recovered from the financial embarrassments of bankruptcy, although new evidence suggests that financial worries persisted, and certainly he was not averse to spending money quite freely.[9] But his son was left more vulnerable and without an occupation. The development of 'Raeburnville' was a means of providing Henry with a steady income, and a useful but not over-strenuous role in life. That this coincided with Raeburn's own amateur interest in architecture made the undertaking not without attraction.

Feuing began in Raeburn Place (1813), followed by Dean Street and then Ann Street (1817) – the first of three intended parallel terraces, each with small front and back gardens, and stretching from the western boundary as far as St Bernards.[10] No pleasure ground was provided apart from a woodland strip alongside the river bank. Who was responsible for this layout? According to Robert Chambers, writing shortly after the artist's death, planning the development became one of Raeburn's new-found hobbies, including 'the architectural elevations of a little group of streets with which the ground was to be occupied'.[11]

We also know that James Milne (fl. 1809–34), 'a thorough bred mason, and . . . well acquainted with the laying out ground for Buildings',[12] became involved from around 1821,

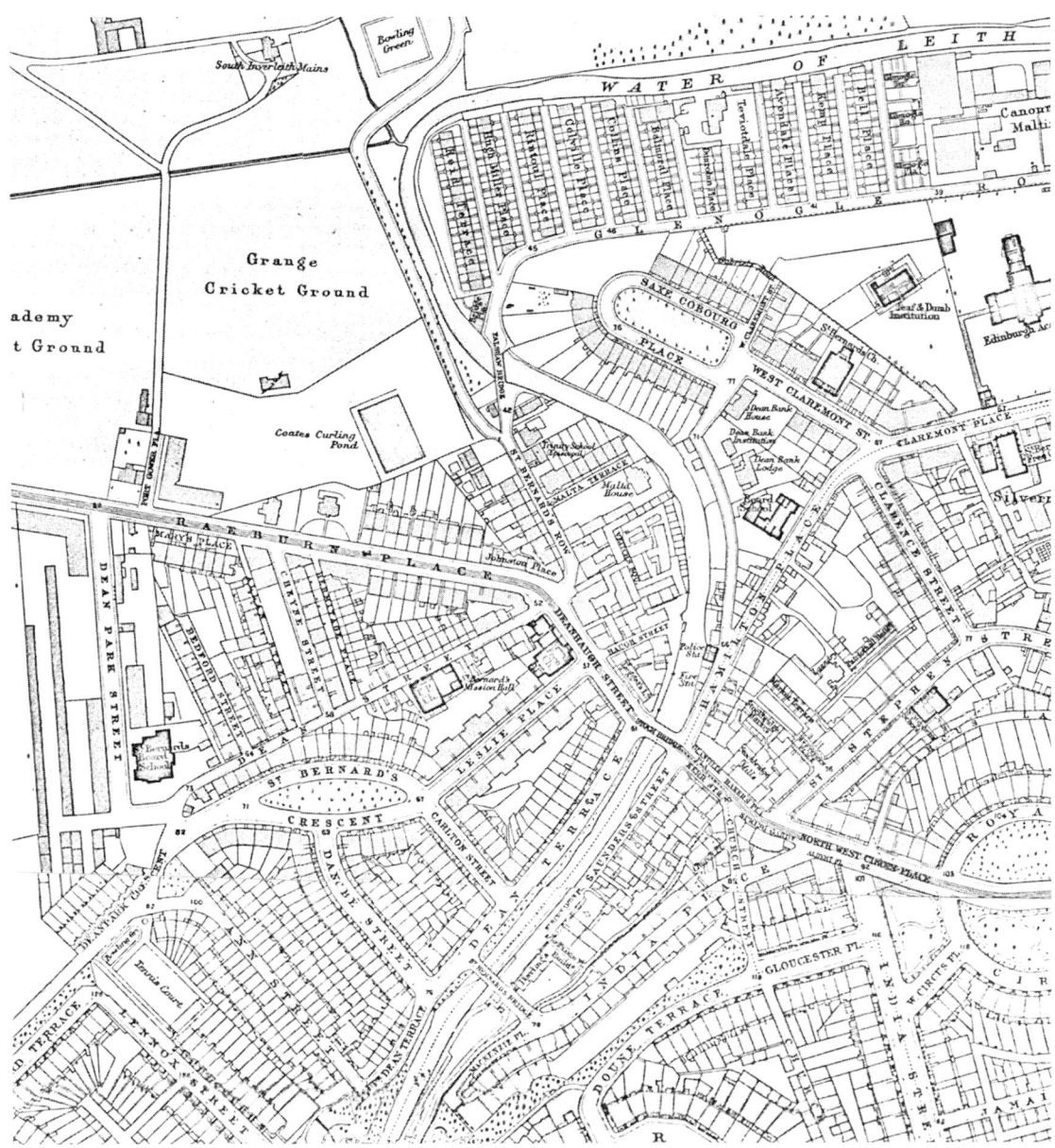

Bartholomew's Edinburgh Map, 1891, showing St Bernard's and Saxe-Coburg Place close to the end of the nineteenth century. Note the underdeveloped plots in Saxe-Coburg Place and the arrival of the model artisans' housing scheme 'the Colonies' to the north.

St Bernard's Stockbridge and Saxe-Coburg Place   365

when he drew up plans for additional parts of the estate.[13] And he might well have assisted Raeburn earlier. Ann Street, for example, has a family likeness to other nearby schemes by Milne – Lynedoch Place (1820–23), also with front and back gardens, and Saxe-Coburg Place (1822–30).

James Milne was an enterprising architect-cum-civil-engineer, possessing both practical and intellectual skills.[14] He had spent his early career superintending the construction of John Rennie's piers and harbours at Queensferry and Newhaven, and the naval offices at Jessfield. This experience, combined with success as one of the competition winners for laying out the ground east of Calton Hill, encouraged him to apply for the post of Superintendent of Works to the City in 1819. Just the sort of man who would have appealed to Raeburn – a person of similar magpie enthusiasms and energies. Their paths certainly crossed, for both served on the committee of the Society of Arts for Scotland (Milne also being one of the founder members).

But why were two terraces scrapped and a crescent and pleasure garden substituted instead? We know from contemporary comment that the appearance of Ann Street had not received wholehearted approval. One citizen, when writing to the press in 1817, admitted to finding fault 'with the plans which are now executing', considering that 'the formal unbroken rows of buildings' were not suited to a site so grand and beautifully romantic. Rather he felt the eye would have been more gratified if 'on ascending this eminence, a number of detached villas had been presented to the view – or a crescent, formed of twenty of thirty houses, had appeared, with a shrubbery or an entire garden in front'.[15] It was a view shared by Raeburn's friend, the artist David Wilkie (1785–1841). When making a visit to St Bernard's, he had been so impressed by the magnificent double row of elms bordering the driveway that he suggested to his host that there should be erected 'on each side of the trees a deep crescent in the purest style of Grecian Architecture'.[16] It fell to Milne to translate these ideas into practice. The result was St Bernard's Crescent, and the streets adjacent – Carlton and Danube Streets. Counter-balancing the massive scale of the crescent with its giant Doric columns was the equally sturdy landscape of tall elms now secured within a pleasure garden.

After Raeburn's death feuing continued under his son. A set of conditions was produced covering both the buildings and the open spaces.[17] No tree, for example, was to be injured or removed, 'even those standing on the carriage ways', unless nine-tenths of the proprietors agreed in writing. The quality of the landscape now became a means of promoting sales and something to be protected. Most of the crescent was built during the 1820s and 1830s, but some gaps remained for several years. In 1842, after living at 17 St Bernard's Crescent for fourteen years, Raeburn's son and family departed.[18] By then James Milne had also left Edinburgh,[19] and without close supervision changes inevitably occurred to the later parts.

Areas of Pleasure Ground

Rights and responsibilities for two areas of pleasure ground were stated in the 1824 Articles and Conditions of Sale. In the first place all the feuars were required to pay 10 guineas towards the cost of building the retaining walls, curb stone and iron railing along the south side of Dean Terrace. The Raeburn family undertook to have the work done, and to meet the expense of planting trees and shrubs along the bank. This strip, it will be remembered, contained a row of fine beech trees. Thereafter it was to be kept as pleasure ground 'in all time coming', the Dean Terrace proprietors being given a common right and made liable for its upkeep 'at their common expense', keeping the ground 'in proper order and condition'. Secondly, those owning property in St Bernard's Crescent were given 'a common right . . . in the large elm trees and pleasure ground in front of said crescents', each paying a proportion towards the cost of enclosing and laying out, as well as for its perpetual upkeep. All the railings were to match those used in West Heriot Row (West Queen Street Gardens); the ones along Dean Terrace still survive. A further area of communal garden ground has been added in recent years and named the Raeburn Garden.

Dean Bank Pleasure Garden

Although too narrow and steep to be formed into walks or terraces, the bank nevertheless has served as an important visual amenity. No management records have been traced, if ever they were in fact kept, and it would appear that few Dean Terrace proprietors are aware of their rights and responsibilities concerning this piece of ground. It remains a thickly wooded bank, containing many elms and self-sown seedlings, a neglected but still attractive area whose progressive decay will eventually force it on the attention of someone. The beech trees have long since disappeared.

St Bernard's Crescent Garden
0.5 acres (0.20 ha)

No garden minutes appear to have survived to tell us about the fortunes of this small garden. Starting life with the stately elms already in place, little else was necessary apart from enclosure, levelling and grass-seeding. Some of the old elms required removal in the 1880s when new planting was added, particularly ash trees. Further tree planting was carried out around the borders during the twentieth century, mostly of lime, sycamore and whitebeam. The last of the Raeburn elms was felled in 1980, having succumbed to Dutch elm disease; it was a sad day for the Crescent.[20] For the most part the Crescent has kept its residential character, although much subdivided; in previous times it was popular amongst legal and military families. About 60 proprietors contribute towards annual upkeep, based on a flat-rate sum. A small committee oversees its management and employs a jobbing gardener; the residents periodically help by removing wind-blown rubbish and litter. A plain iron railing was erected in 1968 to replace those removed in the war years after a determined and substantial fund-raising effort.[21]

The Raeburn Garden

At the west end of Ann Street on the north side there is a small triangular piece of land – one of the residual areas – but never formally made over to the residents. In 1852 it came

View of St Bernard's Crescent and garden. (Edinburgh World Heritage)

into the possession of the Caledonian Insurance Company, a firm which Raeburn himself had helped to found. In recent years some of the people living in the Street began to create a semi-wild woodland patch. In 1973 the Ann Street Society approached the Insurance Company, with the result that the ground was formally made over to them. Since then it has received further protection by a Tree Preservation Order.[22]

Saxe-Coburg Place

Saxe-Coburg Place (named after Prince Leopold of Saxe-Coburg[23]) was built on ground formerly part of the Stockbridge Mill lands and lying between the Water of Leith on the west, and Gabriel's Road to the east. Ownership passed from Heriot's Hospital to various farmers[24] and eventually to James Rose (d. 1823), Depute Clerk of Session. He lived with his family in almost rural seclusion at Dean Bank House, an eighteenth-century villa which still stands at the north-west corner of Saxe-Coburg Street. With so much neighbouring land up for development, Rose understandably was tempted to join the ranks of hopeful speculators.[25] The design drawn up by James Milne was for a rectangular layout (Saxe-Coburg Place), with a central enclosed garden, approached by one long street – Claremont Street – later renamed West Claremont Street. Feuing was delayed by Rose's death, but by 1825 building had started and by 1827 two 'self contained and highly finished houses' were advertised for sale.[26] Besides the very generous accommodation 'particularly deserving the attention of gentlemen with large families', other selling features highlighted included: 'the privilege of walking in the inclosed ground at the front', together with good local amenities such as ' the new church, academy, and Mr Carnegie's markets'.[27]

Even at this early stage Milne's plan was under revision, with a church added to Saxe-Coburg Street. Either in the late 1820s or early 1830s the western end became oval-shaped[28], and the rear stable block was omitted. Milne's departure, coupled with the slow feuing, resulted in less strict control, and consequent alterations to the architect's original design. The north-east flank of the Place was never completed and the land was sold instead to the Town Council for Glenogle Public Baths, built in 1896.

Saxe-Coburg Place Garden
0.06 acres (0.024 ha)

Although amongst one of the smaller New Town Gardens, Saxe-Coburg Place nevertheless gives the impression of greater size and importance by being raised 3 feet (1 m) above street level, the probable result of accumulated soil and spoil conveniently dumped from the house foundations. All the dwellings in the Place were given rights to the garden, the proprietors being made responsible for its enclosure, layout and perpetual upkeep. A flat-rate system of payment now operates with a lower rate for pensioners.

The north side of Saxe-Coburg Place was not completed until the 1850s, and although the central space was enclosed by railings sometime in the 1820s, the interior was left untouched. First evidence of the garden having been formed is seen in the Ordnance Survey map of 1853. This shows the outer border planted with trees (some ash, horsechesnut and sycamore still survive), a perimeter footpath, shrub beds at either end, and the rest grassed. During these years the garden was informally run; for example, although the first set of regulations were drafted in 1859, it took four years to implement them simply because meetings were held so infrequently.[29] For a large part of the garden's life maintenance has been carried out by a jobbing gardener. In 1868, Mr Thomson, gardener at Canon Mills Bridge was employed; he also had charge of Royal Circus Gardens and was probably the same Peter Thomson who became the first Keeper of East Princes Street Gardens. He was paid £3.25 per annum. On Thomson's resignation two years later his successor was Mr McCrosbie who had taken over from Thomson as head gardener at East Princes Street Gardens. This link with the City re-established itself in 1957 when Edinburgh Corporation Parks Department contracted to cut the grass when working on the public open space adjoining Glenogle Lane, an arrangement which continued until the reorganisation of local government in the 1970s. Since then Capability Scotland has taken on the responsibility, with voluntary help by some of the residents.

What makes this tiny garden interesting is the extraordinary number of uses to which it has been put: handball, shuttlecock, bowling, foot racing, leaping, football, cricket, shinty (rounders), pole vaulting and lawn tennis (a court at either end) have all been played at one time or another. Although there were occasions when more vigorous games were banned (particularly football and cricket), strict enforcement was rare. Most times boisterous and sedate activities have managed to co-exist, although always rather delicately balanced.

Thus at a meeting of proprietors in 1927 cricket was given general approval, provided that 'when ladies come out to sit or walk in the gardens, the boys behave as gentlemen and recognise the rights of ladies'. Such concentrated use did cause damage, and when this happened the garden was closed to allow for reseeding and recovery. In more recent times, use of the garden became extended to other nearby residents, but progressive misuse caused unacceptable levels of damage and the policy now is to limit access to proprietors alone.

During the Second World War the ground was made over for twelve vegetable plots; these remained until 1945 when the garden was restored by Dobbie & Co. Because of its height above street level the garden was able to retain its railings. In the mid-1970s there were proposals to redesign the garden area with plans prepared by a local landscape architect showing possibilities for a children's play area at the east end (with swings, slide, climbing frame, sandpit), a central sitting area, dog toilets and a tennis lawn on the west side.[30] But the division of this relatively small space into so many compartments lacked overall support and was consequently abandoned. More successful was the involvement of landscape designer Kate Hawkins, who in 1984, created two new sickle-shaped shrub beds at the eastern end, with shelter provided by beech hedging; the two beds suggested for the west end were not implemented on cost grounds. Then aged 87 years, this must have been one of her last projects (see also St Andrew Square Gardens). Since then a nursery firm have carried out improvements to the central area, renewing the beds, adding gravel to the ground and creating a pleasant sitting area.[31] A number of old diseased elm trees have also been removed and new tree planting added, including plane and ash trees and some 'fun' trees such as maple and mountain ash, intended for removal once the larger trees become established. The garden presents a well-cared-for appearance.

Notes

1. The lands of Stockbridge had formed part of the Dean Estate owned by the Nisbet family, but in 1726 some 12 acres were sold to James McDowell, merchant and brewer in Canonmills. He farmed the land and built for himself Deanhaugh House; see John Geddie, 'Sculptured stones of old Edinburgh', *BOEC*, (1908) Vol. 1, pp. 77–135.
2. *Edinburgh Evening Courant*, 13 February 1794. Advert for the letting of St Bernard's Villa.
3. For details about the St Bernard's Estate and the artist himself, see William Raeburn Andrew, *Life of Sir Henry Raeburn RA* (London, 1886), pp. 22, 55–6. The garden details were based on an account by Mrs Ferrier, eldest daughter of Professor Wilson ('Christopher North ' of *Blackwood's Magazine*), who as a child lived at 29 Ann Street and visited St Bernard's to play with Raeburn's grandchildren.
4. Raeburn's father's cottage stood on the south side of the Water of Leith directly opposite Dean Terrace. The charter for the land was granted in 1754 by Heriot's Hospital in favour of Robert Raeburn, weaver in Edinburgh, (Charter Vol. 2. p. 707, 15 April 1754).
5. Described as a plain, unpretentious building situated a short distance north-west of St Bernard's House.
6. James Skene, *Memoirs of Sir Walter Scott* (London, 1909), pp. 95–101. Skene negotiated the removal of the stones built into the summer-house when the building was demolished prior to completion of Ann Street.

7. Edward Pinnington, *Sir Henry Raeburn RA* (Edinburgh, 1904), p. 77 & 111.

8. *Edinburgh Evening Courant*, 16 January 1808, notice of sequestration relating to 'Henry Raeburn & Co, merchants in Leith; and Henry Raeburn, painter in Edinburgh'. The firm consisted of Henry Raeburn junior, and James Philip Inglis, husband of the artist's step daughter Ann Leslie. The nature of the business was not stated but was probably wholesale trading of some kind.

9. In the bankruptcy proceedings Raeburn made settlement of £17,000, which included all his savings and money raised from the sale of his York Place house and studio; which he continued to rent from the purchaser. He received his discharge in June 1808, but the affairs of Henry Raeburn & Co were not settled until March 1810 (E. Rimbault Dibden, op. cit., p. 62). See also *The Scotsman*, 11 November 1997, p. 13 'Raeburn's letters tell sorry tale of debts'.

10. Named Ann Street, Charlotte Street and Elizabeth Street after Raeburn's first three grand-daughters.

11. Robert Chambers, *Biographical dictionary of eminent Scotsmen* (Glasgow, 1835), p. 126. Chambers once lived in Ann Street.

12. Letter of recommendation by John Paterson, when Milne was applying for the post of Superintendent of Works in 1819; ECA, Bundle, Bay C, shelf 20.

13. Feuing plan for Athole Street (later India Place), the site which had belonged to Raeburn's father; signed by Milne and dated 1822, *SRO, RHP* 812.

14. He was author of *The elements of Architecture*, Vol. 1, published in 1822; a practical guide with an introduction on the principle and theory of good taste in architecture; Vols 2 & 3 were never completed.

15. *The Edinburgh Observer, or Town and Country Magazine*, No 11, 27 September 1817; letter to Editor entitled 'Walks in Edinburgh and its vicinity'.

16. *The Scotsman*, 3 February 1827.

17. St Bernard's, Articles and Conditions of Feu (1824), EPL, YDA 2280.

18. St Bernard's House was demolished in 1826 and the Raeburn family moved to St Bernard's Crescent. Later the son acquired property in Mid Calder and became Raeburn of Charlesfield and a JP for the county.

19. In 1835 Charles Inglis wrote to his step-uncle – Raeburn's son – asking for the elevations of Dean Terrace, Leslie Place, Deanhaugh Street 'for the purpose of Mr Bryce (now architect for Deanhaugh) to make copies of': RHP 818/1+2.

20. *Evening News,* 17 January 1980; & 20 January 1980.

21. Mr J. Hepburn, 26 St Bernard's Crescent, who for many years was secretary of the garden committee. The new railing cost £1,600. The garden was used for air raid shelters.

22. *The Scotsman*, 21 March 1973, Ceremony of Sasine as the garden is formally gifted to the Ann Street Society. The City of Edinburgh (Ann Street) Tree Preservation Order, 19 October 1973.

23. Prince Leopold of Saxe-Coburg had visited Edinburgh in 1819 for the official opening of Regent Bridge. In 1816 he had married Charlotte, only daughter of the future George IV.

24. Robert Montgomery and Thomas Wood of Broughton (both of whom had farm land in the Queen Street garden area), and James Finlay from Wallingford, who also had land in the Coates area: HHA, Charter 28 March 1743.

25. Rose might even have been ahead of his neighbours, for apparently four acres (1.6 ha) at Deanbank were advertised for feuing as early as 1802 to a plan by Robert Burn; *The Buildings of Scotland*, p. 413.

26 *The Scotsman*, 31 January 1827; readvertised, 18 September 1827; the advert concerned house numbers 8 & 9, part of the sequestered estate of James Hope, builder.

27. The church (also designed by Milne), was St Cuthbert's Chapel of Ease in Saxe Coburg Street, now known as St Bernard's parish church.

28. The change was probably to allow a central roadway to be made connecting with another projected housing scheme beyond. This did not materialise.

29. This and the following information is based on the Saxe Coburg Place Garden Minute Book (1863–) held by the Secretary to the Garden Management Committee.

30. A plan had been drawn up in 1974 by Edward Hilliard, an American landscape architect then resident in Scotland, and put forward at a proprietors' meeting in the following year. The general response favoured the status quo rather than seeing the garden divided into smaller activity areas.

31. The work was carried out by Dougal Philip's Walled Garden Centre, Hopetoun Gardens.

PART TEN

LATER EXTENSIONS TO THE NEW TOWN

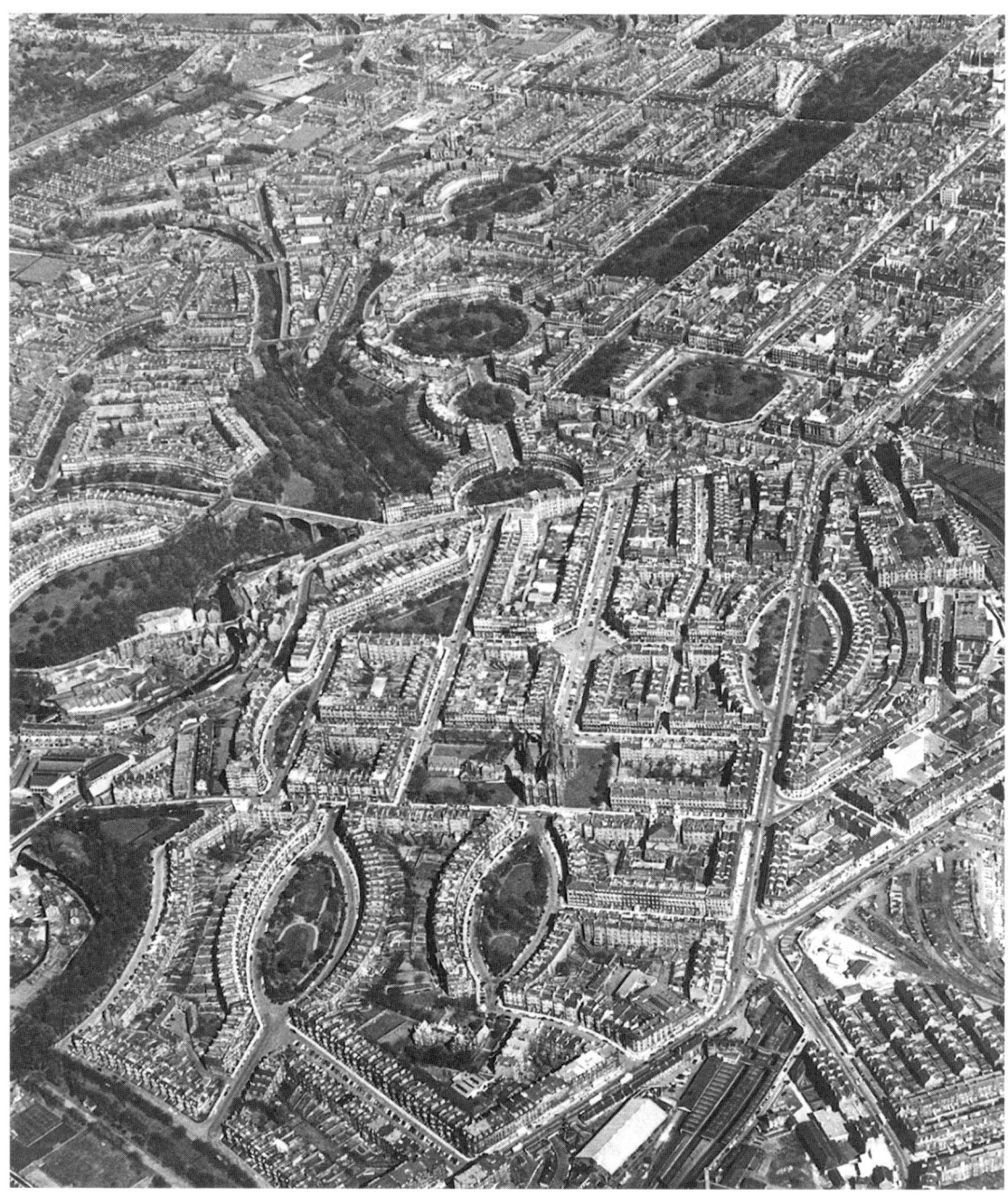

Aerial view of the western end of the New Town, in Edinburgh, showing the later Victorian crescents and gardens. (Edinburgh World Heritage)

CHAPTER 22

GARDENS OF THE DEAN ESTATE

Oxford Terrace, Clarendon Crescent, Dean & Belgrave Crescent

We doubt if there is a single city in the empire increasing in the same rapid proportion at the present time as Edinburgh. We are certain this holds true as to the magnitude and value of the buildings, and we rather imagine it is equally true as to the number of inhabitants. Street has been laid out after street, and square after square . . . The buildings in Moray Place, and the adjacent streets and squares, have extended the town to the deep ravine of the Water of Leith. But the march of improvement is not to stop here. A spirited individual has purchased the extensive range of ground known by the name of Dean, extending westward from Stockbridge and bounded by the river on one side, and the Stockbridge road to Queensferry on the other. It reaches west as far as Bell's Mill road, including upwards of half a mile on the north bank of the river, and measuring nearly 140 acres. The buildings to be erected here may be considered as forming a third New Town fully equal in magnitude, and probably surpassing the splendour, each of the other two old divisions.

The Scotsman, 12 October 1825[1]

The gardens described in this chapter contain the two largest to border the Water of Leith, within the former Barony of Dean, or the Dean Estate; at one time an area of rich agricultural land, used for growing grain crops. The left banks of the river provided rough pasturage, and the site of several corn mills, the best known being Bell's Mill. Since 1609 the land had been owned by the Nisbet's, a venerable family who had produced several successful merchants and two Lord Provosts. Dean House, the family home, was built by William Nisbet around 1614; it was sited near the east gate of the Dean cemetery and was demolished in 1845. It was here that Baron Ord enjoyed his horticultural pursuits before moving to 8 Queen Street, establishing the first private garden plot which eventually became part of East Queen Street Gardens. Sir John Nisbet (d. 1827), the last of the line, lived in America and his affairs were managed by his Edinburgh agents, Smith & Findlay.

Although small parts of the property had occasionally been sold, including a portion which later became the Raeburn estate,[2] most of the Dean land remained intact. Around 1817 ideas for residential development began to surface when Alexander Nasmyth was involved in sketching out ideas for a layout, as well as for a bridge to span the ravine, without which no large-scale development was possible. Nasmyth, a versatile artist with far-ranging interests, had designed Almondell bridge in 1811, and in 1814 had been one of

The lands of Dean advertised for sale, 1819.

the prizewinners for his plan for laying out the grounds north of Calton Hill; so he was not without appropriate experience.[3] Two years later James Gillespie Graham appears also to have been employed to produce draft proposals; his plan was for a villa development – a collection of mini country residences set on the city's doorstep.[4] The bank adjacent to the Water of Leith was, however, set aside as ornamental ground, intersected with serpentine walks: the first hint of Dean Gardens.

In 1825, about the time the Cramond Road Trustees had promised financial assistance towards building a toll-free bridge, the ground was sold. According to *The Scotsman*, a large speculative development was imminent and Edinburgh's expansion looked virtually unstoppable. The account suggested a grid-shaped layout not dissimilar to Craig's plan for the first New Town, with a large elliptical circus at the centre, and a square at either end. The top of the river bank supported a long terrace stretching from Ann Street to Bell's Mills. Too rectangular and sharp-angled for Gillespie Graham's style, the layout was probably by John Tait, architect to John Learmonth, the 'spirited purchaser'.[5]

John Learmonth and the Dean Estate

Earlier in the same year Learmonth had bought the wedge of land that became Rutland Square and Street. He was soon to withdraw from his successful coachbuilding and army contracting business to devote time to managing his ample fortune both made and inherited, and to assume an active role in public life. By the time of his death in 1858 he was described as the largest individual house proprietor and one of the largest feu proprietors in the city.[6] Developing the Dean Estate required his kind of financial muscle, for with the purchase came responsibility for erecting 'a handsome and sufficient bridge over the Water of Leith'. In 1832 the bridge, designed by Thomas Telford and supervised by James Jardine, associate engineer, was opened to traffic.[7] But in spite of the new bridge feuing of the Dean Estate was delayed for several years. The demand for new housing had in fact peaked, and the building trade entering a period of stagnation. Learmonth, however, could afford to wait, but as a result the land was developed in a more piecemeal fashion.

When the economy improved in the 1850s Learmonth commissioned John Tait (his architect for Rutland Square and Street) to design a layout for the area between Ann Street and the Queensferry Road. It included Clarendon Crescent (completed in 1853), Eton Terrace (begun in 1855) and finally Oxford Terrace and Lennox Street (the last not started until the late 1860s, and then under Tait's successor, John Chesser). This layout was also to include a row of houses, named Cambridge Terrace, nearly opposite Holy Trinity Church. Maximum use was made of the site by adopting linked terraces which followed the contours, and provided accommodation, 'mainly of the middle and higher class of "self-contained" houses'[8] with flatted accommodation at the corner ends. The rather solid Victorian architecture was softened by areas of green, the tree-planted strip along Oxford Terrace, a crescent-shaped garden fronting Clarendon Crescent and most significant, the ornamental bank fronting Eton Terrace, extending down to the Water of Leith, and overlooking the Moray Bank pleasure grounds opposite.

Subsequent Developments

The second stage was undertaken after Learmonth's death by his only surviving son, Lieutenant-Colonel Alexander Learmonth (1829–87) whose military and political career drew him away from Edinburgh for most of his adult life.[9] His architect was John Chesser, who, as Heriot's Hospital Superintendent of Works, became involved with other schemes on this side of Edinburgh. Chesser's layout (produced between 1863 and 1865) included the area south of

John Learmonth, Lord Provost, owner and developer of the lands of Dean. (Edinburgh City Libraries)

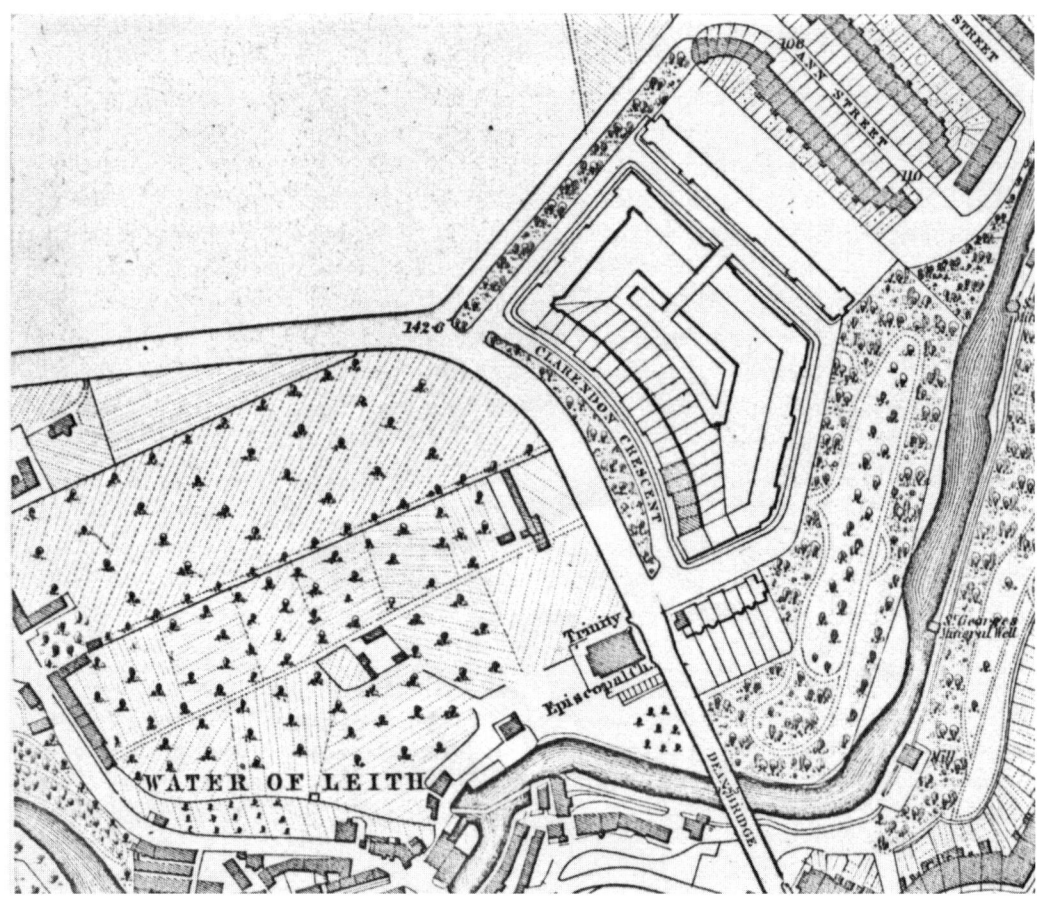

Johnston's map of Edinburgh and Leith, 1851, showing the Dean lands under development, including the proposed Cambridge Terrace.

Queensferry Road, between Dean Cemetery on the west and Dean Bridge to the east, and included Buckingham Terrace, Belgrave Crescent and Belgrave Place. Building was to continue for several years; Belgrave Place, for example, was not begun until 1880 and was then developed by the builder and quarry-master, James Steel (1830–1904) using his own architect. Belgrave Crescent originally included a semicircular garden, but this was later extended. No other open space was provided apart from two narrow tree-belts alongside Buckingham Terrace, serving as a buffer to the busy main road. These small strips remain the responsibility of the terrace proprietors.

A third portion of the Dean Estate between Queensferry Road and Comely Bank Road, consisting of 60–70 acres (24–28 ha), was advertised for feuing in 1874, again to plans by John Chesser. His layout was described as including a series of 'tastefully designed terraces and crescents with intervening pleasure gardens', the 400 or so houses similar in character to those in Belgrave Crescent.[10] Only Learmonth Terrace, parallel to

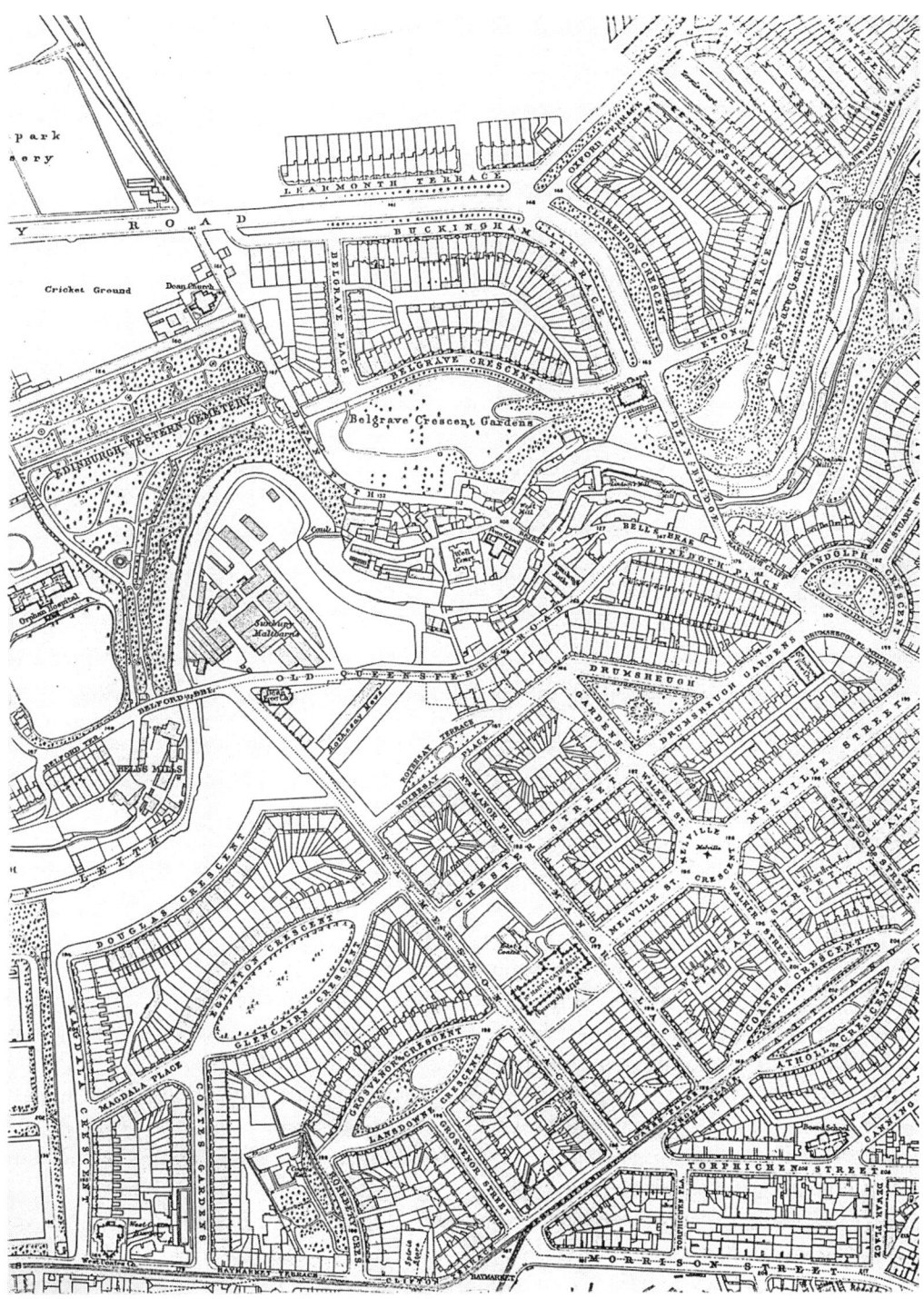

Bartholomew's map of 1891 showing completion of the several garden areas, including the extension of both the Eton Terrace (Dean Gardens) and Belgrave Crescent Gardens.

and separated from Queensferry Road 'by a tastefully laid out shrubbery', was executed according to Chesser's plan. Overall progress was halted by the action of West End residents to try and raise money to buy the land for a 'much needed' West End park (and more immediately to protect their open outlooks!). But although some funding was promised, and Duncan McLaren, the Liberal MP, pledged his support, the council decided that public backing was not justified for a project that would mostly benefit those already privileged.[11]

The Formation of the Cockburn Association

Although the West End park movement slipped into oblivion, it was to have unexpected benefits for this later group of pleasure gardens, and in this way. Although the campaign was unsuccessful, it brought together a number of like-minded individuals concerned about the rapid expansion of Edinburgh and loss of open space. The need for a more permanent group of informed citizens, committed to preserving the City's fine features and acting as watchdogs had become apparent, and one that would work in co-operation with the Town Council. In 1875 the Cockburn Association (Edinburgh's Civic Trust) was born, its remit to focus on preserving Edinburgh's remaining open spaces. Founder member and first treasurer was David Smith, WS, the man who had fought to save the Moray Bank Gardens when land slippages threatened their existence. Smith was to assume an equally spirited role in the setting up of Dean Gardens; and when there were later possibilities of extending them, the Cockburn Association provided a supportive arm, just as they did when West Princes Street Gardens were being transferred to public use. The area north of Learmonth Terrace amounting to around 80 acres was purchased in 1894 by James Steel, now a wealthy builder, whose career was soon to be crowned by his election as Lord Provost in 1900. Only Learmonth Gardens/South Learmonth Gardens (built around the turn of the twentieth century) show any vestige of Chesser's plans to match housing development with areas of communal open space. The era of pleasure gardens had come to an end.

Clarendon Crescent Garden
0.6 acres (0.24 ha)

Clarendon Crescent Garden, together with the tree-planted strips directly opposite, enhances the western approaches to the City centre. The Crescent garden is the oldest attached to the Dean Estate, and the same feuing conditions applied as for Rutland Square. Adjoining owners were made responsible for keeping the parapet walls, railing and garden ground 'in good order and repair in all time coming', payment for upkeep to be based on the 'foot frontage' principle (the 22 houses in the crescent vary in width from 21 to 36 ft (6.40–10.98 m)): a method which still applies, although most of the property is now subdivided. No early garden records survive, but plans indicate that they were formed in the mid-1850s, and most likely by a nursery firm who would have levelled, grassed and planted the borders with trees and shrubs.[12] Like most smaller gardens, it has been run on fairly informal lines.

Clarendon Crescent Gardens, 1939, when used to accommodate two ARP shelters. (Clarendon Crescent minute book)

The Second World War witnessed the removal of the railings and the addition of two ARP shelters; an offensive and much disliked pig bin appeared at the lower end of the garden. Afterwards the ground was reinstated: a chain-link fence was added along Queensferry Road together with privet hedging. The rest remains open and prey to lazy dog owners exercising their pets. The main varieties of trees are sycamore, elm, lime, poplar, ash, yew and whitebeam. Generally the garden is well cared for, although lacking any long-term management plan.

Oxford Terrace Garden
0.35 acres (0.14 ha)

Oxford Terrace Garden dates from the 1860s and under the same conditions as just described. With only half the number of proprietors, their survival has always been somewhat questionable. Consisting of a mixed woodland strip, it received but scant care, and in 1908 the Town Council threatened to take over the garden. Alarmed at this prospect, the residents approached the Dean Gardens with the suggestion that to preserve 'the amenity of the Dean feuars' the larger garden assume responsibility.[13] It was agreed that every Oxford Terrace proprietor would contribute ten shillings (50p) annually towards maintenance costs. But in practice it has proved an unsatisfactory marriage which cannot be easily dissolved. Payments soon became haphazard and a nuisance to collect, bearing little relation to actual expenditure. Rather ironically the Dean Trustees themselves later tried to make the strip over to the City. It continues to receive minimum attention with occasional blitzes, relying on the goodwill of Oxford Terrace proprietors to contribute more generously whenever major work is needed.

Dean Gardens
(formerly Eton Terrace Gardens)
7.20 acres (2.9 ha)

> Sir, – I was much struck the other day, in passing across the Dean Bridge by the contrast exhibited between the cultivated bank of the Water of Leith behind Moray Place, and the neglected aspect of that below Eton Terrace. In the former the fine natural slope of the ground has been fully taken advantage of, and has been diversified by walks, and embellished with trees, shrubs and flowers; in the latter, only so much has been done, that we have neither the wildness of rude nature, nor the cultivation of the landscape gardener – nothing but chaos of stunted grass, overlaid with heaps of rubbish; which is the more to be regretted, as a moderate outlay would place this bank, which possesses natural capabilities quite equal to its opposite neighbour in as high state of cultivation and make it a convenience to the feuars, and an ornament to the town. Surely the proprietor of the ground in question might do something to improve this garden of the sluggard; even in a purely utilitarian point of view, he might find such an outlay a good investment; for if he has other land to feu in the neighbourhood, such a pleasure ground as this might easily be rendered, would form a great attraction to the feuars. At present its appearance is an eyesore to everyone crossing the Dean Bridge; and even if it were in contemplation to cover it with pig sties, like some ground not far distant, it could not be left in a more disorderly and neglected condition. [Signed Edinensis]
>
> *The Courant*, 22 November 1858[15]

Dean Gardens are the largest of the four pleasure grounds to border the Water of Leith and they are now the second-biggest private amenity gardens in Edinburgh. For years the bank had been used as rough grazing for sheep, but when building commenced in the 1850s it also served as a convenient tip for the spoil and rubble from the foundations of the new houses. To convert this tangled wilderness, so scathingly described above, into a pleasure garden of great charm and subtle design proved almost as challenging as forming the Queen Street and West Princes Street Gardens many years before.

Early Stages

Learmonth had placed a servitude on the ground lying between Eton Terrace and the Water of Leith, restricting its use 'for occupation as pasture, nursery, garden or pleasure ground'; this, however, excluded the western end opposite Holy Trinity Church which was reserved for a row of houses named Cambridge Terrace. By 1867 the first stage of the Dean development was nearing completion, and the second well under way. The same year saw two newcomers to Eton Terrace, and both were to play an important role in establishing the Dean Gardens. One was David Smith, WS (10 Eton Terrace), formerly partner in the law firm Smith & Kinnear, and since 1858 Manager of the North British and Mercantile Insurance Company; the other, James Balfour, WS (1815–98) (13 Eton Terrace). Both men were qualified lawyers and shared a commitment to worthwhile causes. Smith, a man of 'very kindly disposition, of courteous manner and goodness of heart'[16] is already known to us in connection with the Moray Bank pleasure gardens. Now at the height of his career, his arrival was indeed auspicious for he possessed the qualities needed to get the gardens off to a good start – persistence, attention to detail, drive, diplomatic skills and sound practical experience. He was appointed convener of the newly formed garden committee, and remained in that position until his death in 1880. Balfour, a younger gentleman and related to the Balfours of Pilrig, went on to serve as Secretary for nearly thirty years, a role fulfilled with great tact and mostly without remuneration.[17] His son, E.S. Balfour Melville, CA, eventually succeeded him, maintaining the tradition of long years of service.

Smith and Balfour's first move was to arrange a 'conference' with Lt-Col. Learmonth, 'to consider the propriety of improving and dressing the bank between Eton terrace and the Water of Leith'.[18] It took place in Edinburgh on 12 November 1867, attended by two other Dean feuars – Mr Fraser Farquharson (5 Eton Terrace), and Mr Dick Peddie, architect (33 Buckingham Terrace): the only occasion the feuars met with the Colonel. He travelled up from Melrose, to which he returned before going on to his London residence at 93 Eaton Place. Acting as the group's spokesman, Smith stated the feuars' belief that the Colonel's late father, and also the Colonel himself, had intended to lay out the bank as a communal pleasure ground. As feuing was now well advanced, the new residents felt that 'the time had come for this being done'; in order to hasten progress they now proposed paying for the costs themselves, and offered to feu the ground, 'on payment of a moderate feu duty'.

The Colonel, while not unsympathetic to the idea, nevertheless thought that the time had 'hardly yet come for making permanent alterations on the bank in case these might possibly affect the street of Eton Terrace which was partly composed of travelled earth'. He would have been aware of the Moray Bank slippages, for indeed it was his father who had provided space on the Dean lands for depositing the surplus earth that had to be removed. Action, he felt, should be postponed for another year or more, but in the meantime he would plant the bank 'pretty extensively'. Rather than see their plans thwarted, the delegation 'after some conversation' proposed taking on a temporary lease, forcing the Colonel to confess that the bank was still useful to him 'as a place to deposit the soil brought from the foundations of the other houses'. So much for concern at the bank's stability! Tact, however, was all the essence. Smith gently reminded the Colonel that such operations were contrary to the spirit of the servitude, but that if a temporary lease was granted, the feuars 'would agree to his reserving a part of the ground as a spoil bank'. The meeting closed amicably with the feuars promising to put their proposals in writing.

Diplomacy was rewarded. A twelve-year lease was granted 'of such part that may not be required to be retained as a deposit for earth' at a nominal rent of £1 per annum (the same as when let for pasturage), and on condition that the feuars 'be at the whole expense of enclosing and laying out the ground as pleasure garden and keeping and leaving the same in proper order'.[19] The portion initially allocated was considered 'too limited'; but to strengthen their case the feuars asked 'one of their number', the architect John Dick Peddie, to 'make a sketch of how he would propose to lay out the grounds and to take estimates of the expense of doing that, and of enclosing them'. Dick Peddie's 'architectural taste', combined with James McNab's planting skills, had not long since transformed the rather dowdy St Andrew Square Gardens. With the architect's sketch to hand, Learmonth agreed to include the whole bank between Eton Terrace and the Water of Leith, with the exception of the portion reserved for Cambridge Terrace. The committee, however, registered their interest in purchasing this additional ground 'on reasonable terms' if and when the opportunity should arise.[20]

These arrangements were approved by the rest of the feuars[21] and it was left to the committee (now enlarged from four to nine members) to raise funds by voluntary subscriptions. Ten pounds was suggested for those living along Eton Terrace and five pounds for other Dean feuars; the Moray feuars overlooking the bank were also circulated for donations. In addition the committee was asked to negotiate with the Raeburn Trustees for a corner of adjoining bank which would allow a gated access between the two estates.[22]

Daniel Mackay & Co. of Cameron Bank Nursery, Dalkeith Road[23] had already supplied estimates for carrying out Dick Peddie's design. This was revised in the light of a detailed planting list supplied by James McNab at the request of David Smith.[24] The overall cost was put at £382. The time for action had finally arrived. In mid-February 1868 Dick Peddie was instructed to see 'that the work was immediately proceeded with'; he was also asked for plans for the additional ground now acquired from the St Bernard's estate, including an opening to Ann Street.[25]

Dick Peddie's plans have not survived, but they received detailed press coverage, and by happy chance the new garden featured in an early photograph taken from the Dean Bridge by Washington Wilson. The following account appeared in *The Scotsman*:

> The plan exhibits two terraces, extending along the whole length of the ground, and dividing the space lying between Eton Terrace and the Water of Leith into three nearly equal portions. The ground is very steep, but by means of these terraces it will be made level to about 30 feet in one case, and to about 40 feet in the other. The centre of each terrace will be a broad walk with a turf margin ornamented with shrubs of various kinds. To connect the terraces a series of winding walks will be formed along the face of the slope. These will be somewhat steep, but the gradients are to be made as easy as the natural acclivity of the grounds will admit of. On the ground between the lower terraces and the Water of Leith, forest trees are to be thickly planted: and the slopes between the two terraces will be studded at intervals with clumps of trees of the same kinds, with shrubs at intersections of the various walks. The slope from the upper terrace to Eton Terrace will be kept clear of trees in order that the view from the houses may not be interrupted, but the whole surface will be closely planted with shrubs of various colours of leaf, and flowering plants, set in masses so as to give variety and richness of effect at all times of the year. The shrubberies will be so dressed as to be allowed to spread without attaining to any considerable height. The work is being rapidly proceeded with under the direction of Messrs Peddie & Kinnear, architects, by whom the plans are furnished; and it will when finished, add considerably to this favoured part of the city and Mr McNab of the Botanic Gardens has been called in to advise as to the kind of shrubs and trees to be planted and the proper arrangement of them.[26]

The *Courant* newspaper avoided lengthy comment, but instead took the credit for having had the idea of turning the 'eyesore' into ornamental garden space. They now recommended

Photograph taken by George Washington Wilson, not long after the first part of the Dean Gardens had been formed, but prior to the acquisition of the western section in 1877 (compare with Ewbank's drawing of 1825 on page 264, top drawing). (George Washington Wilson Collection, Aberdeen University Library)

that the feuars on both sides of the river should grasp the opportunity 'to have the gardens connected by a light and elegant suspension bridge', a notion welcomed by the Dean feuars but meeting with little enthusiasm from their neighbours.[27] By the end of 1868 most of the structural work was complete and the bottom slope planted. The upper banks were allowed to consolidate for several months. In 1870 an avenue of limes was added along the lower terrace walk (just discernible in the photograph – and still surviving – although now in a backward-going state). Clumps of shrubbery were formed and mahonias and cotoneaster planted on the lowest slope.[28]

Costs came to around £576, nearly three-quarters of which went to the contractor. Other items of expense included £25 for the Ann Street boundary wall, £42 for paling for the west-end boundary and £15 to the architect for his plan.[29] Over and above this was the provision of a parapet wall and railing along part of Eton Terrace (Learmonth paid for his end section), so the total expenditure was in the region of £800. It had been hoped that subscriptions from the Dean feuars, together with contributions from the Moray proprietors, would cover everything, but even after reminders had been sent out, the total collected was less than half the amount required. The shortfall had to be met by a long-term bank loan. All subscribers on the Dean Estate were given rights to the garden provided they paid their annual maintenance dues; others from outwith the Dean Estate who had contributed were allowed to rent a key; these were nearly all Moray feuars.

Acquisition of Further Land

By 1875 the new planting was sufficiently well established for tree-thinning to be necessary along the lower terrace, the surplus being distributed 'pretty freely' throughout the rest of the garden, allowing them to be 'clothed and beautified at a slight cost'. Walks which had proved 'most inconveniently steep' had also been adjusted 'and the gradients of some of these materially lessened', thereby adding 'to the convenience and pleasure in the use of the gardens'. Not all was politeness and joy, however; the minutes record 'wanton mischief' and damage to the banks and young trees and ivy on the walls 'from boys that frequent them'. Parents and 'nurses who go with young children' were asked to exercise more control over their charges.[30]

The adjoining piece of wasteland continued to rankle, becoming more of an anomaly as the rest of the bank developed its ornamental character. Circumstances, however, were soon to become more favourable for its acquisition, with the setting up of the Cockburn Association with its declared intention of defending Edinburgh's open spaces. Behind the scenes was of course David Smith, the Association's first convener and surely the man responsible for putting this parcel of land firmly on the Cockburn's agenda. Hence the minutes of their first AGM contain the pertinent observation that no-one crossing the Dean Bridge could not but be struck with 'the unseemly state of the waste ground to the north east of the Bridge as well as its capability of improvement and of being converted into one of the finest parterres in that part of the city'. In April 1876 a sub-committee was appointed to investigate the possibility of buying the land.[31]

Lt.-Col. Learmonth has been rather harshly labelled as 'that hard-hearted warrior', making off 'with his pound of flesh', but there is nothing to indicate that dealings with him (via his agents) were other than civil and helpful.[32] This was a business matter, and if Learmonth was being asked to forgo land with development potential, then he was entitled to compensation. In any case large-scale property developers are rarely portrayed as popular figures.[33] In 1876 Learmonth agreed to sell the western end for £2,250, 'rather higher than anticipated' by the feuars, but nevertheless a fair price; Lord Moray had received £2,000 ten years earlier for a smaller and more limited space at the centre of Randolph Crescent. The existing garden – still held on lease – was bought at the same time for £189: almost a token payment.

Raising the Cash

Reasonably priced or not, quite substantial sums had to be raised. Lord Moray's feuars, overlooking the ground, and with their view now guaranteed, agreed to subscribe half the amount – £1,125. The rest, including existing debts and money for forming the ground, had to be met by 'a united and hearty effort' from the Dean feuars themselves.[34] It was estimated that £1,450 would be required, and of this £1,000 had already been subscribed by the Dean feuars. The shortfall was the sum needed to convert the ground into garden and connect it with the existing one. An appeal was immediately launched for contributions of shrubs – 'such as thorn trees, laburnums, lilacs, ribuses, cotoneaster, guilder roses, mock orange etc, also ferns and other plants for the rockery, garden chairs etc'; the minutes noted optimistically that 'many gentlemen who have country places might easily give such contributions or procure them from friends'.

Waiting in the wings, however, and eager to rise to the challenge, were the ladies of the district: the only known occasion of Edinburgh women uniting in force to raise money for making a pleasure garden: early signs of changes to come. Sanctioned by the all-male committee (relieved that a large sum of money might so be conjured up), a stylish three-day bazaar took place in the Masonic Hall, George Street during April 1877. Military bands and Punch and Judy shows enlivened the proceedings, and amongst the novelties were chocolates brought from Paris, and jewellery from Genoa. An impressive list of nineteen Lady Patronesses, nearly all with titles, supported the venture and no doubt aided the quest for quality donations and generous spending. A team of eighteen others – mostly Dean ladies – with one or two helpers from outside, were responsible for assembling the goods and looking after the stalls. And much must have been collected in order to sustain a three-day sale. Although highly successful – just under £500 profit was made – it was not enough to ensure solvency. Happily, William Wood, CA, one of the committee, agreed to lend the shortfall of around £400 at a low interest rate; the sum was eventually paid off in 1891. The 'exertions of the ladies' were rewarded with a personal letter of appreciation and making over 'for life' a key to the garden.[36]

Laying Out the New Area

Formed between the latter part of 1876 and 1877, the work was undertaken by local nursery gardeners, John Jeffrey & Son, and to their own plan after being approved by McNab.[37] The extra area extended from the parapet wall of Trinity Church Cemetery to the existing garden, and stretched down to the Water of Leith. It provided a reasonably level and extensive area of lawn (the site of the proposed Cambridge Terrace) which became useful recreational space for children and for tennis (another small court was also formed off the lower terrace walk). Tennis was so popular that play had to be rationed to one hour at peak times; a wooden pavilion survives from these days. Footpaths were made to link with existing ones and trees and shrubs were planted along the banks. Several Dean feuars hoped that this might

Notice of the Bazaar, 1877, organised by ladies of the district to raise money towards extending the Dean Gardens. (*The Scotsman*, 3 April 1877)

DEAN GARDENS
A BAZAAR will be held on THURSDAY, FRIDAY, and SATURDAY, the 5th, 6th, and 7th APRIL in the FREEMASONS HALL, 98 GEORGE STREET, to assist in defraying the expense of constructing these Gardens.
The Gardens will not only be a fine feature in the beauty of Edinburgh, but as they are to be open to the Inhabitants generally who contribute to their maintenance, they will be a valuable addition to the Pleasure- Grounds of the City.
It is intended that the Bazaar should be somewhat different from those at which Ladies' Work alone is sold. There will be one Stall devoted to Flowers, Cut and in Pots to which Contributions have been kindly promised from the Duchess of Buccleuch, Lady Louise Wardlaw-Ramsay, Lady Elphinstone, Lady Polwarth, Lady Don Wanchope, Lady Baxter, and many others, besides nearly all the Nurserymen in the neighbourhood of Edinburgh.
There will also be a variety of Works of Art, including Photographs of Rome; China comprising Contributions from Dresden, Valleria, &c- Genoese Jewellery, Pyrenees Work, Fancy and Lawn Tennis Tables, African Goods, Parisian Chocolates, French Coffee, &c, all ordered especially for this Bazaar.
By permission of the OFFICERS, the BANDS of the 78th HIGHLANDERS and 7th QUEEN'S OWN HUSSARS will be present on the AFTERNOONS of THURSDAY and FRIDAY respectively.

provide the opportunity for their enlarged garden to be united with the Belgrave Crescent ones, also in the process of being extended. Balfour and Smith once more assumed the role of ambassadors, hopeful that the spirit of the West End Park movement was still alive; but it was not to be.[38] In recent times the walk beneath Dean Bridge has been re-established with stout steps and balustrade leading down to the river, providing magnificent views across to Dean village and to 'the waterfall' formed by the old weir.

From this time on the pleasure ground became known as Dean Gardens, and the land was vested in five trustees and managed by a committee of seven. Proprietors were deemed to be those who had subscribed £10 towards the setting up of the first garden area, or, after 1876, £25 pounds towards purchasing the adjoining land, provided they paid annual dues. Those contributing from the Moray Estate also qualified as proprietors. Rights and privileges therefore became attached to the property making the initial contributions (99 altogether). But while proprietors had certain constitutional rights, unlike most New Town gardens they were under no obligation to pay any annual assessment – and there are now many 'lapsed' proprietors. This somewhat idiosyncratic spread of proprietors has made record-keeping and control of keys much more difficult. Without a guaranteed source of

Photograph showing the handsome, although ageing, lime trees planted along the lower terrace walk. (Mike Griffiths)

income the financial running of the gardens has also been more precarious, and the gardens more dependent on outside subscribers and local goodwill. Nevertheless, despite various ups and downs the gardens have survived surprisingly well, helped by the fact that most of the neighbouring property remains residential. It has as its ace a wonderfully attractive space, occupying a most outstanding and magnificent site, which, although not the easiest from the maintenance point of view, is able to claim one of the lowest subscription charges in Edinburgh.

The gardens remain faithful to Dick Peddie's original design but the enormous growth in the planting has transformed their appearance. Abercombie & Plumstead in 1949 described the tree planting as 'excessive'; producing 'this gorge-like wilderness' more appropriate for 'tropical parts than northern climes' and obscuring 'the natural features of the river side and its banks'.[39] Little did they appreciate the discontent when the bank was in its 'natural' state, or the sheer magic when within. Dick Peddie's design not only transformed a difficult site to maximum effect, but by making clever use of the several changes in level, challenged the eye with a feast of enchanting and varied sights probably not bettered anywhere in Edinburgh.

Belgrave Crescent Gardens
6.0 acres (2.4 ha)

> The braes of Belgrave Crescent is lovely to see,
> With its beautiful walks and green shrubbery.
> 'Tis health for the people that lives near by there
> To walk along the bonny walks and breathe the sweet air.
>
> Therefore all lovers of the picturesque, be advised by me
> And the beautiful scenery of the River Leith go and see,
> And I am sure you will get a very great treat,
> Because the River of Leith scenery cannot be beat.

William McGonagall, 'The River of Leith'[40]

Belgrave Crescent Gardens were designed to enhance the view from Dean Bridge and create the effect of uninterrupted parkland. But the garden started life more modestly as a crescent-shaped enclosure immediately fronting the houses, similar in character to Clarendon Crescent, and bound by the same rights and responsibilities. The land beyond, amounting to some 5 acres (2.0 ha), was covered with kitchen gardens, ruinous buildings and broken-down fences,[41] and was intended to contain an eastward extension of Belgrave Place. It was soon, however, to attract the interest of the new residents.

A Move to Extend the Garden

Encouraged by their neighbours' success in extending their gardens, the Belgrave Crescent proprietors followed suit in a bid to increase their own and thereby 'preserve the beauty and

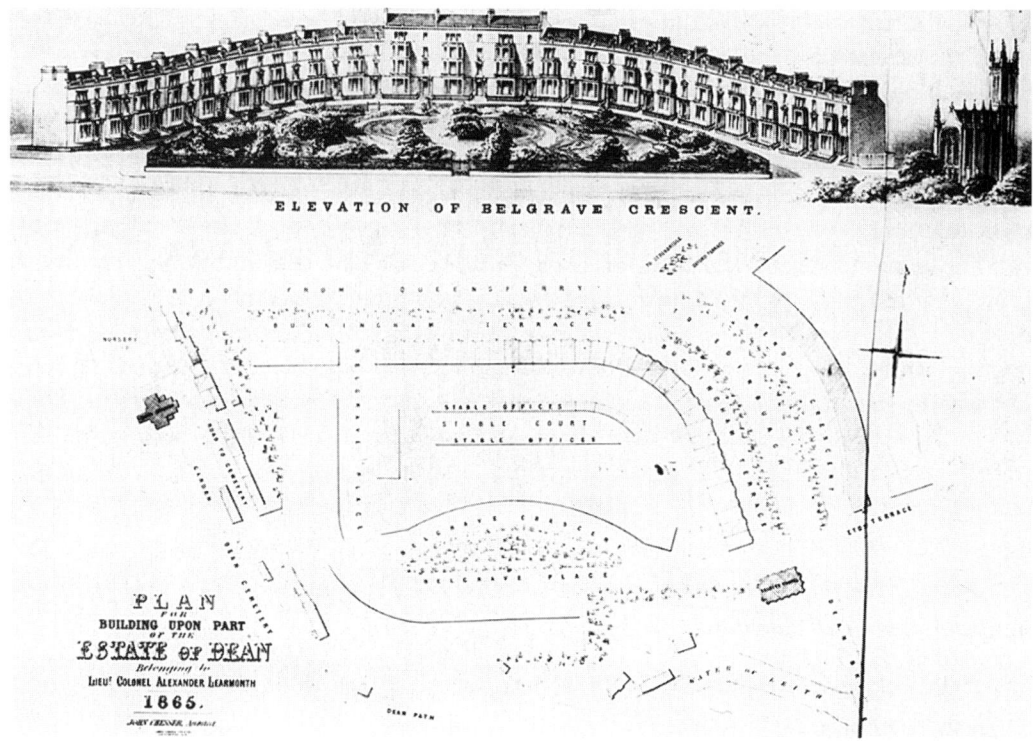

John Chesser's plan of Belgrave Crescent, Edinburgh, 1865, with a crescent-shaped garden area. (ECA, Crown copyright © RCAHMS)

elevation of Belgrave Crescent' as well as 'enhance the amenity of the whole district'.[42] No-one wanted their outlook spoilt by other buildings, and as the the public mood favoured such improvement, this was too good an opportunity to miss. A committee was appointed in July 1876 to negotiate with Lt-Col. Learmonth's agents, and to raise the necessary funds.[43] Taking command was Lord Provost Sir James Falshaw (1810–89), a blunt, no-nonsense Yorkshireman living at 14 Belgrave Crescent. Falshaw, a civil engineer by profession, was a man 'of indomitable energy and firm purpose'.[44] While in office he helped secure two important open spaces for the benefit of Edinburgh's citizens – the West Princes Street Gardens and Inverleith Park.

Focused action produced speedy results. In just six months the details of purchase and the basis for funding had been decided. Learmonth's agents, not long since in negotiations with the other Dean feuars, sought to apply similar procedures in drafting the contract. Hence the asking price of £5,000 (considered by the committee as 'excessive') was reduced by £1,000 on condition that those living in Buckingham Terrace, Clarendon Crescent, Learmonth Terrace and Belgrave Place were allowed equal rights to the gardens provided they contributed towards cost of purchase, formation and upkeep. Provision was also made for the Dean Gardens and Belgrave Crescent Gardens to be united at some stage if so desired.

Sir James Falshaw, Lord Provost, and driving force behind Belgrave Crescent Garden. (Grant, *Old and New Edinburgh*)

The Belgrave Crescent proprietors raised enough subscriptions amongst themselves to meet the cost of the land (£4,435 was collected by this means, with over half giving £250 each); other related costs were to be financed by contributions promised 'from the opposite side of the Water of Leith'. The leap on this occasion was not to the Moray Bank feuars, but a more athletic jump over to Rothesay Terrace, where building work had recently commenced. Such a long shot seems to have been contrived by John Dick Peddie, whose practice, Peddie & Kinnear, were acting as architectural consultants to the Scottish Lands & Building Company, owners of fifteen plots in Rothesay Terrace and surely emanating from his earlier involvement with the Eton Terrace Gardens. Sitings of a pleasure garden were infinitely preferable to further rows of housing, and Dick Peddie offered on behalf of the building company to subscribe £20 for each house built. In return each property was to be given rights to the garden provided contributions were made towards annual maintenance costs. Mr Blyth, CE, and Mr John R. Findlay (of *The Scotsman* newspaper), whose houses were already built, decided to do the same; they agreed to make over a lump sum of £50 each, for which they were granted a key in perpetuity, and without further charge.[45]

Negotiations were successfully concluded on 2 February 1877. The new feu charter, amongst other matters, extended the rights and obligations already applying to the original crescent garden to the extended area,[46] thus setting them at an advantage over the Dean Gardens which lacked any such prior enforcements. Trusteeship of the land was vested in six proprietors from the Crescent and a management committee was appointed (between five and seven proprietors) with full responsibility for having the grounds laid out, levying assessments and with powers to negotiate with Dean Gardens over possible integration.[46]

Forming the Extended Garden

Not surprisingly, James McNab, already known from his association with the Dean Gardens, was approached for a plan to unite the two areas. He was asked to liaise with one of the committee members, William Mowbray (7 Belgrave Crescent), a captain in the Royal Navy with 'an active interest in the arrangements'. Mowbray closely monitored the construction of the new garden, and took responsibility for selecting trees, seats and a horse-driven mowing machine, and maintained his interest over the next few years. This marked McNab's last major involvement with any of the New Town gardens, and it was an appropriate one to bow out from, exemplifying as it did all the characteristics dear to his heart: a romantic and picturesque site, one capable of being enjoyed from both within and without, and presenting a splendid opportunity to create a miniature parkland within a city. It was important both to the committee and McNab that the view from Dean Bridge should be kept simple and uncluttered, relying for effect on broad sweeps of grass and carefully grouped trees. Following McNab's death in 1879, Mr McLeod, Superintendent of the City Parks and Gardens, gave practical advice on completing the walks, further planting and the forming of an embankment on the west side. The garden records contain no evidence of Dick Peddie having liaised with McNab on this occasion, but according to his grandson he did prepare designs for the Gardens which 'perhaps fortunately, were not put into effect, as they included a glorified fun fair'.[47]

John Jeffrey & Son (with premises adjoining at 50 Dean Path), fresh from a similar exercise with Dean Gardens, were appointed to do the work; this started in the spring of 1877 and for the next few years the garden continued under their care. Part of their remit was to integrate the existing garden; hence the former crescent footpath was continued, to skirt gently round the outer edge. The border of lime and holly along the crescent side was also extended (now gone and replaced by privet hedge and poles for climbing roses). The inner area was levelled and grassed, a lawn tennis ground was prepared at the west end and clumps of trees were planted. Work on the walls and railings was carried out by Chalmers & Lawson, builders, and Chesser's original railing on the north side was extended. The section of copestone and railing on the other side was removed and the materials were later used for heightening the wall along Dean Path. An old ruin near the Water of Leith was also demolished.

Just under £400 was spent, including a £65 bill for trees supplied by Lawson & Co. Many more trees were added along the bank areas in 1887: mixed woodland species consisting of birch, sycamore, elm, ash, horse chestnut, willow and others.[48] In 1881 John Anderson was appointed as the first full-time gardener at £55 a year. For a while he lived within the grounds in part of Grove Cottage, which stood in the lower part of the garden practically opposite Lindsay's Mill. This cottage (whose foundations can still be seen near the picnic area) had once housed the manager of East Binny Quarry, but was later subdivided. It gradually deteriorated, was labelled unsanitary and was demolished in the late 1940s. The stone was re-used to build a rockery and sheltered sitting area at the top of the bank.

Further Extension

Increasing the garden's size caused a change in the building plan: while Belgrave Place became foreshortened, Belgrave Crescent was extended by four extra houses at the western end. The builder was James Steel, a well-off councillor (and later Lord Provost) with successful interests in stone quarrying and building.[49] He negotiated for the privilege of the gardens being extended first to his property in Belgrave Crescent, agreeing to pay the committee £850 for such rights provided a new access gate was made opposite Belgrave Place. Most of this money was used to pay Lt-Col. Learmonth for an additional strip of ground alongside Dean Path, which it was rumoured was to accommodate stables or workmens' houses.[50] In 1880 Steel paid a further £750 for a similar transfer of rights to the fifteen houses erecting in Belgrave Place; this had been calculated at a lower rate to take account of Steel's useful work on the newly acquired piece of ground – forming an embankment, heightening and extending the boundary wall and making a connecting pathway, besides adding good top soil rescued from Belgrave Place.[51] These extra properties significantly increased the prosperity of the gardens, which have always been able to afford a higher than average standard of care.

Belgrave Crescent Gardens have benefited from generous gifts of money, plants and equipment by residents, who have also given their own time to carry out garden

Photograph taken by Professor Chrystal of Belgrave Crescent Gardens in the early years of the twentieth century. The outer border is planted with an inner and outer row of well-clipped shrubs. (Crown copyright © RCAHMS)

A more recent view of Bellevue Crescent Gardens. Their park-like appearance would have delighted James McNab. (C. Byrom)

improvements. The committee has seen many long-serving members; but none surpassing John Ross (d. 1933) who served for 46 continuous years. The ladies only made their debut after the Second World War, when the question was tentatively raised as to whether they could legitimately be on the committee! An examination of the feu contract revealed nothing to debar them! Mrs Crabbie (15 Belgrave Crescent) and Lady Grant led the way, with the former elected first lady chairman in 1944, a position she continued to hold for over 20 years. Her son, William Crabbie, WS, served equally long as secretary. These war years saw other changes, as the garden was made available for training and drilling of the 6th Battalion of the Home Guard and the Air Cadets; railings were removed and the flower borders on the north side were converted into vegetable plots, the last one not disappearing until 1960.

When in 1880 it was decided 'to bring the grass into better condition' by hiring a horse and mowing machine, no-one could have foreseen that such an arrangement would last for nearly half a century. The horse belonged to James Stewart, a coach hirer, and came complete with a lad to handle her. In 1927 the horse finally made way for a 17" Pennsylvania lawn mower. The garden in its time has accommodated a range of activities: lawn tennis, a short-hole golf course (licences issued at a cost of 2/6d (25p)) and performances by the band of the 42nd Highlanders (the Black Watch). It continues to be well-used both by proprietors and subscribers, having the advantage of reasonably level areas of lawn, large enough to accommodate play equipment and provide space for the occasional marquee hired for celebrations. Most of the property is now subdivided, so the numbers having rights to the gardens have increased.[52]

Over time the pathways have been extended (the whole resurfaced in 1998) and planting renewed (with rather more variety of tree species than originally planted). In 1970, the lower bank at the south-east end was cleared of scrub and saplings, to create an attractive picnic area, with fine views across to the Dean Bridge and the weir and waterfall by the old West Mill. Only glimpses of the garden can now be seen from the bridge through the dense growth of trees along the lower banks. From the Crescent glimpses of the garden reveal sweeps of well-manicured lawn of park-like appearance, an effect which James McNab would have been proud to be associated with.[53]

Notes

1. The same article was repeated in the *Edinburgh Advertiser*, 1 November 1825.
2. In 1726 for example, the grounds of Deanhaugh house (about 2 acres (0.8 ha)) and St Bernard's (about 10 acres (4 ha)) were sold by Sir John Nisbet to James M'Dowell, merchant and farmer of Canonmills. A useful account of the history of the Dean estate can be found in John Geddie, 'Sculptured stones of old Edinburgh: the Dean group', *BOEC*, Vol. 1, 1908, pp. 77–135.
3. See *James Nasmyth, Engineer, an Autobiography*, ed. Samuel Smiles (London, 1883), p. 43 when his son refers to his father's involvement with the Dean estate and bridge; a small pencil drawing headed 'Laying out of a plott of Dean land for Sir J. Nisbet 1817' appears in a miscellaneous portfolio of work by the Nasmyth family in NLS, MS 3241 f 5. A copy of this sketch appears in A.A. Tait, *The Landscape Garden in Scotland, 1735–1835*, p. 128.
4. Part of Gillespie Graham's feuing plan covering the area which was purchased in 1825 for John Watson's School was found amongst various papers held by the school when purchased by the Crown Agents in 1978.
5. The lands to the west of Bells Mill were sold separately in 1825 to John Watson's Trustees for building John Watson's Hospital (school) designed by William Burn, and now the National Gallery of Modern Art.
6. *The Scotsman*, 22 December 1858.
7. Between 1825 and 1829 there was much discussion between the various interested parties about the design of the bridge. Two useful accounts of the origins and making of the Dean Bridge are: Basil Skinner, 'The Origins of the Dean Bridge Project', *BOEC* Vol. 30, 1959, pp. 166–7; and Roland Paxton, 'Dean Bridge Edinburgh', part of an article from *Our Engineering Heritage: 3 notable examples in the Edinburgh area, Dean bridge, Leith Docks, and Forth Rail Bridge*, Institute of Civil Engineers (Edinburgh, 1978).
8. *The Scotsman,* 13 April 1850, 'Extension of the New Town'.
9. Lt.-Col. Alexander Learmonth, WS was educated at Edinburgh Academy.
10. *The Scotsman*, 14 March 1874, 'Building notes: the feuing of the Dean Estate'; which contains a double-column spread about the further extension to the Dean estate.
11. Col. Learmonth had offered to sell 32 acres (12.8 ha) adjoining Queensferry road as a public park for £48,332.
12. Clarendon Crescent Garden Minute Book No. 1 has disappeared; Book No. 2 (1906–58) is kept by the garden secretary. Amongst other matters it contains a statement of the feuing conditions relating to the gardens.

13. Dean Garden, Minute Book 1 (1867–1909), 24 February 1908. Both Garden Minute Books covering the periods 1867–1909 and 1910–58 are held by the garden secretary.

14. Ibid., Minute, 7 June 1908. For further references to Oxford Terrace Gardens, see Dean Garden Minute Book 2, 28 May 1913, 12 February 1947, 9 October 1950, 12 January 1951, 26 June 1951, 26 July 1954, 28 January 1955.

15. *The Courant*, 23 November 1858, letter to Editor signed Edinensis.

16. *Edinburgh Evening Courant*, 17 December 1880, David Smith's obituary.

17. James Balfour was the fourth son of James Balfour, WS, of Pilrig. He assumed the surname of Melville on succeeding to Mount Melville in Fife in 1893.

18. Dean Garden Minute book 1 (1867–1901), 12 November 1867.

19. Ibid., 11 December 1867, which includes a copy of the letter from Col. Learmonth dated 22 November 1867 and sent from The Pavilion, Melrose.

20. Ibid., 4 January 1868; proposed letter to Col. Learmonth about renting the ground.

21. Fifteen residents were present at the general meeting: 6 from Eton Terrace, 5 from Buckingham terrace and the rest from neighbouring streets. Among those attending were William Brodie, sculptor (10 Oxford Terrace) and Arthur Perigal, landscape painter (7 Oxford Terrace).

22. This proved a straightforward transaction as it was to the benefit of both the Dean and St Bernard's feuars.

23. They had another nursery ground close by at Echo Bank, situated almost opposite Newington cemetery.

24. Dean Garden Minute Book 1, Minute 27 January 1868.

25. Ibid., Minute 14 February 1868.

26 *The Scotsman*, 13 March 1868; *Edinburgh Evening Courant*, 14 March 1868.

27. *Edinburgh Evening Courant*, 14 March 1868; Dean Garden Minute Book 1, 14 March 1868; 20 February 1880; 28 February 1881.

28. Dean Garden Minute Book 1, 19 November 1870.

29. Ibid., 29 March 1869.

30. Ibid., 10 February 1876.

31. Cockburn Association, Report by the Council to the first Annual meeting of the Association, 'Dean Bridge Gardens' (1875–6).

32. Neil Bayne, 'The Dean Gardens', *BOEC*, Vol. 32 (1966). Neil Bayne acted as garden secretary from 1944 to 1948.

33. A poetic protest, 'A lay of Edinburgh', was in fact written by one of the residents, Miss Gracie Wood, whose father/brother? was on the committee. It starts with the verse: Our landlord, Colonel Learmonth/He made a stern decree/ Where now are trees and grassy fields/ Must rows of houses be. It tells of the fight to buy the land, how the ladies 'spake out' to save the bridge and how £1,000 might well be raised by holding a bazaar. A copy of this was given to me by Mr Catford; it was lent to him by B.C. Skinner in 1973.

34. Dean Garden Minute Book 1, 30 June 1876, which gives full details of the transactions including the constitution for the new garden. A copy of the minute was sent to Col. Learmonth for his information. The details were also fully reported in the press, see *The Scotsman*, 3 July 1876, 'Proposed improvements at Dean Bridge'.

35. *Edinburgh Evening Courant* 31 March 1877; *The Scotsman*, 3 April 1877.

36. Dean Garden Minute Book 1, 27 February 1877; 21 April 1877.

37. Ibid., 31 July 1876; 27 February 1877; Jeffries' estimate for the work came to £410.

38. Ibid., 11 May 1878; 14 February 1879; 28 February 1894; 4 March 1895.

39. Patrick Abercrombie & Derek Plumstead, *A Civic Survey and Plan for Edinburgh* (Edinburgh, 1949), captions to Plates 48 & 49.

40. William McGonagall, *Last Poetic Gems* (London, 1968), pp. 69–70. He at least would now rejoice that his sparkling Water of Leith, after many murky years, once more sports trout and even an otter.

41. Grant, *Old and New Edinburgh*, Vol. 3, p. 37.

42. *The Scotsman*, 20 February 1877, 'New Dean Bridge Gardens'.

43. Miscellaneous paper held by the Clerk to the garden from which this and the following information is taken. There are also four minute books relating to the gardens as follows: Belgrave Garden Minute Book 1 (1877–1927); Book 2 (1928–49); Book 3 (1949–66); Book 4 (1967–); in possession of the Clerk to the gardens.

44. *The Scotsman*, 15 June 1889, Obituary, Sir James Falshaw.

45. Belgrave Crescent, Minute Book 1, 23 February 1877.

46. Feu contract between Lt.-Col. Alexander Learmonth & Trustees for Belgrave Crescent feuars of the Gardens opposite the Crescent. Recorded in the General Register of Sasine, 26 February 1877. Over time the role of Trustee and Committee member have become merged.

47. Letter from J.A. Dick Peddie, grandson, to the author, dated 21 March 1974. Dick Peddie's son (12 Belgrave Crescent) was a member of the garden committee from 1904–1921 and gave advice about plans for Grove Cottage.

48. On the advice of Mr Mackenzie, of Thomas Methven & Sons, when he recommended plating between 600 –700 trees along the banks. (Minute Book 1, 19 January 1887).

49. Charles Smith, *Historic South Side*, Vol. 2 (Edinburgh & London, 1979), p. 268. Steel was also responsible for Buckingham Terrace.

50. Belgrave Crescent, Minute Book 1, 29 April 1879; 15 July 1879; 4 November 1879; as part of the sale Lt.-Col. Learmonth gave up the right to the track leading to Grove Cottage.

51. Ibid., 5 February 1880; 14 April 1880.

52. In 1928 the Solicitor General (A.M. MacRobert) gave his opinion following a memorial from the committee on access rights and payment of dues, that each part-owner of a subdivided property was a successor, and liable to pay the annual levy in return for the right to use the garden.

53. For a short history of the garden, see Kenneth W. Sanderson, *The Centenary of Belgrave Crescent Gardens* (Edinburgh, 1977).

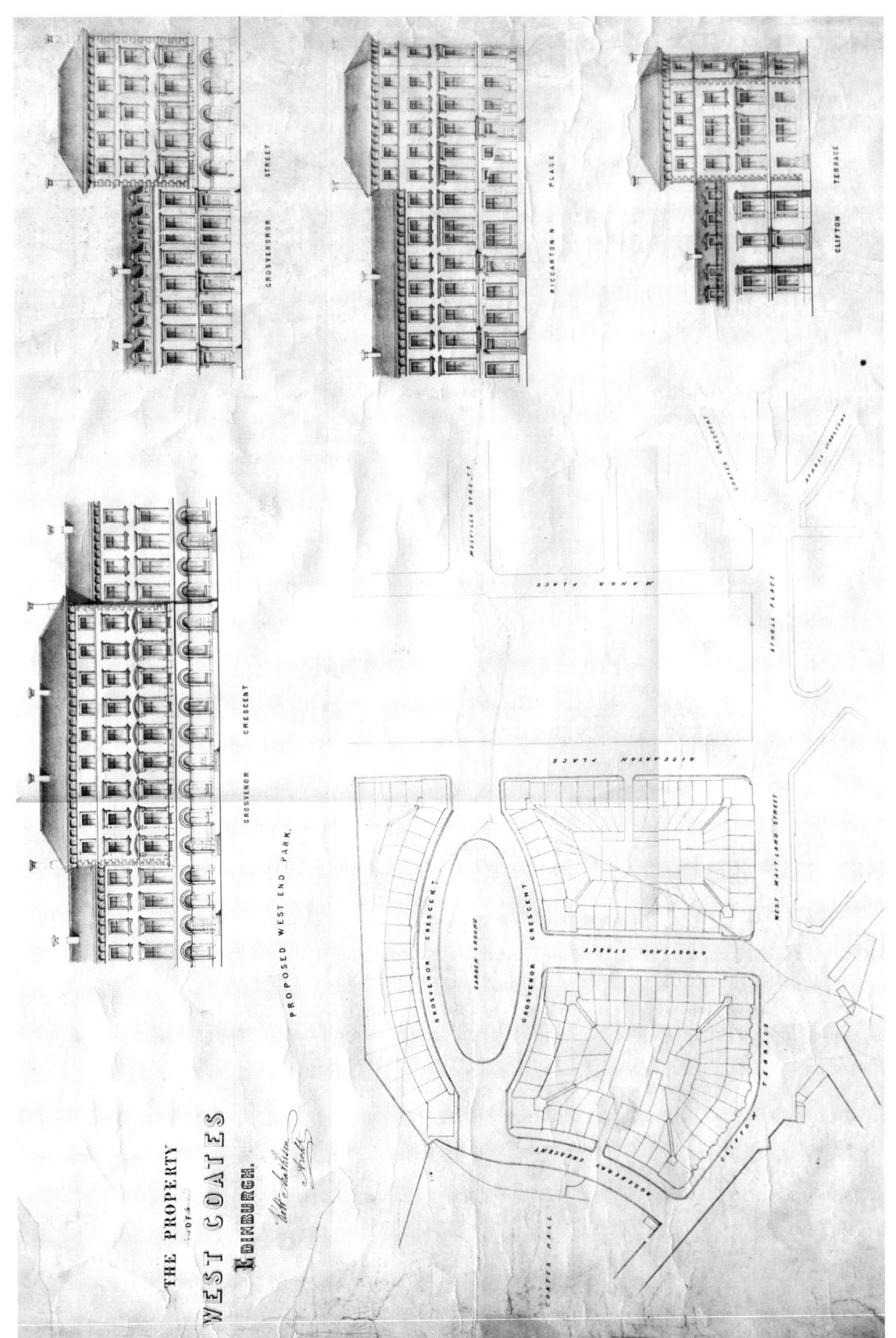

Robert Matheson's plan and elevation for Grosvenor/Lansdowne Crescent, Edinburgh, early 1860s. (NAS RHP 391)

CHAPTER 23

OTHER LATER GARDENS
Grosvenor/Lansdowne Crescent, Magdala,
Eglinton/Glencairn, Douglas Crescent Gardens,
Drumsheugh and Rothesay Terrace/Place

This chapter covers a miscellaneous group of gardens formed towards the end of the nineteenth century, and all situated on the west side of Edinburgh. They consist of two small gardens attached to the final phase of the Walker estate north of Melville Street, an oval-shaped garden within a scheme designed by Robert Matheson to the west of the Walker estate and three gardens within a development designed by John Chesser for Heriot's Hospital, including the last garden to border the Water of Leith. The gardens, although formed so much later, follow very much the established format in layout and planting and are not noticeably different from the earlier ones. We start with the oldest gardens in this group.

Grosvenor and Lansdowne Crescent Gardens
1.20 acres (0.48 ha)

Early in the 1860s Robert Matheson, Architect to Her Majesty's Office of Works bought around 9 acres (3.6 ha) of land, part of the estate of West Coates, for speculative development.[1] His plan and elevations reflected the Georgian character of the neighbouring Walker Estate; and its most distinctive feature was the double-sided crescent designed to line up with Melville Street (this was before the position for St Mary's Episcopal Cathedral had been finalised) and having an oval-shaped garden at its centre.[2] The whole crescent was initially planned to have matching sides. In the event, only the south side – Lansdowne Crescent – built around 1865, and bisected by Grosvenor Street, kept to Matheson's elevations. The north side, dating from 1869 (and named Grosvenor Crescent) became bay-windowed, more ornate and more Victorian in character,[3] and was in part executed by Peddie & Kinnear and the builder John Watherston & Sons. These were substantial family residences for the well-to-do business and professional classes. Wester Coates House had stood close to the middle of the central space but was demolished in 1869; some of the surrounding mature trees were, however, retained to ornament the new pleasure ground. Matheson was no stranger to New Town Gardens and about this time was busy supervising improvements to East Queen Street Gardens.

The proprietors in the two crescents were required in terms of their feu charters to 'maintain the garden ground in good order in all time coming' the cost of upkeep to be based on the width of the individual property (the foot frontage principle; now replaced by a flat rate system). The garden dates from 1870, and was most probably laid out by the local nursery firm of Downie & Laird, suppliers of a large quantity of trees and shrubs during the following year; several of these still survive.[4] Planting was concentrated round the outer border with shrub beds at either end for increased shelter; the inner area was gently mounded (possibly by using some of the material salvaged from Wester Coates House), grass seeded and divided into oval-shaped areas by looping paths. In 1882 Mr Mcleod, the City's Superintendent of Parks, recommended the removal of two large elderly beech trees which 'were dead or nearly so', the work being undertaken by the builders, J. Watherston & Sons, for under £7 (the same job today would cost well over £200). He also advised on 'the preservation of the remaining old trees', and the addition of twenty new ones.

A mostly uneventful history is indicated by the scant detail recorded in the garden minutes apart from listings of routine expenditure on items such as garden seats, tool-house, bulbs, bedding plants and fresh gravel. Management problems were sufficiently rare for the garden to function without any set regulations until 1903 – and then only prompted by a gardener exasperated by the boisterous and uncontrollable antics of children and dogs (the latter theoretically were banned from entry) causing damage to the garden. The rules then adopted followed the usual format, but also covered tennis play and included the rather quaint directive that 'no perambulator, mail cart, or wheeled carriage of any kind' should be taken upon the courts. Croquet was also played.

Over the years different methods of upkeep have operated, ranging from jobbing gardeners to contracts with nursery firms, and also a shared system with Eglinton/Glencairn Crescent during the 1950s; an arrangement which survived for fourteen years until the gardener's retirement. The Second World War witnessed the removal of the railings and the ground made over for air-raid shelters. The driving force behind their restoration was a Mr T.A. Turnbull who, the minutes tell us, died in a railway accident in 1948. His commitment was such as to inspire another resident, Major Douglas, to continue as chairman 'in respect of the memory of the late Mr Turnbull', a role he performed for several more years. Work on restoring the gardens was carried out in 1949 by Maxwell Hart & Co. at a cost of just over £550.

There are now about 60 trees in the garden, made up of sycamore, maple, lime, elm, horsechestnut, whitebeam, oak, rowan, birch, ash, hawthorn, holly, laburnum and some ornamental shrubs. In the 1970s a long-term programme of refurbishment was initiated, and efforts at present are concentrated on improving the borders, now grown patchy with age. In 1995 the wire-mesh fencing, a legacy from post-war years, was finally scrapped and replaced with an iron railing modelled on Matheson's design for the ones surrounding the Botanic Garden; their cost was part-funded by the New Town Conservation Committee. Steps are under way to restore the Victorian Swiss chalet-style tool-shed, also with financial help from the same source.[5]

The Lands Of Wester Coates

Closely following Matheson's scheme were Heriot's Hospital's proposals to feu their remaining land at Coates: the central portion had already been sold for Donaldson's School, built between 1841 and 1851 to a Jacobean design by Playfair. The area beyond

John Chesser's proposed layout of 1865, minus Eglinton/Glencairn Crescent. (George Heriot Trust, Crown copyright © RCAHMS)

was intended for villas, leaving the eastern wedge between the school and the Water of Leith to be developed with terrace housing. Gillespie Graham's proposals for the whole of Wester Coates were now obsolete, but his ideas for keeping the banks of the Water of Leith as ornamental ground saw partial fulfilment in John Chesser's plans. His first proposed layout of 1865 was for a rather prosaic rectangular block, but later revisions produced a more imaginative design containing a large double-sided crescent (Eglinton/Glencairn) and two single crescents (Magdala and Douglas), all with associated areas of pleasure garden.[6]

Magdala Crescent Garden
0.8 acre (0.32 ha)

Magdala Crescent was the first to be feued in 1869; by 1874 the twenty-four houses (now mostly subdivided) had been completed, each supplied with a small front garden. The house charters stated that the proprietors were responsible 'in all time coming' for enclosing, planting and maintaining the strip of land opposite, to which they had a common right 'so far as it may be capable of being used for walking thereon'.[7]

The garden was formed in 1874 by Downie & Laird, to a simple design of grass, trees, and shrubs. Footpaths were not thought appropriate but the northern end was levelled for use as a croquet or tennis lawn, and for children's play. A high stone boundary wall runs the whole length of the western side and provides shelter as well as opportunities for growing climbing plants. The lime trees skirting the crescent were planted in 1887; other trees include sycamores, hawthorn, horsechestnut and cherry, as well as ornamental shrubs. Attempts at herbaceous flower plots have never proved very successful.

This is essentially a decorative strip, with moderate use by children and dog owners (dog loos provided) and run on fairly *ad hoc* lines (small committee, plus unpaid secretary and the services of a jobbing gardener). A flat-rate annual assessment operates with occasional special levies to meet extra-ordinary expenses, such as the erection in 1963 of a plain iron railing.[8]

Eglinton / Glencairn Crescent Gardens
1.9 acres (0.76 ha)

House plots in this double crescent were advertised for sale in 1872, and nearly half were bought by a local builder, James Steel, who was also responsible for much of the building in Douglas Crescent. Building continued until the early 1880s. The houses in Glencairn Crescent were three-storeyed and smaller in scale than Eglinton, with an extra storey, wider frontages, bow and bay windows and a grander, more substantial appearance.

Rights and obligations relating to the central pleasure garden were stated in the individual house charters: the ground was never to be built upon, and was to form 'a pro indiviso inseparable part and pertinent' of each of the building areas on both sides of the crescent. The proprietors were made responsible for enclosing and laying out the garden 'in a suitable and handsome manner' and for its future upkeep. Assessments were to be based on the width of the property, with a fixed upper limit of £2 per annum. The pleasure ground fronting Douglas Crescent was also referred to in the charters, the Eglinton and Glencairn proprietors being given rights to them on certain conditions.[9]

Little is known about the early history of this garden. It probably dates from around 1886 when the first set of rules was circulated 'by order of the Committee', bearing the names of James Steel (Chairman) and J. Hope Finlay (Secretary and Treasurer).[10] No-one by the name of Steel lived in the crescents at that time, so one must presume that the builder himself took an active role in setting up the gardens. This kind of initiative was nothing new, and Steel had already assisted in forming the eastern portion of the Belgrave Crescent Gardens. John Chesser's plan had shown the garden containing a central croquet lawn, with outer footpath and perimeter planting of trees and shrubs. A similar practical layout was adopted, with the new rules making reference to a tennis court.[11] Over time the pathway system was altered to converge at the centre, creating two areas of lawn: one on the west side allocated for tennis and one on the east for croquet (also for putting and tennis quoits). In recent years a small toddlers' play area has been added to the eastern end. Further shrub beds have also been formed at the centre of the north side to provide more shelter. A variety of trees are grown including sycamore, elm, lime, birch, hawthorn, poplar, yew, holly and cherries together with ornamental shrubs such as laurel, privet and red currant.

The garden quickly became established and within half a century had developed a somewhat cluttered appearance. When Robert Scarlett (1888–1979) the Musselburgh market gardener and horticulturalist, surveyed the grounds in 1934, he found them to be in a 'decidedly unattractive condition': most of the large trees overgrown, the shrubs beneath scraggly and the grass and paths in poor shape. Extensive tree maintenance followed, with additional evergreens and shrubs planted from a list prepared by the Royal Botanic Garden. Creating a well-sheltered garden has always been a priority and the outer border has now achieved thickness and height. The Second World War left the gardens relatively unscathed apart from the removal of the railings; these were replaced in 1948 by ones of plain design paid for by voluntary contributions.

The £2 upper limit on assessments was exceeded in 1929, but the shortfall was made good initially by an increase in the number of proprietors following subdivision of property into flats. By 1949, however, the fixed rate was wholly inadequate to meet the high costs of refurbishment after the war years. To meet the shortfall the system was adopted of asking proprietors for additional 'voluntary' contributions over and above the £2. This has worked reasonably well, although it is dependent on the goodwill and co-operation of the proprietors. Some residents from neighbouring streets also subscribe to them.

Douglas Crescent Gardens
4.40 acres (1.76 ha)

> The steep bank between Douglas Crescent and the Water of Leith has now been laid out in grass, intersected by agreeable paths, and when the trees planted have attained a greater size, this will form a worthy link between the natural beauties of the upper reaches of the stream and the Eton Terrace and Moray Place, for which the town is indebted to the good taste which Lord Cockburn did so much to foster. Some further planting would increase the attractions of this bank.
>
> Cockburn Association Annual Report, 1893.[12]

Had Gillespie Graham's intentions for Coates been implemented, a large section of the south bank along the Water of Leith would have become pleasure ground. Instead only a fragment was formed as such, and that along Douglas Crescent. It was enough, however, to attract favourable comment from the Cockburn Association as a worthy addition to the other neighbouring pleasure grounds. This portion had formed part of the farmlands of Coates and was left 'in its natural state', although in 1835 the Heriot's Hospital Works Committee had recommended its enclosure with a six-foot (1.83 m) high wall, planted with trees and with a cottage provided at the eastern end for a farm servant, as an extra measure of security. These plans never seem to have been implemented.[13] It remained rough ground, trodden by tracks leading from Coates to the Old Queensferry Road, and the hamlet and milling centre at Bell's Mills.

A preliminary plan by John Chesser, dated 1865, had shown Douglas Crescent divided by a central road. By the time of the 1872 feuing plan the crescent had become a continuous curve with an oblique eastern wing designed as a continuation of Palmerston Place. The houses in this wing later became part of Douglas Crescent; the wedge-shaped piece of ground directly opposite was intended for stable accommodation. In all the plans, however, the land immediately fronting the crescent was marked as pleasure ground.

In May 1872, 103 lots of land (including Douglas Crescent (22 lots), Palmerston Place (19 lots, some of which later became part of Douglas Crescent – Nos. 23–28), Eglinton & Glencairn Crescent (50 lots) and Magdala Place – part of Coates Gardens (12 lots)) were advertised for sale. Under the conditions of purchase, this area of pleasure ground fronting the Water of Leith was to 'belong to and form a pro indiviso inseparable part and pertinent' of all the property then being sold. Douglas Crescent feuars were made responsible for enclosing the ground along the street side, but it was intended that the whole body of feuars would share the cost of laying out the ground and its future upkeep. In return they were to have sole right to the ground, subject to such regulations being agreed to by a majority at a general meeting set up under the terms of the feu charter. A similar right was conferred on the purchasers of property in Magdala Crescent and Coates Gardens which had been sold earlier, provided application was made 'five years after the term of Martinmas 1872', and on condition that a fair and equal proportion of the expense already incurred was also paid. John Chesser, whose responsibility it would have been for framing these details, was most probably influenced by his experience with the Dean feuars. Extending garden rights to all the proprietors would spread the cost of upkeep while providing an attractive amenity with sales appeal. It was a worthy idea, but not at all practicable.[14] Building began in 1873, and by 1878 twenty-two houses had been completed; the six houses comprising the eastern angle were not started until 1879. These were large houses similar in appearance to Eglinton Crescent but with rather plainer detailing.

A copestone with iron railing matching Chesser's design for the house fronts (a round head with spike) was erected along the top of the bank soon after the new proprietors moved in. Further improvements were discussed at a gathering of Douglas Crescent residents on 8 February 1878 (the first recorded meeting) when it was decided 'to clear, sow with grass and plant with a double row of trees [lime] and shrubs the top of the bank opposite the crescent'. A committee was appointed, and a £2 assessment levied on all the Crescent proprietors.[15] By July, 'Mackay the gardener' (Daniel Mackay & Co of Cameron and Echo Bank nursery) was being instructed to 'cut down the weeds on the bank at least half way down to the river' to limit the spread of windblown seeds and so reduce 'further heavy expense for weeding next year'.

In 1879 Major-General James Furlong (1825–1904) joined the committee, first as secretary and then for twenty-four years as chairman. He was a retired General of the Madras Staff Corps who lived at 11 Douglas Crescent. His substantial contribution to the establishment of the garden was acknowledged in the minutes at the time of his death:

> Mainly by his persevering energy, and great assistance, technical as well as practical, were the proprietors enabled to bring the garden ground from the exceedingly rough waste unprotected state in which it then lay, to its present well planted, protected and cared for condition.[16]

He was well supported by another stalwart committee member, Mr Bennet Clark, WS, who acted as treasurer from 1892 to 1922. Another individual contributing long years

TAKE NOTICE.

The Proprietors of DOUGLAS CRESCENT GARDENS have been under the necessity of summoning, and this day PROSECUTING, A NUMBER OF BOYS, for trespassing on their Gardens, and destroying the young Trees, and this is to give due notice, that all Persons found on these grounds below and adjoining the lands from Bell's Mills Bridge to Donaldson's Hospital will be similarly proceeded against.

BY ORDER.

EDINBURGH, *7th October* 1881.

Warning notice 1881 to would-be trespassers. (Douglas Crescent Garden Minutes)

of service was James Hutchison, appointed secretary in 1885, a post he held for thirty-four years.

Some trial planting was carried out on the bank in 1881, prompted by a letter from the Rev. Dr Rainy (23 Douglas Crescent) to Heriot's, requesting that the ground 'be put in order without delay'; the Hospital referred the matter back to the feuars.[17] In the spring of 1882, Dr Rainy was treated to the sight of 355 forest trees being added to the bank – horsechestnuts, sycamores, elms, beeches and ashes – together with some fast-growing willows, poplars and a number of shrubs. Heriot's Hospital were asked to fence off their land at the north-east end, and notices were erected warning of stern measures should youthful trespassers be caught in the act of causing damage.

Mischievous boys, however, posed less of a threat than unstable land, and in 1881 the first slip occurred towards the middle area, requiring it to be piled and filled. Another and more serious slip took place in 1883. Both were caused, as Chesser reported to the Hospital governors, by large quantities of material excavated from the house foundations being 'thrown over the bank, filling it up to a steep slope, thereby entirely altering its natural gradient', and contrary to the building agreements. Moray Bank Garden, it will be remembered, had likewise suffered an overload from dumped material and with dire effect.[18] To secure the bank and prevent further mishap the committee decided that a strong retaining wall was necessary at the base of the garden. But although James Steel offered to build one at modest cost, and to slope the bank more gently, funds proved insufficient.[19]

A logical move therefore was to rally the feuars of the hundred or so properties specified in the 1872 sale missives, and to encourage them to assume their rights and responsibilities for the pleasure garden. Douglas Crescent Committee was disbanded, and a general meeting called to form a new and broader-based committee. But the plan failed. The only proprietors with any real interest in the ground were the Douglas Crescent feuars themselves (after all, Eglinton and Glencairn Crescent residents were soon to become absorbed with forming their own pleasure garden). Another hurdle was the Heriot's Hospital insistence that no general assessment could be levied without a plan being available showing the ground properly laid out as a garden, and not just as a planted but virtually unusable space (unless written consent of every proprietor was obtained). There was no real option but for the Douglas Crescent proprietors to reappoint their committee and assume full responsibility.[20]

Disappointed but not discouraged, the committee soon became immersed in another project, which fortuitously resulted in a useful meeting with John Chesser, the Hospital's Superintendent. It happened in this way. The committee had been offered a free load of topsoil which they decided to use for raising and levelling the ground at the eastern end. In order to do this some encroachment onto the Hospital's piece of land was unavoidable. While inspecting the site in April 1885, Mr Chesser chanced upon General Furlong and Mr Bennet Clark and a lengthy and productive discussion ensued on 'the advantage to the feuars and proprietors in the neighbourhood if they acquired the ground intended for stable ground so as to throw it into the pleasure ground and keep it free of buildings'. Not long afterwards a formal offer was made by Mr Bennett Clark and Messrs. Watherstons & Sons, builders on behalf of themselves, and the six feuars of property in the eastern wing (Nos. 23–28), to purchase the stable ground for £550. Only this group of proprietors, the ones directly facing the ground, were involved in the transaction, and this extra land, although merged with the rest, was named initially Belford Bridge Gardens (a title which persisted until the beginning of the twentieth century). It was to become a most useful addition.[21]

By May 1886, the newly acquired portion had been laid out according to a plan by Ireland & Thomson of Craigleith nurseries, and financed by a special assessment of £4 levied on the proprietors at the eastern end.[22] Later these proprietors were invited to join with the rest of the Crescent for management purposes, and to be represented on the committee. It was a simple but effective design making maximum use of a steeply sloping

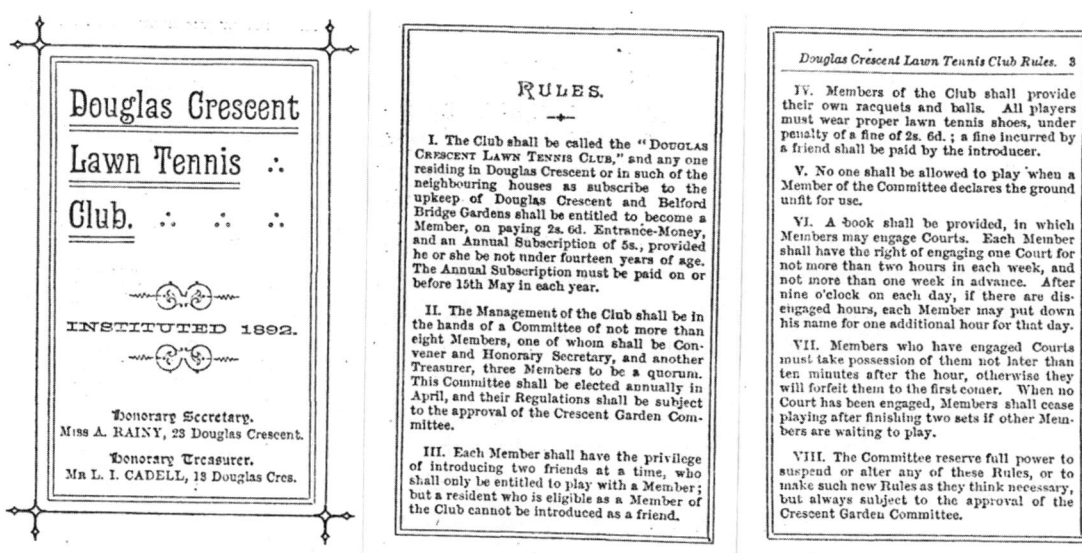

Rules for Douglas Crescent Lawn Tennis Club, instituted in 1891. (Douglas Crescent Garden Minutes)

site by transforming it into a series of grassed terraces; this arrangement provided two lawns suitable for tennis and a third and rather smaller one for croquet and putting. At the same time drain tiles were laid in various parts of the garden to help stabilise the bank. Mackay & Co., who had maintained the ground from the start, were given the contract for the combined area.[23] In 1891, a small portion of ground at the north-east corner by the bridge, owned by the City, was conveyed to the proprietors in exchange for a strip of garden ground at the south-east corner: an adjustment needed when Douglas Gardens and the new Belford Bridge were under construction.[24]

Improvements continued. Once the bank became stable, a series of pathways were made running from east to west across the top and bottom ends of the garden, and connected by intermediary walks. Further substantial planting took place in 1889; on this occasion Methven's Nursery planted 4,000 trees and shrubs, most of which survived.[25] The committee had to wait until 1893 before securing an 8½ foot (2.59 m) stone retaining wall at the foot of the garden, largely the result of a fortuitous agreement struck with the commissioners for the purification of the Water of Leith. Earlier they had negotiated with the garden committee for a strip of land at the bottom, together with the right to build a sewer under Belford Garden for which they offered £300 in compensation – about half the sum required for the wall. Convinced that 'now is the time', the committee launched a successful appeal to cover the shortfall. Without such a wall, the proprietors were reminded, the gardens would remain forever vulnerable, 'as the plantations are invaded by boys and sheep, and the shrubs and trees and grass are burnt down, broken and even bodily uplifted'.[26]

Since then the gardens have grown in maturity, forming a woodland strip of great beauty and providing cover and shelter for a wide range of birds and other wildlife much enjoyed by the locals. The limes along the crescent quickly established themselves, and as early as 1894 complaints were made of their dense growth. Several were removed and others thinned. Similar thinning took place at intervals along the bank under the guidance of Mr Seth from Morningside Nursery and Mr McHattie from the City Parks Department. In the 1990s after 'age and benign neglect were taking their toll' (with about half the trees in their declining years), an extensive and carefully managed programme was initiated to remove diseased trees, replant the gaps and restore the pathways; this was greatly aided by grants from Scottish Natural Heritage (the first ever received by a New Town garden from this source).[27] Notwithstanding, much voluntary effort has been put into the gardens by a group of very committed residents, and the fact that today the gardens are in better shape than twenty years previously testifies to this surge of enthusiasm and hard work.

As at Eglinton/Glencairn Gardens, the £2 maximum assessment has long been inadequate, and has had to be supplemented by additional 'voluntary' contributions.[28] A small income is also derived from the twenty or so outside subscribers. The garden remains a popular space for sitting, children's play and walking the woodland pathways – which continue to extend as obliterated tracks are rediscovered. The terrace slopes at the eastern end have always offered potential for youthful experiment; and for one family the reckless but amusing escapade instigated by one of their forebears has become legendary. The garden minutes of 22 March 1905 report on a meeting called to:

People and ponies. Top: Mrs Hope Scott (1897–1989) *c.* 1906, sitting sidesaddle (as was then deemed proper) on her pony Merrylegs. The photograph was taken by Moffat of Princes Street, Edinburgh, and posed just inside the garden entrance. She and her three brothers often played in the gardens. In later life Hope set up the Hope Scott Trust to encourage young artists and on her death bequeathed her fine-art collection to Edinburgh University. (The late Mrs Hope Scott). Bottom: New Year's Day party when residents and friends celebrate together. (Jean McNab)

discover damage done to river wall of the gardens, Belford Bridge, to the garden roller, and destruction of at least six shrubs and at which was read correspondence with Mrs S (in her husband's absence abroad) whose son with a friend while playing with a roller allowed it to roll away over the steep slope and crash against the wall at the foot; the complaint having been sent by Mrs Y as her children were near the spot at the time and ran some risk of serious injury.

Accompanying the minute was a jaunty sketch neatly portraying the drama of the occasion. But better still has been the discovery of a written account by the main perpetrator of the act recorded later in life as part of his childhood memories.[29] Funny but at the same time poignant, it reflects a boyhood spent in a comfortable, well-off Edinburgh household at the start of the twentieth century. It is well worth the telling:

When David entered Osborne in his thirteenth year, I gave up smoking altogether until I left school. During his absence for the entrance examination, it happened that I got into rather serious trouble in those same gardens which were the scene of our Sunday evening saturnalia. Another friend and I found the garden roller unchained and the gardener absent. We naturally proceeded to play with the roller. When pushing it aimlessly about had palled we tried the experiment of allowing it to run by itself down a short steep bank which separated the top two lawns. This experiment was a compete success, and we determined to repeat it between the second and third lawns. Unfortunately, we failed to take into account that the third lawn was itself on a gentle slope, and accordingly the roller having arrived there continued its progress across the lawn, across the path beyond, and over the crest of the steep hill leading down to the Water of Leith. From the moment it gently breasted the summit, it gathered speed like a live thing. Instead of merely rolling, it proceeded by leaps and bounds. It was at its most impressive during its moment of flight, at its most destructive on its visit to earth, since it contrived to uproot a number of shrubs and bushes, on which an extravagant valuation was subsequently placed by the garden committee. Reaching the bottom at a terrific speed the roller dashed out several yards of solid stone wall, and finally sank to rest in the river. The sight was at once exhilarating and awe-inspiring, but the awe soon dominated the exhilaration. In no time a crowd collected on the bridge, and an officious policeman forced his way into the gardens to take 'full particulars'. I returned home in an unusually thoughtful mood, and my preoccupations were soon increased by the arrival of a communication addressed to my mother by an angry mater familias, who complained that her young daughters and their nurse had nearly been swept to their death by my negligence, while they were taking a harmless walk in the gardens. This, I felt was a quite needless aggravation of my troubles: her children had been nowhere near the roller, or at any rate never directly underneath its transit, and they were disagreeable little things anyway. Also she had lots of others. The roller was eventually retrieved from the bed of the river: two horses were employed, and a number of men with a good deal of tackle. The shrubs were replanted, and the wall rebuilt. For at least 25 years after, it was possible to distinguish the new piece of wall from the old. All this ran to money, and I was the sufferer, or at least one of the sufferers. My father was the other. He was abroad at the time of this regrettable occurrence, and part of my punishment was that I had to break the news to him on his return. The natural thing would have been to divide the bill between the two offenders, but Freddy, my companion on that occasion, had a weak heart and a father addicted to horsewhipping his children. So his father was never told, and mine nobly paid Freddy's share. My own share was duly deducted from my savings bank account, and I have never since pushed a garden roller into a river.

Contretemps with a garden roller. Top: Sketch of the incident recorded in the minute book, 1905. (Douglas Crescent Garden Minutes). Bottom: The runaway roller now permanently at rest: rediscovered during clearing up operations by the bottom fence.

Later Additions to the Walker Estate
Drumsheugh Gardens and Rothesay Terrace/Place Gardens

With the death of Miss Mary Walker in 1870, the last of the line, the remaining family lands of Coates and Drumsheugh (to the west and north of Melville Street – Drumsheugh Gardens, Walker Street, Chester Street, Manor and Palmerston Place etc)) were put up for sale. Money from the estate was left for building St Mary's Cathedral in Palmerston Place, and for the endowment of the Scottish Episcopal Church.

One small problem connected with the development of this land, and recognised from an early date, was the line of Lynedoch Place, developed by Captain Weir to a plan by James Milne and completed in 1823. This gently curved terrace effectively blocked off a whole portion of the Walker Estate from Queensferry Street. Robert Brown overcame this in his 1825 layout by including a crescent to the north-west, with adjoining garden ground (the future Rothesay Terrace/Place) which then linked with a triangular-shaped development at the eastern end (with a similar shaped garden – Drumsheugh Gardens), allowing a somewhat oblique sweep into Chester Street and thence to the main road. This solution was adopted by John Lessels, Brown's successor.

Feuing began on the south side of Drumsheugh Gardens in 1870, the plots purchased by John Watherstons & Sons, a large and prosperous building company who, together with their offshoot – the Scottish Lands & Building Company – built most of the property in the area. Drumsheugh Gardens (west side, Peddie & Kinnear, the rest by Lessels) was completed in the early 1880s, but Rothesay Terrace (mostly Peddie & Kinnear) was still building in 1908. These were all substantial houses built for the well-off business and professional classes. Drumsheugh and Rothesay Terrace/Place Gardens share the same feuing conditions modelled on the ones for Coates Crescent, the first part of the Walker Estate to have a pleasure garden. Surrounding proprietors have a common right to the ground, to be maintained under such conditions as are agreed by a majority, with payment for upkeep based on the amount of feu-duty payable on each property.[30]

Drumsheugh Gardens
1 acre (0.4 ha)

Drumsheugh Gardens provide a further example of a building firm's commitment to forming the associated garden ground, prior to the completion of all the houses. In this case John Watherstons & Sons assumed responsibility for having the triangular area enclosed and laid out, and for its initial upkeep, presumably as a goodwill gesture and to encourage sales. It was formed in 1877, probably by Downie & Laird, nurserymen, who were already involved with several west-end gardens. It was elaborately designed with an outer border of trees and shrubs (mostly English elm, wych elm, sycamore, hawthorn, lime and plane), a perimeter footpath and three linking paths to a central circular walk with inner ornamental plots. The rest was grassed with a scatter of specimen trees. The builders employed a jobbing gardener by the name of Thomas Baxter, 3 Eglinton Street, who was later taken on by the proprietors.

In the Spring of 1878 the surrounding proprietors met to appoint a management committee and to assume responsibility; the first minute book dates from then.[31] These records lack dramatic incident but reveal a garden being carefully and responsibly maintained over the years. Upkeep has mostly been in the hands of jobbing gardeners (although the nursery firm Ireland & Thomson provided care from 1883 to 1895). The original rather fussy design has long since gone, and the garden now consists of grass and trees, with floral display concentrated on spring bulbs. New railings to replace those removed during the Second World War were erected in 1949 for reasons of safety and maintenance, although many had liked the garden's open appearance. Assessments are now based on the former feu-rate system for whole properties, and a flat-rate system for divided property. Cricket, football and tennis, have all been played at one time or another. Tennis made its appearance in 1886 and space was found for two courts. The ground continues to be carefully managed and is mostly used by those exercising their dogs, although a sitting area has now been formed.

Rothesay Terrace/Place Gardens
0.3 acres (0.12 ha)

This was not only one of the smallest but also the last New Town garden to be formed. John Watherstons & Sons also took responsibility for enclosing and laying out the space, and this was done long before the terrace was complete. Surrounded by an attractive stone wall, its main feature was a raised central bed planted with trees and shrubs, the rest being grassed, with rose bed and privet hedge at either end, together with an outer border of trees consisting of sycamore, lime, whitebeam, hawthorn and rowan. In the 1970s the management committee had been defunct for many years, and the costs of basic maintenance were being met by the firm supplying the secretary.[32] The garden was in slow decline.

When the Hydro Electricity Board offices (occupying ten former houses) were advertised for sale in 1993, the selling agents remarked in the press that 'with a Georgian garden in the front and views over the Forth estuary to the rear', the Board had been envied for having the best traditional headquarters in the city.[33] With their departure to Perth, and a lull in the demand for older property for offices, a financially viable opportunity presented itself to convert the premises back to residential use as flatted accommodation.[34]

And what of the garden? This too has seen a remarkable reversal in fortune. A New Town resident left a bequest for its improvement and refurbishment, which has been undertaken by R.A. Brown Associates, garden designers, together with Sinclair Landscaping.[35] The raised central feature had been extended to make a ramped gravelled walkway with raised walled beds and paving around the sides. A number of mature trees were retained and the boundary privet hedge was brought back into shape. Proprietors in Rothesay Terrace and Place once more contribute towards upkeep based on the size of their properties, and under a garden management committee. The garden's regeneration is a triumph, and proof that gardens can still be a valued part of the whole and without too much difficulty can be brought back to life.

Notes

1. George Heriot Trust Chartulary 41, pp. 206–14, disposition of land in favour of Robert Matheson. Recorded on 1 June 1863. The land was bought for £15,750. The Heriot's Hospital were the feu superiors but had previously sold the land to Lady Glencairn.

2. SRO plan 1391, feuing plan of property of West Coates by R. Matheson, n.d., with layout and elevations of Grosvenor Crescent, Grosvenor Street, Riccarton Place (now part of Palmerston Place) and Clifton Terrace (Haymarket Terrace). At this time ideas for an Episcopal Cathedral were still tentative, although the outline for such a building at the near end of Melville Street is indicated on a plan of the whole area by John Chesser dated 1865; in this plan it is shown to line up with Manor Place. (CD/53/3 Lands of Coates, NMBR). The cathedral was not begun until 1874.

3. Charles Kinnear lived at 12 Grosvenor Crescent; the firm Peddie & Kinnear built Nos. 1–3 (1871), 5–6 (1869), 15–20 (1869–70). John Watherston & Sons, builders, worked on 7–10. Watherston's seem to have been linked with the Scottish Lands Building Co for whom Peddie & Kinnear did consultancy work, so there might well have been a tie-up here.

4. This and the following information is based on the Grosvenor/Landsdowne Garden Minute Book, 1870–1963, which is kept by the clerk to the gardens.

5. Information on the railings was supplied by John Fox, present advisor to the garden committee, in succession to Dr John Byrom. The new railing cost £60,000 and was met by a 60 per cent grant from the New Town Conservation Committee (who are also helping to fund repairs to the rather handsome Victorian garden-shed, having about it a hint of the architect James Findlay.)

6. Magdala Crescent had been shown in all the draft feuing plans and was probably why feuing started at the end. There were changes to the elevations however, and the Heriot Trust Minutes record that in November 1868 Chesser presented 'a new plan of a somewhat different elevation' which received approval along with the name of the street. HHM, vol. 48, 12 November 1868.

7. Feu Charter in favour of Misses Jane Scott Anderson & Jemima Anderson, Lot No. 23, Magdala Crescent, 6 &10 November 1873.

8. Information based on the three garden minute books as follows: Magdala Crescent Minute Book 1 (1874–1911); Minute Book 2 (1921–47); Minute Book 3 (1949–74); held by the clerk to the garden.

9. Articles of Roup, 21 May 1872, Heriot Hospital archives; and the clerks papers of Eglinton/ Glencairn gardens; and Contract of Feu between George Heriot's Hospital and James Steel, builder in Edinburgh, Chartulary 46, pp. 478–91.

10. Rules & Regulations to be observed regarding the use of the Pleasure Grounds of Eglinton & Glencairn Crescent, Edinburgh, July 1886; in possession of the Clerk to the gardens. These were referred to later in the minutes as being the only ones available, indicating that they were the first to be drawn up.

11. Information about the garden has been partly based on the Eglinton/Glencairn Garden Minute Book, 1916–65; held by the Garden Secretary. The first book of minutes appears to have been lost.

12. Cockburn Association Annual Report, 1893, p. 5. 'Water of Leith', Cockburn Association archives.

13. HHM, vol. 27, 26 October 1835; possible expense of such improvements put at £250 which included £30 for planting, and £70 for the cottage.

14. Articles of Roup, 1 May 1872; Contract of Feu between the Governors of George Heriot's Hospital and James Steel, Builder, lots 10–20 Douglas Crescent, dated 6th, 8th, 11th April 1876, Chartulary 45, pp. 562–74.

15. Douglas Crescent Minute Book (1878–), held by the clerk to the garden committee. Fifteen proprietors attended the first meeting.

16. Ibid., 25 May 1904.

17. HHM, vol. 46, 2 April 1880.

18. Report as to Douglas Crescent Pleasure Garden, Report by John Tawse & John Chesser to the Governors (February 1885). Clerk's papers.

19. Douglas Crescent Garden Minutes (1878–), 3 February 1883; Steel put an estimate in for £80. The Heriot's Hospital, although asked, declined to help; HHM, vol. 47, 5 April 1883.

20. Ibid., 27 February 1885; HHM, vol. 48, 18 August 1884; 2 January 1885.

21. Ibid., 27 April 1885; HHM, 2 April 1885, v. 48; Feu Charter 27 July 1885, by Governors George Heriot's Hospital in favour of Major-General James Furlong, and others as trustees, one piece of ground at Douglas Crescent to be used as Pleasure Garden.

22. Douglas Crescent Garden Minutes (1878–), 12 November 1885.

23. Ibid., 17 May 1886.

24. Ibid., 28 May 1891; this exchange of land consequent to the new road and bridge had been written into the feu contract when the eastern wedge of land was made over to the proprietors in 1885.

25. Ibid., 5 November 1889.

26. Memorandum as to Douglas Crescent Gardens, 26 November 1890, clerk's papers. Although the wall was substantial it did not provide the complete security hoped for, and in 1925 an 'unclimbable' metal fence with spiked tops was erected on top of the wall, (Minutes, 30 October 1925).

27. A tree-management plan for the garden was initially carried out by Airlie Bruce Jones (RBJ Consultancy Services, Fife) in 1991/92 and was the basis of the grant application. The Scottish Natural Heritage grant was awarded in 1993 and a further grant in 1994 & 1995.

28. As this sum was specified at a time when the 103 lots were up for sale, with stated rights and obligations for all the purchasers to the Douglas Crescent gardens, it is probably no longer legally relevant as only the Douglas Crescent proprietors opted to take on the responsibilities.

29. Sheriff T.B. Simpson, 'Extract from his boyhood memories', supplied by his nephew Patrick Simpson, 1994, and gratefully acknowledged.

30. The Walker Trust, Coates Chartulary vol. 2, 10 March 1885–89; various charters for property in Drumsheugh Gardens.

31. Information for Drumsheugh Gardens is based on The Garden Minute Book, Drumsheugh gardens (1878–1974) in the hands of the Garden Secretary.

32. A.G. Murray & Co., 14 Rothesay Place; information from Mr Ritchie, CA, secretary to the gardens in the 1970s.

33. *The Scotsman*, 19 October 1993.

34. *The Scotsman*, Property Weekly, 12 October 1995; the Walker Group carried out the conversion.

35. *Weekend Scotsman*, 6 October 1994.

ON REFLECTION

Enlightened man in harmony with nature has perhaps come full circle with the present-day 'greening of cities', the creation of 'urban forests' and the provision of 'green corridors'. When this study commenced, the pleasure gardens were not, however, thought of as being particularly special, of having much of a history, or deserving of any great attention. In any case, as I was reminded on several occasions, they were a closed book, hidden behind locked gates and not available to the general public. An air of hostility surrounded them, fuelled occasionally by critical press coverage and local politicians seeking to stir up discontent. No matter that only the exterior of Edinburgh's New Town architecture could be sampled yet the gardens – set up, financed and maintained by the residents as their private outdoor space – should be made freely available. Most gardens in fact are happy to rent out keys, and to open the gardens on occasions. And there seems no reason why Historic Scotland should not follow the practice of English Heritage with their annual London Garden Square open day and organise a similar event.

How myopic and misleading such attitudes have proved! The New Town gardens have yielded, and will no doubt go on yielding rich veins of material not only of interest in their own right, but also adding fresh insights and perspectives to our understanding of the New Town itself. The two really cannot be separated. Unravelling the story behind the gardens was more challenging than expected, but the discoveries have been both fascinating and rewarding. Having spoken to many study groups both from Canada and America, most with no connections whatever with any of the gardens, I have found that their reaction very often has been one of surprise, interest and delight at what they have heard. This growing awareness can only augur well for the gardens and heighten appreciation of them.

Having reached the end of this particular journey, I am left to ponder the many curiosities encountered on the way, from washing women to pig styes, to collapsing river banks, and labourers not only intent on forming ornamental spaces but also on occasion tearing them apart; and on the enormous time, effort and financial commitment channelled into having the gardens made, and nursing them back to health after periods of neglect. All involving a wide range of people, from a variety of backgrounds, acting not solely out of self-interest but also with an eye to enhancing the neighbourhood and the city as a whole. True, many of these individuals were drawn from the well-off professional and upper classes who formed the bulk of the early residents of the New Town. But there were many others not particularly affluent or well connected who willingly devoted time and energy to establishing the gardens. Certainly the contribution of some of the builders was in this respect remarkable and something of surprise. Making the gardens was in fact very much a co-operative enterprise, bringing the New Town residents, the Town, Heriot's

Hospital and other land developers together. It has been satisfying to discover the many dedicated individuals who contributed so much to the gardens but whose names have been obscured with time. Indeed one of the happy features of my study has been the way certain individuals kept reappearing in different places: a reminder perhaps of the village society Edinburgh was in the early days of the New Town. These were times when professional interests overlapped, when membership of clubs and City Improvement Commissions and charitable enterprises brought people into frequent contact with friends and associates; when large and extended families provided all kinds of possibilities and opportunities for networking. This was all to the benefit of the gardens, as people of known skills were easily identified and information and ideas readily exchanged and circulated.

It is perhaps a little fanciful to talk of earthly paradises, garden elysiums and arcadias when one considers the effort and struggle of getting the gardens made; or at all to assume that some grand and noble philosophy underlay it all. Garden minutes focused on day-to-day issues, the practicalities of getting the gardens up and running: negotiating for pieces of land, raising enough cash, getting the work and planting done as economically as possible, revising rules and dealing with misdemeanours, threats from outside and so on. Grand aims or objectives were rarely expressed other than that the garden was intended for the 'embellishment' or 'improvement' of the neighbourhood, and ultimately the City; to protect outlooks, and to provide recreational space for adults and children. Self-interest was a motivating force but it was tempered with the belief that here was an unrivalled opportunity to create something worthwhile and for the benefit of all. The press was rather more fulsome in their praise and used the expression 'picturesque effect' rather more freely.

At the same time it would be foolish to deny that the artists and designers involved in the larger New Town gardens were not influenced by landscape ideals and aspirations of their times, and put them into practice in the gardens they were creating. A late flowering of the picturesque can still be traced in several of the gardens; and certainly the artist Andrew Wilson designed his two Queen Street ones as miniature classical landscapes that he delighted to paint. The development of the lands eastwards of Calton Hill probably best demonstrates attitudes towards these picturesque principles. William Stark drew attention to the outstanding natural qualities of the site which until then had been given rather cursory attention. He prepared the way for William Playfair, and the result was a happy blending of landscape and housing in the best of picturesque traditions. By James McNab's time the gardens had not only become more mature but had also become more ornate with increasing number of flower and shrub beds. McNab probably had a greater single influence on the appearance of the New Town gardens than anyone before or since, curbing the spread of these additional beds, placing emphasis on 'broad spaces of well kept grass, with fine shaped trees standing upon it' and gently chiding committees into adopting a long-term management plan. But whatever the high ideals these had to be tempered with the strict discipline of keeping a tight rein on costs, of providing spaces that not only looked good but were also capable of being put to a variety of uses and working to the utilitarian, sometimes conflicting demands of management committees.

What has also emerged is the arbitrary and fairly random way several of the New Town gardens came into being, requiring a greater push and commitment from the local people to have them established. Pleasure grounds were in any case uncharted territory: there were no set guidelines for either the developer or the new residents. Yet amazingly, despite the haphazard beginnings of some, the gardens did eventually get under way. Edinburgh owes much to the many residents who gave unsparing time and energy to this end; and even now continue to do so.

Gardens, however, evolve, they do not stand still. When the first New Town gardens were formed, large areas of grass had to be cut by scythe, smaller areas by shears; garden labour was cheap and plentiful, polite society kept to the gravel paths, the young were wheeled in or had their hand held by nanny, decisions on management or matters politic were a man's domain. Anything a little unusual such as a bird bath, invalid wheel carriage, putting, bowls, fountains, telescopes or band performances required careful penned application followed by earnest deliberation amongst committees, and usually a cautious response. But boys were still boys and there were railings to be climbed, stones and gravel chips to be thrown, battles to be fought, trees to be climbed, squibs and firecrackers to be thrown, the odd pistol to be fired, the patience of the gardener tested, birds' nests plundered and flower heads assaulted. Girls just waited in the wings and joined in when no-one was looking. No wonder that when tennis arrived it was such a success, for boys and girls and men and women could come out to play, enjoying exercise and fresh air in a purposeful, pleasurable, amusing and approved way. Tennis courts multiplied, methods of grass-cutting improved and the zest for tree planting was temporarily halted. But in all this gardening remained a very physical activity, requiring long hours of dedicated toil and loyalty to more than one master.

And the process of change continues. Who could foresee that one day great monstrous objects called trains would force their way through two of the major pleasure grounds, that some spaces would expand while others contracted, or even disappeared altogether, that some would survive by coming under the care of the City. Who could predict that a World War would cause so much upheaval? Railings disappeared, large holes were dug for water tanks, shelters and huts were erected, vegetable plots were dug and the lawns were used for army units and civil defence corps to practise and parade on. Yet remarkably few signs remain to tell of these invasions and upheavals. Fashion and politics have influenced the gardens in their time, just as in other areas of life. But the grass remains green and trees grow taller, children still play, dogs are still exercised and people sit and lie on the grass whenever the sun shines.

And what of today? Edinburgh learns to live with traffic, more traffic, and re-routed traffic as the bedlam that was Princes Street is pushed closer into residential territory and a mini-motorway now tears along Queen Street, separating man from nature more aggressively than any surrounding wall and rail. What would Robert Chambers or William Playfair say now of the Queen Street gardens pitted against such a roar and bustle? Will sanity return one day when cars are banished to out-of-town car parks? One positive change for the better has been the Weston Link, opened in 2004 to unite the Royal Scottish Academy with the National Galleries of Scotland which successfully provides refreshing views over the East Princes Street gardens and allows a lower level access to them.

The Weston Link, which unites the Royal Scottish Academy with the National Galleries of Scotland, was opened in August 2004. It provides stunning views of the East Princes Street Gardens and allows easy access to and from them and thus opens up an exiciting new era for the Gardens. (C. Byrom)

It is hoped that what has been discovered about the New Town Gardens will provide encouragement to the garden committees, their custodians for so long, to continue their benevolent stewardship. The gardens' survival over many years is a tribute to this ongoing commitment and care, and this local involvement is vital to their health and continuation. Management committees have always fulfilled a useful role as local watchdogs – a vigilante group whenever a threat or crisis occurred. When no amenity or neighbourhood groups existed, this was an invaluable safety net, and it is still a useful mechanism to bring people together. No garden has been without its ups and downs, good committees and not such good ones, times of neglect and times of great activity, but today, despite a reduction in the number of gardeners employed to look after them, the majority are being well cared for. Indeed gardens which over twenty years ago appeared to be in terminal decline have managed to bounce back with unexpected vigour.

Under most circumstances the gardens are happy to remain independent, but where outstanding costs are on occasions unavoidable, for example, repair and renewal of railings, major removal and renewal of old and diseased trees, then outside funding and expertise should be made available. To some extent this has been achieved through grants from the former New Town Conservation Committee (now Edinburgh World Heritage) for railings and structures, but large, old and diseased trees, particularly those in difficult

Hopetoun Crescent Garden, off Leith Walk, has been given a new lease of life after a long period of dereliction. A partnership has been formed between a local group, the Friends of Hopetoun Crescent Garden, and the Council, with horticultural advice and botanical advice from the RBG. The photograph shows the Regius Keeper, Stephen Blackmore, with Ann Hope, a descedent of John Hope (Keeper of the Garden at Leith Walk), looking at an information panel outlining the history of the site. The panel was unveiled in November 2004 and the event was marked by the planting of a Japanese umbrella pine (*Sciadopitys verticilla*). (RBG)

locations such as river banks, are a problem and a worry to many committees with limited financial reserves.

The gardens are a precious component of the Edinburgh New Town, an essential part of this outstanding urban landscape requiring to be cherished and carefully managed in the same co-ordinated way as the buildings. If and when any major re-assessment is required of their planting or layout, then it must be done with an ear to the past and with an eye to the future. The gardens are a resource we all share.

INDEX

Note to index: Names beginning with 'Mac', 'Mc' are placed as spelt. Page numbers in bold indicate a photograph or other illustration. References such as 371 *n23* refer to note 23 on page 371.